BATTLING THE ADMINISTRATION

An Inmate's Guide to a Successful Lawsuit

TM

By David J. Meister

Wynword Press
PO Box 557
Bonners Ferry, ID 83805
www.wynwordpress.com

Cover Art by David Meister

Printed in the US
ISBN 978-1-940638-03-4

PUBLISHER'S NOTE

The Publisher makes no claims, guarantees or warrantees of the information or materials contained herein. The publisher makes no independent review or analysis of the product provided by the author, and disclaims any obligation to provide any information in addition to that which is proved by the author. The Publisher hereby expressly disclaims liability of any kind whatsoever from the reader's use of, or reliance upon, the content herein.

The content of the sample pleadings and figures contained herein are works of fiction. Names, characters, places, and incidents either are a product of the author's imagination or are used fictitiously, and any resemblance to events, locales, or actual persons, living or dead, is entirely coincidental.

For my brother and sister,
and for Mom . . .

TABLE OF CONTENTS

PART 1:
GETTING READY

INTRODUCTION

Those who intend to assert their legal rights in prison should endeavor from the outset to accept that civil liberties come at a price. It has been written and read and said over and again that every right society takes for granted was at some time earned by the blood and toil of those unfortunate enough to have been burdened with the costs of freedom. This burden, this reality, is taken personally; taken, if not from our nation's history, then from our own experiences, for patterns of oppression, from struggle to eventual vindication, abound among us. Each of us has been afflicted by injustice at some stage of life, and each time something inherent in ourselves rose in revolt to caution and sharply remind us of just how deep-seated are the lessons of securing liberty. The price of this education was paid in flesh, in dreadful installments, and those sacrifices are held dear. Dear enough that most of us willingly yield personal freedoms only when absolutely necessary to achieve a greater good. The pain is inevitable, we realize, but justice and liberty are not. Therefore, for those of us brought again for our turn to preserve what is rightly ours, enduring personal sacrifice, to protect or achieve something worthwhile, we should as the best means for overcoming adversity assume a will resolved to the fight.

For prisoners—the antisocial, cast out on the veritable fringes of civilization—the challenge is doubly hard. Who even cares when the government trespasses on inmates' rights? Who protects them?

The *prisoners* do.

The few remaining liberties so tenuously claimed by the ill-fated masses of men and women locked behind a veil of cement and steel were likewise won at great expense. Every right the incarcerated enjoy, like the rights of free persons, was earned by commensurate tribulation—a prisoner suffered, but then a prisoner chose to fight against an injustice that could no longer be tolerated.

The fight, however, never ends. With greater society as with the incarcerated, the struggle for liberty carries on, like the riparian battle between bank and stream. Old issues and new are churned with the eddy of government trend; the people's victory gaining ground by inches, if gaining at all. Yet we carry on for vindication and justice, reckoning ourselves successful when merely preserving our social bedrock as it is. Then we remain anxious, because—sometimes we forget this—our hard-won rights are never to be thought securely fixed, especially so for the rights of prisoners. The next day comes bearing new contests.

For prisoners, one particular contest stands above the others in the threat to personal liberty.

In our age of perpetual innovation and progress, where no market is long left undeveloped, it comes as expected that acquisitive minds have found new and rich avenues from which to wring a dollar, money squeezed from an unavoidable and regrettable part of civilized life, taken from crime and criminals and by extension, their victims. The increasing privatization of the traditionally government-run American penal system has drawn investors while the criminal industry itself has emerged as one of our country's largest industries. A lucrative, job-creating industry, and never mind social balance or justice. Deterrence, retribution, rehabilitation, even restorative justice—all are ancillary, at best, given that more important business is at hand, with money to be made.

Society would have a moral interest, one would presume, in preventing the use of what is essentially a reckless business model premised on increasing the amount of people behind bars. Perhaps society would take an interest if it were sufficiently apprised of the negative aspects of the present course of criminal justice, but the people remain inert as things are today. It seems, therefore, that society is not fully aware of the corpulence of our growing criminal and prison industries. It follows that society does not know that special interest groups and private prison companies aggressively lobby for stiffer, longer prison terms, ever seeking to build more and more institutions; not for correctional goals, but for the profitable internment of human beings. The model: The more bunks that are filled, the more money flows[1].

What does this model mean for prisoners?

Because it makes sound business sense for a company to minimize its costs at every opportunity, private prisons tend to make the financially smart choice to reduce their costs of overhead and operations. But this, of course, entails a reduction in the quantity and quality of prisoner programs—offender counseling, drug treatment, basic education, therapeutic amenities, food quality, medical services, and so on. As program cuts are made, prisoners' prospects for free, healthy lives are correspondingly diminished. Should this pattern of cutting corners continue as it has been, prisoners can expect the likelihood of successful release into the world to concomitantly decrease. After all, under the current business model, it only makes sense that prisons are kept full with a steady and predictable stream of recidivist offenders.

Our government is not offering solutions, either. In fact, the U.S. government has been increasingly turning a blind eye to offender grievances; our Congress has even passed legislation specifically with the intention of limiting prisoners' ability to seek relief from their troubles by court action. That would be obstacle enough, one would think, and yet the courts themselves have compounded the problem. Their recent and relatively recent interpretations of the law have tended to derogate precedents favorable to prisoners. The courts' will be done, what does America say? Well, there, too, is scarce sympathy to be had.

What to do, then?

Sink in your teeth, and hold on! Stubbornly defend what you feel is just, and educate yourself to this purpose. The legal dynamic of America's penal complex is a battlefront in the wider world of civil rights. You are a soldier in hostile country. Such champions of cause who hold the line are, unfortunately, mostly friendless and isolated, laboring in secluded environments where inhabitants are subject to conditions imposed at the whim of a—technically speaking—totalitarian administrative regime. Stalwart souls must, nevertheless, press authorities to respect those rights in danger of corruption, or cede ground that may never again be recovered.

Even with an unsympathetic government, prisoners can, and do, prevail in the courts. But again, a will resolved to the struggle and inconvenience of asserting a legal claim is necessary should hope last for the preservation of civil rights in prison. What are the alternatives, after all?

---

[1] http://www.newyorker.com/arts/critics/atlarge/2012/01/30/120130crat_atlarge_gopnik

http://www.prisonpolicy.org/research/prison_and_the_economy/

The alternatives are grim, not to put too fine a point on it. Prisoners must succeed. Success will come with diligence and the correct mind-frame. A little human decency is not too much to ask—which is what most prisoner lawsuits fundamentally request—and by mustering a sound argument, it might just be possible to persuade others of the same. Common decency, we can agree, comports with society's goal of enhancing quality of life. Prisoners, the argument goes, remain a part of society. Thus, what society does to its incarcerated, it does to itself. If injustice is tolerated in penal institutions, in what other public institutions will it next be allowed? A slippery-slope argument, to be sure, but an argument hard to defeat when predicated on a sobering reality of demonstrable injustice. The *facts* of such injustice will bear the afflicted litigant to success; thus, hard evidence is crucial. Fortunately, by the nature of the beast, being big and powerful, the government is slow and clumsy. The dedicated, attentive inmate can, therefore, catch the monster with its pants down.

I have learned a few important lessons from my time of incarceration. Alarmed but not surprised, I discovered that prison guards can be as evil and vindictive as they were sometimes portrayed in quintessential 1970s prison movies. I learned that prison administrators are expert at implementing impractical and even dangerous policies. I learned that even sensible prison policies can be abusive by uneven or capricious enforcement. Guards and officers, I've found to frequently show lesser regard for policy as it affects their personal conduct, especially when such policy would work to the favor of prisoners. And I searched and I found out that often no one is around or willing to hold an administration accountable when it falls out of sync with the dictates of law. No one, that is, except prisoners who've had enough.

I learned a difficult lesson when it turned out I was to be one of the prisoners to cry foul.

Although a young man when first locked away, nineteen, and full of piss and vinegar, I led a relatively easygoing prison life. I did my share of "hole" time, but otherwise caused few ripples—certainly nothing serious enough to provoke the ill-attention I eventually received from Admin.

It started, as it sometimes does in the prison setting, when I pursued a grievance. I had the temerity (in Admin's view) to complain over the unreasonable censoring of my mail. Not only did prison officials have zero right to confiscate this particular bit of mail, but I was afforded zero due process in the taking—indeed, I wasn't even notified. (I learned of the confiscation through a friendly inmate worker who'd noticed a package addressed to me sitting for months in the prison's property department.) At length, I prevailed in the grievance, but in the process made enemies with the department heads ultimately responsible for the wrongful confiscation.

Angered, certain officials took it upon themselves to make my life more difficult, causing a string of civil violations, from general harassment to retaliatory denial of substantive liberties.

I was forced to demand relief through the courts, and was consequently forced to educate myself on the convoluted theories of U.S. and Idaho civil law and procedure. I took a crash-course in prisoner meatball lawyering (offered by a few sympathetic inmate legal-beagles), endured volumes of dry reading, and eventually completed a paralegal course. But more important, I gained practical experience in pursuing claims against an intransigent prison bureaucracy. And I've learned some tricks.

* * *

This book is designed to guide the uninitiated prisoner through the complicated and sometimes nonsensical legal world of prisoners' rights. I know how difficult prosecuting a claim can be, possessing virtually no legal experience and absolutely no legal training. If you are a prisoner filing a lawsuit for the first time, this book should provide enough information for you to get a lawsuit off the ground. (But do not, by any means, limit research to this single text. Seek help when and where available; read what books are available.)

In addition to sections detailing legal research and writing, court procedure and prisoners' rights, included are practical suggestions for how to logistically manage an inmate lawsuit. Scattered throughout the sections of this book are morsels of info added to give the prisoner-litigant an idea of what to expect, how to deal with eventualities, and some straightforward strategies that may prove useful in pursuing a case. I've tried to address the practicalities.

Finally, to aid the researcher, each chapter is followed by blank, lined pages bearing the designation "Notes." I know well the hassle of keeping one's papers together and organized in a prison system where binders or folders may not be available—a slip of paper here, a scrawled note there, notes lost never to reappear. Researchers can use the blank pages to organize their notes and thoughts under the various topics of each chapter. Laws and precedents change, furthermore, and using the blank space to enter updates as legal trends shift is a good way to keep current your copy of this book.

NOTICE TO THE READER:

I, the author hereof, am not an attorney, and do not intend here to give legal advice. I am not advising you to pursue a course of action, nor am I advising you not to. Be forewarned that readers assume all risks in relying upon the information and/or theories described herein, and be aware that legal authority cited and quoted in this book is current as of October, 2013. I urge that any information or legal theory of consequence to readers be independently verified by standard legal sources. And I shall not be liable for any damages of any and all description, in part or whole, from the use of, or reliance upon, this material. That being said, this text should acquaint readers with the strange world of prisoners' rights, lawsuits, and litigation. Break a leg.

CHAPTER 1: GETTING READY

YOU'VE BEEN INJURED

If you have been denied medical care, or your religious practices have been unnecessarily restricted, or you have been thrown in segregation for no discernible reason, or fed an insufficient diet, or are not provided adequate programs or recreation, or have been assaulted by prison guards, or your prison's environment is generally unhealthy, then you have been injured. Your civil rights have been injured, violated.

Legal injury is defined as the violation of a legal right for which the law provides a remedy. Precisely what remedies are available to inmates are explored below. Study the later sections in this book; learn what your rights are; learn what rights you no longer enjoy as a consequence of your prisoner status; and learn what remedies are available to you. Then get organized.

MAPPING OUT THE ISSUES

Your job as a prisoner-litigant will be tremendously simplified if you take the time to get organized right from the outset. Legal minds and the questions they ask are direly concerned with factual details and with splitting hairs. As your case proceeds from injury to grievance to complaint to hearing and trial, you will increasingly need to be able to pull up precise facts about your case on a moment's notice, under deadlines, and even while on your toes in open court. Cases can be and are lost because of overlooked facts, missed because of poor preparation or disorganization. Unavoidably, prisoner-litigants will spend enormous amounts of time in pursuing their claims. Yet hours upon hours in preparation can be saved if one takes the time to keep complete lists and records of every matter that may plausibly become important in the civil suit.

Notebooks

First, acquire some notebooks or writing tablets or whatever stationary is available. Designate these materials for the sole purpose of pursuing your lawsuit. Do not muddle or otherwise confuse legal files and work product with other business—you don't want to pull out last week's commissary list from an evidence file.

NOTE: Use scratch pads or writing tablets for scribbling out notes while working. Then review those notes when you can spare them the time they deserve, organize your thoughts, and rewrite the important stuff in the notebooks or other papers you've set aside for this purpose. This process may sound tedious (and it is), but time will be saved in the end, and you won't lose an enlightened thought or crucial piece of case law scribbled on some random slip of paper. Also, consider printing your final notes in a clear hand, in all capitals (known as "hand typing") if you can manage it. This is not only for your own ease of reference, but for others who might end up deciphering your handwriting at some stage, such as with an assisting jailhouse lawyer or a deliberating jury.

Who? What? When? Were? Why? How?

You have been forced to petition the courts for relief. The prison has failed to adequately address your concerns, and now the issue must be brought to another level. To do that, you must consider the injury with clear logic and in neutral terms. Sit down with pen and paper, and ask yourself: *Who caused my injury? What, exactly, is the nature of my injury? In what way has the government failed me?* Together, written in plain language, the answers to these questions will paint a concise but complete picture of *what* has happened to you. And that is the beginning.

Next, write out the dates and times of the troubling events, and where they occurred. Write out the full names of each person involved. Were there witnesses? Do you need to learn the identity of any witness? You must learn the name, Department of Corrections (DOC) number, and housing location of each inmate witness. Get the name, rank, title, and badge number of every prison employee or government agent who has knowledge of the circumstances surrounding your case. As you write what you *do* know, any lapse in memory or gaps in information will look up at you from the sheet of paper upon which you've written your mind, and your next task will be to fill those holes.

Now, dispassionately, objectively—why and how did the injurious event happen? Did you, in any way, contribute to your own injury? That question may come up later, and it would be prudent to ponder a response in advance. Then ask yourself the hard question of whether you have a claim worthy of the energy a lawsuit will demand. Is your case strong enough to press in court?

These initial notes can serve as a thumbnail sketch of the circumstances giving rise to your lawsuit. These notes are best made as soon as possible after the incident, even before filing formal grievances (so long as you don't jeopardize any policy-imposed deadlines in the meantime).

Listing the Elements of Your Claim

Once a preliminary outline of the facts and circumstances as you understand them has been drafted, the next stage is to research the legal causes of action under which your problem falls. A **cause of action** is a civil injury that gives one the right to assert a claim based on the breach of a right guaranteed under a constitution (federal and/or state), statute, regulation, or as a matter of due process. For instance, the substantive right to be free from cruel and unusual punishment stems from the Eighth Amendment of the U.S. Constitution. Therefore, the cause of action for cruel and unusual punishment is covered by the Eighth Amendment.

Later sections deal with the manifold legal causes by which prisoners frequently pursue claims. For now, know that every cause of action is defined by specific factual elements that must be satisfied to assert a valid legal claim. For example, a claim of insufficient medical care falls under the Eighth Amendment of the U.S. Constitution. In order to establish such a medical claim, it must be shown that (1) the medical need was sufficiently serious (more than a stubbed toe or headache, in other words); (2) that prison authorities knew about the issue; and (3) that they deliberately failed to provide medical care, causing harm. These are the elements of a Constitutional medical claim. Should the prisoner-litigant fail to provide evidence that meets each of the three elements, no valid cause of action can be said to have arisen—as far as the law is concerned, that is.

Read through this book, assess your issue(s), and then come back to this section.

Charts

Having identified the claim elements, your time will then be well spent by creating some charts in which to list concise summaries of the evidence in your case. Reserve a section in your notebooks for these evidence charts, and make a chart for the individual elements of each claim. A single claim may need a few charts, one for every element, and a single chart will likely need two or three pages.

Start by writing one element of the claim at the head of its own chart. Next, divide the page into three columns. Head the first column with "Evidence Proving." Head the second with "Evidence Disproving," and the third with "Evidence Needed." Under the designated column, write in a brief description of the evidence you have that proves that specific element of your claim, disproves that element, and what evidence you believe to exist but do not yet have in your possession (think about what potentially negative evidence might be in existence). Take a look at how evidence is listed in the sample charts of Figure 1 at the end of this chapter.

Update your charts as and when new evidence and info is received—for practical reasons, consider making your entries in pencil. Persevere past the hassle and make sure your charts are thorough, for evidence charts are hugely convenient when it comes time to write legal briefs and other documents, especially if one is pursing numerous claims involving a varied and extensive collection of evidence.

Catalogs

Evidence charts make it easy to assess the particulars of a claim at a glance. The more complex the case, the more convenient these charts become. But for finding and referencing the parts and pieces of the evidence you've gathered, the prisoner-litigant will find a couple of additional organizational tools very useful. First, consider keeping evidence (which will be mostly if not entirely documents) together in its own files, separated from other paperwork in your cell or property. After arranging the evidence documents in chronological order (earliest date to latest; for example, a prison memo issued on December 12, 2009 would be placed before a cell-search log on January 3, 2010), write a page number in the bottom right-hand corner of every document. For example, a catalog summary for three documents might appear thus:

42. *Population Memo (law library access limited to three hours weekly; signed by Security Chief Wilkinson), dated 12/12/09.*

43. *DOC SOP 320.02.001 (Property permitted inmates, including legal property), 10 pgs, revised 2/23/10.*

53. *Concern Form (Requesting time at the Resource Center), dated 2/23/10, denied by J. Hopkins 2/27/10.*

Note the example's assigned catalog numbers "42" and "43." These numbers correspond with the first page of each document, to the number added on the bottom right-hand corner of each page, meaning that forty-one pages of evidence precede the Population

Memo. Following the page number is a brief description of the item and its content, who signed the document (if known), and on what date the item was issued. Notice that the second entry, number 43, lists a document of ten pages in length—"*10 pgs.*" Each page, of course, does not need to be cataloged; the page where the document begins is enough.

Catalogs not only tell exactly where a document is stashed in a particular file, but also what that document is. The alternative is to try to remember where and what each piece of paper is among hundreds if not thousands of loose pages. Furthermore, as these files expand, think about creating a catalog for the files of evidence themselves:

File No. 1: *Contains pages 1 - 76.*
File No. 2: *Contains pages 77 - 152.*
File No. 3: *Contains pages 153 - 231.*

The second organizational tool is yet another catalog. This one, however, is used for keeping track of dates, including when you've sent and received case-pertinent correspondence, institutional forms, and other important papers such as court documents (pleadings, motions, etc.). Such a catalog is handy for a number of reasons, including the fact that it provides the litigant with an accurate reference in the event that timeline or deadline issues are raised. This catalog may even be offered as proof should a certain date come into dispute. (*See* Figure 2 at the end of this chapter.)

Calendars

Finally, procure a calendar or designate a section in a notebook for use as a calendar (grid out the pages and write in the months and days). Thereon mark every deadline, statute of limitation due date, hearing, trial, deposition—whatever. This is your lawsuit calendar, so don't muddle it with birthdays and anniversaries.

NOTE: The purpose in organizing, using and updating these tools consistently, with case-dedicated files and notebooks, is to facilitate the lawsuit process; that is, to make it easier on yourself. Having clean, organized notes and catalogs all together in a couple-few notebooks is hugely convenient. And though the initial preparation may be tedious, penciling in and updating entries as things proceed is comparatively little trouble once the organizational tools have been properly set up.

ELEMENT TO PROVE: MEDICAL NEED IS "SUFFICIENTLY SERIOUS." (1ST OF 3)

ESTELLE V. GAMBLE, 429 U.S. 97, 97 S.CT. 285, 50 L.ED.2D 251 (1976).

EVIDENCE PROVING: NEEDED:	EVIDENCE DISPROVING:	EVIDENCE
1. ADA CO. JAIL MEDICAL RECORDS (NOV. 14, '10 – MAR. 26, '11)	1. DR. COLLINS' & WARDEN JOHNSON'S STATEMENTS THAT MEDICAL ISSUE NOT SERIOUS ENOUGH TO WARRANT SURGERY.	1. IDOC/ISCF PRISON MEDICAL RECORDS (MAR. 26, '10 – PRESENT)..
2. MEDICAL RECORDS DR. G. MICHAEL (BACK SPECIALIST) (SEPT. 21, '10 BACK INJURY)		2. AFFIDAVIT FROM CELLMATE B. GREY #52407 WHO WITNESSED MY PAIN & RESTRICTED BODY & WEIGHT LOSS.
3. MY STATEMENT & PERSONAL NOTES OF PAIN, RESTRICTION OF BODY MOVEMENT, WEIGHT LOSE, DEGENERATING CONDITION.		3. AFFIDAVITS FROM OTHERS WHO WITNESSED MY PAIN & RESTRICTED BODY MOVEMENT: a. J. MARTINEZ #56702; b. D. MOORE #89001; c. J. LAWSON #55111
		4. AFFIDAVIT FROM DR. MICHAEL (NATURE AND EXTENT OF BACK INJURY; DIAGNOSIS & TREATMENT).
		5. EXPERT WITNESS EXAM AND OPINION.

Figure 1

ELEMENT TO PROVE: PRISON OFFICIALS "KNEW OF MEDICAL NEED." (2ND OF 3)

ESTELLE v. GAMBLE, 429 U.S. 97, 97 S.CT. 285, 50 L.ED.2D 251 (1976).

EVIDENCE PROVING:	EVIDENCE DISPROVING:	EVIDENCE NEEDED:
1. ADA CO. JAIL MEDICAL RECORDS (NOV. 14, '10 – MAR. 26, '11)	1. DR. COLLINS' & WARDEN JOHNSON'S STATEMENTS THAT MEDICAL ISSUE IS NOT SERIOUS ENOUGH TO WARRANT SURGERY.	1. IDOC/ISCF PRISON MEDICAL RECORDS (MAR. 26, '11 – PRESENT).
2. CARBON COPIES OF CONCERNS AND GRIEVANCES :		
a. CONCERN FORMS: DR. COLLINS (5/4/11); WARDEN (5/15/11).		
b. MEDICAL GRIEVANCE #10-0163 (6/3/11).		
3. MY STATEMENT & PERSONAL NOTES OF VERBAL REQUESTS & CONVERSATIONS WITH DR. COLLINS; OF FILING CONCERNS; OF FILING GRIEVANCES.		

Figure 1 (continued)

ELEMENT TO PROVE: PRISON OFFICIALS "DELIBERATELY INDIFFERENT" (FAILED TO ACT, CAUSED HARM).

(3RD OF 3)

EVIDENCE PROVING:	EVIDENCE DISPROVING:	EVIDENCE NEEDED:
1. ADA CO. JAIL MEDICAL RECORDS (NOV. 14, '10 – MAR. 26, '11)	1. DR. COLLINS' & WARDEN JOHNSON'S STATEMENTS THAT MEDICAL ISSUE IS NOT SERIOUS ENOUGH TO WARRANT SURGERY.	1. COPY OF IDOC POLICY CONCERNING PROCEDURE & TIME LIMITS FOR INMATE CONCERNS & GRIEVANCES.
2. CARBON COPIES OF CONCERNS AND GRIEVANCES:		2. COPY OF IDOC POLICY CONCERNING MEDICAL CARE & MEDICAL REQUESTS.
a. CONCERN FORMS: DR. COLLINS (5/4/11); WARDEN (5/15/11).		
b. MEDICAL GRIEVANCE #10-0163 (6/3/11).		3. IDOC/ISCF PRISON MEDICAL RECORDS (MAR. 26, '11 – PRESENT).
3. MY STATEMENT & PERSONAL NOTES OF VERBAL REQUESTS & CONVERSATIONS WITH DR. COLLINS; OF FILING CONCERNS; OF FILING GRIEVANCES.		4. AFFIDAVITS FROM OTHERS WHO WITNESSED MY PAIN & RESTRICTED BODY MOVEMENT:
		a. CELLMATE GREY #52407
		b. J. MARTINEZ #56702;
		c. D. MOORE #89001;
		d. J. LAWSON #45123
		5. AFFIDAVIT FROM DR. MICHAEL (NATURE AND EXTENT OF BACK INJURY; DIAGNOSIS & TREATMENT).
		5. EXPERT WITNESS EXAM AND OPINION.

Figure 1 (continued)

CASE LOG (BACK INJURY)
PAGE 1

3/27/11 –	CARBON COPY OF HEALTH SERVICE REQUEST FORM (I.S.C.I.); REQUESTING EXAMINATION, PAIN MEDICATION, AND TREATMENT. (NO RESPONSE.)
4/8/11 –	CARBON COPY OF HEALTH SERVICE REQUEST FORM (I.S.C.F.); REQUESTING EXAMINATION, PAIN MEDICATION, AND TREATMENT .
4/21/11 – ABUSE);	EXAMINED BY DR. COLLINS (CONDITION DOESN'T WARRANT SURGERY; WILL MONITOR CONDITION; CANNOT PRESCRIBE OXYCODONE – POTENTIAL FOR REC'D RECEIPT OF HEALTH SERVICE REQUEST FORM.
4/23/11 –	CARBON COPY OF CONCERN FORM TO DR. COLLINS (TREATMENT AND PAIN MEDICATION IS INADEQUATE; PLEASE RECONSIDER; PAIN TERRIBLE).
5/4/11 –	RESPONSE TO 4/23/10 CONCERN FORM TO DR. COLLINS (REQUEST FOR ADDITIONAL TREATMENT DENIED; CURRENT MEDICAL ADEQUATE).
5/6/11 –	COPY OF GRIEVANCE FILED (INADEQUATE MEDICAL CARE).
5/15/11 –	SPOKE TO WARDEN JOHNSON ON UNIT (COMPLAINED OF TERRIBLE PAIN & INADEQUATE MEDICAL CARE – "WILL LOOK INTO IT"); CARBON COPY OF CONCERN FORM CONFIRMING CONVO. WITH WARDEN. (NO RESPONSE.)
5/24/11 –	GRIEVANCE (#10-0163) DENIED BY CHIEF OF OPERATION, MR. WILKINSON (HOLDING DOCTOR'S TREATMENT ADEQUATE); COPY OF GRIEVANCE, APPEALED.
6/3/11 –	APPEALED GRIEVANCE (#10-0163) DENIED BY WARDEN JOHNSON (HOLDING STAFF RESPONSES TO BE APPROPRIATE).

Figure 2

NOTES: _____

NOTES: _____

NOTES: _____

CHAPTER 2:
USING ADMINISTRATIVE REMEDIES

THE GRIEVANCE PROCESS

Patience and the PLRA

Before filing anything in court, federal law (and the law of most states) *mandates* that prisoners exhaust *all* administrative remedies reasonably available to redress a wrong. The infamous federal title so burdening inmates is called the Prisoner Litigation Reform Act of 1995 (PLRA), actually passed in 1996, and is discussed in depth in later sections. Suffice it to say that the PLRA severely limits the relief available to inmates; and remember that Rule One under the PLRA is that your prisoner lawsuit *will* be dismissed should you fail to follow the prison's or jail's grievance procedures to the best of your ability. You must include all the information required under prison policy, obey all time limits, and follow through with appeals. Be especially aware of how many days from the date of the troubling event the facility allows for filing grievances or other concern forms.

Administrative processes—especially prison administrative processes—can take a while. And all responses probably will be less than satisfactory, vague, often obtuse, and sometimes even belligerent. Nevertheless, you *must* be patient and follow prison policy, even if it is seemingly pointless to do so; the courts can be unforgiving on this point, bound by the rationale that the purpose of the PLRA exhaustion requirement exists "to reduce the quantity and improve the quality of prisoners suits; to this purpose, Congress afforded corrections officials time and opportunity to address complaints internally before allowing the initiation of a federal case." *Porter v. Nussle*, 534 U.S. 516, 524-25 (2002).

Verbal Requests

Start with a verbal request. Approach those parties responsible for your injury or those who can best address your issue, and tell them your concern; especially do so if prison policy requires this step as a prerequisite before taking further remedial steps. And make sure you jot down the details of any such conversations—date, time, place, what was said, attitude.

Another thing to be conscious of is the prison chain of command. Many prisons require an inmate to attempt to resolve concerns by first submitting them to the lowest ranking officer with power to correct the wrong, and then on up from there. Don't skip any steps.

Administrative Forms

After the verbal request, then comes the written request. Most prisons supply forms for this purpose. Some are called "Concern Forms," or "Staff Request Forms," or are otherwise commonly known as "Kites." Often these forms are "three-in-one"—that is, comprised of three pages, usually white, yellow, and pink. The white is the writing surface and the other two are carbon-copy duplicates. Review your prison policy, but usually that last, pink carbon copy is meant to be torn away and kept as your personal copy and proof that you submitted the form. Be sure to keep this copy. If your prison's forms are *not* three-in-one, see if you can get a copy made down at the law library before you submit the form. Otherwise, you must write out a copy by hand. You *must* keep copies of everything, even if you are forced to copy things by hand.

Grievances

If you receive no action on a written request, or a request is not responded to at all (prison policy should include a provision explaining how long staff has to respond to a written request), then the next step is to file a formal grievance. If policy requires you to attach copies of all relevant staff request forms, do so. Do not attach your originals if you can avoid it. If you have only the copy of an unanswered request, make sure to indicate somewhere in the grievance, or on your copy of the unanswered form, that your written request to staff never received a response. Again, make sure you do not file anything without making a duplicate for yourself.

A grievance ought to be as detailed as possible, ideally including the name of each possible defendant, who did what, and what you want officials to do about it. However, "no administrative system may demand that the prisoner specify each remedy later sought in litigation—for *Booth v. Churner* . . . holds that § 1997e(a) [of the PLRA] requires each prisoner to exhaust a process and not a remedy." *Strong v. David*, 297 F.3d 646, 649 (7th Cir. 2002) ; *Booth v. Churner*, 532 U.S 731 (2001) (the applicability of the exhaustion requirement of the PLRA turns on whether the grievances system will address the prisoner's complaint, not whether it provides the remedy that the prisoner prefers).

However a grievance is posed or composed, should prison officials actually hear and decide the merits of a grievance rather than rejecting it for noncompliance with institutional policy, they cannot later rely on that noncompliance to seek dismissal of a subsequent lawsuit for non-exhaustion. *Riccardo v. Rausch*, 375 F.3d 521, 524 (7th Cir. 2004); *Gates v. Cook*, 376 F.3d 323, 331 n.6 (5th Cir. 2004); *Spruill v. Gillis*, 372 F.3d 218, 234 (3rd Cir. 2004); *Ross v. County of Bernalillo*, 365 F.3d 1181, 1186 (10th Cir. 2004); *Pozo v. McCaughtry*, 286 F.3d 1022, 1025 (7th Cir.), *cert. denied*, 537 U.S. 949 (2002).

Many prisons require prisoners to submit only one issue per grievance form, and then impose further limitations on how many grievances a prisoner may have pending at a single time. Whether this is legally permissible is questionable—what if one has valid concerns beyond the grievance limitations? can such a regulation trump a legal claim?—but do your utmost to follow *their* rules.

If your grievance does not receive a response in a timely fashion, or is not responded to at all, consider grieving the delay or lack of response. Otherwise, it should be possible to appeal the grievance directly, once it becomes apparent that no response will be forthcoming.

Administrative Appeals

Provided the grievance is denied, not responded to, or is unsatisfactorily addressed, one must appeal any and all adverse decisions through the highest institutional appellate authority (usually the warden). Clearly state why staff responses have been insufficient, attaching copies of the adverse decisions. And, once again, because it's vitally important, always hang on to originals, and keep copies of all submissions.

NOTE: If you have done what you are supposed to do by prison policy—pursued concerns/requests, pursued grievances and appeals—and the administration has not responded, then you've done all that can be done at the prison level. Arguably, the courts ought not fault you for failing to exhaust your administrative remedies if the administration is ignoring your pleas for redress. You can only file the papers; you can't force admin to address them.

NOTICE OF TORT

There may be one more step to the administrative-remedy process, requiring a potential plaintiff to seek relief by way of state or federal notice of tort (or notice of claim) procedures. Although the PLRA generally requires exhaustion of administrative remedies *within the prison system* (i.e, internal grievance procedures), administrative tort claims procedures need not, necessarily, be exhausted as well. The Ninth Circuit explained this point:

> The language of the PLRA, as well as the language of the pre-PLRA version of section 1997e, indicates that Congress had internal prison grievance procedures in mind when it passed the PLRA. That is, while Congress certainly intended to require prisoners to exhaust available prison administrative grievance procedures, there is no indication that it intended prisoners also to exhaust state tort claim procedures.

Rumbles v. Hill, 182 F.3d 1064, 1069 (9th Cir. 1999), *cert. denied*, 528 U.S. 1074 (2000).

For instance, those inmates seeking relief under 42 U.S.C. § 1983 or by a *Bivens* action (both discussed in later sections) are not required to submit state or federal notices of tort. *Garrett v. Hawk*, 127 F.3d 1263, 1266 (10th Cir. 1998) (holding that Federal Tort Claims Act is not "available" to prisoner pursuing *Bivens* claim against individual prison staff). And yet, if a particular grievance system refers prisoners to a tort claims system, exhaustion of that procedure and the not the grievance procedure may be required.

However, before filing suit under the Federal Tort Claims Act (also discussed in later sections), a prisoner must first present his or her claim to the federal agency responsible for the civil injury. 28 U.S.C. § 2675. Such a presentment is called a *Notice of Tort* or *Notice of Claim*. Under the FTCA, this notice must be submitted within two years after a claim arises. 28 U.S.C. § 2401. If, within six months after receiving a notice of claim, the Feds return a denial, then a plaintiff has six months from that denial to file suit in federal district court. 28 U.S.C. §§ 2401, 2675. But no period of limitations for filing applies to a plaintiff if the agency fails to act within six months of receiving the *Notice of Tort*. The federal notice must request a specific sum in money damages. 28 C.F.R. § 14.2(a). If it does not, your subsequent lawsuit may be dismissed for failure to exhaust administrative remedies for failing to file a proper administrative claim. (The amount specified will likely be the highest amount permitted to be demanded in the later lawsuit, unless new evidence or circumstances unknown at the time of the administrative notice of claim support an increase in dollar amount. 28 U.S.C. § 2675(b).)

Each state may have more or fewer steps of formal remedies available to prisoners, but, as with the Feds, most states require, under their own various Tort Claims Acts, that the state or municipal government (counties, cities, towns, etc.) be given one last chance to rectify their wrongs. Under these Tort Claims Acts, one must serve a *Notice of Tort* upon the state's Office of the Attorney General *and* Secretary of State if one intends to sue in state court a state office, official, or agent. If one is suing a county, city, town, or other municipality, one must serve the *Notice of Tort* on both the County Clerk and the City Attorney. Sometimes who-all must be served with notice is not so clear-cut. If you are unsure, err on the side of caution and send a *Notice of Tort* to all offices that may have a legal interest. Be sure to read over your state's Tort Claims Act, or the Federal Tort Claims Act if filing against the U.S. government, to make sure of precisely who must be served and other details involved in a *Notice of Tort*.

Usually a *Notice of Tort* ("tort" means "injury," by the way) must contain these four elements:

1. The place where the civil violation occurred, and names and addresses (if you have them) of the people involved;
2. The matter in controversy (what happened)
3. A carefully composed statement explaining what you want the government to do about the matter (in state court you may or may not be required to include a dollar amount for damages, but be aware that any dollar amount that you give, even at such an early stage, may be used against you later should you choose to raise that amount); and
4. The signature of the claimant (you) or that of the claimant's legal representation. *See* C.F.R. § 14.3(e) for federal tort claims

Check your state laws, but usually one can simply mail the *Notice of Tort* to the appropriate offices, without formal service. If so mailed, include a self-addressed envelope and an additional copy of the first page of the notice. Include a cover letter asking that the recipient "conform" this additional copy of the notice cover page and return it to you via the self-addressed stamped envelope. The clerk or whoever receives the document will then stamp the provided copy with the name of the office and date/time of receipt of your *Notice of Tort*. The conformed copy is your proof that you timely served the notice on the correct offices, just in case of a later dispute over proper service of notice.

Again, check your state laws, but usually a notice must be served within six months of the injury—not when you've finished the prison grievance process, but from the date of the actual injury. If a notice is not timely served, a subsequent lawsuit may be barred. Should the government refuse to respond to your notice (and they probably will) in the amount of time prescribed by law (usually ninety days) or their response is unsatisfactory, then the notice is regarded as denied for statutory purposes, and you may file the lawsuit.

NOTE: A *Notice of Tort* should be simple and brief, without legal arguments. Each important fact should be clearly delineated, however, and you should state what you want, concisely. Check with your prison's resource center or law library for stock *Notice of Tort* forms, or send a letter to a local court clerk requesting the same, or you can just write one out.

NOTES: _____
_____
_____
_____
_____
_____
_____
_____
_____
_____
_____
_____
_____
_____
_____
_____
_____
_____
_____
_____
_____
_____
_____
_____
_____
_____
_____
_____
_____
_____
_____
_____
_____
_____
_____
_____
_____
_____
_____
_____
_____
_____
_____
_____
_____
_____
_____

NOTES: _____

_____

_____

_____

_____

_____

_____

_____

_____

_____

_____

_____

_____

_____

_____

_____

_____

_____

_____

_____

_____

_____

_____

_____

_____

_____

_____

_____

_____

_____

_____

_____

_____

_____

_____

_____

_____

_____

_____

_____

NOTES: _____
_____
_____
_____
_____
_____
_____
_____
_____
_____
_____
_____
_____
_____
_____
_____
_____
_____
_____
_____
_____
_____
_____
_____
_____
_____
_____
_____
_____
_____
_____
_____
_____
_____
_____
_____
_____

CHAPTER 3:
EVIDENCE

You need evidence, naturally. Much of the pre-game will be dedicated to digging up facts and documents and gathering witnesses' accounts. Although it can't hurt to collect all the evidence possible—because one never knows where a seemingly insignificant piece of evidence might lead—it is crucial that the prisoner-litigant become at least somewhat familiar with legal definitions of evidence and evidence admissibility, to more effectively investigate a claim. Touched upon here are some of the major aspects of rules of evidence. Evidence and the rules of evidence are complicated subjects, really a distinct species of law in their own right. An in-depth look into this arena is beyond the scope of this book; however, an outline of the basics ought to help along the potential litigant. That is why the subject of evidence is broached in this early section; you will be gathering evidence long before filing anything in court, and knowing what to look for and what may or may not be admissible will economize your endeavors. Further discussion of the rules of evidence can be found in the "Trial" section of "Chapter 12" below.

In this discussion, I refer exclusively to the court rules governing the admissibility of evidence in federal court: The Federal Rules of Evidence (Fed. R. Evid.). State rules are another matter; they routinely differ in subtle and not-so-subtle ways from their federal counterparts, even if the drafters of the state rules have used language identical to that of the federal rules. Nevertheless, the basic theories presented here are fairly universal.

I introduce the reader to a selection of rules in a somewhat disordered sequence (summarizing and clarifying certain points as we go, and often quoting lengthy passages from the actual federal rules). Most of the rules of evidence have been omitted, some are only briefly raised, others are mentioned in later sections. What I've included below is meant to acquaint the reader with those rules bearing most heavily on the investigation of a claim, to give the prisoner-litigant an idea of what to look for. For clarity purposes, consider reading the federal rules of evidence along with this section.

But first, a few definitions are in order:

1. **Circumstantial evidence** is evidence based on inference and not on personal knowledge or observation. Motive or opportunity to commit an act, for example, are two circumstances that could lead one to infer that a person did or did not do something.

2. **Demonstrative evidence** (a.k.a. illustrative evidence) is physical evidence that one can see and inspect (i.e., an explanatory aid, such as a chart, map, or computer simulation). This is evidence prepared and presented at hearing or trial by a witness or litigant, which is usually offered to *clarify* testimony. This type of evidence does not play a direct part in the actual incident in question.

3. **Direct evidence** is evidence that is based on the personal knowledge or observation of a witness that, if true, proves a fact without presuming or inferring any other facts. A prisoner's eyewitness testimony that he or she saw a guard unjustifiably assault an inmate would be an example of direct evidence. Direct evidence is contrasted by circumstantial evidence.

4. **Original evidence** is a witness's statement that he or she perceived a fact in issue by one of the five senses, or that the witness was in a particular physical or mental state.

5. **Real evidence** is physical evidence that played a direct part in the incident in question. A knife wound or a bloody shirt are examples of real evidence.

By the methodical presentation of positive and negative evidence, we theorize that some acceptable version of the truth will duly emerge. Witnesses are called into court, impressed with the gravity of a formal government affair, required to make a solemn vow to tell the truth under the penalty of perjury, and then are asked to provide evidence in open court where their testimony and demeanor can be weighed for credibility and accuracy. Through this process, the facts are developed into a rendering of the events in controversy.

In rare circumstances, however, a fact of consequence can be *presumed* to exist, without the usual presentation of evidence. Where a fact can reasonably be said to exist as a logical consequence of other facts already accepted as true, such presumptions can play an expediting role in the operation of a hearing or a trial. Fed. R. Evid. 301-302. A **presumption** is a rule that requires the trier-of-fact to conclude upon a showing of legally sufficient evidence ("threshold evidence") that an ultimate fact is true. (An **ultimate fact** is a fact essential to a claim or defense, such as, for instance, whether prison officials *knew* of a serious medical need and failed to act, for a prisoner's Eighth Amendment medical claim.)

Most presumptions are **rebuttable presumptions**, meaning that the ultimate fact can be shown to be untrue by contradictory evidence. It can be disputed. There could be a rebuttable presumption that prison officials knew of a serious medical need, had the inmate filed the appropriate forms/requests. Prison officials may, however, effectively rebut this presumption by showing that the inmate actually filed his forms with the wrong department or failed to include important information in his requests. An **irrebuttable presumption** (or "conclusive presumption") requires that an ultimate fact be treated as true once the threshold evidence has been shown. For example, in criminal law, once a child is proven to be under the age of seven, the law says the child cannot commit a felony, based on the theory that young children are incapable of possessing the requisite *mens rea* (guilty mind) necessary to constitute criminal intent. Contrary evidence is of no consequence; the law presumes that the child is incapable of committing a crime.

When reading about evidence or the discovery process (the process whereby the parties to an action furnish each other with the evidence in their possession) or hearings and trials, bear in mind that evidence is most often presented to the trier-of-fact (jury or judge) by in-court witness testimony. Even if, say, a government document is to be admitted to evidence at trial, a foundation for that document's admissibility must still be laid. At the least, the witness will have to testify about the document's source, pertinent dates, chain of custody, and its method of storage.

NOTE: Always think about who will be testifying to lay the foundation for documents and physical evidence that you gather. And always keep in mind that a person must usually have personal, firsthand knowledge of a matter to be able to testify about it. As you collect evidence, make a list of witnesses that might need to be called later to testify about that evidence; making a list as you go will save time in the end.

Evidence Must Be Relevant

For evidence to be admissible at trial it must be relevant to (have some bearing on) the claims asserted in the lawsuit; that is, with respect to the facts alleged as true in your complaint and/or in the defendant's answer to your complaint.

"**Relevant Evidence**" is evidence that "has *any tendency* to make a fact more or less probable than it would be without the evidence; and the fact is of consequence in determining the action [your lawsuit]." Fed. R. Evid. 401 (emphasis added). All relevant evidence is admissible at hearing or trial unless that relevant evidence is *specifically* excluded by operation of other rules of evidence. Fed. R. Evid. 402. This is a broad rule borne on the theory that the trier-of-fact will be better suited to render a verdict after hearing more evidence rather than less. Makes sense, right?

And yet, not all evidence can be used, and for very good reasons. But which evidence? This is where the rules of evidence can get confusing: Which rule controls where two or more rules seem to conflict with each other? One rule says the evidence comes in, yet another seems to say the contrary. Should you face this problem, it is probably your interpretation that is in error, not the rules. Read them over carefully, because on the face of their writing the rules do not conflict, in the legal sense, and you should eventually be able to reason why. If all else fails, ask an experienced legal-beagle for help.

Some relevant evidence is routinely excluded by operation of Federal Rule of Evidence 403:

> The court may exclude relevant evidence if its probative value [its potential to prove or disprove a fact of consequence] is substantially outweighed by a danger of one or more of the following: unfair prejudice, confusing the issues, misleading the jury, undue delay, waste of time, or needlessly presenting cumulative evidence.

Unfairly prejudicial evidence is evidence that has an undue tendency to draw the fact-finder into making a determination based on improper grounds. Suppose an inmate is assaulted by a guard, forming the bases for a cruel-and-unusual-punishment claim. Suppose the prison's medical staff took photos of the resultant injuries, and suppose that depicted in some of the photos is the inmate's swastika tattoo. While the photos are obviously relevant, showing the injuries, the photos containing the swastika reasonably could evoke an unfairly prejudicial emotional response in the fact-finder. The tattoo has nothing to do with the case and poses the danger of inflaming the emotions of the jury, and therefore should be excluded.

Relevant evidence that would likely cause jurors to become confused about what issues they are supposed to decide, or that direct the fact-finders' attention down tangential paths, should be excluded as **misleading evidence**. Such a rule forces the parties to address the material facts simply and clearly, thus restricting the use of the "smokescreen" strategy.

Lastly, a litigant is not allowed to put on needlessly **cumulative evidence**. For a party to bring added attention to a particular fact by putting on cumulative (extra) evidence is not fair; the evidence is unnecessary, essentially reiterating a point already established in full. One may not repeatedly "hit the jury over the head" with a favorable aspect of the case.

Character Evidence

Character evidence is evidence of a person's personality traits. It also encompasses a person's propensity for praiseworthy or blameworthy behavior, evidence which can include one's moral standing in his or her community. Under Rule 404(a), the *character* of a person is not admissible if offered to prove that the person acted in line with (or "in accordance with") his or her character on a given occasion—*"Guard Lese is a real piece of crap; he'd* *do something like this. "* Whether a person is kind or cruel, smart or stupid, a pillar of society or no-account derelict is not regarded as proof that this person would commit a particular act or omission on any given occasion.

Additionally, evidence of crimes, wrongs, or other acts are not admissible at trial if offered to prove that the person acted in line with his or her character on a given occasion—*unless* the evidence of crimes, wrongs, or other acts are not offered for this reason, but for "other purposes." Fed. R. Evid. 404(b). Such "other purposes" include, but are not limited to, crimes, wrongs, or other acts offered to prove the existence of motive, or opportunity to commit an act, or one's intent. *Id.* Such evidence can be offered to prove that a person prepared for some event, or formed a plan, or that the person had knowledge of relevant facts, or to prove someone's identity (*id.*)—but only so long as that evidence is not offered solely to prove an act was committed on a given occasion because of one's character.

However, the rule against character evidence can be waived should a witness elect to offer up character evidence about his- or herself—*"I'm a peaceful person; I would never do that. "* Such a statement could "open the door" for contradictory testimony to that person's trait of peacefulness. Moreover, in all cases where character evidence *is* admissible, proof may be made by evidence of a person's reputation or even by evidence in the form of an opinion—*"In my opinion, Guard Lese is a violent person. "* Fed. R. Evid. 405(a).

Reputation evidence is evidence of how a person is thought of by others— *"Guard Lese is not considered to be a reliable person. "* If such reputation evidence is offered by a witness on direct examination (examination by the litigant who called the witness to court), then later, on cross-examination by opposing counsel, that witness can be asked about specific instances of conduct—*"Sir, when have you witnessed Guard Lese to be unreliable? What precipitated the event? "* Fed. R. Evid. 405(a). Such a line of questioning may expose a bias. If the witness can't summon a memory of an instance to support an opinion . . . well, then, maybe the witness is full of crap, or possibly has an axe to grind. (But be careful of asking questions to which you don't already know the answers!)

Provided that character evidence is *not* offered to prove that a person acted in conformity with his or her character on a given occasion in an attempt to prove a particular event, then character evidence *is* admissible for the more general purpose of attacking the *credibility* of a witness. **Credibility** is the propensity to be either truthful or untruthful. Credibility can be proved by reputation or opinion evidence, but only as to the trait of *untruthfulness*. Fed. R. Evid. 608(a). A witness's testimony cannot be bolstered by additional evidence of the person's trait of honesty. Nevertheless, once a witness is attacked as untruthful—*"Guard Lese is a pathological liar"*—evidence of reputation or of opinion about the *truthfulness* of the witness will then become admissible. *"Guard Lese is the most honest person I've ever known. "* Fed. R. Evid. 608(a).

Again, *specific instances of conduct*, going to a person's propensity for truthfulness or untruthfulness, may be inquired into—*"In 2003, Guard Lese gave false receipts during an audit . . . "* That's permitted; however, "specific instances" may not be proved by extrinsic evidence. Fed. R. Evid. 608(b). **Extrinsic evidence** is evidence that has not been brought out by the examination of a witness in court. If you intend to show a specific instance of truthfulness or untruthfulness, you'd better be able to call a witness with firsthand knowledge of the event.

Unfortunately for those pursing claims from inside prison, specific instances of felony conviction, offered to attack a person's truthfulness, are also admissible. But a felony conviction, to be admissible, must have resulted either in the death penalty or imprisonment for a term exceeding one year. Fed. R. Evid. 609(a)(1). Yet conviction for a crime, regardless of punishment, is, nevertheless, admissible if the crime contained an element of dishonesty. Fed. R. Evid. 609(a)(2). Examples of crimes that are dishonest in nature, by order of relevance and probity, are (1) perjury, (2) fraud, (3) providing false statements to law enforcement or on a government form, and (4) theft.

That being said, evidence of crimes will *not* normally be admissible if the conviction or release from prison (whichever is later) occurred more than ten years in the past. Fed. R. Evid. 609(b). So if the crime is ten or more years old, or one has been out of prison for ten or more years, evidence of that crime is not likely to be admitted in court.

Finally, evidence of a person's or organization's habit or routine is admissible for limited purposes. Rule 406 of the Federal Rules of Evidence reads:

> Evidence of a person's habit or an organization's routine practice may be admitted to prove that on a particular occasion the person or organization acted in accordance with the habit or routine practice. The court may admit this evidence regardless of whether it is corroborated or whether there was an eyewitness.

Therefore, if for some reason it becomes relevant to a claim or defense, evidence that a factory puts its garbage out at 6:00 a.m., or that you eat breakfast at 8:00 a.m. daily, should be admissible under this rule.

NOTE: You can be assured that opposing counsel will attempt to attack the motives and the credibility of every incarcerated witness who supports your case, including yourself. They will attempt to bring up past and present criminal charges (whether or not they resulted in conviction) and institutional history. If they succeed in presenting this kind of character evidence at trial, then your case may be seriously prejudiced by such a misdirection of the jury's attention, and by the jury's inflamed emotions against you. Stay on your toes for this one; though you won't be able to conceal the fact that you are a prisoner, as many of your witnesses may be, try very hard to lessen the impact of this fact by attempting to restrict what the defendants can use against you. Some things in this vein may be admissible, others shouldn't be. Being charged or disciplined for gambling in prison, for example, is irrelevant to whether you are honest. Be prepared to object; become an expert on the admissibility of character evidence.

Hearsay Evidence

Hearsay is a statement that "the declarant [the person who makes the statement] does not make while testifying at the current hearing or trial," and which is offered by a party into "evidence to prove the truth of the matter asserted in the statement." Fed. R. Evid. 801(c). Hearsay is not admissible in court unless other rules of evidence, rules prescribed by the Supreme Court or federal statutes, specifically provide an exception to the general rule excluding hearsay. Fed. R. Evid. 802. The Supreme Court has said that:

> The hearsay rule, Fed. Rule Evid. 802, is premised on the theory that out-of-court statements are subject to particular hazards. The declarant might be lying; he might have misperceived the events which he relates; he might have faulty memory; his words might have been misunderstood or taken out of context by the listener. And the ways in which these dangers are minimized for

in-court statements—the oath, the witness' awareness of the gravity of the proceedings, the jury's ability to observe the witness' demeanor, and, most importantly, the right of the opponent to cross-examine—are generally absent for things said out of court.

Williamson v. United States, 512 U.S. 594, 598-99 (1994).

But note the operative phrase in Rule 801(c)—"a party offers in evidence to *prove the truth of the matter asserted*"—which defines impermissible hearsay statements. Fed. R. Evid. 801(c) (emphasis added). Under this definition, hearsay statements *not* offered to "prove the truth of the matter asserted" may be admissible. For example, Warden Weighty claims that Guard Moore called his office at ten o'clock, reporting that he was on B-Unit. Warden Weighty's statement is impermissible hearsay if offered to prove that Guard Moore was actually on B-Unit. Guard Moore could testify as to his whereabouts, but let's suppose in this scenario that he's in a coma, unavailable to testify. Warden Weighty's testimony *would* be permissible, however, to prove that Guard Moore was able to talk at ten o'clock, if, say, a material fact in dispute was that Guard Moore suffered severe head trauma during a cell extraction, resulting in a coma at nine o'clock, an hour before the alleged phone call. In this case, it does not matter what Guard Moore may have said to the warden, because the fact that he was awake and could talk at ten o'clock, when he was supposedly already in a coma, is not hearsay. The fact that he could talk is admissible.

However, many out-of-court utterances are not considered hearsay. These include greetings, pleasantries, expressions of gratitude, courtesies, questions, offers, instructions, warnings, exclamations, and expressions of joy, annoyance, or other emotion, etc.

If the **declarant**, the person who made the statement, *is* confronted *under oath* with the hearsay version of his or her statement as recounted by another witness, then that statement is not considered hearsay. Fed. R. Evid. 801(d)(1). Question: *"Guard Lese, did you tell Sergeant Hassell that you wanted a reason to take Prisoner-Plaintiff to the hole?"* Answer: *"Yes, I seem to recall a comment to that effect."* Such a statement thus becomes an "in-court" statement at that point—the declarant is in court, and has had the opportunity to explain why the statement was made, or if it was made at all. (Note that it would be unlikely that Sergeant Hassell could be called at this point; Guard Lese admitted to the comment, and so the sergeant's further testimony on the matter would be cumulative.)

However, the testimony of the witness who originally heard the declarant's out-of-court statement would become admissible if the declarant's in-court testimony is contradicted by the witness's version. Question: *"Guard Lese, did you tell Sergeant Hassell that you wanted a reason to take Prisoner-Plaintiff to the hole?"* Answer: *"No, I did not."* Now Sergeant Hassell can be called to impeach Guard Lese. Simply, if a witness says one thing while on the stand, but another person heard that witness make a contrary remark, then that witness would be permitted to testify about those inconsistent out-of-court statements. Fed. R. Evid. 801(d)(1)(A). Had the maker of the out-of-court statement—Guard Lese—not been confronted in court with the "prior inconsistent statement," the version offered by the witness (Sergeant Hassell) would not be admissible. It is hearsay because the declarant was not given the opportunity to explain himself.

Normally, a witness's testimony cannot be bolstered by pointing out that he or she has consistently said the same thing over and over. It cannot be said: *"See, the witness told Neighbor Jane about his reasons; he told Farmer John; he told his sister as well."* The witness himself can testify about his reasons, and the truth can be ascertained through his in-court examination, but he may not testify about every time he told somebody the same thing to show that he has been consistent, and, therefore, is more credible. Neither could Neighbor Jane, Farmer John, nor the witness's sister be called to testify about the witness's prior consistent statements; the witness has testified about his reasons, that's enough.

However, there is an exception to the rule excluding prior consistent statements. Should there be an express or implied allegation that the witness has recently fabricated the substance of his or her testimony, or has been improperly influenced concerning that testimony, or that the witness has an improper motive, then prior consistent statements *will* be admissible to rebut that allegation. Fed. R. Evid. 801(d)(1)(B). Simply, if Witness A testifies that Witness B has recently fabricated his story, then Witness B may testify about his prior consistent statements, and Witness C may also testify that Witness B once told her things consistent with his in-court testimony. To give another analogy, if a witness is accused of suddenly fabricating a story on April 1, 2009, because that's when a motive for the witness to lie manifested, for whatever reason, then that witness or another witness may be called to confirm that the witness has told the story, consistently, before April 1, 2009. Those prior statements, then, are not excluded by the hearsay rule.

Further, an out-of-court statement offered against a person *who is a party to the case at hand* is fair game and not considered hearsay. Fed R. Evid 801(d)(2). This is called a "party-opponent statement." If Warden Weighty told Inmate Jones about such-and-such, the plaintiff can call Inmate Jones to testify about it, without first confronting the warden with the statements, because Warden Weighty is a named defendant in the lawsuit, a party to the case and the plaintiff's opponent. In the previous example where Guard Lese was confronted with his statements to Sergeant Hassell, had Guard Lese actually been a named party to the lawsuit, then Sergeant Hassell could have been called to give his account directly—never mind about confronting Lese on the stand.

Hearsay Exceptions

The rule precluding (forbidding) hearsay evidence is predicated on (supported by; based upon) the theory that it is simply best to have the maker of a statement testify about that statement. Who else could explain? "Nonetheless, the Federal Rules of Evidence also recognize that some kinds of out-of-court statements are less subject to . . . hearsay dangers, and therefore except them from the general rule that hearsay is inadmissible." *Williamson v. United States*, 512 U.S 594, 598-99 (1994).

Rule 803 provides for certain exceptions to the rule against hearsay, whether or not the maker of the statement is available (can be readily called into court) to testify about it. The following are some of the recognized exceptions, admissible in court:

1. **Present sense impressions** are statements "describing or explaining an event or condition made *while or immediately after* the declarant perceived it." Fed. R. Evid. 803(1) (emphasis added).
2. **Excited utterances** are statements "relating to a startling event or condition made while the declarant was under the stress of excitement that it caused." Fed. R. Evid. 803(2).
3. **"A statement of the declarant's then-existing state of mind** [such as motive, intent, or plan] **or emotional, sensory, or physical condition** [such as mental feeling, pain, or bodily health]" is admissible. "[B]ut not including a statement of memory or

belief to prove the fact remembered or believed. . . ." Fed. R. Evid. 803(3). Recall the language of the hearsay Rule 801(c)(2): *"a party offers in evidence to prove the truth of the matter asserted in the statement."* In apparent contradiction, under this rule statements looking forward (of intent) are an admissible exception, while backward-looking statements of a deed done (of memory or of belief) are excluded as hearsay under Rule 801(c) and 802. *"I think I'll go to rec this afternoon,"* would be admissible. *"I went out to rec earlier this afternoon,"* would not be admissible. The idea that forward-looking statements of intent are admissible while backward-looking statements of a deed done are inadmissible hearsay (unless, of course, the declarant is confronted with the statement in court) is predicated on the theory that forward-looking statements do not present the classic dangers of hearsay evidence.

4. **A record** (such as a memorandum, report, or electronic recording) **of a matter that a "witness once knew about"** but now cannot recall well enough to testify fully and accurately about" that "was made or adopted by the witness when the matter was fresh in the witness's memory," and that "accurately reflects the witness's knowledge." Fed. R. Evid. 803(5)(a)-(c). If the record is admitted as evidence, it may be read aloud in court, but may not be taken as an exhibit unless offered by an adverse party—that is, if you as the plaintiff offer such evidence, only the adverse (defending) party would be permitted to offer the document to the trier-of-fact as an exhibit for review during deliberations. Fed. R. Evid. 803(5).

5. **Records of regularly conducted activity** (such as memoranda, reports, records, or data compilations, in any form) of acts, events, conditions, opinions, or diagnoses are admissible if the record was made by someone with knowledge of the matter contained in the records, and if the records were kept in the course of regularly conducted business. This rule applies to all businesses, non-government institutions, associations, professions, occupations, and callings of every kind, whether or not conducted for profit. Fed. R. Evid. 803(6).

6. **The absence of entry in records of regularly conducted activity**, with respect to the above paragraph, is admissible to prove the nonoccurrence or nonexistence of a matter that normally would have been recorded. Fed. R. Evid. 803(7).

7. **Public records, reports, statements, or data compilations of public offices or agencies** that describe or set out the office's or agency's activities; or that reflect a matter observed by a person who is under a legal duty to report his or her observations (but excluding, in a criminal case, the observations of law-enforcement personnel); or that, in a civil case or against the government in a criminal case, reflect "factual findings from a legally authorized investigation." Fed. R. Evid. 803(8)(a). For such public records to be admissible under this rule, "neither the source or information nor other circumstances [may] indicate a lack of trustworthiness." Fed. R. Evid. 803(8)(b). This means that a prison-admin report may be admissible, without someone to testify or to be cross-examined about its contents, unless the report's trustworthiness can reasonably be called into question.

8. **Learned treatises** (scholarly texts, journals, periodicals, or pamphlets) are admissible to the extent that their content "is called to the attention of an expert witness upon cross-examination or relied upon by the expert in direct examination," provided that such learned treatises are "established as . . . reliable authorit[ies] by the expert's admission or testimony, by another expert's testimony, or by judicial notice." Fed.

R. Evid. 803(18)(a)-(b). If a treatise is admitted as evidence, it may be read aloud into the court record but may not be received as an exhibit. *Id.*

9. **Reputation as to character** of a person among the person's associates or in the community. Fed. R. Evid. 803(21).

10. **Judgment of previous conviction** that "was entered after a trial or guilty plea, but not a nolo contendere plea," provided that "the conviction was for a crime punishable by death or by imprisonment for more than a year." Fed. R. Evid. 803(22)(a)-(b). However, the fact of a previous conviction is not admissible for all purposes, but only insofar as this "evidence is admitted to prove a fact essential to the judgment" in the current case. Fed. R. Evid. 803(22)(c).

Under Rule 804, should a witness become unavailable to testify, certain exceptions to the hearsay rule are made that would not otherwise be permitted. A witness may be deemed "unavailable" if he or she is (1) exempt from testifying on the ground of privilege (e.g., attorney-client privilege—consult Article V of the Federal Rules of Evidence for details on privileged statements); (2) persists in refusing to testify despite an order of the court; (3) testifies to a lack of memory; (4) is unable to be present or to testify at the hearing because of death or then-existing physical or mental illness or infirmity; or (5) "is absent from the trial or hearing and the statement's proponent [the party offering the statement as evidence] has not been able, by process or other reasonable means, to procure . . . the declarant's attendance, in the case of a hearsay exception under Rule 804(b)(2),(3), or (4)." Fed. R. Evid. 804(a)(1)-(5).

And, of course, one cannot cause a witness to become "unavailable" so as to have a prior statement admitted under a hearsay exception. That is to say, Rule 804(a) "does not apply if the statement's proponent procured or wrongfully caused the declarant's unavailability as a witness in order to prevent the declarantfrom attending or testifying." *Id.*

Should the witness be unavailable, the following are not excluded by the hearsay rule:

1. **Former testimony** of a witness that "was given . . . at a trial, hearing, or lawful deposition, whether given during the current proceeding or a different one," provided the former testimony is, in the current proceeding, being offered "against a party who had—or, in a civil case, whose predecessor in interest had—opportunity and similar motive to develop it by direct, cross- or redirect examination." Fed. R. Evid. 804(b)(1); *see also* Rule 801(d). (*See about* direct, cross- and redirect examination in "Chapter 17.")

2. **A statement under belief of impending death** is admissible in a civil action or proceeding if the declarant makes the statement while believing his or her death to be imminent, provided the statement concerns the cause or the circumstances of the death. Fed. R. Evid. 804(b)(2).

3. **A statement against interest** may be admissible if at the time of its making it was so far contrary to the declarant's pecuniary (financial) or proprietary (ownership) interest, or so far tended to subject the declarant to civil or criminal liability, or to render invalid a claim by the declarantagainst another, that a reasonable man or woman in the declarant's position would not have made the statement unless he or she believed it to be true. Fed. R. Evid. 804(b)(3).

4. A party may forfeit an objection to the admission of hearsay evidence by wrong-doing if the statement is "offered against a party that wrongfully caused—or acquiesced in wrongfully causing—the declarant's unavailability as a witness, and did so intending that result." Fed. R. Evid. 804(b)(6); *see also* Fed. R. Evid. 804(a).

Statements admitted under the hearsay exceptions are subject to credibility attacks in the same manner as if the person who had made the out-of-court statement had actually came into court and testified: impeaching witnesses can be called and other evidence can be offered. Credibility can be supported in the same way, but only when credibility has first been attacked. And the "court may admit evidence of the declarant's inconsistent statement or conduct, regardless of when it occurred or whether the declarant had an opportunity to explain or deny it [during hearing, trial, or deposition]." Fed. R. Evid. 806. One can fight hearsay with hearsay, in this instance.

Finally, there is a residual-exception rule that allows for a judge to admit hearsay evidence if the court determines there are circumstantial guarantees that the hearsay statement is trustworthy. But a party looking to have evidence admitted under this exception *must* notify the opposing party of this intent sufficiently in advance of hearing or trial, permitting one's adversary time to prepare for and meet the statement. Fed. R. Evid. 807.

When analyzing a statement under the residual-hearsay exception, the court must determine that

(1) the statement has [circumstantial guarantees of trustworthiness equivalent to Rule 803 or 804];

(2) it is offered as evidence of a material fact [which is a fact important to the outcome of the hearing or trial];

(3) it is more probative [tending to prove or disprove a material fact] on the point for which it is offered than any other evidence that the proponent can obtain through reasonable efforts; and

(4) admitting it will best serve the purposes of these rules [of evidence] and the interests of justice.

Fed. R. Evid. 807.

Although hearsay statements can justly be admitted under Rule 807 in some cases, the reader should be aware that to offer a statement under this rule necessarily implies that the statement is not admissible under the firmer hearsay exceptions of Rules 803 and 804, a somewhat tenuous position. Better to explore one's options under the other hearsay exceptions before resorting to a Rule 807 argument.

Expert Witnesses

The use of expert witnesses at trial is governed by Article VII of the Federal Rules of Evidence. When it comes to rendering an opinion at hearing or trial, *regular* witnesses (ordinary, common folk) are generally limited to those opinions or inferences that are (a) rationally based on the perception of the witness—*"In my opinion, he was running around the pool too fast"*—that are (b) "helpful to clearly understanding the witness's testimony or to determining a fact in issue"; and that are (c) "not based on scientific, technical, or other specialized knowledge within the scope of Rule 702." Fed. R. Evid. 701.

Under Rule 702, persons who qualify as experts in a given field, subject, or discipline, whether qualified by knowledge, skill, experience, training or education may testify in the form of an opinion or otherwise if

> (1) the expert's scientific, technical, or other specialized knowledge will help the trier of fact to understand the evidence or to determine a fact in issue;
>
> (2) the testimony is based upon sufficient facts or data;
>
> (3) the testimony is the product of reliable principles and methods; and
>
> (4) the expert has reliably applied the principles and methods to the facts of the case.

Fed. R. Evid. 702.

Under the above rule, two kinds of expert witnesses emerge. The first is of the scientific or technical kind, where a Newtonian system of logic and experimentation, based on tried-and-true principles and methods accepted as reliable in given field of science, is applied to the facts at hand in order to assist the jury in making a decision. The second is of the specialized-knowledge kind, where a witness who has extensive experience in a pertinent field may testify in order to assist the jury in understanding the unfamiliar. For example, Psychologist Smartguy may qualify as an expert to testify on whether overcrowding causes anxiety in prison inmates (an assessment based on established principles of psychology), and Warden Weighty may qualify as an expert on the effectiveness of certain prison administrative practices (an assessment based on extensive experience). But Psychologist Smartguy cannot testify as an expert on prison administration just because he's visited numerous prisons, and Warden Weighty cannot testify about how social conditions may affect the human mind—although, a warden would probably be allowed to testify about his observation of prison culture and sub-cultures and how they are affected by prison conditions. For specifics and the latest developments on the admissibility of expert testimony on both the state and the federal levels, visit www.dauberttracker.com.

Depending on your problem, such as a claim involving medical issues, you may need the services of an expert witness.

First, note that medical experts—psychiatrists, surgical experts, etc.—often provide service at the modest rate of $400 to $500 an hour. Yikes! But don't give up yet; you may be able to figure something out, maybe even find an expert witness to assist *pro bono*. Second, at some point you will have to qualify your expert—that is, demonstrate the witness's expertise to the court in order for his or her testimony to be admissible. To that end, many professionals maintain a list of scholarly degrees, certificates, honors, publications, etc., in a document known as a **curriculum vitae** ("course of life"), which reads somewhat like a long resumé.

Always bear in mind that anything you disclose to an expert that will be used as a basis for that expert's opinion must be disclosed to the opposing party. Fed. R. Civ. P. 26(a)(2) and Fed. R. Evid. 705. The *curriculum vitae* will have to be disclosed as well, as will the expert's eventual report that details his or her findings regarding the particulars of your case. *Id.* You do not have to disclose anything about expert witnesses whom you've merely interviewed, and/or had review your case, if the expert is not going to be used at trial, or is simply offering advice as a consultant. You don't even have to tell your opponents about them.

If you are without resources and no other options are open to you, consider asking the court to shoulder the expenses for obtaining an expert.

At a minimum, a motion for such funding should include the

1. Type of resources sought (concisely);
2. Nature and degree of assistance (concisely);
3. Name and title of the expert, qualifications and costs;
4. Reasonableness of the rates charged and cost;
5. Factual basis for the need of the expert, including your theory of the case;
6. Your observations, knowledge, and insights about the case;
7. Legal basis for the expert in the case;
8. Legal rationale for such resources for the indigent prisoner-plaintiff;
9. Inadequacy or unavailability of current resources; and
10. Supporting evidentiary documentation.

Evidence of Subsequent Remedial Measures

Evidence of subsequent remedial measures is not usually admissible to prove liability. Fed. R. Evid. 407. A **subsequent remedial measure** is any measure taken to fix a problem that, had the measure been taken before, would have made less likely or prevented the harm that resulted in the lawsuit. A shop owner, for example, who installs a handrail on her shop's entry steps *after* a person has slipped and fallen could not have the measure of installing a handrail admitted to prove her liability. One would think a person, by implication, admits liability by taking such measures. Well, that may be true, but the rule has a greater social value. The rule is intended to encourage people to fix a problem—without fear of what that would imply in court—before others are hurt.

Additionally, any evidence of **compromise or offers of compromise** regarding a claim––i.e., settlement discussions or offers—are not admissible to prove liability, nor is such evidence admissible for the purpose of disputing the validity of a claim or a monetary amount in controversy. Fed. R. Evid. 408. This, too, goes for payment of medical expenses or offers to pay medical expenses. Fed. R. Evid. 409. Such gestures are not admissible to prove liability.

Evidence, and its admissibility in court, is a complex subject. The information supplied here should assist the reader in gathering helpful evidence more efficiently. However, in the early stages of building a lawsuit, you have everything to gain in collecting every piece of information and evidence that even remotely bears on your claims. A basic understanding of the rules of evidence, though, will save the reader precious time and energy, because a basic understanding of what is going to be admissible at trial will prevent needless waste of energy in obtaining evidence that will be of no use. More important, it will help you prioritize which evidence you should expend resources to obtain. You may find a single piece of evidence so crucial to your case that it's worth sacrificing your whole budget over its procurement.

Further, one should bear in mind that evidence is usually introduced at hearing or trial by witness testimony. You should always ask yourself, *"How will I lay a foundation for this evidence? Who will testify about it?"*

NOTE: Do not fret if you haven't fully absorbed the above discussion. Give it time and a few more passes, and, of course, read the actual rules for yourself. Your prison's law library should have copies.

NOTES: _____

NOTES: _____
_____
_____
_____
_____
_____
_____
_____
_____
_____
_____
_____
_____
_____
_____
_____
_____
_____
_____
_____
_____
_____
_____
_____
_____
_____
_____
_____
_____
_____
_____
_____
_____
_____
_____
_____
_____
_____
_____

NOTES: _____

CHAPTER 4:
INFORMAL DISCOVERY

Informal discovery is the process whereby a party to a lawsuit personally investigates and gathers evidence without making formal discovery requests to any opposing party (formal discovery is discussed in later sections). By the nature of confinement, prisoners are at a disadvantage in the extent to which they can investigate things personally, but a few strategies are outlined herein. You may also be able to coax some tips from a jailhouse lawyer.

WARNING:

BEWARE PRISON INFORMANTS!!! The government uses informants to defeat prisoner lawsuits in the same way it uses them in criminal actions. If you have done any amount of time in jail or prison, then you have personal knowledge of the havoc that can flow from the informant-government relationship. A sneaky or unusually clever informant will cue on the signs of an inmate preparing a lawsuit (e.g., asking about legal authority, collecting documents, frequenting the law library). So be careful, circumspect, and use discretion. Do not boast to people of your intention to sue the prison, because anything you say can be used against you in a civil case, just like in a criminal case. And, you are no doubt aware, prison informants will *lie*. They will get enough info to make their story plausible, and then you're in trouble.

Seek out help from prisoners experienced in inmate lawsuits, but do so carefully; some legal-beagles (a.k.a. jailhouse lawyers) are more trustworthy than others. A little casual, subtle investigation will reveal whom you can trust.

Staff/Government Written Responses

All the documents, requests, grievances, etc., that you've gathered concerning your issue are evidence. Once an official responds in writing, a commitment to that response has been made, and that response can be used to hold the person accountable. I've observed that written responses account for most of the pivotal evidence in inmate lawsuits. And I've noticed that prison officials often hang themselves if provided the rope. It is also my observation that prison officials on the right hand do not necessarily know what prison officials on the left hand are doing. A savvy prisoner can take advantage, and it is perfectly legal to do so.

Following are few strategies for allowing prison officials to provide you with the ammunition needed for a successful lawsuit. These strategies work best before the filing of a grievance, before warning, before officials have the chance to collaborate and collude and to put up walls.

1. **Engage staff in front of witnesses.** Regular, low-level guards are the most likely to let important information slip (but have the least decision-making authority, so their statements may be less useful) and have the most contact with the population. Consider approaching, nonchalantly, a guard in a public area (say, on the walkway passing by your cell) within earshot of another inmate or inmates (say, your cellmate, who is maybe sitting on his rack within your cell, just out of the guard's view). A seemingly casual conversation with a passing guard might work as a tactic for acquiring information about other

guards, new policies, how admin intends to treat your issue, etc. It also works to pin that guard or official down on his or her version of the facts pertaining to your problem/case. A guard might provide more info in such casual circumstances than otherwise, without the benefit of reflecting on the consequences of revealing sensitive information. If lucky, you'll have a disinterested witness (a witness without a legal, moral, or financial interest in the outcome of your lawsuit) to the guard's statements, as well.

2. **Send a written request to confirm a conversation.** Should an official say anything in your presence that is of concern to your case, consider sending a written request asking confirmation of the substance of the conversation. *"I was just wondering, regarding the conversation about policy we had last Tuesday, would it be okay if I . . ." "I understand your position, but do you think it would be permissible if . . ."* This strategy works especially well if guards and officials are routinely violating their own policies; a casual request will likely be responded to, committing the official to, for example, an erroneous interpretation of the rules and regulations. If nothing else, their response will likely acknowledge (if not expressly then implicitly) that the conversation took place. That acknowledgment might become important in court if, later, there occurs a dispute about the conversation's substance, or whether it happened at all.

3. **Send multiple written requests to numerous departments, offices, staff, etc.** Departments, offices, employee factions, commonly do not communicate between themselves as one might assume. Therefore, by sending multiple written requests to differing recipients, one might be able to obtain conflicting responses. Conflicting statements are useful for a variety of reasons: they can expose a policy as arbitrary or capricious (why is one department using policy differently from others?); one department may provide more information than another; and one department might just throw another under the bus of liability—pointing fingers. (Do not send multiple written requests all at once. Spread them out over a few days or weeks; prisoner requests are stopped and sorted by an intermediate office before being sent on to the addressee, and the sorting officers are looking for exactly this type of activity. They'll look to consolidate your requests, after reviewing the issues, by sending all the forms to a single office that (in the sorting officer's opinion) is the most appropriate office to deal with your concern. Try to avoid this, but note that some prisons have policy prohibiting inmates from precisely this type of conduct. Don't break any rules.)

Again, be careful of informants, but another source of officials' statements is other prisoners. Sometimes the only way to change conditions of confinement is to patiently build a case over years. Some prisoners (usually lifers), who have experience in these matters, will compile large files on prison activity, including collecting staff responses they and other inmates have received. Such inmates will be very careful of talking about this info; they know better. With a little effort and time, it might just be possible to persuade such an inmate to help you out.

Inmate Affidavits and Declarations

Prisoners who've witnessed any of the events surrounding your lawsuit must be tracked down and persuaded to make and sign affidavits. (Concerning lawsuits, your prison should have policy in place that permits *pro se* litigants to contact witnesses in other areas of the prison or at other prisons. This contact will be monitored, and any correspondence read.)

Affidavits are sworn statements that subject the affiant (person making the statements) to the penalty of perjury should he or she lie. Affidavits are of paramount importance during a case's pretrial proceedings, such as during the summary judgment stage. (Summary judgment is discussed in later sections.) They also lock in a witness's story, a prophylactic measure preventing mistaken memories and witness tampering by the opposition.

Affidavits are easy to write. The document is headed by a legal caption, titled as *Affidavit of (Full Name)*. The state and county where the affidavit is sworn should be written under the caption, including the abbreviation *ss* ("*subscripsi*"), indicating that the affiant's signature appears at the end of the document. After that, the affiant writes out his or her story; then the affidavit is notarized. Take a look at Figure 3 for a sample affidavit.

It is perfectly legal for you to draft an affidavit for another person, so long as this person reads it and agrees to its accuracy and truthfulness. You will probably end up writing most of the affidavits you collect. This is in your interest; you know what information is important to your lawsuit and can ask the witness pertinent questions, touching on every point. If you can, prepare beforehand to interview the witness. A good strategy is to ask the witness to walk through what he or she has seen, moment by moment, always letting the witness tell the story. Clarifying questions can be asked of witnesses as interviews proceed, but your questions shouldn't supply them with too many facts about your case—you don't what to influence their recollections, and you don't want them saying that you did when later testifying—but you can ask questions, memory-prompting questions, if necessary.

During the interview, take notes from which to draft the affidavit. The affidavit itself is a plain document, mechanical in tone, with short, numbered paragraphs. If the witness is satisfied with the content, make an appointment to have the affidavit notarized—a process whereby the affiant swears to the truthfulness of the statements and signs the document before a Notary Public. The Notary Public then affixes his or her seal to the document, and then signs and dates it. (*See* Figure 3.) Notary services should be offered at your prison, either by someone at the prison law library or via a case manager.

Dennis P. Smith #50703
I.S.C.F. A-154-B
2334 North Orchid
PO Box 454
Boise, Idaho 83707

Plaintiff, *pro se*

IN THE UNITED STATES DISTRICT COURT

FOR THE DISTRICT OF IDAHO

DENNIS PATRICK SMITH,   )
Plaintiff,   )   Case No. CV-11-08527-S-EJL
vs.   )   **AFFIDAVIT OF BRADLEY B. GREY**
PHILIP J. JOHNSON, et al,   )   **#52407**
Defendants.   )

STATE OF IDAHO)
) ss
COUNTY OF ADA)

I, Bradley B. Grey #52407, duly sworn, state the following to the best of my belief and knowledge:

1. I am over the age of eighteen, and have personal knowledge of the matters stated herein;

2. On April 8, 2011, Dennis P. Smith #50703 was housed on Unit A, Cell 154, Bunk B, at the Idaho State Correctional Facility;

3. Cell 154, Unit A, is a two-man cell in which I was housed (Bunk A) when Mr. Smith arrived on April 8, 2011;

AFFIDAVIT OF BRADLEY B. GREY   Page 1 of 3

4. From that time to the present, Mr. Smith and I have remained housed together in the same cell, and on a daily basis I have observed in Mr. Smith physical manifestations of lower-back pain, including but not limited to grunting, sounds of physical distress (such as moaning and cries of pain), restlessness, inability to sleep, and slow, stiff, and inhibited body movement;

5. I have observed Mr. Smith to regularly miss meal times at the ISCF cafeteria, including breakfast, lunch, and dinner, but have never witnessed Mr. Smith to attend breakfast;

6. I have also observed Mr. Smith to regularly forgo outside recreation;

7. Mr. Smith has explained to me on several occasions that he is often unable to walk to the ISCF cafeteria and recreation yard because of severe lower-back pain;

8. From April 8, 2011, to the present, I have witnessed Mr. Smith to increasingly complain about his physical condition and pain; to increasingly miss meal times and recreation; to increasingly manifest physical signs of pain; and to have lost approximately 30 pounds of body weight, from his approximately 190 pounds in April 2011, to approximately 160 pounds currently;

9. Mr. Smith has explained to me, on numerous occasions, that his back pain is caused by a ruptured disk sustained in a 2010 car wreck, and that his prison-doctor prescribed regimen of ibuprofen does not alleviate his pain.

Further you affiant sayeth not.

AFFIDAVIT OF BRADLEY B. GREY   Page 2 of 3

Figure 3

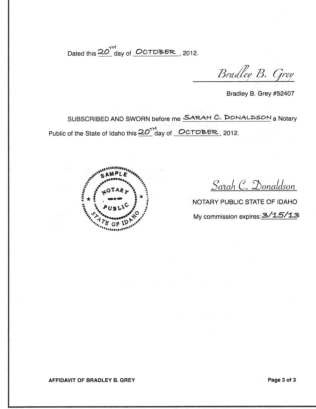

Dated this 20ᵀᴴ day of OCTOBER, 2012.

Bradley B. Grey

Bradley B. Grey #52407

SUBSCRIBED AND SWORN before me SARAH C. DONALDSON a Notary

Public of the State of Idaho this 20ᵀᴴ day of OCTOBER, 2012.

Sarah C. Donaldson

NOTARY PUBLIC STATE OF IDAHO

My commission expires: 3/15/13

AFFIDAVIT OF BRADLEY B. GREY   Page 3 of 3

Figure 3 (continued)

Apart from affidavits, federal law permits one to forego the hassle and formality of notarization, allowing (in federal proceedings) for one to simply "declare" under the penalty of perjury, with nothing more, no notarization. You can write a declaration for another person, just as you can draft an affidavit for another person. A declaration follows the same format as an affidavit (legal caption, numbered paragraphs, etc.), but instead of being called an affidavit it bears the designation of *Declaration of (Full Name) Under Penalty of Perjury* in the caption. And instead of a Notary Public's seal and signature at the bottom, simply include words to the effect of, *"I, (Full Name), have read the foregoing, and declare under the penalty of perjury under the laws of the United States that the statements contained herein are true and correct to the best of my belief and knowledge."* Follow this with the date and the declarant's signature. That's it.

Be aware, asking a witness to make an affidavit or declaration is by no stretch of the imagination the same as asking the witness to testify in court. That could mean for the witness inconvenient transports, stopovers in county jails, and myriad other headaches.

Investigation Notes

Always, always write things down. Any conversation you have with staff or other people, including inmates, that is relevant to your case should be written down, clearly, with detail, and with the date and time. Write down any personal observations as well. Consider using a specific notebook for recording events and conversations. Or, write each piece of evidence on a separate piece of paper, because such investigative or observation notes *are* evidence and may be subject to disclosure. Don't mix investigation notes with general case notes (e.g., research, strategy, work notes), because investigation notes probably will have to be disclosed to opposing counsel and/or submitted as evidence at hearing or trial. You don't want your personal case notes incidentally revealed to others. Each record should be dated, then cataloged and filed with your other evidence in chronological sequence. If possible, copy investigation notes for your working files, leaving the originals alone in their own files, unmarred and in good condition. Better to abuse photocopies while working on your case from day to day.

NOTE: A prisoner pursuing a case involving persistently bad conditions of confinement should endeavor to track and map out both broader trends and individual occurrences. One complaining of a housing unit's low temperatures, for example, would not be amiss to note every day in which the temperature dropped below permissible limits and what the temperature was, even if only by estimation. If you are being harassed with too-frequent cell searches, write down the date and the circumstances of each time your cell is tossed, include the officer's name and the condition of the cell before and after the search. Maybe have your cellie read and sign your notes, too.

Documents and Memos

Other sources of evidence are memos, notices, and other papers prison officials post in the population housing units or common areas. Usually, prison rules do not allow inmates to remove postings, but that doesn't mean one can't record their contents or ask staff to burn off a copy for personal reference. It may even be possible to get a copy of a memo, notice, or other posted document by sending a written request to the office or department that issued the item. One might also obtain a posted item when staff elects to discard the document after it becomes outdated; you will have to be attentive to catch them while doing this.

Documents such as prison polices, in one fashion or another, often become relevant in a prisoner's lawsuit. If you cannot get copies of policy (some prisons don't allow inmates to actually copy policy, but only to review it), consider sending an official request for copies to the appropriate government office. With some exceptions, government departments are legally required to make information about the department, including policy, available to the public. You might have to pay for the copies. And you should probably make the formal request through the U.S. Postal Service, using envelope and stamp, rather than submitting the request through the prison mail system. The cost should be minimal, and less of a bother than attempting to obtain such papers through the prison system itself.

Experiment with using the Freedom of Information Act (5 U.S.C. § 552) and state freedom of information acts or public records acts to obtain relevant information. Such searches are informal and are not subject to ordinary discovery rules, and can be made at any time, given a valid reason for the inquiry. Some information is not subject to disclosure, but a properly placed request cannot be denied, except for certain legal reasons, reasons that must be disclosed to you. Place requests with the agency responsible for controlling the information/records that you are after. Don't give up if a request doesn't work; one can always try another agency, department, or office—though agency record-departments are routinely forwarded such requests, and may end up processing all your requests no matter how extensively you canvass the government with queries.

Keep an Eye on Staff

Finally, depending on your claim, consider keeping an eye on which guards work in the various sectors or areas of the prison, and to which shifts they're assigned. Take notes, because prisons keep logs of inmate as well as staff activity—who's doing what and where. Activity records are made easier to get (later, during the formal discovery process) by making requests as specific as possible. Sometimes a too-disruptive guard, for instance, will be transferred around to numerous posts over a short period; when, where to, and why may become important if such a person is involved in your case.

NOTES: _____

NOTES: _____

CHAPTER 5:
SOURCES OF LAW & RESEARCH

Your prison's resource center is unlikely to have anything approaching an adequate law library. Some states still keep larger selections of legal materials, but others offer only the skeletal minimum required by law, such as penal codes, federal and state court rules, possibly a few legal treatises, and fill-in-the-blank civil and criminal pleading packets. You must make do.

Whatever your prison provides, spend some time getting familiar with what *is* available. Learn to take advantage of what's provided. Your resource center might publish a list of the legal materials it offers. Get it. You'll save time and energy entering the law library already knowing what and where to look for resources for a given research project. And because access to the resource center may be restricted to brief one- or two-hour time slots, two or three slots a week, planning research before entering the library is the best way to make the most out of the time allotted.

Most prisons require inmates to submit formal written requests before access to the law library can be granted. Forms are usually provided for this purpose; but if not, policy dictates how prisoners' resources are used. Obtain a copy of the policy if you can; it should explain law-library/resource-center rules, how to request services from the prison's paralegal or contract attorney (if there is one), and how to checkout law books and other materials.

With the resource center, as with most areas of a prison, inmate workers probably run the show. As a matter of prudence, stay on friendly terms with the workers running the resource center. Throughout the course of a lawsuit, you will have need of reference materials and large quantities of photocopies. A friendly worker may become invaluable if, say, a particular book is needed for checkout, or to ensure copies can be made with little hassle. (Many states are obstinate about making inmate photocopies, even when legally required to do so. Policy controls, so read it, get a copy of it—know your rights.)

Once you understand what resources are available, you can then research with the self-assurance that if something of importance to your case is missed, the prison's limited resources are responsible, not you—no point in worrying over something that can't be changed. Your legal issues, viewed through the lens of your research, can then confidently be placed in their proper legal perspectives.

The proper perspective is how the law, not you, views the circumstances surrounding your case. You can best ascertain what the state of law is regarding a civil injury by researching from the top legal authority on down to the bottom. Start with the federal and your state constitutions, then federal and state statutes, and then federal and state executive orders and regulations. Then read the case law.

The sources of law, from top to bottom, are outlined in following sections. Before moving on to them, however, a basic summary of our government's organization and some of its functions is given here to provide context for further discussion on the sources and interpretation of laws.

BRANCHES AND DUTIES OF GOVERNMENT

The **federal government** is of "expressly limited powers"—that is, its powers are limited to those described in the documents that establish our government. The most important of these documents is the United States Constitution, which grants the federal government jurisdiction over interstate matters such as interstate commerce and travel; over things that appy to all the states, including federal taxation, immigration and naturalization; and over international concerns such as foreign relations, waging war, and so on. The federal government also maintains jurisdiction in all matters dealing with the fundamental rights of people, rights embodied in the U.S. Constitution's Bill of Rights and its Amendments.

In this country, the Bill of Rights is held as near to sacred text as a government paper can be. It is a shield against an abusive government. It is also a prisoner's best friend because no prison rule or regulation, state or federal statute can undermine the basic liberties guaranteed in the U.S. Constitution. Although state and federal legislatures can *expand* those liberties, they cannot diminish them.

Beyond protecting personal liberty and assigning duties and responsibilities to the federal government, as summarized above, the Constitution also provides the schematic plan for the structure of federal government itself, creating the three separate branches of government—executive, legislative, and judiciall—and stating when, under what conditions, and for how long federal officials serve their terms and appointments in office. It also provides for the creation and implementation of laws, investing in the legislative branch—the House of Representatives and the Senate (together known as Congress)—the power to *create* law; assigning the executive branch—the President, the Attorney General, and just about any federal office bearing the words "Department of . . ." in its name—the duty of enforcing or *executing* the law; and making the judicial branch of courts and judges responsible for *interpreting* the law (which is discussed further below).

State governments, regarded as sovereign entities (and yet still subject to federal domain), possess among the fifty states the larger power of governance and power to invent law. Any power of government not *specifically* granted to the federal government in the U.S. Constitution remains with the state governments, or with the people. The majority of laws, it follows, are state laws; and although the federal government does prosecute offenses named in a vast federal criminal code, state government still controls in most matters of criminal law. States, moreover, have almost exclusive domain over matters of personal torts, contract law, trusts, property law, partnerships, and corporations.

State governments are, generally speaking, structured to resemble the federal government. State legislatures are usually bicameral (of two chambers, in the fashion of the U.S. House of Representatives and the Senate). A state executive branch starts with a governor at its top (a state's functional equivalent to the U.S. President), and then onto the many administrative agencies (including your Department of Corrections) tasked with the workaday affairs of conducting a state's business. And finally there are, of course, the state courts—the branch of state government that handles legal disputes.

PRIMARY SOURCES OF LAW

What a government does (federal or state), how it does it, whom it affects, how it executes its policy, and how it upholds the rights of the people, are all matters provided for within the law. Primary sources are sources that contain the actual *letter* of the law itself. Foremost sources are described here in descending order of authority.

Constitutions

The United States Constitution is the land's highest legal authority, prescribing our model of federal government, separating its powers into three branches—executive, legislative, and judicial—and listing, among other things, the inalienable rights (rights that cannot be taken nor *given* away) ensured to the people, i.e., the rights embodied in the Bill of Rights.

Each of the fifty states has its own constitution as well. A constitution does for the state substantially the same things the U.S. Constitution does for the federal government: forming branches of government, prescribing their duties, limitations, and powers; defining terms of representatives and other officials; and listing fundamental rights of the people—which in state constitutions are sometimes expanded beyond the minimum guarantees of the U.S. Constitution.

NOTE: A free copy of your state constitution may be available from your state's office of the Secretary of State. The publication will probably include the U.S. Constitution as well, and will likely have a topic index—very handy. The state's *Blue Book* may also be available, at no cost, from the same office. The *Blue Book* (or your state's equivalent title) contains general background information about the state, including names, bios, and office addresses for state legislators, judges (state and federal), and heads of executive departments. Send a short letter to your Secretary of State explaining your status as a broke inmate (if you're broke) and requesting free copies if available. Ask for recent versions; they usually come out in spring.

Statutes

Federal and state statutes are codified (coherently systematized by topic) enactments of the legislative process. The legislative process starts with a bill. A **bill** is proposed legislation that can originate from many sources, including committees and subcommittees within the legislature itself, or from the people—you could actually submit one yourself. Both houses of the federal legislature (House of Representatives and Senate) can propose legislation. The two houses follow similar, though different, processes in research, in deliberation, and in hashing out the details of new law.

For the Feds, and generally for the states as well, after a bill is introduced, it is referred to a committee specializing in the area of law at which the bill is aimed. The committee holds hearings, debates pertinent issues, and amends the bill as necessary. Then it offers up its results in a report to the full house. The house holds its own debate, modifies and amends the bill, and then sends it back to a conference committee, which is tasked with resolving the differences in opinion between the House of Representatives and the Senate. Differences resolved, another full-house debate is held. Should the bill be passed, it is then given to the President (or governor, in the analogous state process) for a signature and final passage into law. The President has the power to reject ("veto") the law if he or she chooses, but Congress can then override the veto by passing the law again with a two-thirds majority vote in each house.

Federal bills that survive the rigorous legislative process, becoming statutes, are *officially* published for everyone's convenience in the *United States Code* (abbreviated U.S.C., as in 42 U.S.C. § 1983). Federal statutes are also published *unofficially* by proprietary companies, in the *United States Code Annotated* (U.S.C.A) (published by West Group), and in the *United States Code Service* (U.S.C.S.) (published by Reed). Both unofficial publications reproduce exactly the official wording of the laws, but additionally provide copious amounts of citations to cross-reference materials, historical notes, and case notes construing specific Code sections. (For prisoners with limited access to case law and legislative history, annotated unofficial versions are more useful; they offer insight where the official versions won't, and cite important cases interpreting statutes.)

State statutes, too, come in official and unofficial varieties. An official publication bears the state's name in its title—*Idaho Code* or *Washington Revised Code*, for example—as do unofficial versions: *Idaho Code Annotated* (I.C.A.) or *Washington Revised Code Annotated* (Wash. Rev. Code Ann.), published by West Group. Both official and unofficial versions of law can be cited with confidence. Both versions are kept current: each of the many volumes of statutes is updated annually with **pocket parts**, which are paperback supplements stored under the back cover of the volumes they amend.

Executive Rules and Regulations

Laws, of course, have no effect if no one enforces them. That's the job of the executive branch; and the legislature leaves it to the executives, on their own, to make sense of statutes as they read. This is because a government branch is not, theoretically, supposed to micromanage the function of another branch. Therefore, in creating the law, laws are carefully written to be precise about what subjects/areas they cover and the intentions of bill drafters, but are left broad enough in language to sufficiently encompass the intended subject while also allowing room for practical interpretations as to how the law should be applied. Drafters cannot foresee every eventuality; broad language is used in crafting laws to allow their execution as intended in spirit—too-specific language may inadvertently create loopholes defeating the purpose of the law. The actual logistics involved in implementing a law, additionally, are rarely addressed in the statute itself, allowing the executive departments to order their own priorities, and trusting in administrative discretion to implement effective policy, so long as the job gets done.

Where not already established by the Constitution, the legislature, using the same process of enacting law, created every executive department, defined the scope and duties for a department's demarcated area of government, and then invested each department (a.k.a administrative agency) with power to create policies for that department to accomplish its purpose for existing. Such policies are called **administrative rules and regulations**.

Administrative rules and regulations are the primary source of executive law, which, in a narrow sense, has the same weight as the law that the executive policies are designed to implement. Although experience tells us that rules and regulations are taken as somewhat less binding than full-blown statutes, they are, nevertheless, supposed to be followed. Perhaps the casual view can be attributed to the less formal processes prescribed for creating executive policy. Maybe so. And yet, whatever our perceptions, every department or agency is required to abide by specific statutory procedures when promulgating policies, directives, rules, regulations—whatever such policy may be called.

Once passed, federal executive policy, which includes executive orders, is published in a manner resembling the codification of statutes, in the *Federal Register* (Fed. Reg.) and in the

Code of Federal Regulations (C.F.R.). States have similar publications for state executive policies and orders.

The **executive order** is another source of executive law, originating from the executive head—the U.S. President or the state governor—issued from time to time when it becomes necessary, for whatever reason, to direct departments of the executive branch to do or not do something.

NOTE: Your state has on its books a statute called something similar to the "Administrative Procedure Act." This Act controls how administrative/executive agencies/departments go about making rules and regulations. Such laws, unfortunately, often have provisions exempting prison administrators from the strictures of the ordinary, formal process required of other government departments in enacting policy. This means that prison officials can more easily institute policy and policy changes.

If you've spent any appreciable time in prison, you've observed that admin and staff are fond of suddenly conjuring up new rules or interpretations of rules whenever it suits their purposes. Such conduct may or may not be legal under procedural law; study your state's administrative/executive laws to ascertain to what extent admin and staff can informally create rules.

Another thing to look into is whether your state receives federal money for correctional programs (most states do). A state that accepts financial aid for its prison operations may be required, as a condition to receiving those funds, to observe *federal administrative procedures* pertaining to programs benefitting from federal money. Should such a state fail to follow the proper procedures in conducting its operations, it risks losing federal support.

Which programs use federal money? Well, that's a difficult question particular to each state. It'll take a little research on your part to make heads or tails of how federal money impacts your department of corrections, and to learn how federal policy comes into play.

Nevertheless, whatever state or federal administrative policy is used, substantive due process—the rule of fair play—requires that prisoners receive advance notice of any regulation potentially affecting prisoners' liberty interests. (More on "liberty interests" in later sections.) If a rule directing or prohibiting conduct—a rule of conduct that is not otherwise a matter of common sense—can result in prisoners being disciplined for its violation, then prisoners are entitled to notification of the rule *before* it can be applied. (*See* "Rules and Regulations" in "PART 5," below.) Additionally, established rules cannot be arbitrarily deviated or departed from when dealing with prisoners. For prison staff to do so may raise serious questions of due process protection (fair play), even harassment.

Interpretive Law

The legislature creates it, the executives enforce it, but it's up to the judiciary to interpret the final meaning of law. Judicial interpretations are, essentially, quasi-laws. Strictly speaking, the courts are not supposed to create law; but in practice, judicial opinion can be as binding as any statute. And because the lower courts must follow the higher, and because parallel jurisdictions courteously defer to each other, interpretive trends within judicial opinion have wide-ranging and penetrating effect.

Cutting to the meat of it, judges exist to settle disputes and to be obeyed, often absolutely. For a judge to gain this authority, however, a case must first be presented to the court by a person or an organization, using proper procedures, before a judicial opinion may be rendered.

Disputing parties who submit a matter, civil or criminal, to a state or federal court grant that court authority to resolve the dispute.

The lowest courts (trial courts) are responsible for hearing (presiding over) such disputes, where the judge (or jury) sorts out the facts in controversy, then makes the first stab at reviewing, interpreting, and applying the law in a given case. Your criminal case was handled in such a court; your lawsuit, once filed, will also be heard in such a court. The trial court hears the facts, a judge or jury decides the weight of evidence, the state of facts is determined—what happened, and who is responsible for what—and then the judge applies the law to the facts in a final judgment or opinion.

Opinion issued, higher court levels may then get a turn to offer their considered opinions on the matter: if a trial court ruling is disputed by any of the parties involved with a case, an appeal can usually be made to a higher court. Appeal duly made, an appellate court analyzes a case's facts as they already have been developed at the trial or hearing level, and then it examines the lower court's application of law to those facts, searching for factual or legal error. The appellate court then issues a written decision, either "affirming" (approving of) the lower court's ruling, "reversing" (overturning; disagreeing with) the ruling, or "remanding" (returning to the trial court) the case for further action. Cases are remanded when some fact or set of facts important to a final determination of law has yet to be fully developed in evidence. The trial court resumes jurisdiction over the case to conduct the necessary hearings, because appellate courts do not hear new evidence. Then the trial court issues another ruling. If the new ruling is disputed by a party to the case, the appellate process begins anew.

Appellate decisions, in their many of thousands, constitute the main body of interpretive law, and are exhaustively published in what are called **reporters**. Reporters are the primary source of interpretive law. The multitude of cases they publish are known as **case law**.

Case law originating within different court systems is published within different case reporters. The lowest courts of the federal system are the federal district courts (United States District Courts), which hear civil and criminal cases. Over ninety U.S. District Courts are spread throughout the states, each state with at least one federal court. States with more than one federal trial court are divided into judicial districts, each court having federal jurisdiction over a designated state region. (Federal lawsuits, by the way, are usually filed in the federal district nearest to the place where the civil injury occurred.) Federal district court jurisdiction is limited in scope as the federal government itself is limited in scope by the U.S. Constitution, constraining federal courts to handling matters of federal crime, civil cases involving federal questions, cases between the states, cases between the U.S. and foreign nations, and cases between parties from different states when more than $75,000 is at stake. Federal courts *do* sometimes hear cases involving questions of state law (usually all parties must agree to this), but are generally not permitted to meddle in matters better addressed in state courts. Federal district court rulings are published in the case reporters called the *Federal Supplement* (F.Supp.) and the *Federal Supplement Second* (F.Supp.2d).

Parties not satisfied with a ruling at the federal trial court level may appeal to the higher federal circuit courts of appeal. There are thirteen federal circuit courts in all, each circuit presiding over its own region of the United States:

1. **The First Circuit Court of Appeal** covers Maine, Massachusetts, New Hampshire, Puerto Rico, and Rhode Island.
2. **The Second Circuit Court of Appeal** covers Connecticut, New York, and Vermont.

3. **The Third Circuit Court of Appeal** covers Delaware, New Jersey, Pennsylvania, and the Virgin Islands.
4. **The Fourth Circuit Court of Appeal** covers Maryland, North Carolina, South Carolina, Virginia, and West Virginia.
5. **The Fifth Circuit Court of Appeal** covers Louisiana, Mississippi, and Texas.
6. **The Sixth Circuit Court of Appeal** covers Kentucky, Michigan, Ohio, and Tennessee.
7. **The Seventh Circuit Court of Appeal** covers Illinois, Indiana, and Wisconsin.
8. **The Eighth Circuit Court of Appeal** covers Arkansas, Iowa, Minnesota, Missouri, Nebraska, North Dakota, and South Dakota.
9. **The Ninth Circuit Court of Appeal** covers Alaska, Arizona, California, Guam, Hawaii, Idaho, Montana, Nevada, the Northern Mariana Islands, Oregon, and Washington.
10. **The Tenth Circuit Court of Appeal** covers Colorado, Kansas, New Mexico, Oklahoma, Utah, and Wyoming.
11. **The Eleventh Circuit Court of Appeal** covers Alabama, Florida, and Georgia.
12. **The District of Columbia Circuit** covers the District of Columbia.
13. **The Federal Circuit of Appeal** has nationwide jurisdiction in limited matters.

Decisions handed down from the thirteen circuit courts are published in three massive series: the *Federal Reporter* (F.), which includes federal decisions (trial and appellate) from 1880 to 1924; the *Federal Reporter Second* (F.2d), which includes federal appellate decisions from 1924 to 1993; and the *Federal Reporter Third* (F.3d), publishing cases from 1993 to present.

Parties not satisfied with a decision at the circuit level may petition the nation's highest court, the United States Supreme Court—though review is rarely granted (only about a hundred cases a year are accepted). The Supreme Court consists of nine justices. Decisions are settled by the majority of justices, and they are final, the end of the line for any appeal. Supreme Court decisions, furthermore, are of the highest interpretive authority, which means that all lower courts, state and federal, are bound to follow its precedents. Supreme Court decisions are published officially in the *United States Reports* (abbreviated "U.S.," as in *Turner v. Safley*, 482 U.S. 78 (1998)), and published weekly in the *United States Law Week* (U.S.L.W.). Unofficial reporters are the *Supreme Court Reporter* (S.Ct.) (by West Group), and the *Supreme Court Reporter, Lawyer's Edition* (L.Ed.) (by Lawyers Cooperative Publishing).

SECONDARY SOURCES OF LAW

Whereas primary sources of law lay down the letter of the law, secondary sources *describe* and *discuss* the law. Inmate researchers, due to reduced legal materials in prison law libraries, must, pragmatically, rely on secondary sources as their primary reference. Legal scholars would frown on the practice, but most prisoners really have no other choice. Still, secondary sources are universally easier to understand than primary sources, and many offer opinions that carry persuasive weight with judges. And although judges are bound to the letter of the law and court precedent, legal interpretations presented in secondary sources by specialists and scholars can offer lines of insight into legal obscurities where the letter of the law and existing court opinion are silent.

Law Dictionaries

Law dictionaries are an easy-to-use source of information on just about every legal subject, small and large, new and old. Your prison law library is likely to have law dictionaries, even if your state is one of those that has minimized its legal resources. Either *Black's Law Dictionary* or *Ballentine's Law Dictionary* ought to be available. Both provide for spelling of legal terms, pronunciation, definitions, and identify cases defining or using legal words and phrases. Both dictionaries also include summaries of legal canons and doctrines and other principles of law. Spending an afternoon leafing through a law dictionary is a good way to familiarize yourself with the legal fundamentals bearing on your case, and with how legal minds generally work.

Encyclopedias

Legal encyclopedias are essentially juiced up legal dictionaries. They do not cover the number of subjects found in a dictionary, but the subjects they do cover are discussed in far more detail and depth. The subjects are diverse and numerous, each with an article paraphrasing important fundamental points of its subject. Articles are generously footnoted with references to cases and other legal sources, and therefore are an excellent place for researchers to start work. National encyclopedias include the *Corpus Juris Secundum* (C.J.S.) (by West group) and the *American Jurisprudence Second* (Am. Jur. 2d) (by Lawyer's Cooperative Publishing). Legal encyclopedias are produced to cover the law of each state, as well.

A.L.R.s

Annotated law reporters (A.L.R.s) (e.g., *The American Law Reports*, by West Group) are juiced up encyclopedias. They are very, very useful to those looking to gain a working knowledge of an area of law quickly. A.L.R.s select a current legal issue, publish a leading case on the issue, then follow up with a scholarly article. A.L.R.s are a great source for research leads, and include annotations with useful info from sources all over the U.S.

Law Journals and Reviews

Law journals and reviews are usually published by law schools, written and edited by law students. *The Georgetown Law Journal* is a good example of a journal often circulated in prisons: it addresses many legal topics—from commonplace issues surrounding any criminal case, to prisoners' rights—summarizing the current state of law, and punctuating each of its conclusions with copious amounts of citations to controlling and recent cases.

Journals and reviews are sometimes available to prisoners at a discount price, and are otherwise invaluable to prisoners, rich or poor, for learning about current and recent cases. They are continually revised and printed multiple times a year, coming in paperback—advantageous for prisoners in institutions that ban hardbacks.

Treatises

Treatises are scholarly works published on a single or limited range of legal subjects. Each area of law possesses its own array of "authoritative" treatises. Finding them is easy; selecting a good one is not; most are expensive. Treatises come in the form of textbooks, hornbooks (books dealing with a single subject), and loose-leaf services (easily updatable pages in three-ring binders). A treatise provides detailed background and narrative explanations of its subjects, and supports its theories with footnotes indicating the primary and the secondary reference material used by the author in formulating his or her conclusions. Treatises are commonly updated with pocket parts (paperback supplements, stored under the back cover), supplemental publications, revisions, or replacement pages if the treatise is a loose-leaf service.

Legal Newspapers

Chasing the freshest news, legal newspapers offer readers up-to-date commentary on legal events, including what's happening with old and new legislation and court decisions. Some papers publish regionally, some nationally, some specialize. *Prisoner Legal News*, for example, is a handy monthly publication specializing in news impacting the incarcerated. It discusses recent events that may interest both convicted prisoners and pre-trial detainees, and is a great source for news affecting criminal as well as civil law. It's also a great source for prisoners looking to stay up on legal developments in the federal system and states other than their own. (Subscription info for the PLN is given under "Recommended Reading" in the APPENDIX section of this book.)

INMATE RESEARCH

Again, prison law libraries commonly do not stock everything needed to adequately prosecute a claim, and that is unfortunate. Many valid prisoner lawsuits are defeated not on their merits, but for technical missteps no untrained litigant could reasonably be expected to foresee. Insufficient resources are likely the cause. Nevertheless, information crucial to prevail in court *is* possible to gather—the spirit willing, a few research methods remain to the determined inmate.

Talk to a Legal-Beagle

You are not alone. Other prisoners have suffered unjustly, and have filed lawsuits. A little sleuthing around the housing unit may turn up an experienced jailhouse lawyer ("legal-beagle"). Beware the pretenders, however: many inmates have *some* experience with fighting their own legal battles, but only a few have sufficient knowledge of prisoner civil matters to offer advice without the risk of being misleading. If not on your unit, then a capable legal-beagle may be found elsewhere (check the law library; that's the usual hangout); the time spent enlisting this kind of help is worth the expense. Experienced legal-beagles know the directions in which to point you, can answer many practical questions not addressed in books, and probably have useful case law and legal treatises on hand.

State Law Library

Your state law library may be of help, as well. State law libraries are financed and operated by, you guessed it, state governments. Accordingly, their collections of resources are vast and comprehensive, containing all legal sources (save for jailhouse lawyers) and legal publications addressed in the above sections—and much, much more.

Your state law library, before providing services, probably requires prisoners to set up a library account and give a deposit. The deposit keeps the account alive and covers costs of processing requests, copies, and postage and mailing.

Sending a letter to (or otherwise arranging contact with) the state law library is the first step to establish an account. Ask about services for prisoners. If services are provided, and everything besides seems to check out, money from the prisoner's institutional account must then be transferred to the state law library, or the prisoner can arrange for free-world persons to deposit money with the library on his or her behalf.

The account established, requests for legal materials can be mailed to the law library at the prisoner's convenience. Generally, library employees make copies of whatever legal materials are asked for—cases, statutes, encyclopedia articles, etc. Vague requests produce something unwanted, but nevertheless paid for. When fishing for case law by letter correspondence, explain clearly the subject and the reason for a search and ask librarians to search a digest, and then to mail back their findings. Do *not* have them copy cases of their own choosing; even a single case can be expensive. Rather, request copies of the digest findings so you can select the case(s) deemed appropriate by you. Then send the state law library another letter listing your choice(s).

NOTE: Be aware that some state law library employees are more helpful than others (as is common with any personal service business). Some are no help at all. Whatever their disposition, always be polite in letters, and remember to thank these facilitators for their time and services (you know—flies and honey). Finally, some states no longer provide state law library services to prisoners at all. You are out of luck if that's the situation in your state.

Digests

Digests are publications designed to help researchers find case law. A digest is an index of case **headnotes** (an editor's summary of legal holdings in a court decision, added to the beginning of the published case), but not entire cases. Digests are topically and alphabetically organized, and are quite handy: simply look up a topic—say, "civil law" or "prisons"––then scan subtopics until narrowing the search to a collection of case headnotes addressing the desired subject.

Internet Research

The Internet, of course, is a great and ever-expanding source of information. The problem, however, is how reliable Internet info is, because law researchers must be able to trust their sources. Some Internet sites are accepted in the legal world as more reliable—and complete—than others, and are frequently used by legal professionals of all varieties. Notable sites are Westlaw (West Group), at www.westlaw.com, and LEXIS (Reed), at www.lexis.com. Other useful websites are www.findlaw.com, www.lawcrawler.com, and www.lectlaw.com, and www.scholar.google.com.

As a general rule, prisoners do not have access to the Internet; however, prisoners can arrange for friends or family to search the Internet on their behalf. (Some prisons do not allow inmates to do Internet research at all, even through free-world third parties. Disturbingly, some courts have upheld such policies as serving some "legitimate" government interest.) But, alas, even if Internet research *can* be managed, it is still prohibitively expensive, which is the major drawback to the otherwise most expedient method of legal research. Cost can be minimized by first determining, as much as possible, which reference materials are needed before entering a website—lengthy fishing expeditions are sure to quickly consume a prisoner's budget.

NOTE: A good method for finding pertinent authority is to get a single recent case dealing with the subject of your claim. In writing their opinions, judges usually detail—indeed, carefully enumerate—relevant sources of law and controlling precedent influencing their conclusions. Even cases not directly on point of your issue should at least provide a few citations to useful materials.

Family Research or Professional Research

If you are a prisoner lucky enough to have friends or family willing to help out, send a letter to see if they wouldn't mind doing a little legal research for you. Even a quick scan of the Internet, without logging onto expensive law sites, can uncover tons of useful info.

Prisoners with or without friend/family support can make use of a few small companies, some existing solely to assist prisoners, that are not only knowledgeable about common issues afflicting inmates and how to economically do research, but can mail thick packets of print media into prisons, where private sources may not.

Most prisons limit the amount of photocopies allowed a prisoner in any single mailing from a personal, nonbusiness address. Print media originating from a company, on the other hand, usually is permitted in larger quantities under policy allowing for the receipt of literature/books sent from publishers or other businesses. Packets of materials from businesses, law libraries, or legal organizations should not, therefore, be subject to a prison's five-photocopies-per-letter rule.

Prisoner-friendly research companies such as those described above, depending on the company, provide a number of services in addition to legal research. Many provide clerical services (such as converting handwritten papers into neatly typed documents), transcribe audio/video recordings, and perform general Internet searches of any topic. These services may include, say, finding a warden's home address, associations, business ventures, and *assets*—especially important data when it comes time in a lawsuit to calculate money damages.

E-mail is another service sometimes offered. Those who so offer will set up prisoner e-mail accounts through their own company, mail copies of e-mails addressed to account owners, and e-mail messages sent from the prisoner to the company for this purpose. This feature is useful for communicating with the world at large. Some people simply won't spend the time to respond to a prisoner's letter by snail mail, whereas they may respond via a convenient e-mail.

These services are, of course, not free, but prices are reasonable; these companies seem to appreciate that, as a rule, prisoners don't have much money. Some accept stamps and/or embossed stamped envelopes for payment.

How to hire a professional researcher? A good place to find service advertisements and current contact info is the *Prison Legal News* monthly newspaper. Hunt down the nearest legal-beagle to review a copy—it's a popular publication and easy to find in any prison. Or you can send a letter to *Prison Legal News*, P.O. Box 1151, Lake Worth, FL 33460, for subscription info.

Shepardizing

"Shepardizing" is a term that has come to mean, broadly, "researching the history and treatment of a case, statute, or administrative opinion."

Originally the term "Shepard's" referred only to the publications called *Shepard's Citations*, which complement, update, and supplement information regarding the cases contained in companion reporters and other types of legal publications. *Shepard's Citations* come in series sets of volumes that give information about cases, statutes, or administrative decisions and regulations published in a corresponding publication. A state's court of appeals case reporter, for example, would be found on a law library's shelves next to its companion volumes of *Shepard's Citations*.

Case citations to the appellate case reporter are listed in the *Shepard's Citations* in the barest citation form (e.g., *456 Idaho 34*—which means volume 456 of the *Idaho Reporter* at page 34, where the case begins). Directly under the bare citation are listed in column form a number of additional bare case citations to cases that discuss or interpret or apply the holdings in the case under which they have been placed in the *Shepard's Citations*. Each citation in the list includes codes that indicate that particular case's **history** (that is, what happened to this case on appeal) and how it treats the case being shepardized. The term **treatment** refers to whether holdings in the shepardized case have been followed, disregarded, criticized, distinguished, harmonized, or overruled.

A prison is not likely to supply *Shepard's Citations* for any of the legal materials it provides, but look around the resource center, anyway. Should a prison have *Shepard's Citations*, don't worry if you don't understand their use and utility based on the description herein. *Shepard's Citations* come with instructions, each series with a key or a booklet demonstrating and explaining exactly how and why case citations are given, how codes are assigned, and what the codes mean.

Under the broader definition of "shepardizing," any case you intend to rely on must be checked for history and treatment; to build a case around legal perceptions that are no longer valid would be most unfortunate. Luckily, even if *Shepard's Citations* are unavailable, the history and treatment of cases, statutes, orders and regulations can speedily be verified through the Internet on LEXIS, by way of "Lexcite," or Westlaw, by way of "Keycite."

Send a list of case citations to your state law library (provided you have a library account), your support on the street, or professionals hired to help with research, asking them to Lexcite or Keycite or otherwise shepardize the cases. Remember that using law websites is costly—choose wisely the cases for shepardizing in this fashion.

If shepardizing by website, a case in question will turn up a list of positive and/or negative cases (or other sources beside cases, such as articles and statutes) that impact or refer to the shepardized case in some way. Similar, though different, to *Shepard's Citations*, pertinent cases are individually ascribed codes or symbols that convey information about their relevance to the case shepardized. Major companies providing such shepardizing services offer easily understood instructions for using their systems, systems that are themselves simplified for the user. For example, Westlaw's Keycite feature organizes cases by how they relate to the case shepardized. Negative cases—which dispute, disregard, or overturn one or more of the shepardized case's holdings—are sensibly listed under the heading "Negative Cases." Under the heading "Positive Cases" are cited cases implementing or adopting the views expressed by the court in the shepardized case. Each case citation, under either heading, is given symbols to indicate its own treatment and to what degree it discusses the case shepardized. For instance, a red flag "▶" means at least one point among the case's holdings has been reversed or overruled. A yellow flag "▷" means *caution*, because the case may be called into question or pending legislation may affect its validity on at least one substantive point. Stars "★ ★ ★ ★ " indicate how extensively the case discusses the shepardized case—4 stars means *examined*, 3 stars means *discussed*, 2 stars means *cited*, and 1 star means *mentioned*.

Again, tracking the treatment and the history of your legal sources is a necessary burden. Set aside some money and figure out a way to get your important cases shepardized, whether through friends or family, professionals, law libraries, or however it can be managed. It must be done. Should a case of interest receive a Keycite red flag—or a red flag equivalent in other shepardizing forums—you must acquire the negative case(s) overturning the case you'd planned to use. Such negative cases may enlighten you as to the probability of prevailing in the prosecution of your claim.

NOTES: _____

NOTES: _____

_____

_____

_____

_____

_____

_____

_____

_____

_____

_____

_____

_____

_____

_____

_____

_____

_____

_____

_____

_____

_____

_____

_____

_____

_____

_____

_____

_____

_____

_____

_____

_____

_____

_____

_____

_____

_____

_____

CHAPTER 6:
LEGAL ANALYSIS

Once you have a solid notion of the type of legal problem(s) you're facing and where to find corresponding law, you then must make a legal analysis to determine how the current state of law impacts your claims.

Legal analysis involves a careful, logical process of reading—and understanding—controlling legal sources *individually*, deciding how each of those sources complements others, and then reasoning how those sources combine to *state the law*. Legal analysis may be difficult for novices at first, but as a prisoner becomes familiar with how the law is written, and how the legal minds conjuring it up are thinking, with time, it becomes easier.

But of course, legal analyses require comprehension of legal sources, and the reader should be aware of the fact that all legal writings are not cut of the same cloth. Of the many sources of law, there emerge two distinct forms of legal writing, and neither is defined so much by its source as by what it *does*.

The first form—**legislative form**—is written to direct future conduct, prescribing what can and cannot be done under the law. This includes writings from all three branches of the government, including statutes, executive regulations and orders, and court rules. The second form of writing—**adjudicative form**—applies existing legal principles and laws to past conduct, or, rather, to the facts of a case under consideration. Adjudicative writings do not direct conduct, but establish whether past conduct was lawful or not (essentially the same as interpretive law, discussed previously). Both the executive and the judicial branches of government issue adjudicative writings, and sometimes, in special circumstances, the legislature will also have cause to do the same—in making findings of fact and conclusions of law as to whether it has become necessary to impeach a U.S. President, for example.

There are basic rules to observe when interpreting both legislative and adjudicative writing.

Interpreting Legislative Writings

Soon after starting research, you will notice that every statute and most executive orders and administrative regulations are written in consistent and generic patterns. Pay attention to this structure—beginning, middle, and end, and how all the pieces are put together. Awareness of how laws are written will provide a sense of direction when wading through lengthy writings, without wasting too much time searching back and forth through the material.

Legislative writings start with the title; the title provides information about the authors' intention in creating the law. *Pennsylvania Dep't of Corr. v. Yeskey*, 524 U.S. 206, 212 (1998) (indicating that although title of a statute cannot limit the statute's plain meaning, it can clear up otherwise ambiguous language). After the title comes the **preamble**, which is a statement by the authors that describes what the law is and what it's for, and will often contain a summary of what the law requires, permits, or prohibits. The preamble is followed by the main body of the law, the "language of the law" itself. This is the actual word of law.

Often the statute or executive order or regulation will be annotated, directing the reader to case law that interprets specific portions of the law, and to other cross-reference materials. Pay attention to the annotation (either in the main body of the writing or in the footnotes) that refers you to other statutes, orders, or regulations; one piece of legislative writing may depend on another for meaning (such as in defining words), or have exemptions and/or restrictions enumerated in *other* statutes or regulations.

Finally, you can find federal legislative history (early bill versions, committee and house debates, presidential actions) published in the U.S.C., U.S.C.A., and U.S.C.S. (historical data), among many other publications. State legislative history will be published as well. (Finding legislative history is an excellent task for your friends/family to do on the Internet.)

Construction

When reading legislative writings, ask yourself:

1. **What is the plain language of the law?** (Law directs conduct—what is the law telling you to do or not to do?)
2. **What are the specific definitions of operative words used by the drafters?** (In legal writing, some seemingly plain words and phrases take on subtle connotations in meaning that can alter the essence of the entire writing. So beware, and perhaps checkout a law dictionary from your prison law library.)
3. **What is the legislation *not* saying?** (Have certain subjects, definitions, limitations, time lines, etc., been omitted? If so, it was for a reason.)
4. **How is the language in a portion of the legislation used with respect to the rest of the writing, or in other statutes and regulations?** (Often, an ambiguous provision can be cleared up by reading it in light of other, related sections.)
5. **How do executive rules and regulations interpret the statute?** (How is the law being enforced?)
6. **What is the legislative history and intent?** (Simply, why did the drafters create the law in the first place? Is it being used for that reason? Consider the answers you've received from answering question No. 5, above.)

Pay attention to modal and auxiliary verbs, as well. Deceptively simple, these terms are routinely used without any qualifying explanation or obvious indication as to their heightened value in legal writing, and they are easy to overlook, too. For example, the words "shall," "must," and "will" express the authors' intention that the section be strictly adhered to (which is called *mandatory* or *imperative* language). *Salahuddin v. Mead*, 174 F.3d 271 (2nd Cir. 1999) ; *U.S. v. Myers*, 106 F.3d 936 (10th Cir. 1997) (it is a basic canon of statutory construction that the word "shall" indicates mandatory intent). For example, the *Prisoner Litigation Reform Act* states: "No action *shall* be brought with respect to prison conditions . . . by a prisoner confined in any jail, prison, or other correctional facility until such administrative remedies as are available are exhausted." 42 U.S.C. § 1997(e)(a) (emphasis added). (So, by the operative word "shall," all administrative remedies had better be exhausted before filing an action.) The words "may," "should," and "can" indicate that the directive of the provision is propositional, not mandatory (of *discretionary* or *permissive* language).

Canons of Statutory Construction

The Canons of Statutory Construction are rules followed by the legislature when creating law. The idea is that universally adopted modes for writing laws will lead to consistent interpretation.

Generally speaking:

1. **Statutes (and regulations) concerning criminal matters, licensing, or that are in derogation of the common law, must not be construed beyond their plain language.** For example, the Seventh Circuit Court of Appeals held that the PLRA provision that bars prisoners from bringing suit for mental or emotional injury without a prior showing of physical injury did not apply to a suit filed by an inmate *after* he was released on parole. *Kerr v. Puckett*, 138 F.3d 321 (7th Cir. 1998). Strictly speaking, "[n]o action shall be brought with respect to prison conditions . . . by a prisoner *confined* in any jail, prison, or other correctional facility. . . ." 42 U.S.C. § 1997(e)(a) (emphasis added). The plain language is clear—for the PLRA to apply, the person who files a complaint must actually be in prison or jail. To construe § 1997(e)(a) to apply to claims arising from prison conditions, but where the injured person has been released from custody, would be an impermissible expansion of the PLRA's scope.

2. **The rule of construction *expressio unis est exclusio alternus* (expression of one context requires denial of other contexts) suggests that for the legislature to express or include one thing implies the exclusion of another, or of the alternative.** For example, the rule that a "prisoner confined in any jail, prison, or other correctional facility" suggests that free citizens are not bound by the provisions of the PLRA. Another example is the U.S. law providing that "each citizen is entitled to vote," implying that non-citizens are not entitled to vote.

3. **The rule of construction *in pari materia* (related to the same subject) provides that statutes should be consistently interpreted when dealing with similar subject matter.**

4. **The rule of construction *Noscitur a sociis* ("it is known by its associates") requires that the meaning of an unclear word or phrase be interpreted by the words immediately surrounding it.**

5. **The rule of construction *ejusdem generis* (of the same kind or class) requires that when a word or phrase of general meaning follows a list of specifics, then the general word or phrase should be interpreted to include only items of the same type as those listed.** For example, *carrots, radishes, and other products*, would indicate that the catchall phrase—"and other products"—applies only to items of the same class. Vegetables, in this case.

Interpreting Adjudicative Writings

Like statutes, court and administrative decisions are written with a uniform structure. Administrative and court decisions start, at the head of the first page, with a caption containing the document's abbreviated citation form (e.g., *Spear v. Sowders*, 71 F.3d 626 (6th Cir. 1995)), followed by the full, unabbreviated citation information. This information includes the full name of each party involved in the case, the date the case was decided, the name of the administrative agency or of the court and the judges or justices presiding over the matter, which judge wrote the opinion, and whether there is a dissenting (disagreeing) opinion following the majority opinion.

An editor-prepared syllabus then follows, which summarizes the background and the holdings in the case. (Note that the syllabus and other headnotes are not written by the court deciding the case; they are written by an editor in order for readers to quickly assess the court holdings. Don't quote the syllabus and headnotes, as they are not the official opinion.) Following the syllabus is the actual opinion written by a judge or judges.

The senior judge or senior judge voting with the majority on the case assigns one member of the panel to write the opinion. A *per curiam* **opinion** means the decision represents the opinion of the entire panel without specifying an authoring judge. More often, an opinion is signed by the authoring judge, and by the others voting in the majority.

Court opinions start with a summary description of the facts that surround the issue, including also a summary of the procedural history (when and before which courts the matter had previously been heard). The court will state the question(s) of law examined in the opinion, and following that will be a complex analysis of the issue(s). Then the final opinion of the court is given.

Occasionally, judges elect to include additional thoughts not included in the main section of the majority opinion. Such **concurring opinions** emphasize *different* arguments in support of the same, majority decision. Merely another avenue for reaching the same conclusions. Judges voting in the minority (disagreeing with the majority of the judges on the panel) may add their **dissenting opinions**, following the concurring opinions. Dissenting opinions do not create binding precedent, but can provide a window into the mind of the entire court, shedding light on the issue in question beyond the language of the majority opinion. You can quote a dissenting opinion as persuasive authority, but not binding authority—if citing, remember to include a "dissenting opinion" citation signal. (The use of citation signals is discussed below.)

All appellate courts have methods for excluding cases from publication that raise no new issue of law or clear error of law. This is done to avoid publishing multiple cases stating substantially the same thing. So it follows that if an appellate decision *is* published, it indicates a change in the law, such as (1) a new common law, (2) a new interpretation of law, (3) a new application of law, or (4) a restating of old law due for a modern reiteration.

Take your time when reading adjudicative writings; make sure you understand them. Keep in mind that the logic applying to the construction and the interpretation of legislative writings already discussed in the "Canons of Construction" section, above, relates, also, to how courts go about writing their opinions. Proper prudence dictates that a court—though permitted to use colorful or expressive language, unlike with statutes—remain cautious of what is said in an opinion, and *how* it's said. One should not presume that a court would arbitrarily and capriciously render an opinion. The same rationale applies to decisions made by administrators.

Therefore, when reading interpretive law, ask yourself:

1. What is the question of law, and how was it answered?
2. What are the specific definitions of operative words or technical terms used by the author?
3. What is the administration or the court *not* saying?
4. How have other administrators or courts interpreted the opinion?
5. How has the opinion been treated by other administrators or courts in other cases?

THE PECKING ORDER OF LEGAL AUTHORITY

In our system of laws and governments, there exists a hierarchy controlling whose directives should be obeyed over others. Exactly how the authority of the different parts of government are divided up is not always clear. But there are a few broad, easily-recognizable distinctions.

Legislative

Almost holy writ, the U.S. Constitution is the highest legal authority in the United States of America. Nothing trumps the Constitution. Under that, federal statutes reign. (But remember, the federal government only has jurisdiction in certain areas such as interstate commerce and interstate travel, limited penal matters, things managed on behalf of all the states (e.g., federal taxation, immigration, and naturalization), international matters (e.g., waging war, foreign relations, etc.), and, of course, in guaranteeing those fundamental rights retained by the people, rights flowing from The Bill of Rights. However, the federal legislature has, from time to time, imposed on the states, through Congress's spending clause of the U.S. Constitution, statutes expanding the civil liberties of the people, laws that the states must follow if they would like to receive federal money for state programs.

Continuing down the line, under the federal statute is the state constitution, followed by the state statute. (Remember, any power not specifically granted to the federal government in the U.S. Constitution remains with the states, or with the people. And state governments have almost exclusive domain over matters of criminal law, torts, contract law, trusts, property law, corporations and partnerships, etc.)

Should there arise a conflict between state and federal law, then pursuant to the Supremacy Clause of the U.S. Constitution, federal law trumps state law. *Boomer v. AT&T Corp.*, 309 F.3d 404 (7th Cir. 2002) ; *Ace Auto Body & Towing Ltd. v. City of New York*, 171 F.3d 765 (2nd Cir. 1999); *Broad v. Sealaska Corp.*, 85 F.3d 422 (9th Cir. 1996). However, should they find themselves interpreting state law, federal courts are bound to accept the interpretation of a state's law by the highest court of that state. *Hillside Enterprises, Inc., v. Continental Carlisle, Inc.*, 147 F.3d 732 (8th Cir. 1998) . So, if the state Supreme Court defines what a state law means, so long as it doesn't impinge on any federal laws, even the U.S. Supreme Court will be required to defer to that opinion.

Regulations

Federal rules and regulations that control an executive or an administrative department are promulgated under the authority the Federal Administrative Procedure Act (5 U.S.C. § 551, *et seq.*) and the statute creating and defining the purpose of the executive department itself. Therefore, rules and regulations have the force and the effect of their parent statutes, though they may not be extended beyond the statutes' scope. Where a state law conflicts with a federal regulation, the federal regulation has authority (it is, after all, an extension of a federal statute). Where a federal regulation is in conflict with a federal statute, the statute has authority (this is a generality; however, there are exceptions).

The same logic goes for state regulations, on their own state level. And when a state regulation is in conflict with federal law, federal law wins.

The Courts

Unless a law is deemed unconstitutional or otherwise unlawful, all courts are bound to uphold every law in the U.S. of A. Further, a court is required, whenever possible, to give force to each word in every statute and constitutional provision, and to resolve conflicting laws in favor of legislative intent, that the spirit of these laws be upheld.

On *federal* matters, the Supreme Court of the United States is the highest judicial authority, followed by the circuit courts of appeals, followed by the federal district courts. The circuits, though bound only by the precedent of the Supreme Court, must give due consideration to the opinions originating in the other circuits, and seek to resolve conflicting authority whenever possible. District courts are bound by the precedent of the appeals circuit (there are 13 separate federal appeals circuits, dividing and having jurisdiction over specific regions of the U.S.), but must follow the precedent of the circuit appellate court directly above them when conflicting opinions occur among the circuits.

District courts are further subdivided into two parts: the Federal District Court and the Federal Magistrates Court. The magistrate court is under the district court.

Each state has a similar pecking order in their own court systems, and follow similar rules. The highest state court is the highest authority on state law; all lower state courts are bound by its precedent. Yet even the opinion of the *highest* state court can be overturned by the *lowest* federal court, on federal questions.

NOTE: In practice, the order of authority regarding judicial precedent is not so clear-cut as described here. Often, federal and state questions overlap, and it can be quite difficult to make heads or tails as to which authority controls. To further confuse the issue, federal courts often defer to state precedent and state law. For example, a federal court will generally refer "to state law for tolling rules [suspending, for good cause, the time limit for pursuing a legal matter] . . . [as well as] for the length of statutes of limitation." *Wallace v. Kato*, 549 U.S. 384, 394 (2007).

Muddling the issue further, if you've found a federal case within your circuit of appeals that discusses a case *not* from your state—yet seemingly directly on point of one of your issues—do *not* presume the opinion to hold sway in your state. When federal courts review and interpret the law of a state, they view this law through a lens of jurisprudence (science of law) developed in *that* state. Suppose you find a Ninth Circuit Court of Appeals case that struck down an Arizona law as unconstitutional. Now, your state, let's say Washington, is in the same circuit as Arizona and has a law very similar, if not identical, in language on its books. The law in Washington then *may be questionable*, in light of Arizona's law being held unconstitutional, but don't presume it to be unconstitutional without first researching the question thoroughly by the law of your own state, because Washington may use and interpret its version of the law with a slight difference, different enough so that the Washington's law passes constitutional muster where Arizona's law did not.

ANALYSIS

Harmonizing Your Sources

Once the preliminary research is completed, what do all your references say? A pattern should emerge from the gathered source material. If you've discovered conflicting sources, authority from higher up in the legal pecking order supersedes that of the lower. If conflicting sources are on the same level of authority—say, differing interpretations of a law by the same court but from separate cases—search for the commonalities between opinions. On which points do they agree? Also, look for what both cases *do not* say. Between what is agreed on and that which can be gleaned by what is not mentioned in either case, you should be able to compose a fair argument for the overall state of law by emphasizing similarities between the cases. The overall state of law may not be apparent at first glance, however. Sometimes a bit of logical gymnastics becomes necessary when synthesizing legal sources into a cohesive interpretation.

NOTE: Carefully contemplate opposing rationale and plausible legal interpretations that dispute your lawsuit's position. You'll find portions of a law—sometimes even in the same piece of law—that are favorable to your cause, and portions that are not. Unfavorable aspects are likely to found part of your adversary's opposing arguments. You must explain to the court, in detail, why such an unfavorable interpretation doesn't apply in your case. In addition, you should explain why the favorable portions of a law are the strongest basis for a final court ruling. Moreover, even if you possess case law that wonderfully demonstrates the validity of an argument, which seemingly settles on your side all questions of law, still look at what the case does not mention or seems to skip over; a good lawyer can tease out of a judicial holding at least one theory for why the believed-to-be favorable case should not actually be applied in your situation. While in the early process of preparing a lawsuit, try viewing the facts and the law at issue through the eyes of your adversary. Try to uncover ways to dispute or disprove your own claims, and always question your conclusions. A trustworthy legal-beagle may be able to provide an objective insight in this regard.

Plainly Stating a Clear-Cut Point of Law

A complex analysis of the law is not always needed to make a persuasive argument, especially if the subject is peripheral to a larger question, or if it simply states the obvious. Sometimes the application/function of a law *is* crystal clear, and an uncomplicated reference by a brief citation, perhaps accompanied by a small quotation from the law/case, will suffice to support a conclusion—still, it is not recommended that you neglect marginal issues. Should you find a case from another court with jurisdiction comparable to the court hearing your case, and which says substantially the same thing that you want to persuade your judge of, then analogize its logic to the circumstances surrounding your case, telling the judge you should prevail for the same reasons articulated in the previous case. However, for prisoners with meager legal resources, it may not be possible to find a case *exactly* on point of law and of fact to a case such as yours. In that event, a prisoner's recourse is to perform a more complex synthesis of the sources that are available, making the best interpretation. And, if you locate a case that is similar to yours but not right on, you must supply an argument to bridge the gaps in order to construe the existing conclusion of law in your favor.

Negative Case Law

If you repeatedly run into case law that seems to oppose your theories, you will have to distinguish the substantive facts in those cases from the facts in yours. Then, you must reason why those negative cases—with the same law that is applicable in your case—resulted as they did, and argue that the law is favorable to your opinion of the controversy because of the uniqueness of your case's underlying facts. In other words, you must show the court why the law actually leans in your favor, even though it did not support seemingly similar previous cases. This is a tricky argument to make.

Arguing for a Change in the Law

If your desired conclusion is unsupported by current law, you can nevertheless argue for a change in the present interpretation of law, that the law should be changed to agree with a recent *trend in the law*. This type of argument borrows a trajectory of rationale from a different, though related, area of law. For example, although recent judicial interpretations seem to increasingly diminish prisoners' rights to, say, nutritious meals, prisoners may nevertheless overcome this negative trend by finding logic sympathetic to prisoners' causes within existing laws concerning, say, dietary minimums for public-school lunches or military chow, which ponder the question of how much nutritional value should justifiably be borne on the government's dollar.

Arguing for a change in the law is tantamount to arguing that society is changing for the better, as exhibited in recent legal trends; and that, in the interests of fairness and justice, the old law must be retired because it is no longer useful, or has become harmful in modern applications. Such an argument is difficult to make—an uphill battle—made on legal as well as broader philosophical grounds of societal interest, and each element of constructive logic must be based on concrete evidence. Research is necessary. Statistics, also—in which case, the services of an expert to perform and analyze a survey might be crucial. And your reasoning must be strong. If you must, crack open a book of philosophy from the prison library; a sound bit of philosophy, even if seemingly not *compelling* a specific interpretation of a particular law, can oftentimes be argued as having broader or universal applications that extend to persuasively support your new legal theory.

NOTES: _____

_____

_____

_____

_____

_____

_____

_____

_____

_____

_____

_____

_____

_____

_____

_____

_____

_____

_____

_____

_____

_____

_____

_____

_____

_____

_____

_____

_____

_____

_____

_____

_____

_____

_____

_____

_____

_____

_____

_____

NOTES: _____

NOTES: _____

PART 2:
ENGLISH & LEGAL WRITING

CHAPTER 7:
QUICK ENGLISH REFRESHER

By its nature, legal work involves lots and lots of writing, from research notes and case summaries to formal correspondence and legal papers. And while you don't have to be an English professor to prosecute a lawsuit, you should make an effort to write as correctly and *clearly* as you are able. Punctuation and grammatical errors can be forgiven, though they annoy and may cause readers to lose respect for the writer. Diluted or underdeveloped or confused ideas (usually caused by poor or lazy composition) can lose a lawsuit.

Prisoners considering filing a civil complaint, who are in the process of assessing their rights and claims, can skip over this chapter. When it comes time to put pen to paper, though, return to this chapter for a thorough read.

SPELLING AND GRAMMAR

The Parts of Language

Vowels are "a, e, i, o, u," and sometimes "y." **Consonants** are every other letter in the English alphabet. **Syllables** are units of pronunciation within a word that have one vowel sound (e.g. i*n-mate*, two syllables; *gua*rd, one syllable). A **noun** is a person, place, or thing (e.g., *bartender, home, book*). **Pronouns** are words used as a substitute for nouns (e.g., *it, them, she*). **Proper nouns** are names and tiles. **Verbs** describe an action, state, or occurrence (e.g., *write, writing, and written*). An **adverb** is a word or a phrase (a short combination of words) that modifies a verb by providing it a sense of place, time, circumstance, manner, cause, degree, etc. (e.g., *gently, thoroughly, slightly, then, there,* and *where*). An **adjective** is a word or a phrase describing an attribute, added to or grammatically related to a noun to modify or describe it (e.g., "brown" in *a brown house*; "silly" in *silly dog*). **Prepositions** connect nouns or pronouns to other words or elements within a clause (e.g., *the creamer* in *the coffee*; *an envelope traded* for *a ramen*; *a ramen confiscated* by *a guard*). **Conjunctions** connect clauses to other clauses or sentences (e.g., *and, but, if, for, because—I would go,* but *he offered to go first*).

The Parts of a Sentence

A **phrase** is two or more words linked together in sense and regarded as a single conceptual unit, which is to say that a phrase acts like a noun, an adjective, a verb, or an adverb. *"He was talking of politics and economy,"* is an example of a sentence containing a group of words that act together as an adverb modifying the word "talking." The phrase "of politics and economy" serves as a single unit of meaning that explains what "He" was talking about. The first part of the sentence, "He was talking," is not a phrase, because it has both a subject (the pronoun *he*) and a verb (*talking*). For a group of words to be defined as a phrase, the group must not contain both subject and verb—notice that "of politics and economy" has neither subject nor verb. A group of words such as "He was talking," having subject and verb, is called a **clause**. *Words* by themselves, *phrases* without subject or verb or both, and *clauses* with their verbs and subjects, are used together in innumerable combinations to create sentences.

A **sentence** is a set of words—words, phrases, clauses—developing an idea in a statement, question, exclamation, or command. An idea is completed when a sentence consists of a subject and a predicate. A **subject** (noun or pronoun) is what a sentence is about—the subject is described as doing or not doing something, or is described to be in a particular state. The **predicate**, which usually follows the subject, is the sentence part containing a verb and stating something about the subject. Most predicates consist of a verb and a direct object. The **direct object** (also a noun or a pronoun) receives the action of the verb; that is, it is that at which the verb is aimed. In standard English form, the majority of sentences proceed from subject to verb, then to direct object (though a predicate need not contain an object):

We gave the warden our grievances.

The idea in the example is stated in a simple sentence expressing that the subject (the pronoun "We") did something (the verb "gave") with the direct object (the noun "grievances"). The words "gave the warden our grievances" form the predicate of the subject. (Notice, too, that the noun "warden" also receives the action of the verb "gave." The warden, therefore, is also an object of the verb, and yet is not a direct object. The warden, rather, is what is called an **indirect object** because the warden is not the *primary* recipient of the verb: the subject "We" did not *gave* the warden; it *gave* the grievances.) The example statement is called a **simple sentence** because it contains only one subject and one verb (though either subject or verb, or both, can be compound—containing more than one subject and/or more than one verb—and the sentence still be considered simple).

A simple sentence is also an independent clause. Since all **independent clauses** consist of a subject and its predicate, all independent clauses can be written as simple sentences; however, all sentences are not simple sentences, and not all sentences include only independent clauses.

Specifically, there are four types of sentences: simple (already discussed), compound, complex, and compound-complex. **Compound sentences** consist of two or more independent clauses, but do not include any subordinate clauses. A **subordinate clause** (also called a **dependent clause**), as with every clause, consists of a subject and a predicate; but, unlike independent clauses, it cannot stand on its own as a sentence, because it is reliant upon another clause in a sentence to complete its meaning.

We gave the warden our grievances, and he seemed affable and receptive to our concerns.

The above sentence is compound—two independent clauses joined by a comma and the conjunction "and"—because each clause, if separated at the conjunction, could stand alone to express a complete idea in itself.

We gave the warden our grievances. He seemed affable and receptive to our concerns.

However, if one of the clauses would not make sense if it were separated from the rest of the sentence, then that clause is not independent, but subordinate.

If one or more subordinate clauses are combined with *one* independent clause, the sentence is not called compound; it is called a **complex sentence**:

The warden appeared to be a little distracted, his eyes and feet shifting anxiously.

The example's first clause, preceding the comma, is independent because it makes sense on its own. The second clause—"his eyes and feet shifting anxiously," which contains the compound subject "his eyes and feet" and predicate "shifting anxiously" (which is an example of a predicate without a direct object)—would make no sense if not connected to the first clause. It is subordinate, being dependent on the independent clause to complete its meaning.

The final sentence type is the **compound-complex sentence**. A sentence is compound-complex if it consists of two or more independent clauses *and* at least one subordinate clause:

> *Chow would be called soon, and I assumed he intended to finish his unit business and be off before the corridors filled with hungry inmates in transit.*

The clauses "Chow would be called soon" and "I assumed he intended to finish his unit business and be off" are both independent; each could stand alone as a complete sentence. The clause "before the corridors filled with hungry inmates in transit" could not stand alone; it is dependent on the second independent clause to justify its construction: to explain why the warden seems anxious to leave the unit.

Basic Spelling Rules

There are six easily remembered rules for spelling:

1. The general rule is that *i* comes before *e* except when they come after *c* and have a long *eee* sound, or when *i* and *e* are pronounced in the long *a* sound (e.g., long *e*: *perceive*; long *a*: *weight*; *i* before *e*: *grievance*). However, this rule has numerous exceptions (e.g., *either, sleight, sovereign*, etc.).

2. When a word ends in a *y* that is preceded by a consonant, the rule is to change the *y* to *i* when a suffix is added, unless the suffix begins with *i* (as in *ing*) (e.g., *lazy + ness = laziness*; *bully + ing = bullying*). The rule does not apply to words ending with a *y* that is preceded by a vowel (e.g., *attorneys, obeying, essays*).

3. Words ending with the silent *e* usually drop the *e* before a suffix beginning with a vowel (e.g., *divide + ing = dividing*; *fortune + ate = fortunate*; *negate + ive = negative*). Exceptions to this rule are (1) words that contain the soft sounds of *g* or *c,* which retain the *e* before the suffix "able" or "ous" (e.g., *peace + able = peaceable*; *courage + ous = courageous*); (2) words retaining the *e* if they can be mistaken for another word (e.g., *dye + ing = dyeing*); and (3) words ending in *ie* that drop the *e* and change the *i* to *y* when the suffix "ing" is added (e.g., *die + ing = dying*).

4. The silent *e* at the end of a word usually remains before a suffix beginning with a consonant (e.g., *forgive + ness = forgiveness*; *safe + ty = safety*). However, there are numerous exceptions to the rule (e.g., *argue* to *argument, whole* to *wholly*, etc.).

5. One-syllable words that end in one consonant that is preceded by one vowel must double their ending consonant when a suffix beginning with a vowel is added (e.g., *big + est = biggest*; *hot + er = hotter*). However, this rule does not apply to words ending in two consonants, or to words ending in one consonant that is preceded by two vowels (e.g., two consonants: *yard + age = yardage*; two vowels before final consonant: *swear + ing = swearing*).

6. If a word of two or more syllables that ends with one consonant preceded by one vowel is pronounced with stress on its ending syllable, then the ending consonant is doubled before adding a suffix beginning with a vowel (e.g., *defer + ing = deferring*; *regret +*

able = regrettable; accent not on last syllable: *benefit + ed = benefited*.) This rule does not apply to words ending in two consonants, or to words where the ending consonant is preceded by two vowels, or to words that shift their stress from the ending syllable when the suffix is added (e.g., two consonants: *reform + ing = reforming*; two vowels: *appeal + ing = appealing*; accent shifts: *refer + ence = reference*).

Forming Plurals of Nouns

Forming plurals of nouns is a simple matter, described as follows:

1. An *s* is used to form plurals of most nouns and proper nouns (e.g., *dogs, papers, Smiths*). Nouns ending in a *y* preceded by a consonant change the *y* to an *i* before adding the *es* (e.g., *century* to *centuries*); but the *y* remains if preceded by a vowel (e.g., *stays, plays, valleys*).

2. Nouns and proper nouns ending in *ch*, *sh*, *ss*, *s*, *x*, or *z* are pluralized by adding *es* (e.g., *marches, boxes, Joneses*).

3. Nouns ending in *f*, *ff*, or *fe* are pluralized by adding an *s* (e.g., *chefs, safes, wharfs*). Many words with these endings, however, drop the *f* in exchange for a *v* before the *es* is added (e.g., *wolf* to *wolves*, *dwarf* to *dwarves*, *life* to *lives*).

4. When a word ends in an *o* that is preceded by a vowel, the rule is to pluralize the word by adding *s* (e.g., *studios, ratios, pistachios*), unless the *o* is preceded by a consonant, in which case *es* is added (e.g., *tomatoes, echoes, heroes*).

5. Pluralizing compound nouns (nouns created by combining two or more words) is a little trickier. Compound nouns are pluralized by adding an *s* or an *es* to the important part of the compound. For example, "brothers" in *brothers-in-law* is the most important word in the compound; it is not correct to say "brother-in-laws." An *s* or an *es* is always placed at the end, however, when compounds end in *ful* (e.g., *bucketfuls, handfuls, mouthfuls*), or when the words of the compound are of equal importance (e.g., *bathrobes, shirtsleeves, clotheslines*).

6. Some nouns are pluralized not by adding an *s* or *es,* but by changing their spelling (e.g., *man* to *men*, *louse* to *lice*, *cactus* to *cacti*); and some nouns have the same spelling in both singular and plural forms (e.g., *deer, fish, corps*).

Forming Possessives

Forming possessives is just as simple as forming plurals:

1. Singular nouns and proper nouns are made possessive by adding an apostrophe (') and an *s* (e.g., *woman's, child's, Santa Claus's*). Plural nouns and proper nouns ending in an *s* add only the apostrophe (e.g., *wolves', elves', Joneses'*—The Joneses' *family company is doing well*). But plural nouns and proper nouns not ending in an *s* are given both the apostrophe and the *s* (e.g., *sheep's, fish's, deer's*).

2. Apostrophes are not given to form the possessives of personal pronouns (e.g., *my* to *mine*, *your* to *yours*, *who* to *whose*, *it* to *its*) (note: "it's," with an apostrophe, is a contraction of *it is*, not the possessive of *it*). Indefinite pronouns do, however, get an apostrophe and an *s* (e.g., *someone's, everybody's, anyone's*).

3. Compound words, regardless of which of their parts are plural, are given the possessive form by adding the apostrophe and *s* at their ends (e.g., *brothers-in-law's, passersby's, rubbernecker's*).

Capitalization

Words are capitalized by the following rules:

1. The first letter of the first word of a sentence or direct quotation is usually capitalized:

   Ramens are the staple of the prison commissary diet. (Narrative sentence.)
   He said, "The commissary staple is ramen noodles." (Sentence with direct quotation.)

2. Capitalize the names or the titles of places, persons, literature, works of art, films, musical pieces, events, particular things (e.g., awards, monuments, memorials), calendar events, and vehicles/vessels (e.g., planes, ships, trains):

   Thomas Jefferson (name), America (place), *A Man in Full* (novel, by Tom Wolfe), the *Mona Lisa* (painting), *Ghost Busters* (film), "Schism" (song, by Tool), World War II (event), Lincoln Memorial (particular thing), Sunday and October and Labor Day (calendar events), and the *Titanic* (ship).

   Do not capitalize words that follow, or are a substitute for, a person's name, unless the title is that of a national government's head or that of a person attributed a special respect. And do not capitalize prepositions or other unimportant words in a title unless they start or end the title, or are of five or more letters:

   President Thomas Jefferson (nation's head); *Thomas Jefferson, President* (title following name, remains capitalized); *Reverend Ben Smith* (title and name); *Ben Smith, reverend* (title following name, not capitalized); *a reverend stopped by this morning* (substitution for name); *the Reverend stopped by this morning* (title given respect); *"The Stone of the Star and Moon"* (*of*, *the*, *and*—unimportant words).

3. Titles of direct address are capitalized; titles of indirect address are not:

   Thank you, Reverend, for coming by this morning. Did you know, Dad, that a police officer called? (Direct address.) *My dad intends to assert his right to silence.* (Indirect address.)

4. The names of seasons are not capitalized unless personified, nor are the names of directions, unless used to designate a particular region:

   Next summer should be warmer. They captured Summer in their fragrant candle. We'll be moving south of the lake. We're moving to the South.

   However, if the name of a season or a direction is part of a proper noun, it is always capitalized:

   The Summer Fair will start late this year. We saw the Northern Lights when we visited Alaska.

PUNCTUATION

The Period

The period (.) is used by these four rules:

1. Declarative sentences (statements announcing something) and imperative sentences (statements giving a command) are ended by using a period:

    > *My cellie cleaned the cell yesterday.* (Declarative.) *Clean your cell immediately.* (Imperative.)

2. Instead of using a question mark after courteous requests, use a period:

    > *If you would, please send me a copy of the case.*

3. Use the period after abbreviations and initials:

    > *Ph.D.   Mrs.   U.S.A.*

    A single period will suffice to finish a sentence that ends in an abbreviation:

    > *Direct all inquires to the customer service department of Shady & Hustler, Inc.*

4. Three successive periods (. . .), called "ellipses marks," are used to indicate that a part of a quoted passage has been left out:

    > *"If a man is thought-free. fancy-free, imagination-free . . . unwise rulers and reformers cannot fatally interrupt him."*
    > —*Henry David Thoreau,* Civil Disobedience

    Sometimes ellipses marks are added to indicate the omission of words at the end of a quotation (which is the usual practice in legal writing):

    > *"It is not many moments that I live under a government. . . ."*

    But this is not, strictly speaking, always necessary:

    > *"It is not many moments that I live under a government."*

    Ellipses marks are obligatory, however, when the end of a sentence, or entire sentences, are omitted within a paragraph:

    > *"It is not many moments that I live under a government. . . . If a man is thought-free, fancy-free, imagination-free, that which* is not *never for a long time appearing* to be *to him, unwise rulers and reformers cannot fatally interrupt him."*

The Comma

The rules governing the use of the comma (,) are manifold. Some rules are flexible, used or not according to one's style of writing; other rules, most of them, are obligatory. The rules listed below are a fair selection of the common usages of the comma:

1. A clause that depends on an adverb is usually set off by a comma if that adverbial clause precedes the main clause:

    > <u>*After the Warden read over yesterday's reports*</u>, *he called a special security meeting.* (Depends on the adverb "after.")

2. Use a comma to set off an introductory clause of four or more words that begins with a preposition (e.g., *in, at, by, with, of, from*):

> *In the back room, we built a small gym.* (Four words.) *In the back we built a small gym.* (Less than four words.)

3. A comma is used after a participle phrase or an absolute that begins a sentence. A **participle phrase** is a group of words along with a verb participle that work together in one sense, in the sense of an adjective—that is, a participle phrase modifies a noun in the main clause of the sentence. An **absolute** begins with a noun followed by a participle and modifies the entire clause rather than any particular word within the clause:

    > *Seeing the Sergeant walk in, we hastily stashed our tattoo gear.* (The participle phrase dependent on the participle *seeing* modifies the subject "we," which begins the main clause.) *The Sergeant taking forever to leave, we finally got back to work.* (The absolute "The Sergeant taking" modifies equally the rest of the words in the introductory clause, and is not linked grammatically to any specific word in the main clause other than to provide the clause general context.)

4. A comma is used after an introductory infinitive phrase (a phrase is **infinitive** if its verb is not bound to a particular subject or given a sense of time—past, present, or future tense):

    > *To be at peace, you must forgive the small stuff.* ("To be" is the infinitive verb.)

5. The comma is used to set off words expressing doubt or choice, transitional words, parenthetical expressions, explanatory expressions, modifying phrases and clauses, and introductory expressions:

    > *Whether or not he was actually guilty, we convicted him just to be sure.* (Expressing doubt.) *She was, so to speak, a major pain in the backside.* (Modifying phrase.) *Moreover, the back exit let in a significant draft.* (Transitional words; e.g., *therefore, furthermore, consequently.*) *Inmate Jones, we believe, has been informing on the tier.* (Modifying clause.) *The line for medical was too long, inmates wrapped clear around the side of the building, and I didn't feel like waiting.* (Parenthetical expression.) *Inmate Blacke says commissary profits would increase, so far as we can determine, if they reduced the price of ramen noodles by ten cents.* (Explanatory expression.) *Yes, I'll make sure it happens. Indeed, you are correct. No, get someone else to do it.* (Introductory expressions.)

6. Commas are used to set off nonrestrictive clauses. Similar to parenthetical expressions, nonrestrictive clauses add information but are not needed to complete the essential meaning of a sentence:

    > *Inmate Blacke, who works commissary, says profits would increase if the price of ramen noodles was reduced by ten cents.* (The clause "who works commissary" is nonrestrictive because it can easily be omitted without changing the meaning of the sentence.) *The inmate who works commissary says profits would increase if the price of ramen noodles was reduced by ten cents.* (The clause "who works commissary" is restrictive, and therefore not set off by commas, because it is essential to identify which inmate is being discussed. In the example previous to this one, the inmate is sufficiently identified by the use of his name, "Blacke.")

7. Commas are used to set off appositive words or phrases. An **appositive** is a word or phrase used to rename or otherwise define or identify the noun it follows:

    Jim Corbin, <u>our CEO</u>, is running things well. ("Jim Corbin" is the same person—and thus means the same—as "our CEO.")

    An appositive phrase following at the end of a sentence is also set off by a comma:

    The original society fragmented into widely divergent sects, <u>each with its own agenda</u>. (The appositive phrase begins with the pronoun "each," representing the noun "sects.")

8. Words of direct address are set off by commas:

    It is imperative, <u>Mrs. Smith</u>, that you send the memorandum today.

9. Words, phrases, or clauses in a successive series of three or more are set off by commas:

    I need some ramens, beans, and a sausage. He came out of the cell, walked to the end of the tier, looked Jason square in the eye, then punched him in the nose. By this time next week, we hope to have (1) finished our working lesson plan, (2) arranged a time for services in the chapel, and (3) informed all interested parties of the above.

10. Coordinate adjectives that modify the same noun are set off by a comma:

    It was an old, comfortable chair. (*Old* and *comfortable* modify "chair.") The test is whether the clause would still make sense if the word "and" was used instead of the comma: *It was an old* and *comfortable chair.* If "and" wouldn't be used to separate the adjectives, a comma is unnecessary: *The bright white lights in the cell keep me up at night.* You wouldn't say "bright *and* white lights" keep me up at night.)

11. Use a comma to separate independent clauses of a compound sentence joined by a coordinate conjunction (i.e., *and, but, for, or, nor, because*; and *while* and *yet* when they mean the same as *but*):

    Properly used, Universals are good for toning and strength training, but free weights are the way to go for building mass.

    Do not connect two independent clauses by a comma without using a conjunction:

    Properly used, Universals are good for toning and strength training, free weights are the way to go for building mass. (Sentence is incorrect.)

    So long as the conjunction is used, the comma may be omitted in short compound sentences if the absence of a comma does not confuse the meaning of the sentence (note: this exception does not extend to include the use of the conjunctions *for* and *yet*; they must be preceded by a comma when used to connect two independent clauses):

    Universals are good for toning but free weights are better for building.

    The conjunction can be omitted if a semicolon is used instead of a comma:

    Properly used, Universals are good for toning and strength training; free weights are the way to go for building mass.

    Or you can break the independent clauses into two sentences:

Properly used, Universals are good for toning and strength training. Free weights are the way to go for building mass.

12. Words expressing contrast are set off by commas:

    You were supposed wash the dishes, not break the dishes.

13. Use the comma to set off a definite place, month, or year:

    The meeting will be held on May 23, 2012, at 565 Oak Street, Fairland, Oregon.

14. Direct quotations are set off by commas:

    The Warden said, "As far as I'm concerned, inmates have no rights."

15. A declarative clause is set off from interrogative clause by a comma. An **interrogative clause** is a clause that asks a question:

    People often form rash opinions with little to no forethought, isn't that so?

16. A comma can be used to indicate where a word has been omitted:

    Reading leads to an introspective person; introspection, to a thoughtful person; thoughtfulness, to an understanding person.

17. Use the comma to set off a proper noun from following degree or honorific titles; to set off separate sets of figures; and to separate two identical words:

    Joseph P. Fleming, A.B., M.A., Ph.D. (Proper noun separated from academic degrees.) *In 2005, 1,301 cars were stolen from the county area.* (Two sets of figures.) *We have much, much more inventory than we should.* (Two identical words.)

The Semicolon

The semicolon (;) is used to indicate a separation between words or parts of a sentence when the use of a comma could cause the meaning of the sentence to be confusing:

1. Independent clauses (one or both of which) having commas or other punctuation are sometimes set off by a semicolon before a coordinate conjunction, to avoid confusion between the parts of the sentence:

    Assuming a putative view of the facts, some feel they can discover offhand whether an inmate has a reasonable cause to pursue in court; but a common-sense assessment of the facts, no matter how seemingly correct, is often faulty in light of what the law actually intends.

2. Two independent coordinate clauses can be connected by a semicolon when a conjunction is not used. (Same as Rule 11 under commas.)

3. Coordinate clauses are set off by a semicolon when the clauses are connected by a transitional word or phrase (e.g., *however, moreover, in fact, thus,* etc.):

    The Wheel of Times series is an excellent fantasy epic; in fact, it is one of the best I've ever read.

4. Words and phrases—such as "for example," "that is," "namely," "for instance," and "specifically"—that are used to introduce a list, series, or example are set off from the main clause by a semicolon:

    The facility's policy violates a number of constitutional provisions; namely, the First, Eighth, and Fourteenth Amendments.

5. Semicolons are used to separate the parts of a list when commas do not provide a strong enough separation to prevent the parts of the list from being confused with each other:

    The inmates who didn't make it out to recreation are Conner, cell 234A; Jamison, cell 156A; Dickson, cell 214B, he was at school; and Franks, cell 117A.

The Colon

The colon (:) is used by these rules:

1. The colon is used at the end of an independent clause that introduces a list, enumeration, or details:

    When first arriving in prison, one needs to buy the following items: T.V., hotpot, and radio.

    Do not break an independent clause with a colon:

    When first arriving in prison, one needs to buy: T.V., hotpot, and radio. (This construction is incorrect because the clause "one needs to buy" lacks a direct object before the placement of the colon, and the clause is therefore incomplete. In the example previous to this one, the direct object of the verb "buy" is the pronoun phrase "the following items," which stands in for the nouns "T.V., hotpot, and radio," which receives the action of *buy*.)

    If you are set on using a construction like that in the above example, revise the sentence to eliminate the colon:

    When first arriving in prison, one needs to buy a T.V., hotpot, and radio.

2. Appositive clauses and phrases can be set off by a colon (note: an appositive phrase or clause defines or identifies the subject of the preceding clause):

    This old truism is as valid today as it was in the past: No matter how much you polish a turd, it's still a turd. ("This old truism" is the subject defined by the appositive.)

3. Colons can also be used, similar to the usage of appositives, to connect a second independent clause when it is meant to be a clarification or a consequence of the first independent clause:

    Redwald was ecstatic: someone had bungled his discharge papers and he was to be released six months early.

4. Colons are used after the salutation of business or other formal letters (commas are used in informal letters; semicolons are never used after a salutation):

    Dear Ms. Wright: Dear Sir or Madam: Dear Mom, (Informal.)

Parentheses

Parentheses ( ) are used by these three rules:

1. Parentheses are used to add comments or explanations or translations into sentences (though they also can surround complete sentences that stand alone), which are meant to alter the sense or clarify the main text (note: compare this rule to Rule 5 and 6 under "The Comma," above, and Rule 1 under "The Dash," below):

    Inmates may pursue legal claims (with great impediment from the government) insofar as a cause of action exists. You can ask the court to apply nunc pro tunc *("now for then") a newly-risen claim by filing an amended complaint, if the statute of limitation has not run out.*

2. Letters, symbols, or numerals, when used as appositives, are set off by parentheses:

    There were five (5) carefully enumerated requests for relief. Use the semicolon (;) to indicated a stronger break than a period.

3. Parentheses have no grammatical effect on the sentence they modify—that is, a sentence in which parentheses appear is punctuated as it would be if the parentheses were not there:

    Inmates may pursue legal claims (with great impediment from the government) insofar as a cause of action exists. (Correct.) *Inmates may pursue legal claims, (with great impediment from the government), insofar as a cause of action exists.* (Incorrect.) *Inmates may pursue legal claims (With great impediment from the government.) insofar as a cause of action exists.* (Incorrect.)

    Punctuation within a clause always comes after the ending parenthesis:

    Inmates may pursue legal claims (with great impediment from the government), and authorities must not interfere with this process (unless it can be done without detection). (The comma is needed to connect the second independent clause, beginning with "and," to the first independent clause. The parenthetical "(with great impediment from the government)" adds information to the first clause and thus appears to the left of the comma. If it had come after the comma, it would have been separated in sense from the first clause and confusingly attributed in meaning to the second clause.)

    However, if a punctuation mark applies only to the text contained within parentheses, then the punctuation mark is enclosed inside the ending parenthesis. This is also true of parentheticals meant to stand alone as complete sentences:

    Don't take your time (and I mean, hurry!) in placing the order. (The comma and exclamation mark apply only to the parenthetical text.) *Early detection of symptoms of arrhythmia is crucial to prevent cardiac arrest. (See about cardiac arrest under Section 12.)* (The parenthetical referring the reader to "Section 12" stands as its own sentence.)

The Dash

The dash (—) may be used for visual emphasis in places where commas or parentheses or colons ordinarily are used:

> *The new prison has plenty of amenities—pool, weight room, larger cells—that this inmate plans to make full use of.* (Appositives referring to "amenities" could also be set off in parentheses.) *I need copies of my two grievances, disciplinary policy, the August 10th letter—you know what, forget the whole thing.* (The dash here indicates an abrupt change in thought. Such a construction, though rarely used, is more typical of an informal writing style or written dialogue; it would not be used in formal legal writing.) *I said you could have one burrito—one burrito—not three!* (The dashes are used here to set off words repeated for emphasis.) *Nirvana, Pearl Jam, and Stone Temple Pilots—these are, in my opinion, the greatest examples of early '90s Alternative Rock bands.* (The dash is used to emphasize the statement about the compound subject.)

The Question Mark

The question mark (?), of course, indicates a question, and is used by three basic rules:

1. Questions, which are called "interrogative statements" by pedantic grammarians, are followed by a question mark (courteous requests, however, are not; see Rule 2 under "The Period," above):

    > *Are you going to meet me out on the ball field?*

2. The question mark is sometimes used after sentence fragments that depend on a preceding interrogative sentence, or after each part of a sentence that asks more than one question:

    > *Do you think the current cabinet has even an ounce of accountability? Or honesty? Or wherewithal? He didn't ask the important questions—where is the money? how was it shipped? who was involved?—and only circuitously touched on the other big concerns.*

    Do not, however, use a question mark after every part of a compound question, if the question is not actually complete until the end of the sentence. Use only one question mark at the end of the sentence:

    > *Do you think we should act now, without being sure, or tomorrow, when we can be certain?*

3. Where only part of a sentence is a question, the question portion is always set off by a comma, semicolon, colon, or dash, and placed at the end of the sentence:

    > *This is the issue: What can we do to improve the conditions here?*

The Exclamation Mark

Exclamation marks (!) are used after sentences that express surprise, emotion, or emphasis, and after interjections or statements calling for quick action:

> *Wow!* (Interjection.) *Get on board! Quick!* (Need for action.) *That's terrible!* (Emotion.) *Holy crap! Aah!* (Surprise.) *That was incredible!* (Emphasis.)

The Quotation Mark

Quotation marks (" ") are used by these six rules:

1. Use quotation marks to enclose a direct quotation (capitalize the first word of the direct quote):

   The Warden shouted, "We have a zero tolerance policy, and I don't have to listen to your excuses!" "It is possible," he went on, "that you'll spend the next three years in seg."

   Do not use quotation marks or capital letters for indirect quotations (note: **indirect quotations** do not give an exact representation of the original words, but are meant to paraphrase only, and are often introduced by the word "that"):

   The Warden shouted that he has a zero tolerance policy and doesn't have to listen to your excuses.

2. If more than one paragraph is quoted, quotation marks are used at the beginning of each paragraph; however, each paragraph is not ended in a quotation mark, but the last paragraph only:

   "People are universally poor fact witnesses because the human memory is subject to variable forms of corrupting influence. This is a problem nearly impossible to overcome.

   "Nevertheless, our system of justice is mostly reliant upon the in-court testimony of fact witnesses to provide as evidence the content of their memories. Even what is perceived as conclusive, unassailable scientific evidence is admissible, in most circumstance, only on the predicate testimony of an expert."

   (Longer quotations of about fifty words or more are usually set off from the main body of text by indenting the passage in a quotation block; see "Rules for Legal Writing" at "Quotation Blocks," below.)

3. Quotation marks are used to enclose the titles of essays, articles, chapters, songs and poems. The titles of books, magazines, journals, newspapers, operas, music albums, works of art, ships, spaceships, airplanes, and trains are either <u>underscored</u> or *italicized* (note: underscoring in type or handwriting signifies the use of italics for final printing; underscoring is the grammatical equivalent of italicizing):

   The "Quick English Refresher" section from <u>Battling the Administration: An Inmates' Guide to a Successful Lawsuit</u> was instructive. Alternative form: The "Quick English Refresher" section from *Battling the Administration: An Inmates' Guide to a Successful Lawsuit* was instructive.

   "The Red Wolf" is one of my favorite poems.

4. Words, phrases, or clauses that are directly referred to within a sentence are set off by quotation marks:

   The term "pro se" means that one is proceeding on his or her own behalf, without a lawyer.

5. Words, phrases, or clauses that you disagree with may be set off by quotation marks:

> *The prison's newsletter described the "facts" supporting Admin's decision to cancel our program.*

Do not use quotation marks to set off your own colloquialisms, slang, or figurative speech:

> *He's either shy or thinks himself "too cool" for the crowd.* (Use words confidently, or don't use them at all. Wrapping words in quotation marks, such as "too cool" in the example, tells the reader that the writer is distancing him- or herself from the particular usage because of some insecurity about the idiom.)

6. Quotation marks are used with other punctuation marks as follows:

Always place commas and periods before the ending quotation mark:

> *She said, "They left yesterday." "They left yesterday," she said. One of the most overused redundancies is the expression "personally, I."*

Question marks and exclamation marks are placed after the ending quotation mark, unless the question mark or exclamation mark is part of the quotation:

> *She asked, "When do you get out of prison?" Did he actually say, "You're going to the Hole"?*

The semicolon and the colon are placed after the ending quotation mark:

> *He said, "You're going to the Hole"; therefore, I packed up all my personal stuff, getting ready.*

When using parentheses or brackets for in-text citations to footnotes or endnotes, the citation comes after the ending quotation mark; the period, comma, or other punctuation mark then comes after the citation:

> *Dr. Farnsworth was "surprised to discover a colony of Alaccians settled on the northern island" [17], commenting that the "temerity of the journey [was] unmitigated for the ingenuity of the watercraft employed" [18].*

NOTES: _____
_____
_____
_____
_____
_____
_____
_____
_____
_____
_____
_____
_____
_____
_____
_____
_____
_____
_____
_____
_____
_____
_____
_____
_____
_____
_____
_____
_____
_____
_____
_____
_____
_____
_____
_____
_____
_____

NOTES: _____
_____
_____
_____
_____
_____
_____
_____
_____
_____
_____
_____
_____
_____
_____
_____
_____
_____
_____
_____
_____
_____
_____
_____
_____
_____
_____
_____
_____
_____
_____
_____
_____
_____
_____
_____
_____
_____

NOTES: _____

_____

_____

_____

_____

_____

_____

_____

_____

_____

_____

_____

_____

_____

_____

_____

_____

_____

_____

_____

_____

_____

_____

_____

_____

_____

_____

_____

_____

_____

_____

_____

_____

_____

_____

_____

CHAPTER 8:
LEGAL CITATIONS

CITING TO REFERENCE MATERIAL

Following are numerous examples of how to properly cite to legal materials typically seen in the legal publications any inmate is likely to come across in prison. At least one example is given for how to cite the below-featured sources of law. Then, for clarity, each example citation is followed by a parenthetical explanation, which breaks down in specific terms the individual components of the citation.

This section discusses how to properly cite to legal materials by using correct citation forms. How to actually incorporate citations into a body of text, and to punctuate (support) a piece of writing with such citations, is discussed in "Rules of Legal Writing," below.

Form of Citations

Citations are written in sentence form and according to the ordinary rules of grammar. Most citations, though not all, are written as independent sentences that come directly after the written proposition they support. And, even though standing alone as an independent sentence, a citation should not be separated from the text to which it refers. Take the example:

> The Ninth Circuit has held that when a government employee "invoke[s] the power of [his or her] office to accomplish the offensive act," that act "clearly relates to the performance of official duties," and the employee acted under color of state law for the purposes of a § 1983 action. *McDade v. West*, 223 F.3d 1135, 1140 (9th Cir. 2000).

Citing Statutes

Statutes are cited by (1) statutory code/title number (for federal statutes), (2) abbreviated name of statutory code, (3) section (or subdivision), and (4) year of code, in parentheses (year of publication is often left out; however, if citing from an older version, the date should be indicated to avoid misleading readers about currency):

Federal statutes:
42 U.S.C. § 1983 (2010).

(**Code number:** 42; **name of code:** U.S.C. (*United States Code*); **section (§):** 1983; **year of code:** 2010. (Note: the "year of code" is not the year the law was enacted; it is the year the volume containing the law was published. Use the date of the volume.))

State statutes:
Wash. Rev. Code § 12-22-125 (2003);
I.C. § 67-5201 (2010).

(**Name of code:** I.C (*Idaho Code*); **section and subsection (§):** 67-5201; **year of code:** 2010.)

Unofficial annotated versions:
42 U.S.C.A. § 1983 (West 2010);
42 U.S.C.S. § 1983 (Reed 2010);
Wash. Rev. Code Ann. § 12-22-125 (West 2003);
I.C. Ann. § 67-5201 (West 2010).

(Notice that the name of the publisher is indicated in parentheses with the date.)

Citing Procedural Court Rules

Court rules vary from jurisdiction to jurisdiction, but are usually cited by (1) the abbreviated name identifying the rule, and (2) the rule number.

Fed. R. Civ. P. 65(a).

(**Name:** *Federal Rules of Civil Procedure*; **rule:** 65(a). Note that rules of court procedure are revised and republished each year; be careful to use the current version.)

Citing Administrative Decisions

Per the Federal Administrative Procedure Act (5 U.S.C. §§ 551, *et seq*.), and your state's analogous laws, administrative agencies are required to publish their official decisions for review by the public. Federal decisions are officially published by the Government Printing Office (GPO) in a myriad of publications covering the separate areas of government. However, because of the informal nature of administrative decisions (state and federal), publishing is inconsistent.

Administrative decisions are cited by (1) name of the first party listed (underscored or *italicized*), (2) volume number, (3) abbreviated name of publication, and (4) year of decision, in parentheses:

Aaron C. Wright, 73 I. & N. Dec. 503 (1984)

(**Name:** *Aaron C. Wright*; **reporter volume:** 73; **name of reporter:** I. & N. (*Immigration and Nationalization*); **decision number:** Dec. 503; **year of decision:** 1984.)

Citing Administrative Regulations

Regulations are cited by (1) title/code number, (2) abbreviated name of publication, (3) section number of regulation, and (4) year of latest publication (year of publication is often left out; however, if citing from an older version, the date should be indicated to avoid misleading the reader about currentness):

15 C.F.R. § 138 (2000).

(**Code number:** 15; **name of code:** C.F.R. (*Code of Federal Regulations*); **section (§):** 138; **year of code:** 2000. (Note: the "year of code" is not the year the law was enacted; it is the year the volume containing the law was published. Use the date of the volume.))

Citing Case Law

Cases are cited by (1) case title (underscored or *italicized*), (2) reporter volume number, (3) abbreviated name of reporter, (4) page number where the case begins, (5) abbreviated name of the court, and (6) year of decision, in parentheses along with the abbreviated name of the court:

> Wright v. Enomoto, 462 F.Supp. 397 (N.D. Cal. 1976); *or Wright v. Enomoto*, 462 F.Supp. 397 (N.D. Cal. 1976).

> (**Title:** *Wright v. Enomoto*; **reporter volume:** 462; **name of reporter:** F.Supp. (*Federal Supplement*); **starting page:** 397; **court name:** N.D. Cal. (Northern District of California); **year of decision:** 1976.)

In citing case law, when possible, you should also include the "parallel citations" to other reporters that publish the same case. U.S. Supreme Court cases are published officially in the *United States Reports* (U.S.), and unofficially in the *Supreme Court Reporter* (S.Ct.) and *Supreme Court Reporter, Lawyers Edition* (L.Ed., and L.Ed.2d for the second series ("2d") of volumes). Each of the *unofficial* reporters publishes the same cases as the *official*. When giving parallel citations, give the official reporter first, and then cite where the same case can be found in the unofficial versions (this is for your readers' ease of reference). For example:

> *Devlin v. Scardelletti*, 536 U.S. 1, 122 S.Ct. 205, 153 L.Ed.2d 27 (2002).

> (It is not strictly required that you cite all three reporters—your case is not going to be dismissed for a citation error. Do not, however, give only a *S.Ct.* or *L.Ed.* citation without also giving the official *U.S.* citation, unless the decision has not yet been reported in the *U.S.*, or if you cannot find the *U.S.* citation. If this happens, cite the case as: *Devlin v. Scardelletti*, __U.S.__, 122 S.Ct. 205, 153 L.Ed.2d 27 (2002).)

You may be able to get your hands on a legal newspaper called the *United States Law Week* (U.S.L.W.), published weekly. The U.S.L.W. publishes cases from federal courts before they appear in the reporters. A Supreme Court citation from this newspaper looks like this:

> *Wallace v. Kato*, 75 U.S.L.W. 4107 (U.S. Feb. 21, 2007) (No. 05-1240).

There are no notable reporters beyond the *Federal Supplement* (F.Supp. and F.Supp.2d) for federal district court cases, and no notable reporters beyond the *Federal Reporter* (abbreviated F., F.2d, or F.3d) for federal circuit decisions. So cases cited from any of these reporters are not usually given with parallel citations:

> *Wright v. Enomoto*, 462 F.Supp. 397 (N.D. Cal. 1976); *Huchings v. Corum*, 501 F.Supp. 1276 (D.Neb. 1980); *Davenprt v. DeRobertis*, 844 F.2d 1310 (7th Cir. 1988), *cert. denied*, __U.S.__, 109 S.Ct. 260, __L.Ed.2d__ (1989).

State appellate cases are officially and unofficially published in state reporters, and unofficially published in regional reporters, each covering different groups of states. Specifically:

1. *Atlantic Reporter* (A., A.2d.), covers Connecticut, Delaware, Maine, Maryland, New Hampshire, New Jersey, Pennsylvania, Rhode Island, and Vermont.
2. *North Eastern Reporter* (N.E., N.E.2d.), covers Illinois, Indiana, Massachusetts, New York, and Ohio.
3. *North Western Reporter* (N.W., N.W.2d.), covers Iowa, Michigan, Minnesota, Nebraska, North Dakota, South Dakota, and Wisconsin.

4. ***Pacific Reporter*** (P., P.2d, P.3d), covers Alaska, Arizona, California, Colorado, Hawaii, Idaho, Kansas, Montana, Nevada, New Mexico, Oklahoma, Oregon, Utah, Washington, and Wyoming.

5. ***South Eastern Reporter*** (S.E., S.E.2d.), covers Georgia, North Carolina, South Carolina, Virginia, and West Virginia.

6. ***Southern Reporter*** (So., So.2d), covers Alabama, Florida, Louisiana, and Mississippi.

7. ***South Western Reporter*** (S.W., S.W.2d., S.W.3d), covers Arkansas, Kentucky, Missouri, Tennessee, and Texas.

When citing state cases, always cite the official reporter first, followed by the unofficial parallel citation:

> *State v. Alger*, 115 Idaho 42, 764 P.2d 119 (1988); *State v. Johnson*, 166 N.J. 523, 766 A.2d 1126 (2001); *Taylor v. Maile,* 146 Idaho 705, 201 P.3d 1282 (2009).

If citing only to the regional reporter, you must indicate the state from which the case originated:

> *State v. Lawhorn*, 762 S.W.2d 820, 823 (Mo. 1988); *State v. Johnson*, 766 A.2d 1126 (N.J. 2001); *Taylor v. Maile,* 201 P.3d 1282 (Idaho 2009).

When citing multiple cases, you should list the cases originating from the higher courts down to lower, and then by opinion date, in reverse chronological order:

> It is well established that prisoners retain those Constitutional rights that are not inconsistent with incarceration. *Bell v. Wolfish*, 411 U.S. 520, 99 S.Ct. 1800, 60 L.Ed.2d 447 (1979); *Procunier v. Martinez*, 416 U.S. 396, 94 S.Ct. 1800, 40 L.Ed.2d 224 (1974); *Pell v. Procunier*, 417 U.S. 817, 94 S.Ct. 2800, 41 L.Ed.2d 495 (1974); *Brown v. Nix*, 33 F.3d 951 (8th Cir. 1994).

> (*Brown v. Nix*, though it is the most recent case, is listed last because it comes from a court lower in authority than the others, which are all Supreme Court cases.)

Citing Unpublished Cases

You can often get new cases from companies providing Internet services for legal research. If the case is so new that it hasn't made it into a reporter yet, you can cite the unpublished decision by (1) case title (underscored or *italicized*), (2) year of decision, (3) abbreviated name of company, (4) company case number, (5) abbreviated name of the court, and (6) month, day, and year of decision, in parentheses with the abbreviated name of the court:

> *Bell v. Ercole*, 2008 WL 2484585 (E.D. N.Y. Jun 20, 2008); *Young v. Vaughn*, 2000 WL 1056444 (E.D. Penn. Aug. 1, 2000); *Hamilton v. Schriro*, 1994 LEXIS 14885 (W.D. Mo. Sept. 13, 1994).

> (**Title:** *Hamilton v. Schriro*; **year:** 1994; **company name:** LEXIS; **company case number:** 14885; **court name:** W.D. Mo. (Western District of Missouri); **date of decision:** September 13, 1994.)

NOTE: Not every case is officially reported, and your local court may not allow the use of unpublished decisions; check the local court rules. If unpublished cases are permitted, you should, if possible, submit to the judge a courtesy copy of the case when submitting the motion or other papers citing the case, for the court's ease of reference. Consider sending a copy to your adversaries as well, so you will be in a better position to insist that they extend you the same courtesy in the future.

Further, you can cite to cases that haven't appeared in a reporter, newspaper, website, etc., by listing (1) case title, (2) official case number (the docket number), and (3) the name of the court and date of decision, in parentheses:

> *Boothe v. Procunier*, No. C-70-1990-ACW (N.D. Cal. Sept. 29, 1970).

Citing Restatements

Restatements are treatises detailing and discussing a given area of the law. Restatements are written by judges and lawyers to, essentially, clarify the law and guide its development—though the opinions are not binding on courts (unless officially adopted by a jurisdiction's highest court), Restatement opinions are, nevertheless, quite persuasive. Restatements are published by the American Law Institute, and can be cited by (1) full name of the Restatement and the edition (underscored or *italicized*), (2) section number, and (3) year of publication:

> *Restatement (2d) of Torts* § 899 (1977).

> (**Name:** *Restatement (Second Edition) of Torts*; **section (§):** 899; **year:** 1977.)

Citing Legal Treatises and Books

Treatises and books are cited by (1) volume number (if there's more than one), (2) name of author or editor (if given), (3) title of publication (underscored or *italicized*), (4) edition or series number, and (5) year of publication, in parentheses with edition or series number:

> 2 H. Wood, *Limitations of Actions* (4th ed. 1916).

> (**Volume:** 2; **author/editor:** H. Wood; **title:** *Limitations of Actions*; **edition/series:** fourth; **date of publication:** 1916.)

Citing Legal Encyclopedias

Encyclopedias are cited by (1) volume number, (2) abbreviated publication name, (3) topic (underscored or *italicized*), (4) section number, and (5) year of publication, in parentheses:

> 54 C.J.S. *Limitations of Actions* § 112 (2005).

> (**Volume:** 54; **publication:** C.J.S. (*Corpus Juris Secundum*); **topic:** *Limitations of Actions*; **section (§):** 112; **date of publication:** 2005.)

Citing Annotated Law Reporters

Annotated law reporters are cited by (1) author's name, (2) the word "Annotated," (3) title of annotation, (4) volume number, (5) abbreviated name of publication and series, (6) page where annotation begins, and (7) year of publication, in parentheses:

> Damian E. Okasinski, Annotated, *Attorney Malpractice in Connection with Services Related to Adoption of Child*, 18 A.L.R. 5th 592 (1994)

> (**Author:** Damian E. Okasinski; "Annotated"; **title:** *Attorney Malpractice in Connection with Services Related to Adoption of Child*; **volume:** 18; **publication:** A.L.R. 5th (*American Law Report Fifth Series*); **page:** 592; **date of publication:** 1994.)

Citing Law Reviews and Journals

Law reviews and journals are cited by (1) author's name, (2) title of article (underscored or *italicized*), (3) volume number, (4) abbreviated title of publication, (5) page where article begins, and (6) year of publication, in parentheses:

> Stephen K. Stark, *Idaho Government Immunity Doctrine in the Wake of Sterling v. Bloom*, 14 Idaho L. Rev. 291 (1988).

> (**Author:** Stephen K. Stark; **article title:** *Idaho Government Immunity Doctrine in the Wake of* Sterling v. Bloom; **volume:** 14; **publication:** Idaho L. Rev. (*Idaho Law Review*); **page:** 291: **year:** 1988.)

Citing From Supplements

If you use a supplement or **pocket part** (the paperback booklet or pages published to update the material, usually stored under the volume's back cover) be sure to indicate that you have used a supplement, and include the date of its publication:

> 28 U.S.C. § 1326(b) (Supp. 2012);
> 15 C.F.R. § 138 (Supp. 2009).

Citing Transcripts

Transcripts are cited by (1) identifying the subject and date, (2) the abbreviation for transcript, "Tr.," (3) page number, and (4) line:

> Deposition of Henry J. Charles, August 15, 2007, Tr., p. 57, Ls. 4-13 (note: "Ls." (lines) is the plural form of "L." (line)). Deposition Tr., pp. 23-31 ("pp." (pages) is the plural form of "p." (page)); Deposition Tr., p. 4, L. 17 - p. 5, L. 4 (page 4, line 17, thru page 5, line 4); Deposition Tr., pp. 55-56; pp. 73-75; p. 84, L. 20 - p. 85, L. 2.

CITATION SIGNALS

The novice may at first be a bit confused by the liberal use of abbreviations and short signals found throughout legal works, but never fear. In short time the meaning of each signal and what an author intends by using a particular form of citation will be obvious at a glance. Below are listed the more common examples of signals that one inevitably encounters with legal citations. And remember, when it comes time for you to pen citation signals such as the below, any words or phrases here appearing in *italics* may instead be underscored. An inmate writing out documents by hand can readily use the underscoring method.

E.g.

The citation signal "*e.g.*" means "for example," indicating that the cited material is among authorities clearly stating the principle for which the citation was given.

See; See, E.g.; See Also

The citation signals "*see*," "*see, e.g.*," and "*see also*" indicate that the cited material clearly supports the principle being expressed. For example:

> A determination of whether the sought injunctive relief goes "no further than necessary to correct a violation" and is "narrowly drawn and the least intrusive means to correct the violation" will rest upon case-specific factors; namely, the extent of the current and ongoing constitutional violations. ***See, e.g.****, Morales Feliciano v. Rullan*, 378 F.3d 42, 54-55 (1st Cir. 2004); ***see also*** *Armstrong v. Davis*, 275 F.3d 849, 870 (9th Cir. 2001) (noting that a "few isolated violations affecting a narrow range of plaintiffs" will not provide a basis for systemwide injunctive relief).

Accord

The signal *"accord"* is used to introduce one or more cases clearly supporting a point or proposition for which *another* case is being directly quoted or referred.

See Generally

The signal "*see generally*" means the cited material is providing nonspecific background information for the expressed principle.

Supra v. Infra

The term "*supra*" ("above") means that a subject or a piece of authority has already been discussed and/or cited earlier in the document. Opposite is the term "*infra*" ("below"), which means that a subject will be further addressed in later sections.

No Citation Signal

Should a citation appear without a corresponding signal—that is, no *see, see, e.g., see generally,* etc.—then the authority cited either clearly states the principle expressed in the instant passage, identifies the source of quotations in the directly preceding text, or identifies authority contained in the foregoing text. The citation ending the example passage below lacks a signal because in this context the author intends to communicate that the citation is unequivocally the source of the paragraph's quoted clause.

> A district court's decision will constitute an abuse of judicial discretion if it makes an error of law or clear error of fact, but "[r]eversal will not be granted unless prejudice is shown." *City of Long Beach v. Standard Oil Co.*, 46 F.3d 929, 936 (9th Cir. 1995).

Explanatory Parentheticals

It is often a good idea to clarify a point by providing the reader with a brief summary or excerpt from the cited material. Take the example: "*Armstrong v. Davis*, 275 F.3d 849, 870 (9th Cir. 2001) **(noting that a 'few isolated violations affecting a narrow range of plaintiffs' would not provide a basis for systemwide injunctive relief)**." The summary is always placed between parentheses "( )" and contained in the same sentence as the citation itself—such is called an "explanatory parenthetical."

A determination of whether the sought injunctive relief goes "no further than necessary to correct a violation" and is "narrowly drawn and the least intrusive means to correct the violation" will rest upon case-specific factors; namely, the extent of the current and ongoing constitutional violations. *See, e.g., Morales Feliciano v. Rullan*, 378 F.3d 42, 54-55 (1st Cir. 2004); *see also Armstrong v. Davis*, 275 F.3d 849, 870 (9th Cir. 2001) **(noting that a "few isolated violations affecting a narrow range of plaintiffs" will not provide a basis for systemwide injunctive relief)**.

Other explanatory parentheticals indicate how the author has altered quoted text, or that seemingly-altered portions of the quotation actually have appeared in the original passage. Briefly, the term **emphasis added** means the author has emphasized some portion of the quoted passage to further signify an important feature of the quotation (usually done by *italicizing* or underscoring). **Emphasis in original** means that an emphasized word, clause, or larger part of a quotation, appeared in the original text and was not added by the person quoting the material; **alterations in original** means that alteration signals appeared in the original material; **citation omitted** means the author has elected to leave out a citation originally included in the quoted passage. There are a number of these signals; their usage and meaning are usually clear within the context of where they appear. For example:

> "Without requiring *some evidence* that prison policies are based on legitimate penological justifications . . . 'judicial review of prison policies would not be meaningful.'" *Walker v. Sumner,* 917 F.2d 382, 386 (9th Cir. 1990) (emphasis added) (citation omitted).

Compare

The signal "*compare*" or "*compare* [citation] *with* [citation]" indicates that the cited authority compares supporting authorities or authorities exemplifying (giving a typical example of) the principle. The "*compare*" signal should be supported with a clarifying explanatory parenthetical.

> ***Compare*** Spain v. Procunier*, 600 F.2d 189, 192, 199-200 (9th Cir. 1979) (it is impermissible to completely deny outdoor exercise for a particular category of inmates, even when inmates within the category are being disciplined for violent acts while in prison) ***with*** LeMaire v. Maass*, 12 F.3d 1444, 1458 (9th Cir. 1993) (upholding denial of exercise privileges for a particular inmate deemed a "grave security risk" who had previously attacked corrections officers).

Cf.

The signal "*cf.*" indicates that the cited authority supports a different, yet analogous principle:

> Denying inmates access to all outlets for religious worship offers no "alternative means of exercising the right," as called for under the second prong of *Turner. Turner v. Safely,* 482 U.S. 78, 89-90, 107 S.Ct. 2254, 96 L.Ed.2d 64 (1987); *cf. O'Lone v. Estate of Shabazz,* 482 U.S. 342, 107 S.Ct. 2400, 96 L.Ed.2d 282 (1987) (concluding that prison rules which prohibited Muslim inmates from engaging in Friday afternoon prayer services were reasonable, and relying in part on the fact that the inmates were allowed to participate in other weekly religious services).

Contra; But See; But Cf.

The signals "*contra*," "*but see*" and "*but cf.*," indicate authority contrary to the stated principle.

> The Tenth Circuit court, considering a prison's budget constraints, found that indigent inmates do not enjoy a right to unlimited free postage for legal mail. *See, e.g., U.S. v. Gray*, 182 F.3d 762, 766 (10th Cir. 1999); **but see** *Smith v. Erickson*, 884 F.2d 1108, 1109-11 (8th Cir. 1989) (holding the right of access to courts was violated when prison officials refused to provide indigent inmates with free postage or supplies for legal mail, because officials must furnish inmates with basic materials to draft and mail legal documents).

History/Treatment Signals

Other signals indicate the history and the treatment of the authority cited. When referring to a decision that has been appealed, you should indicate the decision made on appeal and cite the case name along with the ruling court's reporter citation.

> *Gilmore v. Lynch*, 319 F.Supp. 105 (N.D. Cal. 1970), *aff'd sub nom Younger v. Gilmore*, 404 U.S. 15 (1971).

The **affirmed** or **aff'd** means the decision in the cited case has been upheld by the appeals court. The phrase **sub nom** or **sub nomine** (under the name), a rather rare signal, means there has been a name change from one stage of the case to another. In the above example, Younger had replaced Lynch as the Attorney General defending against the case, and Gilmore had his name listed second because he was now defending against Younger's appeal of the federal district court's opinion.

Often a case on appeal will end up partially reversed (**rev'd**) and partially affirmed. When this happens, the citation looks like this:

> *Toussaint v. McCarthy*, 597 F.Supp. 1388 (N.D. Cal. 1984), *aff'd in part, rev'd in part on other grounds* 801 F.2d 1080 (9th Cir. 1986), *cert. denied*, 481 U.S. 1069 (1987).

Should the Supreme Court be asked to review the holdings of a lower court, whether the request was granted should be indicated:

> *Freeman v. Flake*, 448 F.2d 258 (10th Cir. 1971), *cert. denied*, 405 U.S. 1032, 92 S.Ct. 1292, 31 L.Ed.2d 489 (1972).

Cert. is the abbreviation for "*writ of certiorari*," which is the writ the Supreme Court issues upon granting a review of a lower court's opinion. The highest state court can likewise agree or not agree to review lower-court decisions. Instead of the "*cert. denied*" or "*cert. granted*" signals, a state may use the *cert.* equivalent of **rev. denied** or **review denied**. If for whatever reason the appeal was granted but later dismissed, the signal would look so:

> *Baker v. Nelson*, 291 Minn. 310, 191 N.W.2d 185 (1971), *app'l dism'd* 409 U.S. 810, 93 S.Ct. 37, 34 L.Ed.2d 65 (1972).

As society evolves, so, consequently, does the law. Even when court rulings have been previously affirmed as valid, or as otherwise withstanding appellate scrutiny, they can still be overruled in the future. Old trends and legal precedents are routinely retired because they are no longer useful or have become obsolete. Look for the signal **overruled.**

Bounds v. Smith, 430 U.S. 817 (1977), *overruled in part by Lewis v. Casey*, 518 U.S. 343 (1996).

The signal **en banc** means that *all* the judges of a court participated in the decision:

Mauro v. Arpaio, 188 F.3d 1054 (9th Cir. 1999) (en banc).

The citation signal **per curiam** indicates that the decision was given by the whole court without naming the authoring judge.

Flittie v. Solem, 827 F.2d 276 (8th Cir. 1987) (per cuiriam).

NOTE: Remember that judges don't expect you, as an inmate, to submit flawlessly drafted legal briefs with perfect citations. And irregular methods of citation construction do occur in actual practice, even some of the forms listed herein can be varied. What has been provided is not an exhaustive list of citation usage and variety, but is sufficient to familiarize prisoners with common methods and to help them understand why citations appear as they do in legal materials. That being said, apply what you've learned here to the best of your ability; accurate citations with regular form will show the judge that you have made an effort to follow the rules.

NOTES:

NOTES: _____
_____
_____
_____
_____
_____
_____
_____
_____
_____
_____
_____
_____
_____
_____
_____
_____
_____
_____
_____
_____
_____
_____
_____
_____
_____
_____
_____
_____
_____
_____
_____
_____
_____
_____
_____
_____
_____

NOTES: _____
_____
_____
_____
_____
_____
_____
_____
_____
_____
_____
_____
_____
_____
_____
_____
_____
_____
_____
_____
_____
_____
_____
_____
_____
_____
_____
_____
_____
_____
_____
_____
_____
_____
_____
_____
_____

CHAPTER 9:
LEGAL COMPOSITION

RULES FOR LEGAL WRITING

Use the Formal Style of English

The environment of a court of law is the epitome of formality, a strict convention that reaches the writing style that legal professionals are supposed to adopt—in theory. In practice, however, legal professionals tend to refine their writing styles in the interest of effectiveness and advantage, rather than in rigorous attention to traditional forms of grammar. Some secondary sources of law—such as legal newspapers, reviews, and treatises, in addition to trial-level papers, including legal briefs—are sometimes written in a semi-formal style that inclines in tone toward the conversational, rather than the mechanical. That is not to say, however, that this more casual approach may extend to the informality of, say, a personal letter to one's folks. Writers assuming the semi-formal tone generally walk the safer course by leaning toward the formal, in preference to the informal style of writing. But even so, function takes priority over form; this is why primary sources of law—constitutions, statutes, regulations, etc.—are always drafted in sparse, cautious terms with slavish deference to traditional grammatical rules, whereas trial lawyers and prisoner-litigants enjoy more freedom of style in making persuasive argument. (Legal sources must be painstakingly clear; legal briefs must be clearly painstaking.)

Due consideration in choice of style is advised. And while you should always remember that legal papers are written for a readership of lawyers and judges, do not be intimidated by these professionals into hesitating to express a point as you see fit; the substance and purpose of a piece of writing is more important than a writer's observation of rigid grammatical form. Tell your story; write clearly and with a mind for brevity, avoiding overly expressive language and embellishment. But above all, submit papers written in a tone of frank assertiveness and unwavering confidence.

A formal, efficient, and effective style can be confidently utilized by the adoption of the following rules:

1. **Do not use contractions.** A contraction is created by combining together two or more words. Common examples are "don't" (do not), "aren't" (are not), "wouldn't" (would not), "isn't" (is not), "it's" (it is), and so on. This book is replete with violations of this rule, but I've assumed a casual style for the most part, leaning in the direction of semi-formal/formal in the more technical sections detailing law and procedure. In strict formal style, however, contractions aren't used.

2. **Avoid beginning sentences with conjunctions.** Beginning a sentence with a conjunction—e.g., *and*, *but*, *because*—is considered by many grammarians to be technically incorrect. Even so, the fact of the matter is that many writers *do* begin sentences with conjunctions. The naysayers hold that a sentence beginning with a conjunction does not express a complete thought in itself, and therefore is better written

as a subordinate or independent clause attached to a preceding sentence, or rewritten to develop an idea without relying on a beginning conjunction. The yeasayers hold that beginning sentences with conjunctions is convenient and, if used properly, does not confuse readers. The choice is left to you—but if sentence-starting conjunctions are used, the prevailing opinion is that they should be used sparingly.

3. **Avoid ending sentences with prepositions.** Prepositions are words such as "to," "by," "with," "for," "in," "against," "across" that combine in meaning with a noun or pronoun to form a phrase: *go to the store*; *eaten with a spoon*; *given by James*. Some grammarians hold inviolate the rule against preposition-ended sentences. Other writers disregard the rule when it would cause a sentence to sound unnatural; still other writers reject the rule altogether. A stickler for the rule might write, *"That is not a path across which I have come,"* but other writers would say, *"That is not a path I have come across."* (This particular problem could be circumvented by saying, *"I have never come across this path."*) Still, the rule holds if the preposition can be moved from the sentence's end without causing an odd-sounding construction. *"I flipped the warden off,"* is properly rewritten as, *"I flipped off the warden."*

4. **Do not write in the first person.** The **first person** (*I, me, myself, we, us*) is used in a narrative to give a personal account—*"I filed my lawsuit on the 13th"*—and is not used in motions or briefs. The *first person* is used in letters, reports, and affidavits; whereas motions and briefs are written in the **third person** (*he, him, her, she, they, them*) to affect an impersonal recounting or third-party observation—*"The Plaintiff, acting* pro se, *filed his lawsuit on the 13th."* The **second person** (*you, your, yourself, we, us*) addresses the reader directly, and is almost never used in formal writing. In the legal world, second-person usage is found mainly in correspondence and documents meant to directly address an audience or reader, such as with Jury Instructions.

Avoid the Passive Voice

We say that a sentence is in the **passive voice** when the subject is affected by the action of the verb. (You'll recall that the subject of a sentence is the noun or pronoun that the rest of the sentence describes as doing or not doing something, or as being in a particular state or condition.) When the subject effectuates the verb, we say the sentence is in the **active voice**, because the action of the verb is attributed to the subject, the subject *does* something. In *"the guard confiscated my commissary,"* the subject "the guard" does the confiscating (the verb), and thus is written in the active voice. Active becomes passive when the subject, instead of doing, has something done to it. In *"my commissary was confiscated by the guard,"* "my commissary" has become the subject and *was confiscated*; it does not do the confiscating, and thus is written in the passive voice.

Passive voice is not grammatically incorrect; it is merely a variant of style used at the discretion of a writer. Passive voice, however, is regarded as somewhat of a writer's finishing tool, selected from one's repertoire to achieve a deliberate effect. It is used sparingly.

In the legal world of candid opinions and stark reason, passive voice is nearly useless—even disadvantageous. If a judge uses it, he or she is probably couching a harsh truth in polite terms to spare someone's feelings. When lawyers employ the device, they are usually trying to distance a client from some action/event, so that *"Mr. Johnson was alleged to have been stabbed by his cellmate."* Whereas the opposition assumes the active voice, saying, *"Aaron Hanson brutally stabbed his cellmate."* Active voice is pithy and assertive, and therein lies its advantage. Passive voice concedes this benefit, and is further subject to three major problems:

1. **Passive voice is wordy.** It takes longer to say anything in passive voice than it does in active. We could say, *"Mr. Johnson was alleged to have been stabbed by his cellmate,"* or we could say, *"The State accuses that Mr. Johnson stabbed his cellmate."* We see that the second example is the stronger version of the statement, efficient and pithy. Notice, too, in the second sentence the absence of the verbs "was" and "have been," and the preposition "by"—passive writing is permeated with such unnecessary uses of small words; they add up to a lot of wasted space and time.

2. **Passive voice betrays insecurity.** As already mentioned, passive voice is sometimes used to distance a subject from the action of a verb. The idea is to rob the verb of its force as it relates to the subject, so that Mr. Hanson didn't *stab his cellmate*, but rather Mr. Johnson *was stabbed by his cellmate.* The ruse does not work, however. The same idea is completed in the passive as well as the active voice, and the passive voice simply colors the message with a shade of insecurity—if confident about a message, why use wordplay?

3. **Passive voice can be vague.** Although passive voice is not necessarily vague in and of itself, vagueness can arise if a subject is not adequately identified when using a passive composition style. Take the example: *"A surplus of thirty thousand packages of ramen noodles was ordered for the Idaho prison commissary."* The sentence leaves us to wonder "Who messed up? Computer error, possibly?" But worse, especially so in legal writing, such a sentence leaves the reader to entertain the possibilities that (1) the writer does not know how the surplus ramens were ordered, and therefore has not done the requisite homework; or that (2) the writer has been vague intentionally, which leaves us to ask, "What are you hiding?" or, "What are you protecting?" We have too many questions for this bit of prose to be effective. Better to eschew the passive voice and commit to the statement with confidence. For example: *"Investigators discovered that Warden Weighty directed prison commissary employees to order a surplus of thirty thousand packages of ramen noodles from a wholesaler/distributor identified as the Warden's brother-in-law,"* or, *"Representatives of the Idaho Department of Corrections have revealed a surplus order of thirty thousand packages of ramen noodles, but have yet to identify the source of the mistake."*

Despite the intrinsic drawbacks of passive style, authors of case law, legal treatises, and scholarly article *do* sometimes include the passive voice in their rhetorical style, and to great effect. (**Rhetorical**: terms expressed in a way that is intended to persuade or impress.) Before you attempt to emulate these sources, however, review again this section and recall that standard sources of law are written by practiced legal minds, then reviewed by professional editors. You, at the trial level, are in the trenches, under fire, prosecuting a case without having the benefit of a law degree. Confident, active language—easier to write, easier to read—is for you the superior method of writing, which avoids altogether the hazards of passive voice.

Composing Sentences

Sentences should express a single thought in no more than fifteen to thirty words, though the rule is flexible. Content and clarity are more important than how long or short a sentence is, because the issue ultimately comes down to readability. Writers who keep in mind that longer sentences can lose readers or dilute an idea, whereas shorter sentences can lead to choppy, mechanical reading, generally have an easier time of producing readable prose. We've all worked to the end of a half-page sentence, only to realize we've somehow missed the point. Shorter sentences pose less risk of losing or confusing readers, but too many short sentences, written in succession, can be annoying, causing a reader to start and stall. For example:

> *We were on the housing unit. The warden entered to conduct a watch tour. We approached and gave him our grievances. He seemed affable and receptive to our concerns. But he did appear a little distracted. At least, I supposed he was distracted. This was because his eyes and feet had shifted anxiously. I assumed he intended to finish his unit business and be off. Lunch would be called soon. He probably wanted to avoid passing through corridors filled with inmates in transit to the chow hall.*

Although the meaning of a short sentence is usually clear, overuse does detract from the flow of the piece of writing. Moderation and balance, then. Use a short sentence after a long sentence, break too-long sentences into shorter ones, and combine short sentences by subordinating one to another, for example:

> *We approached the warden while he was doing a watch tour of our unit. He seemed affable and receptive to our concerns when we handed him our grievance forms, though his eyes and feet shifted anxiously—a little distracted, perhaps. At least, I supposed he was distracted; lunch would soon be called and I assumed he wanted to finish his unit business and be off before the corridors filled with inmates in transit to the chow hall.*

The example's first sentence is fairly short; the last, fairly long; the second, not so much; and it all makes sense. And yet, while the structure of each sentence plays its part, the *transition* of ideas between the sentences takes priority in writing a cohesive paragraph.

Notice the flow of ideas from one sentence to another. Each idea is developed individually, yet still adds to the overall idea of the whole paragraph: The subject handed grievances to the warden, who then began to act funny. In the first sentence, the writer and unspecified others approach the warden. In the second, the warden is given grievance forms and the writer notices the warden's strange body language. In the third, the writer develops his thoughts about the warden's behavior.

The trick of good transition or unity of sentences is to select a particular idea, noun, pronoun, or verb from one sentence to repeat in the next. In the above example, the first sentence introduces the "warden." The second, referring to the warden by using the pronoun "he," develops the idea of why the warden was introduced and provides some observations. The third sentence actually repeats the verb "distracted" from the second sentence, then develops the writer's suppositions about the warden's behavior. It's as easy as that—when uncertain of how to write the next sentence, look to the preceding sentence for a word or an idea to repeat or develop.

Another method for drawing readers into your prose is to construct sentences with alternate sentence forms. We've talked about alternating sentence length, so I won't belabor the point other than to offer that alternating sentence length combats monotonous prose—especially so for dry subjects. Alternating how you begin sentences, which are easily varied, works just as well to break the monotony, providing a pleasing change of sentence form.

Roughly eighty percent of sentences begin with the subject. Look back to the last set of example sentences and notice that the first sentence starts with the subject "We." The second sentence starts with the subject "He." But the third sentence—and I realize this example departs from the eighty-percent theory—does not begin with the subject. The subject is the personal pronoun "I," and it follows the words "At least." So, if not with the subject, how does the sentence begin?

"At least," in this instance, is an introductory phrase—an adverbial phrase, to be specific, which means "anyway" and modifies the verb "supposed." Sentences that do not begin with the subject are usually introduced by some kind of adverb, adverbial phrase, or adverb-dependent clause:

> *At the outset* we knew it would be difficult. *In the beginning* we had full confidence. *After* the Yule Tide my diet returned to normal. *There* are two candies I like best: butterscotch and peppermint. *When* we started the club, there was no telling how long it would last.

Beyond adverbial openers, sometimes sentences are opened with a participle phrase or clause—*"Possessing the muscle and nerve my friend did not, I chose to confront his bully on the ball field after school"*—though this variety of opener is seldom used, and only then after considering its rhetorical advantage.

Rarer still are the one-word modifiers, for example:

> *Angry*, she stomped off to bed. *Unfortunately*, the brown bear had returned. *Sighing*, Mr. Hanson resigned to his fate.

If the subject began sixteen out of twenty sentences, then adverbs would begin the seventeenth and eighteenth. Participle and one-word openers would complete for the last two places. That's the theory, anyway. And, although keeping this guideline in the back of one's mind is useful during the writing process, good composition—sometimes disregarding the rules—remains a matter of artful expression. "But," you may be thinking, "I'm filing legal documents, not writing a novel." Which is correct, and is why the basic rules of composition are provided here, to prevent you from worrying about whether irregularities in your prose might cause a reader to hang up. Beginning most, if not all, sentences with the subject, and transitioning from one sentence by elaborating on a word or an idea in the next, is a simple strategy for straightforward, readable, and *effective* legal writing.

Composing Paragraphs

A paragraph of three to eight sentences is usually enough to develop an idea. At their longest, paragraphs should go no further than half a page in handwriting or double-spaced typeface. Any longer and you run the risk of detracting from your prose; the same drawbacks to using long sentences also applies to long paragraphs: they can lose or confuse readers. Short paragraphs, as with short sentences, are not subject to the problems of long paragraphs, but may fail to fully convey the intended meaning behind the paragraph. And, as with short sentences, too may short paragraphs, written one after another, make for difficult, halting prose. Again, varying composition style is key.

Unity—the smooth transition between paragraphs—is in level of importance right next to variation of composition. Paragraphs should build upon each other, linked in a chain of sense. The easiest way to draft a strong, smooth link between paragraphs is to first examine the main idea of an ending sentence, and then to repeat or develop the idea in the first sentence of the next paragraph. An efficient method is to select a prominent noun, pronoun, or verb from an ending sentence of one paragraph to repeat at the beginning of the next paragraph. The main idea of any sentence usually turns on one or two key words—find them; they're your springboard into the next paragraph.

> *We approached the warden while he was doing a watch tour of our unit. He seemed affable and receptive to our concerns when we handed him our grievance forms, though his eyes and feet shifted anxiously—a little distracted, perhaps. At least, I supposed he was distracted; lunch would soon be called and I assumed he wanted to finish his unit business and be off before the corridors filled with inmates in transit to the chow hall.*
>
> *I supposed wrongly, as it turned out. The warden had been anxious for action, true, but not to avoid a hallway rush. He had gone by the time we returned from chow, and in his stead awaited two sergeants and four peons. Each of the six officers had chosen a cell to toss. Each of the cells belonged to one of us, those who'd filed grievances. The cells were a mess, but we would be spared the fuss of clearing up our things, for we would be cuffed and dragged to new habitations in Seg.*

The first example paragraph develops the idea that the writer and unnamed associates approached their warden to deliver grievances, and that the warden thereafter began to act funny. The paragraph's ending sentence develops a theory about the warden's behavior, and uses the word "suppose." The second paragraph repeats this word and runs with the idea of the first paragraph's ending by commenting on the writer's original supposition about the odd behavior. The rest of the second paragraph builds on this thought while also giving a factual account describing the warden's behavior and connecting it to what the writer believes was a series of consequences following from the filing of grievances. Both paragraphs, we see, develop different yet related ideas; the transition between which is assisted by the simple method of repeating a word.

This method doesn't always work, however. If your writer's block can't otherwise be overcome, if after a couple revisions it seems the two paragraphs just aren't compatible, then consider, that the underlying ideas of each paragraph may not be related enough to be sequenced together. In that event, the paragraph you want to write might be better placed elsewhere. This can sometimes be a hassle, or impracticable, which is why it's a good practice to first compare the main ideas of both paragraphs before moving on or committing to a particular revision. Look to the topic sentence of each paragraph, if there is one, to assure yourself that the disagreement in paragraph content cannot somehow be resolved.

A **topic sentence** consists of a general statement that expresses, outright, the main idea of the paragraph in which it appears. A topic sentence may appear anywhere in a paragraph but is usually at its beginning. The telltale of a topic sentence is in whether other sentences of the paragraph all seem to refer and rely on the same, single sentence. That's your topic sentence. In the example paragraphs above, neither possesses a strong topic sentence; their sentences express a general idea collectively, rather than build on an idea given firmly in any one sentence. The sentences of these paragraphs, therefore, must be read together to communicate their overall idea. If a paragraph is not properly composed, extracting its idea in this way may be difficult, a good indicator that the paragraph needs rewriting. Extracting the idea of a paragraph with a strong topic sentence, however, is much easier:

The warden retaliated against us for submitting grievances. He personally took our forms on the unit, and seemed affable and receptive. However, when we later returned from chow, all six of our cells had been tossed and officers awaited us on the tier, cuffs at the ready. We were then escorted to Segregation.

The example's first sentence is the topic sentence. It makes a general allegation of retaliation, which is then supported by the events described in the subsequent sentences. Most paragraphs, however, lack a strong topic sentence, though many have something approaching one, even if vaguely so. As long as sentences are unified, contribute to the paragraph's underlying message, and don't stray too far from the central thought, whether a topic sentence is used makes no difference, as far as concerns grammatical correctness. A topic sentences *does* cut right to the point, though; *and* can simplify complex paragraphs.

Concluding sentences, too, work well to frame a point in unmistakable terms. **Concluding sentences**, also known as "clinchers," appear at a paragraph's end, summarizing or emphasizing its content:

The warden retaliated against us for submitting grievances. He personally took our forms on the unit, and seemed affable and receptive. However, when we later returned from chow, all six of our cells had been tossed and officers awaited us on the tier, cuffs at the ready. We were then escorted to Segregation. The fact that our cells were searched, and that we were all thrown in the Hole immediately after we filed grievances, suggests strongly that the warden, despite outward appearances, did not receive our concerns well.

Concluding sentences such as in the above paragraph—though actually unnecessary in this particular example—are especially useful for clarifying the message of a long paragraph. They are useful in legal writing, as well: evidence or opinions can be summarized, and/or a specific course of action can be suggested to the judge.

Whether using clinchers or strong topic sentences or distinguished sentences united in meaning, any single paragraph should be committed to developing a central thought. And it should develop the thought well, before transitioning to the next thought. Thought to thought to thought in compact units—*units*, that is, instead of an unbroken block of information. Thus the writer makes strong points and sets a comfortable pace for readers to digest the material, allowing pauses between ideas. Ideas made all the more interesting by the advantage paragraphs provide to vary composition style, which grants writers freedom to manipulate the reading pace of text or to abruptly alternate tone of voice and/or sentence structure to draw attention to a particular paragraph, keeping the reader stimulated.

NOTE: Compare the first two example paragraphs in this section to the third paragraph. Notice that the third paragraph says essentially the same thing as the first two, though it doesn't elaborate as much on the writer's theories about the warden's odd behavior. The third paragraph begins with a brief, assertive topic sentence that sets the tone of the whole paragraph. It is also much more efficient than the first two paragraphs. The difference between the examples is that the first and second paragraphs are more stylized, whereas the third is more pithy—the fat has been trimmed, so to speak. The style of the third paragraph, for this reason, is suitable for legal composition, whereas the style of the first two examples might justifiably appear in a biography or a novel.

Legalese and Latin

The use of legalese (e.g., *hereinunder*, *forthwith*, *aforesaid*, etc.) is better avoided in inmate legal writing. In fact, legalese is used less and less among legal professionals generally. The use of Latin is on its way out as well; avoid using it. The necessity of a few Latin words and phrases, however, persists, and these words are used frequently. Below are common examples of such (their definitions are given in the glossary at the end of this book):

> *Certiorari, amicus curia, estoppel, ex parte, ex post facto, de novo, in limine, in forma paupris, prima facie, quid pro quo, per se, res judicata, stare decisis.*

Formatting Rules for Legal Papers

Most jurisdictions require that all papers drafted for court use (e.g., complaints, motions, briefs, etc.) leave at least a one-inch margin around the text of the page. Text should appear in 12-point typeface, and spaces between lines should be doubled. But check your local court rules for specifics on formatting.

Handwritten papers are sometimes subject to the double-spaced rule. Since a handwritten, double-space page is equal to about half a page of typeface with double-spaced lines, consider asking the court to make an exception to the double-spaced rule on the grounds of fairness. Or you can, in the alternative, request a standing page-length extension on all papers (an ordinary protocol of many courts is to limit brief length). Your adversaries have the benefit of computer-generated papers, and can, by way of typeface, include more info per page than can be given in a handwritten page. Point this out to the judge.

Quotation Blocks

Quotations of fewer than fifty words can simply be included within the main body of text without being set off by indentation. Passages of more than fifty words, however, should appear in indented blocks, using single-spaced lines rather than the double of the main body. Take the following example:

> In *Bell v. Wolfish*, 441 U.S. 520, 99 S.Ct. 1861, 60 L.Ed.2d. 447 (1979),
>
> the Supreme Court explained that the determination of whether a particular
>
> government-imposed condition or restriction imposes punishment—in the
>
> constitutional sense—will generally turn on whether an alternative, justifiable
>
> purpose is reasonably assignable to the imposition:
>
>> [I]f a particular condition or restriction of pre-trial detention is reasonably related to a legitimate governmental objective, it does not without more, amount to "punishment." Conversely, if a restriction or condition is not reasonably related to a legitimate goal—if it is arbitrary or purposeless—a court permissibly may infer that the purpose of the governmental action is punishment that may not constitutionally be inflicted upon detainees *qua* detainees.

Bell, 441 U.S. at 529, quoting *Kennedy v. Mendoxa-Martinez*, 372 U.S. 144, 168-69, 83 S.Ct. 554, 9 L.Ed.2d 644 (1963).

The *Bell* court further noted that a *de minimus* level of imposition is generally permissible, *id.*, at 441 U.S. 539 n.21, and that legitimate non-punitive governmental objectives include "maintaining security and order" and "operating the [detention facility] in a manageable fashion." *Id.,* at 540, n.23.

Note that the citation sentence "*Bell*, 441 U.S. at 529. . . ." that follows directly after the indented quotation block is itself *not* indented. This is because the citation does not begin a new paragraph, remaining part of the paragraph divided by the quotation block. The citation sentence is set below and apart from the quotation block because it is not part of the quoted material. Take another example:

> In 1992, the Ninth Circuit observed that:
>
> > litigation necessarily requires some means of accurate duplication because the court and parties need to refer to the same documents . . . photocopying is a reasonable means of providing the necessary copies of petitions, complaints, answers, motions, affidavits, exhibits, memoranda and briefs, including attachments and appendices, material needed for discovery and investigation, including interrogatories and freedom of information requests.

Gluth v. Kangas, 951 F.2d 1504, 1510 (9th Cir. 1992).

Gluth, directly addressing an inmate's right to photocopy legal materials, suggests a non-exclusive list of legal materials prison facilitators can reasonably be expected to encounter and duplicate on behalf of prisoners pursuing legal actions. Despite his numerous requests, Plaintiff was denied . . .

Quotation blocks should be used sparingly; too many dense tracts of quotations tend to disrupt the flow of a piece of writing. Large quotations, furthermore, may cause a reader to disengage, to skim over the quote so as to resume more quickly with the main body of writing. If a passage is essential to an argument or conveys a point best made in the original words of the source, don't hesitate to incorporate the quotation into your writing. Passages of lesser significance can be summarized in your own words. Passages of shorter length can be quoted within the main body of text, without indentation, lessening the risk that a reader might only skim it.

Short Citing

Once a source has been fully cited in a writing, the author may elect to shorten later citations to the same source. The signals *id.* and *id., at* [page#] refer to the *immediately* preceding citation—that is, *no* other citations appear between the use of the full citation form and the subsequent use of its short-cite *id.* signal. The signal "*id.*" is the abbreviation for the Latin word "*idem,*" which means "same." Notice the short citing of *Bell v. Wolfish* and the use of *id.* in the writing example of the previous section.

Citation Clauses

"Citation clauses" are citations that are imbedded *in* a sentence, set off by commas, rather than following the text in a separate sentence, as is more common. For example:

> Our state's tort claims act, I. C. § 6-901, *et seq.*, has no express provision waiving Idaho's Eleventh Amendment immunity from actions brought in federal courts.

In the alternative, citation clauses may be set off by using parentheses.

> Our state's tort claims act (I. C. § 6-901, *et seq.*) has no express provision waiving Idaho's Eleventh Amendment immunity from actions brought in federal courts.

Numerous Citations Are Listed in One Sentence

Numerous citations appearing together should be written in a single sentence, each clause––each citation—separated by a semicolon, as so:

> *See generally Wardell v. Maggard,* 470 F.3d 954 (10th Cir. 2006); *DeMallory v. Cullen,* 885 F.2d 442 (7th Cir. 1988); *Jones v. Smith,* 784 F.2d 149 (2d Cir. 1986).

Pinpoint Citations

The extra page numbers **54-55** and **870** in the below example *pinpoint* the specific page(s) to which the writer is referring.

> *See, e.g., Morales Feliciano v. Rullan,* 378 F.3d 42, **54-55** (1st Cir. 2004); *see also Armstrong v. Davis,* 275 F.3d 849, **870** (9th Cir. 2001) (noting that a "few isolated violations affecting a narrow range of plaintiffs" would not provide a basis for systemwide injunctive relief).

Using Brackets "[ ]"

Brackets inserted into a quotation indicate that the writer has altered the original passage where the brackets appear. For instance, the bracketed lowercase "[r]" in the word "[r]eversal" appearing in the below-provided example signals that the writer has changed the uppercase *R* in the original passage to the lowercase *r*. The uppercase letter in this example, which indicated the beginning of a sentence in the original passage— *"Reversal will not be granted unless prejudice is shown."*—is changed to the lowercase to grammatically fit the passage to the writer's own paragraph.

> A district court's decision will constitute an abuse of judicial discretion if it makes an error of law or clear error of fact, but "[r]eversal will not be granted

unless prejudice is shown." *City of Long Beach v. Standard Oil Co.*, 46 F.3d 929, 936 (9th Cir. 1995).

Other examples:

When determining whether legitimate, non-punitive reasons exist, a "court should not . . . blindly [defer] to [a prison official's] bare invocation of security concerns" without requiring some evidence that prison policies are based on legitimate penological justifications. *Pierce v. County of Orange,* 526 F.3d 1190, 1211 (9th Cir. 2008) (citation omitted).

The original sentence read:

"The district court should not have blindly deferred to the County's bare invocation of security concerns, when the County has failed to even establish that there is regular access to religious services for administrative segregation detainees, much less that interruptions in such access are on account of security." *Pierce v. County of Orange,* 526 F.3d 1190, 1211 (9th Cir. 2008) (citation omitted).

Using Footnotes

Footnotes are used to explain, clarify, or direct the reader's attention to some matter of special consideration in the main body of text. If the writer wishes to make comment or provide further clarification, but to do so would interrupt the natural flow of discussion, then footnotes can be used. Footnotes are listed at the bottom of the page, each being assigned assigned a number (usually in superscript [1,2,3,4,5] or in brackets/parentheses) or a symbol (usually *, †, ‡) that appears in the main body of text next to the sentence, clause, or word to which the footnote refers.

The advantage of using footnotes is that they can be single-spaced and printed in a smaller font, saving the writer precious briefing space should a page limit be imposed. Consult your local court rules for instruction on the use of footnotes and document formatting.

Tips for Editing

Prisoners without word-processor assistance, relegated to preparing papers by hand, are better off using pencil to write first drafts. Pencil marks are easily altered, where an inked draft is soon cluttered with indelible scribbles and revisions. Should an entire sentence or paragraph need rewriting, inked pages may have to be completely redone before the final proofing, whereupon the piece of writing will again have to be rewritten to complete the final draft. Early pencil-written versions are more amenable to later proofing and editing.

First drafts, especially, justify a rigorous once- or twice-over revision. Most writers, while writing first drafts, are less concerned about grammar and punctuation than they are about getting thoughts onto paper while inspiration strikes. Writers begin a piece of writing——as you should—already intending to refine their work at a later time.

The *later time* for draft revisions does not suggest that revisions be done as soon as a draft is completed, either. Take at least a night and a day before revision in order to disengage and reset your mind frame. Less than that and the writer may not be sufficiently distanced from the writing to view it with the objectivity that another reader would bring to the work.

Simple matters of checking spelling and punctuation are readily dealt with at any time, having less to do with the essence of the composition than they do with the basic mechanics of grammar. Revising for overall readability and effectiveness generally, as mentioned, should wait at least a day or two, or longer, and perhaps until after a friend (or a jailhouse lawyer) can be solicited for his or her thoughts about your work. Erasing and then pencilling in spelling or other relatively trivial corrections does not demand the creative power of actually converting ideas into words, and can be done as you go, during or after the initial writing process. Perhaps review the "Quick English Refresher" chapter to reassure yourself of grammar basics before beginning a piece of work.

After a sufficient period of reflection, and refreshed by a new day and a rundown on the rules of grammar, you can approach your raw prose with your mind newly invigorated and alert, ready to pounce on any error in your composition. If another person has examined your early draft, you can edit with the security that your expression is passible in at least some places, and consider the ideas of your peer where he or she has located problems. Commit to the inevitability that, necessarily, you may have to rewrite, amend, relocate, or even eliminate entire problem sections. A decided mind for efficient and readable prose should attenuate the pain of eliminating passages that may represent hours of creative labor.

Editing early drafts takes time. Dedicate, if you can, the same amount of time for editing and revising as you originally spent in creating the entire first draft. Yes, this all amounts to a whole lot of work, I know—but no one said writing was easy. Although, recalling these few tips, mercifully, should help you along in the editing process:

1. **Watch for errors in parallelism.** The rule of **parallelism**: Thoughts that are similar should be written with similar structure. The rule allows for balanced sentences, for example:

   We brought the car home at noon and left the house at eight. (Correct.)
   We brought the car home at noon and left home at eight. (Incorrect; the verb, "brought," in the first example is followed by the definite article "the"; the verb, "left," in the second clause is missing the article, going straight to the noun "home.")

   Imbalances in enumerations or lists are more common than imbalances between clauses, as with the above example, but are more easily detected:

   We drove home, had lunch, and left by one o'clock. (Correct.) *We drove home, had lunch, and we left by one o'clock.* (Incorrect; the second "we" is unnecessary and disturbs the flow from the second element of the enumeration to the third.)

   Parallelism errors in longer lists, with longer elements, occur even more frequently. A careful eye, however, should have no trouble detecting an imbalanced sentence structure if it is recalled that each element of a list should look the same. Examine this list:

   If my time in prison has taught me anything, it is to
   (1) mind personal business;
   (2) trust no person; and
   (3) avoid attention.

   Compare the three elements in the list. Notice that each is a phrase (as opposed to a word or a clause) beginning with a verb. Each element is written in the active voice, and each element independently corresponds with the introductory "it is to." The structure of this list is balanced.

Other common imbalances tend to involve the usage of three particular words: *neither*, *either*, and *both*. When using the word "neither" as a correlative conjunction with the word "nor," the practice is to place the two words so that they balance and mirror each other. For example, we would write *"prisoners are perceived as neither friendly nor forgiving,"* rather than *"prisoners neither are perceived as friendly nor forgiving."*

The word "either" poses a similar concern. For example, the structure of *"I am going to either the library or chapel after count time"* is imbalanced because "either the" is not mirrored by "or chapel." The proper structure reads: *"I am going to either the library or the chapel after count time."* Notice "either the" and "or the."

Similar to the usage of *neither/nor* and *either/or*, the usage of "both" as a correlative conjunction with "and" should be written symmetrically. We would write that *"both the library and the chapel are closed today,"* but not that *"both the library and chapel are closed today."* The former of the two sentence structures is clearer and stronger.

2. **Watch for misplaced modifiers. Modifier** is a term of general meaning that pertains to a word, phrase, or clause that restricts or adds to the sense of another word, phrase, or clause. The rule is that modifiers should appear as close as possible to the word(s) they modify. This is to avoid confusion about which part of a sentence a modifier is actually modifying. If we read that *"hanging on the doorknob, Kevin saw the sock announcing that his roommate had a guest,"* are we to believe that Kevin was hanging on the doorknob? Probably not. To avoid confusion the sentence should say, *"hanging on the doorknob, the sock announced that Kevin's roommate had a guest."* The participle phrase "hanging on the doorknob" modifies "the sock," and therefore should appear next to it in the sentence. This is an example of how to correct what is called a "dangling modifier," so called because the modifier "dangles" by a comma at the beginning of the sentence, without sensibly modifying the adjoined clause. The dangler in the example became a correct modifier by the simple rearrangement of the main clause, placing modifier and word modified closer in the sentence. This is an easy correction to make because danglers are easy to spot. Other misplaced modifiers, not so much. Take these examples:

> *I bought a sheet for my bed made of silk.* (Is the bed made of silk? Better rewrite it, "I bought a silk sheet for my bed.") *We heard about the prisoners who escaped on the radio.* (Were the prisoners riding the radio? Better rewrite it, "We heard on the radio about the prisoners who escaped.")

3. **Avoid wordiness.** When a thought is expressed in more words than necessary, we call that expression "wordy." Writers, of course, have wide latitude in how they elect to string words together, but readers possess the greater discretion in what they choose not to read. And readers, particularly in the legal world, do not want their time wasted. Economical use of words, then, is crucial to effective writing; and is, fortunately, largely achieved by these simple guidelines:

   i. **Avoid using throat-clearing phrases. Throat clearers** are phrases, usually beginning sentences, which do not actually add anything to the clauses they introduce. Most are used purely for rhetorical purposes, or as a device to smooth the transition between sentences or paragraphs. Prime examples of throat clearers that can be completely eliminated from most prose are as follows:

> *Considering the fact that . . . In a position to . . . It may be concluded . . . It is possible that . . . One of the things that . . . Take into consideration* [or *account*] *. . . Voice* [or *I'm of*] *the opinion . . . With regard* [or *respect*] *to . . .*

ii. **Avoid using intensifiers. Intensifiers** are adverbs that are used to give extra force of emphasis to a thought. The adverb "really" in *"he was really careless"* emphasizes what *he was*, but is *really* unnecessary. *"He was careless,"* works just fine. Used sparingly, however, intensifiers *can* add a pleasing variety of rhetorical effect to a piece of writing, yet this virtue is nonetheless diminished by overuse. Use of the following words as intensifiers ought to be avoided:

> *Absolutely, assuredly, basically, certainly, definitely, dreadfully, essentially, fabulously, fantastically, horribly, incredibly, immensely, intensely, marvelously, perfectly, positively, quite, rather, simply, terribly, utterly, and very.*

iii. **Avoid beginning sentences with "it is," "there is," and "what was."** Using any of these three phrases at the beginning of a sentence often leads to belabored sentenced structures. The phrase "it is" in *"it is unusual for inmates to complete their terms without receiving some kind of institutional infraction"* can be eliminated entirely in the simpler construction, *"inmates usually receive some kind of institutional infraction before completing their prison terms."* The phrase "there is" (also "there are," "there was," "there were") offers the same type of problem as "it is." We could say, *"There is a strange car parked in front of the house,"* but it's easier to say, *"A strange car is parked in front of the house."* ("There is" *is* acceptable to begin a sentence, however, if the only other option is to use the word "exist"—*"there is a concern"* is preferable to *"a concern exists."*) A sentence that starts with "what was [or *is*]" may also be faulted for wordiness. This phrase, like its companions listed above, frequently appears when writers try to affect in their prose an eloquent tone or "learned" style, so that we get sentences such as this one: *"What was important to sick inmates was getting treatment."* The simpler and therefore stronger construction is, *"Getting treatment was important to sick inmates."*

iv. **Avoid elegant variation.** Problems with elegant variation often afflict writers who are, perhaps, a little too concerned with finding different ways to express a word or an idea that must be repeated. These writers hold that expressing similar ideas in a pleasing variety prevents readers from becoming bored—which *is* the prevailing theory. In practice, writers, especially novice writers over-burdened by the idea of variation, can sometimes end up using phrases such as *"due to the fact"* instead of "because." So long as things stay in hand, variety is good; but saying things like *"prior to"* instead of "before" may resound falsely with readers and clog prose. Repeating words like "because" and "before" won't diminish the style of a piece, but ever-evolving variations of a similar thought might. If you find that you've resorted to using *"particulate matter in a colloidal suspension"* instead of repeating the word "mud," or if you've written that a person has an *"aversion to profitable labor"* instead of just saying he's "lazy," then, dear reader, things are worse than we thought.

v.   **Eliminate redundancies. Redundancies** are parts of speech that are *both* repetitious *and* unnecessary. A phrase such as *"aid and abet"* is a perfect example. "Aid" means the same as "abet," which is to say, *help*. One or the other may be used; using both is redundant. Particularly watch for redundancies in expressions of time—*"six a.m. in the morning,"* for example, should be written "six o'clock in the morning" or "six a.m."

NOTES: _____

NOTES: _____

_____

_____

_____

_____

_____

_____

_____

_____

_____

_____

_____

_____

_____

_____

_____

_____

_____

_____

_____

_____

_____

_____

_____

_____

_____

_____

_____

_____

_____

_____

_____

_____

CHAPTER 10: WRITING LEGAL BRIEFS

Legal briefs, also called "memoranda," are used to persuade a trial judge into taking one course of action over another.

Ordinarily, the people reading the briefs are the lawyers involved with the case, the judge, and the judge's law clerk, all of whom will come to your brief already possessing a fair understand of the procedural status of the case and facts and issues involved. Nevertheless, it remains necessary to follow the usual rules of brief writing, which include summarizing all relevant information. Sometimes this can be tedious, and seem redundant. Do it anyway.

Content and Form of Brief

The rules that govern the particulars of memoranda form and order of content differ among jurisdictions. Review your local rules of court for specifics, but most jurisdictions share the requirement that a persuasive legal brief be headed with a formal caption, followed by a short introduction, a summation of the facts, the argument, and a concluding section.

1. **Caption.** The "caption" heads just about every legal document you will receive or file with the court (e.g., pleadings, briefs, affidavits, even discovery requests). The form varies depending on the jurisdiction, but all contain the same basic information: (1) title of trial court, (2) names of plaintiffs and defendants, (3) case number, and (4) title or "designation" of the document itself. (Caption examples are given in other places throughout this book.)

2. **Introduction.** The introduction provides the reader with context. In the introduction the writer tells the court why the brief was filed and its purpose. Is the memorandum in support of a motion? Or is it in opposition to a motion filed by an adverse party?

3. **Statement of facts.** The statement of facts section is what it sounds like, a detailed account of the facts surrounding the case. The facts section of a memorandum is usually divided into two parts: (1) procedural facts and (2) substantive facts. The procedural part concerns how and when the case has been brought to the attention of the government, including its disposition at administrative levels, how and when it travelled to the court, and current procedural status. The substantive part of the statement of facts concerns the underlying facts of the case, what happened to whom. (In simple cases it is usually okay, and beneficial, to combine the introduction section with the statement of facts section. This method saves space and helps with readability. Whatever the chosen method, litigants should be certain to summarize the underlying facts consistently throughout the pleadings and all memoranda. That is, how the facts are portrayed should remain substantively the same in all tellings, because any inconsistencies in retelling can be construed to cast doubt on your overall credibility. And don't gloss over facts that hurt your case; you can be assured the opposition won't. Facing them head-on, negative aspects of argument or fact can be minimized or explained away in the argument section.)

4. **Argument.** The argument is, of course, where a brief gets interesting. It is also the hardest part of legal writing. The goal is to persuade the reader to your way of thinking, which

can be difficult for *pro se* prisoners contending with trained legal professionals experienced in making counter-arguments. Prisoners, however, can be consoled by the fact that the best legal arguments are simple and straightforward, and that one of the most effective argumentation methods for legal novices is the easy-to-use IRAC method, which is detailed in the next section. (Give yourself plenty of preparation time, to research and write and revise. Don't stress yourself. Recall the rules for legal writing. Write with confidence and use an assertive tone. Pithy sentences are better than flamboyant sentences. Finally, revise, revise, revise. Find someone to look over your draft; they will spot inconsistencies, weak writing, and other hang-ups. Sense and readability are the objectives.)

5. **Conclusion.** At the end of the memorandum, there should be a concise summary of the overall conclusions and recommendations argued in the body of the brief. A paragraph or two should do the trick, but go longer if you must. And don't worry if a concluding section seems a bit redundant—coming as it does after a rigorous delineation and argument of the issues—because it *is* redundant. But it's expected, and useful as well. First, the conclusion allows the author to reiterate the thrust of his or her main points and state what is desired in no uncertain terms. Second, it allows a reader to flip to the back pages of a brief to understand quickly what the writer is ultimately saying and what he or she wants.

Idea Rule Application Conclusion (IRAC)

The easiest way to draft a persuasive legal argument is by following these four steps: (1) illustrate a clear idea of what the issue is and what you want to say; (2) list clearly the pertinent law or rule; (3) apply that law to the facts surrounding the idea; and (4) form a clear and concise conclusion as to why the idea is supported by the law. This process is called the Idea-Rule-Application-Conclusion method, IRAC for short, and can be used for most types of legal argument. Start with a short outline like the following example, and go from there.

Idea: Inmate Smith is being denied necessary prescription pain medication and orthopedic back surgery. He suffers chronic pain caused from a ruptured disk and inflamed tissue. (Include a brief but complete factual summary of condition and diagnosis.)

Rule: The prison is legally required to provide inmates with adequate medical care. (Cite and discuss the legal authority establishing an inmate's right to medical care.)

Application: Describe the severity of the medical condition, the denial of medical care (when, where, who by), include all steps in requests/grievances, and cite/discuss supporting legal authority.

Conclusion: Succinctly summarize the legal conclusion(s) and state relief/decision sought from the court.

Before starting a legal brief draft, determine exactly which points are to be covered in the brief, and then write an IRAC outline like in the above example for each of those important points. Make sure to look over, carefully, the reference materials (legal and evidentiary) that you intend to rely upon in the brief. For longer memoranda, separate the major points into individual sections, each following its own mini IRAC argument. Set off each section by using a boldface header that indicates both the topic and the purpose of the section. (See Figure 7 in

"What to Expect After Filing" of "PART 3," below, for an example of the IRAC method in practice.)

Common Types of Arguments

Unlike ordinary arguments offered by one's peers around the poker table, offering an argument to a court of law is rarely ever as easy as stating baldly a personal opinion or observation. Indeed, even on the exceptionally rare occasion when a set of facts and the law regarding those facts *can* be stated outright as self-evident, a judge may *still* require a demonstration of the logical steps that led the proponent to such a seemingly obvious truth. Judges want to hear reasoning. They want those who posit a conclusion to show their work. Legal writers, therefore, cultivate early on in their careers a habit of carefully noting (at least briefly) each fact, inference, or principle that they rely on to build a chain of reason.

Reason is the process whereby a premise (the foundation of an argument or theory) is established by observable facts or by apparent truths that, when taken together (viewed to have some kind of relationship), culminate in some belief. This process is divided into two broad, though overlapping categories of "deductive reasoning" and "inductive reasoning."

Deductive reasoning is characterized by the inference of a fact resulting from the comparison of two or more facts, laws, or principles. The first of the accepted facts, laws, or principles is called the "major premise." To the major premise is applied the "minor premise," which is also some belief already established as valid. Comparing the minor premise to the major, a logical conclusion may then be derived; for example:

Major premise:	*All reptiles are cold-blooded.*
Minor premise:	*All snakes are reptiles.*
Conclusion:	*All snakes are cold-blooded.*

If the premises are true (the argument goes), the conclusion must be true. The obvious problem with this form of reasoning lies in whether the major and the minor premises are actually correct—which provides two avenues for attack. Disputing that snakes are in fact cold-blood, an opponent has the choice of undermining either the major or the minor premise, or both. *"Well, Your Honor, recently an Amazonian species of lizard—also a reptile—has been discovered to maintain its body temperature above that of its environment by the same homeothermic means of warm-blooded animals." "Your Honor, we submit a recent article from the peer-reviewed journal,* American Zoology, *which describes strong evidence that at least one Australian species formerly classified as a snake has more genetically in common with a chicken than any reptile."* Should one or both of these counterpoints prove true, the conclusion that snakes are cold-blooded, if not totally defeated, would have to be revised as *"most* snakes are cold-blooded."

Inductive reasoning is characterized by the process in which events are observed until a relationship or a pattern between or among the events emerges to supply a basis for some kind of conclusion. If on no other day but Tuesday our subject leaves her house—the first Tuesday, going to the store; the second, to the bank; the third, to the post office; the fourth, to the store again—then we can inductively reason that, for this particular month, Tuesday is the subject's errand day.

The way to attack this type of argument is to (1) question the process and protocol involved in making the observations of the subject (e.g., how was the subject watched? what technology was use? how were findings and observations recorded? who was on the surveillance team? was the subject observed twenty-four hours a day?), and to (2) inquire after the credibility of the observers themselves (e.g., what are their qualifications? do they have moral or financial interests in the outcome of the observation? have any ever been accused of falsifying data?).

Both deductive reasoning and inductive reasoning have their innate pros and cons; there's no escaping it. The trick to pressing either argument is to prepare assiduously to defend the weaker points, as a chess player assiduously protects one game piece with another. Which is to say, don't let the opposition poke holes in a good theory because you've been lazy about verifying your sources, or about completing research. (Note: Look for such failings in the opposition's arguments.) Knowing that each component of an argument is well-reasoned and well-supported by some kind of evidence, you can then assert your opinions with confidence.

Recognizing whether each of your arguments is based primarily on deductive or inductive reasoning is crucial to ascertaining the support needed to marshal the argument's defense. In practice, most arguments have elements of both the deductive and the inductive forms of logic, but the presence of one form is always stronger than the presence of the other. Of arguments themselves, five common types are most often used in the legal world:

1. **Arguing *a fortiori*.** The Latin phrase means "from the stronger," and the argument, stripped to its essence, says that if the greater of two related things (facts, events, ideas) is true, it is even more likely that the lesser is also true. For example, if in a time of economic freedom, state legislators refuse to pass a measure for correctional reform as too costly, it is even less likely to pass in a time of economical constraint.

2. **Arguing from cause to effect.** This argument is often used to understand something that has already happened—that an event or effect of some kind was caused by a preceding and apparently connected occurrence. For example, we could argue that high rates of lung cancer in smokers are caused by the toxins in tobacco smoke. Problems with looking backward in this way to identify a cause (or looking forward to predict a likely event, which is arguing effect to cause) arise when we jump immediately to an "obvious" cause (or obvious effect) without carefully eliminating other reasonable possibilities. On its face, an argument holding that when an escalation in prison violence coincides with an increase in prison gangs, prison gangs are the cause. But, one could counter, has the issue been thoroughly considered? Perhaps the increase in violence also coincided with prison overcrowding? Have prison jobs and/or programs been reduced, causing thousands of prisoners to be idle and therefore ripe to cause trouble?

3. **Arguing from necessity.** This argument simply says that a certain course of action *must* be taken because no other viable choice exists. If we accept that the earth's atmosphere is warming because of human-caused carbon emissions, and that a rise in temperature is likely to cause humanity and the earth's ecosystems critical trouble, then we can argue that reducing air pollution is necessary. This type of argument, however, is vulnerable to attack on two fronts. First, the underlying facts can be disputed—*"There is no evidence connecting global warming with human-caused carbon emissions."* Second, conceding the underlying facts as true, the proposed solution to the problem is false—*"Instead of reducing carbon emissions, it's more feasible to construct carbon filters to gradually clean the air."* Whether such counterpoints are successful depends on the overall state of evidence bearing on the question. In this example, we would point to the multitude of scientific data connecting humanity's carbon emissions to global warming. Whether fil-

tering the atmosphere as the singular solution is actually a realistic alternative for combatting the effects of pollution is a question resolved with evidence demonstrating the impossibility of building enough filters to cycle out emissions at the rate in which they are dumped into the air.

4. **Arguing from the similitude.** This argument says that people, things, or events that are similar in some ways are probably similar in other ways, too. By this reasoning we may predict that, since a positively charged particle of one type veered to the left after entering a strong magnetic field, then a positively charged particle of another type will also veer to the left. In the harder sciences, such as physics and geology, arguing from the similitude makes practical sense and produces workable solutions. For the softer sciences, which deal with animal behavior and mental process, the similitude argument can sometimes lead to stereotypes or other over-generalizations that do not, by their nature, account for irregularities or individual characteristics.

5. **Arguing from authority.** This type of argument is less a process of reason than a reference to existing arguments, ideas, or examples made by someone else who is deemed persuasive by virtue of his or her authority. Such arguments tend to start with some variety of "Thomas Jefferson wrote . . ." or "Abraham Lincoln once said . . ." or "Albert Einstein postulated that . . ." which then continue on to provide an old argument or example as a supporting analogy for a new argument. The argument is more persuasive depending on the authority attributed to the person(s). Some people are perceived as credible sheerly on the basis of their charisma, sensibilities, or good reputation. Others we believe because of their experience, credentials, references, degrees, certificates, etc. (In the legal world, the authority argument—which is given a special, prominent role by legal professionals—has evolved into a rigid system of judicial deference, i.e., *precedence.* Judges operate under the presumption that prior judicial opinions were reasoned correctly by sound, objective minds. And this presumption will persist, sometimes when it shouldn't, unless conclusively invalidated by new evidence or by strong logic to the contrary. Which is why—especially for a prisoner-litigant without adequate legal resources to build new arguments—comparing the facts of your case to those of an existing, favorably decided case is the easiest, most effect scheme for persuading a judge. The argument goes, *"Judge, the facts of these cases are very similar; and in the earlier case, the court decided that the law is on my side. You should, too."*)

NOTE: Recall the ordinary components of a legal brief—Caption, Introduction, Statement of Facts, Argument, Conclusion. In writing the Argument section, instead of repeating facts over and over, the factual part of arguments may be supported by a reference back to the Statement of Facts section. However, first determine whether the facts you refer to are so complex or obscure that they would interrupt a reader's attention, causing him or her to flip back to review your facts section. Are you okay with that? If not, perhaps briefly repeat the pertinent facts within the written body of the argument as the argument is being made, or maybe include a summarizing footnote.

NOTES: _____

_____

_____

_____

_____

_____

_____

_____

_____

_____

_____

_____

_____

_____

_____

_____

_____

_____

_____

_____

_____

_____

_____

_____

_____

_____

_____

_____

_____

_____

_____

_____

_____

NOTES: _____
_____
_____
_____
_____
_____
_____
_____
_____
_____
_____
_____
_____
_____
_____
_____
_____
_____
_____
_____
_____
_____
_____
_____
_____
_____
_____
_____
_____
_____
_____
_____
_____
_____

PART 3:
FILING & LITIGATING

CHAPTER 11:
SECTION 1983, *BIVENS*, OR TORT?

THE RIGHT VEHICLE

In the legal world, the term **vehicle** is used as technical jargon for the mode of pleading by which a legal claim or motion can be brought into court for judicial consideration. That a claim or motion can be asserted in more than a single way, or indeed in more than a single type of court, is not unusual. Selecting the right method—the right "vehicle"—is crucial to a favorable outcome. One vehicle may avail you where another may not; carefully consider your options.

Constitutional and Federal Claims

The majority of prisoner claims raise federal questions, and therefore are filed in federal courts. By far, most prisoners seek redress by filing under **42 U.S.C. § 1983**. This is because the majority of prisoners in this country are state prisoners, and § 1983 provides a cause of action against those who deprive prisoners of federally guaranteed rights while acting under color of *state* law. (*See generally* "PART 4" for discussion of prisoners' rights.)

> The statute reads:
>
> Every person who, under color of any statute, ordinance, regulation, custom, or usage, of any State or Territory or the District of Columbia, subjects, or causes to be subjected, any citizen of the United States or other person within the jurisdiction thereof to the deprivation of any rights, privileges, or immunities secured by the Constitution and laws, shall be liable to the party injured in an action at law, suit in equity, or other proper proceeding for redress, except that in any action brought against a judicial officer for an act or omission taken in such officer's judicial capacity, injunctive relief shall not be granted unless a declaratory decree was violated or declaratory relief was unavailable. For the purposes of this section, any Act of Congress applicable exclusively to the District of Columbia shall be considered to be a statute of the District of Columbia.

This title is broader in scope than it may appear at first blush. Most pointedly, state prison officials and companies or company employees contracted to provide prison services (such as medical or catering companies, or private prisons) are almost always considered to be acting "under color of state law" for the purposes of a § 1983 action, and thus are liable for deprivations proscribed against by federal law. For the gray areas arising as to whether the misdeeds of a *private* person, company, or institution fall within the purview of § 1983, the courts have established a two-prong analysis for ascertaining whether questionable conduct was perpetrated "under color of state law." The courts ask (1) whether the alleged civil injury was caused by an exercise of authority conferred or imposed by the state, and (2) whether the private party can reasonably be said to have acted as a state agent. *Lugar v. Edmondson Oil Co.*, 457 U.S. 922, 937 (1982).

Such actors have been held liable under § 1983 when they have misused official power, power possessed by virtue of state law and made possible only because the wrong-doer is clothed with the authority of state law; when the actor was a willful participant in joint activity with the state or its agents, though not actually an officer of the state; or when the act or omission is committed by a private person who was authorized to exercise state authority. Accordingly, § 1983 suits may not be brought against private parties who possess *no* connection to the government. For instance, a prisoner would not be able to sue another prisoner under § 1983 for assault, though a suit could be filed in state court under the common-law tort action for assault.

However, private *companies* operating prisons or providing services to prisoners cannot automatically be imputed liability for the wrongful conduct of their agents or employees. For § 1983 liability to extend to a company for the performances of its agents or employees, the conduct in question must have occurred as the result of a company policy or custom. Acts or omissions not motivated by a company policy cannot found the basis of a § 1983 action against the company; although, the individual actors themselves can probably be held liable in state court under state tort law. (Note that *Bivens* actions, discussed in later paragraphs, may not be used against private companies contracted with the federal government. *Correctional Services Corp. V. Malesko*, 534 U.S. 61, 70-74 (2001).)

Clearly, § 1983 is a significant weapon in the inmate arsenal, though it doesn't create any *new* substantial rights in itself. What it does create is a means for *asserting* federal rights *already* established under the Constitution or federal statutes, and allows a plaintiff to file directly in the federal courts, without having had to first pursue and exhaust a lawsuit in state court. An exception occurs should another federal law expressly preempt § 1983, requiring the exhaustion of state remedies. For example, the Prisoner Litigation Reform Act requires prisoners to exhaust all state administrative remedies where they exist—which necessarily includes full compliance with institutional grievance and, possibly, notice-of-tort procedures. (*See generally* "PLRA" section, below.)

Section 1983 may *not* be used, however, to challenge a criminal conviction or the duration of a sentence, and will not be available where a plaintiff's § 1983 complaint, if successful, would logically imply the invalidity of criminal conviction or sentence duration. Such challenges are usually brought by a petition for a writ of *habeas corpus*. However, if the plaintiff can show that his or her conviction or sentence has already been reversed on direct appeal, expunged by executive order, invalidated by an authorized state tribunal, or called into question by a federal court's issuance of a writ of *habeas corpus*, well, then, the plaintiff may pursue a § 1983. (*See* "Heck v. Humphrey" subsection in "Chapter 18," below.)

In most states the statute of limitations (the time limit for filing) for bringing a § 1983 or a *Bivens* action is two years—BUT CHECK THE LAWS OF YOUR STATE. Section 1983 and *Bivens* actions have no statutes of limitation of their own; therefore, federal courts look to state statutes of limitation controlling personal injury claims. Federal courts will also adopt your state's tolling rules (rules temporarily suspending the statutes of limitation). A common example of equitable tolling occurs when a prospective plaintiff is unable to bring a suit because of temporary physical or mental incompetence.

Still, federal law controls when the statute of limitations actually *begins* to run, if not the length of the statute itself. The action accrues (commencing the statute of limitations) for the purposes of § 1983 and *Bivens* when the plaintiff has a "complete and present" cause of action. (*See* the discussion of *Wallace v. Kato* under the "*Heck v. Humphrey*" subsection in "Chapter 18," below.)

Keep in mind that § 1983 is not the exclusive remedy for all federal claims. Section 1983 is the proper vehicle for claims of wrongful acts or omissions perpetrated under color of *state* law. But when a person acting under color of *federal* law (i.e., federal employees) deprives a person of a Constitutional or other federal right, a plaintiff may pursue an action against the U.S. government official under the theory of a *Bivens* action, or against the U.S. government under the Federal Tort Claims Act.

The **Federal Tort Claims Act** (FTCA), at 28 U.S.C. §§ 1346(b), 2671-2680, is the statute by which prisoners and other citizens are able to sue the federal government directly. Under this statute, the only relief available is compensatory damages, *id.*, at § 1346(b), and such claims will be tried by a judge only, no jury. 28 U.S.C. § 2402. Although the doctrine of sovereign immunity shields the federal government from most kinds of liability, the FTCA makes a few exceptions for compensatory damages suits arising from torts as defined and limited in the statute. (Damages suits arising from violations of the Constitution, however, are not actionable under the FTCA.) Under the FTCA, the United States may be held liable "for injury or loss of property, or personal injury or death. . . ," provided the injury is

> caused by the negligent or wrongful act or omission of any employee of the government while acting within the scope of his office or employment, under circumstances where the United States, if a private person would be liable to the claimant in accordance with the law of the place where the act or omission occurred.

28 U.S.C. § 1346(b).

Thus, the FTCA makes the U.S. liable for the torts of its employees to the extent that private employers are liable under state law for the torts of their employees, so long as those torts are committed by employees acting "within the scope of [their] office or employment," *id.*, and provided statutory administrative notice requirements are followed by tort claimants (see "Notice of Tort" section in "Chapter 2," above.) There are, however, some exceptions to this liability.

First, the *Feres* doctrine, as in *Feres v. United States*, 340 U.S. 135 (1950), prohibits suits by military personnel for injuries sustained in service, and is not particularly relevant to prisoners' rights actions. Second, the **discretionary function exception**—most relevant—shields the U.S. from claims "based upon the exercise or performance or the failure to exercise or perform a discretionary function." 28 U.S.C. § 2680(a). It precludes liability even if a federal employee acted negligently in the performance or nonperformance of his or her discretionary duty. In *Dalehite v. United States*, 346 U.S. 15 (1953), the Supreme Court said that the discretion protected by the exception

> is the discretion of the executive or administrator to act according to one's judgment of the best course. . . . It . . . includes more than the initiation of programs and activities. It also includes determinations made by executives or administrators in establishing plans, specifications or schedules of operations. Where there is room for policy judgment and decision there is discretion. It necessarily follows that acts of subordinates in carrying out the operations of government in accordance with official directions cannot be actionable.

Id., at 34, 35-36 (footnotes omitted).

To be clear, the FTCA provides a cause of action against the U.S. government when its employees cause injury resulting from conduct that cannot be fairly characterized as discretionary. (A federal prison guard, for instance, does not have the discretion to ignore policy governing health and safety.) In determining the applicability of the discretionary exception,

> a court must first consider whether the action is a matter of choice for the acting employee. . . . [C]onduct cannot be discretionary unless it involves an element of judgment or choice. . . . Thus, the discretionary function exception will not apply when a federal statute, regulation, or policy specifically pre-scribes a course of action for an employee to follow. In this event, the em-ployee has no rightful option but to adhere to the directive. . . . The [discre-tionary function] exception . . . protects only governmental actions and deci-sions based on considerations of public policy.

United States v. Gaubert, 499 U.S. 315, 536-537 (1991).

Some acts are clearly discretionary, others are clearly not, and yet others may depend on circumstance. This question might end up being a hotly debated in your case. As to that, the Supreme Court has provided us a bit more insight, which may prove useful in coming to a resolution:

> [I]t is unnecessary—and indeed impossible—to define with precision every contour of the discretionary function exception. From the legislative and judi-cial materials, however, it is possible to isolate several factors useful in deter-mining when the acts of a Government employee are protected from liability by § 2680(a). First, it is the nature of the conduct, rather than the status of the actor, that governs whether the discretionary function exception applies in a given case. . . . Second, whatever else the discretionary function exception may in-clude, it plainly was intended to encompass the discretionary acts of the Gov-ernment acting in its role as a regulator of the conduct of private individuals.

United States v. Varig Airlines, 467 U.S. 797, 813-814 (1984).

A third major exception to liability is the **intentional tort exception**, which provides that the FTCA does not apply to claims

> arising out of assault, battery, false imprisonment, false arrest, malicious pros-ecution, abuse of process, libel, slander, misrepresentation, deceit, or interfer-ence with contract rights.

However, the United States may be held liable for any of the first six torts in the above-given list—assault, battery, false imprisonment, false arrest, malicious prosecution, abuse of process—if committed by an "investigative or law enforcement officer of the United States Government." 28 U.S.C. § 2680(h).

Furthermore, the United States may not be held liable under a state law imposing strict liability (**strict liability** is liability that does not depend on negligence or intent to harm, but that is based only on the breach of an absolute duty to make something safe); it may not be held liable for interest accumulated prior to a court judgment or for punitive damages (28 U.S.C. § 2674); for the act or omission of an employee exercising due care while following the directive of an invalid statute or regulation (28 U.S.C. § 2680); for claims "arising out of the loss, miscarriage, or negligent transmission of letters or postal matter" (28 U.S.C. § 2680); for claims arising in respect to the assessment or collection of any tax or customs duty (28 U.S.C. § 2680); for claims caused by the fiscal operations of the Treasury or by the regulation of the monetary system (28 U.S.C. § 2680); for claims arising out of combatant activities; for claims arising in a foreign country (28 U.S.C. § 2680); or for damages claims for mental or emotional suffering, absent a prior showing of physical injury or sexual assault:

> No person convicted of a felony who is incarcerated while awaiting sentencing or while serving a sentence may bring a civil action against the United States or an agency, officer, or employee of the Government, for mental or emotional injury suffered while in custody *without a prior showing of physical injury or the commission of a sexual act* (as defined in section 2246 of title 18).

28. U.S.C. § 1346(b)(2) (emphasis added).

> Title 18 U.S.C. § 2246 defines a sexual act as

> (A) Contact between the penis and the vulva or the penis and the anus, and for purposes of this subparagraph contact involving the penis occurs upon penetration, however slight;

> (B) Contact between the mouth and the penis, the mouth and the vulva, or the mouth and the anus;

> (C) The penetration, however slight, of the anal or genital opening of another by a hand or finger or by any object, with an intent to abuse, humiliate, harass, degrade, or arouse or gratify the sexual desire of any person; or

> (D) The intentional touching, not through the clothing, of the genitalia of another person who has not attained the age of 16 years with an intent to abuse, humiliate, harass, degrade, or arouse or gratify the sexual desire of any person.

One more point should be clarified. While the FTCA allows us to sue the the U.S. government for the conduct of its employees, the employees themselves are protected from liability under the Federal Employees Liability Reform and Tort Compensation Act of 1988, P.L. 100-694 (a.k.a. the Westfall Act, so-named for the superseded *Westfall v. Erwin*, 484 U.S. 292 (1988)). Basically, this act amended the FTCA to make it the exclusive remedy for torts committed by federal employees within the scope of their employment. It immunizes federal employees from actions arising under *state tort law*.

Federal employees may nevertheless be held personally liable for torts infringing upon Constitutional rights. Another type of action, a ***Bivens* action**, allows federal employees to be sued for damages for their violations of the U.S. Constitution. 28 U.S.C. § 2679(b)(2).

In *Bivens v. Six Unknown Named Agents*, 403 U.S. 388 (1970), federal agents, without a warrant, entered and searched the plaintiff's apartment and arrested the plaintiff for alleged narcotics violations. The Court held that the plaintiff could sue the federal agents for damages directly under the Fourth Amendment. However, a *Bivens* action may only be brought where Congress has not provided an otherwise adequate legal remedy. In *Wilkie v. Robbins*, __U.S.__, 127 S. Ct. 2588, 2598, __L.Ed.2d__ (2007) , the Supreme Court explained that:

> [T]he decision whether to recognize a *Bivens* remedy may require two steps. In the first place, there is the question whether any alternative, existing process for protecting [a constitutionally recognized] interest amounts to a convincing reason for the Judicial Branch to refrain from providing a new and freestanding remedy in damages. But even in the absence of an alternative, a *Bivens* remedy is a subject of judgment: "the federal courts must make the kind of remedial determination that is appropriate for a common-law tribunal, paying special heed, however, to any special factors counseling hesitation before authorizing a new kind of federal litigation."

(Citations omitted.)

In addition to § 1983, FTCA, and Bivens (and in addition to the federal titles creating avenues of redress concerning religious practices and medical issues, discussed later in "Chapter 19"), you might consider a cause of action under these federal laws:

- **Section 1985.** The federal title 42 U.S.C. § 1985 covers both private and government conduct, provided the terms in the statute creating liability are met. Under the first clause of § 1985(2), those who conspire to deter any party or witness from attending or from testifying truthfully in federal court, whether force, threat, or intimidation is used, may be held liable, and damages and injunctive relief are available. The second clause of § 1985(2) provides a cause of action against those who conspire to deter or obstruct actions in state court, with the intention of denying protections of laws, or with the intention of retaliating against persons who enforce their equal protection rights. Section 1985(3) then allows for the recovery of damages against such conspirators. (The title 42 U.S.C. 1986, moreover, allows for damages suits against those who knew of a § 1985 conspiracy and failed to act to prevent it.) To bring a claim under either § 1985(2) or § 1985(3), a plaintiff must allege that the discriminatory motive behind the conspirators' actions or omissions to violate the equal protection of law was based on race or class. *A&A Concrete, Inc. v. White Mountain Apache Tribe*, 676 F.2d 1330, 1333 (9th Cir. 1982); *see generally Gillespre v. Civiletti*, 629 F.2d 637 (9th Cir. 1980) (section 1985 is a civil-rights statute that is derived from the Thirteenth Amendment to the U.S. Constitution, and covers all deprivations of equal protection of law and equal privileges and immunities under the law).
- **The Privacy Act.** The federal title 5 U.S.C. § 552a creates an obligation for federal agencies to ensure that the records they keep concerning individual persons are accurate. Under this Act, known as the "Privacy Act," officials must respond to requests to correct errors in their records, or be subject to civil action for either enforcement of this requirement or judgments of money damages, or both. Only the federal agency, and not individual persons, may be sued under this Act.
- **The Inmate Accident Compensation Act.** The federal title 18 U.S.C. § 4126(c), the Inmate Accident Compensation Act (IACA), is the exclusive remedy for recompense from the U.S. government for work-related injuries of federal prisoners. (The FTCA is not available in such cases, 28 C.F.R. § 301.319; however, *Bivens* and other vehicles that allow for suits against individuals are still available.) Under the IACA, a federal inmate may file for work compensation if he or she suffers "any injury, including occupational disease or illness, proximately caused by the actual performance of the inmate's work assignment." 28 C.F.R. § 301.102(a). Although, compensation must be based on the federal minimum wage, 28 C.F.R. § 301.314(c), and

will not be paid until the inmate is released. 28 C.F.R. § 301.301(a). The amount in compensation will also be based on the degree of impairment suffered by the inmate at the time of his or her release. 28 C.F.R. § 301.314(a). And pain and suffering will not be compensated under this Act (an award in damages for pain and suffering may, however, be available through other vehicles, such as *Bivens* or the FTCA).

- **The Administrative Procedures Act.** The federal title 5 U.S.C. § 702, the Administrative Procedures Act (APA), allows judicial review of the questionable acts or omissions of administrators. Under the APA prisoners may seek the enforcement of federal regulations, statutes, and the Constitution, but they may not seek an award of money damages.
- **Writ of Mandamus.** A mandamus is a court order issued to direct government officials or agencies to carry out duties that, under their official government stations, they are required to do by law (State statutes allow for similar petitions.)

State Tort Claims

State courts ordinarily have jurisdiction to hear claims substantively similar to actions that are commonly brought under § 1983 or *Bivens* in federal court. However, you should consider your options carefully before bringing federal issues before a state court. Generally speaking, federal courts have been more friendly to prisoners' complaints. With a little sleuthing and research, you might discover the general predisposition of judges presiding in local courts (state and federal) who are likely to be assigned to your case. If state judges in your venue have been sympathetic to prisoners' complaints in the past, consider giving them a shot. However, where a judge is an untested shooter and an elected official (as opposed to an appointed official), he or she may be more politician than impartial referee. Come election day, a judge might jeopardize reelection because of a history of appearing sympathetic to prisoners' complaints.

Remember that Constitutional claims, whether brought in state or federal court, prevail only upon the satisfaction of tough judge-made standards of evidence and a demonstration of the severity of civil injury (discussed in later sections). You might have better luck foregoing the federal claims and bringing an action under your state's Tort Claims Act. The problem with suing officials under this type of state law is that a plaintiff must usually prove that an official's tortious (injurious) conduct was motivated by "malicious" or "criminal intent." This is a heavier burden than the breach-of-a-legal-duty-to-use-due-care standard of a simple negligence claim, or the wrongful-application-of-force standard of a property or personal claim of trespass. If it can be shown that the official was *not* "acting in the course and in furtherance" of a governmental duty, then the official's tortious conduct will not be protected under the heightened standard of the state Tort Claims Act, and he or she may then be sued for negligence or trespass (technically, trespass includes assault and battery) under the standards of proof applicable to private citizens.

A plaintiff who brings a trespass tort action against a private person accused of assault or battery or false imprisonment/arrest must show an *unjustified* use of force. To prove negligence (for example, a T.V. carelessly broken, smashed during, say, a malicious cell search), three elements must be satisfied:

1. That the defendant had the duty to exercise reasonably prudent care;
2. That that duty was breached; and

3. That the plaintiff sustained injury.

Still, there is a "rebuttable presumption" that officials are "acting in the course and in furtherance" of their governmental duties when questionable conduct occurs at a place of employment, such as at a prison. This means one must *clearly* demonstrate that the official was not acting in the course and in furtherance of his or her governmental duties. (Was the guard out of his or her assigned area when the incident occurred? Was the guard acting beyond the scope of duty?) If it cannot be shown that the official was acting outside of employee/policy limits, the malicious/criminal-intent standard under the Tort Claims Act will hold sway. A plaintiff must then show that:

1. A cause of action exists by which one can recover for a tort under state law;
2. There exists no exception to liability under the Tort Claims Act (here enters the burden of proving "malicious" or "criminal" intent); and
3. The plaintiff is entitled to recovery based on the merits of the claim.

Simply put, if you are suing over an isolated incident and are looking to recover money damages, you might be better off pursuing a claim in state court under the common law or the state's Tort Claims Act. If dealing with persistent problems that more squarely fall under the category of a constitutional violation, go with a civil rights suit in federal court. Moreover, should there be a federal or a state statute that provides a specific vehicle for recovery or other relief regarding your particular problem, include in your complaint a separate cause of action brought under that statute, naming that statute specifically.

Joint Plaintiff Action

If more than one prisoner is injured by the wrongful conduct of prison officials, those prisoners can combine their claims in a single lawsuit. This is called a "joint-plaintiff action," and is initiated by simply adding each of the multiple plaintiffs' names and signatures to the complaint. A joint action may not be appropriate if the facts surrounding the prisoners' issues differ significantly from one inmate to another, or if individual causes of action or damages claims are likewise significantly different.

An advantage of pursuing a joint-plaintiff action is in the distribution of expenses and resources among all the plaintiffs. A disadvantage is that, should the plaintiffs be separated, which is very common, it becomes very difficult for them to collaborate in the joint endeavor. And although prison officials are supposed to facilitate the legal work of joint litigants, odds are that officials will flatly refuse to make accommodations, or will make accommodations very difficult to obtain.

Class Action Suits

You might consider pursuing a class-action should widespread violations of constitutional rights continue. Class-action lawsuits allow large groups of people with essentially the same issue—called a "class"—to unite and press a claim in a single court action. Once a single suit or a number of suits are filed, plaintiffs can ask the court to certify the case or multiple cases (combining them in one action) as a class action under Fed. R. Civ. P. 23.

Gaining certification is more involved than a mere request, however. Rule 23 of the Federal Rules of Civil Procedure allows class-action status to be granted and maintained only when the prerequisites of subsection (a) of the rule are satisfied (i.e., numerosity, commonality, typicality, and representativeness), and only when "the party opposing the class has acted or refused to act on grounds that generally apply to the class, so that final injunctive relief or corresponding declaratory relief is appropriate respecting the class as a whole." Fed. R. Civ. P. 23(b)(2).

However, even if the above criteria are met, courts are still reluctant to grant class-action status to *pro se* litigants. This is because there remains, at the head of a list of questions a court will consider before granting class-action status, a doubt as to whether the named plaintiff(s) possesses the ability to adequately represent the entire class. The answer to this question depends on too many variables to list; but generally comes down to whether *pro se* litigants are *actually* competent to serve/protect the interests of the entire class. If you feel that you cannot adequately represent the class for whatever reason, consider combining a motion for class action certification with a motion for appointment of counsel, either to assist or to fully take on the case as attorney of record. You may also think about asking organizations like the ACLU to represent the class; after all, these are the types of cases such pro-liberty organization are usually interested in pursuing.

Necessary criteria met, with capable minds to litigate the suit, Fed. R. Civ. P. 23(b)(3) provides that class actions may be maintained in cases where "the court finds that the questions of law or fact common to class members predominate over any questions affecting only individual members, and that a class action is superior to other available methods for fairly and effectively adjudicating the controversy."

The short of it is, if the problem is widespread, affecting many inmates, or a specific class of inmate (e.g., wheelchair-bound prisoners, prisoners with a special security classification, etc.), then a class-action lawsuit may be appropriate. On the other hand, even if a number of prisoners are affected by a problem, but individual injuries and claims and damages are diverse and divergent, the court may decide that separate, individual actions are better suited for addressing the problems of each plaintiff, and that class relief is inappropriate.

COURT ORDERED RELIEF

Injunctive and Declaratory Relief

Injunctive relief—often referred to as "prospective relief"—is awarded to correct an ongoing violation of civil rights. An "injunction" is a court order directing a party to do or cease doing something. For example, should a prisoner-plaintiff succeed in a claim that a prison lacks adequate facilities to accommodate the number of prisoners it houses, the court may order officials to install additional toilets, sinks, showers, etc. However, relating to prison conditions, injunctive relief is only available under the conditions imposed by the PLRA. (*See* the discussion of the PLRA, below.) And courts will not usually grant an injunction where an award of money damages is sufficient to redress a wrong.

Other forms of injunctive relief are the **preliminary injunction** and the **temporary restraining order** (TRO), which are injunctions issued very soon after the filing of the complaint, issued without waiting for final adjudication as to the facts or law surrounding the case. Such early injunctions are *only* issued on the condition that an early judicial order is needed to prevent "irreparable harm"—harm that will occur and cannot be fixed should an order be postponed until after the case has developed by the slower rate of ordinary court progress. Preliminary injunctions are tough to get, tough to justify, granted usually under emergency circumstances only. (*See* "Preliminary Injunctions and Temporary Restraining Orders (TROs)" subsection in the next chapter.)

Before an injunction is issued, the court must first examine whether "declaratory relief" would be enough to prevent or fix the problem. **Declaratory relief** is essentially what it sounds like—the court *declares* (in writing) that the plaintiff's civil rights are being or have been violated. Such a declaration definitively states the plaintiff's legal rights and the defendant's duties with respect to those rights. Often, declaratory relief is accompanied by injunctive relief, but declaratory relief may be issued on its own, leaving the defendants to comply with the law as the court declares, without its having to issue an order directing conduct. However, if declaratory relief is granted and the defendants still persist in violating the law, the plaintiff can then ask the court to issue an injunction to force compliance. If the defendants fail to comply with the order, the plaintiff can ask the court to hold the defendants in contempt, which may warrant money sanctions or, in some extreme circumstances, criminal charges.

Monetary Relief

In 1996, Congress, enacting the PLRA, dramatically restricted the legal remedies available to prisoners under federal civil rights actions (discussed more below). However, monetary relief, including nominal, compensatory, and punitive damages, still remains available to successful litigants.

Nominal damages usually $1.00, are available for the successful plaintiff who has asserted a violation of a civil right but has suffered no significant loss. Why bother with a claim for nominal damages, then? Two reasons. First, a claim for nominal damages will prevent a suit from being rendered moot if the plaintiff is transferred from the offending prison. Second, a nominal victory is nevertheless a victory, and other prisoner-litigants may be able to follow the logic of your case to their own success.

Compensatory damages are awarded to compensate a plaintiff for a loss caused by the wrongful conduct of the defendant(s). A prisoner-plaintiff may be compensated for many types of injury, from damaged property to emotional suffering. However, per the PLRA and FTCA, in federal actions, in order to recover for mental or emotional injury suffered while in custody, one must also establish that he or she suffered a non-*de minimus* physical injury or a sexual assault.

Punitive damages are not awarded to compensate the plaintiff for a loss but to punish a defendant who intentionally violated a plaintiff's rights. Usually it must be shown that the defendant acted with malice, criminal intent, or with recklessness. Punitive damages are awarded against individuals only. Government entities are not usually liable in punitive damages. This includes local entities such as municipalities. *Cook County v. U.S. ex rel Chandler*, 538 U.S. 199 (2003).

In addition, and subject to certain limitations, courts may award **attorney's fees** to the party ultimately prevailing on its claims. Even a plaintiff awarded only nominal damages of a dollar is a "prevailing party," but because a nominal-damages award is only a partial or limited success for the plaintiff, an award of attorney's fees will not likely be granted. When a case is settled before trial, the plaintiff may qualify as a "prevailing party" for the purposes of an award of attorney's fees, if the settlement is effected by a court-ordered "consent decree" (which is a court-ordered settlement agreed to by the parties).

But attorney's fees will not be awarded in the absence of a judicially-ordered change in the legal relationship of the parties—that is, a change resulting in a *substantial* shift in the status quo between the parties.

And note, to save yourself time and energy, that attorney's fees in suits against judicial officers (e.g., judges, clerks, prosecutors, etc.) whose wrongful conduct occurred when acting in their official capacities are not permitted in most circumstances.

Finally, a prevailing *defendant* in a civil-rights case may also recover attorney's fees (from you, the plaintiff) when the suit is frivolous or brought to harass the defendant, but such an award is not usually appropriate where the suit is dismissed for other reasons.

PRISONER LITIGATION REFORM ACT (PLRA)

Before even thinking of mailing off a federal complaint, you *must* make yourself familiar with the Prisoner Litigation Reform Act of 1995 (PLRA), at Pub. L. No. 104-134 §§ 801-810, 110 Stat. 1321-66 to 1321-77 (1996), codified in the scattered provisions of 11 U.S.C. § 523; 18 U.S.C. §§ 3624, 3626; 28 U.S.C §§ 1346, 1915, 1915A, 1932; and 42 U.S.C. §§ 1997a-1997h.

Unfortunately, as you will learn, the PLRA strictly limits prisoners' civil rights complaints in federal court. (*See generally* "PLRA" subsection under "PART 5," below.) The law was passed on the premise that the government has a legitimate interest in conserving judicial resources by placing limitations on what legislators see as intolerably numerous inmate lawsuits—never mind that the prison environment, under basically totalitarian administrative control, intrinsically gives rise to numerous cases of civil injuries, and never mind that the judiciary's hands-off policy of deferring to prison officials' expertise practically invites administrators to abuse their discretion over inmates. Despite all complaints, the PLRA is, nevertheless, here to stay, having been upheld again and again as okay by the Constitution.

Read over, then re-read, the PLRA provisions summarized here and in previous and later sections; these provisions must be borne in mind when preparing a case and when reading about the theories concerning prisoners' rights under "PART 4," below. Additionally, most states have in place legislation that restricts prisoners' complaints, many using very similar language to the PLRA. Get your hands on that law, too.

Filing In Forma Pauperis

Most prisoners simply do not have the money to pay the fees and costs associated with litigating a lawsuit. If one is in poverty (*in forma pauperis*), courts are authorized to waive fees and costs where appropriate in order to facilitate claims brought by the poor. By any definition, prisoners are usually considered "poor" for these purposes.

However, in an effort to curtail prisoner lawsuits, Congress passed the PLRA to make it more difficult for the incarcerated to bring civil actions *in forma pauperis*. Courts are now required to deny *in forma pauperis* status to prisoners who have personally brought three previous actions that were dismissed because the claims were frivolous or malicious or failed to state a claim upon which relief could be granted. 28 U.S.C. § 1915(g). But whatever the number of previously dismissed lawsuits, this PLRA limitation does *not* apply if the prisoner is in imminent danger of serious physical injury. 28 U.S.C. § 1915(g). If filing your first prisoner lawsuit, don't worry about this particular provision.

If a court allows you to proceed *in forma pauperis*, initial filing fees will *still* be required. 28 U.S.C. § 1915(b). (Check with your local district court for current filing fees.) Should your funds be insufficient to pay the whole fee at filing, the court will issue an order to deduct a *partial* filing fee of 20% of your average monthly inmate-account deposits *or* of the average monthly balance in your account for the prior six-month period, whichever of the two is greater. 28 U.S.C. § 1915(b)(1). You must include with your motion for *in forma pauperis* status an account statement covering all financial activity for the six-month period directly preceding the date on which your complaint is filed. (*See* "Motion for *In Forma Pauperis* Status" subsection in the next chapter.)

Following the initial fee payment, the court will require additional monthly payments of 20% of the preceding month's income to your inmate account. 28 U.S.C. § 1915(b)(2). The court will issue an order to this effect, directing the prison agency to forward payments from your account to the clerk of the court each time the amount in the account exceeds $10, until the filing fee is paid in full. 28 U.S.C. § 1915(b)(2). However, under no circumstances can a prisoner without the cash to pay the initial filing fee be prevented from filing suit. 28 U.S.C. § 1915(b). If you don't have the money, you don't have the money—but you're still entitled to justice.

Procedural Hurdles

The PLRA prohibits prisoners from taking legal action *with respect to prison conditions* until "such administrative remedies as are available are exhausted." 42 U.S.C. § 1997e(a). "Administrative remedies" include institutional grievance procedures (which may include a notice of tort to both your state's Attorney General and Secretary of State). Prison administrative procedures—requests, concerns, grievances—*must* be followed to the letter, appealed through the highest institutional appellate authority, or otherwise *totally* exhausted with the department per *its* policy. And exhaustion must occur *before* the initiation of the lawsuit.

A grievance ought to be as detailed as possible, ideally including the name of each possible defendant, who did what, and what you want officials to do about your problem. However, "no administrative system may demand that the prisoner specify each remedy later sought in litigation—for *Booth v. Churner* . . . holds that § 1997e(a) [of the PLRA] requires each prisoner to exhaust a process and not a remedy." *Strong v. David*, 297 F.3d 646, 649 (7th Cir. 2002); *Booth v. Churner*, 532 U.S 731 (2001) (the applicability of the exhaustion requirement of the PLRA turns on whether the grievances system will address the prisoner's complaint, not whether it provides the remedy that the prisoner prefers).

Administrative remedies duly exhausted and complaint filed, the court then will make a preliminary screening of your claims—before docketing (officially registering your case and assigning a case or *docket* number)—to determine if the complaint should be dismissed outright as frivolous, malicious, failing to state a claim upon which relief can be granted, or for one of the other PLRA catches. 28 U.S.C. § 1915A(b). The court will then issue an opinion/order granting you leave to proceed on the issues, or not, dismissing your complaint or allowing you the option of amending the complaint so that it may survive for the time being, or anywhere in between. Further, it is not uncommon for a judge to order early mediation before docketing a case or requiring a plaintiff to pay filing fees. Mediation is an ordeal in itself, and is addressed in later sections.

A formal reply to your complaint is not required of the defendant(s) until the court orders a reply based on its initial finding that you, the plaintiff, have a reasonable chance of prevailing on the merits of the complaint. 42 U.S.C. § 1997e(g). Still, courts must dismiss an action if, *at any time*, it determines that the suit is frivolous or malicious, fails to state a claim upon which relief can be granted, or seeks monetary relief against an immune defendant. 28 U.S.C. § 1915(e)(2)(B). In addition, courts dismiss complaints that are brought by inmates who lack standing—that is, the complaint must implicate *your* rights; you would not have legal standing to pursue a claim on behalf of another inmate, for instance.

Should the complaint pass the initial hurdles, then the fun begins—disputes, discovery, disputes, depositions, disputes, motions and briefs, disputes, and hearings. You probably won't spend much time in a courtroom. If practicable, the PLRA requires that pretrial proceedings in prisoners' civil-rights cases be conducted over the phone to prevent removing the prisoner from his or her housing facility. 42 U.S.C. § 1997e(f)(1). The PLRA also allows hearings to be conducted at the prison, with counsel participating by phone, if practicable. 42 U.S.C. § 1997e(f)(2).

Finally, you should be aware that if the court eventually finds that (1) the claim was filed for a malicious purpose, or (2) the claim was filed solely to harass the defendant, or (3) the plaintiff testified falsely or knowingly presented false evidence, then a *federal* prisoner's good-time credits may be revoked. 28 U.S.C. § 1932. *State* prisoners may also lose good-time credits (or be otherwise disciplined) for the same reasons under state statutes similar to the PLRA.

Damages, Injunctions, and Attorneys Fees

The PLRA imposes even more restrictions on prisoners by limiting the availability of monetary relief in two important ways.

First, a prisoner may not recover for mental or emotional injury suffered while *in* custody without also establishing that a non-*de minimus* physical injury was suffered, or that the prisoner was the victim of a sexual act. 42 U.S.C § 1997e(e). The same goes for suits filed under the FTCA or as *Bivens* actions against federal officials. 28 U.S.C § 1346(b)(2). (*See* "Constitutional and Federal Claims" under "Chapter 11," above.) Nominal and punitive damages are still available without a showing of physical injury or sexual assault.

Second, damages awards are to be paid directly to satisfy outstanding restitution orders. Pub. L. No. 104-134, Stat. 1321 § 807 (April 24, 1996) (not codified; appears after 18 U.S.C.A. § 3626). The prisoner may keep what remains of the award after restitution is settled.

Along with limiting the circumstance under which damages may be awarded, the PLRA makes further restrictions on what an inmate can potentially achieve in court by restricting the availability of prospective injunctive relief. 18 U.S.C § 3626; 28 U.S.C. § 1932. For instance, preliminary injunctions and TROs shall expire after only ninety (90) days, 18 U.S.C § 3626(aX)(2), and the PLRA mandates that:

1. Injunctive relief must be narrowly tailored to extend *no further* than to address the issues of the particular plaintiff (18 U.S.C. § 3626(a)(1));
2. The court must give substantial weight to any adverse impact on public safety that may result from the relief (18 U.S.C. § 3626(a)(3)); and

3. Injunctions providing for prisoner *release orders* may not be granted unless (a) the court has previously entered a less intrusive order and the order has failed to remedy the federal violation, and (b) the defendant has had a reasonable amount of time to comply with the prior court order (18 U.S.C. § 3626(a)(3)).

Yet, unlike their preliminary kin, regular injunctions are longer lived—two years. After which time, courts are required to terminate prospective injunctive relief governing prison conditions on a showing by the defendant or other legally interested party that the injunction is no longer needed to correct an ongoing violation of federal rights. 18 U.S.C. § 3626(b).

> In any civil action with respect to prison conditions in which prospective relief is ordered, such relief shall be terminable upon the motion of any party or intervener: (i) two years after the date the court granted or approved the prospective relief; (ii) one year after the date the court has entered an order denying termination of prospective relief; or (iii) in the case of an order issued on or before the date of enactment of [the PLRA in 1996], two years after such date of enactment.

18 U.S.C. § 3626(b)(1)(A).

However:

> Prospective relief shall not terminate if the court makes written findings based on the record that prospective relief remains necessary to correct a current and ongoing violation of the Federal right, extends no further than necessary to correct the violation of the Federal right, and that the prospective relief is narrowly drawn and the least intrusive means to correct the violation.

18 U.S.C. § 3626(b)(3). And, of course, injunctive relief may be terminated or modified by mutual agreement between the opposing parties. 18 U.S.C. § 3626(b)(1)(B).

You should be aware that the PLRA's restrictions on injunctive relief apply to consent decrees as well. 18 U.S.C. § 3626(c). A consent decree is essentially a settlement agreement, stipulated by the parties and then ordered by the court without, in most cases, any adjudication of fact or law (i.e., no assignment of blame or liability).

As far as attorney's fees go, the PLRA is something of a hinderance in this regard as well. Specifically, the court may award attorney's fees for court actions on behalf of prisoners only if (1) the fees are directly and reasonably incurred in proving an actual violation of the plaintiff's rights, and (2) the fee amount was proportionally related to the relief awarded by the court for the violation *or* the attorney's fees were incurred in enforcing a court's order of relief. 42 U.S.C. § 1997e(d)(1).

The PLRA provides that up to 25% of the judgment awarded to the successful plaintiff *must* be applied to satisfy the amount of attorney's fees. 42 U.S.C. § 1997e(d)(2). So, no matter what, 25% of your monetary compensation for civil injury will go toward paying off your attorney. The remaining attorney's fees should then be covered by the defendants. But wait, there's more. While the PLRA does require the defendant to pay the remaining attorney's fees (what remains owed to the attorney after you've already paid the 25% of your award), it only requires a defendant to pay up to 150% of the overall judgment amount. 42 U.S.C. § 1997e(d)(2). So an award of $100 will only support an award of attorney's fees up to $150, for example. And, though plaintiffs can always agree to pay more from their award (so enticing an attorney to take the case), the defendant can *not* be required to pay beyond the PLRA limitation. 42 U.S.C. § 1997e(d)(4).

Moreover, pursuant to 42 U.S.C. § 1988, the PLRA limits the hourly fees charged by your attorney to 150% of the hourly rate paid to court-appointed counsel under the Criminal Justice Acts 42 U.S.C. § 1997e(d)(3); 18 U.S.C. § 3006A. So, if—per their employment agreement with the government—court-appointed counsel make $100 an hour, your attorney can hope to collect at most $150 an hour for an award of attorney's fees. This cap does not apply, however, if the court orders injunctive relief *as well as damages*. *Dannenberg v. Valadez*, 338 F.3d 1070, 1074-75 (9th Cir. 2003).

NOTES: _____

_____

_____

_____

_____

_____

_____

_____

_____

_____

_____

_____

_____

_____

_____

_____

_____

_____

_____

_____

_____

_____

_____

_____

_____

_____

_____

_____

_____

_____

_____

_____

_____

_____

_____

_____

NOTES: _____

CHAPTER 12:
FILING THE COMPLAINT

WRITING THE COMPLAINT

Writing a complaint is not too difficult. At least the writing part. Identifying exactly what your rights are, then writing an effective complaint under the correct legal theories—trying to anticipate all contingencies and affirmative defenses that may result in the dismissal of part or all of your suit—is a little more difficult. Luckily, courts are required to construe prisoner complaints liberally. Judges don't expect you to write like an attorney, quite the opposite, but you should nevertheless do your best.

To that end, follow along with the sample complaint provided in this section. Each component of a complaint is explained in turn and then referenced to the corresponding page of the sample § 1983 *Complaint* provided below.

Bear in mind that a complaint is not a legal brief or memorandum—that is, you are not making a complex legal argument, punctuating every other sentence with a piece of legal authority. Heavy citation to legal authority is improper for this initial pleading. The singular exception, however, is the "Cause of Action" section of the complaint, where you *will* allege the violation of your rights under specific legal theories (i.e., constitutional provisions, statutes, regulations), but even there your legal conclusions should be concise.

NOTE: In the sample *Complaint* below and other samples provided herein, I have chosen to refer to the fictional parties by their legal roles rather than by their names. And while personalizing legal writings by using first and last names may evoke a judge's empathy for a *real* person, I nevertheless refer to the plaintiff as "Plaintiff," and to a defendant as "Defendant." The reason for this is threefold. First, *pro se* plaintiffs draft their own papers, and for one to use his or her own name when referring to oneself, instead of using the pronoun "I," can sound as strange in the written word as it does when talking aloud about oneself in the third person. Second, it is simply more convenient to refer to multiple defendants as "the defendants," rather than identifying each person by name. Third, when referring to a single defendant, I combine his legal role with his name—*Defendant Johnson*—for consistency and for clarity purposes. If a plaintiff refers to him- or herself as "Plaintiff," then the prose is balanced by referring to a defendant as "Defendant."

Caption
The "Caption" heads the document—the legal caption is contained in nearly every legal document you will receive or file with the court (e.g., pleadings, briefs, affidavits, even discovery requests). Captions can vary in form depending on the jurisdiction, but all conventionally contain the same type of information.

Dennis P. Smith #50703
I.S.C.F. A-154-B
2334 North Orchid
PO Box 454
Boise, Idaho 83707

Plaintiff, *pro se*

IN THE UNITED STATES DISTRICT COURT

FOR THE DISTRICT OF IDAHO

DENNIS PATRICK SMITH,   )
)
        Plaintiff,   )   Case No. _____
)
vs.   )   **CIVIL RIGHTS COMPLAINT**
)   **[§1983]**
PHILIP J. JOHNSON, Idaho State   )
Correctional Facility Warden; DANIEL K.)
COLLINS, Idaho State Correctional   )   **Trial by Jury Demanded**
Facility Medical Doctor; sued in their   )
individual and official capacities,)
)
        Defendants.   )

COMES NOW, Dennis P. Smith #50703, plaintiff *pro se*, who presents the following civil-rights complaint and claim for compensatory, declaratory, and injunctive relief as follows:

I. INTRODUCTION

1.   This action places before the Court a lawsuit involving the administration of the Idaho State Correctional Facility (a prison facility of the Idaho Department of Correction, charged with the custody and control of approximately 2000 inmates), and

CIVIL RIGHTS COMPLAINT [§1983]   Page 1 of 11

---

the private medical practitioner contracted with the State of Idaho to provide ISCF inmates with medical care.

2.   This complaint alleges that adequate medical care has been and is being refused to Plaintiff by the Idaho State Correctional Facility in concert with its contracted resident physician and partner to the Valley Medical Group, LLC.

II. PARTIES

Plaintiff:

3.   DENNIS P. SMITH #50703 ("Plaintiff") is presently serving a criminal sentence in the custody of the Idaho Department of Corrections. At all times relevant to this action, Plaintiff was housed at ISCF, 2334 North Orchid, Boise, Idaho 83707, where he currently resides.

Defendants:

4.   Defendant PHILIP JOSEPH JOHNSON ("Warden Johnson") at all times relevant to this action was/is employed as Warden of the ISCF, 2334 North Orchid, Boise, Idaho 83707, charged with the custody and care of Plaintiff. Warden Johnson is the facility's highest authority responsible for the appointment, employment, and oversight of facility staff, and oversight of facility operations generally, and is the final appellate authority over inmate institutional grievances and concerns. At all times relevant to this complaint, Warden Johnson acted under the color of state law. He is hereby sued in his individual as well as official capacity, jointly and severally, for those acts and omissions described fully below.

5.   Defendant DANIEL KEVEN COLLINS, M.D., ("Dr. Collins") at all times relevant to this action was/is a partner of Valley Medical Group, LLC., 783 North

CIVIL RIGHTS COMPLAINT [§1983]   Page 2 of 11

Figure 4-1

First, head the document with your name and address, followed by the name and district of the court in which the complaint is filed. Directly under the name of the court should appear a two-column layout-split. The left column must contain the full name(s) of the plaintiff(s), followed by the full name (and government office, if applicable) of the defendant(s). The caption of the complaint must include the full name of every defendant. In subsequent papers, instead of writing out full names and titles of numerous defendants, you can choose to state the name of the *first* defendant and follow it by the Latin phrase *"et al."* (which means "and others"). The right column must contain the case number (a blank space for the case number must be provided in the caption of the complaint; the court clerk will write in the number once the complaint is docketed) followed by the title of the document (e.g., *Complaint,* or in other papers *Affidavit of John Smith, Request for Admissions,* etc.) (*See* Figure 4-1.)

Introduction

The "Introduction" section is the first opportunity in the complaint to explain the problems you've submitted for the court to resolve (use a couple of brief paragraphs at most). Strictly speaking, an introduction is not necessary in a complaint. In the interest of brevity, you may elect to leave out this section. The benefit of using an introduction, however, is that you can quickly familiarize the judge with the issues, and further clarify and describe and impress the judge with your problem. (*See* Figure 4-1.)

Parties - Official v. Personal Capacity, Joint v. Several Liability

The "Parties" section is the part of the complaint where you formally state your name and address, and identify yourself as the Plaintiff. Following should be listed the name, title, and address of each defendant, along with a brief overview of his or her official duties. (*See* Figure 4-1 and 4-2.) You must also explain (1) whether each defendant was acting under the color of state law (for a § 1983 complaint); (2) whether each defendant is being sued in the official or individual (personal) capacity, or both; and (3) whether each defendant is being sued jointly or severally, or both. "Jointly" means a defendant will share the liability for dama ges with the other defendants. "Severally" means an individual defendant may be held personally liable for damages, without joining the other defendants. "Joint and several liability" means that liability may be apportioned between two or more defendants, or one only (or a few select defendants), at the discretion of the plaintiff. For example, a guard may be held liable, along with his supervisor, in an excessive force claim, but the guard would be *severally* liable in punitive damages for the battery, which he alone committed, whereas the supervisor would not.

Jurisdiction and Venue

"Jurisdiction" is a court's power to hear and decide a matter and issue a decree. Federal district courts have subject-matter jurisdiction to hear civil rights complaints based on federal law. The courts of your state may be divided into numerous levels and domains, each with prescribed areas of jurisdiction. If filing in state court, check with a legal-beagle or your resource center about which state court has jurisdiction over civil rights complaints—usually such a court is styled as a *District Court* or *Superior Court*. Some courts have jurisdiction only if the amount of money damages in controversy exceeds a set statutory limit. A claim falling short of that jurisdictional amount may be consigned to a court of small claims, or to a court in that vein. However, a prisoner filing a civil rights complaint in federal court does not need to satisfy a jurisdictional monetary amount.

In addition to substantive jurisdiction, a court must have *personal* jurisdiction over a person in order to hear a complaint against that defendant—that is, the court must have the power to tell the defendant to do or cease doing something. Usually this is a question of venue.

Venue (the county or judicial district in which a case may be heard) depends on where the tortious event took place and where the liable parties are located. For instance, a party seeking redress in federal court under § 1983 may file only in the judicial district in which all the defendants reside *or* in which a substantial part of the events leading to the complaint occurred. If no judicial district exists in which the action may otherwise be brought, the action may

---

Franklin, Suite 4, Boise, Idaho 83707, contracted to provided medical care to the inmates of ISCF, 2334 North Orchid, Boise, Idaho 83707, charged with the duty of providing professional medical services of General Practitioner to the inmate population. At all times relevant to this complaint, Dr. Collins acted under the color of state law. He is hereby sued in his individual as well as official capacity, jointly and severally, for those acts and omissions described fully below.

III. JURISDICTION AND VENUE

6. Jurisdiction is asserted pursuant the United States Constitution and 42 U.S.C. § 1983, to redress the deprivation of those rights secured by the United States Constitution, deprived by persons acting under color of state law. The Court has jurisdiction over these matters pursuant to 28 U.S.C. §§ 1331, 1343(a)(3).

7. Plaintiff's claim for injunctive relief is authorized pursuant to 28 U.S.C §§ 2283, 2284.

8. The United States District Court for the District of Idaho, in the County of Ada, City of Boise, is the appropriate venue for trial pursuant to 28 U.S.C. § 1391(b)(2); the County of Ada is where the events complained of have occurred.

IV. PREVIOUS LAWSUITS

9. Plaintiff has never before filed a civil suit, nor has there been previous litigation regarding any of the issues described in this complaint.

V. STATEMENT OF FACTS

10. On September 21, 2010, Plaintiff suffered severe physical trauma as a result of a vehicle collision. Among other injuries, Plaintiff sustained damage to his spine.

CIVIL RIGHTS COMPLAINT [§1983]   Page 3 of 11

---

11. Plaintiff was taken by ambulance to the Valley General Hospital, where he received medical treatment and referral to Gregory J. Michael, M.D. ("Dr. Michael"), a specialist in spinal injuries and reconstructive orthopedic surgery.

12. Examination revealed Plaintiff to have suffered damage to the ligature and surrounding tissues of both the fourth and fifth lumbar vertebrae (lower back), and rupture of the fourth and fifth lumbar intervertebra disk. Specifically, Plaintiff suffered a tear in the *annulus fibrosis*, which in healthy disks tightly encloses the soft, spherical *nucleus pulposus.* (The *annulus fibrosis* itself in healthy bodies is securely held between the vertebrae by the anterior and posterior longitudinal ligaments, among other tissues.) Plaintiff suffered a slight tearing of the anterior longitudinal ligament, and severe tearing of the posterior longitudinal ligament and *annulus fibrosis* itself, resulting in the rupture of the *nucleus pulposus* between the fourth and fifth lumbar vertebrae.

13. Dr. Michael diagnosed Plaintiff's condition as degenerative, necessitating invasive surgical treatment. In his diagnosis/prognosis, Dr. Michael concluded that the injured tissues would continue to worsen by ineluctable strain on the damaged ligaments and facet joint capsules of the fourth and fifth lumbar posterior spinal column. Dr. Michael concluded that the affected vertebra themselves would remain in a state of severe subluxation (misalignment), and would continue to pressure the damaged tissues and surrounding cerebro-spinal and sympathetic ganglionic nerves. Over time, Dr. Michael concluded, the pressure would increase and accelerate deterioration.

14. Dr. Michael opined that as spinal integrity degrades, Plaintiff's pain would become increasingly severe, and mobility would become increasingly restricted. Dr. Michael projected that spinal movement (including axial rotation (twisting), lateral flexion

CIVIL RIGHTS COMPLAINT [§1983]   Page 4 of 11

Figure 4-2

(side bending), extension, and, particularly, flexion (bending over) would diminish to the degree of inhibiting normal body movement, eventually consigning Plaintiff to a wheelchair if his condition remained untreated. Additionally, Dr. Michael held, as subluxation of the fourth and fifth lumbar vertebrae continued to pressure surrounding nerves and musculature, painful spasms and swelling could be expected with regularity.

15.   Plaintiff was presented with two possible remedies, both surgical. First, the ruptured disk could be removed and the fourth and fifth lumbar vertebrae surgically fused. This remedy, while relieving immediate nerve, ligament, and joint strain, would inevitably increase stress on the adjacent disks, ligaments, and joints between the third and fourth lumbar vertebrae, and between the fifth lumbar and sacral. Even granted a successful vertebrae fusion, Plaintiff would nevertheless be faced with other potential complications associated with the abnormal stress on connective tissues and vertebrae adjoining the fused portion of the spine. The second option was to simply replace the ruptured disk with a disk of synthetic material, and then repair the damaged ligaments. This remedy would allow for natural inter-vertebra movement, drastically reducing the potential for short-term and long-term degenerative effects.

16.   Either surgical option could potentially remedy Plaintiff's ailment, the second was held by Dr. Michael to be the superior method, and therefore recommended; Plaintiff concurred.

17.   Plaintiff was scheduled for surgery at the Valley General Hospital on December 15, 2010. However, Plaintiff was arrested on November 14, 2010. (Plaintiff was placed into the custody of the Ada County Sheriff's Office, housed at the Ada County Jail, until March 26, 2011, when he was transferred into the custody of the Idaho

CIVIL RIGHTS COMPLAINT [§1983]   Page 5 of 11

Department of Corrections following sentencing and the imposition of confinement for six years fixed and ten years indeterminate, for a total prison term of sixteen years.)

18.   In the days following his mid-November arrest, Plaintiff made numerous transfer and furlough requests to the Sheriff's Office in an attempt to keep his December 2010 surgical appointment. Plaintiff motioned the court in this regard, and eventually requested a reduction in bail. All administrative requests and motions were denied, on the grounds of security concerns. Plaintiff ultimately was unable to post bail, and thus unable to receive medical care.

19.   Prior to his arrest, Plaintiff was prescribed a regimen of three daily doses of twenty milligrams of oxycodone pain medication and five hundred milligrams of the anti-inflammatory medication, naproxen, to manage his severe lower-back pain. Plaintiff was additionally proscribed fast-acting five-milligram oxycodone medication, consumed as needed for painful flare-ups.

20.   After his arrest, Plaintiff's prescribed regimen was altered against his will by order of the medical provider contracted in service to the Ada County Jail. Specifically, Plaintiff's oxycodone prescription was replaced with a regimen of three daily doses of ibuprofen, eight hundred milligrams, and five hundred milligrams of the naproxen anti-inflammatory.

21.   Starting from his initial incarceration on November 14, 2010, Plaintiff made repeated requests that his original pain-management regimen be resumed, and that the county arrange or otherwise facilitate Plaintiff's needed reconstructive spinal surgery. The County of Ada refused Plaintiff's requests.

CIVIL RIGHTS COMPLAINT [§1983]   Page 6 of 11

Figure 4-3

---

be brought in any judicial district where *any* defendant can be found. Prisoners don't usually face problems over personal jurisdiction and venue.

Federal courts have substantive jurisdiction to hear civil rights claims brought under section § 1983 by 28 U.S.C. §§ 1331 and 1343. They may issue declaratory relief under 28 U.S.C. §§ 2201 and 2202; injunctive relief under 28 U.S.C. §§ 2283 and 2284; and, additionally, have supplemental jurisdiction over claims arising via state law under 28 U.S.C. § 1367. (*See* Figure 4-2, above.)

Supplemental Jurisdiction under 28 U.S.C. § 1367 allows federal courts to hear claims arising under the laws of a state, so long as the state-law claim arises from the same facts that also gave rise to a violation of federal law. The PLRA's "prospective relief" provision, however, prohibits federal courts from issueing injunctive relief for violations of state law. 18 U.S.C. 3626(a)(1). Thus, only damages are available under a supplemental jurisdiction claim. (The PLRA, of course, has no effect on state claims filed in state court.) Moreover, the Eleventh Amendment precludes lawsuits against states and state officials sued in their official capacities. This means that supplemental jurisdiction applies only for suits in which state officials are sued personally, in the individual capacity, unless the sate has expressly waived its Eleventh Amendment immunity (giving consent to be sued in federal court) with regard to your type of civil injury. (Again, actions in state court are not subject to these limitations on federal jurisdiction.)

Previous Lawsuits

Whether a prisoner has previously filed lawsuits is a question considered by a court when deciding if a prisoner may proceed with a lawsuit *in forma pauperis*, without first paying the initial filing fees. Because of the three-strikes provision of the PLRA, an inmate will not be allowed to pursue a claim without first paying the filing fee if the inmate, on three prior occasions, had claims dismissed as frivolous, malicious, or for failing to state a claim for which relief may be granted. Some jurisdictions require prisoners to describe previous lawsuits and their final dispositions. For the first-timer, a short statement that you have never before filed a civil rights complaint, and that the factual issues and questions of law have never before been adjudicated, should suffice. (*See* Figure 4-2.)

Statement of Facts

The "Statement of Facts" section is the part of the complaint where you tell your story. It must be detailed—stating what, when, and where with precision. Each party must be identified, describing who did what to whom, describing events in chronological order. Be careful not to make allegations—or not-so-subtle insinuations—of wrongs which you have no evidence to support. If you later obtain evidence to support an additional claim, the court will probably permit an amendment of the original complaint. Be brief but precise, as a rule; however, it is imperative that enough facts are alleged to support each of your legal causes of action. So, when drafting a complaint, bear in mind *each and every* element that must eventually be proven for you to succeed on each legal claim. Lastly, the "Statement of Facts" section is not the place to argue the legal merits of your case; stick to the facts. (*See* Figure 4-2 to 4-5, above and below.)

Exhaustion of Remedies

By now you should be aware of the requirement to exhaust all available administrative remedies before commencing a federal lawsuit. Such remedies include institutional grievances, and may include state or federal *Notice of Tort* claims as well. Under the PLRA, a complaint must be dismissed if all available administrative remedies haven't been fully undertaken and exhausted; however, it is not necessary for you to assert in the complaint that you have exhausted all remedies. A court has no reason to assume that you haven't followed the rules. For exhaustion to become an issue for judicial consideration, the defense must raise the question as an affirmative defense. Accordingly, the "Exhaustion of Remedies" section is optional in most jurisdictions, but it can't hurt to supply a preemptory assertion in the complaint that such remedies have been properly completed. (*See* Figure 4-5, below.)

Cause of Action

The "Cause of Action" section is the part of the complaint where you specifically allege who violated which rights. You must identify the defendants, their

22. On March 26, 2011, after his sentencing, Plaintiff was given into the care and custody of the Idaho Department of Corrections, and transferred to its Receiving and Diagnostic Unit (RDU) at the Idaho State Correctional Institution, where Plaintiff would receive a physical examination, security classification, and then permanent housing assignment. Soon after arriving at RDU, Plaintiff made prison authorities aware of his medical condition; he was directed by prison staff to submit a Health Service Request Form to the Medical Department detailing his ailment.

23. On March 27, 2011, Plaintiff submitted a detailed Health Service Request Form via the institutional mail system. Before receiving a response, Plaintiff was transferred to the Idaho State Correctional Facility (ISCF) on April 8, 2011. On the same day of this transfer, Plaintiff submitted another detailed Health Service Request Form to the ISCF Medical Department.

24. On April 21, 2011, Plaintiff was examined in the ISCF's Medical Department by one Daniel K. Collins, M.D., a physician partner with Valley Medical Group, LLC., contracted to provide medical care to the ISCF inmate population. Dr. Collins performed a brief physical examination and reviewed Plaintiff's medical records on file, including X-rays of Plaintiff's spinal injury and prior diagnosis by Dr. Michael. Plaintiff informed Dr. Collins of his need for corrective surgery and the then more urgent need for adequate pain medication. Dr. Collins held that Plaintiff's condition did not require surgery at that time, and held that the current eight hundred milligram dose of ibuprofen, three times daily, was sufficient to manage Plaintiff's pain, explaining that prison policy "discourages" the prescription of "narcotic-level" drugs because of the potential for inmate abuse.

CIVIL RIGHTS COMPLAINT [§1983]   Page 7 of 11

---

25. On April 23, 2011, Plaintiff submitted to Dr. Collins an institutional Concern Form asking him to reconsider his decision to deny Plaintiff medical care, and reiterating the extent and nature of Plaintiff's suffering.

26. On May 4, 2011, Dr. Collins responded to Plaintiff's Concern Form, denying his request.

27. On May 6, 2011, Plaintiff filed an institutional Grievance (Grievance #10-0163) with the ISCF administration, concerning the denial of medical care.

28. On May 15, 2011, Plaintiff approached ISCF's Warden Johnson while in Plaintiff's housing unit. Plaintiff informed Warden Johnson of the nature of his back injury, pre-arrest diagnosis and recommended treatment, current insufficient treatment, and of the extent and nature of Plaintiff's suffering. Warden Johnson responded with words to the effect of, "I'll look into it." On the same day, Plaintiff submitted to Warden Johnson a Concern Form to confirm the substance of this conversation. The Concern Form never received a response.

29. On May 24, 2011, Plaintiff received notice that his Grievance #10-0163 had been denied by the Chief of Operation, Greg W. Wilkinson; Plaintiff submitted an appeal the same day.

30. On June 3, 2011, Plaintiff's Grievance on appeal was denied by Warden Johnson, stating only that, "Staff responses are appropriate."

31. Resulting from lack of adequate medical care—from time of injury, continuing while incarcerated, to present—Plaintiff has increasingly suffered restricted spinal and bodily motion. His condition is current and ongoing, and has resulted in Plaintiff's inability to sleep, exercise, or even walk any distances greater than a few feet

CIVIL RIGHTS COMPLAINT [§1983]   Page 8 of 11

Figure 4-4

without experiencing excruciating pain. Plaintiff's current ibuprofen prescription has been and is wholly inadequate for his pain management.

32.   Further, because of restricted mobility, Plaintiff is forced to routinely forego meals, being at times unable to walk the several hundred yards to the prison's cafeteria. As a result, from approximately late March 2011, to the present, Plaintiff has suffered a loss of thirty pounds in body weight and increased physical weakness.

33.   By the absence of adequate medical treatment, Plaintiff's spinal injury and overall physical condition has deteriorated. With the physical pain and incapacity has come a general loss of life's amenities and privileges. Plaintiff is now unable to attend religious services, school classes, rehabilitation programs, or even to go outside for fresh air and sunshine. Plaintiff now succumbs to severe and prolonged spells of depression, while at the same time suffering from a prevailing and deep-seated anxiety over his condition, future, and inability to defend himself within the hostile prison environment.

VI. EXHAUSTION OF ADMINISTRATIVE REMEDIES

34.   Plaintiff has timely exhausted all available administrative remedies prior to filing this complaint.

VII. CAUSE OF ACTION

35.   Defendants Warden Philip J. Johnson and Daniel K. Collins, M.D., acted with deliberate indifference to Plaintiff's serious medical needs, violating Plaintiff's rights, constituting cruel and unusual punishment under the Eighth Amendment of the United States Constitution.

CIVIL RIGHTS COMPLAINT [§1983]   Page 9 of 11

VIII. PRAYER FOR RELIEF

WHEREFORE, Plaintiff respectfully prays that this Court enter an order:

36.   Issuing declaratory relief, declaring that the acts and omissions of the defendants have violated Plaintiff's rights, and stating the defendants' duties with respect to those rights;

37.   Issuing injunctive relief, commanding the defendants to (1) provide Plaintiff with adequate pain medication, and to (2) provide for or otherwise facilitate the reconstructive spinal surgery necessary to remedy Plaintiff's medical condition;

38.   Awarding Plaintiff compensatory damages for the unnecessary deterioration of his physically condition and consequential pain and emotional suffering, in an amount as yet to be deduced from the evidence, but in no event in an amount less than $100,000.00; and

39.   Any other relief that this Court may deem just an proper.

40.   Trial by jury is hereby demanded on all claims alleged herein, and the parties are hereby given notice, pursuant to Fed. R. Civ. P. 38(a)-(c).

Respectfully submitted this 4th day of November, 2011.

Dennis P. Smith

Dennis P. Smith #50703

CIVIL RIGHTS COMPLAINT [§1983]   Page 10 of 11

Figure 4-5

wrongful conduct (you can refer to the "Statement of Facts" section to support your conclusions about cause of action), and exactly which rights have been violated, also stating the legal source from which those rights stem. (*See* Figure 4-5.)

Prayer for Relief

The "Prayer for Relief" section is the part of the complaint where you ask the judge for what you need. If you need more than one thing, it is permissible to ask for different kinds of relief at the same time. For example, you may ask the court to enter an order declaring your rights and the duties of a defendant with respect to those rights (declaratory relief), followed by a request for an injunction directing that defendant in some course of action (injunctive relief). If you ask for an injunction, be specific about what you want the defendant(s) to do or cease doing.

Remember that an injunction may not be issued when money damages will suffice in redress of a deprivation; be careful about demanding damages for past wrongs that overlap areas in which prospective relief (injunctive relief) is sought. This does not mean one cannot ask for both injunction and damages in the same lawsuit. For instance, damages may be appropriate to compensate the plaintiff for prior injury, where an injunction is still necessary to correct an ongoing wrong.

Be careful about asking for huge amounts of money, but don't sell your claim short. Put some thought into the number; once you demand a specific dollar amount, it might be difficult to justify an increase at a later time—you can be sure that the defense will object. If unsure of the amount you require at the time of filing, then instead of giving a specific dollar amount, consider stating that you "request an amount to be deduced from the evidence at trial." (That may not fly for long, however; the defense is likely to attempt to pin you down on a dollar amount via discovery requests. If your damages are certain, say, the cost to replace damaged property, that dollar amount will have to be disclosed. Punitive damages and damages for pain and suffering are harder to determine in exact dollar amounts, and will probably be left for determination by the jury.) You may also make a statement to the tune of, *"Plaintiff anticipates the discovery of documents and other evidence within the control of Defendant that* *must be reviewed before any meaningful calculation of damages, but in no circumstance will the amount in demand be less than $150,000.00.* " Another matter to contemplate when framing a number, attorneys will not take a case if they cannot expect a respectable payoff—and recall the PLRA's cap on attorney's fees. To entice an attorney to take the case, you might have to demand an award larger than first anticipated, an award large enough to first impress and then share with an attorney, while personally retaining what you deem fair considering your civil injury.

If demanding a jury trial (as opposed to a bench trial, where the judge acts as the sole fact-finder), be sure to include a clause clearly stating this in this part of the complaint. Fed. R. Civ. P. 38. (But remember that suits brought under the FTCA are tried without a jury, 28 U.S.C. § 2402, as are tort actions brought under many state laws.) And be sure to include a clause asking the court to order "any additional relief as the court deems just and proper." (*See* Figure 4-5.)

Verification

Federal courts allow for the verification of a complaint under 28 U.S.C. § 1746. (*See* Figure 4-6.) This is optional, but a good idea, because a verified complaint is treated as an affidavit for the purposes of summary judgment (see below about summary judgment). A verified complaint is like an affidavit because it is treated as sworn testimony: it subjects one to the laws of perjury. If you intend to file in state court, and your state does not have a statute allowing for verification without notary, then you may have to either get the complaint notarized at your prison's resource center (or however the prison facilitates notary services), or submit an affidavit affirming the content of the complaint as true and correct. Check your local rules on this point.

Attachments

Federal courts permit complaints to be attached with exhibits—should you have reason to include them. Review your options before submitting copies of documents or evidence with a complaint, for two reasons. One, you should be careful about what evidence is disclosed to your adversaries at such an early stage; there's no sense in giving up advantages until you must. Two, copies are expensive. Whether or not you finally decide to submit attachments with the complaint, make sure to provide the judge enough info to communicate the magnitude of your problem. Sometimes exhibits may assist a judge in understanding your position. If including attachments, make sure to cite each exhibit within the body of the complaint where appropriate. Don't just attach a bunch of documents. This is done in much the same way as one would cite legal authority in a brief. For example, to support with an exhibit a point made in a paragraph or sentence, you would cite the material: "See

IX. VERIFICATION

Pursuant to 28 U.S.C. § 1746, I, Dennis P. Smith, declare and verify, under penalty of perjury under the laws of the United States of America, that I have read the foregoing and that it is true and correct to the best of my belief and knowledge.

Dated this 4th day of November, 2011.

Dennis P. Smith
Dennis P. Smith #50703

CIVIL RIGHTS COMPLAINT [§1983]   Page 11 of 11

Figure 4-6

DENNIS P. SMITH #50703
I.S.C.F. A-154-B
2334 NORTH ORCHID
PO BOX 454
BOISE, IDAHO 83707

NOVEMBER 4, 2011

UNITED STATES DISTRICT COURT
550 WEST FORT STREET, MSC 039
BOISE, ID. 83724-0039

RE: FILING OF CIVIL RIGHTS COMPLAINT

DEAR CLERK OF COURT:

PLEASE FIND ENCLOSED:

1. A CIVIL RIGHTS COMPLAINT [§ 1983];

2. PARTY SUMMONS;

3. MOTION FOR IN FORMA PAUPERIS STATUS;

4. MOTION FOR APPOINTMENT OF COUNSEL; AND

5. FOUR ADDITIONAL COPIES OF THE ABOVE.

ALONG WITH THE ORIGINALS, A COURTESY COPY FOR THE COURT'S EASE OF REFERENCE HAS BEEN ENCLOSED; THE OTHER TWO COPIES ARE TO BE SERVED UPON THE DEFENDANTS WITH SUMMONS; AND THE FOURTH COPY IS SUBMITTED FOR ENDORSEMENT AND RETURN IN THE SELF-ADDRESSED STAMPED ENVELOPE. I ANTICIPATE THAT MY MOTION FOR IN FORMA PAUPERIS STATUS WILL BE GRANTED, AND THUS ANTICIPATE THAT A FEDERAL MARSHAL WILL BE DIRECTED BY THE COURT TO PROCESS SERVICE. FOR THE SAME REASON, I HAVE NOT ENCLOSED THE $350 FILING FEE AT THIS TIME.

THANK YOU FOR YOUR TIME IN THIS MATTER.

SINCERELY,

Dennis P. Smith

Figure 5

(document description) *attached hereto as Exhibit A and incorporated into this* Complaint *by this reference."*

Exhibits should be attached at the end of the complaint itself, in an order corresponding to the order in which the exhibits are first cited in the body of the complaint. Following the attachments should be another signed verification (declaration) or affidavit affirming the truthfulness and accuracy of the submitted copies of documents or other records attached to the complaint as exhibits.

Filing and Extra Copies

When submitting a complaint and other attached papers to the court, include a cover letter addressed to the Clerk of Court, explaining what it is you are filing (listing each item one by one). (*See* Figure 5, above.) With the cover letter must follow the original complaint and attachments, and originals of any motions, to be filed with the court. Also, you ought to include for the judge an additional courtesy copy of the complaint and each motion, and a copy of each document to be served upon each of the defendants (unless court rules direct otherwise). You should also include a summons for each defendant (*See* Figure 6.)

Finally, include with your submission one more copy of each of the papers for the court clerk to endorse and then return to you. Such an **endorsed copy** is your official copy of the document, a copy endorsed on the cover page with the clerk's official stamp, which reflects the date and time and place of filing.

If the federal lawsuit survives the initial procedural hurdles, and *in forma pauperis* status is granted, the clerk of the court will then forward to the Federal Marshals the summons and copies of the pleadings that you have already submitted (or will submit when the court directs you to) for each of the defendants. The marshals then formally serve these papers upon each defendant. States have their own procedures in this respect. Check your local court rules; they may require you, the broke prisoner, to hire a process server or otherwise arrange for formal service.

A defendant can waive formal service if he or she chooses. In federal cases, if the defendant waives formal service, an extra forty days beyond the usual twenty (for a total of sixty days) is permitted for the defendant to file an answer to the complaint. If formal service is waived, the clerk will either send you back the copies of the complaint so you can simply mail them to the defendants, or mail the copies him- or herself.

MOTIONS TO FILE WITH THE COMPLAINT

Filing Motions and Other Papers

Certain motions are appropriately filed at the same time as the complaint. Below are three examples of motions commonly filed with a complaint, or soon thereafter. Include in the cover letter to the Clerk of Court a description of each motion being submitted with the complaint. Your local court rules may provide for specifics, but generally include with a submission the following:

1. The original motions (to be retained in the court file);
2. Enough copies of each motion for service upon each defendant; and
3. An extra courtesy copy of each motion for the judge.

The judge will eventually deal with each of your motions in turn, but not before an initial finding that your complaint sufficiently asserts viable claims.

After the initial service and summons, where your complaint and first motions are formally delivered to the defendants, you may submit only two copies of each subsequent document filed with the court—an original and a courtesy copy for the judge (three copies if you include one for endorsement and return to you). Additional copies for adverse parties can simply be mailed to their defense attorneys, formal service no longer being necessary. Be sure to mail those copies; the defense is entitled to copies of most things you file with the court.

However, before a motion or a brief or other legal document is filed, the requisite *Certificate of Service* must be attached. The certificate need not be fancy because it merely verifies that you have indeed mailed accurate copies of the documents to each of the defendants or their attorneys. For an example mailing certificate, turn to the last page of Figure 7 in the next chapter. (Note that some states require a legally disinterested third party—that is, a person not in any way involved in your lawsuit—to sign the certificate and make the mailing; check your state rules.)

IN THE UNITED STATES DISTRICT COURT

FOR THE DISTRICT OF IDAHO

DENNIS PATRICK SMITH,

    Plaintiff,

        Case No. _____

vs.

        SUMMONS

PHILIP J. JOHNSON, Idaho State Correctional Facility Warden; DANIEL K. COLLINS, Idaho State Correctional Facility Medical Doctor; sued in their individual and official capacities,

    Defendants.

        TO: PHILIP JOSEPH JOHNSON, Idaho State Correctional Facility, 2334 North Orchid, Boise, Idaho 83707:

        A lawsuit has been filed against you.

        Within twenty-one (21) days after service of this summons on you (not counting the day you received it), you must serve on the plaintiff an answer to the attached complaint or a motion under Rule 12 of the Federal Rules of Civil Procedure. The answer or motion must be served on the plaintiff, Dennis P. Smith #50703, I.S.C.F. A-154-B, 2334 North Orchid, PO Box 454, Boise, Idaho 83707. If you fail to do so, judgment by default will be entered against you for the relief demanded in the complaint. You also must file your answer or motion with the court.

        Dated this ___ day of _____, 20___.

                    _____

                    Clerk of Court

SUMMONS

Figure 6

Adapted from Form 3, SUMMONS, of the Fed. R. Civ. P

Motion for In Forma Pauperis

The PLRA limits the ability of prisoners to file lawsuits *in forma pauperis* without first paying filing fees. Although judges can waive the fee in whole, it is more likely that prisoners will be held responsible for paying at least partial fees, depending on a prisoner's financial resources. Eventually the entire fee will have to be paid. As provided for in the PLRA, if the fee is not initially paid in full, the judge will probably issue an order to the Department of Corrections directing the withdrawal of a percentage (usually 20%) from all monies coming into your prison account, including wages earned from a prison job. The 20% withdrawals continue until the filing fee is satisfied.

But regardless of the payment status of the filing fee, *in forma pauperis* litigants, *pro se*, are usually entitled—at no cost—to (1) process issued and served (Federal Marshals usually handle this); (2) notice of any motion made by the defendant or the court to dismiss the complaint, and the basis for the motion; (3) an opportunity to at least submit a memorandum in opposition; (4) in the event of dismissal, a statement of the grounds for the decision; and (5) an opportunity to amend the complaint to overcome the deficiencies, unless it clearly appears the deficiencies cannot be overcome by amendment. *Noll v. Carlson*, 809 F.3d 1446 (9th Cir. 1987).

However, process and service at no charge to the plaintiff depends on a prior granting of *in forma pauperis* status. First-time litigants need not worry, but under the PLRA, prisoners who've filed three claims dismissed as frivolous, malicious, or for failing to state a legal claim are barred from litigating further suits *in forma pauperis*. This "three-strikes" provision may nevertheless be suspended if a prisoner seeking *in forma pauperis* is in imminent danger of serious physical injury. (*See* discussion of PLRA, above, and "PLRA" subsection in "PART 5," below.)

Your prison resource center might have pre-made *pauperis* motions in stock. If not, they are easy to draft. Start with the proper legal caption, then tell the judge that you are a poor inmate who is requesting the status of *in forma pauperis*. Ask the court to waive filing fees in whole, or, failing that, permission to proceed on partial payments. If you possess no significant assets, cash, or valuables, tell this to the judge. A couple hundred bucks, or even a couple thousand, is not enough to prosecute a lawsuit, and should not be considered significant enough to preclude *pauperis* status. On the other hand, inmates with a bit of money—or property or assets that can be liquidated—will have to list their potential resources in detail. Expenses that support the *in forma pauperis* motion also should be listed.

You can file a motion together with an affidavit in support, or you can simply file a single motion/affidavit combination—basically this is a notarized motion. Whichever method is chosen, your claims about your financial status must be sworn, and the motion and affidavit must be accompanied by a verified printout of the preceding six-month's activity on your inmate account. Ask the resource center facilitator or your case manager about such an account statement.

Motion for Appointment of Counsel

Before a complaint is filed, a prisoner should make an effort to obtain legal representation, whether by an offer of terms of fees, of contingence, or of *pro bono* service. A prisoner is far more likely to successfully pursue a claim, and damages awards are exponentially higher, if the prisoner-plaintiff is represented by counsel. However, indigent prisoners may petition a federal court for appointment of counsel. 28 U.S.C. § 1915(e)(1). Whether counsel will be appointed is a matter of judicial discretion. Before a court will exercise its discretion to appoint counsel, it will first determine whether the petitioner-plaintiff's claims are legally plausible. Following that, the court will generally inquire about the

1. Merits of the case, that is, the likelihood of the plaintiff's claims to succeed at trial;
2. Complexity of the underlying facts (must there be substantial discovery and investicagtion of facts? are there numerous witnesses who will give conflicting testimony? are expert witnesses necessary?) and the legal theories involved (do the claims invoke obscure applications of the law, or fall into an area of law still unsettled by jurists?); and the inmate's ability to litigate in light of the foregoing considerations (inquiring also into education level, literacy, and ability of the inmate to speak or advocate on his or her own behalf); and
3. Ability of the inmate to acquire counsel by is or her own efforts and, if able, whether and to what extent the search was made.

Hodge v. Police Officers, 802 F.2d 58 (2nd Cir. 1986)

Refer to your local court rules, but as a matter of practice it is unnecessary to file a separate supporting brief with a *Petition for the Appointment of Counsel*. That is, you can make a motion *and* a legal argument in one document. But don't shy away from filing a separate, longer brief if necessary to build a persuasive argument. In addition to addressing the elements of the above list, consider emphasizing your poor education (if applicable); the lack of available legal resources at your facility (if applicable); whether it's necessary for you to depose numerous witnesses; your inability to gather evidence and investigate; the fact that inmate witnesses are housed in different facilities; your inability to investigate prison officials' hiring, training, and supervisory practices; your inability to review policy not accessible to inmates; and any reason that may support the appointment of counsel in the interest of justice and fair play.

Follow the IRAC method for legal writing when drafting the brief. Support your conclusions/assertions with evidence, and include copies of the letters you've sent to attorneys to solicit their representation. And support any factual assertion by an affidavit in support of your petition for appointment of counsel.

Counsel will not be appointed on a bare-bones petition; you'll have to be convincing as to why it is impossible or unfair for you to proceed without representation.

NOTE: The fact of a well-crafted motion for appointment of counsel may be viewed as evidence of an inmate's ability to adequately represent his or her cause in court. If using the services of a jailhouse lawyer in drafting an appointment motion, it may, therefore, be prudent to point out in the motion (or during the subsequent hearing on the motion) that you've had help drafting your papers but remain unable to prosecute your claims without professional assistance.

Preliminary Injunctions and Temporary Restraining Orders (TROs)

If you are faced with a threat of harm, a harm that could fairly be characterized as irreparable, it is possible to ask the court to issue a preliminary injunction to prevent this "irreparable harm" from happening. If, for example, your health is directly at risk or you are at risk of losing a limb or eyesight, a preliminary injunction will likely be granted. "Preliminary" means *preceding* or *in preparation for*, it means the injunction is issued *before* a matter is fully litigated, as opposed to a regular injunction, issued only after a final finding of fact and adjudication of law (years after the occurrence of the injury).

A *Temporary Restraining Order* (TRO) is a preliminary injunction ordering a party to refrain from some action. For example, if a prison guard continues to harass you for, say, filing a lawsuit, you may be able to get a TRO directing the officer to stay away.

Unfortunately, the availability and usefulness of preliminary injunctions is now, thanks to the PLRA, quite limited for the incarcerated. Read over the discussion of the restrictions imposed by the PLRA in the previous chapter. As it is, preliminary injunctions and TROs are ordered subject to exceptional circumstances and conditions. To obtain a preliminary injunction, you must demonstrate that:

1. You will, at trial, likely be able to show the defendants violated your rights;
2. You are likely to suffer irreparable harm (unfixable damage) if a preliminary injunction is not issued;
3. The threat of harm to you is greater than the harm the defendant(s) will face should you be granted the preliminary injunction; and
4. A preliminary injunction will serve the public interest (or at least not negatively affect it).

Rule 65 of the Federal Rules of Civil Procedure governs preliminary injunctions and TROs. For state actions, look up the state's equivalent court rule. Make sure you understand the rules and what you're asking the court to do. And be prepared to back up your assertions, because if your motion has sufficient merit on its face, the court will hold a hearing *very soon* after the motion is filed.

Do not file for a preliminary injunction just because you can. Should it be denied, you will only have prejudiced yourself at this early stage, by (1) giving your adversaries advanced knowledge of your legal theories and evidence, and (2) by giving the judge a foul impression as to the overall merits of your claims. One always wants to appear composed and conscientious; hasty or meritless motions will demonstrate the opposite. File a motion if necessary, but make sure that you include (1) a detailed summary of the problem (your situation, what the "irreparable harm" will be, and what preservative/preventative measures you have *already* taken), (2) sufficient legal grounds (cite pertinent statutes, case law, and court rules), (3) an analysis under the four-prong standard for preliminary injunctions listed above; and (4) sufficient evidence to back your claims (include your own affidavit). A supporting affidavit should include, in addition to a factual description of the imminent harm, a complete summary of the steps you've taken on your own to prevent the "irreparable harm."

NOTES: _____

NOTES:_____

_____

_____

_____

_____

_____

_____

_____

_____

_____

_____

_____

_____

_____

_____

_____

_____

_____

_____

_____

_____

_____

_____

_____

_____

_____

_____

_____

_____

_____

_____

_____

_____

_____

_____

_____

_____

_____

NOTES: _____

CHAPTER 13:
WHAT TO EXPECT AFTER FILING

FIRST OFF

Initial Review

After the clerk receives the complaint, the action is assigned a case number and then a judge. The judge, per various laws, is required to make an initial finding of whether your complaint alleges facts (events and circumstances) sufficient to support a viable legal claim. When making this determination, the court must view all facts in your favor, taking your allegations as true (unless obviously false). Then must determine if the complaint can go forward under current legal theory. The court must construe prisoner complaints liberally, to state a viable cause of action wherever possible. If the complaint is insufficient, the court should give notice and provide an opportunity for the plaintiff to amend the complaint before dismissing the suit. If the suit *is* dismissed at this early stage, the dismissal will likely be "without prejudice," meaning that the complaint can be re-filed—provided the statute of limitation has not run. If the suit is dismissed "with prejudice," meaning that the complaint cannot be re-filed, the only recourse is then to appeal the negative decision to a higher court of appeals.

If claims *are* sufficiently stated under the law, the court will issue an *Initial Review Order*, or its like, specifically addressing your claims, granting leave to proceed with each and stating why. The judge (or, more likely, a law clerk) will punctuate his or her opinion with legal authority. This authority is helpful; it may provide a window into what the judge views as the standard of law controlling each claim. Most definitely you should try to get your hands on any authority so cited.

(In making the order, if the court has misread the complaint or otherwise missed or misunderstood something, you can file what is called a *Motion for Clarification*. In this motion you must explain the cause of confusion or where the judge has made error. Such motions can be filed at any time, concerning any confusion, not just for complaints.)

In the same *Initial Review Order*, the court may rule on any or all motions you've submitted with the complaint, if any. The court may defer (postpone) ruling until the defendants have been formally served, or order a hearing (usually telephonic), or any combination of proceedings.

Frequently, the court will order what is called **early mediation**, in an effort to give the parties one last chance to settle the dispute before the lawsuit commences. If this happens, the court will direct the plaintiff not to file anything more until after mediation, and direct the defendants not to file an answer to the complaint. A mediator is then assigned to the case (usually a magistrate judge), and a date for mediation is set. The mediator reviews the complaint and possibly researches the underlying legal questions. During negotiations the mediator acts as a go-between for the opposing parties, lubricating the settlement process, and in some cases expresses his or her opinion about the strengths and weaknesses of the case on each side of the dispute. The mediator then submits a report to the judge, explaining whether or not an agreement has been reached.

Should early mediation fail, resulting in no agreement, the court will order the lawsuit to proceed, deal with any outstanding motions, and then enter an order directing the Department of Corrections to begin deducting funds from your inmate account to satisfy the initial filing fee (per PLRA), usually 20% of all incoming funds over ten dollars is deducted at a single time. (It should be noted that if early mediation is ordered, all pending motions—e.g., motions for appointment of counsel, *in forma pauperis*, etc.—are normally not ruled upon until after mediation is concluded, which can be months after the initial filing of the complaint. Essentially, an order for early mediation stays (pauses) the proceedings.

Service and Summons - Waiver Option
Following mediation (even though the defense has already received copies of the complaint before mediation), the defense (or its attorneys) may, per court rules, still be entitled to formal services and summons. If early mediation was not ordered, formal service and summons directly follows the *Initial Review Order*, which permits the case to advance. However, in both scenarios the defendants are, in federal court, given the option of waiving formal service and summons, to consent instead to service and summons via mail service (as opposed to hand delivery). Fed. R. Civ. P. 4(d). Defendants who waive formal service are granted additional time in which to file a formal *Answer* to your *Complaint*. If formal service is not waived, defendants must answer a complaint or file another responding motion within twenty-one days of receipt; they get sixty days, however, should they waive formal service. Fed. R. Civ. P. 12(a)(1)(A). Your state may have similar rules in this respect.

A summons for each defendant should be filed along with the initial filing of the complaint. Federal courts are accustomed to managing inmate lawsuits, and upon a granting of *in forma pauperis* status they will direct the Federal Marshals to serve a prisoner-litigant's papers, routinely without a plaintiff having to ask formally. They know the drill. If the inmate is not granted *pauperis* status, the court clerk will sign the summons, affixing the seal of the court, and mail it back to the inmate, to make his or her own arrangements for formal service. This process is much the same in state courts. You can choose to hire a professional to serve the papers, but anyone over the age of eighteen (and not a party to the suit) can serve legal papers. After service, the process server must file an affidavit with the court, affirming that he or she has actually handed the correct papers to the correct people, detailing the time and place of delivery. Such an affidavit is as simple as it sounds.

A ***Summons*** is a simple document as well, containing the same legal caption used with all your other court papers and a paragraph commanding a defendant to appear. (*See* Figure 6 in the previous chapter.) The document specifically "summons" the defendant to whom it's addressed and provides information about where and when to answer the complaint. You can write your own, following the sample form provided in your local court rules; you can follow the sample *Summons* already provided herein; or you can send off a letter to the court clerk's office, asking for copies of their stock summons form.

Magistrate or District Judge?

At some point in the early stages of the lawsuit, in federal court, you will receive from the clerk of court a form asking whether you are willing to have the case heard in the lower magistrates division of the district court. Both you and the opposing party must consent to this.

Whether to make this choice is a matter of strategy. Before filing of the complaint, it is wise to spend some time researching the attitude and predisposition of the judges and magistrate judges presiding in your area. This kind of information is usually only circulated by word of mouth, so consult with more experienced inmates who might be in the know. Another method is to get hold of published case opinions from the local judges.

By the time the consent form arrives after the commencement of the lawsuit, one's options are between the district judge already assigned the case and the magistrate judges who preside in your division of the Federal District Court. You can go with the magistrate's division, but you don't get to select which magistrate, so you'll be rolling the dice. Consider your options. Does the presiding district judge fancy him- or herself a constitutionalist? This specialty may bode well for a constitutional claim. Is the judge known to frequently crack down on the procedural errors of inexperienced *pro se* prisoner-litigants? Such an attitude may signify an underlying prejudice against prisoner complaints.

Another thing to be aware of is that district judges generally have more experience with inmate lawsuits, and they're aware and possibly more accommodating of the difficulties and logistical problems accompanying *pro se* suits. However, an inexperienced judge may give your case more attention, based on the sheer novelty of a subject with which he or she has had few dealings. So, think to over.

Notice of Appearance

Very early in the proceedings, defense attorneys will file what is called a *Notice of Appearance*. This document tells the court and all interested parties who the defending attorney is—name, contact info, bar number. Once an attorney has made a formal appearance, he or she is then the defendant's attorney of record and must be served by the plaintiff with copies of all pleadings, motions, letters, and other papers. The plaintiff is no longer obligated to mail the defendant(s) a personal set of copies, but rather a single set to the defense attorney(s) only. State governments are represented by the state's Office of the Attorney General. Private prisons, and sometimes private companies contracted to a prison, have in-house attorneys who specialize in everything prison related, including defeating inmate lawsuits.

Defendant's Answer

After the initial procedural matters are concluded, the defense must file an answer to your complaint—the document is actual titled *Answer*. In the *Answer*, defense counsel will address every paragraph, if not every sentence, in your *Complaint* specifically denying, re-characterizing, admitting, or objecting to each line in turn. They will also assert certain affirmative defenses—such as arguing that a cause of action is barred by the doctrine of estoppel, or that the statute of limitations has expired, or by asserting more specific defenses, such as lack of the "deliberate indifference" element in a medical or other Eighth Amendment claim; or for failure to exhaust administrative remedies, etc.

Read the *Answer* carefully, for obvious reasons, and because it will indicate how your adversaries plan to defeat your claims.

Notwithstanding local or state court rules, the *Answer* constitutes the final stage for the initial "pleadings"; therefore, you must not file a *Reply* to the *Answer* unless the court so orders or in other limited circumstances provided for in the court rules of civil procedure.

Technically, if a defendant does not timely answer the complaint by submitting an opposing motion or formal answer, then, theoretically, a plaintiff may prevail on a claim for a clear sum of money damages, by entry of default judgment under Fed. R. Civ. P. 55(b), or by a similar rule in state cases. However, default judgments are not favored and are extremely unlikely in prisoners' lawsuits. Moreover, for federal civil actions, the PLRA allows defendants in prisoner-plaintiff cases to "waive the right to reply." And "[n]o relief shall be granted to the plaintiff unless a reply has been filed." The court may require a reply "if it finds that the plaintiff has a reasonable opportunity to prevail on the merits." 42 U.S.C. § 1997e(g). Under this law, defendants don't have to answer your complaint until the judge tells them to do so.

NOTE: Defense counsel commonly files a dispositive motion (a motion asking the court to dismiss the action in part or whole) before filing an *Answer* to the *Complaint*. If this happens, you must respond to this motion by filing a brief in opposition, and you'll have to make lucid legal arguments. Such motions are discussed in the next section.

Scheduling

Once the *Complaint* and *Answer* are filed, the next phase involves planning how to proceed with discovery, pretrial motions, and trial. Under Fed. R. Civ. P. 16, or your state's equivalent rule, the parties must collaborate in a "scheduling conference." Together, the parties and the judge will hammer out the particulars of deadlines for discovery requests and responses and motions for summary judgment, and set the trial date. Under Rule 26(f), the parties should confer and attempt to form a discovery plan before the scheduling conference is to take place. The parties may agree to a schedule, submitting it to the court, or disagree, in which case each side submits its own report for the judge's consideration. The court then resolves any scheduling disputes and issues a final *Scheduling Order*. Provided a sufficient reason, you may file an objection, telling the court how the existing schedule prejudices you and/or your case.

If, at a later time, circumstances develop so that the existing schedule is simply not practicable, you can file a *Motion to Vacate and Reset Scheduling Order*, explaining your problems and proposing, with detail, a new schedule. Before filing such a motion, one should first make an effort to collaborate with and obtain the consent of defense counsel. If the opposition objects to the proposed schedule change, one is then forced to overcome this objection by briefing or hearing in front of the judge. If the defense consents, ask whether it's willing to submit a joint motion called a *Stipulated Motion to Vacate and Reset Scheduling Order*.

Because of the logistical hassles in arranging pretrial conferences and court hearings with *pro se* prisoners, many federal district courts have a custom, if not a written rule, of simply issuing a scheduling order *sua sponte* (of their own volition) without following the process described above—don't be surprised to find that trial has been set one or even two years out, by the way. Such *sua sponte* scheduling orders may or may not place restrictions on discovery procedure. Whatever the situation, the parties are required to follow the court's order, unless one can change the judge's mind via formal objection, stipulation between the parties (which is not binding on the court, but judges often cede to a stipulation), or other motion. If an order does not address how discovery is to be managed, then the Rules of Court control. (*See* "Court Rules and Discovery," below.)

Having Your Lawsuit Lumped In with Others

Although unlikely, a judge may deem it expedient to combine your lawsuit with another, or others, in order to conserve judicial resources (or defense resources). If your suit involves the same defendants (e.g., employees of the Department of Corrections) and similar questions (e.g., overcrowding, insufficient food, lack of programs) as other pending cases, then your case is at a greater risk of being lumped in with other existing lawsuits seeking the same results as yours.

Should your case be combined with another, the case then proceeds, basically, as a joint-plaintiff or class action suit.

EARLY MOTIONS TO DISMISS

Rule 12 Motions to Dismiss

Rule 12(b) of the Federal Rules of Civil Procedure (and similar state rules) provides for the assertion of certain dispositive motions that should be made by the defense before filing the *Answer*. Specifically, under Rule 12(b)(1)-(7), a complaint may be challenged for

1. Lack of subject-matter jurisdiction;
2. Lack of personal jurisdiction;
3. Improper venue;
4. Insufficient process;
5. Insufficient service of process;
6. Failure to state a claim upon which relief can be granted; and
7. Failure to join a party under Fed. R. Civ. P. 19.

With the exception of Number 6, none of the defenses listed above actually deal with the merits of the complaint—that is, they are dilatory motions looking to defeat or postpone the lawsuit on procedural grounds. A properly pled complaint, filed in the judicial district in which the wrongful, injurious acts occurred, is likely to defeat most of the above defenses. Number 6––failure to state a claim upon which relief can be granting (Rule 12(b)(6))—is only granted if it is obvious to the court that the prisoner-plaintiff is not legally entitled to relief, because the complained facts, even if true, do not constitute a viable cause of action. In other words, there's been no civil/criminal violation.

On a Rule 12 motion of this kind, where the facts alleged in the prisoner's complaint are not reasonably in dispute (everyone agrees on what happened), the court might interpret the Rule 12 motion as a Rule 56 motion for summary judgment. Under Rule 12(c), "[a]fter the pleadings are closed—but early enough not to delay trial—a party may move for judgment on the pleadings." Judgment on the pleadings is a final adjudication based on the pleadings with nothing more, no witness testimony, no trial. If, however, "on motion under Rule 12(b)(6) or 12(c), matters outside the pleadings are presented to and not excluded by the court, the motion must be treated as one for summary judgment under Rule 56. All parties must be given a reasonable opportunity to present all the material that is pertinent to the motion." Fed. R. Civ. P. 12(d).

Should you face summary judgment at this early stage, you have a couple of options. First, you can argue that the material facts *are* still in dispute, and that you reasonably expect to obtain evidence through discovery to support this position; therefore, summary judgment should be denied or deferred (postponed) until the parties have had the opportunity to complete discovery. This is essentially an objection to the fact that the defense has filed a summary judgment motion too early, and you need more time to gather evidence. Your second option is to directly attack the motion by submitting a formal brief in opposition, addressing every point in the defense's brief, and attaching pertinent evidence where appropriate. In effect, such a response waives any objection that the motion for summary judgment was prematurely filed, and you'd better be ready to back the claims in your complaint with evidence and logic.

NOTE: Speaking generally, when it becomes necessary to respond to an opponent's brief, it is important to keep in mind your case's strengths and weaknesses. Arguments should focus on your strengths. Do not allow an opponent to draw you into squabbling over minor issues or details. Of course, merely ignoring negative arguments is not advisable, but you are better off not fighting on the enemy's terms.

Apart from dispositive motions, under Rule 12(e) a party can request that a more definite statement be made in the opposition's initial pleading. Defendants can ask that a vague or ambiguous portion of the *Complaint* be clarified, and a plaintiff may ask for an *Answer* to be more clearly stated, in part or whole. Additionally, under Rule 12(f), "[t]he court may strike from a pleading [*Complaint*, *Answer*, *Reply*, etc.] an insufficient defense or any redundant, immaterial, impertinent, or scandalous matter." The court can do this on its own, or on the motion of any party, provided the motion to strike is made before the formal response to the pleading is actually filed.

Claims May Be Barred

In some instances the doctrines of *res judicata*, collateral estoppel, and judicial estoppel may bar a civil action. **Res judicata** bars the parties to an action from litigating a second lawsuit on the same set of facts, or from litigating a claim that could have or should have been raised in a previous lawsuit, but was not. **Collateral estoppel** bars actions essentially re-litigating a particular question or set of facts already decided in a previous proceeding, even if the new action is significantly different from the prior affair. **Judicial estoppel** bars claims that contradict declarations made by the court during the same or earlier proceeding if the change would adversely affect the current proceeding or constitute fraud on the court.

One who is bringing a lawsuit for the first time shouldn't worry too much about these kinds of procedural bars. However, problems of system- or prison-wide magnitude are more likely to have been previously litigated. An outstanding order or adjudication may prevent new parties from re-litigating the old issue. Those pursing a claim of legal scope that affects a class or entire prison system may be able to obtain information from jailhouse lawyers about whether your issue has been previously fought, and lost or won in local courts

NOTES: _____

_____

_____

_____

_____

_____

_____

_____

_____

_____

_____

_____

_____

_____

_____

_____

_____

_____

_____

_____

_____

_____

_____

_____

_____

_____

_____

_____

_____

_____

_____

_____

_____

_____

_____

_____

NOTES: _____

_____

_____

_____

_____

_____

_____

_____

_____

_____

_____

_____

_____

_____

_____

_____

_____

_____

_____

_____

_____

_____

_____

_____

_____

_____

_____

_____

_____

_____

_____

_____

_____

_____

_____

_____

_____

_____

NOTES: _____

CHAPTER 14:
SUMMARY JUDGMENT & IMMUNITY

RULE 56 MOTION FOR SUMMARY JUDGMENT

If a case is destined for pre-trial dismissal, it will occur at the summary judgment stage. Rule 56 of the Federal Rules of Civil Procedure reads, in part, that:

> A party may move for summary judgment, identifying each claim or defense—or part of each claim or defense—on which summary judgment is sought. The court shall grant summary judgment if the movant shows that there is no genuine dispute as to any material fact and the movant is entitled to judgment as a matter of law.

Fed. R. Civ. P. 56(b).

A party who moves for summary judgment (the "movant") is effectively telling the court that a trial of fact (via jury or judge) is unnecessary because there is no genuine dispute of the facts surrounding the case; there's nothing for the jury or judge to resolve in favor of one party or the other, and therefore the court can render judgment. Either party can bring a summary judgment motion.

Really, most of your legal research and amassing of legal authority has been done in an effort to survive the summary judgment stage. Now is the time to shine; you must swiftly become a legal expert. Read over the court rules regarding the exact response procedure, and also check your local rules. If nothing else, at least confer with other prisoners experienced with summary judgment motions. But, to survive summary judgment, the rule of thumb is to *maintain the disputed facts*. If the facts are not reasonably in dispute—i.e., the defendants agree with the facts as you've alleged them in the "Statement of Facts" section of your *Complaint*—then the bulk of your argument should be confined to interpreting the law so as to illustrate why/how the acts and/or omissions of the defendants have caused injury (civilly, physically, or monetarily) in violation of your rights. Be sure to attach supportive affidavits, discovery responses, or other evidence to your *Brief in Opposition to Summary Judgment*. A verified complaint, in federal court, is viewed as an affidavit (sworn testimony) for the purposes of summary judgment, but you may consider submitting an additional affidavit specially tailored in response to the defense's summary judgment motion and its brief in support. You should also submit an affidavit affirming the accuracy and truthfulness of any copies of documents, photos, or other evidence submitted with your brief. (*See* Figure 7 at the end of this chapter for a sample motion in opposition to summary judgment.)

Tactics to Watch For

Some tactics attorneys employ to defeat prisoner claims at the summary judgment stage are (1) to attack certain facts alleged in the complaint that *are* reasonably in dispute as immaterial (of no consequence to a final adjudication of fact or law), and thus irrelevant to a determination of summary judgment; (2) to attack the relevance and/or admissibility of the evidence backing your claims; and (3) to attack your assertion as to the state of the law controlling the legal claims listed in your complaint. You must prepare to meet these arguments by becoming thoroughly familiar with the law impacting your claims and how evidence is legally defined as relevant and *admissible* in court. Read over the discussion of evidence in "PART 1," above, and read religiously the State or Federal Rules of Evidence, depending on the court in which the complaint was filed.

NOTE: At the soonest opportunity, consider sending a letter to opposing counsel requesting that they supply you with any and all case law upon which they intend to rely, whether in summary judgment or in other motions and briefs. Responding to the logic of a contentious legal theory is most difficult if its case law or other authority is unavailable. Should you find yourself in the position of having to respond to a motion or brief citing authority unavailable to you, and you have previously asked opposing counsel to supply you copies of authority in such circumstances, as a matter of courtesy, then object to the use of such authority. Inform the court of your earlier, standing request that counsel send you copies of all authority relied upon in their papers; that you cannot properly respond to the opposing motion or brief without reviewing that authority, and therefore object to the motion or the brief until such a time that the pertinent material is obtained, reviewed, and properly considered in formulating a response.

Strictly speaking, opposing counsel is not legally required to send you copies of their authority (if a piece of case law is *unpublished*, however, they may be so required by court rules). Nevertheless, the parties are supposed to participate in the legal process with good faith, and sometimes it is just *fair* that opposing counsel furnish the resource-limited, *pro se* prisoner-plaintiff with copies. Should you make an objection to the use of certain authority by your opponents, be ready to explain why you couldn't obtain copies by your own means.

Finally, summary judgment motions are often combined with other dispositive motions. Most notably, when suing governmental officials, the immunity question is frequently raised. If an immunity defense has not been asserted in previous motions, it will be brought up at the summary judgment stage. If so, the court must deal with the immunity question before deciding whether summary judgment is proper.

THE IMMUNITY QUESTION

Government defendants almost always assert an immunity defense of one kind or another. **Immunity** means that a party cannot be sued, regardless of whether the facts in the complaint are true—as a body can be immune from a disease, a government can be immune from a lawsuit. Yet some limitations and exceptions exist.

Of the many types of immunity defenses, four are particular to civil actions against the government and its officers:

1. **Absolute Immunity:** Judges, prosecutors, probation/parole officers, public defenders, and others performing judicially related acts are absolutely immune from liability in damages for conduct closely associated with court procedure, and injunctive relief will not be permitted unless declaratory relief is insufficient to redress a wrong.

2. **Sovereign Immunity**: Under older rules, States were totally immune from lawsuits for money damages brought directly against the state by its own citizens, and the

United States government was likewise immune from lawsuits brought by its citizens for money damages; however, the FTCA and parallel state laws waive much of this immunity, permitting damages claims under limited conditions.

3. **Eleventh Amendment Immunity:** A state is immune from lawsuits brought by residents of another state, and a state is immune from lawsuits brought in federal court by its own residents.

4. **Qualified Immunity:** Public officials exercising due discretion and acting reasonably within the confines of what they believe their legal duties to be are immune from lawsuits for money damages.

Absolute immunity protects judges, prosecutors, probation/parole officers, public defenders, and others who perform judicially related acts. So long as these officials are exercising a discretionary, judicially-related function (e.g., making determinations of fact, deciding to use one process/procedure or another, conducting hearings, and just about anything relating to court procedures) they are entitled to absolute immunity—meaning that no lawsuits may be brought against them for anything but injunctive or declaratory relief. Injunctive relief in a § 1983 action against a judicial officer is not granted unless declaratory relief is either unavailable or has proved ineffective. Federal Courts Improvement Act of 1996, Pub. L. No. 104-317, 110 Stat. 3847 § 309(c). Judicial officers, furthermore, cannot be held *personally* liable for costs—including attorney's fees—associated with the prosecution of a § 1983 claim, *unless their actions were clearly in excess of their jurisdiction (id.,* at § 309(a)); but in no case can judicial officers, sued in their official capacities, be held liable for attorney's fees. *Id.,* at § 309(b). (Testifying witnesses, too, are considered integral enough to the judicial process that they may also be held absolutely immune from liability for the content of their deposition or in-court testimony.)

However, judicial officers acting in either a *ministrative* capacity (not involving acts of discretion, but of merely following instructions) or an *investigative* capacity do not enjoy absolute immunity, but qualified immunity only. Suppose, for instance, that a prosecutor elects to charge a person with first- rather than second-degree murder (even if the case facts better fall under the second-degree category). The prosecutor is absolutely immune from lawsuits concerning that decision. Yet if the prosecutor acts in an investigative capacity— say, processing a crime scene—he or she then enjoys qualified immunity only, the same as other investigators. Should a prosecutor destroy evidence, for example, that prosecutor may be held liable. Moreover, there is no immunity of any kind for improper acts committed outside a protected government function or capacity—if a judge punches you in the nose at a BBQ, you can sue that judge for money damages, just like anyone else can be sued for a battery tort.

Sovereign immunity and Eleventh Amendment immunity together forbid lawsuits against the government itself, without the government's consent—that is, the federal government cannot be sued directly by a U.S. citizen, and a state likewise cannot be sued by one of its own citizens in its own courts. Eleventh Amendment immunity also expressly prohibits citizens from suing a state in which they are not residents, or suing their home state in federal courts.

Sovereign immunity/Eleventh Amendment immunity, where it exists, protects the government itself against claims for any type of relief. It does not, however, prevent claims for injunctive or declaratory relief against persons sued in their *official* governmental capacities.

Further, a suit for money damages can *still* be brought under a *Bivens* action or § 1983 action, or other title creating a legal remedy, where a government actor is sued in the *individual* capacity, as opposed to the *official* capacity as a government instrument. There is an important distinction here: To sue a person in the official capacity is the same as suing the government itself; to sue in the individual capacity is to sue the person him- or herself. Official-capacity suits are brought for prospective/injunctive/declaratory relief; individual-capacity suits are brought for money damages. And yet, officials can be sued in *both* official and individual capacities, so long as the plaintiff is careful to demand only injunctive/declaratory relief regarding a defendant's official capacity as a government agent, and only monetary relief regarding that defendant's personal, civilian status.

Moreover, Congress has waived much of its sovereign immunity under the Federal Tort Claims Act (meaning the government *can* be sued directly for money damages) for injuries arising from a federal agent's tortious conduct. (*See* about the FTCA in the "Chapter 11: Section 1983, *Bivens*, or Tort?" above.) Many states have passed similar legislation bearing a "Tort Claims Act" styling of one fashion or another that permits the recovery of money damages from the state government itself. Under a state's Tort Claims Act, *official* capacity as well as *individual* capacity suits can be brought for monetary relief in state court. But you should note that, unless the state statute expressly waives its *Eleventh Amendment* immunity, it is unlikely that a money-damages suit can be brought *in federal* court for *official* capacity suits or suits directly against the state government.

There is another important exception to Eleventh Amendment immunity. Certain federal statutes are made applicable to the states via Congress's authority to legislate under the "spending clause" of the U.S. Constitution. This means that if a state receives federal money by virtue of a federal law providing for state programs, the state must adhere to federal policy concerning those programs. Should a state run afoul of the controlling federal law, a state citizen may be able to bring a suit under that federal law directly against the state government in federal court, because in accepting federal money the state effectively waives its Eleventh Amendment immunity with regard to the programs it is supposed to operate with the federal funding in question.

Qualified immunity protects prison guards and other officials performing executive/administrative functions from lawsuits arising from injuries that have occurred in the course of executing a governmental duty—but only insofar as the official has undertaken a "discretionary function," and provided that this conduct has not violated a "clearly established," constitutionally protected right. A function is "discretionary" if it combines the right or power to act with the freedom to exercise judgment. Whether or not such actions/decisions are immunized under the common-law discretionary-function exception to liability is a matter of

> varying scope, . . . the variation being dependent upon the scope of discretion and responsibilities of the office and all the circumstances as they reasonably appeared at the time of the action on which liability is sought to be based. It is the existence of reasonable grounds for the belief formed at the time and in light of the circumstances, coupled with good-faith belief, that affords a basis for qualified immunity of executive officers for acts performed in the course of official conduct.

Scheuer v. Rhodes, 416 U.S. 232, 247-248 (1974).

Rationalizing by the common-law exception to liability afforded *state officials* in *Scheuer*, the Supreme Court later contemplated the availability of qualified immunity for the actions of *federal officials* without parting markedly from its earlier opinion, except to hold applicable the *Scheuer* standard for immunity defenses in actions against federal officers:

> [I]n a suit for damages arising from unconstitutional action, federal executive officials exercising discretion are entitled only to the qualified immunity specified in *Scheuer*, subject to those exceptional situations where it is demonstrated that absolute immunity is essential for the conduct of public business.

Butz v. Economon, 438 U.S. 478, 507 (1978).

NOTE: In performing an act of discretion, should a federal official violate the constitutional rights of a person, that official may be personally held liable in damages, even though the statutory "discretionary function exception" of the FTCA would preclude suits against the federal government itself. Review "The Right Vehicle" in "Chapter 11" in this regard.

If tortious events cannot reasonably be characterized as having resulted from an act within the discretion of the official, the offending official might not be entitled to a defense of qualified immunity. For officials who act outside *prescribed* or *obligatory* responsibilities or directives, for instance, neither the common-law not the FTCA discretionary-function exception to liability may be available. So, was a prison guard doing something he or she shouldn't have, or didn't have the authority to do? Was the guard complying with policy throughout the incident? For example, should a prison nurse withhold prescribed medication from a prisoner who suffers medical complications as a result, a constitutional claim of inadequate medical care may thus be created. A common nurse does not have license—and therefore has no discretion—to alter or interfere with doctor-prescribed treatment.

Moreover, an act within the discretion of an officer can *still* be constitutionally actionable if the conduct is in violation of a prisoner's rights, of which a person performing the duties of a particular government office *should* have been aware. It follows that, even if an official caused a civil injury, harmful conduct will not give rise to liability if the official couldn't reasonably have been expected to know his or her actions violated civil law. This exception to liability is based on the idea that competent government actors should be free to fulfill their duties unburdened by the fear of facing legal repercussions for every official act. Qualified immunity, therefore, seeks to protect all but intentionally tortious conduct (there is no immunity for malicious acts) and the plainly incompetent.

Whether a defendant can assert a successful qualified immunity defense is typically tested by the two-part query of whether the alleged misconduct violated (1) a Constitutionally protected right that was (2) clearly established at the time of the incident under review. The first question is usually easier answered than the second, which is often a focus of debate in disputes about immunity.

Many rights are retained by prisoners, and cannot be genuinely disputed, including those guaranteed under the U.S. Constitution and other federal and state rights assured to the people via the application of constitutional substantive due process. (*See* "PART 4" for discussion of prisoners' rights and due process.) However, a right or application/interpretation of a right might not be considered "clearly established" if it is very new (say, a right created under a brand-new law or policy), or if no controlling legal authority existed in the particular judicial jurisdiction at the time of the alleged violation that can show a reasonable officer should have known his or her conduct was unlawful. Judges are encouraged to use their sound discretion in resolving this issue, free to adopt the traditional two-part test as a useful analytical tool. *Pearson v. Callahan*, __U.S.__, 129 S.Ct. 808, 818 (2009).

The immunity question is slightly different with regard to local governments and their officers. Municipalities (local governments, such as counties, cities, townships, etc) are not considered "arms of state" within the reach of sovereign or Eleventh Amendment immunity protection. They are "persons" (like a corporation is a legal "person") who may be sued for money damages as well as for other forms of relief that are cognizable under § 1983—though they may enjoy absolute or qualified immunity by the same conditions providing exception to liability for federal and state officers, as discussed above.

However, to hold a municipal official liable in damages, the conduct forming the basis of a § 1983 complaint *must* have occurred *as a result of municipal policy or custom*. That is to say, the official must have acted by the prevailing practices/protocols of a municipal entity, in order for that entity (and/or its agent) to be liable under § 1983, which, to reiterate, is a federal statute that allows persons acting under color of *state law* to be sued in federal court for violations of federal law. Accordingly, tortious conduct of municipal officials is not actionable under § 1983 if that conduct cannot fairly be characterized as an expression or result of municipal policy (although the same conduct may nevertheless create a viable cause of action in state court, under ordinary principles of tort law).

An exception, however, arises should the complained misconduct occur at the hand of a municipality's chief policy-maker, who is a person (or persons) cloaked in state authority, being a source of policy by state leave, and therefore falling within the purview of § 1983 for redress of deprivations of federal rights. This is true even if the policy-maker's acts or omissions do not necessarily occur as a consequence of existing municipal policy or custom.

Lastly, private citizens and private companies (such as private prison companies) may be held liable under § 1983 for violations of federal law that are perpetrated against prisoners, insofar as the activity was perpetrated "under color of state law." The immunity defenses discussed in this section are not usually available for private actors. (*See* "Constitutional and Federal Claims" under "Chapter 11" for discussion of private-person liability under § 1983.)

NOTE: Remember that injunctive and/or declaratory relief are always available against government officials in their official capacities, to correct a continuing wrong. Anything less would give the government license to do whatever, whenever it chose, without fear of correction. Immunity defenses come into play when defendants seek to dodge liability in *money damages*. And note that an *individual* person can always be held liable in money damages for civil injuries caused while *not* acting in the role of a government agent/official/employee, just like any other private person. A prison guard would be hard-pressed to summon an immunity defense for, say, an unprovoked spray of mace into your cell while you lay asleep on your rack—certainly the guard had no discretion in making the assault, and was hardly acting in the course of governmental duties. In such a scenario, a simple tort action in state court would probably be the better vehicle and forum for achieving redress.

Dennis P. Smith #50703
A-154-B
2334 North Orchid
PO Box 454
Boise, Idaho 83707

Plaintiff, *pro se*

IN THE UNITED STATES DISTRICT COURT

FOR THE DISTRICT OF IDAHO

DENNIS PATRICK SMITH,	)	Case No. CV-11-08527-S-EJL
Plaintiff,	)	
	)	**PLAINTIFF'S BRIEF IN RESPONSE**
	)	**TO DEFENDANTS' MOTION FOR**
vs.	)	**SUMMARY JUDGMENT**
	)	
PHILIP J. JOHNSON, *et al*,	)	
	)	
Defendants.	)	
_____	)	

COMES NOW Dennis P. Smith #50703, plaintiff *pro se*, and submits this *Plaintiff's Brief in Response to Defendants' Motion for Summary Judgment.*

I. INTRODUCTION

On October 17, 2012, defendants filed a *Motion for Summary Judgment.* Plaintiff submits this brief in response, that the defendants' motion be denied. Defendants have failed to demonstrate that summary judgment is appropriate as a matter of law, i.e., (1) Plaintiff's claim of inadequate medical care is cognizable under federal law; (2) defendants are liable for their failure to provide adequate medical care; and (3) material facts remain in genuine dispute for resolution at trial.

**PLAINTIFF'S BRIEF IN RESPONSE TO
DEFENDANTS' MOTION FOR SUMMARY JUDGMENT**   **Page 1 of 29**

Figure 7 p. 1

II. STATEMENT OF FACTS

On September 21, 2010, Plaintiff suffered severe injury to his lower back as a result of a vehicle collision. Plaintiff was taken by ambulance to the Valley General Hospital, where he was treated for numerous injuries and was discovered to have suffered a ruptured disk between the fourth and fifth lumbar vertebrae, along with related ligament and nerve damage. Plaintiff was scheduled to undergo reconstructive spinal surgery on December 15, 2010. Plaintiff was, however, arrested and taken into police custody on November 14, 2010, and, being confined, was unable to make his surgical appointment. To date, Plaintiff's spinal injuries have not healed, nor have his injuries received adequate medical treatment. Plaintiff endures continual lower-back muscle spasms and nerve pain, both of which restrict his mobility generally, in addition to causing acute surges of pain.

Plaintiff is currently housed at the Idaho State Correctional Facility (I.S.C.F.), where he is within the care and custody of defendant Philip Johnson and defendant Daniel Collins, M.D. While in the care of the defendants, Plaintiff has repeatedly requested, through institutional channels, that the defendants provide for him the medical care necessary to relieve him of his lower-back condition—that is, the type of care considered, and determined by a medical specialist to be, the only efficacious remedy for Plaintiff's severe spinal injury and his chronic lower-back pain. The defendants have refused to provide this treatment.

On November 4, 2011, Plaintiff filed a *Complaint* with the Court, requesting from the Court an order directing the defendants to provide for Plaintiff's much-needed pain medication and reconstructive surgery, as well as an order awarding

Figure 7 p. 2

monetary relief for the unnecessary physical deterioration and the suffering caused by the defendants' program of inadequate medical treatment and inadequate pain management. Defendants filed an *Answer* on March 12, 2012; the parties completed discovery on October 5, 2012; and the defense filed a *Motion for Summary Judgment* on October 17, 2012, submitted with a *Brief in Support of Motion for Summary Judgment.*

III. DEFENDANTS ARE LIABLE FOR FAILING IN THEIR DUTY TO PROVIDE PLAINTIFF ADEQUATE MEDICAL CARE

A. INTRODUCTION

Defendants propose two theories to dispute their liability. First, Defendant Johnson contends that there is no recognized doctrine of respondent superior in 42 U.S.C. § 1983 actions and, because he is not responsible for choosing the course of medical treatment prescribed for Plaintiff, he therefore cannot be held liable in damages for the conduct of his employee. *See Brief in Support*, at 3-5. Second, Defendant Johnson (proposes in the alternative) and Defendant Collins offer a defense of qualified immunity, asserting specifically that they have acted reasonably, in light of the protections granted Plaintiff under the U.S. Constitution. *Id.*, at 5-10.

B. SUPERVISORY OFFICIALS MAY BE HELD LIABLE FOR FAILING TO PREVENT THE ACTIONS OF THEIR SUBORDINATES

1. **The Doctrine of Respondent Superior Is Inapplicable. Defendant Johnson Is Nevertheless Liable for Failure to Fulfill His Duties as Prison Warden**

"Under Section 1983, supervisory officials are not liable for actions of subordinates on any theory of vicarious liability." *Hansen v. Black*, 885 F.2d 642, 645-

Figure 7 p. 3

646 (9th Cir. 1989). A supervisor may, however, be liable "if (1) he or she is personally involved in the constitutional deprivation, or (2) there is 'a sufficient causal connection between the supervisor's wrongful conduct and the constitutional violation.'" *Snow v. McDaniel*, 681 F.3d 978, 989 (9th Cir. 2012), *quoting Hansen*, 885 F.3d at 646. "A supervisor may be liable for constitutional violations . . . if the supervisor . . . knew of the violations and failed to act on them." *Barry v. Ratelle*, 985 F.Supp 1235, 1239 (S.D. Cal. 1997); *accord Taylor v. List*, 880 F.2d 1040, 1045 (9th Cir. 1989).

Circumstantial evidence may suffice to indicate that a defendant had knowledge of a violation when allegations are supported by corresponding evidence such as institutional appeals forms. *Barry*, 985 F.Supp at 1239. Prison grievances may also serve to establish a supervisor's knowledge of a medical need. *Snow*, 681 F.3d at 989 (finding that prison grievances were sufficient notice of prisoner's need of hip-replacement surgery and that prison officials' failure to prevent further harm precluded a grant of summary judgment).

2. Defendant Johnson Failed to Act When the Law Required Him To

That Defendant Johnson is the highest I.S.C.F. authority charged with the care and custody of Plaintiff is not in dispute. *See Philip J. Johnson's Response to Plaintiff's Request for Admissions*, No. 8, attached hereto as Exhibit A and incorporated by this reference. That prison officials have an affirmative duty under the Eighth Amendment of the U.S. Constitution to provide adequate "medical care for the prisoners within their care and custody is also indisputable. *See Estell v. Gamble*, *infra*. For a supervisor such as a prison warden to be liable for an Eighth Amendment

Figure 7 p. 4

medical care violation, resulting from the actions of subordinates (or of those contracted with the state to fulfill obligations charged to the supervisor), the supervisor must have been aware of a sufficiently serious medical need and failed to take measures to address it, resulting in harm. *Estell, infra; Barry,* 985 F.Supp at 1239.

Defendant Johnson has admitted, through discovery answers, that during the time of the events concerning this lawsuit he was fully aware of Plaintiff's severe spinal injury. *See* Exhibit A, Nos. 11-13. Defendant Johnson has acknowledged the occurrence and content of a May 15, 2011, conversation in which Plaintiff informed the defendant of the nature of Plaintiff's back injury and explained the inadequacy of the medical treatment he was currently receiving at I.S.C.F. *Id.,* Nos. 1-4. Defendant Johnson has admitted that during the May conversation he agreed to investigate Plaintiff's concerns. *Id.,* at No. 4; *see also Compl.,* at 8, para. 28. Defendant Johnson has also admitted that, despite his agreement to investigate and his subsequent review of Plaintiff's institutional Concern Form (*see* Exhibit B attached hereto and hereby incorporated, a concern form which Defendant Johnson failed to answer in violation of IDOC policy, *see* Exhibit A, Nos. 5-6), and despite the resulting grievance submitted by Plaintiff (*see* Exhibit C attached hereto and hereby incorporated) he has, in fact, taken no measures to determine the veracity of Plaintiff's claim of inadequate medical treatment. *See Philip J. Johnson's Response to Plaintiff's Request for Interrogatories,* No. 7, attached hereto as Exhibit D and incorporated by this reference; *see also Compl.,* at 8, para. 25-30. Because Defendant Johnson has failed to act to prevent the harm to one entrusted into his care, knowing fully of the substantial risk to Plaintiff's health, Defendant Johnson cannot escape liability for his

PLAINTIFF'S BRIEF IN RESPONSE TO
DEFENDANTS' MOTION FOR SUMMARY JUDGMENT   **Page 5 of 29**

Figure 7 p. 5

participation in causing Plaintiff's injuries when failing in his supervisory duties as warden of I.S.C.F.

C. NEITHER DEFENDANT JOHNSON NOR DEFENDANT COLLINS IS ENTITLED TO QUALIFIED IMMUNITY

1. Standard for Qualified Immunity

Qualified immunity protects government officials from damages claims arising out of civil injuries occurring in the course of performing an executive duty, so long as the duty can fairly be characterized as "discretionary." *Alexander v. Perrill*, 916 F.2d 1392, 1396 (9th Cir. 1990); *cf. U.S. v. Gaubert*, 499 U.S. 315, 336-337 (1991) ("[T]he discretionary function exception will not apply when a federal statute, regulation, or policy specifically prescribes a course of action for an employee to follow. In this event, the employee has no rightful option but to adhere to the directive. . . ."). Officials who are permitted under law the discretion to exercise their judgment are generally shielded "from liability for civil damages insofar as their conduct does not violate clearly established [federal] statutory or constitutional rights of which a reasonable person would have known." *Harlow v. Fitzgerald*, 457 U.S. 800, 816 (1982); *see, e.g., Beck v. City of Upland*, 527 F.3d 853, 870-872 (9th Cir. 2008) (reasonable officers would have known arresting plaintiff in retaliation for staging protest violated the First Amendment, precluding a grant of summary judgment to the defendants).

The doctrine of qualified immunity seeks to ensure that officials "reasonably can anticipate when their conduct may give rise to liability," by attaching liability when "[t]he contours of the right [violated are] sufficiently clear that a reasonable official would understand that what he is doing violates the right." *U.S. v. Lanier*, 520 U.S. 259, 270 (1997); *see also Elder v. Holloway*, 510 U.S. 510, 511 (1994) (officials lose immunity if

PLAINTIFF'S BRIEF IN RESPONSE TO
DEFENDANTS' MOTION FOR SUMMARY JUDGMENT   **Page 6 of 29**

Figure 7 p. 6

"their conduct was unreasonable in light of clearly established law."). "This is not to say that an official action is protected by qualified immunity unless the very action in question has been held unlawful; but it is to say that in the light of preexisting law the unlawfulness must be apparent." *Anderson v. Creighton,* 483 U.S. 635, 640 (1987). Whether the contours of a right are reasonably apparent may be determined in view of preexisting statutory or constitutional law or case law originating within the particular jurisdiction, though "closely analogous preexisting case law is not required to show that a right was clearly established." *White v. Lee*, 227 F.3d 1214, 1238 (9th Cir. 2000).

Accordingly, once a government function is established as discretionary,[1] a determination of whether qualified immunity exists "generally turns on the 'objective legal reasonableness' of the action. . . ." *Anderson*, 483 U.S. at 639, *quoting Harlow*, 457 U.S. at 819. Objective reasonableness is normally tested by a two-part inquiry: (1) whether the facts alleged constitute a violation of federal law, and (2) whether the federal right was clearly established at the time of the violation. *Saucier v. Katz*, 533 U.S. 194, 201 (2001). Which of the two prongs should be addressed first is left within the sound discretion of the trial court. *Pearson v. Callahan*, __U.S.__, 129 S.Ct. 808, 818 (2009).

After the court concludes that a right was clearly established, an officer is not ordinarily entitled to qualified immunity, because a reasonably competent public official is charged with knowing the law governing his or her conduct. *Harlow*, 457 U.S. at 818-819. In rare circumstances, however, an official may nevertheless qualify for immunity protection if the violation of the clearly established right occurred while

---

[1] That Defendant Johnson has discretion as I.S.C.F. Warden to choose the way in which he will provide adequate medical care is uncontested.

**PLAINTIFF'S BRIEF IN RESPONSE TO
DEFENDANTS' MOTION FOR SUMMARY JUDGMENT** Page 7 of 29

Figure 7 p. 7

the official "reasonably but mistakenly believed that his . . . conduct did not violate the right." *Jackson v. City of Bremerton*, 268 F.3d 646, 651 (9th Cir. 2001).

2. Defendant Johnson Knew His Conduct Violated a Clearly Established Right.

Prisoners retain those federal rights that are not inconsistent with the station of a prisoner and legitimate penological objectives. *Procunier v. Martinez*, 416 U.S. 396 (1974). Although in punitive incarceration for their offences against society, "there is no iron curtain drawn between the Constitution and the prisoners of this country." *Bell v. Wolfish*, 482 U.S. 520, 545 (1979), *citing Wolf v. McDonnell*, 418 U.S. 539 (1974); *see, e.g., Morrison v. Hall*, 261 F.3d 896 (9th Cir. 2001) (should a prison regulation or practice infringe upon a prisoner's Constitutional right, the federal court may order such remedies as necessary to protect the right).

The United States Supreme Court has explicitly stated that prisoners are entitled to adequate medical care under the United States Constitution. *See generally Estell v. Gamble*, 429 U.S. 97 (1979) (plurality opinion). And because prisoners "must rely on prison authorities to treat [their] medical needs . . ." (*id.*, 429 U.S. at 103), the Constitution requires the government to meet those needs by imposing an affirmative duty on officials to provide prisoners with medical care. *See, e.g., Dickworth v. Ahmed*, 532 F.3d 675 (7th Cir. 2008). Should officials fail in this duty, they may be held liable in a 42 U.S.C. § 1983 action. *Estell*, 429 U.S. at 105; *see, e.g., Snow*, 681 F.3d at 989 (reversing grant of summary judgment to prison warden and assistant warden; holding cognizable § 1983 Eighth Amendment claim when officials failed to provide inmate with hip-replacement surgery).

Mere negligence or accidents or inadvertence, however, will not support a

Figure 7 p. 8

federal constitutional claim; but only

> [d]eliberate indifference to serious needs of prisoners constitutes the unnecessary and wanton infliction of pain proscribed by the Eighth Amendment. This is true whether the indifference is manifested by prison doctors in their response to the prisoner's needs or by prison guards in intentionally denying or delaying access to medical care or intentionally interfering with treatment once prescribed. Regardless of how evidenced, deliberate indifference to a prisoner's serious illness or injury states a cause of action under section 1983.

Estell, 429 U.S. at 104-105 (quotations and citation omitted); *accord Farmer v. Brennon*, 511 U.S. 825, 837 (1994).

Plaintiff has brought a § 1983 claim, alleging a violation of the Eighth Amendment arising from inadequate medical treatment, proposed on a theory of deliberate indifference to serious medical needs. Our Circuit's test for deliberate indifference to a serious medical need is of two parts:

> First, the plaintiff must show a serious medical need by demonstrating that failure to treat a prisoner's condition could result in further significant injury or the unnecessary and wanton infliction of pain. Second, the plaintiff must show the defendant's response to the need was deliberately indifferent.

Jett v. Penner, 439 F.3d 1091, 1096 (9th Cir. 2006) (internal quotations and citation omitted).

Plaintiff's spinal injury and resulting deterioration of overall physical condition is a serious medical need. "An injury or illness is sufficiently serious if the failure to treat a prisoner's condition could result in further significant injury or the '. . . unnecessary and wanton infliction of pain.'" *Lyons v. Busi*, 566 F.Supp.2d 1172, 1191 (E.D. Cal. 2008), *quoting McGuckin v. Smith*, 974 F.2d 1050, 1059 (9th Cir. 1992). "Factors indicating seriousness are: (1) whether a reasonable doctor would think that the condition is

Figure 7 p. 9

worthy of comment; (2) whether the condition significantly impacts the prisoner's daily activities; and (3) whether the condition is chronic and accompanied by substantial pain." *Lyons*, 566 F.Supp.2d at 1191, *citing Lopez v. Smith*, 203 F.3d 1122, 1131-1132 (9th Cir. 2000) (en banc). That Plaintiff's spinal injury is worthy of medical comment is specifically supported by a specialist in spinal injuries and orthopedic surgery:

> Mr. Smith exhibits acute subluxation of the L4 and L5 vertabrea, a rupture of the nucleus pulposus and severe posterior herniation to the L4/L5 intervertabrea disc, tearing of multiple attendant ligaments, and neural abnormalities. . . .

Affidavit of Gregory J. Michael, p. 3, para. 7, February 9, 2012, attached hereto as Exhibit E and incorporated by this reference.

Defendant Collins himself acknowledged Plaintiff's injury when he prescribed Plaintiff a regimen of three daily eight-hundred-milligram doses of ibuprofen and five-hundred-milligram doses of Naprosyn anti-inflammatory. *See Dr. Daniel K. Collins's Response to Plaintiff's Request for Admissions*, No. 6, attached hereto as Exhibit F and incorporated by this reference; *see also Compl.*, at 7, para. 24.

Whether Plaintiff's condition is chronic and causing substantial pain is affirmatively answered and amply evinced in the September 21, 2010, diagnosis and February 9, 2012 affidavit of Dr. Michael (*see* Exhibit E, at 3-4, para. 7-11), and is further supported by Plaintiff's own statements (*see Compl.*, at 8-9, para. 31-33) and those of four disinterested witnesses who have had opportunity to observe Plaintiff exhibit signs of physical distress for significant periods of time relevant to this lawsuit.[2]

---

[2] *See Affidavit of Bradely B. Grey #52407*, October 20, 2012; *Affidavit of Jose R. Martinez #56702*, February 10, 2012; *Affidavit of Damon D. Moore #89001*, February 10, 2012; and *Affidavit of James J. Lawson #55111*, February 12, 2012; marked respectively as Exhibits G, H, I, and J, and incorporated by this reference.

PLAINTIFF'S BRIEF IN RESPONSE TO
DEFENDANTS' MOTION FOR SUMMARY JUDGMENT   **Page 10 of 29**

Figure 7 p. 10

The evidence on record together with the affidavits attached hereto, taken as true and drawing all inferences in the light most favorable to Plaintiff,[3] demonstrate that Defendants' failure to provide adequate medical care has resulted "in further significant injury . . . [and] the '. . . unnecessary and wanton infliction of pain,'" satisfying the first part of the Ninth Circuit's deliberate-indifference test. *Lyons*, 566 F.Supp.2d at 1191, *quoting McGuckin*, 974 F.2d at 1059.

The second part of the test[4] requires a plaintiff to demonstrate "(a) a purposeful act or failure to respond to a prisoner's pain or possible medical need and (b) harm caused by the indifference." *Jett*, 439 F.2d at 1096. A purposeful act or failure to respond "may appear when prison officials deny, delay or intentionally interfere with medical treatment, or it may be shown by the way in which prison physicians provide medical care." *Id.* (internal quotations omitted). The "harm" caused by deliberate indifference, moreover, need not be "substantial." *Id.* ("A prisoner need not show his harm was substantial"); *see also McGuckin*, 974 F.2d at 1060 ("[A] finding that the defendant's activities resulted in 'substantial' harm to the prisoner is not necessary.").

Defendant Johnson does not dispute that he was aware of Plaintiff's medical condition. *See* Exhibit A, Nos. 1-7, 11-13. Defendant Johnson has admitted that he took no reasonable measures to investigate or address Plaintiff's complaints and grievances of inadequate medical care. *See* Exhibit D, No. 7. Plaintiff's own statements, the eye-witness accounts of fellow inmates in a position to observe Plaintiff's physical condition,

---

[3]   For a determination of summary judgment, the evidence of the non-moving party is to be believed. *Anderson v. Liberty Lobby, Inc.*, 477 U.S. 242, 255 (1986). And all reasonable inferences that may be drawn from the facts on record or indicated in the pleadings or briefs must be drawn in favor of the non-moving party. *Matsushita Elec. Indus. Co. v. Zenith Radio Corp.*, 475 U.S. 574, 587 (1986).

[4]   "Second, the plaintiff must show the defendant's response to the [medical] need was deliberately indifferent." *Jett*, 439 F.3d at 1096.

PLAINTIFF'S BRIEF IN RESPONSE TO
DEFENDANTS' MOTION FOR SUMMARY JUDGMENT   **Page 11 of 29**

Figure 7 p. 11

and the testimony of a medical specialist are heavily probative of the severity of Plaintiff's medical needs, all of which statements describe manifest deterioration and significant pain suffered by Plaintiff while entrusted to the care and custody of Defendant Johnson. *See Compl.*, at 3-4 and 8-9; Exhibit G, at 2; Exhibit H, at 2; Exhibit I, at 2; Exhibit J, at 2; and Exhibit E, at 3-4, para. 7-11. These facts, taken as true, easily satisfy the second part of the Ninth Circuit's deliberate-indifference test.

Defendant Johnson does not dispute that prison officials have an affirmative duty under the Constitution to provide inmates with adequate medical care (*see* Exhibit A, No. 9), and prisoners' right to medical care is clearly established. *See Estell, supra.* His claim to qualified immunity focuses instead on essentially what amounts to a good-faith defense. He argues that "immunity is available when an official 'reasonably but mistakenly believed that his . . . conduct did not violate a clearly established right. . . .'" *See Brief in Support*, at 6, *quoting Jackson v. City of Bremerton*, 268 F.3d 646, 651 (9th Cir. 2001). Specifically, Defendant Johnson argues that he should not be personally held accountable in damages when he relied on the professional judgment of Defendant Collins to select for Plaintiff the appropriate course of medical treatment. He argues that his reliance on the expertise of Defendant Collins was reasonable, even if Defendant Collins's choices ultimately proved to be mistaken, as contemplated by the *Jackson* court.

This argument, valid, perhaps, in circumstances of a diligent supervisory prison authority, is unfounded in this case. Defendant Johnson has not acted in good faith to ensure Plaintiff's health needs were met. Defendant Johnson was aware of Plaintiff's significant spinal problems and complaints of inadequate treatment; he has admitted as much. *See* Exhibit A, Nos. 1-7 and 11-13. And aside from the manifest deterioration of

Figure 7 p. 12

Plaintiff's overall physical condition—in itself sufficient indication of inadequate medical care for an otherwise surgically easily-operable back injury (*see* Exhibit E, at 5, para. 12-13)—the fact that Defendant Johnson agreed to investigate Plaintiff's concerns of inadequate treatment when personally speaking with Plaintiff about his ailment and surgical recommendation and then failed to follow up with any meaningful inquiry, either after the conversation or after Plaintiff's subsequent grievances, precludes Defendant Johnson from a grant of qualified immunity. A reasonable prison warden, charged with knowing the law governing his conduct (*Harlow*, 457 U.S. at 818-819), would have known it was his duty to investigate a credible allegation of misconduct on the part of a medical provider contracted to serve the prison he supervises, and a "supervisor may be liable if the supervisor knew of [a] violation [of federal law] and failed to act to prevent [it]." *Snow*, 681 F.3d at 989, *citing Taylor*, 880 F.2d at 1045.

3. Defendant Collins Is Not a Government Official Entitled to a Defense of Qualified Immunity

The doctrine of qualified immunity stands to immunize government officials from damages claims arising from the performance of official business, in which is necessary the exercise of reasonable discretion. *Alexander v. Perrill*, 916 F.2d 1392, 1396 (9th Cir. 1990). Officials enjoy qualified immunity protection while performing discretionary functions, and will not be held liable for discretionary acts insofar as their conduct does not violate clearly established federal "rights of which a reasonable person would have known." *Harlow*, 457 U.S. at 818. This rationale is grounded on the theory that government officials must be free to prefer one course of action over another, without fear of civil litigation arising from mistakes made when acting in good faith. In other words, the interests of society are served in the efficient execution of government duties.

**PLAINTIFF'S BRIEF IN RESPONSE TO
DEFENDANTS' MOTION FOR SUMMARY JUDGMENT**   **Page 13 of 29**

Figure 7 p. 13

Defendant Collins, however, is not a government official; and while certainly performing a discretionary function when formulating a medical plan for Plaintiff, he was not, in fact, a government employee within the purview of the doctrine traditionally immunizing government conduct. Qualified immunity is not available to protect non-government actors. *See generally Wyatt v. Cole*, 504 U.S. 158, 167-169 (1992); *see also Richardson v. McKnight*, 521 U.S. 399 (1997) (holding defense of qualified immunity unavailable to private prison employees). This is because there has never been a firmly rooted tradition of immunity for private actors who perform government functions. *Richardson*, 521 U.S. at 47. The purpose of qualified immunity is to ensure the vigorous operation of the government by allowing officials to act decisively, unfearing of legal consequence for mistakes made in the course of fulfilling what they believe in good faith to be their duty. The Supreme Court has instructed that this societal interest is not served by extending traditional government immunity protection to private employees. *Id.*, 521 U.S. at 407-412.

Rather, so long as there remains a private interest in obtaining contracts with the government, there is incentive for private actors to vigorously fulfill the government function they are employed to perform, without timidity for fear of litigation. *Id.*, 521 U.S. at 405-406. Defendant Collins is contracted with the I.S.C.F. to provide medical services to prisoners. *See* Exhibit F, No. 10. He has not argued that circumstances diminish the incentive to fulfill his contractual duties with the I.S.C.F.—a contract that was won over numerous other competing private bids (*see* Exhibit D, No. 20)—and therefore is not entitled to a defense of qualified immunity. *Richardson*, 521 U.S. at 407-408 (noting in dicta that unless the private incentive is absent, when, for example, private actors fulfill an

Figure 7 p.14

"essential" government role at the directive of officials or act under the direct supervision of officials, qualified immunity is not to be extended to protect private actors).

IV. DEFENDANTS ARE NOT ENTITLED TO A GRANT OF SUMMARY JUDGMENT AS A MATTER OF LAW

A. INTRODUCTION

Defendants argue in their *Brief in Support* that there is no genuine dispute of material fact in this case, and that there is insufficient evidence on record to satisfy the subjective element of an Eighth Amendment medical claim, a burden of proof Plaintiff would bear at trial. *See Brief in Support*, at 11-25. They argue that the facts entitle them to a grant of summary judgment as a matter of law. *Id.*, at 25. Defendants, however, have inaccurately portrayed the current state of law defining the deliberate indifference standard used within our Federal Circuit, and have understated the nature of the evidence and the dispute between the parties concerning what constitutes adequate medical care, as contemplated under the Constitution.

B. STANDARD FOR SUMMARY JUDGMENT

"A party may move for summary judgment, identifying each claim or defense—or the part of each claim or defense—on which summary judgment is sought. The court shall grant summary judgment if the movant shows that there is no genuine dispute as to any material fact and the movant is entitled to judgment as a matter of law." Fed. R. Cir. P. 56(a). A fact is "material" if it could affect the outcome of trial, and a dispute is "genuine" when on the record is "sufficient evidence supporting the claimed factual dispute . . . to require a jury or judge to resolve the parties' differing versions of the truth at trial." *Hahn v. Sargent*, 523 F.2d 461, 463 (1st Cir. 1975), *cert. denied*, 425 U.S. 904

Figure 7 p. 15

(1976), *citing First Natl. Bank v. Cities Serv. Co.*, 391 U.S. 253, 289 (1968).

On a motion for summary judgment, the moving party

> always bears the initial responsibility of informing the district court of the basis for its motion, and identifying those portions of "the pleadings, depositions, answers to interrogatories, and admissions on file, together with the affidavits, if any," which it believes demonstrate the absence of a genuine issue of material fact.

Celotex Corp. v Catnett, 477 U.S. 317, 323 (1986) (quoting former Fed. R. Cir. P. 56(c), substantively unchanged by 2010 amendments). If movants meet this initial responsibility, the burden shifts to the non-moving party to show that a genuine issue of material fact does actually remain for resolution at trial. *Matushit*, 475 U.S. at 586. If the non-moving party fails to meet this burden, summary judgment should be entered in favor of the movant. *Celotex*, 477 U.S. at 322.

To survive summary judgment once the moving party has met the initial requirement under Rule 56, the non-moving party may not meet its burden of demonstrating a factual dispute by relying only upon the allegations of its pleadings, but is required to offer evidence of specific facts in the form of admissible discovery materials and/or affidavits. *See Matsushita*, 475 U.S. at 586, n.11; *see also Anderson*, 477 U.S. at 266.

This burden on the non-moving party, however, is not so heavy. A material issue of fact need not be demonstrated conclusively in its favor—it is enough that "the claimed dispute be shown to require a jury or judge to resolve the parties' differing versions of truth at trial." *T.W. Elec. Serv., Inc. v. Pacific Elec. Contractors Ass'n*, 809 F.2d 626, 631 (9th Cir. 1987). In determining whether the non-moving party has met its burden on summary judgment, the judge should not attempt to resolve conflicting evidence of

Figure 7 p. 16

material facts in dispute, nor should the judge engage in determinations of credibility. *Anderson*, 477 U.S. at 254. The purpose of summary judgment, rather, "is to pierce the pleadings and to assess the proof in order to see whether there is a genuine need for trial." *Matsushita*, 475 U.S. at 587 (internal quotations omitted).

The judge must not ask himself whether he thinks the evidence favors one side or the other, but whether a reasonable jury could return a verdict for the non-moving party on the evidence presented. *Anderson*, 477 U.S. at 250. In making this determination, the evidence presented by the non-moving party is to be taken as true. *Id.*, 477 U.S. at 255. And all reasonable inferences that may be drawn from the evidence on record are to be drawn in the light most favorable to the non-moving party. *Matsushita*, 475 U.S. at 587; *Anderson*, 477 U.S. at 254; *T.W. Elec. Serv.*, 809 F.2d at 631.

C. NEITHER DEFENDANT JOHNSON NOR DEFENDANT COLLINS IS ENTITLED TO A GRANT OF SUMMARY JUDGMENT

1. The Elements to an Eighth Amendment Medical Claim

To successfully state a claim under the Eighth Amendment of the U.S. Constitution, a plaintiff must allege a violation that satisfies both the objective injury threshold and the subjective intent necessary to constitute "cruel and unusual punishment." The objective element asks whether there has been a "sufficiently serious" deprivation of a life's necessity. *Wilson v. Seiter*, 501 U.S. 294, 298 (1991). The subjective element asks whether "a sufficiently culpable state of mind" existed behind the deprivation. *Id.*

Figure 7 p. 17

In an Eighth Amendment medical claim, the objective element is satisfied if the medical condition is "sufficiently serious" (*Estell*, 429 U.S. at 104-105) that failure to treat it "could result in further significant injury or the '. . . unnecessary and wanton infliction of pain.'" *Lyons*, 566 F.Supp.2d at 1191, *quoting McGuckin*, 974 F.2d at 1059. The subjective element of sufficiently culpable state of mind is satisfied upon a showing of "deliberate indifference".[5] (*Estell*, 429 U.S. at 104-105: *see also Farmer* 511 U.S. at 828; *see generally* III(C)(2), *supra*. This standard is, however, less stringent than in other Eighth Amendment claims of cruel and unusual punishment because in prisoners' medical cases "'the State's responsibility to provide inmates with medical care ordinarily does not conflict with competing administrative concerns.'" *McGuckin,* 974 F.2d at 1060, *quoting Hudson v. McMillian*, 503 U.S. 1, 6 (1992) (alterations omitted). And therefore, courts need not defer to the judgment of prison officials in matters concerning medical needs. *Hunt v. Dental Dep't*, 865 F.2d 198, 200 (9th Cir. 1989); *cf. Sandin v. Conner*, 515 U.S. 472, 482 (1995) (discussing general concerns of prison order and security, stating in dicta that "federal courts ought to afford appropriate deference and flexibility to state officials trying to manage a volatile environment.").

2. Defendant Johnson Was Deliberately Indifferent to Plaintiff's Serious Medical Needs

Originally, Defendants' *Answer* disputed whether the seriousness of Plaintiff's spinal injury satisfied the objective constitutional minimum. *See Answer*, at 9, para. 31. Were the law not so clear that arguments of counsel are not evidence, Plaintiff would point to such reasoning as substantive evidence of deliberate indifference. *See Estell*,

---

[5]   "Deliberate indifference" is identical to "subjective recklessness" under common-law principles of criminal law. *Farmer*, 511 U.S. at 835.

Figure 7 p. 18

429 U.S. at 105-106 (referring to "evolving standards of decency"). Both defendants appear to have abandoned this line of defense. *See generally Brief in Support*, at 11-12.

Defendants now focus instead on the subjective deliberate indifference element of an Eighth Amendment medical claim. Defendant Johnson, in particular, argues that (1) the requisite subjective intent cannot exist behind his reliance upon Defendant Collins's professional judgment as a physician, and that (2), in any case, a difference of medical opinion between Defendant Collins and Plaintiff, or Plaintiff's medical expert, cannot amount to deliberate indifference. *Id.*, at 17.

Both arguments fail. Defendant Johnson, as I.S.C.F. Warden, has an affirmative duty to provide his prisoners with adequate medical care.[6] However, Defendant Johnson, advancing an argument similar to his defense of qualified immunity (*supra*, at III(C)(2)), contends, essentially, that he is neither qualified nor in a professional position to second-guess the decisions of a medical doctor, and any medical injury arising from his reliance on the doctor's opinion is a matter of "inadvertence," not deliberate indifference. *See Brief in Support*, at 16, *quoting McGuckin*, 974 F.2d at 1060 (internal quotations omitted) ("[A]n *inadvertent* failure to provide adequate medical care" cannot by itself amount to deliberate indifference for the purposes of a § 1983 claim).

This assertion is incorrect; a defense of inadvertence is not available under the circumstances of this case. Defendant Johnson was amply notified of Plaintiff's back injury, complaints of inadequate medical care by current providers, and a specialist recommendation for surgery. His failure to act on this knowledge precludes any

---

[6] *See, e.g., Estell v. Gumble, supra; Erickson v. Pardus*, 551 U.S. 89, 92-94 (2007); *Johnson v. Meltzer*, 134 F.3d 1393 (9th Cir. 1998); *Jett v. Penner, supra; Goebert v. Lee County*, 510 F.3d 1312 (11th Cir. 2007); *Brown v. D.C.*, 514 F.3d 1279 (D. C. Cir. 2008); *Smith v. Smith*, 589 F.3d 736 (4th Cir. 2009); *Flanary v. Born*, 604 F.3d 249 (6th Cir. 2010).

Figure 7 p. 19

inadvertence defense when considered in view of a prison warden's duty under the Constitution and other laws to ensure the orderly and safe operation of the prison and the services it provides. The law does not allow officials to insulate themselves from liability by instituting policies of neglect. *McElligott v. Foley*, 182 F.3d 48, 54 (11th Cir. 1999) (prison officials cannot protect themselves from Eighth Amendment liability by instituting a policy of ignorance). And Defendant Johnson has not proposed any theory of law to contradict the settled principle that a supervisory official may be held liable when the official "knew of [constitutional] violations and failed to act on them." *Barry*, 985 F.Supp at 1239; *see generally* III(B), *supra*.

The secondary line of defense under this rationale, then, is to dispute the extent to which Defendant Johnson was actually aware of Plaintiff's serious medical need. *See Brief in Support*, at 18. Again, the evidence on record herein is more than sufficient to suppose that a reasonable jury could find deliberate indifference; however, when the disposition of a claim turns on an element of extent of knowledge or state of mind, courts should ordinarily refrain from entry of summary judgment (*Frederick S. Wyle P.C. v. Texaco, Inc.*, 764 F.2d 604, 608 (9th Cir. 1985)), because questions involving defendants' state of mind are generally factual issues inappropriate for resolution at summary judgment. *Braxto-Secret v. A.H. Robbins Co.*, 769 F.2d 528, 531 (9th Cir. 1985).

Defendant Johnson's second argument is equally unimpressive. He states that Plaintiff's Eighth Amendment cause of action is incomplete because "Plaintiff, if his evidence is to be believed, has shown 'nothing more than a difference of medical opinion as to the need to pursue one course of treatment over another,' which is 'insufficient, as a matter of law, to establish deliberate indifference'" *Brief in Support*, at

Figure 7 p.20

19, *quoting Jackson*, 90 F.3d at 332. This characterization of the facts and the law defining deliberate indifference is inaccurate.

A mere disagreement between a prisoner and a doctor, or between two doctors, in itself, is not enough to satisfy the subjective element of an Eighth Amended medical claim. *Id.* Deliberate indifference, rather, is actionable under the Constitution when, as in this case, "the course of treatment the doctors chose was medically unacceptable under the circumstances" and when defendants "chose this course in conscious disregard of an excessive risk to [the] plaintiff's health." *Jackson*, 9 F.3d at 332 (internal citations omitted). (Deliberate indifference as contemplated here is discussed further under the next subheading.) If a medical plan is unacceptable under the circumstances, resulting in injury cognizable under federal law, the prison officials responsible for implementing the plan, or for failing to rectify the unacceptable plan, can be held legally responsible for their acts or omissions. *See generally* III(B), *supra.*

Over the seventeen months since May 2011 when Defendant Johnson first became aware of Plaintiff's medical need (*see* Exhibit B), Plaintiff's back injury and overall physical condition has dramatically worsened. *See Compl.*, at 8-9, para. 31-33; Exhibit E, at 3-4, para 7-11; Exhibit G, at 2: Exhibit H, at 2; Exhibit I, at 2: Exhibit J, at 2. Defendant Johnson himself has acknowledged that he was informed on multiple occasions that Plaintiff's physical state was deteriorating and that Defendant Collins was refusing to heed the medical recommendations of a treating specialist in spinal injuries. *See* Exhibit D, Nos. 6-7; *see generally* Exhibits B and C. Based on these facts and the unchallenged medical records (drawing all inferences in favor of Plaintiff), a reasonable jury could conclude that the decision of a non-specialist physician to persist for a year and a half in

Figure 7 p. 21

an ineffective course of medication, rejecting out-of-hand specialist recommendations for surgery, was medically unacceptable under all of the circumstances. *See, e.g., Snow*, 681 F.3d at 987-988 (finding a reasonable jury could find denial of surgery by non-treating, non-specialist physicians medically unacceptable). That Defendant Johnson failed to intervene on Plaintiff's behalf precludes a grant of summary judgment. However, where a matter is of material dispute—the medically acceptable course of treatment in this case— the question is unsuited for determination at summary judgment, but properly preserved for resolution at trial. *Anderson*, 477 U.S. at 254.

3. Defendant Collins Was Deliberately Indifferent to Plaintiff's Serious Medical Needs

As a result of a vehicle collision on September 21, 2010, Plaintiff "suffered damage to the ligature and surrounding tissues of both the fourth and fifth lumbar vertebrae (lower back), and rupture of the fourth and fifth lumbar intervertebrea disk." *See Compl.*, at 4, para. 12-13; Exhibit E, at 3, para. 7. The treating specialist in spinal injuries and orthopedic surgery, Dr. Gregory J. Michael, concluded that Plaintiff's injury was acute, that the injury would not mend if left untreated, and that the affected vertebrae would remain in a state of severe misalignment, continuing to place pressure on the damaged tissues and surrounding cerebrospinal and sympathetic ganglion nerves. *See Compl.*, at 4, para 13; Exhibit E, at 3, para. 8. The only viable remedy: invasive surgical procedure, in which the ruptured disk was to be replaced by a synthetic substitute and the damaged ligaments repaired. *See Compl.*, at 4-5, para. 13- 15; Exhibit E, at 4, para. 9. Plaintiff was scheduled to undergo surgery on December 15, 2010. To manage his pain in the interim, Plaintiff was prescribed by Dr. Michael a regimen of three daily doses of twenty milligrams of oxycodone pain medication and five

Figure 7 p. 22

hundred milligrams of Naprosyn anti-inflammatory medication. *See Compl.*, at 6, para. 19; Exhibit E, at 5, para. 15.

Plaintiff was incarcerated before surgery could take place. On April 21, 2011, Defendant Collins, a medical doctor board-certified to practice family medicine, examined Plaintiff at the Idaho State Correctional Facility's Medical Department. He digitally palpitated the swollen and inflamed region of Plaintiff's back injury and reviewed Plaintiff's medical file, which contained the X-rays, radiology report, and diagnosis/prognosis of Dr. Michael. *See* Exhibit F, No. 4, and *Dr. Daniel K. Collins's Response to Plaintiff's Request for Interrogatories*, No. 3, attached hereto as Exhibit K and incorporated by this reference. Over Plaintiff's protests and Dr. Michael's expert opinion, Defendant Collins refused at that time to recommend Plaintiff for surgery; he refused to refer Plaintiff to a specialist; and he refused to authorize for Plaintiff the prior-to-incarceration prescription of oxycodone and naproxen medication, preferring instead a pharmaceutical plan of ibuprofen and naproxen only and commenting that prison policy "discourages" the use of "narcotic-level" drugs because of potential inmate abuse. *See Compl.*, at 6-7, para. 21-24; Exhibit F, No. 7; Exhibit K, No. 6.

Over the eighteen months, to date, since the April 2011 examination by Defendant Collins, Plaintiff's medical condition has progressively worsened. *See Compl.*, at 8-9, para. 31-33; Exhibit E, at 3-4, para. 7-11. Plaintiff's cellmate, in perhaps the best position to remark the extent to which Plaintiff's condition has affected his life, gives a sobering portrayal of pain and suffering:

> From [April 8, 2011, to this date, October 20, 2012]. . . , Mr. Smith and I have remained housed together in the same cell, and on a daily basis I have observed in Mr. Smith physical manifestations of lower-back pain, including but not limited to grunting, sounds of physical distress (such as

PLAINTIFF'S BRIEF IN RESPONSE TO
DEFENDANTS' MOTION FOR SUMMARY JUDGMENT Page 23 of 29

Figure 7 p. 23

moaning and cries of pain), restlessness, inability to sleep, and slow, stiff, and inhibited body movement;

I have observed Mr. Smith to routinely miss meal times at the I.S.C.F. cafeteria, including lunch and dinner, but have never witnessed Mr. Smith to attend breakfast;

I have also observed Mr. Smith to routinely forgo outside recreation;

Mr. Smith has explained to me on several occasions that he is often unable to walk to the I.S.C.F. cafeteria and recreation yard because of severe lower-back pain;

From April 8, 2011, to the present, I have witnessed Mr. Smith to increasingly complain about his physical condition and pain; to increasingly miss meal times and recreation; to increasingly manifest physical signs of pain; and to have lost approximately 30 pounds of body weight, from his approximately 190 pounds in April 2011, to approximately 160 pounds currently.

Affidavit of Bradely B. Grey #52407, at 2, para. 4-8 (Exhibit G), October 2, 2012; *see generally* Exhibits H, I, and J.

Despite Plaintiff's numerous complaints of worsening condition and inadequate medical care subsequent to the April 2011 examination, Defendant Collins maintains then, as he does now, that the course of treatment he chose for Plaintiff was medically acceptable. *Brief in Support*, at 22. He argues that any difference of opinion between him and Plaintiff or him and Dr. Michaels as to proper course of treatment cannot give rise to an Eighth Amendment claim. *Id.*, at 22-23.

There is clearly a difference of medical opinion here, which, if that were the extent of the dispute, would not be actionable under the Constitution. *Jackson*, 90 F.3d at 332; *Sanchez v. Valid*, 891 F.2d 24, 242 (9th Cir. 1989). "Even proof that a physician has committed medical malpractice does not necessarily violate the Eighth Amendment." *Snow*, 681 F.3d at 987-988, *citing Estell*, 429 U.S. at 106.

PLAINTIFF'S BRIEF IN RESPONSE TO
DEFENDANTS' MOTION FOR SUMMARY JUDGMENT   **Page 24 of 29**

Figure 7 p. 24

However, a constitutional violation may "be shown by the way in which prison physicians provide medical care." *Jett*, 439 F.3d at 1096 (internal quotations omitted). Nor does a plaintiff need to "prove that he was completely denied medical care" in order to prevail. *Lopez v. Smith*, 203 F.3d 1122, 1132 (9th Cir. 2000). When care is provided, deliberate indifference may be shown in doctors' persistence with an ineffective course of treatment. *See Greeno v. Daley*, 414 F.3d 645, 655 (7th Cir. 2005); *White v. Napoleon*, 897 F.2d 103, 109 (3rd Cir. 1990). When medical opinions conflict, to show deliberate indifference the plaintiff must show that the course of treatment was chosen in "conscious disregard of an excessive risk to plaintiff's health," a choice which was also, under the circumstances, medically unacceptable. *Jackson*, 90 F.3d at 332. Whether a prescription of ibuprofen and naproxen is medically acceptable to treat spinal trauma is the question here. That Plaintiff's spinal injury poses an excessive risk to his health is not in dispute. *See Brief in Support*, at 11-12.

Protection under the Eighth Amendment "embodies broad and idealistic concepts of dignity, civilized standards, humanity, and decency." *Estell*, 429 U.S. at 102. Thus, the level of medical care provided to prisoners must be that which is commensurate with modern medical science, and in accordance with limits acceptable under the professional standards required generally of health services and medical providers. *Fernandez v. U.S.*, 941 F.2d 1488, 1493 (11th Cir. 1991); *U.S. v. DeCologero*, 821 F.2d 39, 43 (1st Cir. 1987).

Dr. Michael is prepared to testify that in Plaintiff's case, "there is no option here other than surgery for relief." *See* Exhibit E, at 3, para. 9. He is prepared to discuss the basis of his expert opinion and the prevailing medical literature in the area of spinal

Figure 7 p. 25

injury, a sampling of which Dr. Michael has attached to his affidavit for the Court's review on summary judgment. *See* Appendices 1, 2, and 3 of Exhibit E. Defendant Collins, on the other hand, has offered no medical argument, cites no medical authority, in support of the indefinite ibuprofen/naproxen-only course of treatment he chose for Plaintiff. Defendant Collins, board-certified only in the practice of family medicine, provides no medical rationale (1) for his failure to refer plaintiff to a specialist when he discovered that Plaintiff's medical records revealed questions of medical science surpassing his level of training to answer, and (2) for his disregard of the advice of a treating expert in spinal injury and reconstructive orthopedic surgery.

The evidence on record (viewed in the light most favorable to Plaintiff) and the undisputed medical records prove this is not a case of mere negligence, misdiagnosis, or inadvertence. Defendant Collins examined Plaintiff, heard his complaints, reviewed his medical records, and chose a *totally* unacceptable form of treatment in deliberate indifference to Plaintiff's serious medical needs. A decision, Dr. Michael is prepared to testify, that did not even approach professional standards for pain management, let alone for the treatment of the spinal injury itself. *See* Exhibit E, at 7, para. 20. A decision that "was in fact reckless." *Id.*, at para. 21. However, because it is a controverted issue of fact, it should be for the jury to decide whether Defendant Collins's decision to treat Plaintiff pharmacologically rather than surgically was medically acceptable.

The choice in pharmaceuticals, itself, is another question incorrectly answered by Defendant Collins. Dr. Michael opines that Plaintiff's original regimen of forty milligrams of oxycodone, three times daily, and five hundred milligrams of naproxen, three times

PLAINTIFF'S BRIEF IN RESPONSE TO
DEFENDANTS' MOTION FOR SUMMARY JUDGMENT   **Page 26 of 29**

Figure 7 p. 26

daily, was sufficient to manage Plaintiff's pain and inflammation in September 2010; but, due to one and one half years deterioration, would be insufficient to provide Plaintiff pain and inflammation relief in his current state. *See* Exhibit E, at 7, para. 22. Why Defendant Collins would persist with ibuprofen and only five hundred milligram doses of naproxen is not understood by Dr. Michael. *Id.*, at 7, para 20.

Defendant Collins's own comment, however, provides us some insight into the motivation behind the choice. On April 21, 2011, Defendant Collins denied Plaintiff's request for his original oxycodone and Naprosyn regimen, explaining that prison policy "discourages" the use of narcotics because of potential inmate abuse. He has admitted to giving this explanation (*see* Exhibit F, No. 7), though he now explains it away as merely a tongue-in-cheek remark. *See* Exhibit K, No. 6. Yet Defendant Collins *did* persist in what Plaintiff complained to him as an ineffective pain-management plan. This is particularly disturbing in light of the fact that prior to the first examination of Plaintiff, Defendant Collins had in fact prescribed narcotic-level drugs in extreme cases of pain. *See* Exhibits F, No. 11, and K, No. 10. A reasonable jury could conclude, therefore, that Defendant Collins's refusal to authorize the use of stronger pain medication was motivated by prison policy or custom and not medical science, and/or was motivated by a belief that Plaintiff would abuse the medication, which would be a conjecture entirely devoid of foundation. "Evidence of an improper motive can support a conclusion that a defendant acted with deliberate indifference." *Snow*, 681 F.3d at 987, *citing George v. Sonoma County Sheriff's Dep't.*, 732 F.Supp.2d 922, 937 (N.D. Cal. 2010) (*citing Jackson*, 90 F.3d at 332).

PLAINTIFF'S BRIEF IN RESPONSE TO
DEFENDANTS' MOTION FOR SUMMARY JUDGMENT Page 27 of 29

Figure 7 p. 27

V. CONCLUSION

Defendant Johnson and Defendant Collins are not entitled to a defense of immunity from Plaintiff's claims for damages; both defendants have acted in clear disregard of their respective duties under the law. Nor have the defendants offered persuasive reasons for an entry of summary judgment as a matter of law. They have not successfully refuted the facts supporting both the objective and the subjective elements of Plaintiff's medical claim nor have they met their burden under Rule 56 of the Federal Rules of Civil Procedure in demonstrating no genuine dispute of material fact.

For the reasons articulated above, Plaintiff respectfully requests that the Court deny the defendants' motion for summary judgment.

Dated this 28th day of October, 2012

Dennis P. Smith
Dennis P. Smith #50703

Figure 7 p. 28

CERTIFICATE OF SERVICE

I, Dennis P. Smith, hereby certify that I have caused to be served to the below named true and correct copies of the foregoing document via the ISCF prison mail service and U.S. Postal Service.

William B. Franklin, ISBN 4233
Deputy Attorney General
Idaho Department of Corrections
1299 N. Orchard St., Suite 110
Boise, ID 83707

Dated this 28th day of October, 2012

Dennis P. Smith
Dennis P. Smith #50703

**PLAINTIFF'S BRIEF IN RESPONSE TO
DEFENDANTS' MOTION FOR SUMMARY JUDGMENT**   **Page 29 of 29**

Figure 7 p. 29

NOTES:

NOTES:

NOTES: _____

CHAPTER 15:
COURT RULES & DISCOVERY

COURT RULES GENERALLY

Court rules, or rather "Rules of Court," are judicially promulgated regulations that have the force of law, governing the practice and procedure in both federal and state courts. These rules are made to govern and simplify civil, criminal, and appellate court practice. These rules are also created to control the use of evidence in court—e.g., the Federal Rules of Evidence—along with myriad other practice-and-procedure concerns. Each of the several and distinct sets of rules for a particular jurisdiction are published together in one or two soft-bound volumes, and often include standards of judicial and attorney ethics. Your prison resource center or law library ought to have current sets of both the federal and your state rules of court, criminal and civil. Before filing a lawsuit, it is imperative that you undertake a thorough examination of your trial court's procedural rules.

Intent of Rules
Rules of Court are written and topically arranged in handy softcovers to simplify court practice and procedure. They allow litigants and court officers to quickly access standards that would otherwise be scattered throughout legislative writings, principles from common law, ever-changing interpretive precedent, and custom. In short, the Rules of Court allow for consistent and convenient access to most legal theories controlling court practice and procedure, providing an exoteric body of information that even the non-lawyer can comprehend and use.

Court Discretion
Court rules usually contain provisions to the tune of *"these Rules should be construed and administered to secure the just, speedy, and inexpensive determination of every action and proceeding,"* and/or that *"the court should so interpret the Rules with due discretion in the interest of justice, but not inconsistent with the scope and purpose of these Rules."* This means the judge may fudge the application of, and creatively define, court rules if fair and practical to do so. Appellate courts only disturb a trial court's management of a case if it can be shown that (1) the court abused its discretion, and (2) that a party was actually prejudiced as a result. Accordingly, trial courts possess *wide* discretion over practice and procedure in the jurisdiction over which they preside.

The parties to an action can also consent to specific, *divergent* interpretations of court rules. But such agreement between the parties (stipulation) is not binding on the court. Nevertheless, one should be careful about what is requested or consented to, because the doctrine of **invited-error estoppel** precludes parties from appealing a matter (even if technically in legal error) if they have consented to or caused the error. For example, if you consented at trial to the admission of a piece of evidence that would otherwise have been properly excluded under the Rules of Evidence, and, say, later that piece of evidence opened the door for an unanticipated piece of damaging testimony, then you would not likely be able to appeal successfully the admissibility of that testimony should the trial be lost.

Local Rules and Custom

Beyond the broader state and federal court rules, local districts, state and federal, are permitted to develop and publish rules governing local routine. Usually local rules expound on existing state or federal rules to suit the individual court's peculiar needs. Local rules are not permitted, however, to contradict the broader state or federal versions. Your prison law library should have a copy of the local rules promulgated in your district. If not, you might persuade the nearest Clerk of Court's Office to send you a copy. Failing that, the court rules are available, at a cost, from your State Law Library and/or proprietary services such as Westlaw and LEXIS.

Moreover, each court, invariably, has its own *customs*. Customs, unlike rules, are not as likely to be published, and are usually learned through experience with a particular court or judge. Customs can range from how the clerk schedules hearings to standing or sitting while addressing the judge in court. (One should stand when addressing the judge, in most courts.) Ask around, and don't be afraid to speak with court officers about their unique practices. But, rule of thumb: "When in Rome, do as the Romans do."

THE DISCOVERY PROCESS

Discovery Defined

Discovery is the process by which opposing parties make available to each other information concerning the lawsuit. There are various tools of discovery that may be combined in myriad ways and various strategies to get the information or evidence you want. Not everything is subject to disclosure, however. Work product (your notes from preparing and litigating the lawsuit) is generally not discoverable, for example. Read over the Rules of Evidence concerning what is and is not "privileged" information (info not subject to disclosure).

NOTE: In addition to withholding privileged materials and information, a person can refuse to answer a discovery request, whatever the discovery method involved, if the answer could potentially subject one to criminal prosecution. The Fifth Amendment right to silence surpasses any rights to discovery materials.

When drafting discovery requests, keep in mind that a party can only be asked to disclose information that he or she actually has or can obtain. Of course that makes sense in plain terms, yet some parties may not be in the necessary position to provide certain types of info where common sense would mistakenly suggest they could. (Sometimes this is for legal reasons, sometimes because certain administrative ranks don't have the requisite authority of access, sometimes because an office doesn't manage the records or material sought, and sometimes for many other possible reasons that may not be obvious.) Be aware that undue expense and burden in locating, collecting, and copying evidence *may* provide grounds for a legitimate objection to a discovery request. Whether a discovery objection is sustainable usually depends on how important the sought materials are to the determination of the lawsuit. Such materials, however, do not have to be relevant or admissible to be subject to disclosure, only likely to *lead* to the discovery of relevant information or evidence.

Federal courts generally leave discovery practice to the discretion of counsel and *pro se* parties. That is, it is not usually necessary for the court to be privy to discovery requests or responses, nor is it required that the parties submit the same to the clerk to be registered on the case docket. If, by a previous court order, discovery requests are made by the court's express leave only, then one must file the requests with the court, asking that the defense be directed to respond. Many state courts require the parties to at least file discovery requests with the court for register on the record, if not for leave to make the discovery requests themselves.

Initial Disclosures

Rule 26(a) of the Federal Rules of Civil Procedure provides as follows:

> Except as exempt by Rule 26(a)(1)(B) or as otherwise stipulated or ordered by the court, a party must, without awaiting a discovery request, provided to the other parties:

> the name and, if known, the address and telephone number of each individual likely to have discoverable information—along with the subjects of that information—that the disclosing party may use to support its claims or defenses, unless the use would be solely for impeachment;

> a copy—or a description by category and location—of all documents, electronically stored information, and tangible things that the disclosing party has in its possession, custody, or control and may use to support its claims or defenses, unless the use would be solely for impeachment;

> a computation of each category of damages claimed by the disclosing party——who must also make available for inspection and copying as under Rule 34 the documents or other evidentiary material, unless privileged or protected from disclosure, on which each computation is based, including materials bearing on the nature and extent of injuries suffered. . . .

Fed. R. Civ. P. 26(a)(1)(A)(i)-(iii).

This disclosure is known as the **initial disclosure**. Initial disclosures are made soon after the parties have formed their discovery plan or the issuance of the *Scheduling Order*. Each party has the duty to amend its initial disclosure if it learns that any of its disclosures are incomplete or inaccurate.

When making the initial disclosure, the party should include with the materials a cover page bearing the formal legal caption and the designation *Plaintiff's (or Defendants')* *Initial Disclosures*. A brief categorical description of the disclosures should be included next, followed by the date and signature of the disclosing party. A *Certificate of Service*, dated and signed, should accompany the disclosure as well. Then copies of the disclosed materials themselves must be attached. If your discovery plan, *Schedule Order*, or court rules require that all discovery requests and responses be submitted to the court (as opposed to only between the parties), include an affidavit affirming the accuracy and truthfulness of the copies being disclosed. For ease of reference, you should arrange the documents in chronological order of the dates in which they were created, and number the pages by writing the number in the lower right-hand corner (refer to section "Mapping Out the Issues" in "Chapter 1" about this process)—*don't* write on your originals, just the copies. Hang on to the originals for your records, until and unless they are needed for submission as evidence in court, or as are otherwise required for inspection.

The parties are expected to *cooperate* in discovery. Don't let defense attorneys take advantage of your inexperience. If attorneys are tardy, or make less than the required disclosure, call them on it. Send them a letter demanding compliance.

And know that you do not have to disclose *everything* you have. If you have evidence contradicting the sworn testimony of the defendant or a defense witness, you can use this to impeach that witness (attack credibility). This evidence does not necessarily go to the merits of your complaint, but rather to the credibility of a witness or to the reliability of evidence. Such evidence is impeachment evidence, it is not substantive proof, and does not usually have to be disclosed to the opposing party. (Be aware that the inexperienced prisoner-litigant is playing with fire by not disclosing such materials, however. Should a piece of evidence be withheld that ought to have been disclosed, that evidence might not be allowed to come in at trial.)

Depositions

A **deposition** is an out-of-court session wherein a witness is examined by the parties to an action in order to ascertain the exact nature of the evidence the witness is providing, and so that the witness's testimony can be reduced to transcription for later use at hearing or trial. Rules 27 through 32 of the Federal Rules of Civil Procedure govern in this regard. Your state has explicit rules controlling this discovery tool as well.

Deposition testimony is sworn testimony made in the presence of an officer of the court authorized to administer oaths, subjecting the deponent to the penalties of perjury should he or she lie. The officer can be and often is a court clerk/stenographer, who will also record the deposition testimony. However, Fed. R. Civ. P. 29(a) makes an allowance:

> Unless the court orders otherwise, the parties may stipulate [agree] that:

> a deposition may be taken before any person, at any time or place, on any notice, and in the manner specified—in which event it may be used in the same way as any other deposition. . . .

Just about anyone can be deposed, so long as the witness possesses knowledge pertinent to the pending case. This includes all parties to the action, nonparties, and nonparty organizations. Depositions are routinely initiated with a simple *Notice of Deposition* (specifying date, time, and place of deposition) if the witness is a party to the action. For nonparty witnesses, subpoenas may be necessary to secure attendance. (*See* about subpoenas below.) However, if a nonparty witness is persuaded to consent to the deposition, a simple *Notice of Deposition* will suffice. Whether by notice or subpoena, all parties to the action or their counsel must be notified of the intent to conduct a deposition, and the notice must include

1. The time and place of deposition, and deponent's name and address (if known; otherwise a sufficient description to identify the person must be given);
2. A list of all tangible things to be brought by the deponent (e.g., photos, records, documents, etc.), whether requested by a subpoena *duces tecum* or Rule 34 production request; and

3. The method for recording the deposition (e.g., audio, video, stenographic).

Fed. R. Civ. P. 30(b)(1)-(3)(6).

For prisoners, arranging a deposition may be logistically the most difficult part in prosecuting a lawsuit. Unfortunately, prisoners are required to obtain leave from the court before attempting to conduct a deposition. The court, before granting leave, will want to know how you propose to conduct the deposition—where at? when? who will record the session?—and the name and address of witness(es) to be deposed, and the subject or inquiry necessitating the examination. It is very difficult for prisoners to conduct a deposition—because, well, they are in prison. How do you propose to depose, say, a nonparty witness who is neither a prison official nor an inmate? Will this private citizen be escorted into the prison? Must you request a temporary transfer to the courthouse jail, to examine the witness there, under guard? These are questions needing answers. However, the rules do allow for deposition by telecommunication technology; this may be a reasonable alternative. Fed. R. Civ. P. 30(b)(4).

Another problem with arranging depositions is hiring an officer of the court to administer oath and record the deposition (usually a court clerk/stenographer). These people must be paid for their time, and you must pay for the recording to be transcribed, as well. (Note: The opposing party may agree to split the bill, if the deposition is made in its interest as well.) Provided that *in forma pauperis* status has been granted, one can ask the court to order the district to shoulder these expenses, but there is no guarantee a judge will feel such an order is justified.

Another option is to submit a list of questions in the form of a written deposition, though you must still arrange for a court officer or other, neutral, stipulated party to conduct the deposition at a definite place and time. The deposing officer will ask the witness your written questions verbatim and record the responses. In some circumstances it may be necessary to resort to written depositions; but the problem with written depositions is that you are not present at the deposition to ask follow-up questions or query after the revelation of unanticipated information.

If, before filing the complaint—say, while still exhausting administrative remedies—you reasonably expect that a witness will become unavailable before the filing of the suit, and will remain unavailable thereafter, then you may consider filing a *Petition for an Order to Perpetuate Testimony*. Such a petition must be verified (containing a specific statement signed by the petitioner that the facts as represented in the petition are accurate) and explain that a cognizable action is soon to be filed, why it cannot yet be filed, the name and address of the witness to be deposed, names and addresses of the persons expected to be the adverse parties once the suit is filed, the subject matter to be inquired into under deposition, and, of course, why the deposition cannot wait. Fed. R. Civ. P. 27. This is a rare thing for an inmate to file. And because court rules generally make it more difficult for a prisoner to obtain leave to depose a witness—under the best of circumstances—you'd better be able to explain, persuasively, why the testimony must be taken at that time. Since you've yet to ask for *in forma pauperis* status—as the complaint is not yet filed—you should include a *pauperis* petition and affidavit explaining your impoverished and restricted circumstances as a prisoner, along with a request that the court assist in arranging, financing, and recording the deposition. But you will probably have to manage and finance the deposition yourself, in this extraordinary scenario.

When the day finally comes, the deposition will be conducted in the presence of defense counsel, the witness (the deponent), the court officer, and yourself. Usually a video camera is placed on a tripod on the side of the table opposite the witness, framing only the witness. You will proceed much as if you were to question the witness under the rules of in-court direct examination. (*See* "Trial" section in "Chapter 17," below.) Defense counsel, also, is given the opportunity to cross-examine. And remember that, even though a deposition is not an in-court examination, the rules of evidence still apply, if less stringently in practice. Fed. R. Civ. P. 30(c). The prisoner-plaintiff is well served by becoming familiar with the Rules of Evidence controlling in the jurisdiction. (Read over the sections in this book concerning evidence and objections for a basic orientation.)

Just like at a court hearing, opposing counsel may speak up and object to a question. If this happens, consider the objection and see if the question can't be rephrased. If counsel persists with the objection, the witness can still be questioned, and he or she can be directed to answer, without that answer constituting any waiver of the objection. This is because the testimony is not given before a fact-finder (jury), and inadmissible portions of the deposition can be suppressed and redacted from the transcript before trial, and because court rules encourage the parties to continue depositions over objections. Fed. R. Civ. P. 30(c)(2). (Don't let experienced counsel bully you with objections. Should this happen, halt the session to speak with opposing counsel off the record. Let counsel know that if he or she persists with disruptive or baseless objections, no choice will remain but to ask for the court's intervention, to either direct the witness to answer the question or to referee the deposition itself. Judges do not like dealing with discovery disputes; counsel will know this, and will probably back down at the threat.)

Preparing for a deposition is like preparing to examine a witness in court. Form a plan; review the records; make a list of questions; select and copy pertinent documents and records to bring to the proceeding.

Start the deposition with some basic background questions—name, place of employ, why or how the witness came to have knowledge relating to the pending case. Hit upon all the substantial points, while being careful not to inadvertently tip your hand on matters of trial strategy or impeachment. You can bet that opposing counsel is reading between the lines, analyzing each question to glean advantageous information. But don't hesitate to follow an unanticipated line of inquiry, because one never knows what may fall out of a witness's mouth under direct or cross-examination, and because one can pin a witness down on his or her testimony, leaving no future wiggle-room for a sudden change of story. This ability to ask follow-up questions is why depositions are the superior discovery method, and why, even though inconvenient, the prisoner-plaintiff should press for in-person, oral depositions of key witnesses.

Remember that deponents can be required to bring documents or other tangible evidence with them to the deposition. You must specify such a requirement in your notice or subpoena before the deposition is to take place. *You* can also bring documents and other tangible evidence. Among other reasons, this is done to have the deponent verify the authenticity and accuracy of a particular document, or to confront the witness with previously recorded statements. Each piece of evidence introduced at the deposition should be marked with an exhibit number or letter for easy identification throughout the proceeding, and for later review of the deposition transcript.

Sooner or later, defense counsel will probably depose you. Be ready; and be certain to raise any objections *before* answering a question. An objectionable question usually must still be answered. Say something to the effect of, *"I object to the question on the grounds that I lack personal knowledge. Subject to this objection, and insofar as an answer is required, it is my understanding. . . . "* Objections *must* be made even at the deposition stage.

Failure to do so may be considered by the court as a waiver of the objection, and the testimony may then be admitted at trial.

Interrogatories

Interrogatories are questions. Governed by court rules, each party can be required to answer a set number of interrogatories, usually up to twenty-five. In federal court, Rule 33 of the Federal Rule of Civil Procedure controls interrogatory requests, absent a stipulation, discovery plan, or court order managing this aspect of discovery. (Some jurisdictions limit the total number of interrogatories prisoners can request in multiple-defendant cases, no matter how many defendants are named in the complaint.)

Under the federal rule, a party has thirty days from service to respond to an interrogatory request. The parties have a duty to make good-faith efforts to obtain information necessary to fully and accurately answer each question. When drafting responses, each interrogatory must be individually reproduced in full, then followed by an answer specifically tailored to the single interrogatory request. If the interrogatory is objectionable, the response must clearly but concisely explain why, while still answering the question to the extent possible.

Certain discovery objections are explicitly recognized under Rule 26(b)(B)—that's not to say objections are limited to the letter of the rule; there are many types of objections. Objections must be stated *in* each response, before the interrogatory is answered to the extent possible. Under Fed. R. Civ. P. 26(b)(B)-(C), a party may object to a discovery request generally, including interrogatory requests, if the discovery sought is not reasonably accessible because of undue burden or cost. That does *not* mean a party can avoid discovery because it's a hassle. Discovery is always a hassle; lawsuits are a hassle. A party so claiming undue burden or cost, facing a subsequent motion to compel discovery, will be required to explain its noncompliance. If the discovery sought cuts to a matter at the heart of the case—that is, discovery disclosure could affect the outcome of trial—the party will likely be ordered to comply with the request.

Other objections under the federal rules may be made if (1) the discovery is unreasonably cumulative or

---

Dennis P. Smith #50703
I.S.C.F. A-154-B
2334 North Orchid
PO Box 454
Boise, Idaho 83707

Plaintiff, *pro se*

IN THE UNITED STATES DISTRICT COURT

FOR THE DISTRICT OF IDAHO

DENNIS PATRICK SMITH,   )
)
    Plaintiff,   )   Case No. CV-11-08527-S-EJL
)
vs.   )   **PLAINTIFF'S INTERROGATORIES TO**
)   **DEFENDANT PHILIP J. JOHNSON**
PHILIP J. JOHNSON, et al,   )
)
    Defendants.   )

TO: Defendant PHILIP J. JOHNSON.

COMES NOW, Dennis P. Smith #50703, plaintiff *pro se*, and makes this request under Rule 33 and Rule 26(b)(1) of the Federal Rule of Civil Procedure that Defendant Philip J. Johnson answer the following interrogatories and serve his answers upon Plaintiff within thirty (30) days after receipt of these interrogatories.

After exercising due diligence to secure information, if Defendant is unable to answer any or all of the following interrogatories, in part or whole, Defendant is required under Fed. R. Civ. P. 33(b)(3)-(4) to explain his inability to answer in part or whole, while nevertheless answering to the extent possible.

PLAINTIFF'S INTERROGATORIES TO
DEFENDANT PHILIP J. JOHNSON   Page 1 of 3

Interrogatory No. 1: Please describe, with specific detail, the nature, extent, powers, and duties of your employment position with the Idaho State Correctional Facility.

Interrogatory No. 2: Please provide the name, office and title, telephone number and address, of all persons delegated to preform the specific duties entrusted to or entailed in the position of ISCF Warden. Include in your answer a description of each delegated duty.

. . . . *[List each question in sequence. Be specific about what info you are after, but consider including one or two catchall requests, such as the below.]*

Interrogatory No. 15: Please provide, to the extent of Defendant's knowledge and ability to secure, the name, office and title, telephone number and address, of all persons having knowledge pertaining to the facts alleged in Plaintiff's *Complaint* and the defenses and factual assertions in Defendant's *Answer*. Include in your answer a specific description of the nature of that knowledge.

Dated this 7th day of March, 2012.

Dennis P. Smith

Dennis P. Smith #50703

PLAINTIFF'S INTERROGATORIES TO
DEFENDANT PHILIP J. JOHNSON   Page 2 of 3

Figure 8

CERTIFICATE OF SERVICE

I, Dennis P. Smith, hereby certify that I have caused to be served to the below-named true and correct copies of the foregoing document via the ISCF prison mail service and U.S. Postal Service.

William B. Franklin, ISBN 4233
Deputy Attorney General
Idaho Department of Corrections
1299 N. Orchard St., Suite 110
Boise, ID. 83707

Dated this 7th day of March, 2012.

Dennis P. Smith

Dennis P. Smith #50703

PLAINTIFF'S INTERROGATORIES TO
DEFENDANT PHILIP J. JOHNSON   Page 3 of 3

Figure 8 (continued)

Dennis P. Smith #50703
I.S.C.F. A-154-B
2334 North Orchid
PO Box 454
Boise, Idaho 83707

Plaintiff, *pro se*

IN THE UNITED STATES DISTRICT COURT

FOR THE DISTRICT OF IDAHO

DENNIS PATRICK SMITH,   )
)
          Plaintiff,   )   Case No. CV-11-08527-S-EJL
)
vs.   )   PLAINTIFF'S PRODUCTION
)   REQUESTS TO DEFENDANT PHILIP J.
PHILIP J. JOHNSON, et al,   )   JOHNSON
)
          Defendants.   )
_____)

TO: Defendant Philip J. Johnson.

COMES NOW, Dennis P. Smith #50703, plaintiff *pro se*, and makes this request under Rule 34 and Rule 26(b)(1) of the Federal Rule of Civil Procedure that Defendant Philip J. Johnson produce for copying and/or inspection the below-requested documents and/or tangible things. Production must be made within thirty (30) days after receiving this production request.

After exercising due diligence to secure documents and/or tangible things, if Defendant is unable to comply with any or all of the following production requests, in part or whole, Defendant is required under Fed. R. Civ. P. 34(b)(2)(B)-(D) to explain his

PLAINTIFF'S PRODUCTION REQUESTS TO
DEFENDANT PHILIP J. JOHNSON   Page 1 of 3

Figure 9

duplicative; (2) the discovery can be obtained from some other source that is more convenient, less burdensome, or less expensive; (3) the party has already had ample opportunity for discovery (an objection possibly precluding late or supplemental discovery requests); (4) the burden of providing for a discovery request is substantially outweighed by its likely benefit (in light of the facts and theory of the case); (5) the party does not have the resources to comply with a discovery request; and (6) the discovery sought is not likely to lead to the discovery of admissible evidence.

Consider what information or evidence you realistically believe to exist, and then consider what knowledge you believe a party to possess; then frame your interrogatories as precisely as possible. Vague requests elicit vague answers—don't waste your interrogatories. And remember that lawyers are expert at saying a lot without saying anything at all; try to pin down the defendant (defense counsel, rather, who will likely be the one answering) with carefully tailored questions. Nevertheless, it's not a bad idea to include one or two broad, catchall questions that generally require the defendant to supply all relevant info within his or her possession or ability to access. (*See* Figure 8.)

Production of Documents and Things

Rule 34 of the Federal Rule of Civil Procedure allows for the discovery of documents, electronically stored information, and tangible things. (*See* Figure 9.) It also permits, upon proper request, a party to enter onto another's property for inspection, photographing, examination by an expert, etc.

Defending attorneys frequently just copy and mail back the disclosures requested with little more fuss (providing no objection). They can, however, demand reimbursement for copy costs. *Pro se* prisoners proceeding *in forma pauperis* can often avoid these expenses; but if a defendant is very stubborn, and the plaintiff very poor, one might have to motion the court to sort it all out. Such a dispute probably won't arise in your case, but it's better to mentally brace for it now—better to brace for the worst-case scenario.

One unethical strategy government defendants sometimes employ is to bury the plaintiff under boxes of government paperwork, forcing the plaintiff to spend hours upon hours sifting through irrelevant material in order to find what's needed. A counter tactic is to narrow interrogatory requests, asking the defendant to identify the location, condition, and filing procedures pertaining to the requested material.

Moreover, in addition to mere production, discovery practice allows a party to combine interrogatory requests with production requests in one and the same document. Draft the interrogatory requests first, asking the defendant to identify a document or other discoverable item; then, in later sections, one can request production, referring to the answers already provided to an interrogatory. For example: *"Production Request No.3: Please produce copies of each document identified in Defendant's responses to Interrogatory No.1 and No.2."*

Prisons, like all government departments, are legally required to keep and maintain complete records of department administration and operation. And they are legally required to adopt comprehensible filing systems. Some of the potentially useful things DOCs keep on file are (1) committee or conference notes, motions, recordings, transcripts, minutes; (2) population memos (prison), administrative memos, field memos, interoffice memos, inter-department memos, etc; (3) rules and regulations, standard operating procedures, administrative policy, administrative directives, etc.; (4) inmate case and management files, medical records, disciplinary records, investigative records, etc; (5) staff records (has a guard had any administrative sanctions/infraction/reprimands concerning a matter bearing on your case?).

The list goes on. Additionally, it may be prudent to learn what, if any, information about you the DOC has given other agencies, such as the FBI, NSA, ATF, or local and state law enforcement. Each of these agencies maintains databases of criminal information, and is happy to include info about your activities in prison. If, for example, a prisoner was unjustly labeled as a gang member, it would be prudent to learn what info was given to whom in order to assess degree of civil injury, damages, and what it is going to take to clean up those records, or if that is even possible. The National Communication Information Center (NCIC) is the arm of the FBI that keeps records pertaining to criminally charged and/or convicted persons. And the database is extensive, needless to say.

Some types of information, however, are not subject to disclosure. Anything a defendant intends to use in defense against a lawsuit should be disclosed. But this

---

inability to comply in part or whole, while nevertheless producing documents and/or tangible things to the extent possible.

Production Request No. 1: Please provide copies of, or make available for inspection and copying, Plaintiff's ISCF/IDOC medical records.

Production Request No. 2: Please provide copies of, or make available for inspection and copying, all documents on record with the ISCF bearing Plaintiff's name, physical description, date of birth, Social Security Number, or any other identifier, or otherwise pertaining to Plaintiff.

. . . . *[List each production request in sequence. Be specific about what items you are after, but consider including one or two catchall requests, such as the below.]*

Production Request No. 15: Please provide copies, or make available for inspection and/or copying, any and all documents, photos, recordings, or tangible things pertaining to the facts alleged in Plaintiff's *Complaint* and defenses and factual assertions in Defendant's *Answer*.

Dated this 7th day of March, 2012.

Dennis P. Smith

Dennis P. Smith #50703

PLAINTIFF'S PRODUCTION REQUESTS TO
DEFENDANT PHILIP J. JOHNSON   Page 2 of 3

CERTIFICATE OF SERVICE

I, Dennis P. Smith, hereby certify that I have caused to be served to the below-named true and correct copies of the foregoing document via the ISCF prison mail service and U.S. Postal Service.

William B. Franklin, ISBN 4233
Deputy Attorney General
Idaho Department of Corrections
1299 N. Orchard St., Suite 110
Boise, ID. 83707

Dated this 7th day of March, 2012.

Dennis P. Smith

Dennis P. Smith #50703

PLAINTIFF'S PRODUCTION REQUESTS TO
DEFENDANT PHILIP J. JOHNSON   Page 3 of 3

Figure 9 (continued)

Dennis P. Smith #50703
I.S.C.F. A-154-B
2334 North Orchid
PO Box 454
Boise, Idaho 83707

Plaintiff, *pro se*

IN THE UNITED STATES DISTRICT COURT

FOR THE DISTRICT OF IDAHO

DENNIS PATRICK SMITH,	)	
Plaintiff,	)	Case No. CV-11-08527-S-EJL
vs.	)	**PLAINTIFF'S REQUEST FOR**
	)	**ADMISSIONS TO DEFENDANT PHILIP**
PHILIP J. JOHNSON, et al,	)	**J. JOHNSON**
Defendants.	)	

TO: Defendant PHILIP J. JOHNSON.

COMES NOW, Dennis P. Smith #50703, plaintiff *pro se*, and makes this request under Rule 36 and Rule 26(b)(1) of the Federal Rule of Civil Procedure that Defendant Philip J. Johnson admit or deny the following admissions and serve his answers upon Plaintiff within thirty (30) days after receipt of this discovery request.

After exercising due diligence to secure information, if Defendant is unable to admit or deny any or all of the following admission requests, in part or whole, Defendant is required under Fed. R. Civ. P. 36(a)(4)-(5) to explain his inability to admit or deny in part or whole, while nevertheless admitting or denying to the extent possible.

PLAINTIFF'S ADMISSIONS REQUESTS
TO DEFENDANT PHILIP J. JOHNSON   Page 1 of 3

Admission No. 1: Please admit or deny that on May 15, 2011, in the day room of Unit A, ISCF, Plaintiff and yourself engaged in conversation.

Admission No. 2: Please admit or deny that on May 15, 2011, in the day room of Unit A, ISCF, Plaintiff and yourself engaged in conversation concerning the Plaintiff's requests that he be provide medical care with respect to his back injury.

Admission No. 3: Please admit or deny that you received a Concern Form addressed to you from Plaintiff, dated May 15, 2011.

Admission No. 4: With reference to Admission No. 3, please admit or deny that the copy of the document attached hereto as Exhibit A is an accurate copy of Plaintiff's May 15, 2011, Concern Form addressed to you.

Admission No. 5: With reference to Admission No. 3 and No. 4, please admit or deny that you did not respond to Plaintiff's May 15, 2011, Concern Form addressed to you.

Admission No. 6: Please admit or deny that Idaho Department of Corrections Standard Operating Procedure requires IDOC/ISCF staff and administration to respond to inmate Concern Forms within seven (7) working days after receipt.

. . . . [*List each question in sequence. Be specific, asking only one question per each admission request—and try not to allow for any wiggle room!*]

Dated this 5th day of April, 2012.

Dennis P. Smith

Dennis P. Smith #50703

PLAINTIFF'S ADMISSIONS REQUESTS
TO DEFENDANT PHILIP J. JOHNSON   Page 2 of 3

Figure 10

---

generality doesn't help the inmate looking to discover more sensitive kinds of material. Read over your jurisdiction's rules of evidence, and consult the federal or state statutes controlling the release of government information. And remember that a court can ultimately order relevant information to be disclosed, good cause shown. Courts can, however, require that sensitive info remain under seal (not disclosed to anyone but the parties and the jury) and returned upon the case's conclusion.

Special considerations should be given for electronically stored information. With advances in technology have come the ever-increasing convenience of, and dependence on, electronic media. Concomitantly, hard files are diminishing and electronic storage systems are becoming more comprehensive, and thus, more complex.

Electronic discovery requests should be drafted with particular focus on

1. Discovering what information is likely to exist relevant to your case (specific as possible);
2. Learning where the information is located, including backups;
3. Learning who is in control of the electronic information, and who knows how it was created and stored;
4. Learning when the data was created, modified, or deleted, and by whom; and
5. Determining how you would like the data to be complied, delivered, and stored. (Bear in mind that prisoners must make prior arrangements with the facility to store and allow access to electronic or disc-stored information.)

Dan Goldwin, *Effective Electronic Discovery: Who, What, Where, When,* Facts & Findings 54 (May 2004).

If the defendant refuses to comply with a discovery request on the grounds that the information is not subject to disclosure (because maybe it contains the identity of a confidential informant, for instance), ask the defendant to submit the evidence to the court for an *in camera* review. You won't get a copy of the material at this stage, but should at least be entitled to a description of what the documents/records are, if not their content. The judge, in his or her discretion, will order the material to be disclosed upon a finding of its relevance (and probably upon a finding of admissibility, too), disclosed under seal or otherwise. The defense will not, on its own volition, submit such sensitive material for an *in camera* review; you'll have to ask.

Requests for Admissions

Rule 36 of the Federal Rule of Civil Procedure allows a party to ask another party to specifically admit or deny the truth of a matter. This includes questions regarding the material facts necessary to prove or refute a claim. Documents may be attached to the submission, with the request that the defendant either admit or deny the truthfulness and/or accuracy of the item. Requests for admissions are not limited in number under the federal rules, but your jurisdiction might impose a maximum amount, and a court can also, by its discretion, impose further restrictions. Of course, the parties can stipulate to limitations as well. (*See* Figure 10 for sample admissions requests.)

A request for admissions must receive a response within thirty days of service, unless otherwise ordered by the court or stipulated by the parties. Failure to timely respond to a request for admissions is construed as an admission to those requests. Each matter admitted is considered final and binding, and need not be proven by other

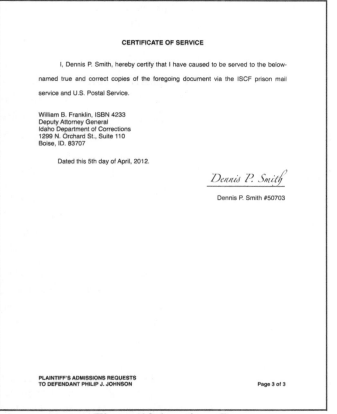

CERTIFICATE OF SERVICE

I, Dennis P. Smith, hereby certify that I have caused to be served to the below-named true and correct copies of the foregoing document via the ISCF prison mail service and U.S. Postal Service.

William B. Franklin, ISBN 4233
Deputy Attorney General
Idaho Department of Corrections
1299 N. Orchard St., Suite 110
Boise, ID. 83707

Dated this 5th day of April, 2012.

Dennis P. Smith
Dennis P. Smith #50703

PLAINTIFF'S ADMISSIONS REQUESTS
TO DEFENDANT PHILIP J. JOHNSON   Page 3 of 3

Figure 10 (continued)

evidence in court. An answer to an admission request, once made, is changed by leave of the court only; a motion to alter the admission would, therefore, have to be filed.

When responding, each admission request must be restated in its entirety and followed by an unequivocal ADMITTED or DENIED. Any objections (*see* discovery objections discussed under the "Interrogatories" subsection, above) must be stated with the response—written *before* the response—or the objection may be considered waived (that you agree the admission request is appropriate). Once an objection is waived, it usually cannot be reasserted at a later time, even if the objection is otherwise well-founded. However, notwithstanding the objection, an answer must still be given if possible, in part or whole. Otherwise the responding party must state in detail why it cannot admit or deny the truth of a matter. Moreover, a party is required to make a good-faith effort to secure the information or materials necessary to provide complete answers. Such is prerequisite to, under the federal rule, an objection based on insufficient knowledge or information.

Motion to Compel Discovery

Discovery requests are answered by defense counsel when possible. Each response, be it to an interrogatory, production, or admissions request, is likely to contain an objection—and probably a very limited response to the request itself. Opposing counsel will probably object to many of the questions asked during a deposition, as well. There are three primary reasons for tactical discovery objections.

First, a party (defendant or plaintiff) must make an objection to a question or a request *when* it occurs, before answering or responding, in order to preserve that objection for later hearing, trial, or appeal. Second, opposing counsel will try to keep from disclosing any and all information that it conceivably can without risking trouble with the court, sometimes unscrupulously. Third, attorneys experienced in defending the government against prisoner-brought lawsuits know inmates have few resources (legal and financial), little legal experience and knowhow, and are easily confused by convoluted legal arguments and objections. Government-defending attorneys often take advantage of *pro se* litigants' ignorance, and may attempt to bully a prisoner-plaintiffinto foregoing an appropriate request or other course of action by using repetitive and vague objections—or by simply not responding to a discovery request at all.

You are likely to find, for example, that,

> *"Defendant objects to Interrogatory No.8 because of undue burden and expense, vagueness, and because the requested information is not likely to lead to the discovery of admissible evidence. Notwithstanding these objections, and insofar as an answer may be required, Defendant is unable. . . ."*

> *"Defendant objects to Production Request No.9 because of undue burden and expense, vagueness, because the requested material is not likely to lead to the discovery of admissible evidence, and because Defendant does not control, have in his custody, nor can obtain the requested materials. Notwithstanding these objections, and insofar as an answer may be required, Defendant responds in part. Attached is. . . ."*

> *"Defendant objects to Admission Request No.10 because of undue burden and expense necessarily incurred in order to truthfully admit or deny the request, and therefore lacks sufficient knowledge and information. Notwithstanding these objections, and insofar as a response may be required, Defendant DENIES the factual assertions contained in this Admission Request, but ADMITS that his name is Iam Recalcitrant."*

Should a request receive a bunch of canned objections like the above, and without appreciable responses, you are not without recourse. The court can be motioned to order the defendant to supplement, amend, or rewrite his or her responses. However, judges are loath to involve themselves in discovery disputes that the parties are supposed to sort out in good faith between themselves—*without* draining court resources. Accordingly, under the federal rules and similar state rules, a party that brings a motion to compel discovery (under Rule 37 of the Federal Rules of Civil Procedure) is *required* to first attempt to resolve any discovery dispute with the adverse party before seeking court intervention.

For the prisoner-litigant, a detailed letter to opposing counsel should suffice. The letter ought to list which discovery responses are inappropriate or insufficient and why, warning that a motion to compel discovery will promptly follow if counsel chooses not to respond to the letter or otherwise supplement the discovery responses in, say, two weeks (it's up to you to decide how much time to allow them). Counsel will probably respond; attorneys know judges are thoroughly annoyed when forced to instruct counsel to observe the rules that a legal professional should already know to follow.

Failing an adequate response or resolution, the only thing left is to file a *Motion to Compel Discovery*. The motion must describe the dispute in detail—e.g., deposition issues, failure to make initial disclosures, insufficient discovery responses—explaining why the information sought is important to the case. Copies of the relevant discovery request/responses must be attached and incorporated by reference into the motion to compel. The motion must be accompanied by an affidavit stating what measures the parties have undertaken in attempting to resolve the discovery dispute before resorting to court action, attaching copies of all relevant documents (e.g., letters).

Be prepared to tell the judge exactly *why* you need the discovery requested. And don't be surprised if the court orders, following a motion to compel discovery, that all subsequent discovery requests be filed and approved by the court before any response is required from the opposing party.

Think long and hard about what you want and why you need it before involving the court in a discovery dispute.

Discovery Strategy

Do *not* submit discovery requests just because you can. Such practice is easily portrayed as harassment and abuse of the discovery process, and the defendant can ask the court to enter a restraining order against you. Better to be sparing with discovery requests than face a restraining order.

Another reason to keep discovery requests short: Should you be forced to file a motion to compel disclosure or discovery, a showing that the sought evidence is admissible at trial may be required before the court grants the requested order. One does not, as a rule, want to deal with questions of admissibility before a case has fully crystalized through the completion of discovery and investigation.

Crucial info is obtained with a little tact. And a plaintiff finds him- or herself in a better position to demand a discovery response if a request is made with greater precision and in view of relevant, existing facts. At the commencement of formal discovery, you should have been able to gather enough information through informal discovery and personal investigation to ascertain what information or evidence can reasonably be expected to exist, who has it, and why it is important to your case.

Before making a discovery request, review your case journal, case log, and evidence charts (covered in "Chapter 1"), to recall the status of evidence and other materials bearing on your lawsuit. This is partly why you've been keeping such detailed notes in the first place—for quick and easy case-theory, case-status, and case-records assessment. Then consider making a request for admissions to pin down the defendant(s) version of the facts and to authenticate important documents. A measure of art is involved in formulating discovery requests, and strategically posed admissions requests ("loaded" admissions, that is) can corner a defendant into admitted the existence of all sorts of beneficial things. Further, an initial round of admissions may negate the need for other forms of discovery, since an admission is considered an established fact, needing no further proof in court.

In light of the answers received in response to your admissions requests, consider submitting a round of follow-up interrogatories. Keep in mind that unless the court otherwise orders, or the parties stipulate, there is nothing in the federal rules that says you cannot submit numerous discovery requests as long as the *total* number of requests pertaining to a discovery-tool limit is not exceeded. For example, the federal rules allow only twenty-five interrogatory requests per defendant. So, ten interrogatory requests can be made of a defendant in May, and then fifteen in July. (Check your local rules, however.)

If the defendant has been tactfully pinned on the issues and the extent of his or her knowledge of those issues by an admissions request, then the defendant has significantly less wiggle-room in which to evade a full response to subsequent interrogatory requests.

Usually it is a good idea to include production requests with interrogatories. If the prison, the government entity itself, is a defendant named in the lawsuit, consider submitting the broader interrogatory/production requests to the government entity, because that entity is an extension of the Department of Corrections. The reason for this is that an *individual* may not possess, control, or have access, or even the authority to disclose what is requested. The *government entity*, on the other hand, possess, controls, can access, and has sweeping authority to disclose department materials. But think about submitting interrogatory/production requests asking about/for evidence *specifically* within the knowledge or control of the individual defendants. Make narrower requests if possible, which will increase the probability of getting what you want.

Another thing to ponder is that defendants can be asked about—and must provide an answer to—what they think has created the legal basis for the affirmative defenses or objections asserted in their *Answer*, and about what forms the legal basis for any factual conclusion asserted in the same. That's right. You can ask the defense about its theory of the case.

Finally, don't let the defense get away with responses like, *"Defendant is currently in the process of investigation and discovery, having yet to (blank), and will supplement these discovery responses as information materializes."* Defendants are required to answer all requests within the time limits prescribed by court rule or order, and can *not* avoid this duty with an indefinite assurance that they'll mail off the discovery to you when they get around to it.

NOTES: _____
_____
_____
_____
_____
_____
_____
_____
_____
_____
_____
_____
_____
_____
_____
_____
_____
_____
_____
_____
_____
_____
_____
_____
_____
_____
_____
_____
_____
_____
_____
_____
_____
_____
_____
_____

NOTES: _____
_____
_____
_____
_____
_____
_____
_____
_____
_____
_____
_____
_____
_____
_____
_____
_____
_____
_____
_____
_____
_____
_____
_____
_____
_____
_____
_____
_____
_____
_____
_____
_____
_____
_____
_____

NOTES: _____
_____
_____
_____
_____
_____
_____
_____
_____
_____
_____
_____
_____
_____
_____
_____
_____
_____
_____
_____
_____
_____
_____
_____
_____
_____
_____
_____
_____
_____
_____
_____
_____
_____
_____
_____
_____
_____

LETTERS AND COMMUNICATION

Stock up on stamps and envelopes; inmate lawsuits inevitably and invariably involve lots of correspondence. Communication by letter is more effective and cheaper than attempting to communicate with the outside world via the prison phone system, as you undoubtedly are aware. Phone calls can be refused, moreover, and messages ignored, but the law presumes, without evidence to the contrary, that a properly mailed letter was indeed delivered to the addressee.

The same logic applies to e-mails, if, as a prisoner, the sending and receiving of e-mails is facilitated by the prison, or can be arranged through an intermediary.

Content

The layout of letters to lawyers and government offices follows the same basic format of a regular business letter. The letter is headed with the sender's contact information, followed by the date, followed by the recipient's name and contact info, followed by a brief statement of the purpose of the letter, followed by the salutation (*Dear Whomever*) and colon (don't use a comma or semicolon), followed by the body of the letter (each paragraph separated by a line space), followed by "Sincerely" or some other formula, and then your signature. (*See* Figure 11.)

Below the signature, include *cc* and list the name (and address, if desired) of each party that will receive a copy of the letter. If documents or other papers are submitted with the letter, include *encl.* and list each item enclosed. Such formalities may seem superfluous, but should a future event re-

DENNIS P. SMITH #50703
I.S.C.F. A-154-B
2334 NORTH ORCHID
PO BOX 454
BOISE, IDAHO 83707

MARCH 31, 2012

WILLIAM B. FRANKLIN, ISBN 4233

DEPUTY ATTORNEY GENERAL

IDAHO DEPARTMENT OF CORRECTIONS

1299 N. ORCHARD ST., SUITE 110

BOISE, ID. 83707

RE: CASE NO. CV-11-08527-S-EJL – DISCOVERY

DEAR MR. FRANKLIN:

I AM IN RECEIPT OF YOUR MARCH 28, 2011, LETTER REQUESTING MORE TIME IN WHICH TO RESPOND TO MY MARCH 7, 2011, INTERROGATORY REQUESTS TO WARDEN JOHNSON AND DR. COLLINS – RESPONSES DUE THE SECOND WEEK OF APRIL, ABSENT EXTENSION.

I HAVE NO OBJECTION TO THE DEFENDANTS TAKING AN ADDITIONAL WEEK TO RESPOND. HOWEVER, SHOULD THIS SITUATION BE REVERSED, I ASK THAT I BE EXTENDED THE SAME COURTESY.

SINCERELY,

Dennis P. Smith

Figure 11

quire an assessment of a letter's purpose or content or enclosures, or who was copied, then these details provide for convenient and easy reference at a glance.

Likely Topics

Prisoner-plaintiffs must communicate with court clerks, attorneys for the defense, the judge in some circumstance, witnesses, etc. It is necessary to communicate with court clerks to schedule hearings, obtain generic legal forms (e.g., subpoenas, pleading packets, local rules, etc.), arrange for copies of hearing exhibits and transcripts, and for a number of procedural matters that cannot be anticipated. Often it is necessary to communicate with opposing counsel, to hammer out procedural details or to air out concerns. A party might communicate with a witness for investigative or procedural purposes, as well. And dealings with expert witnesses engender a whole species of investigative and procedural concerns that swiftly eat up a prisoner's budget.

Don't hesitate to fire off a letter, and don't hesitate to ask for what's needed and proper. Keep copies of all correspondence, and keep notes in your case journal of all spoken communication. Err on the side of caution and send letters to confirm the subject/content of in-person or telephone discussions. Records of such exchanges become of paramount importance if a party feigns ignorance, lack of notification, or asserts a differing version of a conversation.

Copy All Concerned Parties

Any letter to a judge (unless submitted *ex parte* or under seal) should be copied to defense counsel. Any letter to opposing counsel should be copied to the other defense attorneys, if more than one, and if they are in different offices. (In multi-defendant suits, some defendants may be represented by separate counsel from different offices or firms.) Again, keep copies of everything for your own records. Do not send copies of correspondence to the court, as a general rule. Do so only if for some reason it becomes necessary to involve the judge or the clerk.

Reserving for Yourself Benefits that Are Extended to Your Opponent

Finally, reserve for yourself the benefits or courtesies you intend to extend the opposing parties. If, for example, defense counsel asks for an enlargement of time in order to respond to a discovery request, make sure (if granting) to condition that favor on a granting of the same should the situation reverse. If you consent on an evidentiary issue, make that consent contingent on opposing counsel affording you the same benefit, or perhaps secure a promise that counsel will not oppose a bit of your evidence. It is better to acquiesce or cooperate on marginal or trivial concerns. The stubborn, punctilious litigant only makes things more difficult for him- or herself.

PROPRIETY AND OBJECTIONS

One should always strive to maintain objectivity and to conduct him- or herself with cool professionalism. All parties are expected to be calm and composed at all times, and to facilitate the legal process. The parties and their attorneys should attempt to resolve all trifles and procedural disputes between themselves without involving the court, each person participating in good faith, and all investigations, exchanges, communications, etc., are to be conducted "above the table"—that is to say, no shady stuff.

Proper Conduct - Judges and Lawyers - Bar and Judiciary Rules

Each state has rules governing the professional conduct of lawyers and judges; specifically, Rules of Professional Conduct; Bar Commission Rules; and Code of Judicial Conduct. The federal government promulgates such rules as well. Violation of these rules can potentially result in professional reprimand, sanction, or even an attorney's disbarment or a judge's removal from the bench.

Try to get your hands on a copy of these rules. They may be published with the state court rules. If not, check your prison law library for copies. If all else fails, the rules can be purchased—or perhaps the court clerk can be persuaded to send you a copy.

If a judge acts in violation of the rules of professional conduct, a letter can be sent to the jurisdiction's Judicial Council, which investigates all claims of judicial impropriety. Do *not* accuse a judge of misconduct who is currently presiding over your case unless that accusation is unequivocally supported with significant proof. If at all, you should confront the judge with his or her misconduct via a motion for recusal, or a motion to disqualify on the grounds of bias, prejudice, conflict of interest, etc. Even then, be cautious of creating this kind of turbulence. To ask for a judge's disqualification is to say the judge is incapable of being an impartial referee, which is something all judges believe themselves to be. Motions to disqualify should not be made just because one doesn't like the judge.

Attorneys are another matter. Burning bridges with a law firm poses less risk than offending a judge—a judge, even if removed from the current case, may be assigned to a future case, after all. If an attorney is plainly out of line, after you attempt to resolve the issue with him or her personally, consider sending a letter to the Bar Commission explaining the problem. The repercussions implied by sending such a letter, however, may be enough to compel the misbehaving attorney into observing the protocol of proper conduct.

You can fault an attorney for tons of things. For instance, counsel is supposed to act in the interest of conserving judicial resources. If an attorney, say, buries you in paperwork during the discovery process, and could have readily pointed out the pertinent documents, there might be grounds for a motion to compel discovery, judicial sanctions, and official complaint with the Bar Commission. Attorneys are not allowed, additionally, to coach witnesses, or expressly or implicitly suggest potential non-legal repercussions that could result from truthful testimony. Another not-unheard-of example of legal malpractice occurs when counsel suggests to an inmate witness that testifying against the prison or state or U.S. government could compromise parole eligibility.

Don't let opposing counsel get away with failing to give notice, either. The defense should provide due notice of its intent to reschedule hearings, for example, and for numerous other matters of routine governed by court rules. It should give notice of all conferences, in-court as well as out-of-court, although defense counsel is just as likely to show up at the prison unannounced to meet with you for out-of-court conferences. They do this to catch their opponents off guard and unprepared.

Propriety Objections

Always object! It's easy—*"I object to this telephonic conference at this time; I was not given notice that we would, today, be discussing Defendants' insufficient discovery responses, and have thus not prepared. I request that we reschedule this meeting for another time, at the convenience of all parties."* One's reasons must be clear and, as with all arguments, asserted with conviction. This doesn't mean an issue has to be made out of every little thing, but that one should not shy from objecting when necessary. After an objection is made, consider whether acceding the issue will facilitate the legal process or create some advantage. There are always angles to be contemplated; for instance, maybe you can offer to withdraw an objection (off the record, of course) in exchange for something from the opposition. Maybe you withdraw an objection, and maybe counsel agrees not to oppose you in another matter. Such exchanges have been known to transpire.

Keep an Eye on the Docket

Every case is assigned a docket number. This is the same number used in the caption of your legal documents: the Case Number. Every item filed under the case number is docketed chronologically, and given its own docket number. The initial pleading, the *Complaint*, will likely be designated "Docket No. 1." The docket is also known as the "Register of Action" or ROA.

It is a good idea to keep an eye on the docket, because anything filed with court will appear there—if a motion or something else is not served on you, you'll know. Should the defense file anything under seal or *ex parte*, you'll know. The docket can be monitored through the Internet, if a family member or friend can be talked into doing it, or you can periodically ask the clerk to send you a printout.

MOTIONS AND HEARINGS

A motion is a formal request for the court to permit or prohibit some course of action. Motions can be made orally in open court, or submitted in writing. There are many kinds of motions, too many to list here; but the inexperienced prisoner-plaintiff can breath easy with the knowledge that he or she can simply motion the court for what is needed. A judge is not going to penalize a prisoner-plaintiff for a misnamed motion or pleading—a judge may, however, penalize (or at least reprimand) a party who is abusing the legal process by filing a bunch of frivolous motions. Don't hesitate to move the court, but exercise appropriate discretion in doing so.

Pretrial Motions

Any motion—filed during the time leading up to trial, the *pretrial* stage—that involves matters of procedure or major questions of law that could result in the dismissal of any claim or defense is fairly categorized as a **pretrial motion**. Dispositive pretrial motions that are typical to prisoner lawsuits are discussed in "Chapter 13" and "Chapter 14."

Motions In Limine

Motions in limine ("at the outset") are usually filed close to trial, or during trial, and usually deal with the admission or exclusion of evidence. A scheduling order might provide deadlines for motions in limine (not excluding motions pertaining to evidence developed during trial) and deadlines for responding briefs and reply briefs.

By the *in limine* stage, it should be fairly clear what evidence is available and likely to be introduced at trial—subject to motions to exclude said evidence, that is. If the admissibility of a piece of evidence will likely be called into questioned by the opposition, one can preemptively file a motion *in limine* asking for a ruling on admissibility before trial. The benefit, of course, is in obtaining an advanced ruling on the admissibility before the trial starts (as opposed to during trial, in the heat of battle, and possibly with the jury present), removing any doubts that may cause hesitation over an aspect of trial strategy. The benefit in attacking the admissibility of the opposing party's evidence before trial lies in the opportunity to present one's arguments in writing, under thorough analysis that's made at your leisure.

(Some questions are more properly tackled before trial, by the nature of the issue. A motion to exclude an expert witness is an example. Among other reasons, if the witness's qualifications as an expert are challenged, the court might hold a mini-trial to hear the witness's testimony and determine his or her ability to render an expert opinion. This takes time and is best handled before trial.)

A *Motion In Limine* should list the individual pieces of evidence sought to be included or excluded at trial, and state why the evidence ought to be included or excluded, citing the pertinent jurisdiction's rules of evidence or other authority. Attach copies of relevant documents or other evidence addressed in the motion. Check the local rules governing motion practice, but a routine *Motion In Limine* need not be accompanied by a separate brief rigorously delineating and applying the points and authorities upon which the movant has relied. Rather, for brevity, the motion and concise legal argument can appear in a single document, because admissibility arguments are usually straightforward and short. If, however, there *is* a sticky issue, requiring dexterous legal gymnastics, a separate memorandum of points and authorities in support of the *motion in limine* may be appropriate to better attend the argument. One would submit this type of brief (a.k.a. memorandum) on an issue important enough that it could change the course of trial by its own weight—and such a brief will further preserve the issue for appeal, should the motion be denied and the case be lost.

Subpoenas- Subpoena Duces Tecum

A subpoena is a document bearing the seal of the court that commands a person to attend a hearing, trial, or deposition. Every U.S. resident is subject to the imposition of being hailed into court, provided a good reason. Subpoenas can also be issued to legal entities, such as businesses, corporations, and government offices. Subpoenas to entities may demand the appearance of a representative, with peculiar knowledge or authority to speak on issues specified in the subpoena, without specifically naming a particular person in the subpoena.

Subpoenas can be served fairly close to the hearing, trial, or deposition date, but should go out early for experts, physicians, and other busy professionals.

Subpoenas can be issued to the parties of an action and to nonparties, demanding that they or their companies or their offices produce, make available, or bring with them to court, documents or tangible things that you have described in the subpoena or in an attachment to the subpoena. A subpoena demanding the production of documents or things is called

UNITED STATES DISTRICT COURT

FOR THE _____

_____
Plaintiff

v.

_____
Defendant

_____

) Case No. _____
)
) **SUBPOENA TO APPEAR AND TESTIFY**
) **AT A HEARING OR TRIAL IN A CIVIL**
) **ACTION**
)
)
)

TO: _____

YOU ARE COMMANDED to appear in the United Sates district court at the time, date, and place set forth below to testify at a hearing or trial in the civil action. When you arrive, you must remain at the court until the judge or a court officer allows you to leave. If you are an organization that is *not* a party in this case, you must designate one or more officers, directors, or managing agents, or designate other persons who consent to testify on your behalf about the following matters, or those set forth in an attachment:

_____
_____

Place/Address: _____ Courtroom No.: _____
_____ Date and Time: _____

You must also bring with you the following documents, electronically stored information, or object *(leave blank if not applicable)*:

_____
_____

The provisions relating to your protection as a person subject to a subpoena are listed under Fed. R. Civ. P. 45(c). The provisions relating to your duty to respond and the potential consequences of not doing so are listed under Fed. R. Civ. P. 45 (d) and (e).

Dated this ___ day of _____, 20___.

_____
Clerk of Court

_____
Attorney

The contact and mailing information of the party who issues or requests this subpoena is:
_____
_____
_____

SUBPOENA

Figure 12

Adapted from AO 88 (Rev. 01/01) Subpoena to Appear and Testify at a Hearing or Trial in a Civil Action.

a **subpoena** *duces tecum*, governed by Rule 45 of the Federal Rules of Civil Procedure; your state, of course, has a similar rule.

If you plan to elicit the testimony of a person at a hearing, trial, or deposition, a subpoena is usually needed to ensure attendance. Although, this is not always necessary. (Be careful about relying on a bare promise to appear; you could end up high and dry if the witness doesn't show, and with no recourse. You had time to serve a subpoena, after all.)

Normally, an attorney can acquire a blank subpoena, already signed and sealed by the Clerk of Court. The attorney has only then to fill in the blanks—whom it is commanding, and when and where presence is demanded—and arrange for formal service, i.e., hand delivery.

Pro se prisoner-plaintiffs are treated a little differently. A court is likely to have in place a local rule, custom, or to have explicitly ordered that the prisoner-plaintiff first obtain court leave before issuing any subpoenas. In this case, subpoenas are requested by motion, explaining exactly why the witness must be summoned into court or for deposition, and should be accompanied by the completed subpoena you want issued. If the motion is granted, the court then directs the Clerk of Court to sign and seal the subpoena; then directs the Federal Marshals to serve it on the witness. The sheriff's office may handle process of service if your case is pending in state court. Of course, the state or federal government only provides this service if you have already been granted *In forma pauperis* status. Otherwise, the clerk will mail you back the subpoenas, signed and sealed, for you to make the necessary arrangements for formal service. (*See* Figure 12 for a sample subpoena)

NOTE: Prisoner-plaintiffs regularly rely on the testimony of fellow inmates. Every inmate witness must be served with a subpoena, like other witnesses. But there's more. Prisoners cannot just drive up to the courthouse and stroll in and take the stand; therefore, it's crucial that the court is timely asked to enter a transport order for each inmate witness to be brought to the courthouse jail, or other nearby jail, well before the scheduled hearing or trial date. If a party does not both issue a subpoena *and* ask the court to order transportation—*Plaintiff's Motion for Order to Transport Prisoner(s) to (*Jail Name*) to Testify at (*date*) Hearing (or Trial)*—prior statements from absent witnesses are not likely to be admissible in court. Their statements would be considered inadmissible hearsay. If, however, the requisite motions are timely made, and it turns out to be simply impractical to secure the in-court testimony of an imprisoned witness, then that witness is "unavailable" for the purposes of Rule 804 of the Federal Rules of Evidence, and the witness's out-of-court statements may be admitted.

If problems with court attendance are reasonably foreseeable, it's a good idea to attempt to depose the potentially "unavailable" inmate witness(es) should the chance arise—failure to attempt deposition may be argued as a reason to preclude unavailable witness statements from trial. Deposition testimony is sworn testimony, and the parties have had a chance to confront the witness with evidence at the deposition, or otherwise develop testimony by direct and cross-examination. This is why deposition testimony is not considered hearsay evidence, even though the witness is not examined in front of the fact-finder (jury or judge).

Hearings

Hearings are held in order to air out pending issues. Hearings give the judge an opportunity to ask opposing counsel (and/or a *pro se* party) questions. They provide contending litigants with the chance to address each other's arguments face-to-face. Moreover, if necessary, hearings provide a place and time to present witnesses.

For prisoner litigants, most hearings are likely to be held telephonically. For federal civil actions, the PLRA explicitly states that:

> (1) To the extent practicable, in any action brought with respect to prison conditions in Federal court pursuant to section 1983 of this title, or any other Federal law, by a prisoner confined in any jail, prison, or other correctional facility, pretrial proceedings in which the prisoner's participation is required or permitted shall be conducted by telephone, video conference, or other telecommunications technology without removing the prisoner from the facility in which the prisoner is confined.

> (2) Subject to the agreement of the official of the Federal, State, or local unit of government with custody over the prisoner, hearings may be conducted at the facility in which the prisoner is confined. To the extent practicable, the court shall allow counsel to participate by telephone, video conference, or other communications technology in any hearing held at the facility.

42 U.S.C. §1997e(f)(1)-(2).

"To the extent practicable," *id.*, suggests that in some circumstances it simply will not be feasible to exclude the prisoner-litigant's presence from court. By the language of the above-quoted PLRA provisions and traditional common-law theories of due process, whether an incarcerated plaintiff is to be physicaly allowed to attend crucial pretrial proceedings is committed to the discretion of the court. Under the PLRA provisions above, prisoner-litigants in federal civil-rights cases "shall be excluded from court," so long as denial of physical presence is "practicable"—which means so long as denial of physical presence does not violate the inmate's right to due process or right to meaningful access to

Dennis P. Smith #50703
I.S.C.F. A-154-B
2334 North Orchid
PO Box 454
Boise, Idaho 83707

Plaintiff, *pro se*

IN THE UNITED STATES DISTRICT COURT

FOR THE DISTRICT OF IDAHO

DENNIS PATRICK SMITH,   )
)
          Plaintiff,   )   Case No. CV-11-08527-S-EJL
)
vs.   )   **NOTICE OF HEARING**
)
PHILIP J. JOHNSON, et al,   )
)
          Defendants.   )
_____)

          NOTICE IS HEREBY GIVEN that a hearing is scheduled regarding:

          PLAINTIFF'S *"MOTION TO COMPEL DISCOVERY"*

Before Judge: EDWARD J. LAWRENCE

          For the Date: 5/23/12

          At the Time: 9:30 AM

          In Court Room: #2

          Dated this 4th day of May, 2012.

                                        Dennis P. Smith
                                        Dennis P. Smith #50703

NOTICE OF HEARING   Page 1 of 2

CERTIFICATE OF SERVICE

          I, Dennis P. Smith, hereby certify that I have caused to be served to the below-
named true and correct copies of the foregoing document via the ISCF prison mail
service and U.S. Postal Service.

William B. Franklin, ISBN 4233
Deputy Attorney General
Idaho Department of Corrections
1299 N. Orchard St., Suite 110
Boise, ID. 83707

          Dated this 4th day of May, 2012.

                                        Dennis P. Smith
                                        Dennis P. Smith #50703

NOTICE OF HEARING   Page 2 of 2

Figure 13

the courts. A telephonic hearing, for instance, may be improper if a party is planning to examine a witness. Prisoners should not be prevented from attending, in person, proceedings where the outcome may turn on the credibility of witness testimony, including, of course, trial. (The PLRA does not prevent prisoner-litigants from attending trial. *Id.*) To protect inmates' rights, courts may invent or adapt methods for a plaintiff's participation, so long as his or her "allegations and evidence [are] fully and fairly considered." *Poole v. Cambert*, 819 F.2d 1025, 1029 (11th Cir. 1987). In some pretrial contexts, however, physical absence is less prejudicial to the prisoner-plaintiff. For example, the Fourth Circuit authorized psychiatric commitment hearings to be conducted by video, emphasizing that (unlike trials) such decisions are generally based on expert testimony and do not depend much on either the witness's demeanor or the "impression" made by the person being committed, and that the proceeding does not involve fact-finding in the usual sense. *U.S. v. Baker*, 45 F.3d 837 (4th Cir. 1994), *cert. denied*, 516 U.S. 872 (1995).

Make objections when necessary.

Moreover, in a *pro se*-prisoner case, if a judge can get away with it, he or she might elect to make a ruling based solely "on the papers"—that is, based on the papers already submitted on record, without a hearing. This may or may not be objectionable depending on the local rules and whether a hearing would really be of benefit.

Depending on local practice, the clerk may automatically schedule a hearing when a motion is filed, or the moving party might have to request a hearing date via letter or by submitting some other form to the court clerk. It may, in some circumstances, be necessary to file a motion asking the court to schedule a hearing, but this is unusual. If a motion has been properly filed and the proper scheduling routine observed, a motion for hearing may become necessary if it appears the pending motion is being ignored or was somehow overlooked. Finally, a party scheduling a hearing has the obligation to notify the opposition as to subject of hearing, place, date, and time. Fed. R. Civ. P. 6(c)(1). (See Figure 13 for a sample *Notice of Hearing*.)

Objections

Make your objections when problems arise. Should court rules, case law, statutes, or other authority be discussed in open court in regard to an objection, the title and proper citation should be stated aloud for clarity purposes and for preservation on the official record.

A bit of advice: If a significant issue develops during a hearing, and it appears that the judge is going to enter an adverse opinion or order, ask the court to postpone ruling so that you can more properly address the matter in a written brief.

NOTES: _____

NOTES: _____
_____
_____
_____
_____
_____
_____
_____
_____
_____
_____
_____
_____
_____
_____
_____
_____
_____
_____
_____
_____
_____
_____
_____
_____
_____
_____
_____
_____
_____
_____
_____
_____
_____
_____
_____
_____
_____
_____

CHAPTER 17:
SETTLEMENT & TRIAL

SETTLEMENT

Before trial, usually after the summary judgment stage, the parties commonly meet in an attempt to reconcile their differences in order to avoid the ordeal of trial. The parties confer, negotiate, make compromises, and try to come to some agreement to settle the case on terms which no one likes but with which all can live.

As a rule, the best settlement offers come on the verge of trial. Trials are expensive, and take many hours of preparation. However, if one holds out too long, much of that prep work may already be done and opposing counsel may encourage the defendants to go through with trial.

The courts encourage settlement. Larger social interests insist that people settle their own disputes if possible, to conserve judicial (taxpayer) resources and to encourage self-reliance within the public. So, the parties to an action are *expected* to make good-faith attempts to devise some solution to their problems without resorting to trial. In the event trial does occur, when later dealing with an award for money damages, the court might inquire about whether the prevailing party has attempted to discuss settlement in avoidance of trial (which may or may not be a proper question for the court to consider—a question depending on unique case factors and jurisdictional precedent—but there you have it). If, upon this inquiry, it seems to the court that the prevailing party has eschewed settlement negotiations, perhaps declining *reasonable* offers to settle, the court may view such reluctance as stubbornness in bad-faith, perhaps warranting a reduction in money damages.

Be careful about initiating negotiations, however, because the gesture may be interpreted as doubt about the strength of your claims. Don't hesitate to make compromises when acquiring what you really want or need, but remember that settlement means compromise on *both* sides.

Don't make the mistake of being caught unprepared at the negotiation table. Refer to your evidence charts and the legal authority you've amassed to carry your complaint past the summary judgment stage. Put a list together, including strengths and weaknesses of the case on both sides of the controversy, and the items, privileges, or dollar amounts estimated or determined to be indispensable to settlement. You don't want to forget to ask for something important, or neglect the existence of a compelling piece of evidence that could have been leveraged to your favor during negotiations.

Take notes on the things opposing counsel say. Although the content of settlement negotiations is not usually admissible at trial, you can glean much about the opposition's case during negotiations. For the same reason, be careful of what *you* reveal; there is no guarantee that negotiations will end in settlement; don't show your cards.

If a deal eventually is struck, make sure you *explicitly* ask if anything else needs to be disclosed or discussed—before signing anything. Maybe even ask this question repeatedly while running through the settlement elements for the final contract. Note the answers.

Arbitration vs. Mediation

Beware the word "arbitration." **Arbitration** is a process by which a court officer or some other person is appointed to the capacity of Arbitrator, who is to preside as a quasi-judge-mediator. Arbitrators hear the opposing parties' arguments, take evidence, and then render an opinion that decrees the compromises on both sides, settling the case. Arbitration is essentially a formal mediation, but where the findings of the arbitrator are binding on the parties. Both parties must consent to arbitration.

Mediation on the other hand, as discussed in previous sections, is a semiformal session in which an appointed mediator facilitates negotiation between the parties. This method is far preferable to arbitration; the parties are not forced into any agreement or finding or order that results from the mediation. Only the parties can bind themselves.

Contracts and Consent Decrees

Attorneys who routinely deal with prisoner lawsuits keep ready-made contracts or "releasors" on hand (on computer, actually), which contain all the requisite boilerplate language expected of legal documents, awaiting only the insertion of the paragraphs or provisions of the settlement agreement. Such contracts are accompanied by a *Stipulated Motion for Dismissal With Prejudice.* Note the words "with prejudice." They mean that none of the alleged facts contained in the complaint can be reasserted as a cause of action in future claims. Word to the wise, don't give away anything for free, even an agreement to dismiss your case with prejudice.

Invariably, government counsel include in their contracts or releasors a provision for the forfeiture of benefits should the plaintiff show or discuss with others the content of the settlement terms. This is required because administrators do not want prisoners telling each other what they were able to get by pursuing a lawsuit against DOC employees, especially so when concerning money amounts. Admin does not want a settlement contract awarding a large amount of money to form any institutional or system precedent.

Leverage this. For example, if opposing counsel insists that the complaint be dismissed *with* prejudice then demand that in return you be allowed to show the settlement contract to others. You get the idea.

In any case, a stipulated motion to dismiss the complaint must *not* be submitted to the court, if avoidable, until the conditions of the settlement are fulfilled, or significant steps toward fulfillment have been made. If the case is dismissed, and afterward a defendant reneges on his or her duties under the contract, you will have to file in state court—with new filing fees and lawsuit hassles—a whole new action, this one for breach of contract.

Another option is to negotiate for a consent decree. A **consent decree** is a stipulation between the parties made binding by order of the court, but without any final adjudication of fact or law—that is, no formal finding that the government was wrong and you were right. A consent decree reads something like a cross between a court order and a settlement contract. Each element of the settlement/agreement is listed unambiguously, and the duties of the parties are stated, ideally, with crystal-clear precision. However, the Prisoner Litigation Reform Act restricts the utility of consent decrees, just as it does for injunctive relief. (*See* the discussion of the PLRA in previous sections.)

Consent decrees are the way to go if one is looking for relief not easily or immediately obtainable. Suppose one has sued over problems of overcrowding. Remedies may include the construction of an entire facility. That takes time, and there may be a number of unpredictables that the defendant(s) can interpret as an excuse to renege on the agreement. Consent decrees, unlike contacts, are immediately enforceable in court because the case is still live—a whole new court action need not be initiated. Upon a mere motion, the court can order further injunctive relief or hold a defendant in contempt for failing to meet the terms of the consent decree, which is, after all, an order of the court. Again, beware of the word "arbitration"; defense counsel might try to sneak a clause in the decree that would cause a later settlement dispute to be resolved through arbitration, before court intervention can return as an option to sort things out between the parties.

TRIAL

As trial draws near, consider making another request for appointment of counsel. By trial's eve, your claims have overcome the pretrial hurdles of dispositive motions and the judge may now be more open to a request for appointment of counsel, or for "assistance" of counsel (not full-blown representation) to help with routine and logistical eventualities and concerns appurtenant to trial. Among other trial concerns, counsel can help manage and instruct witnesses summoned to court, collect "dailies" (a less formal transcript of the day's proceedings), prepare and handle exhibits, communicate with defense counsel, generally assist the plaintiff, and help to avoid the all-around courtroom headaches associated with *pro se* litigation.

Should you be forced to proceed *pro se* and without assistance, make efforts to learn the particulars of trial procedure in your jurisdiction. Below is a basic discussion of the major stages of a civil trial, each stage offering its own challenges and demands on your time.

Spend some time preparing a trial notebook, with section-divisions dedicated to each stage of trial. Include the information, documents, memoranda, rulings, etc. that are important enough to have at your fingertips in court; maybe include the not-so-important stuff, too. One never knows what might suddenly become significant. As to the content of the notebook itself, create sections for the following:

1. Jury selection, listing *vior dire* questions and leaving space to note potential jurors' answers, bios, an other info;
2. Opening statements;
3. Questions for the direct examination of each of your witness;
4. Questions for the cross-examination of defense witnesses; and
5. Closing arguments.

NOTE: Only the Federal Rules of Evidence and the Federal Rules of Civil Procedure are mentioned and cited below. The theories and practices presented, however, are fairly universal. For further discussion of the admissibility of evidence at trial under the Federal Rules of Evidence, refer to "Chapter 3: Evidence," above.

Jury Selection
At some point in the pretrial stages, a decision must be made about whether it is best for a jury to decide the facts of the case (a jury trial), or if it would be better to have the judge alone act as the fact-finder (a bench trial). One may demanded a trial by jury in the complaint, because one has that right (except for claims brought under the Federal Tort Claims Act and many state

tort actions), but one can also, later, consent to have the case tried by the judge instead of a jury. Fed. R. Civ. P. 38(d). All parties must consent, however. Fed. R. Civ. P. 39.

There are some pros and cons with either option. Juries are unpredictable, for one con, and may bear prejudice against a prisoner-plaintiff simply because he or she is a prisoner, for another con. Judges are sometimes biased by their political ambitions—they can't appear to the public to sympathize with criminals. Juries are more likely to grant larger awards of money, but judges are better suited to decide cases involving complex legal questions.

Should you decide to go with the trial by jury, consider making a motion that asks the judge to permit you and the other plaintiffs, if any, to wear street clothes during the jury-selection and trial process. It is a reasonable presumption that a party may be prejudiced by the attention that an aggressively orange jumpsuit will draw, which is why defendants are allowed to wear street clothes during criminal trials.

So, discovery completed, pretrial motions and motions *in limine* all wrapped up, other preliminary matters sorted out, the next step is jury selection. **Jury selection** is the process whereby neutral, unbiased people are rounded up from the county in which the lawsuit is pending in order to be evaluated on their ability to serve as jurors. Who qualifies as a potential juror is ascertained simply by asking questions. The objective of this inquiry is to learn whether the members of the jury panel can render a fair and impartial verdict, giving the potential jurors a chance to be heard and to raise any concerns. This Q-and-A process is called *voir dire*.

Jury selection will probably occur on the same day or the day before the presentation of evidence is set to begin. A group of potential jurors (called the **venire** or **array**), likely between twenty-five and fifty people, will arrive at the courthouse, having previously received the dreaded notice of jury duty. An initial group is then summoned into the courtroom and seated in the jury box. As potential jurors are called, each is given a number—*"Mr. Sanderson, you are Juror Number One, please take the seat in the upper left-hand corner of the jury box."* (Keep careful notes of names and juror numbers; as the *voir dire* process continues and people are dismissed, names and numbers change.)

After the potential jurors are impaneled in the jury box, the judge asks a series of preliminary question concerning things such as prior jury service, occupations/professions, and other general background questions. Then the judge asks if, for any reason, any concerns of the jury could interfere with their ability to be fair jurors. Responding veniremen or -women will raise their hands or numbered placards. After a brief discussion, the judge will dismiss those who give unsatisfactory answers or who state that they cannot be fair—which does happen, with regularity. Fresh people from the larger pool are then brought in to replace those dismissed. Depending on local practice, you and your adversary may be allowed to separately pose more specific questions to the members of the panel about their eligibility to serve. However, in a case prosecuted by a *pro se* prisoner-plaintiff, the court might elect to do all the questioning. If that is the practice, you should be given the opportunity to submit a list of questions to the court before jury selection.

As with every other part of a lawsuit, effective *voir dire* takes extensive preparation. Think long and hard about any occupation or profession or life status that would lead a potential juror to be biased or otherwise prejudiced against you, whether personally or because of the circumstances surrounding your case. Consider asking the panel as a whole: *"Have any of you ever worked in law enforcement?"* If a potential juror raises a hand, you can ask that person follow-up questions: *"Juror Number 4, in what branch of law enforcement have you been employed?"* A convicted felon would probably want to disqualify (or "challenge") a police officer or corrections officer. Consider asking the panel a few questions such as these: Could you find in favor of a convicted felon currently serving a criminal sentence? Would you be inclined to believe a corrections officer more than you would any other witness? Do you feel that a witness currently serving a prison term is less credible than any other witness? Should an undesirable answer be given, you can challenge and have the undesired juror dismissed.

There are two ways to challenge a potential juror. One, the parties can request the court to dismiss a potential juror via a **challenge for cause**. For instance, if a potential juror answers that she cannot find in favor of a convicted felon, then there is no way the juror could be fair and impartial. She will be dismissed. Two, one can also have a potential juror dismissed for no articulated reason, and with no further demonstration that a legal cause for dismissal exists. This is called a **preemptory challenge**.

In federal civil trials, each party is permitted *only three* preemptory challenges—to be used wisely. 28 U.S.C. § 1870. Do not waste them on jurors that can be dismissed for legal cause, such as the juror who said she would not be able to find in favor of a convicted felon. It *may* be possible to persuade the judge to dismiss a potential juror for cause if the juror (or the juror's spouse or close family member) is connected with law enforcement, detention staff, or corrections, including probation and parol officers. Anyone who has been a victim of the type of crime for which you are currently serving time, or who has had a close involvement with a person who has, could conceivably be challenged for cause.

Again, do not waste your preemptory challenges. Eventually, you and opposing counsel will run out of preemptory challenges and viable challenges for cause; what's left is the jury that will hear the evidence at trial, between six and twelve people in federal civil cases, Fed. R. Civ. P. 48.(a), a number which will be predetermined based on the complexity of the case and estimated trial length.

After selection, the jurors are asked to rise, raise their right hands, and are sworn in; then the judges instructs them not to discuss the case, even with one another, until explicitly told to do so. Any objections to the selection process or final panel must be made before the jury is sworn in.

The details of the *voir dire* process differ from court to court. Ask the judge (or a court clerk, if you can get his or her attention while off the record) how to proceed in this regard. However, federal judges are painfully aware that prisoners are ill-informed on the finer details of litigation, and likely will give a brief *sua sponte* summary of how everyone will be proceeding. (That is, if these things haven't already been hammered out in pretrial conference.)

NOTE: Be prepared to take exhaustive notes on how each potential juror answers questions under *voir dire*. Record each juror's name and corresponding juror number, and where each is seated in the jury box. Pay attention to body language. When they answer questions, note hesitancy, tone of voice, posture, with whom eye contact is made (are they avoiding your eye?), and how they respond to you and opposing counsel, both verbally and nonverbally. Once the jurors are selected, keep observing them for clues indicating which way they are leaning and to whom they are responding more. This information may prove crucial in deciding whether to call reserve witnesses, alter tactics, or adjust closing arguments.

Opening Statements

Opening statements are not strictly necessary, and thus are optional. Should you choose to forego this step—say, if your case is very simple—inform the judge that you are waiving the opening statement. Otherwise, you must prepare a speech.

The purpose of an opening statement is not to argue the points of your case, or to point out the flaws in your opponent's case (that comes later during closing arguments), but to give the jury an idea of what the issues in controversy are and how you intend to present evidence. This gives the jury a contextual framework in which to place the pieces of evidence as they receive them during the trial. The presentation of evidence is often disjointed and non-sequential, like a book with the chapters out of order, and this is true under the best of circumstance. An opening statement can attenuate this problem.

Acquainting the jury with yourself while making an opening statement, telling them who you are and why you and they are in court, is perfectly fine. You can touch on evidence you intend to show—*"You will hear testimony that . . ."*—but be careful not to mention evidence that may ultimately be ruled inadmissible, if there remains any question about admissibility. If you expect that opposing counsel plans to object to the admissibility of a piece of evidence, then maybe avoid that evidence in the opening statement, just in case. Juries remember facts mentioned in opening statements but not presented in evidence, and they wonder why and who caused them to go missing.

It is permissible to explain what the evidence is intended to show, but it is not okay to draw inferences for the jury, to address the credibility of a witness, or otherwise argue your case. To be safe, keep the opening statement brief, twenty minutes at most, and endeavor to establish a basic sketch of the issues that the jury must decide; try to keep it simple. You may also tell the jury what you want from them, in plain terms: *"Ladies and Gentlemen, I hope that you will find the defendant's actions were in violation of my rights. I hope that, after hearing the evidence, you will find that my injury was and remains serious, and order the Defendant to compensate me in the amount of $150, 000."*

Remember, the defense, too, will have a chance to lay out its theory in opening statements. Pay attention; you might deduce the defense's case strategy, or parts thereof.

Presentation of Evidence - Case in Chief

Both sides having made their opening speeches, the court will say something like: *"Plaintiff, you may call your first witness."* This signifies the beginning of the plaintiff's case-in-chief.

The **case-in-chief** is the heart of trial. The plaintiff calls his or her witnesses, examines them methodically under the rules of direct examination, offers exhibits for identification and admission into evidence, and essentially tells the story of what happened through the combined accounts of each witness, one by one.

Always try to hold the jury's focus on what a witness is saying; don't let the jury zone out. Some say that a jury's attention begins to wane after a mere twenty or so minutes of a witness's testimony (especially during expert testimony). One method to inspire a jury's attention is to change the pace of questioning, by altering questions that elicit longer responses with those that elicit shorter, rapid responses. You can vary the manner in which questions are asked as well, by speeding or slowing your rate of speech. Another method is to use demonstrative evidence (e.g., charts, props, PowerPoint presentations) when at all possible. Take the following:

1. Attention is highest at the beginning and very end of a witness's presentation of testimony. If possible, introduce props or other illustrative aids between these times, when a jury's attention can be expected to waver; or, conversely, at the expected height of attention, to drive home a key point.
2. Larger displays/aids, of course, are easier to see than smaller ones, and are better to impress a message upon the subconscious mind of the jurors.
3. Black-and-white displays work well when black stands in large, bold contrast to a white background, but color generally is more engaging, especially for photos and renderings.
4. Key information is better placed at the top of a page display or chart, because the top tends to receive more notice than the bottom, as does the left side of a display over the right side.
5. Uniform, unvaried displays lack features whereon jurors can find a focus; color contrast and font or graphic/image variety aid attention; movement is even better—a display element that is animated to move across a stationary background is most effective.

Before trial, one must prepare to call and examine witnesses in an order consistent with trial strategy—how you want to tell the story. Key testimony should be elicited (drawn out of the witness by carefully crafted questions) in accordance with your view of the facts. A witness's testimony can be controlled to a large degree by artful inquiry. In the trial notebook or elsewhere, you should have ready (1) a list of questions for each witness, and (2) copies of any and all documents pertinent to the presentation of your witnesses' testimony. The documents are important for two reasons.

First, a witness may review a writing to refresh his or her memory (either while on the stand or before being called in to testify). Fed. R. Evid. 612. Any document a witness so reviews must be shown to opposing counsel (you might want to prepare an extra copy for this purpose). Even work product, not normally discoverable, must be shared with the adverse party if it is reviewed by a witness in preparation for testifying. A document used to refresh a witness's memory while on the stand may have to be marked as an exhibit (this process is discussed below). However, writings used to refresh a memory are not ordinarily permitted to be admitted into evidence, nor are they shown to the jury (the testimony of the witness is enough), but may nevertheless be required to be marked as an exhibit for identification purposes—*"Is the witness finished reviewing Plaintiff's Exhibit 12?"* As a rule, one should prepare four copies of any such document—one for the defense, one for the witness on the stand, one for you, and one for the judge. Local practice controls. If anticipated that the document *will* be admitted into evidence, given to the jury for review, you may be required to use the original document, if you have it, but that is not the routine practice.

Second, you should have ready all documents/records needed to impeach each witness—which includes your own witnesses—in case of a sudden change in story. The old legal maxim "Don't ask a question you don't already know the answer to" remains a practical bit of conventional wisdom. One can anticipate a witness's likely answer by reviewing existing evidence—letters, writings, reports, recordings, transcripts of prior proceedings—without the existence of which the witness wouldn't have been called into court in the first place. Therefore, you should have in court with you all prior witness statements, reports, letters, and affidavits so that you can refresh a recollection as the need arises, or shove a prior inconsistent statement under the nose of a vacillating witness.

Broadly speaking, documents and photos are admitted to evidence upon minimal foundation and with little fuss, and copies in place of originals will suffice for the record, so long as there is no genuine dispute about authenticity. Some documents are authenticated by a government seal or other certificate (e.g., notarized documents, certified copies of public documents, certified transcripts, etc.). Fed. R. Evid. 902. Although not usually required, original documents and photos might be demanded by the opposition, and the judge might order their production if the demand is not unreasonable. In this event, the original item then must be submitted, unless it no long exists or is not feasibly obtainable. If an original is not available, a copy ought to suffice, provided it can be authenticated by the right person with pertinent knowledge of the item. This requirement is called the **best-evidence rule**. Fed. R. Evid. 1001-1004.

Other physical evidence—like a shirt or an implement—usually requires a bit more foundation in order to be admissible. A foundational witness must have personal knowledge, not hearsay knowledge, in order to identify an item as what it is purported to be, or to establish a chain of possession to show that another item hasn't been substituted for the original item.

After the direct examine of each witness, the defense then has its turn to question the witness under cross-examination. Direct then cross, over and again, person by person. The processes continues, presenting the jury with each of your witnesses, examining each in turn, and then, finishing with your last witness, you will rest your case—*"The Plaintiff rests, Your Honor."*

The plaintiff having presented evidence, and having rested, the defense then steps up to put on its case-in-chief. The defense does not have to prove a thing—the burden of proof is on you, the plaintiff—but it would be, frankly, crazy to forego examining witnesses in its defense. The defense *will* put on a case, be assured.

The rules of direct examination dictate how defense counsel can elicit testimony, just as it does for the plaintiff's case-in-chief. Witnesses testify, exhibits are introduced, subject to any objections that you may assert, and then you are given the chance to cross-examine each defense witness in turn.

The plaintiff presents his or her case, and then the defendants present theirs. In most civil cases, this is the end for the presentation of evidence. However, after the defense rests, a plaintiff can, if the evidence exists, rebut defense witnesses by putting on additional testimony to specifically dispute the accounts of defense witnesses. This is called "rebuttal." After the plaintiff's rebuttal case, the defense, too, may be provided an opportunity to call additional witnesses on "surrebuttal." The rebuttal and surrebuttal process is discussed below.

Testimony/Evidence - Direct and Cross

Most evidence is *witness* evidence; even tangible things are introduced at trial based on a *foundation* of witness testimony. (However, even without the rigors of hearing testimony, a court can take judicial notice of some types of evidence, if a matter is of common knowledge or public record, requiring no further proof. Fed. R. Evid. 201.)

Foundational evidence is evidence that determines the admissibility of other evidence. Material evidence (evidence proving or disproving a fact of consequence to a claim or defense), whether an object, record, or witness account, *must* be shown to be relevant and admissible by the party seeking its admission in court. Fed. R. Evid. 401; 402; 602; 701; 802 and 901. This is accomplished by offering the evidence after first illustrating how the evidence falls into the context of the case. How did a person come to possess an object? How, why, and when did a witness acquire relevant knowledge? For example, witnesses are asked to tell the court or jury who they are, spell their names for the record, and then are asked foundational questions leading up to why they have relevant knowledge. A witness who took a photo, for instance, might be asked why he or she was in a position to take a photo in the first place, what was observed, the date of that observation, lighting conditions, what type of camera was used, etc. Then the witness would be handed the photo (marked as an exhibit), asked if the photo accurately depicts what the witness observed, and maybe even asked about the process involved in getting the film developed. Only after the foundation is laid would the photo be admissible and submitted to the jury. (Note that the requisite foundation for a photo, in practice, is whether the image—original photo not being strictly necessary—"fairly and accurately" depicts what was seen.)

Although sometimes tedious, the foundational process is, nevertheless, necessary. Proper foundation not only demonstrates relevance, admissibility, and reliability, but it also provides a place for evidence within entire scheme of the case.

Should a foundational dispute arise, the court might deal with the question before trial, upon the motion of a party (see the discussion of motions *in limine* in previous sections), or excuse the jury to air out the parties' concerns, listening to objections outside the jury's presence. Should a dispute manifest while the jury *is* present, in the natural course of trial, ask to approach the bench (the judge) with opposing counsel—*"Your Honor, may we approach?"*—then, out of the jury's hearing, voice the problem. If the disagreement is not resolved in the short, bench-side conference, ask for the jury to be excused so the parties can freely argue on the record.

Should you, the plaintiff, testify as a witness, you will have to narrate from the stand (unless you have assisting counsel to ask questions). Evidence you intend to tell the jury, as with other witnesses, must be admitted based on a proper foundation. Consider making a bullet-point list to keep you on track while testifying, but remember that notes taken to the stand will probably have to be disclosed to the defense. Reiterate who you are and how you came to be injured. Walk through your testimony, step by step, beginning to end, hitting all the points that support the legal elements of your claims. Speak clearly and naturally. (Measured speech in low tones is thought to be better than quick speech in high tones.) Then you must submit to cross-examination by opposing counsel. (Listen to each question, think about the answer, and calmly and truthfully reply.)

Should a witness who previously gave sworn testimony, at a deposition or prior proceeding, become unavailable (by the strict legal definition of "unavailability" under the rules of evidence), the transcript of that testimony can be read into the record, in front of the jury. The judge instructs the jury that they are not to give this testimony more or less weight than any other; then a "reader" is sworn to read truthfully and accurately, after which he or she takes the stand, transcript in hand. (Inadmissible portions of a transcript, if any, should already have been redacted in preparation for the reading.) Everyone plays his or her role. Defense counsel reads aloud the lines spoken by defense counsel during the original proceeding; the judge reads the judge's part, and the plaintiff reads the plaintiff's part. (Those intending to introduce this kind of read-in testimony must first procure the services of a

```
                                              2/13/13
                                              (1 OF 2)

                                              DR. COLLINS,  DIRECT-EXAMINATION

                                  MEDICAL TRAINING AND BACKGROUND?                    □
                                         - SCHOOL AND DEGREES?                        □
                                         - MEDICAL SPECIALTIES?                       □
                                         - ASSOCIATIONS (GOVERN'T, BUSINESS, OTHER)?  □

                                  IDOC/ISCF EMPLOYMENT?                               □
                                         - HISTORY WITH STATE?                        □
                                         - SPECIAL TRAINING?                          □
                                         - NATURE OF CONTRACT WITH STATE?             □
                                         - DUTIES UNDER CONTRACT?                     □
                                         - PROFESSIONAL DUTIES GENERALLY?             □

                                  INMATE CARE (SUBSTANCE & PROCEDURE) ?               □
                                         - INMATE REQUESTS?                           □
                                         - INMATE TREATMENT?                          □
                                         - INMATE PRESCRIPTIONS?                      □
                                         - SPECIALIST REFERRAL?                       □
                                         - CONDITIONS UNDER WHICH SURGERY IS FACILITATED?  □
                                         - PROCEDURE FOR FACILITATING SURGERY?        □
                                         - CONCERNS OVER NARCOTIC PRESCRIPTIONS?      □
                                         - RECEIPT OF PLAINTIFFS MED. REQUEST?        □

                                  APRIL 21, 2011 MEDICAL EXAM OF PLAINTIFF?           □
                                         - RECORDS EXAMINED?  (EXHIBIT 2)             □
                                         - PHYSICAL EXAMINATION?                      □
                                         - DIAGNOSIS?                                 □
                                         - COMMON TREATMENTS (NON-PRISONERS)?         □
```

Figure 14

reader, who can be anyone willing to read in front of the court and jury. Expect to pay $50 to $100 for a day's service.)

The foundation is brought out by the examination conducted by the party who *called* (subpoenaed) the witness to the stand. The party who calls the witness is responsible for eliciting pertinent answers and avoiding improper evidence. Such examination conducted by the calling party is called "direct examination." Take a look at Figure 14 for sample questions in preparation for the direct examination of a witness.

Under **direct examination**, the witness is walked through what he or she has seen or heard, touched or tasted, or even smelled, building a foundation not only for the witness's testimony, but for any exhibits the examining party intends to offer. The idea is to draw out facts without eliciting irrelevancies or digression. Under direct examination, the witness is supposed to give a personal account without undue prompting or leading by examining counsel (or *pro se* party)—that is, counsel may not attempt to influence the witness's testimony. (But, of course, they do.)

As a prophylactic measure against improper influence, the types of questions counsel may ask are restricted for direct examination. Generally, there are four types of questions used to examine witnesses: (1) leading, (2) open, (3) narrative, and (4) closed.

Leading questions are not usually permitted on direct examination because leading questions impermissibly suggest the answer counsel wants the witness to give. Fed. R. Evid. 611(b). For example: *"Sir, you did not actually see Guard Lese strike the Plaintiff, did you?"* This question is leading; it requires only a yes-or-no answer with no further explanation — essentially, it's counsel's statement, merely seeking confirmation by the witness.

However, despite the general rule against leading questions on direct, leading questions may be asked on direct concerning marginally important and undisputed matters, such as preliminary questions about a witness's background—*"And you graduated from the University of Idaho, is that correct?"* One should let witnesses tell their stories as they occur to them, even on such preliminary matters; but if for some reason counsel (or the court) is looking to save time, then leading questions are permitted to quickly get through the small stuff and to the meat of a witness's testimony. Furthermore, on direct, leading questions are sometimes asked to quickly reorient the witness (and the jury) to the place where the witness left off in the story before a recess or break— *"Before we broke for the afternoon recess, you testified that you've worked for the Idaho Department of Corrections for five years, is that right?"*

Notwithstanding the

2/13/13
(2 OF 2)

DR. COLLINS, DIRECT-EXAMINATION

- WHY ARE PRISONERS TREATED DIFFERENT? ☐
- STATE/PRISON FINANCIAL CONCERNS? ☐
- PRESCRIBED TREATMENT / MEDICATION? ☐
- WHY NO OXYCODONE? ☐
- IN WHAT CIRCUMSTANCES WILL OXY. BE PRESCRIBED? ☐
- WHY WAS OXYCODONE PRESCRIBED ORIGINALLY TO PLAINTIFF? ☐
- WHY IS OXY. NO LONGER REQUIRED? ☐

RECEIPT OF APRIL 23, 2011, CONCERN FORM? (EXH. 3) ☐
- REVIEW OF MEDICAL REQUEST? ☐
- WHY THE DENIAL? ☐

REVIEW OF GRIEVANCE #10-0163, MAY 6, 2011? (EXH. 4) ☐
- REVIEW PROCEDURE? ☐
- WITH WHOM? ☐
- CONCLUSION? ☐
- CONSIDER DOING FURTHER EXAMS? ☐
- CONSIDER DOING MRI AND/OR X-RAYS? ☐
- FINAL DECISION (WHO MADE IT)? ☐
- REVIEW OF GRIEVANCE ON APPEAL? (EXH. 5) ☐

ANY POST-GRIEVANCE REVIEWS OR MEDICAL EXAMINATIONS? ☐
- ANY POST-GRIEV. MEDICAL CONSULTATIONS? ☐
- MEDICAL REVIEWS IN PREP. FOR TRIAL? ☐
- RECORD REVIEWS IN PREP. FOR TRIAL? ☐
☐

Figure 14 (continued)

few exceptions for leading questions, counsel is mostly limited to open and closed questions during direct examination. An **open question** invites the witness to testify in her own words, usually about her specific impression of an event or condition. They ask the witness to tell the jury what happened, in her own words, and, though sometimes calling for longer answers, an open question still asks for *less* than an answer on a whole series of events. *"Ma'am, what was Guard Lese's physical condition when you arrived at the housing unit?"* is a permissible open question. *"Ma'am, what did you observe on B-Unit after responding to Guard Lese's distress call?"* is an improper narrative question asking the witness to walk through a series of events.

Narrative questions are broad, open-ended questions that invite a witness to given an answer about numerous matters all at once. These types of questions are not usually permitted because they pose the risk of inviting the witness (1) to refer to improper evidence or (2) to digress or otherwise stray into irrelevancies. This is why attorneys are expected to direct the course of a witness's testimony through carefully designed questions.

On direct examination, open questions are counsel's primary tool for getting at the heart of testimony without unduly influencing the witness or eliciting improper responses. The secondary tool is the closed question.

A **closed question**, like a leading question, does not invite the witness to expand on an answer; but, unlike a leading question, a closed question elicits a specific piece of information, rather than a yes-or-no answer. *"Ma'am, when you first arrived at B-Unit, what was the time?"* is a permissible closed question, asking for a specific piece of info: the time.

Cross-examination comes after direct. Cross is conducted by the party who did *not* call the witness. The principle tool of cross-examination is the leading question, though open and closed questions are used as well. Fed. R. Evid. 611(c). Leading questions are used because the witness already has said what she came to say. The substance of the testimony has already been voiced for the jury on direct and there is now little risk that the witness will be improperly influenced in her recollection of events by follow-up leading questions. This is also why cross-examination is limited to the *scope* of direct. Fed. R. Evid. 611(b). Which means, on cross, counsel may only inquire about matters already testified to on direct, or matters reasonably connected to that testimony. (Although in practice this rule is loosely enforced.) If one wants to put on testimony about a certain matter not elicited on direct, then let that party re-call the witness during its presentation of evidence.

Although cross-examination is not required, there are two good reasons why it should be done. First, it's a good idea to follow up on any points in the witness's testimony that are beneficial to your case. Second, you are allowed to attempt to undermine the credibility of the witness herself, or her version/perception of events. This is called **impeachment**.

Impeachment is of two varieties. One, the examiner can attempt to cast doubt on the witness's account of the facts by asking loaded questions intended to expose inconsistencies, lack of knowledge on certain points, or lack of memory. Two, the examiner can confront the witness with evidence contradicting her testimony. You should be prepared to do this; the defense should have furnished you with a list of witnesses it intended to call at trial, including a brief statement about what each witness is supposed to testify (this will probably be obvious from discovery materials and case circumstances, anyway).

A lot of evidence that would not otherwise be admissible because of the hearsay rule or other rules often becomes admissible for impeachment purposes. Fed. R. Evid. 607. The most common type of impeachment evidence is prior *in*consistent statements. Fed. R. Evid. 613(b). If a witness has been reported to have said something different from what she said in court, then that witness may be confronted with the alleged prior inconsistent statement. The same is true if a witness suddenly claims a lack of memory. Lack of memory is sufficient to support the admission of impeachment evidence.

Following is an example of the impeachment process on cross:

> YOU: *Ma'am, do you recall making the prior statement that you were not on B-Unit when Guard Lese was supposedly assaulted?*
> WITNESS: *I—I don't recall.*
> YOU: *It is your testimony that you* did *see me assault Guard Lese, is that correct?*

WITNESS: *Yes . . . I believe it was you.*

YOU: *Could you be mistaken?*

WITNESS: *I don't think so; I'm pretty sure it was you.*

YOU: *Ma'am, do you recall answering an institutional Concern Form sent by me in March of 2011?*

WITNESS: *I, uh . . . vaguely.*

YOU: *Your Honor, may the witness be shown the Concern Form? I have copies for the Court and opposing counsel.*

COURT: *Yes . . . Bailiff, please hand that to the witness.*

YOU: *Thank you, Your Honor.*

YOU: *Ma'am, please read the document to yourself. Take your time.*

WITNESS: [and so doing] *Okay, I'm finished.*

YOU: *Do you recognize that document as an ISCF institutional Concern Form?*

WITNESS: *Yes.*

YOU: *Did you write the paragraph in the response portion of that Concern Form?*

WITNESS: *Yes.*

YOU: *Do you recognize your signature at the bottom of the page?*

WITNESS: *Yes.*

YOU: *Did you also write in the date next to your signature.*

WITNESS: *Yes.*

YOU: *What is that date.*

WITNESS: *March 10, 2011.*

YOU: *And you testified earlier that you witnessed the injuries to Guard Lese's face in the B-Unit foyer after he was extracted from the B-Unit day room, is that correct?*

WITNESS: *Yes.*

YOU: *And that was on March 3, 2011?*

WITNESS: *Yes.*

YOU: *Take a look at the Concern Form. At about mid-paragraph, and I'll quote: "I'm sorry, Mr. Inmate-Plaintiff, but I cannot provide you with the names of the responding officers. I did not arrive to B-Unit until after Guard Lese was assaulted." Did I read that correctly?*

WITNESS: *Yes*

YOU: *And you wrote that?*

OPPOSITION: *Objection, Your Honor; asked and answered.*

COURT: *Sustained.*

YOU: *Ma'am, I'm done with the Concern Form, so if you'll just set it face down . . .*

To impeach the witness with a prior inconsistent statement, ask the witness to read the inconsistent statement from the earlier record, or quote it yourself; then ask. . . [pause for dramatic effect] . . . why the change in testimony? If you have evidence of an *out-of-court* statement, ask the witness being impeached if he or she will admit to making the inconsistent statement—if so, why? If the witness denies making the out-of-court statement, then you may later be permitted to call the person who heard the out-of-court statement, to rebut the denial. Following cross, the court will ask counsel if there's anything further to be asked on redirect examination.

Redirect examination occurs under the same rules as direct, but with the limitation that redirect questions concern only those matters brought out under cross. Technically, on redirect counsel may not attempt to rehash the substance of the witness's earlier testimony. Counsel should not beat the jury over the head with repetitive testimony in order to distinguish a particular piece of evidence for emphasis. Rather, redirect is allowed to clarify testimony, and for rehabilitation purposes. Counsel is permitted to attempt to undo or mitigate the damage sustained to the witness's credibility during cross-examination. This is called "rehabilitating the witness."

Following redirect, opposing counsel is offered the opportunity to examine the witness yet again on recross-examination. **Recross-examination** is limited to the scope of redirect, allowing only questions going to what was elicited under redirect.

Should counsel forget to ask a witness something on direct examination, even after the back-and-forth of cross, redirect, and recross, counsel may ask the court for permission to **reopen direct**. *"Your Honor, I just reviewed my notes and noticed that I forgot to ask the witness a question. Will the court briefly reopen direct?"* The court will say either no or yes, or might summon you and opposing counsel to the bench to quietly, discreetly find out what you want to ask, and whether opposing counsel has any objection. If direct is reopened, opposing counsel is again offered the chance to follow up with cross.

Finally, if a witness is hostile—uncooperative—ask the court for permission to treat this person as a **hostile witness**. Do this quietly during a sidebar conference, out of the hearing of jurors. If permission is given, then counsel (or the *pro se* litigant) may use leading questions on direct examination. You might be faced with this situation when calling an adverse witness, such as a named defendant. Additionally, should a witness at any point become reluctant to answer a question or is not properly responding—*"The witness is non-responsive."*—to your question, ask the court to direct the witness to answer the question. If the witness still refuses to answer, you have two options: (1) ask the court to hold the witness in contempt, (2) or ask that the witness's prior testimony be stricken from the record (rendering it of no weight and disregarded totally).

Objections

The purpose of trial is to get the facts in front of the fact-finders so they can make an informed finding as to who did what. Generally, courts tend to let in as much evidence as possible, unless that evidence is *plainly* improper. The parties are left to go about putting on their cases; the judge usually won't micromanage that process, and it is up to the parties to make any objections to improper proceedings or evidence or courtroom conduct. If an objection to the exclusion or the admission of evidence is not made when the question first becomes apparent, then that objection may be forever waived, and may not be preserved for a later appeal. Fed. R. Evid. 103(a)(1).

Once an objection is made, the court either overrules it (denies the objection) or sustains it (supports the objection), and then directs conduct accordingly. Sometimes it's tactful to forego an objection so as not to place emphasis on a damaging subject. Objections prick up the ears of jurors; it is not wise to incidentally emphasize parts of the opposition's case. Moreover, one does not want to appear too confrontational or aggressive in front of the jury. Too many objections will communicate truculence, and cast doubt on one's power of reason, and thus credibility. Additionally, jurors sometimes interpret an overruled objection as the judge's endorsement of the evidence in question. Not good.

Should a witness begin to give improper evidence, the witness can be interrupted with an objection—*"Excuse me, sir. Your Honor, speculation."* If the judge sustains the objection, you can then ask the judge to strike the improper testimony—*"Your Honor, I move to strike the witness's testimony in response to the last question."* Fed R. Evid. 103(a)(1). (To **strike** testimony is to render it of no force or weight, nor a subject for consideration during the deliberations of the fact-finders. The court will say something like, *"The jury is not to consider the testimony they just heard for its possible effect on this case, or for any other purpose."*)

Whatever you do, don't argue the merits of your objection without court permission. State the objection concisely, in one sentence, in one breath—*"Objection! Hearsay."* But be prepared to explain yourself, because the judge might ask you to argue the merits of your objection.

There are two broad categories of objections: (1) objections to the form of a question (how it is phrased), and (2) objections to the content of the testimony that question elicits or to which the witness is already testifying. Below are listed some of the more common objections to the form of a question.

OBJECTION!

- **The question is vague** (or ambiguous or unintelligible) (common law). Consider this objection if the question is so unclear that one cannot reasonably anticipate what information the witness will give in response.
- **The question is compound** (common law). Consider this objection if the question is, in actuality, more than one question or calls for an answer on more than one point.
- **The question calls for a narrative answer** (common law). Consider this objection if the question, like a compound question, invites an answer on multiple points or on a whole series of events.
- **The question was asked and answered** (Fed. R. Evid. 403). Consider this objection if the question asks the witness to reiterate testimony already given on a point of significance.
- **Counsel is misquoting the witness** (common law). Consider this objection if, while wording the question, counsel misquotes the witness's prior testimony or the testimony of another witness. An attorney may intentionally misquote, spin, or shade the context of prior testimony in order to either influence the witness's answer or cast the substance of a quote in a positive or negative light (such conduct borders on being argumentative).
- **The question is leading** (Fed. R. Evid. 611(c)). Consider this objection if, under direct examination, the question appears to lead the witness to a specific answer or improperly suggests what counsel *wants* to hear in response.
- **The question is argumentative** (common law). Consider this objection if the question does not ask for information or facts, but is really an argument in question form—*"So, there's no way you could have seen what you've just said you witnessed, could you?"*
- **The question assumes facts not in evidence** (common law). Consider this objection if, while asking the question, counsel refers to evidence that has not properly been brought out before the court or jury. Listen for references to evidence yet to make an appearance as a marked exhibit, or to witnesses who have yet to testify.

Along with the objections concerning question *form*, the actual *content* a question elicits, regardless of whether the question is properly posed, may be objectionable, for myriad reasons; below are listed some of the more common.

OBJECTION!

- **Beyond the scope of direct** (Fed. R. Evid. 611(b)). Consider this objection if a question on cross-examination ventures into new areas of information not addressed during direct.

- **Lack of foundation** (Fed. R. Evid. 901; common law). Consider this objection if a witness testifies about an event without counsel having first laid the proper foundation for its admissibility. (If you find yourself wonder why the testimony is relevant, you may have a foundational objection.) Listen for facts that seem out of sequence with the witness's testimony up to that point, or out of sequence with the progress of the entire trial up to that point. Listen also for abrupt breaks in context. If you suddenly think to yourself, "Wait a minute, how did we get to this point in the story?" then a foundational question may have somewhere been overstepped.

- **The testimony is cumulative** (Fed. R. Evid. 403). Consider this objection if counsel attempts to elicit cumulative evidence on a point significant to the outcome of the case. For example, if opposing counsel calls the warden of a prison to testify about the volatile nature of the prison environment in order to, say, justify the utility of disputed policy, then the point is completed by the warden's testimony. Opposing counsel would not then be permitted to call five additional prison officials to testify to the same thing.

- **The witness lacks personal knowledge** (Fed. R. Evid. 602). Consider this objection if the witness testifies about a matter he or she did not personally learn by one of the five senses—*"He was holding a newspaper, so I assumed he'd read the article."* How could that be known? Is it even the right newspaper in question?

- **The witness is speculating** (or giving an improper opinion) (Fed. R. Evid. 701). Consider this objection if the witness forms conclusions or makes assumptions that are or were beyond the witness's powers of observation, or if hypothesizing, giving an impermissible opinion of technical or scientific matters, or making a legal conclusion.

- **Hearsay** (Fed. R. Evid. 802). Consider this objection if the witness testifies about his or her own or another person's out-of-court statement, if offered to prove the truth of the matter asserted in that statement. For example: *"Inmate Jones said he lied in his affidavit to help his friend's lawsuit."* Inmate Jones, not this witness, would need to be called and examined about the supposed statement; such evidence wouldn't likely be permitted to come in as hearsay.

- **Unfairly prejudicial** (Fed. R. Evid. 403). Consider this objection if the testimony sought is relevant but outweighed by its likely prejudicial effect on the jury. Relevant evidence may be excluded if it is of slight-to-moderate importance and would otherwise influence the fact-finder to render an opinion based on improper grounds.

- **Improper character evidence** (Fed. R. Evid. 404(a)). Consider this objection if opposing counsel elicits improper evidence about a person's character trait, or personal propensities, in order to prove this person acted in conformity with that trait on a particular occasion—that is, this person committed an act on a particular occasion because, apparently, it was already in his or her nature to act so. You can object should witnesses stray into this realm of testimony of their own accord, as well.

The reader should become familiar with the common objections listed above and their theoretical premises under the rules of evidence (and/or whatever case law or legal source is available from prison resources). And remember that these objections are used against the prisoner-plaintiff, as well.

If the court sustains an objection to evidence that you want admitted, or the court permits the opposition to offer evidence you want excluded (before or during trial), consider asking the court to issue a limiting instruction.

Limiting instructions are used when a piece of evidence is admissible for one purpose but not for another. Fed. R. Evid. 105. This is not uncommon, and the judge may attempt to resolve an evidentiary dispute by opting for the compromise of an instruction to the jury that it must consider and weigh the evidence for its *proper* purpose only and completely ignore it for any other purpose, thus "limiting" the scope of admissibility. For example, in an excessive-force claim against a prison guard, a witness may testify, *"Guard Lese told me that he hates inmates who file grievances and has 'whipped whiny inmates' before."* This testimony may not be admissible to show that Guard Lese actually assaulted inmates before; the statements would be hearsay for that purpose. But the testimony may be permitted to show that Guard Lese had a motive (or malicious intent) to assault an inmate who filed a grievance against him. (This would qualify as a question of mental state falling under Fed. R. Evid. 803(3).) The judge might tell the jury, *"You may consider the witness's statement only for its possible effect as to the Defendant's state of mind, but you may not consider the testimony as evidence that the Defendant assaulted inmates on prior occaisions."*

The value of limiting instructions is, well, limited. You can't un-ring a bell, so to speak; and even if the jurors have the mental power to distinguish the differing purposes of the same piece of evidence, their overall view has, nevertheless, been influenced. A limiting instruction, however, is better than nothing, if your back's against the wall.

Exhibits

While examining witnesses in court, you will have the opportunity to introduce tangible evidence, charts and calendars for illustrative purposes, as well as photos and documents, including transcripts of prior proceedings. **Tangible evidence** is evidence that can be touched. **Demonstrative evidence** (or "illustrative evidence") is evidence that a witness or attorney prepares before trial (or during) to aid or orient the witness on important parts of testimony, or to aid the jury in understanding the same. A chart or large calendar used to assist a witness in recalling a time frame and sequence of events is an example of demonstrative evidence. Attorneys often have a witness mark a calendar to lay out clearly dates and times of events for the jury's benefit and to help keep witnesses on mark within a timeline while telling their stories. If an exhibit is marked or written on by a witness, it is routine practice for counsel to request that the demonstrative evidence then be marked as an exhibit (if it was not already) and admitted into evidence. Note that many courts do not admit demonstrative evidence—that is, it will not be submitted to the jury as material evidence for its review during deliberations. Nevertheless, mnemonic or other visual aids can be highly useful, especially during closing arguments.

The most common types of evidence introduced as exhibits in prisoner civil cases are department records and policies, photos, transcripts, and audio/video recordings. Other types of evidence may materialize in your case. If it's relevant, do not hesitate to offer into evidence what you feel is needed. Opposing counsel is sure to object to most of your important evidence, even if the evidence is obviously proper; that's just lawyering. Stay calm and remember that, for the most part, exhibits that are relevant and not merely cumulative ought to be admitted, so long as not offered solely for impeachment purposes (which is not offered as substantive proof, but to call into question the credibility of a witness only).

Before it is offered, however, each exhibit must first be marked for identification. Plaintiff's exhibits are customarily assigned numbers (affixed to an exhibit by a red sticker), whereas defense exhibits get letters (with blue stickers). Depending on local practice, exhibits may need to be marked beforehand, or you may be required to have each exhibit marked by the court clerk one by one as and when you offer the exhibit during hearing or trial. Following is a brief example of how to quickly lay an exhibit's foundation, use of the exhibit, and admission of the exhibit during direct examination:

> YOU: *Sir, you've testified that you went to the ISCF Medical Department after responding to the emergency code on B-Unit, is that right?*
>
> WITNESS: *Yes.*
>
> YOU: *Do you recall what time that was?*
>
> WITNESS: *Approximately Ten p.m.*
>
> YOU: *What was your purpose in going to the Medical Department?*
>
> WITNESS: *I was directed by the shift commander to observe and photograph the injuries sustained by Guard Lese from the assault.*
>
> YOU: *And did you do that?*
>
> WITNESS: *I did.*
>
> YOU: *And how many photos did you take?*
>
> WITNESS: *One.*
>
> YOU: *How many injuries did you observe?*
>
> WITNESS: *One.*
>
> YOU: *Your Honor, may I have an exhibit marked? I have copies for the Court and opposing counsel.*
>
> COURT: *You may. Madam Clerk . . . ?* [pause for marking]
>
> COURT: *The item has been marked as Plaintiff's Exhibit Five for identification purposes.*
>
> YOU: *Thank you, Your Honor. May the witness be shown the exhibit?*
>
> COURT: *Yes, he may. Bailiff, please hand the exhibit to the witness.*
>
> YOU: *Sir, please take a moment to review the exhibit.*
>
> WITNESS: [and so doing] *Okay.*
>
> YOU: *Do you recognize Exhibit Five?*
>
> WITNESS: *Yes. This is a close-up photo of a slight abrasion over Guard Lese's left eye.*
>
> YOU: *Did you take that particular photo?*
>
> WITNESS: *Yes.*
>
> YOU: *Does the image fairly and accurately depict what you witnessed?*
>
> WITNESS: *Yes.*

YOU: *Your Honor, may Exhibit Five be admitted into evidence?*

COURT: *Any objections?*

OPPOSITION: *No objection, Your Honor.*

COURT: *Exhibit Five is admitted.*

YOU: *And I'm finished with the exhibit; may it be shown to the jury?*

COURT: *Yes, it may. Bailiff, please hand the exhibit to the jury.*

This brief rundown of the exhibit-offering process ought to hold true for most tangible pieces of evidence.

With documents, transcripts, or audio/video recordings, should they be offered as exhibits, one should always bear in mind that these materials will in all probability be admitted in their entirety—that is, without removing, striking, or otherwise redacting content, even if containing irrelevant or prejudicial portions. This is because the general **doctrine of completeness** permits a fact-finder to view the evidence in

Ex. #	DESCRIPTION		OFFERED	ADMIT.
1	ISCF HOUSING ASSIGNMENT RECORDS	2/4/13	2/4	
2	IDOC EMERGENCY RESPONSE POLICY	2/4/13	2/4	
3	ISCF SHIFT SCHEDULE, 3/3/12	2/4/13	2/4	
4	ISCF CELL-SEARCH LOG, 10/1/11-4/1/12	2/5/13	2/5	
5	PHOTO (LESE, CUT ABOVE LEFT EYE)	2/5/13	2/5	
6	PHOTO (B-UNIT DAYROOM)	2/5/13	2/5	
7	PHOTO (A, B, C FOYER)	2/5/13	2/5	
8	PHOTO (BLOOD ON FLOOR)	2/5/13	2/5	
9	DIAGRAM (PLAINTIFF'S CELL, B-UNIT DAYROOM, AND FOYER)	2/5/13	2/7	
10	TRNSCPT (G. LESE DEPOSITION)	2/6/13		2/6
11	PHOTO (PLAINTIFF, FACE INJURIES)	2/7/13	2/7	
12	PHOTO (PLAINTIFF, CHEST BRUISES)	2/7/13	2/7	
13	PHOTO (PLAINTIFF, KNUCKLES)	2/7/13	2/7	

PLAINTIFF'S EXHIBIT LIST

Figure 15

its proper context. Fed. R. Evid. 106. Yet the rule is *not* an absolute. You may object to the admissibility of portions of an exhibit if it's proper and prudent to do so. Such issues are usually settled upon the motion *in limine* of one party or the other before trial, or when the jury is not present during the trail.

Near to trial, but allowing enough time for careful preparation, compile a list of exhibits, listed in the order you intend to offer them at trial. (*See* Figure 15, below.) Without venturing into specifics, it is necessary, for myriad reasons, that you track when an exhibit is offered, admitted, or rejected. (When an exhibit is offered, whether or not it is ultimately admitted or rejected, it becomes part of the official court record, and therefore remains in the custody of the court.) Preparation of a list shouldn't prove too burdensome when balanced against its usefulness, and it is probable that a plaintiff's exhibit list will be required by the court clerk and defense, anyway. The defense will likewise prepare such a list, and should supply you a copy. Ask them for a copy at the soonest opportunity if it appears that defense counsel are not intending to provide you one. In the margin of the defense's exhibit list, keep track of when and whether defense exhibits are offered, admitted, or rejected.

When an exhibit is first offered to a witness on the stand, the jury must be prevented from viewing its nature or content before it has been officially admitted into evidence by the judge; the parties should take care not to leave yet-to-be-admitted materials in plain sight. After its admission, the exhibit can be shown to other witnesses or left in view of the jury without worry.

Plaintiff's Rebuttal

Plaintiff goes (case-in-chief); Defendant goes (case-in-chief); Plaintiff goes again (rebuttal); Defendant goes again (surrebuttal)—that is the order of evidence presentation. Following the defense's case-in-chief, the plaintiff may put on additional evidence to rebut (contradict or discredit) the evidence brought out during the defense's main presentation. However, a plaintiff cannot recall witnesses to essentially say over what's already been said; rebuttal testimony must be in regard to new issues that have come out during the defense's case-in-chief.

Since witnesses are supposed to testify about a matter of consequence once only, rebuttal is therefore limited to *new* issues or new points that come out *during* the defense's case-in-chief, or to attack the credibility of defense witnesses, or to support the credibility of one of your witnesses whose credibility was attacked during the defense's case-in-chief. If a defense witness testified that one of your witnesses has a reputation for being dishonest, then on rebuttal you should be permitted to put on evidence to support the character trait of honesty in that discredited witness.

So, rebuttal is a plaintiff's time to attack the defense's witnesses, to impeach its witnesses, directly or indirectly, with contradictory evidence. Testimony about prior inconsistent statements can be used to attack a defense witness directly, or evidence made relevant during the defense's main presentation may be introduced to impeach defense witnesses indirectly.

Defendant's Surrebuttal

Then the defense gets another turn. The defense is not allowed to rehash its entire case on surrebuttal, just as the plaintiff cannot rehash his or her case on rebuttal. The defense is limited to addressing the points touched on during plaintiff's *rebuttal* case, and rebuttal case only. Even so, there is a surrebutal tactic opposing counsel may use to recap substantive evidence.

Suppose two witnesses—Witness A and Witness B—observe the same events. Witness A testified about the matter at length during the defendant's case-in-chief, where Witness B did not. Suppose Plaintiff, during rebuttal, undermines Witness A's recounting of events with an impeaching witness. The defense might then attempt to rehabilitate Witness A's account during surrebuttal by calling Witness B to reiterate and bolster Witness A's earlier testimony. The defense is then essentially repeating favorable evidence under the thin veneer of surrebuttal. If the defense wanted to offer material evidence by Witness B, it should have called her during its case-in-chief. Nevertheless, the defense might just get away with this type of repetitive surrebuttal. However, don't forego an objection to the cumulative nature of the testimony, or as otherwise not within the scope of surrebuttal. Rebuttal and surrebutal are primarily intended for clarity and impeachment purposes, not for putting on substantive proof going to the merits of a claim or a defense.

A possible tactic for avoiding this scenario is to draw out the testimony of both Witness A *and* Witness B earlier in the proceedings, during *your* case-in-chief. Better to get that information out in the open earlier on, rather than allowing the defense to repeat its case under the guise of surrebuttal.

Closing Arguments, Jury Instructions, and Verdict

Once the parties have completed their presentation of evidence—"resting" their respective cases—it is time for the plaintiff to make an epic and persuasive speech, tying flawlessly all the evidence into a cohesive and compelling portrayal of how the defendant(s) have run afoul of the law and caused injury: the **closing argument**. Actually, a better strategy for the legal novice is to speak to the jury in plain and simple terms, drawing reasonable inferences as to what the evidence as a whole has shown to be the truth. And confidence is vital. This is the time for last impressions, and it is crucial that the plaintiff's theory of the case be delivered with unwavering conviction.

Using calm tones and a measured delivery, walk through the facts as you and the jury heard them develop through the presentation of evidence. (Do not speculate about or refer to facts not presented to the jury.) Explain how the facts prove each element of your legal claims, why some facts are more probative than others, and why some witnesses are more credible than others. You can argue why the jury ought to return a favorable verdict, but be careful about showing anger or contempt for the opposing party when so doing. Don't be afraid to handle and discuss exhibits to illustrate your points, and always, always maintain good eye contact with the jurors.

Take the time to point out that the burden of proof for a plaintiff in a civil trial is not proof beyond a reasonable doubt, but rather the **preponderance of the evidence**. That is to say, if after totaling the evidence, the evidence weighs in favor of the plaintiff by the slightest margin (51% to the defense's 49%), then the jury *must* find in favor of the plaintiff.

After your closing arguments, the defense is permitted its turn to argue the facts in its favor.

After all closing arguments, the court then administers instructions to the jury. These **jury instructions**, at a minimum, inform the jury of the controverted facts to be resolved by the jury and the legal elements that must be satisfied in order to prove each claim (and amount of damages) in the complaint. The details of the jury instructions should have been hashed out between the court, opposing counsel, and yourself well before trial, though last-minute amendments are not unusual.

Typically, the court instructs the jury about direct and circumstantial evidence and any permissible inferences; presumptions; credibility of witnesses and impeachment; the right of the jury to accept or reject the opinions of expert witnesses; and how to treat demonstrative evidence. The court will cover the procedure of the deliberation process, including the election of a foreperson, restrictions on items to be taken into the jury room, communications between the judge and the jury, and restrictions on juror conversations outside the deliberations. Objections to an instruction or omission of an instruction must be made before the jury retires to deliberate.

Following the jury instructions, the case is then turned over to the jury for the duration of deliberation and decision of the verdict. The jurors resign to the jury room to privately discuss the evidence, review the admitted exhibits, and argue their individual opinions. Eventually they will come to a conclusion about who is right and who is wrong, rendering a verdict. The **verdict** is the jury's combined opinion in favor of one party or the other—*"We find in favor of the Plaintiff."* That's a good sign. If the jurors cannot agree one way or the other, then you have what's known as a deadlock, and the judge will declare a mistrial, which means the trial must be done over, in front of a new jury.

Upon a verdict favorable to the plaintiff, the judge orders the relief requested in the complaint, or as the judge deems otherwise necessary. Should the verdict go the other way, the court dismisses the complaint. The recourse in that event is to file an appeal.

APPEAL

Higher courts of appeals exist to correct errors made at the trial court level. They correct errors of fact and errors of law. Errors of law included questions such as these: Did the judge exclude crucial evidence that should properly have been admitted at trial? Would the inclusion of that evidence likely have changed the outcome of trial? Did the judge dismiss the case before trial, based on an erroneous interpretation of law? Was a faulty jury instruction given? Did the judge fail to appoint counsel when it was necessary and fair that counsel be appointed? Errors of fact are rarer, involving the judge's mistake as to the existence or purpose of evidence relied upon in the making of some important decision.

What constitutes a viable issue for appeal is determined by simply asking oneself, *Had the judge's decision been different, would it have* actually *made a difference?* In other words, was the error harmless? A **harmless error** is a trivial error that did not prejudice the rights of the appealing party and did not affect the outcome of trial. An appeals court will not remand or overturn a case on a harmless error. A number of such errors, however, amount to a trial rife with fault, and can cumulatively be cause for a successful appeal.

A party may **appeal by right**—without seeking permission—to the court level just above the trial court. The United States Courts of Appeal listen to appeals from United States District Courts. At the state level, appeals by right go to intermediate appellate courts; in a few states, the appeal may go directly to the state's highest court. A subsequent appeal to the highest court is granted at the discretion of that court; such permission must be sought by a petition for review or *certiorari*.

A detailed discussion of appeals is beyond the scope of this book; however, a couple of points should be made. First, one can appeal most final decisions, whether a final judgment entered after the jury has returned a verdict is based on a flawed trial (in the appellant's view), or whether the judge improperly dismissed the action in the pretrial stages. Second, for each issue on appeal, one is required to have made timely objections to each adverse opinion or order, thus preserving the issue for appeal. This is why a party *must* object to all things it feels improper. Exceptions are sometimes made for actions considered to be **plain error**, which is an obvious error that merits review even if not objected to at trial.

Notice of Appeal
Every objection made, of whatever nature, should have been noted in your case/trial notes––including date filed and title of any motions denied, date of hearing, date of order denying the motion (whether written or in open court)—because this information is necessary for

the preparation of a *Notice of Appeal.*

Read your local appellate rules for appellate fees, time for filing the notice of appeal, and content of notice. Typically, a notice of appeal must be filed within thirty days or less of the final judgment, and must contain (1) a legal caption (court title, parties' names, case number); (2) a statement of intent to appeal, identifying the name of the court and the name of the judge whose actions or omissions are the subject of appeal; and (3) a concise but specific list of each issue being brought on appeal. For instance, *"Whether the Court erred in denying Plaintiff's motion* in limine *to exclude Plaintiff's criminal history. (*Plaintiff's Motion In Limine, *section 2, para 3, filed on February 13, 2012; hearing was held on February 17, 2012; and order of denial was entered orally in open court February 17, 2012.)"*

Each issue for appeal must be identified, lest a legally interested party be misled about what that appeal is to encompass. Identifying each issue is also necessary for the the trial court clerk to ascertain which portions of the record need to be transcribed or otherwise made ready for appellate review. In either the *Notice of Appeal* or an additional document accompanying the notice, one should specifically make a request that the court clerk prepare the record for appeal, listing the portions of the proceedings, if not the entire record, that need transcription. Such a request should be accompanied by a motion for waiver of transcription fees and filing fees upon appeal. This must be done even if you've already been granted *in forma pauperis* status at the trial level.

Under Rule 4(b) of the Federal Rules of Appellate Procedure, the *Notice of Appeal* must be filed within ten days of the final judgment or order. Another thirty days may be permitted if a motion for expansion of time is filed. State time limits vary. This deadline must be met, or you risk forever being barred from appealing the particular case. Appellate courts are sticklers for procedure; follow the court rules. The notice is filed with the clerk of the district/appellate court (or clerk of the court in some jurisdictions; check your rules).

Eventually, the trial court clerk will transfer the pertinent records to the appellate court and lodge a certified copy of the trial transcripts. The delivery of the transcripts starts the deadline clock for filing briefs, usually sixty days.

Reading a few appellate briefs will provide a window into the complex world of appellate procedure and the expected depth and extent of legal arguments made at the higher court levels. State and federal level briefs are available for purchase from www.westlaw.com, www.lexis.com, www.briefreport.com, www.briefserve.com; some are available for free from

www. flcourts.org/pubinfo/summaries/ archives.html
www.nku.edu/~chase/library/kysctbriefs.htm www.court.state.nd.us
www.supreme.courts.state.tx.us/ebrief/current.htm http://library.law.wosc.edu/elecresources/databases/wb
www.ca7.uscourts.gov/briefs.htm www.ca8.uscourts.gov/brfs/brFrame.html
http://supreme.lp.findlaw.com/supreme_court/briefs

Motion for Appointment of Counsel on Appeal

Consider making a motion for appointment of counsel on appeal. There is no freestanding right to counsel on appeal in civil cases, but the court can appoint an attorney in the interest of justice. The form and content of a *Motion for Appointment of Counsel on Appeal* is substantially similar to a motion for appointment of counsel usually filed with the complaint at the outset of the case. (Discussed in "Chapter 12," above.) In this appellate version of the appointment motion, however, consider pointing out the increased complexity of the legal questions submitted on appeal, questions made more complicated through the additional witness evidence developed during hearing or trial. Consider pointing out the complex and strict nature of court procedures on appeal, and the procedural impracticality of having a *pro se* prisoner-litigant bungling around in the higher courts, figuratively speaking.

NOTES: _____
_____
_____
_____
_____
_____
_____
_____
_____
_____
_____
_____
_____
_____
_____
_____
_____
_____
_____
_____
_____
_____
_____
_____
_____
_____
_____
_____
_____
_____
_____
_____
_____
_____
_____
_____
_____
_____
_____
_____

NOTES: _____

NOTES: _____

PART 4:
YOUR RIGHTS

CHAPTER 18: MAJOR PRISONERS' RIGHTS PRECEDENT

A court of law exists to resolve disputes. The field of law under which a dispute falls depends on the circumstances of a particular case, e.g., the field of Prisoners' Rights, which concerns the deprivations of civil liberties secured to the incarcerated. After the circumstances that gave rise to a legal dispute are determined, a determination of evidence and finding of facts made either by judge or by jury, the court then issues an order or opinion explaining what the current state of law within the subject legal field has to say about the facts surrounding the case, resolving the dispute.

If the law is unclear, a court must base its decision on standards it thinks most appropriate to formulate an answer to the undecided legal question. The standards and the logic supporting a conclusion of law may be derived from different but closely related areas of law or invented by the court. In such situations it is likely a higher court of appeal will be asked to review the lower court's opinion for error of application of law.

The higher court and the parties involved thoroughly research the questions of law submitted on appeal, the opposing parties advocate their differing interpretations, and then the court renders its opinion, clarifying the law, creating precedent. This precedent provides guidance for future decisions of lower courts.

In any given field of law there are at least a handful of authoritative court precedents (usually those of a jurisdiction's highest court) that establish the criteria by which a trial court must adjudicate. Finding, reading, and thoroughly understanding these cases is indispensable to a general, yet solid, foundation of legal theory, upon which can then be laid additional, more specific research to address the details of a particular case. As a general rule of study, the current theory of an *entire* area of interest should be the primary focus of research for persons preparing to advocate a legal proposition concerning the subject field of law.

Below are summaries of important prisoners'-rights precedents. The researcher should ultimately obtain, read, and re-read each case bearing on his or her claim; but for now, a familiarity with the case summaries presented here may serve for a basic foundation that can be built upon as research progresses.

Procunier v. Martinez

In *Procunier v. Martinez*, 416 U.S. 396, 94 S.Ct 1800, 40 L.Ed.2d 224 (1974), the Supreme Court explained that prisoners are not stripped of constitutional protections at the prison gates. Prisoners retain all the rights of free-world persons, except for those rights taken expressly by law or that necessarily are implicated as a consequence of legitimate penological objectives. However, the Court failed to expand on this notion, side-stepping the Constitutional questions of what this means for the rights remaining to prisoners, and focused instead on how the prison's policies for censoring mail affected the rights of free-world persons to communicate with the incarcerated rather than the rights of prisoners to communicate with free-world persons. *Id.*, 416 U.S. at 408.

So reasoning, the *Procunier* Court held invalid a California prison regulation prohibiting inmate correspondence containing complaints about prison life. Such prohibitions on speech where found unnecessary to further any valid government interest. *Id.,* 416 U.S. at 413-416. A policy of restricting speech merely because it is unflattering or unwelcome or that it is obviously inaccurate is contrary to United States' notions of free speech, and any prison policy so prohibiting, the Court imparted, must run afoul of the First Amendment of the United States Constitution.

The *Procunier* court, however, held censorship of prisoner mail to be justified (1) if the regulation or practice in question furthers an *"important or substantial governmental interest"* unrelated to the suppression of expression, and (2) if the limitation of First Amendment freedoms is no greater than is *"necessary and essential"* to the implementation of the governmental interest involved. *Id.,* 416 U.S. at 413 (emphasis added). The court also explained that unnecessarily broad policies may be invalid, requiring, in this case, that California prison officials show with certainty that adverse consequences would result from the failure to censor a particular letter. *Id.,* 416 U.S. at 416. The officials could not meet this burden even though prison administrators are allowed some leeway in designing policy in anticipation of probable consequences for failing to censor. *Id.*, 416 U.S. at 414.

Procunier was later overruled, in part, by ***Thornburgh v. Abbot*, 490 U.S. 403, 109 S.Ct. 1874, 104 L.Ed.2d 459 (1989)**. In *Thornburgh*, the Supreme Court overruled the more prisoner-friendly "substantial government interest" standard set forth in the *Procunier* decision, in favor of the more government-friendly "legitimate government interest" standard articulated in *Turner v. Safely*, discussed below.

The *Thornburgh* decision permits prisons to censor incoming correspondence provided the four-prong test under *Turner* (see below) is satisfied; with the reservation that *outgoing* mail is still to be held to the less restrictive substantial/important government interest standard of *Procunier*.

Should correspondence be censorable under either standard, due process then requires that (1) the prisoner be notified when officials refuse to send a letter or if they reject an incoming letter; that (2) the author of the letter be afforded an opportunity to contest the decision; and that (3) the decision controversy be heard by a person other than the person who originally disapproved the letter. *Id.*, 490 S.Ct. at 1878; *Krug v. Lutz,* 329 F.3d 692 (9th Cir. 2003).

Wolff v. McDonnell

In *Wolff v. McDonnell*, 418 U.S. 539, 94 S.Ct. 2963, 41 L.Ed.2d. 935 (1974), the Supreme Court found a petitioner's claim for damages and injunctive relief to be cognizable (within the jurisdiction of the court) under § 1983, when the prisoner-petitioner alleged the unconstitutionality of disciplinary proceedings affecting his good-time credits. *Id.*, 418 U.S. at 554-55. Prisoners retain the right to due process of law, the Court held, subject to reasonable restrictions stemming from the nature of incarceration. *Id.*, 418 U.S. at 556. The court explained that the due-process guarantees of the Fifth and Fourteenth Amendments prohibit the government from depriving an inmate of life, liberty, or property without exercising the appropriate procedural process that the law requires. *Id.*, 418 U.S. at 558.

The Court set out due-process minimums for disciplinary procedures affecting a liberty interest, such as that as a prisoner may hold in receiving good-time credit, requiring the following:

1. A written notice of charges;
2. A written statement of reasons for the disciplinary action taken; and
3. The opportunity to call witnesses and present evidence if doing so will not jeopardize institutional order or safety.

Id., 418 U.S. at 563-569. However, because of the real threat of inmate retaliation and institutional disruption (*id.,* at 568-569), whether to allow inmates to confront and cross-examine an accuser is a matter entrusted to the discretion of prison officials (*id.,* 418 U.S. at 567-569).

The *Wolff* court, moreover, observed that, in order for deprivation procedures to be meaningful, due process requires that neutral officers conduct all hearing and appellate proceedings. This means that no person who participated in the case as an investigator or reviewing officer may serve in any capacity responsible for determining the outcome of the case. *Id.,* 418 U. S. at 572 n.20.

What, exactly, constitutes a "liberty interest" invoking these due-process protections was not explored in this opinion. Neither did the Court specifically determine if prisoners had a "right" to be free from solitary confinement, finding only that solitary confinement "represents a major change in the conditions of confinement and is normally imposed only when it is claimed and proven that there has been a major act of misconduct." *Id.,* 418 U.S. at 571 n.19. (Thus the question was left open, and it was determined in subsequent cases that prisoners do not usually have a due-process protected liberty interest, without more, against being segregated. *Touossaint v. McCarthy*, 801 F.2d 1080, 1100-1101 (1986), *cert. denied*, 481 U.S. 1069 (1987)).

Twenty-one years later, the Supreme Court, in **Sandin v. Conner,** 515 U.S. 472, 115 S.Ct. 2293, 132 L.Ed.2d 418 (1995), limited the application of the *Wolff* procedural due-process protections to cases that not only allege an infringement of a liberty interest (such as loss of good-time credits, lengthy placement in segregation or transfer to significantly different and harsher facilities), but also that allege an "atypical and significant hardship." *See* the discussion of *Sandin v. Conner,* below.

Additionally, due-process claims are not permitted under §1983 or *Bivens* where a successful claim would necessarily imply the invalidity of a prison disciplinary action that affects the length of confinement. *See **Edwards v. Balisok,** 520 U.S. 641, 117 S.Ct. 1584, 137 L.Ed.2d 906 (1997)* (procedural defects in prisoner's disciplinary hearing may be challenged under § 1983, and a successful plaintiff is entitled to at least nominal damages upon showing that insufficient hearing procedures violated due process, provided that the result of the disciplinary hearing as to the merits of the charge was not also proven wrong, requiring reinstatement of good-time credits, *id.,* 520 U.S. at 645; claims alleging only *defective procedures* and not seeking reversal of a disciplinary-board decision and reinstatement of good-time credits are not barred by the standard under *Heck v. Humphrey* prohibiting civil actions that would necessarily imply the invalidity of conviction or sentence duration without a prior showing that the same has been invalidated). *See Heck* discussion, below.

Bounds v. Smith

In *Bounds v. Smith*, 430 U.S. 817, 97 S.Ct. 1491, 52 L.Ed.2d 72 (1977) (plurality opinion), the Supreme Court reaffirmed prisoners' constitutionally protected right to access of the courts. *Id.*, 430 U.S. at 821, 828. The Court, discussing access rights of indigents and other prisoners generally, stated that there can be no question that:

> inmates must be provided at state expense with paper and pen to draft legal documents, notarial services to authenticate them, and with stamps to mail them. . . . This is not to say that economic factors may not be considered, for example, in choosing the methods used to provide *meaningful* access. But the cost of protecting a constitutional right cannot justify its total denial. Thus, neither the availability of jailhouse lawyers nor the necessity for affirmative state action is dispositive of respondents' claims. The inquiry is rather whether law libraries or other forms of legal assistances are needed to give prisoners a reasonably adequate opportunity to present claimed violations of fundamental constitutional rights to the courts.

Id., 430 U.S. at 824 (emphasis added).

Meaningful access to courts applies evenly to prisoners' right to challenge conditions of confinement *as well as* judicial proceedings challenging convictions or sentence duration. *Id.*, 430 U.S. at 827. Because physical incarceration necessarily reduces the legal resources otherwise available to free-world persons, this right to challenge cannot be vindicated without the affirmative assistance of prison officials in the preparation and filing of prisoners' legal papers, by either supplying an adequate law library or providing adequate assistance from persons trained in the law. *Id.*, 430 U.S. at 825. However, prison officials do retain some latitude in the methods used to provide prisoners "reasonably adequate opportunity to present claimed violations of fundamental constitutional rights to the courts." *Id.*, 430 U.S. at 825. As long as measures are taken to ensure that access to the courts is "adequate, effective, and meaningful" (*id.*, at 822), both law library *and* trained legal assistance need not be provided. *Id.*, 430 U.S. at 828.

Nearly twenty years after *Bounds*, the Supreme Court, in **Lewis v. Casey, 518 U.S. 343, 116 S.Ct. 2174, 135 L.Ed.2d 606 (1996)**, expanded on its prior decision in *Bounds* when it held improper a federal district court's injunction mandating systemwide changes in prison law-library and legal-assistance programs. The *Lewis* Court explained that the right of access as contemplated in *Bounds* does not extend so far as to permit prisoners to "transform themselves into litigating engines capable of filing everything from shareholder derivative actions up to slip-and-fall claims. . . ." *Id.*, 518 U.S. at 355. The Court rejected the plaintiff's argument that law libraries that supply clerks and other assistance are necessary to satisfy *Bounds*' definition of access to courts under the First Amendment, finding instead that it is the capability of filing non-frivolous claims that determines whether court access is meaningful, not the ability of turning pages in a law library. In other words, there is for prisoners no "abstract free-standing right to a law library or legal assistance." *Id.*, 518 U.S. at 351. The prison-provided legal resources and assistance required under *Lewis* are those that prisoners need in order to challenge their *criminal convictions*, directly or collaterally, or to challenge their *conditions of confinement*. So long as access is meaningful, this right to challenge does not necessarily mean a full panoply of legal resources are needed, and impairment to "any other litigating capacity is simply one of the incidental (and perfectly constitutional) consequences of conviction and incarceration." *Id.*, 518 U.S. at 355.

Whatever the assistance supplied prisoners, however, the Constitution is not offended by a dearth of legal resources or ineffective assistance programs unless a prisoner can show an **actual injury** to a contemplated or existing non-frivolous litigation. *Id.*, 518 U.S. at 349. (Such injuries may include, for example, dismissal of a complaint, or delay resulting in the frustration of a claim.) To show actual injury, it is not necessary to prove a claim would have ultimately prevailed at trial, but only that a viable claim existed.

Estelle v. Gamble

In *Estell v. Gamble*, 429 U.S. 97, 97 S.Ct. 285, 50 L.Ed.2d 251 (1979) (plurality opinion), the Supreme Court observed that prisoners are entitled to adequate medical care and that prison officials may be held liable should they fail to so provide. Because of the fact of incarceration, a prisoner "must rely on prison authorities to treat [his or her] medical needs. . . ." *Id.*, 429 U.S. at 103. And since the Eighth Amendment is concerned with protecting prisoners from the infliction of needless physical pain and injury (*id.*), prison authorities may be liable under federal law for failing in their duty to prevent the same. This is not to say, however, that officials need to provide the best possible medical care, but *adequate* care, only. Nor does the occurrence of trivial or superficial medical concerns suffice for a cause of action under the Constitution. The Court stated that:

> Deliberate indifference to serious needs of prisoners constitutes the unnecessary and wanton infliction of pain proscribed by the Eighth Amendment. This is true whether the indifference is manifested by prison doctors in their response to the prisoner's needs or by prison guards in intentionally denying or delaying access to medical care or intentionally interfering with treatment once prescribed. Regardless of how evidenced, deliberate indifference to a prisoner's serious illness or injury states a cause of action under section 1983.

Id., 429 U.S. at 104-105 (quotations and citation omitted).

By this rationale, only "deliberate indifference" and not accidents or inadvertent failure to provide medical care violates the Eighth Amendment. *Id.*, 429 U.S. at 105-106. The difference between actionable and non-actionable medical injury depends on a criteria of three parts. Under the Eighth Amendment, a medical claim is stated if it can be proved that:

1. A serious medical condition exists or existed;
2. Prison or medical personnel were aware of the condition; and
3. They failed to adequately treat the condition, causing the prisoner injury.

Id., 429 U.S. at 103, 104-105.

Bell v. Wolfish

In *Bell v. Wolfish*, 441 U.S. 520, 99 S.Ct. 1861, 60 L.Ed.2d 447 (1979), the Supreme Court made a categorical distinction between the rights of convicted prisoners and the rights of pretrial detainees, stating explicitly that Eighth Amendment protections against cruel and unusual punishment apply to prisoners only after the government has "secured a formal adjudication of guilt." *Id.*, 441 U.S. at 537 n.16. Pretrial detainees, on the other hand, "are protected by the Fourteenth Amendment's Due Process Clause, as well as specific substantive guarantees of the federal Constitution, such as the First and Eighth Amendments." *Id.*, 441 U.S. at 535-537 (emphasis added). Under the Due Process Clause, moreover, pretrial detainees retain *at least* those constitutional rights that are enjoyed by convicted prisoners (*id.*, at 545); and, unlike convicted prisoners, pretrial detainees may not be punished for crimes of which they have yet to be, or may not be, found guilty, and therefore are protected against jail conditions or restrictions that "amount to punishment." *Id.*, 441 U.S. at 537.

What conditions, exactly, amount to punishment is not always clear, though the *Bell* court has provided some guidance for the analysis. "The determination of whether [jail] restrictions and practices constitute punishment in the constitutional sense depends on whether they are rationally related to a legitimate non-punitive governmental purpose and whether they appear excessive in relation to that purpose." *Id.*, 441 U.S. at 561. Such an "inquiry of federal courts into prison management must be limited to the issue of whether a particular system violates any prohibition of the constitution . . . ," but it must be kept in mind that "[t]he wide range of 'judgment calls' that meet constitutional and statutory requirements are *confided to officials outside the judicial branch of government*." *Id.*, 441 U.S. at 562. (Here the Court expounded on the judiciary's role in the operation of jails and prisons, reiterating that courts ought not micromanage or undermine administrative decisions lightly.)

Turner v. Safely

In *Turner v. Safely*, 482 U.S. 78, 107 S.Ct. 2254, 69 L.Ed.2d 64 (1987), prisoners in Missouri brought a class-action suit challenging a regulation that limited both the ability of prisoners to correspond with other prisoners and the right of prisoners to marry while incarcerated. The Supreme Court used the case to definitively establish that prison officials may impose certain restrictions on the constitutionally protected rights of the inmates they confine, provided those restrictions are reasonable in light of the liberties impinged. Since the Missouri mail rule implicated only the rights of prisoners to communicate with one another, and not those of free-world persons, the Court held that the *Procunier* standard requiring an "important or substantial government interest" (*see Procunier*, above) to justify a restriction on inmate-to-free-person correspondence did not apply.

The distinction was made primarily by the rationale that unrestrained communications among inmates posed significant challenges to prison security, and that "separation of powers concerns [between the different branches of government] counsel a policy of judicial restraint." *Id.*, 482 U.S. at 85. The stricter judicial scrutiny that must necessarily follow from the standard set forth in *Procunier* would create an overstressed role of the federal judiciary in the administration of state prisons, hampering prison officials' "ability to anticipate security problems and to adopt innovative solutions to the intractable problems of prison administration." *Id.*, 482 U.S. at 85. The Supreme Court, therefore, created a new, more government-friendly standard by which courts must assess policies imposing on the First Amendment liberties of prisoners. Under *Turner*, courts ask the following:

1. Whether there are "valid, rational connections" between the regulation and a legitimate government interest put forward to justify it;
2. "[W]hether there are alternative means of exercising the right that remain open to prison inmates";
3. Whether accommodation of the constitutional right would have a significant impact on guards and other inmates; and
4. Whether ready alternatives to the regulations, at minimum cost, are absent (a determination that bears on the reasonableness of the regulation)

Id., 484 U.S. at 89-91.

Under this criterion, the *Turner* court found a legitimate government interest in the Missouri ban on inmate-to-inmate correspondence, but struck down the ban on marriage as unconstitutional, explaining that a regulation or practice cannot be sustained where the logical connection between the practice and the asserted penological goal is so remote as to render the policy arbitrary or irrational. *Id.*, 484 U.S. at 89-90. A regulation may be demonstrated as unreasonable or as an "exaggerated response" to penal concerns if there exists a viable alternative regulation that accommodates the rights of prisoners. *Id.*, 484 U.S. at 90. The reasons advanced by the state supporting the ban on marriage were found not "reasonably related" to security or rehabilitation interests, the ban sweeping broader than was necessary to address these concerns. *Id.*, 484 U.S. at 98.

Wilson v. Seiter

In *Wilson v. Seiter*, 501 U.S. 294, 111 S.Ct. 2321, 115 L.Ed.2 271 (1991), the Supreme Court observed that the Eighth Amendment prohibits cruel and unusual punishment. Punishment is cruel and unusual when "[t]he infliction of punishment is a deliberate act intended to chastise or deter. . . . If the pain inflicted is *not formally meted out as punishment by the statute or the sentencing judge*, some *mental element* must be attributed to the inflicting officer before it can qualify" as cruel and unusual punishment under the Constitution. *Id.*, 501 U.S. at 300 (emphasis added).

Whether a type of state or federally imposed sentence is lawful is not the question here. Rather, *Wilson* discusses punitive conditions imposed by prison officials *beyond* that which is imposed by a sentencing judge. Should conditions exceed the boundaries of punishment as contemplated under the Eighth Amendment, there must still exist a sufficiently culpable (guilty) mind or motivation behind the deprivation of the protected right. The Court stressed that "[i]t is obduracy and wantonness, not inadvertence or error in good faith, that characterize the conduct prohibited by the Cruel and Unusual Punishments Clause."*Id.*, 501 U.S. at 299, citing *Whitley v. Albers*, 475 U.S. 312, 314 (1986).

Under *Wilson*, two elements form the standard for determining whether a prisoner has suffered cruel and unusual punishment. The first element, the objective element, derived from *Rhodes v. Chapman*, 452 U.S. 337, 347 (1981), asks whether there exists a "sufficiently serious" deprivation of life's necessities. *Wilson*, 501 U.S. at 298. The second element, the subjective element, asks whether there exists a "sufficiently culpable state of mind" behind said deprivation (*id.*), a standard that varies according to the facts of the alleged violation. (Which asks, in view of the facts surrounding the conduct in question, was the punishment inflicted with "obdurance and wontonness"? The answer depends on the unique facts of the case.) The motivation behind the deprivation, however, does not need to rise to the level of maliciousness. *Id.*, 501 U.S. at 306.

The Court held, moreover, that the second element, of culpable mind, is always required to establish a cruel and unusual punishment claim, for isolated incidents as well as for continuing or systematic conditions. *Id.*, 501 U.S. at 301. "Deliberate indifference"—that a violation is known to exist, yet remedial measures are not taken, resulting in harm—is sufficient to satisfy the second element. *Id.*, 501 U.S. at 301-303; *see also Farmer v. Brennon,* below.

However, "only those deprivations denying 'the minimal civilized measure of life's necessities'. . . are sufficiently grave to form the basis of an Eight Amendment violation." *Id.*, 501 U.S. at 248, quoting *Rhodes*, 452 U.S. at 347. "Life's necessities" were described to include "food, warmth, or exercise." *Wilson*, 501 U.S. at 304. (Accordingly, the deprivation of a prisoner's T.V., even if a malicious deprivation, will not amount to a constitutional cruel and unusual claim.) Lesser incidents, if individually not violative of the Constitution, can combine to create Eighth Amendment issues (*id.*, at 304), though "[n]othing so amorphous as 'overall conditions' can rise to the level of cruel and unusual punishment when no specific deprivation of a single human need exists." *Id.*, 501 U.S. at 304-305.

Farmer v. Brennan

In *Farmer v. Brennan*, 511 U.S. 825, 114 S.Ct. 1970, 128 L.Ed.2811 (1994), acknowledging that prisoners have the right to be free from cruel and unusual punishment (*id.*, 511 U.S. at 832), the Supreme Court discussed the appropriate standard for determining whether the Eighth Amendment is violated by inmate-on-inmate violence. The Court rejected the proposal of an objective standard under which a prison official who was unaware of a substantial risk of harm to an inmate would nevertheless be held liable under the Eighth Amendment, even if the risk was obvious and a reasonable prison official would have been aware of it. The Court preferred the subjective approach: officials must actually be aware of a risk to be held liable for failing to prevent the risk.

By the subjective approach, "[w]hether a prison official had the requisite knowledge of a substantial risk is a question of fact subject to demonstration in the usual ways, including inference from circumstantial evidence, and a fact finder may conclude that a prison official knew of a substantial risk from the very fact that the risk was obvious. For example, if an Eighth Amendment plaintiff presents evidence showing that a substantial risk of inmate attacks was long-standing, pervasive and well-documented, or expressly noted by prison officials in the past, and the circumstances suggest that the defendant official being sued had been exposed to information about it, then such evidence could be sufficient to permit a trier of fact to find that the defendant official had actual knowledge of the risk." *Id.*, 511 U.S. at 842. However, "the official must both be aware of facts from which the inference could be drawn that a substantial risk of serious harm exists, and he must also draw the inference." *Id.*, 511 U.S. at 837. (In other words, even if a threat was obvious from the circumstances, the prisoner-plaintiff must still prove that the official was actually aware of the risk.)

The *Farmer* court remanded the case to the district court to determine if prison officials acted with "deliberate indifference" when the transsexual inmate, who projected feminine characteristics, was placed in general population, where he was beaten and raped by another inmate. *Id.*, 511 U.S. at 838-842. The Court instructed that the "subjective recklessness" standard used in criminal law was the appropriate standard for demonstrating deliberate indifference. *Id.*, 511 U.S. at 839-840. (Criminal recklessness is defined as conduct "whereby an actor does not desire the harmful consequence but nonetheless foresees the possibility and consciously takes the risk." *Black's Law Dictionary* (3rd Pocket ed. 2006)).

This subjective standard, however, does *not* require a prisoner seeking a remedy for unsafe conditions to await injury, *if injury is imminent*, before obtaining court relief. *Id.*, 511 U.S. at 845.

Heck v. Humphrey

In *Heck v. Humphrey*, 512 U.S. 477, 114 S.Ct. 2364, 129 L.Ed.2d 383 (1994), a state prisoner filed suit under § 1983 raising claims that, if true, would have established the invalidity of his standing conviction. The Court compared the suit to one for malicious prosecution, an element of which is the favorable termination of criminal proceedings. *Id.*, 512 U.S. at 484. The Court instructs us that:

> in order to recover damages for allegedly unconstitutional conviction or imprisonment, or for other harm caused by actions whose unlawfulness would render a conviction or sentence invalid, a § 1983 plaintiff must prove that the conviction or sentence has been reversed on direct appeal, expunged by executive order, declared invalid by state tribunal authorized to make such determination, or called into question by a federal court's issuance of a writ of habeas corpus, 28 U.S.C. § 2254. A claim for damages bearing that relationship to a conviction or sentence that has *not* been so invalidated is not cognizable under § 1983.

Id., at 486-487 (emphasis in original) (footnote omitted).

The Court came to this conclusion by invoking the aged "principle that civil tort actions are not appropriate vehicles for challenging the validity of outstanding criminal judgments." *Id.*, 512 U.S. at 486. Rather, *habeas corpus*, the Court explains, is the proper vehicle, in federal court, for challenging a criminal conviction or sentence. *Id.* 512 U.S. at 482. Under federal law, therefore, a cause of action for damages resulting from an unconstitutional conviction or sentence accrues only when the conviction or sentence is reversed, expunged, invalidated or impugned by grant of writ of *habeas corpus*. *Id.*, 512 U.S. at 489-490.

More recently, in **Wallace v. Kato, 549 U.S. 384, 127 S.Ct. 1091, 166 L.Ed.2d 973 (2007)**, the Supreme Court expounded upon the application of the *Heck* rule, which bars civil suits impugning standing criminal conviction or sentence, with specific attention to when, exactly, § 1983 actions may be brought:

> While we have never stated so expressly, the accrual date of a § 1983 cause of action is a question of federal law that is *not* resolved by reference to state law . . . [and aspects] of § 1983 which are not governed by reference to state law are governed by federal rules conforming in general to common-law tort principles.

Id., 549 U.S. at 338 (emphasis in original); citing *Heck*, 512 U.S. at 483. "Under those principles, it is standard rule that [accrual occurs] when the plaintiff has a complete and present cause of action . . . that is, when the plaintiff can file suit and obtain relief." *Id.*, 549 U.S. at 338 (alteration in original) (internal quotations and citation omitted).

In *Wallace*, the plaintiff, in 2003, brought suit for a 1994 false arrest (among other claims) that formed the basis of his successful appeal, resulting in dismissal of charges on April 10, 2002. *Id.* 549 U.S. at 386-387. The district court held Wallace's suit to be untimely, barred by the two-year Illinois statute of limitations, which, it held, began to run not at the 2002 dismissal of charges, but in 1994 when the false arrest ended, reasoning that Wallace was thereafter lawfully detained when he was arraigned and bound over for trial. At which point, Wallace's cause of action for the false arrest for the period up until arraignment accrued for the purpose of a § 1983 action and the Illinois statute of limitations.

Wallace unsuccessfully argued that the decision in *Heck v. Humphrey* barred the civil action until his conviction was reversed in 2002. The Court of Appeals, and subsequently the Supreme Court, affirmed the district court's granting of summary judgment to the defendants. *Id.*, 549 U.S. at 391-392. The Supreme Court explained as follows:

> If there is a false arrest claim, damages for that claim cover the time of deten-
> tion up until issuance of process or arraignment, but not more. From that point
> on, any damages recoverable must be based on a malicious prosecution claim
> and on the wrongful use of judicial process rather than detention itself.

Id., 549 U.S. at 390 (citation omitted). (Here, the Court distinguished Wallace's false-arrest claim—a species of false imprisonment—from that of Fourth Amendment malicious prosecution, but expressly declined to explore the contours of a malicious prosecution claim under § 1983; Wallace did not assert a malicious prosecution claim. *Id.*, 549 U.S. at 390, n.2.)

The Court held Wallace's claim to have accrued for statute of limitation purposes when the false arrest ended at arraignment, when Wallace could have immediately filed suit, even with criminal charges pending, as he was not yet convicted. The Court rejected the idea that "an action which would impugn *an anticipated future conviction* cannot be brought until that conviction is set aside." *Id.*, 549 U.S. at 393 (emphasis in original). Such a principle, the Court held, goes well beyond the intentions of *Heck*. *Id.* Rather, with criminal charges pending, the civil action should be stayed until disposition of the criminal case. *Id.*, 549 U.S. at 393-394. "If the plaintiff is ultimately convicted, and if the stayed civil suit would impugn that conviction, *Heck* will require dismissal; otherwise, the civil action will proceed, absent some other bar to the suit." *Id.*, 549 U.S. at 394 (citation omitted).

However, the Court advised that in § 1983 actions federal courts "generally refer[] to state law for tolling rules, just as [they do] for the length of statutes of limitations." *Id.* Had the state put in place rules tolling the time limitations for civil actions during the pre-conviction phase of criminal proceedings, then the action might have been timely. Illinois, the Court pointed out, did not have in place any such tolling rules (*id.*, at 394), nor are there any such tolling rules under federal law. *Id.*, 549 U.S. at 394-395.

Sandin v. Conner

In *Sandin v. Conner*, 515 U.S. 472, 115 S.Ct. 2293, 132 L.Ed.2d 418 (1995), the Supreme Court severely limited circumstance in which due-process claims that implicate a "liberty interest" may be pursued under § 1983. (A protected "liberty interest," the *Sandin* court explained, can be created by the Due Process Clause itself, by state statutes, or by regulations. *Id.*, 515 U.S. at 483-484.)

The prior precedent under *Wolff v. McDonnell*—which required that prisoners be given (1) advanced written notice of charges, (2) written statement of reasons for the disciplinary action taken, and (3) opportunity to call witnesses and present evidence if doing so will not jeopardize institutional safety—was narrowed by *Sandin* to apply only in those cases where not only a "liberty interest" is implicated but also where a prisoner has suffered an "atypical and significant hardship," offering the rationale that "federal courts ought to afford appropriate deference and flexibility to state officials trying to manage a volatile environment." *Id.*, 515 U.S. at 482.

An atypical and significant hardship occurs when a prisoner is subject to conditions much different from those ordinarily experienced by large numbers of inmates serving their sentences in a similar way. The Court failed to provide guidance beyond this short definition, except to opine that confinement in disciplinary segregation is not an atypical and significant hardship because conditions in disciplinary segregation are similar to those in administrative segregation and protective custody. *Id.*, 515 U.S. at 484-486. The Court was clear, however, that due process must be afforded if a state action will inevitably affect the duration of a prisoner's sentence, but noted that duration of sentence is not inevitably affected by a prisoner's housing in disciplinary segregation. *Id.*, 515 U.S. at 487.

Sandin unequivocally reduces the extent of due process protections available to convicted prisoners (however, the limitations of *Sandin* do not apply to pre-trial detainees, *id.*, at 484), though the Court made it clear that it did not intend to foreclose other avenues by which prisoners may challenge prison conditions or official conduct: "Prisoners such as Conner, of course retain other protection from arbitrary state action even within the expected conditions of confinement. They may invoke the First and Eighth Amendments and the Equal Protection clause of the Fourteenth Amendment where appropriate, and may draw upon internal prison grievance procedures and state judicial review where available." *Id.*, 515 U.S. at 487 n.11.

NOTES: _____

_____

_____

_____

_____

_____

_____

_____

_____

_____

_____

_____

_____

_____

_____

_____

_____

_____

_____

_____

_____

_____

_____

_____

_____

_____

_____

_____

_____

_____

_____

_____

_____

_____

NOTES: _____

_____
_____
_____
_____
_____
_____
_____
_____
_____
_____
_____
_____
_____
_____
_____
_____
_____
_____
_____
_____
_____
_____
_____
_____
_____
_____
_____
_____
_____
_____
_____
_____
_____
_____
_____

CHAPTER 19:
YOUR RIGHTS IN THEORY

This section is comprised of summary descriptions of prevailing theories covering what a prisoner can expect as a matter of legal right. Some supporting authority is cited throughout, but as with most other sections in this book, case citations have been kept at a minimum for easier reading. When searching for point-specific pieces of case law, refer to "PART 5" of this book following this chapter. In "PART 5," extensive lists of citations are given, along with explanatory parentheticals, under major prisoner-related topics, which are conveniently arranged in alphabetical order.

You Have the Right to Access the Courts

Prisoners have a constitutional right to complain, to petition the government in redress of grievances, which includes the right of reasonable, meaningful access to the courts. ***Johnson v. Avery***, 393 U.S. 483, 89 S.Ct. 747, 21 L.Ed.2d 718 (1967). A person's status or custody level does not diminish this right, which applies evenly for minimum custody as well as for segregated inmates. *Alston v. DeBruyn*, 12 F.3d 1036 (7th Cir. 1994). The right of access stems from the First Amendment and the Due Process Clause of the Fourteenth Amendment, to embrace court petitions and other actions, and to protect those who pursue institutional grievances. *Davis v. Goord*, 320 F.3d 346 (2nd Cir. 2003).

Because of the lack of opportunity that comes along with physical incarceration, prisoners have the right to active assistance from prison officials in the preparation and filing of legal papers. This right imposes on officials the duty to establish either a law library or a program allowing for assistance from persons trained in the law. Prisons are not required, however, to provide both trained legal assistance *and* a law library, so long as access to either is meaningful; and prisons may experiment with a combination of methods such as employing jailhouse lawyers, supplying preformed pleading packets, offering limited legal publications, providing paralegal services, etc. The question of sufficient court access turns on whether the prison provides "meaningful" access. Courts have held that this does not mean prisons must enable prisoners to become full-blown litigating machines, able to file on and research every point of every legal theory, but rather that prison resources must be sufficient to allow prisoners to file papers and subsequently pursue their claims.

If a law library *is* provided, "meaningful access," unfortunately, is not usually interpreted to mean that a prison must supply a *complete* law library, or even any case reporters. And, if security is an issue, denial of access to legal materials for short periods of time won't necessarily amount to a constitutional violation.

Other legitimate administrative concerns may prevail over prisoners' access rights. These concerns tend to involve institutional security and internal order, the prevention of contraband, budget constraints, and the prevention of regular users from dominating the law library. Prisons are usually permitted to require prisoners to store excessive amounts of legal papers in the facility's property department or resource center, legal mail may be inspected in the presence of the recipient, and access to law libraries may be limited.

Prisoners may help other prisoners with their legal matters, but such activity is provided no more protection than other First Amendment speech, and may be restricted provided a legitimate penological reason exists. *See generally Shaw v. Murphy*, 532 U.S. 223 (2001). However, an inmate may have a protected access-to-the-courts right to legal assistance from fellow inmates if that inmate would without it be denied meaningful access. A Spanish-speaking inmate, for example, may have the right to help from another Spanish-speaking inmate should the prison provide legal services in English only.

Some access-to-court rights are more settled. Prison officials must provide for mailing, notary services, and photocopies, as "litigation necessarily requires some means of accurate duplication because the court and parties need to refer to the same documents . . . [and] photocopying is a reasonably means of providing the necessary copies of petitions, complaints, answers, motions, affidavits, exhibits, memoranda and briefs, including attachments and appendices, material needed for discovery and investigation, including interrogatories and freedom of information requests." *Gluth v. Kangas*, 951 F.2d 1504, 1510 (9th Cir. 1992). But even these accommodations are not limitless. Courts have held that indigent prisoners are not entitled to unlimited free copies and postage for legal materials, though budgetary constraints do not justify denial of meaningful access rights.

Denial of access alone is not actionable under the Constitution, however. Prisoners must also demonstrate "actual injury" resulting from a denial of access to the courts in order to establish a cognizable constitutional claim. *See Lewis v. Casey* under "Bounds v. Smith" in the previous chapter. Successful access claims have involved insufficient facilities or resources, or interference by prison staff, such as when officials delay delivery of papers that demand immediate legal attention, causing a claim, defense, or privilege to become frustrated or barred by time limits. The exception to the otherwise strict "actual injury" rule arises with the fundamental deprivation of access rights, such as when a prison or jail is devoid of virtually any legal assistance programs or if officials conspire to forestall a prisoner's claim. *Canell v. Lightner*, 143 F.3d 1210, 1213 (9th Cir. 1998). Moreover, Sixth Amendment claims—usually arising from interference with the attorney-client privilege—also do not require a showing of "actual injury" to a non-frivolous claim; the violation of the Sixth Amendment alone is injury enough to state a claim.

In addition to legal assistance from prison officials, prisoners can expect certain accommodations from the courts once claims are filed. Judges recognize that prisoners face practical difficulties in exercising the right of legal access and usually relax procedural hurdles in some circumstances to allow prisoners to file and prosecute claims. Judges know prisoners are not trained in legal theory and procedure, and thus should "liberally construe" pleadings favorably to prisoner-plaintiffs when possible. (*See generally* "Access to the Courts" section in "PART 5," below.)

You Have the Right to Freedom of Expression and Association

If a legitimate penological interest can be shown (recall the language of *Turner* in the previous chapter), prison officials may permissibly interfere with the exercise of First Amendment rights by the inmates in their control. In no circumstances, however, may officials retaliate against an inmate who exercises his or her protected First Amendment rights, which include, but are not limited to, pursuance of institutional grievances, religious expression, and familial or political association. However, certain associations, especially political associations, may give rise to legitimate security concerns. Nevertheless, the First

Amendment protects a prisoner's **right to express political beliefs**, no matter how unpopular they may be, so long as legitimate security concerns do not dictate otherwise. Expression of ideas and groups advocating or advertising ideas that could cause violence or institutional disruption have been lawfully suppressed. In fact, group organization, circulation of petitions, and dissemination of leaflets in prison have been held lawfully prohibited, for security reasons, no matter the beliefs or objectives behind the expression or association.

Prisons may not adopt policies that, intentionally or not, have a "chilling effect" on protected conduct. A *chilling* policy or custom is one that *discourages* privileged conduct without prohibiting it. For example, a prison custom of searching the cells of jailhouse lawyers more frequently than others could be said to "chill" the exercise of protected speech. (*See* "First Amendment" and "Retaliation" sections in "PART 5.")

Inmates also have the right to receive and send information, though prisons may limit the amount of postage an inmate can possess at any one time, which may curtail the amount of information an inmate can send at that time. Inmate-to-inmate correspondence, in addition, can be prohibited outright, and usually is. Bans on inmate-to-inmate communications have generally been upheld for the "legitimate security concerns" of combating development of escape plans, coordination of security-threat-group activity, introduction of contraband, and orchestration of violent acts, to name a few reasons. Inmates may have a protected right to communicate with each other if they are parties in the same legal action, criminal or civil. Prison authorities, however, can and likely will monitor such communication.

Correspondence between inmates and free-world persons, of course, may not be restricted absent some legitimate threat to security, good order, institutional discipline, or if the correspondence would contribute to criminal activity. If mail is, for whatever reason, withheld or censored, inmates enjoy the procedural due process rights of notification and opportunity to be heard. These rights include notice of why the material is being prohibited and from whom and where it came, and the chance to be heard on appeal by officials not responsible for the original censorship. *Procunier v. Martinez*, 416 U.S. 396 (1974); *King v. Lutz*, 324 F.3d 692 (9th Cir. 2003).

Both incoming and outgoing mail are subject to search for contraband. The *Turner* standard applies to incoming mail—that is, a legitimate penological interest may prevail over the right to receive a particular item of mail—but does not apply to the censorship of *outgoing* mail. Rather, the less restrictive (to inmates) important/substantial government interest test under *Procunier* is used. (*See* "Turner v. Safely" and "Procunier v. Martinez" in the previous chapter.) This is because, concerning content and subject, outgoing correspondence usually poses less threat to prison security. A simple disagreement over the content of a letter, for example, is not "important" or "substantial" enough to justify the infringement of First Amendment liberties.

"Privileged mail" such as **attorney-client correspondence** and court correspondence may not to be delayed, censored or prohibited, and almost without exception must be opened and inspected for contraband—but not read—in the presence of the recipient inmate. Such correspondence, to gain this protection, must be clearly marked as "legal" or "privileged" mail, or it may be subject to search just as regular, non-legal correspondence. (*See generally* "Mail & Legal Mail" in "PART 5," below.)

The right to speak freely, in addition to protecting mail correspondence, entails the right not only to speak but also to be heard and to hear others. Accordingly, courts have upheld inmates' rights to address the media and to author books and articles (though these rights may nevertheless be abridged provided a legitimate penological interest exists). And because free speech means nothing if it does not incorporate the right to be informed, prison officials must allow inmates **access to print media** such as newspapers, magazines, and books. Access to televised media alone, courts have held, cannot suffice as a substitute for the deeper coverage and broader scope of the printed word.

Some prohibitions of print media do prevail, however, and usually center around fire-code issues that involve the amount of flammable material any one inmate may possess, and the risk of makeshift paper weapons or of books being wielded as clubs. Courts look at institutional security levels when determining whether there is a legitimate security interest in limiting print media, which may include a total ban on hardcover publications.

Most prisons place some kind of restriction on the amount of paper material allowable in an inmate's cell, often setting a specific number limit on books and magazines. Most prisons, including high-security and medium-security prisons, allow both hard- and soft-bound books, though many others do not admit hardcovers or hardcovers over a certain size. (Current trends in this area of law are, discouragingly, not in favor of prisoners. An inmate pursuing a claim along these lines might consider arguing for access to electronic forms of media such as the Kindle electronic book as a viable alternative that would accommodate both the prison's security interests and the prisoners' right to free speech—an especially strong argument in the case where a facility already permits electronic typewriters or video-game consoles or MP3 players, as many do.)

Policy restricting the receipt of print media to materials sent only from publishers, bookstores, or book clubs is legally permissible under the Constitution. (The concern is that publications sent from private, non-business sources pose a higher risk of being used for the purpose of introducing contraband.) Prisons may also restrict certain subjects (e.g., marshal-arts, wilderness survival, weapons manufacturing) and publications advocating violence, or that could reasonably lead to violence (e.g., inflammatory racial or politically radical views) or disobedience to prison rules, or that compromise legitimate penological objectives such as rehabilitation (e.g., publications depicting drug use or manufacture). Bans on sexually explicit material—i.e., images showing genitalia or female nipples—are being upheld as well.

Prisons may not *arbitrarily* prohibit print media. They must have specific reasons, and general bans limiting media access to only specified subjects or only through selected publishers, or that limit inmates to items purchased themselves (as opposed to orders placed by friends or family), have been struck down as unconstitutional. However, a general ban on access to the Internet is permissible, even, according to a few recent decisions, to the extent of preventing inmates Internet access through third parties, such as family or friends who would be willing to post and communicate e-mails or do research on an inmate's behalf.

The First Amendment also guarantees prisoners a measure of **freedom of communication and association**, including the opportunity for inmates to receive visitors and to use telephones.

Courts have held that inmates possess no absolute right to visitation, while at the same time implying in their decisions that the Constitution must protect visitation to some extent, or render meaningless the constitutional provisions of the First Amendment. Extent of visitation rights are unsettled. Attorneys must be provided physical access to their clients, unless a necessary restriction on visitation will not interfere with attorney-client privileges or the ability of an attorney to effectively represent his or her client. In this vein, paralegals and law students working under an attorney possess a derivative right to visit inmates within their housing facilities.

With other members of the public, however, restrictions on visitation will be sustained if in advancement of legitimate penological concerns.

Generally, courts have upheld policies limiting visitation times, duration and dates, and that require visitors to undergo security screening before admission into the facility. Visitors can be required to wear only clothing items of a modest description. Most jails (as opposed to prisons) allow exceedingly short visitation periods and completely ban contact visits, yet often relax visitation hurdles such as clothing protocols and visitor pre-approval. Prisons and jails are not at liberty, however, to impose hardships on disabled visitors or to ignore the important needs of visitors, which includes the need to access toilet facilities.

The law surrounding prisoners' right to use the phone is as unsettled as the law around the right to visitation. Implicit in the Constitution is the right of communication and association, though it is not absolute in regard to prisoners. Courts have been consistent in ruling that there must be some right of access to phone services reserved to inmates, but have been inconsistent as to the range of this right. Attorneys must be permitted phone contact with clients, or prisons risk offending the Fourteenth and Sixth Amendments, but otherwise, restrictions of phone usage may be perfectly constitutional given legitimate penological interests. Prison officials may charge inmates for phone calls, even at exorbitant rates, as long as costs to the inmate do not, in effect, amount to denial of meaningful access to phone services. Duration of calls may be limited also, but again, so long as meaningful access is not denied. Five to ten minutes, courts have held, is sufficient to survive constitutional scrutiny. Suspension of phone privileges—as well as visitation privileges, for that matter—have been allowed as a reasonable disciplinary tool. (*See*"Phones" and "Visitation sections in "PART 5," below.)

Marriage is protected under the right to associate. The courts have decisively held that **prisoners have the right to marry**, yet legitimate prison concerns may dictate how and when. Some states still allow conjugal visits, but even then a prison may require the couple to have been married before conviction and imprisonment to receive this benefit. Most state policies completely banning conjugal visits or sexual contact of any kind have been held lawful, in accord with prison safety concerns. Prisons may also have legitimate concerns in preventing inmates from providing specimens for use in artificial insemination. (*See* "Marriage" section in "PART 5," below.)

You Have the Right to Practice Religion

Prison officials must afford inmates a reasonable opportunity to practice religion. (*See generally* "Religion" section in "PART 5," below.) Yet common prison concerns often trump an inmate's religious desires, though any prison concern interfering with a prisoner's free exercise of religion must be related to legitimate penological interests. Whether an interest is legitimate is ascertained by viewing the facts surrounding the infringement or prohibition of religious expression through the four *Turner* factors. *O'Lone v. Estate of Shabazz*, 482 U.S. 342, 349 (1987) (expanding *Turner* standard to apply in determinations of whether administrators may restrict prisoners' right to freely express religion under the First Amendment).

Unfortunately, many have disingenuously beat the drum of "religious entitlement" in order to gain the benefits uniquely permitted to religious groups in prison, i.e., feast days, religious accoutrement, personal time in the chapel. So, unsurprisingly, courts may require prisoners complaining of a violation of religious liberty to demonstrate that the claimed liberty is (1) religious in nature and (2) sincerely held. The burden remains on prison officials, however, to prove the contrary, and there is no presumption, solely because a religion is under court scrutiny, that a belief is falsely maintained or insincerely held.

When it is disputed whether a prisoner's beliefs are religious in nature, a court might approach the question in one of two ways: the objective approach focuses on the purported religion itself; the subjective approach seeks to examine the mind of the prisoner, i.e., the belief behind the asserted religious right. By the objective approach, a court may ask three questions: (1) do the beliefs address *fundamental and ultimate questions*? (2) is the religion *comprehensive in nature*, consisting of a belief system? (3) are there *formal and external signs or symbols*? *Africa v. Pennsylvania*, 662 F.2d 1025, 1032 (3rd Cir. 1981). By the subjective approach, a court may simply ask if the plaintiff "conceives of the beliefs as religious in nature." *Patrick v. LeFerre*, 745 F.2d 153, 159 (2nd Cir. 1984). Under the subjective test, it is usually necessary for a court or jury fact-finder to examine the prisoner's inner attitudes toward his or her purported beliefs. *Id.*, at 159. (But bear in mind that neither the objective nor the subjective standard given here is exclusive; they are merely analytical tools that your jurisdiction may adopt. Stricter or more liberal analytical methods may be used in your jurisdiction, and therefore one should carefully check local precedent.)

For a court to determine whether beliefs are religious in nature, by whatever method, is as far as the Constitution permits judges to make decisions about purported religious beliefs. (To this point, an inmate building a religious suit would be wise to compile religious literature in support of, and for citation in, his or her arguments, and it would be prudent to become versed enough in the germane religious ideals to prepare to withstand a court's pointed examination at hearing.) A court may determine whether a belief is, indeed, religious in nature—a chess club, even claiming philosophical analogy of game strategy to the "strategy of life," will not likely be afforded protection as a religion—but it may not delve into the *validity* of a religious belief. *Thomas v. Review Bd. of Indiana Employment Sec. Div.*, 450 U.S. 707, 715 (1981); *Employment Div., Dep't of Human Resources of Oregon v. Smith*, 494 U.S. 872, 887 (1990) ("It is not within the judicial ken to question the centrality of particular beliefs or practices to a faith, or the validity of particular litigant's interpretations of those creeds.").

Sincerity of belief is another matter. Provided a belief is established as a bona fide religion, does the plaintiff sincerely hold to the belief? Absent evidence otherwise, a plaintiff's affirmation of his or her professed beliefs should be all the evidence a court or jury fact-finder needs. However, should an inmate claiming the right to a specific religious diet, for example, be discovered consuming or ordering food prohibited by his or her religious beliefs (evidenced by, say, commissary sales records), the case could be dismissed for failure to demonstrate a sincerely held belief. However, departure from particular articles of a belief system is not necessarily dispositive to a religious claim: it is not required that a religious practitioner strictly adhere to every religious tenet in fervent orthodoxy in order to gain the protection of the Constitution. Should sincerity genuinely come under dispute, a claim of sincerity may be supported by evidence of long practice—though recent conversion or adoption of religion is not, itself, fatal to a suit—by providing study notes or personal writings, or simply by being able to articulate one's religious views to the court or jury fact-finder with consistency and confidence.

Once legitimacy of religion and sincerity of belief is established, a few ways exist for prisoners to bring religious claims. The most obvious is a First Amendment claim arising from interference with freedom of expression. Under the First Amendment, the government must justify a deprivation of religion by the "legitimate penological interest" standard laid out in *Turner*. This is a tough standard for prisoners to overcome. (Review the "Turner v. Safely" discussion in the previous chapter.) A claim brought under the Establishment Clause of the First Amendment, therefore, might allow a better cause of action in some circumstances.

Under the **Establishment Clause**, the government is prohibited from creating laws or policies that (1) establish or adopt a religion, (2) prefer one religion over another, or (3) force religion upon the unwilling. Suppose, for example, a prison allocates program resources disparately to a preferred faith group while other faith groups are neglected. In such a scenario exits a viable Establishment Clause claim, for the prison is favoring one religious group over others. (Such favoritism need not be proved by showing of written, ironclad policy, but may be demonstrated by circumstantial evidence.) Establishment Clause questions are not analyzed under the cumbersome *Turner* standard, either; presumably because the government can have no "legitimate penological interest" in establishing a religion.

In *Lemon v. Krutzman*, the Supreme Court ventured a different analytical method by which to judge First Amendment Establishment Clause claims. Under the "*Lemon* test," government practice does not violate the Constitution provided the following:

1.   The policy has a secular (non-religious) legislative purpose;
2.   The policy's primary effect neither advances nor impedes religion; and
3.   The policy does not foster an excessive government entanglement with religion.

Lemon v. Krutzman, 403 U.S. 602, 612-613, 91 S.Ct. 2105, 2111, 29 L.Ed.2d 745, 755 (1971).

The *Lemon* test seems most suitable to the resolution of Establishment Clause questions affecting religious opportunities generally. However, there is another, coercion-based test more pointedly concerned with whether the government forces religion upon unwilling persons. In 1992, the Supreme Court forewent the *Lemon* test when rejecting a policy permitting invitation of clergy to say prayers at school graduation ceremonies, instead applying a "bright line rule" focused on coercion. *Lee vs. Weisman*, 505 U.S. 577, 587 (1992): accord *Zelamn v. Simmons-Harris*, 536 U.S. 639, 688-690 (2002). (A **bright-line rule** is a decision rule that seeks to impose a simple, straightforward resolution to ambiguous issues.) In *Lee*, the Supreme court simply asked whether persons are being coerced into prac-ticing a religion; that is, (1) has the government acted? (2) does the action amount to coer-cion? (3) is the purpose of the coercion religious or secular? Government action that would not survive this test, for example, occurs when an inmate is required to complete a faith-based program as a prerequisite to parole. On this point, *Lee* has been elaborated upon, the Eight Circuit holding the Establishment Clause violated if a faith-based government pro-gram (1) indoctrinates recipients with religion, (2) defines program recipients by their ad-herence to religion, or (2) causes the government to become excessively entangled in mat-ters of religion. *Americans United for Separation of Church and State v. Fellowship Min-istries*, 509 F.3d 406, 415 (8th Cir. 2008).

Whether a faith group receives more or less benefits than other faith groups within a prison, to continue with the example, could also constitute a violation of the **Equal Protection Clause of the Fourteenth Amendment**. To succeed on a claim under the Equal Protection Clause, a prisoner must show that his or her religious practice is "similarly situated" to another faith group and that this other group is receiving some advantage the disfavored practitioner or group is not, or that the government is imposing the practice of one faith group upon dissimilar groups.

Most faith groups are "similarly situated" in that they require a place to congregate in worship, in fellowship with other practitioners. If a disfavored group is not allowed a time-slot at the prison chapel where other groups are, there may exist a viable Equal Protection claim. Equal Protection is not violated, however, when prisons must accommodate different religious practices/groups in different ways when such activities pose different demands on prison resources. Prison officials are permitted to take into account the nature of a particular religious service, including the number of inmate practitioners, when making decisions such as how to allocate time for use of chapel facilities and access to chapel services, so long as the distinction made between faith groups is not irrational. *Cruz v. Beto*, 405 U.S. 319, 322 (1972). (Equal Protection claims are further discussed below).

In addition to the avenues of redress available under the Constitution, two pieces of legislation exist specifically to allow inmates to pursue their religious claims in court. In 1993, Congress passed—with the intention of expanding prisoners' religious liberties—the Religious Freedom Restoration Act (RFRA), 42 U.S.C. § 2000bb, *et seq.*, in which the legislature provided that a government may not "substantially burden" prisoners' religious practice without a "compelling government interest," which the government must further by the "least restrictive means" only. Thus was enacted a more liberal standard whereby prisoners may assert their religious rights, to supersede the stricter "legitimate penological interest" standard of *Turner v. Safely,* which still controls on purely Constitutional claims brought under the First Amendment. *Warsoldier v. Woodford*, 418 F.3d 989, 994 (9th Cir. 2005).

Under the newer RFRA standard, a prisoner must show that:

1. The government imposed a substantial burden on a sincerely held religious practice;
2. The government had no compelling interest in doing so; or
3. The government has not used the least restrictive means in furthering its interest, should a compelling interest exist.

In 1997, however, the Supreme Court struck down the RFRA as it applied to the states. Accordingly, federal prisoners may bring claims under the RFRA, but state prisoners may not. Congress responded by enacting the Religious Land Use and Institutionalized Persons Act of 2000 (RLUIPA), 42 U.S.C. § 2000cc, *et seq.*, using very similar language to the RFRA so that claims brought under RLUIPA are likewise analyzed under the three-part standard listed above. *Cutter v. Wilkinson*, 544 U.S. 709, 722-723 (2005). Unlike the RFRA, the RLUIPA has been upheld by the Supreme Court in its application to state prisoners, but only insofar as to protect programs that receive the assistance of federal money. *Id.*, 544 U.S. at 715-716. This means that the RLUIPA applies to almost all state prisons and jails. *Id.*, 544 U.S. at 725, n.4 ("Every State . . . accepts federal funding for its prisons."). (However, a few local correctional agencies may not accept federal funding, and thus, won't be subject to the RLUIPA.) Private companies contracted to state or local agencies that accept federal funding are also bound by the strictures of the RLUIPA.

The type of relief available to prisoners under both the RFRA and the RLUIPA has not been firmly settled by the courts. The law on this point is complicated; read carefully:

- Punitive damages are not available in suits against a government entity or the official capacity of a government agent. *City of Newport v. Fact Concerts, Inc.*, 453 U.S. 247 (1981).

- Money damages are not available against a state or an arm-of-state, though nominal or compensatory damages may be available against municipalities (e.g., counties, cities, towns).
- Individual capacity suits are not available under either the RFRA or the RLUIPA. *See, e.g., Rendelman v. Rouse*, 569 F.3d 182, 187-189 (4th Cir. 2009).
- The PLRA restricts awards of compensatory damages to cases where physical injury or sexual assault is shown in addition to emotional injury (violations of religious rights are emotional injuries, by recent court trend). It does not however, restrict awards of punitive or nominal damages.

From the above enumeration, it follows that RFRA or RLUIPA claims connot be brought against individual persons, but only against government entities or persons in their official government capacities. Under these two statutes, only injunctive relief is available against the federal government (RFRA) or the states or arms-of-states (RLUIPA), though municipalities may be subject to both injunctions and nominal damages (compensatory damages would be available, too, if, somehow, the deprivation of religious liberty—an emotional injury—is accompanied by physical injury or sexual assault as well.

NOTE: Don't forget to **check your state statutes**. Many states have enacted legislation very similar to the RFRA and the RLUIPA. Consider combining multiple claims. For example, you can bring a First Amendment claim and separate RLUIPA claim in the same lawsuit. You may also assert a claim under a state statute similar to the RFRA and the RLUIPA, because federal courts have supplemental jurisdiction to hear state claims arising under the same set of facts that give rise to federal claims. The strategy here is that where one claim may not survive for determination at trial, another might.

The specifics of what, precisely, may be allowed in a given prison to accommodate prisoners' right to practice religion varies on a case-by-case basis. The protections summarized and the standards for analyzing religious claims described in this section are interpreted and applied differently jurisdiction to jurisdiction, state to state, even institution to institution. An anticipated faith-based claim must therefore be built upon research of authority generated in a particular jurisdiction—look at what federal courts have been permitting prisoners in your federal circuit of appeals. Remember, also, that what one prison allows for religious accommodation can depend on many security concerns that may or may not be present at other facilities. Because a prison can justify a prohibition of a religious practice does not automatically mean others can, too.

This inconsistency makes it difficult to pin down what prisoners can expect as a matter of religious freedom. A broad picture can be painted, however. Courts have generally held prisoners to enjoy the following:

1. The right to meet with a personal spiritual advisor;
2. The right to religious accouterment such as religious medallions or beads, prayer oils, headgear, robes, prayer rugs, runestones, tarot cards, candles and incense (the use of which is often supervised);
3. The right to wear religious hair and facial-hair styles;
4. The right to religious name changes. (Although the law surrounding this right is unclear. Prisoners may change their names for religious purposes, and generally may not be prevented from using their new names when completing commissary, sick-call,

grievance, and other institutional forms. However, administrators need not amend existing inmate files to reflect the name change, nor are they required to use the name when its use would cause confusion for administrative operations. And prison staff may address inmates by the names under which they were first committed to prison; courts will not force guards to address inmates in any particular way.)

5. The right to group services and participation in special religious events;

6. The right to special religious diets. (For small faith groups, this accommodation can be problematic from a legal standpoint. So long as the accommodation of the diet does not cause a significant administrative difficulty and costs are not prohibitive, then, under the Constitution and federal statutes, prisoners ought to be provided the diets their faith demands. But prisons usually aren't required to accommodate numerous religious diets for numerous religious sects.)

7. The right to the above-listed for inmates housed in segregation, if safety or security issues do not dictate otherwise. (Whether prisoners in disciplinary segregation retain the right to attend religious services is unsettled. Many courts have upheld bars for the duration of segregation; others have not. The legal justification seems to turn on whether a particular inmate poses security dangers warranting isolation even from the group services of his or her preferred faith.)

You Have Limited Rights to Privacy and Against Search and Seizure

The Fourth Amendment forbids "unreasonable searches and seizures." Yet it is conclusive: Prisoners have little reasonable expectation of privacy within their cells. Cells may be subject to search without a warrant. *Hudson v. Palmer*, 468 U.S. 517, 104 S.Ct. 3194, 60 L.Ed.2d 447 (1984). Prisoners do not have the right to monitor the search of their cells. *Bell v. Wolfish*, 441 U.S. 520, 555 (1979). And cell searches may be conducted at random, though the Eighth Amendment protects against searches that would rise to the level of harassment. With regard to pretrial detainees, however, there is case law to support the proposition that, even though prison officials may, for security reasons, conduct cell searches without fear of infringing upon inmates' protected rights, warrantless cell searches initiated by prosecutors or law enforcement for the purpose of obtaining evidence in a criminal investigation can violate the Fourth Amendment. *U.S. v. Cohen*, 796 F.2d 20 (2nd Cir. 1986). But this nevertheless leaves little room for personal right to privacy while incarcerated, for cells and common areas may be subject to electronic eavesdropping and video monitoring, and inmate informers may be planted without risk of violating the Fourth Amendment. *U.S. v. White*, 401 U.S. 745 (1971); *Shell v. U.S.*, 448 F.3d 951 (7th Cir. 2006). Even private phone conversations may be recorded and monitored (except calls with attorneys) when notice of recording or monitoring is given.

Seizure of an inmate's property by prison officials does not constitute a Fourth Amendment violation if the seizure serves legitimate institutional interests. Should a correctional officer elect to confiscate an inmate's property with no just cause, a viable Fourth Amendment claim may arise. (A common scenario is when a guard confiscates property that is old and no longer sold through the prison commissary. If the property is taken despite the prisoner's proof of ownership and prison policy or custom of "grandfathering" such items, a claim may be stated. However, a simple state tort for theft might be more expedient than a constitutional claim.) (*See* "Deprivation of Property" under "You Have the Right to Procedural Due Process," below, for more on rights concerning inmate property.)

Prisoners do enjoy a reasonable expectancy of privacy over the content of their legal papers, criminal and civil. If privileged attorney-client or court papers are read during a search, not just inspected for contraband, this may give rise to a First Amendment violation of the attorney-client privilege. If the search (particularly in cases of confiscation) interferes with the inmate's ability to file or prosecute a legal action, a viable access-to-courts claim may exist. Other privileged documents such as medical records are also protected, under the Fourth Amendment, yet this protection may yield to a legitimate penological goal.

Physical privacy is another issue often raised, and the courts have upheld inmates' rights to some degree in this regard. The right to privacy under the Fourth Amendment, insofar as it still exists for incarcerated persons, does not extend to prevent prison staff from conducting body cavity searches of inmates, if, considering the prison environment and circumstances in question, the search is *reasonable*. "The test of reasonableness under the Fourth Amendment is not capable of precise definition or mechanical application. In each case it requires a balancing of the need for the particular search against the invasion of personal rights that the search entails. Courts must consider the scope of the particular intrusion, the manner in which it is conducted, the justification for initiating it, and the place in which it is conducted." *Bell*, 441 U.S. at 559.

By this standard of "reasonableness," physical body cavity searches, such as rectal or vaginal cavity searches, are not permitted as a matter of prison routine, but when justified on a particular basis only. Such invasive procedures have been found justified when (1) prison staff have a reasonable cause to search an inmate; (2) the search served a valid penological goal; and (3) the search was undertaken in a reasonable way. *Wiley v. Serrano*, 37 Fed.Appx. 252 (9th Cir. 2002).

Pat- and strip-searches, on the other hand, may be conducted by prison staff on a freer basis, though not a liberal basis. Male inmates may be pat- and strip-searched by male guards *and* by female guards, who may also have regular access to prison areas in which they would see male inmates use the toilet and shower facilities. Male guards, however, may not so broadly infringe upon female inmates' right to personal privacy where avoidable (*Jordan v. Gardner*, 986 F.2d 1521 (9th Cir. 1993)), unless, of course, emergency circumstances justify such searches. *Lee v. Downs*, 641 F.2d 1117 (4th Cir. 1981). While conducting a pat-search, whatever the gender of the inmate or officer, prison officers may not unnecessarily fondle inmates' genitals—if suspected that contraband is hidden in the genital region, a strip-search may be appropriate, not a groping. Additionally, during a visual cavity search, to expect inmates to first manipulate their genitals (lifting or spreading), and then to insert their fingers into their mouths is unreasonable; a guard can easily inspect the mouth before the genitals.

Finally, prisons are allowed to require inmates to produce urine samples for drug testing, and may take blood or cell samples for DNA records. Seizures of cell samples for use in creating DNA databases have generally been upheld in cases of violent offenders and sex offenders. Some courts have upheld this practice for prisoners charged with lesser crimes, under the rationale that the government has a legitimate interest in identifying recidivist offenders. (*See generally* "Privacy, Search & Seizures" in "PART 5," below.)

You Have the Right to Be Safe and to Be Housed Under Humane Conditions

Harsh prison conditions and rough disciplinary treatment are expected (and are constitutional) as a matter of course in federal and state penological systems, so long as this punishment does not reach the level of cruel and unusual, as prohibited by the Eighth Amendment. *Rhodes v. Chapman*, 452 U.S. 337, 346 (1981). To determine if conduct is constitutionally cruel and unusual, courts must first distinguish (1) conduct that is part of the penalty formally imposed for a crime against society from (2) conduct that is not part of a criminal penalty but instead relates to conditions of confinement.

1. *Formally imposed* **punishment is cruel and unusual** if it involves "the unnecessary and wanton infliction of pain" ("wanton" means malicious or uncalled-for) such as punishment "totally without penological justification" or "grossly out of proportion to the severity of the crime." *Gregg v. Georgia*, 428 U.S. 153, 173, 183, (1976). This standard relates to criminal sentences and the government's imposition of criminal sentences. Under this standard, the government cannot, for instance, require prisoners to serve their terms manacled to a wall, and inmates cannot be sentenced to death for stealing a candy bar. Legal claims concerning formally imposed punishment are usually challenged during criminal proceedings, either before sentencing or after sentencing, through direct appeal or *habeas* proceeding. Such a claim must show that
    i.   the punishment is unnecessary or malicious; or
    ii. grossly out of proportion to the severity of the crime.

2. *Prison-official-imposed* **punishment or conduct that is not part of the formal penalty** imposed for a crime violates the Eighth Amendment when (1) a "sufficiently serious" deprivation has occurred (the objective test), and (2) officials have acted with a "sufficiently culpable [guilty] state of mind" (the subjective test). This standard controls prisoners' claims challenging conditions of confinement. The successful prisoner-litigant must show that:
    i.   Under the objective test: A sufficiently serious deprivation or injury; and
    ii. Under the subjective test: A sufficiently guilty mind. (Guilty mind may be established by a showing of "deliberate indifference," discussed below.)

Under the objective test, only factual evidence of a sufficiently serious deprivation will support an Eighth Amendment **conditions of confinement** claim. What types of deprivations are "sufficiently serious"? The Supreme Court has instructed that "only those deprivations denying the minimal civilized measure of life's necessities . . . are sufficiently grave to form the basis of an Eighth Amendment violation." *Wilson v. Seiter*, 501 U.S. 294, 298 (1991) .

Overcrowding, for example, a major problem most prisons currently face in the United States, does not, itself, violate the Eighth Amendment, unless *specific* deprivations of life's necessities are also alleged to be caused by prison overfill. Actionable deprivations include, but are not limited to, consequences of overcrowding such as increase of violence or of anxiety among inmates, or diminished essential services such as medical care. Lack of adequate food or water, shower or toilet facilities, hygiene, sanitation, clean bedding or clothing, physical exercise or time out-of-doors, lighting, ventilation or endurable air conditions; lack of protection from fire hazards or hazardous substances, gases, fungi, smoke, or radiation have also supported successful court actions. (Although *brief* deprivations of some of the above causes, such as clean clothing, won't create a constitutional violation.)

Double-celling, like general prison overcrowding, has been much litigated and determined to be constitutional, unless it can be shown that the cell was originally designed for a single inmate and that it is, indeed, too small to house two inmates without causing a deprivation of a life's necessity. This determination turns on case-specific factors, including dayroom access, time spent in cell, space to exercise, and other aspects in this vein relating to cell life.

Nothing so amorphous as "overall conditions" can support an Eighth Amendment claim. But, where one or two encumbrances or inconveniences may not be sufficient for a cause of action, multiple smaller issues can add up to a single, identifiable and actionable harm. *Wilson*, 501 U.S. at 305. Uncomfortable conditions are allowed, however, which can include lengthy periods of punitive segregation, though excessive periods of segregation can violate the Eighth Amendment if duration is greatly disproportionate to the inmate's offense or other cause for isolation. Prisoners do not need to first endure this type of extreme treatment before filing an action with a court, nor, indeed, do they need to await a deprivation of life's necessities if it can be shown that serious risks exist and harm will likely occur in the future. *Helling v. McKinney*, 509 U.S. 25 (1993) ("It would be odd to deny an injunction to inmates who plainly proved an unsafe, life-threatening condition in their prison on the ground that nothing yet had happened to them.").

Along with the objective requirement of a sufficiently serious harm (or risk of harm), to complete an Eighth Amendment claim evidence must be produced that demonstrates either (1) officials' intent to harm the prisoner(s) or (2) officials' knowledge of a risk of harm, which they failed to act to prevent. Either of the two satisfies the subjective requirement of an Eighth Amendment claim—yet it must be noted that conduct on the part of prison officials in furtherance of legitimate penological interests will not usually reflect the required culpable state of mind. The **deliberate indifference** test is generally dispositive to conditions-of-confinement cases, and must be satisfied in cases alleging deprivation in isolated incidents of harm as well as in cases alleging deprivations in overall prison conditions. Deliberate indifference is shown by proving that officials

1. knew of the risk of harm; and
2. failed to take reasonable steps to prevent it.

Excessive force is another much-litigated species of Eighth Amendment violation. Excessive-force claims frequently arise in the prison context when officials are required to use physical means to restore order. This ranges from shooting an escapee or rioter to forcing cell extractions, macing mutual combatants, or to the force used in placing on restraints. Excessive-force claims, as with other Eighth Amendment claims, are comprised of an objective and a subjective element.

Although similar to the objective element of harm in Eighth Amendment prison-conditions claims or claims of inadequate medical treatment (discussed in the next section), the objective element in excessive-force claims need not rise to the level of "significant" injury. *Wilkins v. Gaddy*, 559 U.S. 34 (2010), 130 S.Ct 1175, 1178 (2010). (Whether prison officials acted with culpable state of mind is key to an excessive-force injury, not whether the prisoner has suffered a certain degree of injury.) Otherwise, officials could permissibly inflict any amount of "physical punishment, no matter how diabolic or inhuman," so long as injury is less than some arbitrary quantity. *Hudson v. McMillian*, 503 U.S. 1, 9-10 (1992).

The subjective element of excessive-force claims, too, departs from that of other Eighth Amendment claims in that the deliberate indifference standard does not apply. Rather, the excessive-force standard of culpability asks whether force was applied "maliciously and sadistically." *Id.*, 503 U.S. at 7. Provided a sufficient injury (less than a significant injury) to satisfy the objective element, courts ask the following when determining if the necessary guilty mind existed behind the infliction of harm:

1. What was the need behind the application of force?
2. Was the amount of force used justified by the need?
3. What was the extent of the threat to the safety of prisoners or staff as reasonably perceived by the officers applying the force?
4. What efforts were employed by officers to use as little force as necessary?

Id., 503 U.S. at 7; citing *Whitley v. Albers*, 475 U.S. 312, 321 (1986). Simply put, the courts look to ascertain whether prison officials acted reasonably under the circumstances—were their actions unnecessary or conducted with malice? (*See generally* "Eighth Amendment" in "PART 5," below.)

Lastly, recall that the PLRA does not allow for money damages in compensation for emotional or mental injuries without showing physical injury or sexual assault also was suffered. Conditions-of-confinement cases pose challenges (though not insurmountable challenges) to damages awards of this kind. The injury sustained to establish an excessive-force claim may satisfy the injury requirement of the PLRA. (*See* PLRA discussion in "Chapter 11.")

You Have the Right to Adequate Medical Care

It would also be cruel and unusual to refuse medical care to prisoners who, while incarcerated, cannot obtain this service for themselves. And since medical care would be meaningless without treatment to sufficiently attend or remedy a particular medical issue, the Eighth Amendment must then impose on prison administrators an affirmative duty to provide inmates with adequate medical care. (This care need not be free-of-charge—usually, prisons charge between $5.00 and $10.00 per medical visit—so long as inability to pay does not deprive inmates of adequate medical care.) "Adequate" medical care is that which is on a level with modern medical science, and that which is provided within limits acceptable under the professional standards required generally of health service and medical providers. *Fernandez v. U.S.*, 941 F.2d 1488, 1493 (11th Cir. 1991); *U.S. v. DeCologero*, 821 F.2d 39, 43 (1st Cir. 1987). "Adequate medical care" is well-settled to cover the following:

- Non-*deminimus* physical injuries or acute bodily ailment or disabilities;
- Eye and dental issues;
- Dangerous diseases such as HIV and hepatitis;
- Medically necessary diets;
- Pre- and post-natal issues; and
- Psychological issues, including but not limited to depression, PTSD, schizophrenia, and gender identity disorder (GID).

In addition, prison officials must take prophylactic measures to prevent reasonably foreseeable medical risks, such as to isolate inmates known to have dangerous infectious diseases from the general population or to prevent sick inmates from exposure to circumstances or substances that could worsen their illnesses.

Prison officials cannot, however, be held in violation of their constitutional duty to provide prisoners medical care if the officials did not know of a medical problem. Constitutional medical claims are judged under the deliberate-indifference standard, which requires a successful showing that:

1. A serious medical condition exists or existed ;
2. A prison official, or doctor, or medical company was aware of the condition;
3. The official or provider failed to adequately treat the condition, causing harm.

(*See* "Estell v. Gamble" in the previous chapter.)

The second and third elements of the above list form the subjective deliberate-indifference component necessary to an Eighth Amendment medical claim (which is commonly evinced later in court by documents such as denied prison grievances and administrative appeals). Consequently, wardens and other supervisors are not deliberately indifferent when they act in reliance upon the judgment of qualified medical personnel. *Spruill v. Gillis*, 372 F.3d 218, 236 (3rd Cir. 2004) (prison officials cannot be held liable for medical mistreatment unless they have reason to believe, or actual knowledge of, mistreatment or non-treatment). Medical personnel, however, are usually contracted to the government to provide an essential service to prisoners and therefore may be held liable under the Eighth Amendment. The Eight Amendment, unfortunately, does not create a cause of action for mere negligence or medical malpractice, though a series of such or continuation with an ineffective course of treatment may amount to constitutional deliberate indifference. *Greeno v. Daley*, 414 F.3d 645, 655 (7th Cir. 2005); *White v. Napoleon*, 897 F.2d 103, 109 (3rd Cir. 1990).

Negligence or malpractice, though not actionable under the Constitution, is usually actionable under state tort law, provided evidence can be mustered to prove a breach of professional duty. The United States may be held liable under the specific substantive cause of action for medical malpractice of the Federal Tort Claims Act. *McNeil v. U.S.*, 508 U.S. 106 (1993).

In addition to tort law and constitutional guarantees, two pieces of federal legislation grant greater protection to inmates who suffer disability. The public entity section of Title II of the Americans with Disabilities Act (ADA) provides that

> no qualified individual with a disability shall, by reason of such disability,
> be excluded from participation in or be denied the benefits of the services,
> programs, or activities of a public entity, or be subject to discrimination
> by any such entity.

42 U.S.C. § 1232. Section 504 of the Rehabilitation Act (RA), the second piece of legislation, says much the same as the ADA. 29 U.S.C. § 794(a). Both titles grant protection to disabled inmates; the difference between the ADA and the RA is that federal agencies and prisons are not subject to the ADA, but to the RA.

A "qualified individual" under the ADA (and the RA has a similar definition for "handicapped" persons, 29 U.S.C. § 706(7)(8)) is a person with a physical or mental impairment that substantially limits one or more major life activities. 42 U.S.C. § 12102(1). This definition embraces many forms of disability and has been interpreted to reach addiction to drugs. "Drug addiction that significantly limits a major life activity is a recognized disability under the ADA," provided the individual is not currently using illegal drugs and has completed, or is in the process of completing, a supervised rehabilitative drug program. *Thompson v. Davis*, 295 F.3d 890, 896 (9th Cir. 2002).

Injunctive relief and compensatory damages are available under both the ADA and the RA, but not punitive damages. *Barns v. Gorman*, 536 U.S. 181, 188-189 (2002). However, damages are generally unavailable in official capacity suits, but not in individual capacity suits. ADA suits against states or arms-of-stats raise Eleventh Amendment immunity questions that may preclude an award of damages (though damages should be available against other government entities like counties, cities, towns and other municipalities). If state or arms-of-state conduct violates both the ADA and the Constitution, compensatory damages are generally permitted. *U.S. v. Georgia*, 546 U.S. 151, 155-160 (2006). To recover damages under either the ADA or the RA (if damages are available), a successful plaintiff must demonstrate a discriminative motive behind a deprivation. The plaintiff will have to prove that defendants acted with deliberate indifference or the intent to discriminate. *Garcia v. S.U.N.Y. Health Services of Brooklyn*, 280 F.3d 98, 112 (2nd Cir. 2000).

You Have the Right to Procedural Due Process

Prisoners, like other U.S. citizens, are assured by provisions of the Fifth and Fourteenth Amendments to the U.S. Constitution that they cannot be deprived of life, liberty, or property without due process of law. (*See generally* "Due Process" in "PART 5," below.)

The right of "due process" exists in two forms: substantive and procedural. The substantive component of the Fifth and Fourteenth Amendments' Due Process Clause bars arbitrary government conduct, regardless of the ultimate fairness of the procedures involved. The procedural component of the right to due process (of most interest to our discussions here) requires implementation of adequate procedural process before the government may deprive one of life, liberty, or property, regardless of the ultimate fairness or lawfulness of the deprivation itself. Courts ask two fundamental questions when first evaluating a procedural due process claim:

1. Has the government deprived (or does it intend to deprive) a protected life, liberty, or property interest?
2. Are the procedural safeguards currently in place sufficient to avoid erroneous deprivations?

Precisely what procedural safeguards are sufficient to meet constitutional minimums is a question that depends on the circumstances of a particular case. Courts must balance a private right with government interests (which include the practicality of proposed measures, efficiency, and costs of implementing new policy) and the *usefulness* of additional procedures. Determining the usefulness of additional procedures involves a determination of whether existing procedures are inadequate to prevent erroneous deprivations. *Mathews v. Eldridge*, 424 U.S. 319, 96 S.Ct. 893, 47 L.Ed.2d 18 (1976) (the process due depends on (1) the effect on the private interest at issue; (2) the effect on government interests should a particular procedure be used; and (3) the usefulness of the particular procedure to the process, with regard to potential error should the procedure not be adopted).

The right of inmates to send and receive letters, for example, has been balanced against the government's interest in safe and orderly prison operations. Provided a legitimate government interest, letters may be censored or rejected. However, due process requires—regardless of whether such deprivation is ultimately lawful—that prison officials ensure (1) prisoners are notified when letters, in-coming or out-going, are refused; (2) a letter's author is afforded an opportunity to challenge the decision; and (3) disputes over such decisions are resolved by officials other than the officials who originally denied or confiscated the correspondence. (*See* "Procunier v. Martinez" in the previous chapter.) Should any of these three steps be omitted, a procedural due process claim may arise.

However, the right of prisoners to correspondence is one of only a few liberty interests to have received this kind of specific delineation of procedural due process protections. The due process ambiguities surrounding other rights start with whether a right is entitled to due process protection under the Constitution. That prisoners have a right to live is, of course, well-settled, and there are many specific due-process safeguards to prevent wrongful deprivations of this right. Deprivation of property, too, has been discussed at length by the judiciary and is addressed later in this section.

The major source of uncertainty is the term "liberty" or "liberty interest." Some liberties are easily identified, such as those specifically named in the Constitution; others are harder to nail down. There are three broad sources of procedurally protected liberty interests:

1. The Due Process Clause itself;
2. A court order; or
3. State statutes and/or regulations.

Substantive rights under the Due Process Clause protect prisoners from arbitrary or capricious government conduct and thus involve questions of fundamental fairness. For example, it is clear law that prison authorities may isolate inmates as punishment for institutional infractions, and that inmates are not entitled to comfortable housing conditions as a matter of right. If, however, such punitive conditions are exceptionally harsh, when "qualitatively different from the punishment characteristically suffered by a person convicted of crime," due process guarantees may be invoked. *Sandin v. Conner*, 515 U.S. 472, 115 S.Ct. 2293, 2297 (1995). Which is to say that such conditions must go beyond the criminal "sentence in such an unexpected manner as to give rise to protection of the Due Process Clause of its own force." *Id.*, 115 S.Ct. at 2300.

Court orders are issued to direct conduct, that is, to require a specific course of action (or non-action). If the conditions of a standing court order directing the conduct of government officials are not met, a due process claim may arise. The provisions of the court order themselves create the "liberty interest"; should the interest face government interference, the court will evaluate whether procedures protecting the interest are adequate to prevent undue deprivation of the rights created under the order.

The state-created liberty interest provides a greater variety of protections, but also a greater cause of uncertainty in definitions of due process. Whether prisoners can claim constitutional due process protection of an interest created under state law depends crucially upon the wording of the particular piece of legislation creating the liberty. For a state statute or regulation to create a protected liberty interest under the U.S. Constitution, two things must be true: (1) the statute or regulation must set rules to govern the decisions of officials, and (2) the language of the statute or regulation must *explicitly* direct official conduct (i.e., a definite "shall" or "must" directive to the decision-maker, which mandates a certain outcome and thus removes the possibility of an outcome based on the discretion of the official). *Kentucky Dep't of Corr. v. Thompson*, 490 U.S. 454, 462-463, 109 S.Ct. 1904, 104 L.Ed.2d 506

(1989). (*NOTE:* The state statute or regulation creating the liberty interest *must* be specified in the body of a due process complaint.)

There is another catch for a successful due process claim. The Supreme Court decided in *Sandin v. Conner* (discussed in the previous chapter) to narrow the protections of the Due Process Clause as it applies to the incarcerated. After *Sandin*, in addition to demonstrating both a state-created liberty interest and a deprivation of adequate procedural process, prisoners must also show an **atypical and significant hardship**. Due process protections, therefore, are only available when a restriction or deprivation of a state-created liberty interest does either of the following:

1. Creates an "atypical and significant hardship"; that is, conditions imposed on the prisoner are very different from the ordinary conditions experiences by the general population of prisoners; or
2. Affects the duration of the prisoner's sentence.

The first requirement is a tough standard to meet, and it applies to just about anything having to do with institutional disciplinary matters, which is a concern often forming the basis of prisoner due-process claims. If an "atypical and significant hardship on the inmate in relation to the ordinary incidents of prison life" cannot be shown to pertain to a state-created liberty interest, then the prisoner simply cannot expect to prevail on a due-process action under the U.S. Constitution. For example, brief stays in the hole, courts have held, do not depart greatly from normal prison life, and will not usually give rise to a cognizable due-process claim, though the law in this area is unsettled. Whether a hardship is "atypical" is a question of law for the court to determine (however, the jury, or the judge in a bench trial, must resolve the facts surrounding the denial of due process, if reasonably in dispute, before the law can be applied). And courts have been inconsistent in this application. Some courts have held ninety days in disciplinary segregation sufficient to invoke due process protections; other courts, six months to one year. A few courts have even surpassed the year mark. Administrative segregation, on the other hand, must be imposed only upon the satisfaction of due process minimums. Although conditions of administrative (or protective) segregation commonly parallel those of disciplinary segregation, duration of inmate isolation is often much longer—year upon year, in fact. Therefore, the Supreme Court has identified in such lengthy segregation both liberty interest and atypical and significant hardship, warranting the due process protections of the Constitution. *Wilkinson v. Austin*, 545 U.S. 209 (2005).

If government conduct (e.g., disciplinary action) will eventually affect the length of a prisoner's criminal sentence, due process protections are implicated. Prisoners have a well-established liberty interest in being released from prison as provided within the court-imposed sentence for their criminal convictions, whether or not date of release is contingent upon good-time credit, pre-parole requirements, or full-term completion. However, deprivations of due process that affect fact of or duration of a criminal sentence are not normally cognizable through a federal civil-rights action, but usually only through a petition for writ of *habeas corpus*. This means that a due-process claim arising from, say, the withdrawal of good-time credits as a result of an institutional infraction cannot be redressed under the federal laws (e.g., § 1983 and *Bivens*) commonly used in prisoners' civil-rights cases. *Habeas corpus*, rather, is the proper vehicle for such challenges. (*See* "Heck v. Humphrey" in the previous chapter.) To be clear, this does not mean that all institutional disciplinary actions cannot be challenged by use of § 1983, *Bivens*, or FTCA. Purely procedural due-process claims, which do not necessarily require the reversal of a disciplinary decision affecting length of criminal sentence, are not banned by *Heck v. Humphrey* and may proceed as ordinary civil-rights actions.

Where state law contains mandatory language that entitles prisoners to release on parole provided the requisite conditions for parole are satisfied, prisoners then have a liberty interest in parole for the purposes of due process protection. *Greenholtz v. Inmates of Nebraska Penal & Corr. Complex*, 442 U.S. 1, 11-12, 14-16 (1979). Where state law contains discretionary language—the parole board "may" instead of "must" or "shall"—no liberty interest is created. *Bd. of Pardons v. Allen* 482 U.S. 369, 378-379 and n.10 (1987). Once parole is granted, however, a parolee has a protected liberty interest in remaining free and is entitled to certain procedural due process protections, which are "(a) written notice of the claimed violations of parole; (b) disclosure to the parolee of evidence against him; (c) opportunity to be heard in person and to present witnesses and documentary evidence; (d) the right to confront and cross-examine adverse witnesses (unless the hearing officer specifically finds good cause for not allowing confrontation); (e) a 'neutral and detached' hearing body such as a traditional parole board, members of which need not be judicial officers or lawyers; and (f) a written statement by the fact-finders as to the evidence relied on and reasons for revoking parole." *Morrissey v. Brewer*, 408 U.S. 471, 489 (1972) (citation omitted). The standard of evidence in parole revocation proceedings is the *preponderance of evidence*, rather than the *some evidence* standard required in institutional disciplinary proceedings.

Due process does not usually require that counsel be appointed to represent a parolee during revocation proceedings, unless a parole agency, in its discretion, finds substantial reason or circumstance that mitigates or refutes a parole violation, and where the parolee has requested counsel. *Gagon v. Scarpelli*, 411 U.S. 778, 790 (1973). Federal parolees, however, are always entitled to appointed legal representation as a matter of federal law. Parole Commission and Reorganization Act of 1976, Pub. L. 94-233, 90 Stat. 219 (1976).

The Supreme Court, in addition to the due process minimums described for revocation of parole, has, to date, specifically addressed the procedural floor in four other prisoner-related contexts:

1. Should the government intend to forcibly administer antipsychotic drugs to an unwilling inmate, the inmate is entitled to
    i.   notice of this intention;
    ii. opportunity to be present when the psychiatrist presents his or her findings to the hearing officials; and
    iii. opportunity to cross-examine adverse witnesses.

2. Should the government intend to non-consensually transfer an inmate to a mental hospital, the inmate is entitled to
    i.   written notice of this intention;
    ii. meaningful opportunity to speak in his or her own defense during the hearing on the matter;
    iii. reasonable opportunity to offer evidence and to call and cross-examine witnesses;
    iv. written statements detailing the evidence and the reasons relied upon by the fact-finders in support of the decision to transfer the inmate;

     v. limited right to assistance, where assistance is necessary to satisfy the protections of due process; and

    vi. precise notice of these rights.

3. Should the government intend, as a disciplinary measure, to deprive an inmate of a protected liberty interest, a deprivation creating an atypical and significant hardship, the inmate is entitled to

     i. twenty-four-hour advance written notice of the hearing to determine the alleged violation of institutional rules;

    ii. meaningful opportunity to speak in his or her own defense during the hearing on the matter;

   iii. reasonable opportunity to offer evidence and to call and cross-examine witnesses (but only if cross-examination would not be inconsistent with correctional goals or institutional safety); and

   iv. written statements detailing the evidence and the reasons relied upon by the fact-finders in support of disciplinary action.

4. Should the government intend to place an inmate in administrative segregation, the inmate is entitled to

     i. written notice of institutional charges or reasons for the segregation;

    ii. an informal hearing (which does not include the right to call and cross-examine witnesses) within a reasonable time after segregation;

   iii. meaningful opportunity to speak in his or her own defense during the informal hearing; and

   iv. meaningful periodic review (every 120 days is constitutionally sufficient) to determine whether segregation remains appropriate.

The observance of these steps must, of course, be meaningful. Empty gestures in which officials merely move through a protocol without genuine deliberation at each stage are antithetical to acceptable notions of meaningful due process. This concept of "meaningfulness," it follows, excludes biased or prejudiced fact-finders and board members from serving as hearing officers, and prohibits decisions based only upon conjecture or speculation. Officers who are involved in the making of *disciplinary* charges should be ineligible to serve on the hearing board ultimately responsible for deciding the veracity of the charges. And evidence, while it need not be admissible under the strictures of court rules of evidence, must still be reliable evidence. *See generally Sira v. Morton*, 300 F.3d 57 (2nd Cir. 2004). The amount of evidence, furthermore, must be enough to allow a decision to stand on a rational basis. This does not entitle a prisoner to a beyond-a-reasonable-doubt standard of proof, but does grant a prisoner the assurance that a disciplinary decision cannot, judiciously, be upheld without that decision being based upon "some evidence." *Superintendent v. Hill*, 472 U.S. 445, 454 (1985).

The burden of some reliable evidence is not, however, very difficult for administrators to bear. Hearsay and the testimony of prison informants can constitutionally support an adverse decision, provided the testimony has passable indications of reliability, generally that there exists corroborating evidence (even if only statements of another informant), and that the informant has been independently determined by the hearing board to be reliable. Whether officials must allow a prisoner to cross-examine his or her accusers depends on whether there is an overriding reason not to. If refused, prison officials must give an explanation, either on the hearing record or later in court, that is reasonably related to institutional safety or correctional goals. That a prison informant's identity will be, of necessity, revealed if officials permit his or her cross-examination by the accused prisoner is usually sufficient reason to prevent the confrontation, in view of the very real possibility of inmate-on-inmate retaliation.

NOTE: Forewarning, when preparing a defense to institutional charges, remember that the Supreme Court, in *Baxter v. Palmigiano*, 425 U.S. 308 (1976), held that inmates are not protected by the Fifth Amendment right to silence in prison disciplinary matters, and that a hearing board can, indeed, use the fact of an accused inmate's silence against him or her. *Id.*, 425 U.S. at 319-320. However, should the inmate be compelled by authorities to speak at a disciplinary proceeding, he or she is entitled to at least use immunity at any subsequent criminal prosecution. *Id.*, 425 U.S. at 316. The prosecution may be commenced, even if premised significantly on the evidence revealed in the compelled testimony, though that evidence itself may not be admissible at the criminal trial. *Kastigar v. U.S.*, 406 U.S. 441, 92 S.Ct. 1653, 32 L.Ed.2d 212 (1972).

A prisoner unlawfully **deprived of property** may bring a procedural due-process claim against the government. Destruction, loss, or damage to property is actionable under the Due Process Clause of the Fourteenth Amendment when state officials/agents act intentionally and abusively. This cause of action includes interference with property rights in existence before incarceration. *King v. Federal Bureau of Prisons*, 415 F.3d 634 (7th Cir. 2005) (although inmates can be prohibited from conducting business while in prison, prisoners cannot be prevented from protecting property interests already in existence at the time of incarceration). Mere negligence, it must be stressed, is not enough to support a constitutional claim; specific intention to deprive must be shown. *Daniels v. Williams*, 474 U.S. 327 (1986). But in any case, Fourteenth Amendment due-process claims are not actionable unless state law does not itself provide adequate procedural remedies by which a prisoner might challenge the unauthorized or intentional deprivation of personal property. Should a state's post-deprivation remedies be wholly lacking or ineffectual, a Fourteenth Amendment due-process claim may be permitted. *Hudson v. Palmer*, 468 U.S. 517, 104 S.Ct. 3194, 60 L.Ed.2d 447 (1984). In many federal circuits, a state tort action is often viewed as an adequate post-deprivation remedy, which means a prisoner may not bring a federal suit without first attempting to resolve his or her claims in state court, under state law. (If, for instance, your TV is intentionally broken during a cell search, you will likely have to sue under tort principles in state court.)

There is an exception. The substantive component of due process protection—as opposed to the procedural component regarding property deprivation, addressed previously— allows for a constitutional cause of action when a deprivation of property is the result of a wider prison policy. The Due Process Clause is implicated if a property deprivation occurred as a result of "an affirmatively established or de facto policy, procedure, or custom, which the state has the power to control." *Abbot v. McCotter*, 13 F.3d 1439, 1443 (10th Cir. 1994) (citation omitted); *see also Bernardino Physicians' Serv. Med. Co., Inc. v. San Bernardino County*, 825 F.2d 1404, 1410 (9th Cir. 1987).

Pretrial Detainees May Not Be Punished

The Supreme Court has explained that the rights of pretrial detainees stem from the Fourteenth Amendment's Due Process Clause, as well as from the other substantive guarantees of the Constitution; and that detainees enjoy at least as much protection under the Due Process

Clause as convicted prisoners enjoy under the Eighth Amendment. (*See* "Bell v. Wolfish" in the previous chapter.) The major difference between rights of convicted prisoners and rights of pretrial detainees is that pretrial detainees may not receive punitive treatment; they have not been convicted of a crime. Detainees may, however, receive jail infractions, because jails generally have overriding interests in maintaining discipline, order, and security.

Judicial standards of review that apply to convicted prisoners generally apply to pretrial detainees also. For instance, courts usually defer to the experience of prison officials when deciding whether a particular regulation is reasonably related to a legitimate government interest. This defense, therefore, can be expected in determinations of whether a jail policy serves a legitimate interest other than punishment, holding inapplicable any heightened standard of review beyond that which the claims of convicted prisoners receive. Simply put, courts determine whether impositions on pretrial detainees comport with the substantive protections of the Due Process Clause by ascertaining whether the jail action is *punitive* or whether it is *reasonably related to a legitimate and non-punitive governmental purpose.* Legitimate, non-punitive governmental interests have been held to include random cell searches, pat- and strip-searches, restrictions on visitation (even banning contact visits altogether), restriction on phone use, disciplinary segregation, suspension of privileges such as access to commissary, and other matters related to jail security and internal order.

The Due Process Clause, like the Eighth Amendment in cases of convicted prisoners, mandates that pretrial detainees be housed under humane conditions (which includes prevention of inmate-on-inmate violence), and imposes on the government an affirmative duty to supply detainees with adequate medical care. *City of Revere v. Mass. General Hospital,* 463 U.S. 239, 244 (1983). Similar to Eighth Amendment claims brought by convicted prisoners, in substantive Due Process claims, "deliberate indifference" on the part of jail officials, not mere negligence or inadvertence, must be proved to successfully pursue a federal claim of inhumane living conditions or inadequate medical care.

Prisoners Do Not Usually Have the Right to Assistance of Counsel
Criminal defendants have an indisputable Sixth Amendment right to appointment of counsel, which extends to prisoners facing criminal prosecutions while already incarcerated for previous charges. However, the right to counsel strictly applies to criminal prosecutions proper (one must be criminally charged). The Sixth Amendment right to counsel does not apply in disciplinary- or administrative-segregation proceedings.

In parole revocation proceedings, parolees may have a due process right to appointment of counsel if a parole agency, or judge in subsequent court proceedings, finds substantial reason or circumstance that mitigates or refutes an alleged parole violation. (*See* "You Have the Right to Procedural Due Process," above.)

Pro se litigants pursuing civil-rights claims under federal law do not normally have a right to appointment of counsel. Whether counsel is appointed is within the discretion of the court, and is only appointed in the fundamental interest of justice and fair play where it is clear a litigant is incapable of representing him- or herself. And even if counsel is appointed, attorneys are under no obligation to accept an appointment by the court. (*See* subsection "Motion for Appointment of Counsel" in "Chapter 12," above.)

You Have the Right to Equal Protection

The Equal Protection Clause of the Fourteenth Amendment requires that the government treat similarly situated people the same, that one person or group not receive more nor less treatment than other persons of a similar circumstance. Prisoners retain *some* equal protection rights while incarcerated; however, prisoners' equal-protection claims that challenge prison policy or action are usually entitled only to the lesser "rational basis" examination.

The "rational-basis test" is a standard for the judicial analysis of a disputed statute or regulation or custom that does not implicate a fundamental right or a "suspect class," but, rather, implicates the lesser rights of the public or general prison population. (A **suspect class** is a group defined by race, national origin, or alienage (non-citizens) identified or particularly affected by statute or policy. An example of a law creating a suspect class of aliens is one that permits only U.S. citizens the advantage of welfare benefits. Such laws are subject to strict scrutiny for their lawfulness under the equal protections of the Constitution.) Under the rational-basis test, a court will uphold a law or a policy if it bears a reasonable relationship to a legitimate government interest.

Contrasting the rational-basis test, under the "strict scrutiny" standard a court can only uphold a law or a policy implicating a fundamental right (such as free speech) or a suspect class (such as a racial group) in an equal protection analysis if the government has established a "compelling interest" to justify its policy. Very few laws that have come under strict constitutional scrutiny have survived.

Prisoners, alas, consistently have been held not to be a suspect class for equal protection purposes. There were questions, once, of whether the PLRA created a suspect classification for inmates—which thus would require strict scrutiny of the PLRA's limitations on prisoners' federal civil-rights claims—but the issue has been resolved, and the prisoners lost. This loss goes for prisoner subclasses as well (e.g., indigent inmates, homosexual inmates, protective-custody inmates, etc.)

Under the lesser protection of the rational-basis test, prisoners may prevail on an equal-protection claim if they can establish two things:

1. That the government has treated them differently from similarly situated inmates; and
2. That no rational government interest exists for the dissimilar treatment.

Racial discrimination of prisoners, however, is a firm exception to the rational-basis standard. Racial issues are especially sensitive to public interest and courts are more prone to listen to claims of racially motivated discrimination. A federal claim of racial discrimination will prevail unless the government can prove that dissimilar treatment is "narrowly tailored" (extending no further than absolutely necessary) to advance a *compelling government interest*—the strict-scrutiny test. (This heightened test, to be clear, does not normally apply in claims of unequal treatment of prisoners based on religious preference, gender, or disability.)

NOTES: _____
_____
_____
_____
_____
_____
_____
_____
_____
_____
_____
_____
_____
_____
_____
_____
_____
_____
_____
_____
_____
_____
_____
_____
_____
_____
_____
_____
_____
_____
_____
_____
_____
_____
_____
_____
_____
_____
_____
_____

NOTES: _____
_____
_____
_____
_____
_____
_____
_____
_____
_____
_____
_____
_____
_____
_____
_____
_____
_____
_____
_____
_____
_____
_____
_____
_____
_____
_____
_____
_____
_____
_____
_____
_____
_____
_____
_____
_____
_____

PART 5:
CASE LAW

INTRODUCTION

The following section is a collection of topically arranged case citations, each of which is accompanied by a brief explanatory parenthetical summarizing the main point for which the material is being provided. The citations provided should in themselves be sufficient to familiarize the reader with the body of pertinent interpretive law for common issues arising within the prison setting. The reader will bear in mind that the case summaries herein are the interpretations of the author. Any cases intended to be relied upon should be obtained in their full published form, read carefully, and then shepardized. It is not enough to make legal conclusions based on brief parenthetical summaries. If you are unable to obtain copies of needed cases, do your best to cross-reference any findings or conclusions in this publication with other sources in your prison law library or resource center, or draft a list of citations to review with your local legal-beagle.

HOW TO READ CITATIONS:

Dannenberg v. Valadez, 338 F.3d 1070, 1074-75 (9th Cir. 2003)

"*Dannenberg v. Valadez*" is the name of the case. "338" is the volume in which the case is found. "F.3d" is the abbreviation for the *Federal Reporter Third Series*, the reporter publishing thousands of cases in thousands of volumes over three series. "1070" is the page where this particular case starts within the volume. "1074-75" is a pinpoint citation to two specific pages of the case. "(9th Cir. 2003)" indicates that the case was decided by Ninth Circuit Court of Appeal in the year 2003.

Lemon v. Krutzman, 403 U.S. 602, 612-613, 91 S.Ct. 2105, 2111, 29 L.Ed.2d 745, 755 (1971)

"*Lemon v. Krutzman*" is the name of the case. "403" is the volume in which the case is found. "U.S." is the abbreviation for the official reporter *United States Reports*. "602" is the page where this particular case starts in the volume. "612-13" is a pinpoint citation to two specific pages in the case. "91 S.Ct. 2105, 2111" and "29 L.Ed.2d 745, 755" are parallel citations to volume, beginning page, and pinpoint page in unofficial reporters also publishing this particular case, respectively the *Supreme Court Reporter* and the *Supreme Court Reporter, Lawyers Edition Second Series*. "(1971)" indicates that the United States Supreme Court decided the case in the year 1971.

ACCESS TO THE COURTS

Johnson v. Avery, 393 U.S. 483, 89 S.Ct. 747, 21 L.Ed.2d 718 (1967) (prisoners have a constitutional right to petition the government for redress of grievances, including a reasonable right of access to the courts).

California Motor Transport Co. v. Trucking Unlimited, 404 U.S. 508, 513, __S.Ct.__, __L.Ed.2d__ (1972) (the right of court access "is part of the right of petition protected by the First Amendment.").

Bounds v. Smith, 430 U.S. 817, 97 S.Ct. 1491, 52 L.Ed.2d 72 (1977) (plurality opinion) (prisoners have constitutional right to access of the courts, and must be provided with sufficient law libraries or sufficient assistance from persons trained in the law), *overruled in part by Lewis v. Casey*, 518 U.S. 343, 116 S.Ct. 2174, 135 L.Ed.2d 606 (1996).

Carter v. Hutto, 781 F.2d 1028 (4th Cir. 1986) (access-to-courts claim stated where prison officials confiscated and destroyed legal material).

Smith v. Erickson, 884 F.2d 1108 (8th Cir. 1989) (finding right of access to courts violated when prison officials refused to provide indigent inmates with free postage or supplies for legal mail because officials must furnish inmates with basic materials to draft and mail legal documents).

Gluth v. Kangas, 951 F.2d 1504, 1510 (9th Cir. 1992) ("[L]itigation necessarily requires some means of accurate duplication because the court and parties need to refer to the same documents . . . photocopying is a reasonably means of providing the necessary copies of petitions, complaints, answers, motions, affidavits, exhibits, memoranda and briefs, including attachments and appendices, material needed for discovery and investigation, including interrogatories and freedom of information requests.").

John L. v. Adams, 969 F.2d 228, 235 (6th Cir. 1992) (although prisoners do not enjoy state assistance in all civil matters that may arise under state law, "states may not erect barriers that impede the right of access of incarcerated persons.").

Alston v. DeBruyn, 13 F.3d 1036 (7th Cir. 1994) (segregated prisoners entitled to access the courts).

Lewis v. Casey, 518 U.S. 343, 116 S.Ct. 2174, 135 L.Ed.2d 606 (1996) (inmate alleging violation of right of access to courts held required to show "actual injury"; federal district court's injunction mandating systemwide changes in prison law library and legal assistance programs held improper).

Higgason v. Farley, 83 F.3d 807 (7th Cir. 1996) (viable § 1983 action stated when inmate transferred for exercising right of access to courts, or assisting others in the same).

Rand v. Rowland, 154 F.3d 952 (9th Cir. 1998) (*pro se* litigants enjoy right of access to courts).

Chriceol v. Phillips, 169 F.3d 313 (5th Cir. 1999) (prisoners have constitutional right of access to the courts; undue delay or similar obstruction may impugn this right).

U.S. v. Gray, 182 F.3d 762 (10th Cir. 1999) (considering a prison's budget constrains, the court found that indigent inmates do not enjoy a right to unlimited free postage for legal mail).

Herron v. Harrison, 203 F.3d 410 (6th Cir. 2000) (a prisoner has the right to legal assistance from another prisoner when prisoner would otherwise have been unable to pursue legal matters).

Akins v. U.S., 204 F.3d 1086 (11th Cir. 2000) (where lockdown for legitimate disciplinary and security concerns caused motion to be untimely filed, no access to courts violation because officials' conduct reasonable under *Turner*).

Shaw v. Murphy, 532 U.S. 223, 121 S.Ct. 1475, 149 L.Ed.2d 420 (2001) (prison inmate's right to provide legal assistance to other prisoners held not to receive protection under First Amendment beyond protection normally accorded prisoners' speech).

Gomez v. Vernon, 255 F.3d 1118 (9th Cir. 2001) (access to courts entails prisoners' right to access legal materials and prisoner law clerks).

Toolasprashad v. Bureau of Prisons, 286 F.3d 576 (D.C. Cir. 2002) (meaningful access to courts necessarily involves the ability to file legal papers and the use of accessories required to prosecute legal claims).

Bear v. Kautzky, 305 F.3d 802 (8th Cir. 2002) (a prison admin may provide its inmates the services of law libraries, jailhouse lawyers, lawyers, or a combination thereof, provided right to access the courts is not harmed).

Tarpley v. Allen County, Indiana, 312 F.3d 895 (7th Cir. 2002) (officials must not impede prisoners' right to access the courts).

Davis v. Goord, 320 F.3d 346 (2nd Cir. 2003) (First Amendment protections extend to include the pursuance of prison grievances).

Chappell v. Rich, 340 F.3d 1279 (11th Cir. 2003) (the First Amendment guarantees prisoners the right of access to courts).

Lehn v. Holmes, 364 F.3d 862 (7th Cir. 2004) (Illinois prisoner was denied access to Maryland legal materials while facing charges in Maryland, and so stated a valid access-to-courts claim).

U.S. v. Cooper, 375 F.3d 1041 (10th Cir. 2004) (prisoners have constitutional right of access to courts, and must be provided with sufficient law libraries or sufficient assistance from persons trained in the law).

Bourdon v. Loughren, 386 F.3d 88 (2nd Cir. 2004) (prisoners have constitutional right of access to courts, and must be provided with sufficient law libraries or sufficient assistance from persons trained in the law).

Peoples v. CCA Detention Ctrs., 422 F.3d 1090 (10th Cir. 2005) (where prisoner was provided access to person trained in the law, but denied access to prison law library, no violation of the right of access to courts occurred).

Marshall v. Knight, 445 F.3d 965, 969 (7th Cir. 2006) (prisoner stated viable access-to-courts claim when law library access was reduced to "non-existent" level and prisoner was unable to prepare for hearing, which resulted in a loss of good-time credits).

Trujillo v. Williams, 465 F.3d 1210 (10th Cir. 2006) (denial or delay of access to courts must actually harm or prejudice a legal claim to constitute an access-to-courts violation).

Barbour v. Haley, 471 F.3d 1222 (11th Cir. 2006) (prisoners have a constitutional right of access to courts).

Entzi v. Redmann, 485 F.3d 998 (8th Cir. 2007) (where prisoner was represented by counsel on direct appeal, official's denial of access to law library did not constitute an access-to-courts violation).

White v. Hantzky, 494 F.3d 677 (8th Cir. 2007) (meaningful access to courts necessarily involves government assistance in preparation and filing of legal papers by providing prisoners adequate law libraries or adequate assistance from persons trained in the law).

Hartsfield v. Nichols, 511 F.3d 826 (8th Cir. 2008) (a non-frivolous claim must actually be impeded or frustrated for prisoner to establish viable access-to-courts claim).

Bridges v. Gilbert, 557 F.3d 541 (7th Cir. 2009) (plaintiff may not rely on another plaintiff's injury to support a claim of personal access-to-courts injury; plaintiff lacked standing).

Cohen v. Longshore, 621 F.3d 1311 (10th Cir. 2010) (although prison officials are required to assist prisoners only in pursuing legal matters concerning conditions of confinement or criminal conviction and sentence, they may not interfere with prisoners' pursuit of other types of legal actions).

Whiteside v. Parrish, 387 Fed.Appx. 608 (6th Cir. 2010), *cert. denied*, 131 S.Ct. 1575, 179 L.Ed.2d 479 (2011) (right of access to courts extends to protect direct and collateral criminal appeals and civil-rights claims only).

Ball v. Hartman, 396 Fed.Appx. 823 (3rd Cir. 2010) (child support action does not challenge sentence, conviction, or conditions of confinement and therefore is not subject to access-to-courts constitutional protection).

Kennedy v. Bonevelle, 413 Fed.Appx. 836 (6th Cir. 2011) (confiscation of inmate's legal documents that would have been used to pursue legal claims is sufficient to state a violation of right of access to courts).

Cooper v. Sniezek, 418 Fed.Appx 56 (3rd Cir. 2011) (where inmate failed to show actual injury resulting from prison's denial of free copies, no viable access-to-courts claim stated).

In re Maxy, 674 F.3d 658 (7th Cir. 2012) (prison's limitation on use of copy machine, which resulted in delays, insufficient to state viable access-to-courts claim where no actual injury was also alleged).

Alvarez v. Attorney General of Fla., 679 F.3d 1257 (11th Cir. 2012) (where denial of evidence did not affect inmate's ability to litigate post-conviction claim, no viable access-to-courts claim was stated).

NOTES: _____

NOTES:

"ACTUAL" INJURY REQUIRED

Sowell v. Vose, 941 F.2d 32 (1st Cir. 1991) (finding no Constitutional violation when prisoner was denied access to legal property kept in storage because of failure to show "actual injury").

Lewis v. Casey, 518 U.S. 343, 116 S.Ct. 2174, 135 L.Ed.2d 606 (1996) (inmate alleging violation of right of access to courts held required to show "actual injury"; federal district court's injunction mandating systemwide changes in prison law library and legal assistance programs held improper).

Kerr v. Puckett, 138 F.3d 321 (7th Cir. 1998) (holding that the PLRA provision barring prisoners from bringing suit for mental or emotional injury without prior showing of physical injury did not apply to a suit filed by an inmate after he was released on parole, because the PLRA "physical injury" provision only applies to *confined* prisoners).

Benefield v. McDowall, 241 F.3d 1267 (10th Cir. 2001) (finding that viable Eight Amendment claim was stated when prisoner alleged psychological injury for fear of harm, absent actual physical injury, in alleging that prison officials deliberately labeled him as a "snitch," thus exposing him to harm).

Phillips v. Hust, 477 F.3d 1070 (9th Cir. 2007) (the guarantees of the Constitution held violated when prison librarian refused to allow prisoner to combine [bind together] petition for writ of *certiorari* which caused the petition to be rejected as untimely), *vacated and remanded on other grounds*, 129 S.Ct. 1036 (2009).

Hartsfield v. Nichols, 511 F.3d 826 (8th Cir. 2008) (finding no Constitutional violation when prisoner was limited in access to law books and legal assistance because prisoner did not show any "actual injury").

Bridges v. Gilbert, 557 F.3d 541 (7th Cir. 2009) (plaintiff may not rely on another plaintiff's injury to support a claim of personal access-to-courts injury; plaintiff lacked standing).

Cooper v. Sniezek, 418 Fed.Appx 56 (3rd Cir. 2011) (where inmate failed to show actual injury resulting from prison's denial of free copies, no viable access-to-courts claim stated).

In re Maxy, 674 F.3d 658 (7th Cir. 2012) (prison's limitation on use of copy machine, which resulted in delays, insufficient to state viable access-to-courts claim where no actual injury was also alleged).

NOTES: _____
_____
_____
_____
_____
_____
_____
_____
_____
_____
_____
_____
_____
_____
_____
_____
_____
_____
_____
_____
_____
_____
_____
_____
_____
_____
_____
_____
_____
_____
_____
_____
_____
_____
_____
_____
_____
_____
_____
_____

NOTES: _____
_____
_____
_____
_____
_____
_____
_____
_____
_____
_____
_____
_____
_____
_____
_____
_____
_____
_____
_____
_____
_____
_____
_____
_____
_____
_____
_____
_____
_____
_____
_____
_____
_____
_____
_____
_____
_____
_____
_____

ADMINISTRATIVE RULES & REGULATIONS

Connally v. General Construction Co., 269 U.S. 385, 391, __S.Ct.__, __L.Ed.2d__ (1926) (a statute or rule under which persons can be punished for its violation must not "forbid . . . or require . . . the doing of an act in terms so vague that men of common intelligence must necessarily guess at its meaning and differ as to its application.").

Ruiz v. Morton, 462 F.2d 818 (9th Cir. 1972) (administrative rules and regulations must comport with the purpose and scope of their progenitorial statute; they may not extend or outreach statutory authority).

Mathews v. Eldridge, 424 U.S. 319, 96 S.Ct. 893, 47 L.Ed.2d 18 (1976) (to determine whether an administrative procedure warrants due process protection, the following should be considered: (1) the nature of the private interest that is affected by the government action, (2) the risk of wrongful deprivation should the procedure be used, (3) the value of additional or alternative procedural safeguards, (4) the government function involved, and (5) the burden and expenses involved in creating a new procedure).

U.S. v. Morton, 467 U.S. 822, 834, 104 S.Ct. 2769, 81 L.Ed.2d 680 (1984) (where Congress has authorized the promulgation of regulations for implementation of a statute, such regulations are given "legislative and hence controlling weight unless they are arbitrary, capricious, or plainly contrary to the statute.").

Caldwell v. Miller, 790 F.2d 589, 609-10 (7th Cir. 1986) ("[A]n agency must conform its actions to the procedures that it has adopted, . . . [because inmates have] the right to expect prison officials to follow [agency] policies and regulations.").

Turner v. Safely, 482 U.S. 78, 107 S.Ct. 2254, 69 L.Ed.2d 64 (1987) (prison officials must show a legitimate government interest to justify a regulation impinging on constitutional rights of inmates, and must provide evidence that the governmental interest proffered is the reason why the regulation was adopted or enforced).

Rios v. Lane, 812 F.2d 1032 (7th Cir. 1987) (sparsely worded rule not otherwise substantiated or explained by other available sources held impermissibly vague where prisoners could not ascertain what conduct the rule prohibited).

Walker v. Sumner, 917 F.2d 382 (9th Cir. 1990) (without requiring "some evidence" that prison policies are based on legitimate penological justifications, judicial review of prison policies would not be meaningful).

Griffin v. Lombardi, 946 F.2d 604 (8th Cir. 1991) (prison officials must show a legitimate government interest to justify a regulation impinging on the constitutional rights of inmates, and must provide evidence that the governmental interest proffered is the reason why the regulation was adopted or enforced).

Gillette v. Delmore, 979 F.2d 1342, 1349 (9th Cir. 1992) (a custom can be shown or a policy can be inferred from widespread practices by "evidence of repeated constitutional violations for which the errant municipal officers were not discharged or reprimanded.").

Reeves v. Pettcox, 19 F.3d 1060 (5th Cir. 1994) (prison officials violated due process because disciplinary procedures were undertaken without giving prisoner fair warning or opportunity to know his conduct was unlawful).

U.S. v. Kirvan, 86 F.3d 309 (2nd Cir. 1996) (federal regulations cannot undermine acts of Congress).

May v. Baldwin, 109 F.3d 557, 564-65 (9th Cir. 1997) ("[W]here a prisoner challenges the [prison's] justification, prison officials must set forth detailed evidence, tailored to the situation before the court, that identifies the failings in the alternatives advanced by the prisoner.").

Calder v. J.S. Alberici Construction Company, Inc., 153 F.3d 1381 (Fed. Cir. 1998) (federal regulations cannot undermine acts of Congress).

U.S. v. Marolf, 173 F.3d 1213 (9th Cir. 1999) (administrative regulations cannot sanction the violation of constitutional or statutory rights).

Warren v. Crabtree, 185 F.3d 1018 (9th Cir. 1999) (Federal Bureau of Prison's program statements are entitled to only some deference because they are not adopted with respect to the strictures of the Administrative Procedure Act).

FCA Health Plans of Texas v. Lachance, 191 F.3d 1353 (Fed. Cir. 1999) (if a regulation can reasonably be interpreted to have more than one meaning, it is ambiguous).

Hells Canyon Alliance v. U.S. Forest Service, 227 F.3d 1170 (9th Cir. 2000) (where an agency has not itself provided a reasoned basis for its actions, a court should refrain from providing its own rationale).

Desert Citizens Against Pollution v. Bisson, 231 F.3d 1172 (9th Cir. 2000) (administrators must supply a reasoned basis for their conclusions in light of their finding of fact).

Sweet v. Sheahan, 235 F.3d 80 (2nd Cir. 2000) (administrators have the power to promulgate rules, to the extent that Congress has authorized, and no further).

Flagner v. Wilkinson, 241 F.3d 475 (6th Cir. 2001) (courts should not defer to administrative decision or policy when substantial evidence demonstrates prison officials have exaggerated their response).

Ester v. Principi, 250 F.3d 1068 (7th Cir. 2001) (administrators must supply a reasoned basis for their actions).

Nadell v. Las Vegas Metro. Police Dep't, 268 F.3d 924 (9th Cir. 2001) (a custom can be shown or a policy can be inferred from widespread practices of repeated constitutional violations for which the offending officers were not discharged or reprimanded).

Johnson v. Ashcroft, 286 F.3d 696 (3rd Cir. 2002) (an action of an agency that deviates from its policy without supplying a reason for the action, may be considered arbitrary, capricious, or an abuse of discretion).

Bieber v. Dep't of Army, 287 F.3d 1358 (Fed. Cir. 2002) (the strictures of due process are not diminished for proceedings by virtue of their administrative nature).

Delta Foundation, Inc. v. U.S., 303 F.3d 551 (5th Cir. 2002) (officials must not disregard evidence in order to reach a preferred conclusion).

Doe v. Tenet, 329 F.3d 1135 (9th Cir. 2003) (officials must not ignore administrative policy).

R&W Flammann GMBH v. U.S., 339 F.3d 1320 (Fed. Cir. 2003) (a regulation cannot preempt a statute).

Earth Island Institute v. U.S. Forest Services, 442 F.3d 1147 (9th Cir. 2006) (administrators must supply a reasoned basis for their conclusions in light of their findings of fact).

NOTES: _____

NOTES:

CONSTITUTIONAL RIGHTS

Lee v. Washington, 390 U.S. 333, __S.Ct.__, __L.Ed.2d__ (1968) (per curiam) (equal protection of laws extends to the incarcerated).

Procunier v. Martinez, 416 U.S. 396, 94 S.Ct. 1800, 40 L.Ed.2d 224 (1974) (prisoners are not stripped of constitutional protections at the prison gates, retaining all those rights an ordinary citizen enjoys, except those taken expressly by law, or by necessary implication not inconstant with penal objectives).

Bell v. Wolfish, 441 U.S. 520, 99 S.Ct. 1800, 60 L.Ed.2d 447 (1979 (prisoners are not stripped of constitutional protections at the prison gates, retaining all those rights an ordinary citizen enjoys, except those taken expressly by law, or by necessary implication not inconstant with penal objectives).

Brown v. Nix, 33 F.3d 951 (8th Cir. 1994) (prisoners are not stripped of constitutional protections at the prison gates, retaining all those rights an ordinary citizen enjoys, except those taken expressly by law, or by necessary implication not inconstant with penal objectives).

Smith v. Campbell, 250 F.3d 1032 (6th Cir. 2001) (officials must not retaliate against a prisoner for exercising his or her Constitutional rights).

Morrison v. Hall, 261 F.3d 896 (9th Cir. 2001) (prison walls do not form a barrier separating prisoners from protections of the Constitution; should a prison regulation or practice infringe upon a fundamental constitutional right, federal courts may order such remedies as are necessary to protect those rights guaranteed under the Constitution).

Fogle v. Pierson, 435 F.3d 1252 (10th Cir. 2006) (officials must not retaliate against a prisoner for exercising his or her Constitutional rights).

NOTES: _____

NOTES: _____
_____
_____
_____
_____
_____
_____
_____
_____
_____
_____
_____
_____
_____
_____
_____
_____
_____
_____
_____
_____
_____
_____
_____
_____
_____
_____
_____
_____
_____
_____
_____
_____
_____
_____
_____
_____
_____
_____
_____

COUNSEL

Baxter v. Palmigiano, 425 U.S. 308, 96 S.Ct.1551, 47 L.Ed.2d 810 (1976) (Sixth Amendment right to counsel does not include prison disciplinary proceedings, even if proceedings involve questions of criminal conduct, unless adversarial judicial proceedings have also commenced against the prisoner/defendant).

Polk County v. Dadson, 454 U.S. 312, __S.Ct.__, __L.Ed.2d__ (1981) (for the purposes of § 1983, public defenders do not act under color of state law).

U.S. v. Gouvcia, 467 U.S. 180, __S.Ct.__, __L.Ed.2d__ (1984) (Sixth Amendment right to counsel remains to prisoners during incarceration, but only in criminal prosecutions where adversarial judicial proceedings have commenced against the prisoner/defendant).

Hodge v. Police Officers, 802 F.2d 58 (2nd Cir. 1986) (to determine whether counsel should be appointed in federal civil-rights cases, courts should consider (1) merits of the case; (2) complexity of facts and legal theories, and inmate's ability to litigate; and (3) ability of inmate to acquire counsel by self efforts, and whether and to what extent the inmate sought counsel).

Castillo v. Cook County Mail Room Dep't, 990 F.2d 304 (7th Cir. 1993) (prisoner entitled to appointment of counsel considering viability of claim and inability of presenting his own claim because of language barrier).

Farmer v. Haas, 990 F.2d 319 (7th Cir. 1993) (no constitutional right to appointment of counsel in federal civil cases).

Murphy v. Walker, 51 F.3d 714 (7th Cir. 1995) (per curiam) (suspension of phone privileges may violate Six Amendment if revocation impedes right to access counsel).

Rand v. Rowland, 113 F.3d 1520 (9th Cir. 1997) (appointment of counsel may be appropriate when a plaintiff can show a likelihood of success on the merits of the claim and complexity of the legal issues involved).

Lewis v. Lynn, 236 F.3d 766 (5th Cir. 2001) (appointment of counsel was not appropriate because plaintiff showed the ability to adequately represent himself, factual and legal issues where not complex, and plaintiff made no claim of exceptional circumstances warranting the appoint of counsel).

Mongomery v. Pinchak, 294 F.3d 492, 499, 501-05 (3rd Cir. 2002) (appointment of counsel may be appropriate considering: (1) plaintiff's inability to present his or her own case; (2) complexity of the legal issues involved; (3) necessity of and plaintiff's inability to investigate factual issues; (4) plaintiff's inability to retain counsel; and (5) necessity of expert testimony).

Alston v. Parker, 363 F.3d 229 (3rd Cir. 2004) (indigent prisoner was entitled to appoint of counsel considering the legal and factual merits of his cruel and unusual punishment and involuntary commitment claims).

Johnson v. Doughty, 433 F.3d 1001 (7th Cir. 2006) (finding appointment of counsel to be inappropriate when plaintiff appeared able to represent himself and because case was not overly complex).

Sash v. Zenk, 439 F.3d 61 (2nd Cir. 2006) (no constitutional right to assistance of counsel in prison disciplinary matters).

Butler v. Fletcher, 465 F.3d 340 (8th Cir. 2006) (when prisoner's claim was defeated as a matter of law based on the undisputed evidence, appointment of counsel was inappropriate).

Watson v. Hulick, 481 F.3d 537 (7th Cir. 2007) (there was no constitutional right to counsel when prisoner confessed to murder while in police custody because he was not indicted, charged, nor had formal adversarial proceedings initiated against him; right to counsel had not yet attached).

Pruitt v. Mote, 503 F.3d 647 (7th Cir. 2007) (when determining whether appropriate to appoint counsel on § 1915(e)(1) motion, a court should first make a threshold finding of whether the *pro se* litigant has made a reasonable attempt to obtain counsel, or the inability to do so, and then consider complexity of case in view of litigant's literacy, communication skills, education level, litigation experience, intellectual capacity, and psychological history).

Vt. v. Brillion, __U.S.__, 129 S.Ct. 1283, __L.Ed.2d__ (2009) (for the purposes of § 1983, public defenders do not act under color of state law).

Palmer v. Valdez, 560 F.3d 965 (9th Cir. 2009) (counsel will not be appointed to represent prisoner in § 1983 claim absent a showing of exceptional circumstances warranting appointment).

NOTES: _____

NOTES: _____

_____

_____

_____

_____

_____

_____

_____

_____

_____

_____

_____

_____

_____

_____

_____

_____

_____

_____

_____

_____

_____

_____

_____

_____

_____

_____

_____

_____

_____

_____

_____

_____

_____

_____

_____

_____

_____

_____

_____

COURTS, JUDGES & TRIALS

Jones v. N.C. Prisoners' Labor Union, Inc., 433 U.S. 119, __S.Ct.__, __L.Ed.2d__ (1977) (the decisions of prison authorities should be regarded with due deference by the courts).

U.S. v. N.Y. Telephone Co., 434 U.S. 159, 172, 98 S.Ct. 364, __L.Ed.2d__ (1977) (courts have the authority to issue the writs "necessary or appropriate to [effectuate] and prevent the frustration of the court orders previously issued.").

Bd. of Regents v. Tomanio, 446 U.S. 478, __S.Ct.__, __L.Ed.2d__ (1980) (state's tolling rules apply to § 1983 claims, so long as rules are not inconsistent with purposes of § 1983).

Arizona v. California, 460 U.S. 605, 103 S.Ct. 1382, 75 L.Ed.2d 318 (1983) (a court's decision on rule of law generally remains binding on the proceedings of the case throughout its later stages, such as on remand following an appeal; although, this doctrine of the "law of the case" does not then restrict the court's jurisdiction or power to revisit its rulings).

James v. Kentucky, 466 U.S. 341, 104 S.Ct 1830, 80 L.Ed.2d 346 (1984) (state statutes do not take precedence over constitutional law; judge required to give jury instructions in accordance).

Block v. Rutherford, 468 U.S. 576, 584-85, __S.Ct.__, __L.Ed.2d__ (1984) (courts should defer to "expert judgment" of prison officials, unless "substantial evidence" demonstrates an exaggerated response to prison event).

Whitley v. Albers, 475 U.S. 312, 321-22, __S.Ct.__, __L.Ed.2d__ (1986) (officials' judgment in responding to prison violence or disturbances should be deferred to and given "special weight" by courts).

Poole v. Lambert, 819 F.2d 1025, 1029 (11th Cir. 1987) (to protect an inmate's due-process and access-to-courts rights, judges may invent or adapt methods for the prisoner-plaintiff's participation in court proceedings, so long as his or her "allegations and evidence [are] fully and fairly considered.").

Hardin v. Straub, 490 U.S. 536, __S.Ct.__, __L.Ed.2d__ (1989) (state's tolling rule suspending statute of limitation for duration of legal disability consistent with purposes of § 1983).

Lyons v. Fisher, 888 F.2d 1071 (5th Cir. 1989) (the doctrine of the "law of the case" is based on the idea that a litigation should eventually end).

Monotype Corp. v. Int'l Typeface Corp., 42 F.3d 443, 451 (9th Cir. 1994) (on appeal, when a trial court's management is challenged, it must be shown that "there was harm incurred as a result" of the challenged decision).

Sandin v. Conner, 515 U.S. 472, 482, 115 S.Ct. 2293, 132 L.Ed.2d 418 (1995) ("[F]ederal courts ought to afford appropriate deference and flexibility to state officials trying to manage a volatile environment.").

City of Long Beach v. Standard Oil Co., 46 F.3d 929, 936 (9th Cir. 1995) (a district court's decision will constitute an abuse of judicial discretion if it makes an error of law or clear error of fact, but "[r]eversal will not be granted unless prejudice is shown.").

Williams v. Benjamin, 77 F.3d 755 (4th Cir. 1996) (although a court should defer to the expertise of prison officials concerning matters of administration, this does not give prison officials constitutional license to torture inmates but is limited to what is necessary for internal prison security).

U.S. v. Josleyn, 99 F.3d 1182 (1st Cir. 1996) ("venue" regards place of trial, whereas "jurisdiction" regards the authority by which a court may hear a case).

U.S. v. Myers, 106 F.3d 936 (10th Cir. 1997) (basic canon of statutory construction: the word "shall" indicates the author's intent that the provision be mandatory).

Rodriguez v. Marshal, 125 F.3d 739 (9th Cir. 1997) (a single improperly influenced juror may warrant a new trial).

Pennsylvania Dep't of Corr. v. Yeskey, 524 U.S. 206, 212, 118 S.Ct. 1952, 141 L.Ed.2d 215 (1998) (although title of statute cannot limit the statute's plain meaning, it can shed light on otherwise ambiguous language).

Hillside Enterprises, Inc. v. Continental Carlisle, Inc., 147 F.3d 732 (8th Cir. 1998) (the interpretation of state law by the state's highest court requires deferential interpretation in federal court).

Dyer v. Calderon, 151 F.3d 970 (9th Cir. 1998) (a biased juror introduces a trial defect that may warrant a new trial, regardless of actual prejudice; harmless-error analysis inappropriate upon a determination of juror bias).

Wellons v. Northwest Airlines, Inc., 165 F.3d 493 (6th Cir. 1999) (absent express purpose otherwise, it is presumed Congress does not intend that its legislation preempt state law).

Salahuddin v. Mead, 174 F.3d 271 (2nd Cir. 1999) (basic canon of statutory construction: the word "shall" indicates the author's intent that the provision be mandatory).

Sealey v. Giltner, 197 F.3d 578 (2nd Cir. 1999) (the jury must resolve the factual circumstances surrounding an alleged denial of due process when facts are reasonably in dispute; however, the ultimate issue of whether a hardship is atypical is a question of law determined by the court).

City of Auburn v. Quest Corp., 260 F.3d 1160 (9th Cir. 2001) (the Supremacy Clause requires state courts to fairly apply federal law and fairly adjudicate federal claims presented to them).

Navellier v. Sletten, 262 F.3d 923 (9th Cir. 2001) (on appeal, challenges to trial court management and denial of class certification is reviewed for abuse of discretion).

U.S. v. Capars, 271 F.3d 962 (11th Cir. 2001) (a biased juror introduces a trial defect that may warrant a new trial, regardless of actual prejudice; harmless-error analysis improper upon a determination of juror bias).

Piggie v. McBride, 277 F.3d 922 (7th Cir. 2002) (determinations made by prison officials in prisoner disciplinary cases are not presumptively correct).

Boomer v. AT&T Corp., 309 F.3d 404 (7th Cir. 2002) (federal law preempts state law, whether by implication, express provision, or by conflict between federal and state law).

Silveira v. Lockyer, 312 F.3d 1052 (9th Cir. 2002) (courts must, when possible, interpret each word of a law so as to give it meaningful effect).

Discovery House v. Consol. City of Indianapolis, 319 F.3d 277 (7th Cir. 2003) (to correct a wrong, federal courts can use any available remedy).

Hubbord v. Taylor, 399 F.3d 150 (3rd Cir. 2005) (absent evidence that prison officials exaggerated the legitimacy of their actions, courts should give due deference to the expert judgment of prison officials).

Fields v. Brown, 431 F.3d 1186 (9th Cir. 2005) (a biased juror introduces a trial defect that may warrant a new trial, regardless of actual prejudice; harmless-error analysis improper upon a determination of juror bias).

U.S. v. Blood, 435 F.3d 612 (6th Cir. 2006) (a faulty jury instruction that incorrectly portrays the law may constitute cause for new trial).

Amerisource Bergen Corp. v. Dailyist West, Inc., 465 F.3d 946 (9th Cir. 2006) (courts should permit amended pleadings when justice requires).

Wallace v. Kato, 549 U.S. 384, 127 S.Ct. 1091, 166 L.Ed.2d 973 (2007) (federal courts defer "to a state law for tolling rules [suspending, for good cause, the time limit for pursuing a legal matter] . . . [as well as] for the length of statutes of limitation.").

Baptist Health v. Smith, 477 F.3d 540 (8th Cir. 2007) (pleadings should be allowed amendment).

U.S. v. Allomon, 500 F.3d 800 (8th Cir. 2007) (continuances should be allowed upon a showing of compelling reason only).

Erickson v. Pardus, 551 U.S. 89, __S.Ct.__, __L.Ed.2d__ (2007) (courts should liberally construe *pro se* complaints).

Davington v. Hadgen, 524 F.3d 91 (1st Cir. 2008) (courts should recognize a jury's conclusions as to whether a person acted under color of state law for purposes of § 1983).

Hannon v. Beard, 524 F.3d 275 (1st Cir. 2008) (a case cannot be heard by a court without personal jurisdiction over the parties).

Pierce v. County of Orange, 526 F.3d 1190, 1200 (9th Cir. 2008) (holding that the district court did not abuse its discretion when it decertified the "damages class" of impaired pretrial detainees, rejecting statistical sampling as a useful tool for computing damages in this circumstance, because the class size (estimated at 180,000) and the array of variables related to claims, causation, and damages are poorly addressed through sampling).

Duffield v. Jackson, 545 F.3d 1234 (10th Cir. 2008) (prisoner's objections to magistrate's findings untimely where prisoner informed of time for objections and consequences for not doing so in a timely manner).

Thompson v. Connick, 553 F.3d 836 (5th Cir. 2008) (section 1983 claim against district attorney office for deliberate indifference to training and supervision of its employees accrued for statute of limitation purposes under federal law on the date when plaintiff's conviction was vacated).

Porter v. Dep't of Treasury, 564 F.3d 176 (3rd Cir. 2009) (*in forma pauperis* status does not totally exempt litigants from all costs associated with prosecuting a lawsuit, including cost of filing, copies, process of service, expert witness fees, and court-ordered sanctions).

Douglas v. Noelle, 567 F.3d 1103 (9th Cir. 2009) (plaintiff's § 1983 claims not tolled for duration of confinement because state provision did not allow tolling on basis of incarceration).

McGregor v. Thurlow, 435 Fed.Appx. 779 (10th Cir. 2011) (where state court had ruled on matter of state law, federal proceeding improper because federal courts cannot disturb holdings of state courts on matters of state law).

NOTES: _____

NOTES: _____
_____
_____
_____
_____
_____
_____
_____
_____
_____
_____
_____
_____
_____
_____
_____
_____
_____
_____
_____
_____
_____
_____
_____
_____
_____
_____
_____
_____
_____
_____
_____
_____
_____
_____
_____
_____
_____
_____

DISCOVERY & DEPOSITIONS

Hickman v. Taylor, 329 U.S. 495, 67 S.Ct. 385, 91 L.Ed.2d 451 (1947) (information within the possession of a party's attorney or that which is supplied to a party by others is discoverable).

Societe Internationale Pour Participations Industrielles Et Commercials, S.A. v. Rogers, 357 U.S. 197, S.Ct. 1087, 2 L.Ed.2d 1255 (1958) (documents within a party's possession are discoverable, even though they may be owned by third parties).

De Vita v. Sillis, 422 F.2d 1172 (3rd Cir. 1970) (parties to a civil action retain their Fifth Amendment right to silence in matters that could expose them to criminal prosecution).

Gordon v. Federal Deposit Ins. Corp., 427 F.2d 578 (D.C. Cir. 1970) (the Fifth Amendment right to silence concerning matters that could incriminate a party remains to that party even when subject of interrogatories, requests for admissions, and requests for production of documents).

Bradshaw v. Thompson, 454 F.2d 75 (6th Cir. 1972) (facts proven but denied in response to a request for admissions may support an award of expenses and fees incurred in proving the facts).

In re Folding Carton Antitrust Litigation, 609 F.2d 867 (7th Cir. 1979) (the Fifth Amendment right to silence concerning matters that could incriminate a party remains to that party during civil depositions).

Guidry v. Continental Oil Co., 640 F.2d 523 (5th Cir. 1981) (sanctions for a party's failure to attend its own deposition, serve answers to interrogatories, or respond to a request for inspection may be issued under the Federal Rules of Civil Procedure without a prior court order based on a motionto compel discovery).

Asea, Inc. v. Southern Pacific Transp. Co., 669 F.2d 1242 (9th Cir. 1981) (answers to requests for admissions may be a simple "admitted" or "denied," or may be a longer statement, so long as the response is not evasive).

Rainbow Pioneer No. 44-18-04A v. Hawaii-Nevada Investment Corp., 711 F.2d 902 (9th Cir. 1983) (the documents requested must be adequately identified when business records are provided in response to an interrogatory request).

Seattle Times Co. v. Rhinehart, 467 U.S. 20, 104 S.Ct. 2199, 81 L.Ed.2d 17 (1984) (under the federal court rules, evidence does not have to be admissible to be discoverable, only relevant).

Farnsworth v. Procter & Gamble Co., 758 F.2d 1545 (11th Cir. 1985) (the Federal Rules of Civil Procedure require full discovery absent exigent circumstance).

Cipollone v. Liggett Group, Inc., 785 F.2d 1108 (3rd Cir. 1986) (discovery orders and protective discovery orders are interlocutory, appealable only upon a conclusion of the lawsuit).

United Coal v. Powell Construction, 839 F.2d 958 (3rd Cir. 1988) (requests for admissions must be written in such a way so as to allow a party to admit or deny without having to explain its answer or to qualify the admission or denial).

Cain v. Lane, 857 F.2d 1139 (7th Cir. 1988) (*pro se* prisoner-litigants have the right under First Amendment to investigate and document claims, including obtaining affidavits from other prisoners).

Dean v. Barber, 951 F.2d 1210 (11th Cir. 1992) (courts should defer ruling on a motion for summary judgment when a genuine discovery dispute exists between the parties; summary judgment may be inappropriate when a party has not had adequate opportunity for discovery).

U.S. v. Kalter, 5 F.3d 1166 (8th Cir. 1993) (the materials sought via subpoena *duces tecum* must be relevant, reasonable, and specifically described).

ACLU v. The Florida Bar, 999 F.2d 1486 (11th Cir. 1993) (an answer to a request for admissions is binding on the answering party, but only in the action in which the admissions were served).

Marchard v. Mercy Medical Center, 22 F.3d 933 (9th Cir. 1994) (admissions requests may ask a party to admit or deny the existence of facts and the application of law to facts).

In re Bankers Trust Co., 61 F.3d 465 (6th Cir. 1995) (for discovery purposes, a party has control of documents if the party has a legal right to demand them).

Helfand v. Gerson, 105 F.3d 530 (9th Cir. 1997) (failure to bring a motion to compel discovery may be deemed a waiver of objection).

In re Perrigo Co., 128 F.3d 430 (6th Cir. 1997) (whether work product is exempt from discovery disclosure is a qualified right, not an absolute privilege).

U.S. v. Lot 41, Berryhill Farm Estates, 128 F.3d 1386 (10th Cir. 1997) (interrogatories may be requested of parties to the action only).

Klonoski v. Mahlab, 156 F.3d 255 (1st Cir. 1998) (pretrial disclosures under the Federal Rules of Civil Procedure must be supplemented if the disclosing party learns of an incomplete or incorrect disclosure).

ATD Corp. v. Lydall, Inc., 159 F.3d 534 (Fed. Cir. 1998) (where only part of an admissions request is objectionable the responding party must still answer, stating the objection and answering the non-objectional portion).

Pacitti v. Macy's, 193 F.3d 766 (3rd Cir. 1999) (the Federal Rules of Civil Procedure permit broad disclosure and liberal discovery practice).

United Kingdom v. U.S., 238 F.3d 1312 (11th Cir. 2001) (work product is subject to discovery disclosure if it is shown that there is reasonably no other source for the information).

U.S. v. Philip Morris, Inc., 347 F.3d 951 (D.C. Cir. 2003) (a discovery request must be responded to specifically, in writing, even if only to state an objection).

Cummings v. General Motors Corp., 365 F.3d 944 (10th Cir. 2004) (parties are not required to disclose witnesses or documents they do not intend to use at hearing or trial).

International Broth. Of Elec. Workers, Local Union No. 545 v. Hope Elec. Corp., 380 F.3d 1084 (8th Cir. 2004) (disclosures or answers that are incomplete or evasive may be deemed a failure to disclose or answer).

Hammel v. Eau Galle Cheese Factory, 407 F.3d 852 (7th Cir. 2005) (evidence to be used solely for impeachment purposes is not required to be disclosed under Fed. R. Civ. P. 26(a)(3)).

Gagnon v. Teledyne Princeton, Inc., 437 F.3d 188 (1st Cir. 2006) (information and evidence improperly withheld from disclosure may be excluded from motion, hearing, or trial).

Shcherbakovsky v. Da Capo Al Fine, Ltd., 490 F.3d 130 (2nd Cir. 2007) (for discovery purposes, information within control of a subsidiary is also within the control of the corporation).

Wegener v. Johnson, 527 F.3d 687 (8th Cir. 2008) (under Fed. R. Civ. P. 26(a)(2)(C)(ii), evidence a party intends to use to impeach an expert witness must be disclosed).

Nilssen v. Osram Sylvania, 528 F.3d 1352 (Fed. Cir. 2008) (the party seeking discovery of experty testimony may be required to pay the fees incurred in the expert's response to the request, unless the imposition of fees would cause a manifest injustice, such as may become the case with indigent parties).

Agiwal v. Mid. Island Mortg. Corp., 555 F.3d 298 (2nd Cir. 2009) (per curiam) (*pro se* complaint properly dismissed for failure to comply with discovery order; litigant warned that non-compliance could be cause for dismissal).

U.S. Aviation Underwriters, Inc. v. Pilatus Business Aircraft, Ltd., 582 F.3d 1131 (10th Cir. 2009) (a party has a duty to supplement its response to a discovery request when it learns the disclosure was incorrect or incomplete at the time it was made).

Garcia v. Berkshire Life Ins. Co. of America, 569 F.3d 1174 (10th Cir. 2009) (an untruthful response to a discovery request may result in the exclusion of evidence or the dismissal of the case).

Praetorian Ins. Co. v. Site Inspection, LLC, 604 F.3d 509 (8th Cir. 2010) (whether an admission response is insufficient or an objection is unfounded is determined by the court upon a Motion to Determine Sufficiency).

In re Violation of Rule 28(D), 635 F.3d 1352 (Fed. Cir. 2011) (an order protecting a party from discovery must only be made on a showing of good cause for its entry).

N.L.R.B. v. Interbake Foods, LLC, 637 F.3d 492 (4th Cir. 2011) (a party claiming privilege or work product protection must describe the withheld information in a manner that permits the parties to assess the nature and extent of protection).

AMCO Ins. Co. v. Inspired Techs., Inc., 648 F.3d 875 (8th Cir. 2011) (admissibility of answers to interrogatories is subject to the rules of evidence).

Siggers v. Campbell, 652 F.3d 681 (6th Cir. 2011) (courts generally grant Rule 56(d) motions to postpone summary judgment when a party files for a summary judgment very early in the proceedings, before the parties have had an opportunity for discovery).

In re Taylor, 655 F.3d 274 (3rd Cir. 2011) (requests for admissions are deemed admitted should the party fail to timely respond).

Josendis v. Wall to Wall Residence Repairs, Inc., 662 F.3d 1292 (11th Cir. 2011) (the victor of a motion to compel discovery is entitled to an award of expenses and reasonable attorney's fees incurred in bringing the motion).

Doe v. Young, 664 F.3d 727 (8th Cir. 2011) (parties must disclose witnesses and documents they intend to use).

R & R Sails, Inc. v. Ins. Co. of Penn., 673 F.3d 1240 (9th Cir. 2012) (unless provided for by court order or stipulation, initial disclosures must be made within the fourteen-day limit of Fed. R. Civ. P. 26(f); when a sanction of exclusion of documents or evidence would result in the disposition of a claim the court must scrutinize the appropriateness of the sanction).

Mulero-Agbreu v. Puerto Rico Police Dep't, 675 F.3d 88 (1st Cir. 2012) (failure to respond to a discovery request in a timely manner may be considered a waiver of objections to the request; when discovery requests are objectionable, specific objections must be provided in response to the particular discovery request).

In re MSTG, Inc., 675 F.3d 1337 (Fed. Cir. 2012) (courts may impose limits on discovery).

Gov't of Ghana v. ProEnergy Servs., LLC, 677 F.3d 340 (8th Cir. 2012) (materials relevant to any claim or defense are discoverable under Fed. R. Civ. P. 26(b)(1)).

Jones v. Secord, 684 F.3d 1 (1st Cir. 2012) (on motion to postpone ruling on summary judgment, the movant generally must make a Rule 56(d) motion describing the discovery sought, explaining how the discovery would preclude summary judgment, and state why this discovery could not have been obtained earlier).

Pensacola Motor Sales, Inc. v. Eastern Shore Toyota, LLC, 684 F.3d 1211 (11th Cir. 2012) (admissions may be withdrawn or amended with permission of the court).

NOTES:

NOTES: _____

DISMISSAL OF COMPLAINTS & SUMMARY JUDGMENT

Copper v. Pate, 378 U.S. 546, 84 S.Ct. 1733, 12 L.Ed.2d 1030 (1964) (a court must view all allegations in pleadings as true).

Adickes v. Kress & Co., 398 U.S. 144, 90 S.Ct. 1598, 26 L.Ed.2d 142 (1970) (at summary judgment stage, a court is required to resolve all ambiguities and draw all factual inferences in favor of the party against whom the summary judgment is sought).

Haines v. Kerner, 404 U.S. 519, 92 S.Ct. 594, 30 L.Ed.2d 652 (1972) (*pro se* litigants' pleadings are to be construed liberally and held to a less stringent standard than pleadings drafted by lawyers; if a court can reasonably interpret *pro se* pleadings to state a cognizable claim on which litigant could prevail, it should do so despite failure to cite proper legal authority, confusion of legal theories, poor syntax and sentence structure, or litigant's unfamiliarity with pleading requirements; and unless it appears beyond doubt that a plaintiff can prove no facts in support of his claim, which would entitle him to relief, a complaint should not be dismissed).

Hahn v. Sargent, 523 F.2d 461, 463 (1st Cir. 1975), *cert. denied* 425 U.S. 904, 96 S.Ct. 1495, 47 L.Ed.2d 754 (1976) (an issue is "material" if it affects the outcome of litigation, and "genuine" when on the record is "sufficient evidence supporting the claimed factual dispute . . . to require a jury or judge to resolve the parties' differing versions of the truth at trial.").

Allen v. McCurry, 449 U.S. 90, __S.Ct.__, __L.Ed.2d__ (1980) (claims brought under § 1983 are subject to the procedural bars of *res judicata*, collateral estoppel, and judicial estoppel).

Western Reserve Oil & Gas Co. v. New, 765 F.2d 1428 (9th Cir. 1985) (upon a motion to dismiss, allegations of material fact must be considered true and all inferences drawn therefrom are to be construed in the light most favorable to the non-moving party).

Anderson v. Liberty Lobby, Inc., 477 U.S. 242, 106 S.Ct. 2505, 91 L.Ed.2d 202 (1986) (on summary judgment, evidence offered by the non-moving party must be taken as true, with all reasonable inferences drawn favorably to the side of the non-moving party; however, the non-moving party must provide significant probative evidence tending to support a claim, over the mere allegation of misconduct).

T.W. Electrical Service, Inc. v. Pacific Electrical Contractors Ass'n, 809 F.2d 626 (9th Cir. 1987) (courts should not attempt to resolve conflicting evidence of disputed material facts, nor should they engage in determinations of credibility; however, disputes over irrelevant or unnecessary facts will not preclude a grant of summary judgment).

Celotex v. Catrett, 477 U.S. 317, 106 S.Ct. 2548, 91 L.Ed.2d 265 (1986) (summary disposition is proper if the non-moving party fails to demonstrate evidence sufficient to establish an element essential to its case upon which it would bear the burden of proof at trial).

Forte v. Sullivan, 935 F.2d 1 (1st Cir. 1991) (per curiam) (finding the district court to have erred when dismissing the *pro se* complaint without affording the plaintiff an opportunity to amend his complaint to include the defendant in her individual capacity).

Murphy v. Kellar, 950 F.2d 290 (5th Cir. 1992) (district court erred when it dismissed the plaintiff's case for failing to identify defendants because identities could have been learned through the discovery process).

Dean v. Barber, 951 F.2d 1210 (11th Cir. 1992) (courts should defer ruling on a motion for summary judgment when a genuine discovery dispute exists between the parties; summary judgment may be inappropriate when a party has not had adequate opportunity for discovery).

Swoboda v. Dubach, 992 F.2d 286 (11th Cir. 1993) (prisoner who alleged no specific injury lacked standing to assert claims on behalf of other prisoners).

Ingram v. Becher, 3 F.3d 1050 (7th Cir. 1993) (courts should afford a party the opportunity to amend the complaint before dismissing for failure to state a claim).

Justice v. U.S., 6 F.3d 1474 (11th Cir. 1993) (dismissing an action for a court sanction is a last resort, proper when there is a clear record of delay or willful contempt).

Hamm v. Groose, 15 F.3d 110 (8th Cir. 1994) ((1) a court must view all allegations in pleadings as true; (2) where prisoners were not unable to bring claims themselves, jailhouse lawyers lacked standing to assert access-to-courts claim on their behalf).

City Management Corp. v. U.S. Chemical Co., Inc., 43 F.3d 244 (6th Cir. 1994) (at the summary judgment stage, a judge may not weigh the evidence, but only determine whether there exists a genuine issue of material fact to be resolved at trial).

Schroader v. McDonald, 55 F.3d 454 (9th Cir. 1995) (a verified complaint is treated as an affidavit for summary judgment purposes).

Yerdon v. Henry, 91 F.3d 370 (2nd Cir. 1996) (at the summary judgment stage, a court is required to resolve all ambiguities and draw all factual inferences in favor of the party against whom the summary judgment is sought).

Johnson v. Baptist Medical Center, 97 F.3d 1070 (8th Cir. 1996) (hearsay evidence alone is insufficient to preclude a grant of summary judgment).

U.S. ex rel Thompson v. Columbia/HCA Healthcare Corp., 125 F.3d 899 (5th Cir. 1997) (a complaint should not be dismissed unless the plaintiff has failed to demonstrate facts that, if proven, would entitle him to relief).

Crawford-El v. Britton, 523 U.S. 574, 118 S.Ct. 1584, 140 L.Ed.2d 759 (1998) (prisoner—who sought damages in a constitutional claim against a prison official, a claim that required a showing of improper motive on the part of the official—was not required to show "clear and convincing evidence" [a legal burden of proof greater than "preponderance of the evidence" but less than "reasonable doubt"] of improper motive in order to defeat the motion for summary judgment).

Danzer v. Norden Systems, Inc., 151 F.3d 50 (2nd Cir. 1998) (at summary judgment, all factual inferences must be resolved in favor of the nonmoving party).

Bazrowx v. Scott, 136 F.3d 1053 (5th Cir. 1998) (*pro se* plaintiffs should be afforded an opportunity to amend their complaints before dismissal).

Hernandez v. City of El Monte, 137 F.3d 393 (9th Cir. 1998) (only extreme circumstances warrant the penalty of dismissal).

AMOCO Oil Co. v. U.S., 234 F.3d 1374 (Fed. Cir. 2000) (a complaint should not be dismissed unless the plaintiff has failed to demonstrate facts that, if proven, would entitle him to relief).

Nodine v. Shiley, Inc., 240 F.3d 1149 (9th Cir. 2001) (should material facts persist for resolution at trial, summary judgment is not proper).

Vanderberg v. Donaldson, 259 F.3d 1321 (11th Cir. 2001) (district court did not err when it denied prisoner's motion to amend his complaint because the motion was filed after the complaint was dismissed and alleged no new facts that would support his claim or reasons why the court should grant the amendment).

Wood v. Kesler, 323 F.3d 872 (11th Cir. 2003) (section 1983 claim in federal court was barred by the doctrine of collateral estoppel because state court had previously rendered a finding on the issue).

McQuillion v. Schwarzenegger, 369 F.3d 1091 (9th Cir. 2004) (*pro se* complaint properly dismissed because amendment could not cure procedural bar of collateral estoppel).

Fonseca v. Sysco Food Servs. of Arizona, Inc., 374 F.3d 840 (9th Cir. 2004) (when plaintiff failed to file a motion showing good cause for delay, the district court erred in dismissing *pro se* complaint for late discovery disclosure because the court had failed to notify the plaintiff of the requirement).

Beard v. Banks, 548 U.S. 521, 529, 126 S.Ct. 2572, 2578, 165 L.Ed.2d 297 (2006) (summary judgment is precluded unless (1) there is no genuine dispute (2) as to any material fact, and (3) the moving party is entitled to judgment as a matter of law; if the non-moving party fails to come forward with sworn evidence sufficiently establishing a genuine issue in dispute, summary judgment must be granted to the moving party).

Stringer v. St. James R-1 School District, 446 F.3d 799 (8th Cir. 2006) (liberally construed complaint properly dismissed because no facts alleged to support claim),

Johnson v. Johnson, 466 F.3d 1213 (10th Cir. 2006) (district court erred in dismissing *pro se* complaint when the court failed to permit plaintiff to amend where he erroneously named the city as responsible under § 1983 false arrest claim and not the individual officers).

Barreto-Rosa v. Varona-Mendez, 470 F.3d 42 (1st Cir. 2006) (section 1983 claim barred by the doctrine of *res judicata* when the action was previously dismissed with prejudice in state court).

Scott v. Harris, 550 U.S. 372, 127 S.Ct. 1769, 167 L.Ed.2d 686 (2007) (on summary judgment, courts are not required to accept a party's assertions in the face of blatantly contradictory evidence).

Robinette v. Jones, 476 F.3d 585 (8th Cir. 2007) (section 1983 claim in federal court was barred because prior suit, though voluntarily dismissed, was sufficiently litigated concerning officials' defense of immunity and constituted a final judgment).

Zinkand v. Brown, 478 F.3d 634 (4th Cir. 2007) (doctrine of judicial estoppel did not bar § 1983 claim where plaintiff's plea bargain for probation, which did not include an admission of guilt, and § 1983 claim were not inconsistent).

Abbas v. Dixon, 480 F.3d 636 (2nd Cir. 2007) (reversing the district court's decision to dismiss prisoner's complaint for failure to state a claim upon which relief can be granted because the court based its decision solely on the complaint and did not afford prisoner the opportunity to be heard on the merits of his claims).

Sealed Plaintiff v. Sealed Defendant, 537 F.3d 185 (2nd Cir. 2008) (courts should liberally construe *pro se* complaints, offering wider latitude despite legal deficiencies and errors in formating).

Arreola v. Godinez, 546 F.3d 788 (7th Cir. 2008) (courts should grant leave to amend *pro se* complaints where there is no dilatory motive, undue delay, repeated failure to cure deficiencies, bad faith, no prejudice to defense, and amendment could cure deficiencies).

SBT Holdings, LLC v. Town of Westminister, 547 F.3d 28 (1st Cir. 2008) (where previous state proceedings did not end in final adjudication as to merits of claim, and where claims not "virtually identical" to those asserted in state forum, the doctrine of *res judicata* did not bar § 1983 claim in federal court).

Guragosian v. Ryan, 547 F.3d 59 (1st Cir. 2008) (where plaintiff voluntarily brought claim in state and federal forum and state court found in favor of defendants, § 1983 complaint in federal court was precluded).

Laurence v. Wall, 551 F.3d 92 (1st Cir. 2008) (per curiam) (dismissal of *pro se* complaint for untimely service of process held improper because *in forma pauperis* status entitles prisoner to service of process by U.S. Marshal without also requiring request for the same).

Kaemmerling v. Lappin, 553 F.3d 669 (D.C. Cir. 2008) (*pro se* complaint of RFRA, First, Fourth, and Fifth Amendment violation, liberally construed, not supported by provable facts and therefore properly dismissed).

Crawford v. Metropolitan Gov't of Nashville & Davidson County, 555 U.S. 271, 274 n.1, 129 S.Ct. 846, 849 n.1, 172 L.Ed.2d 650 (2009) (on summary judgment, courts must take as true the evidence of the non-moving party, resolve all doubts and construe all evidence in the light most favorable to the non-moving party, and draw all inferences as may be reasonable in favor of the non-moving party).

Pettus v. Morgenthau, 554 F.3d 293 (2nd Cir. 2009) (where complaint failed to allege personal responsibility, claim for money damages properly dismissed).

Cardinal v. Metrish, 564 F.3d 794 (6th Cir 2009) (Rule 56(d) of the Fed. R. Civ. P. provides the non-moving party the opportunity for fair discovery).

Best v. City of Portland, 554 F.3d 698 (7th Cir. 2009) (state court's denial of suppression motion and prosecutor's voluntary dismissal of charges did not amount to judgment on the merits; therefore, subsequent § 1983 claim in federal court not barred by doctrine of collateral estoppel).

Bridges v. Gilbert, 557 F.3d 541 (7th Cir. 2009) (retaliatory disciplinary charge that was later dismissed insufficient grounds for constitutional claim under § 1983).

Ortiz v. Downey, 561 F.3d 664 (7th Cir. 2009) (where complaint did not allege actual injury in connection with access-to-courts deprivation, complaint properly dismissed).

Cardinal v. Metrish, 564 F.3d 794 (6th Cir. 2009) (*pro se* complaint properly dismissed because amendment would be futile exercise).

San Diego Police Officers' Association v. San Diego City Employees' Ret. Sys., 568 F.3d 725 (9th Cir. 2009) (where plaintiffs' released claims in settlement of prior lawsuit, plaintiffs barred by claim preclusion from litigating new § 1983 action against new defendants).

Abdulhaseeb v. Calbone, 600 F.3d 1301 (10th Cir. 2010) (summary judgment proper because *pro se* plaintiff did not allege sufficient facts to preclude summary judgment).

Ortiz v. Jordan, __U.S.__, 131 S.Ct. 884, 178 L.Ed.2d__ (2011) (courts must deny motion for summary judgment if genuine dispute of material fact exists for resolution at trial, and order of denial is generally not appealable until after an ultimate determination of the case, unless the order constitutes a "final order" or involves questions of immunity from suit).

Coble v. City of White House, 634 F.3d 865 (6th Cir. 2011) (on summary judgment, courts are not required to accept a party's assertion that is obviously a fiction).

Edwards v. Briggs & Stratton Ret. Plan, 639 F.3d 355 (7th Cir. 2011) (courts must view facts and draw reasonable inferences in favor of the non-moving party, even when reviewing cross-motions for summary judgment, where each motion must be evaluated on its merits under the standards of Fed. R. Civ. P. 56).

Karuk Tribe of Cal. v. U.S. Forest Serv., 640 F.3d 979 (9th Cir. 2011) (should the denial of a motion for summary judgment effectively resolve all issues of claims, constituting a final judgment, it is immediately appealable).

Seng-Tiong Ho v. Taflove, 648 F.3d 489 (7th Cir. 2011) (on summary judgment, both parties are obligated to cite pertinent points of the case record, either supporting or opposing, for the court's consideration).

J.S. ex rel Snyder v. Blue Mountain Sch. Dist., 650 F.3d 915 (3rd Cir. 2011) (on summary judgment, the moving party must make a *prima facie* showing that the record does not factually support the claims of the non-moving party, a showing which then shifts the burden to the non-moving party to demonstrate that such fact does exist; however, should the moving party bear the ultimate burden of proof at trial on an element for which it seeks summary judgment, then the *prima facie* burden is elevated, requiring the movant to demonstrate that it can meet its burden of proof for all essential elements of its claim(s) or defense(s)).

Siggers v. Campbell, 652 F.3d 681 (6th Cir. 2011) (courts generally grant Rule 56(d) motions to postpone summary judgment when a party files for summary judgment very early in the proceedings, before the parties have had an opportunity for discovery).

Everett v. Cook County, 655 F.3d 723 (7th Cir. 2011) (a party must establish an element essential to its case in order to survive a motion for summary judgment).

Marcatante v. City of Chigago, 657 F.3d 433 (7th Cir. 2011) (the fact of cross-motions, the fact that opposing parties have both filed for summary judgment, does not itself necessitate an entry of summary judgment).

Balser v. Int'l Union of Elec., Salaried, Mach. & Furniture Workers (IUE) Local 201, 661 F.3d 109 (1st Cir. 2011) (evidence, not hopes and conjectures, must be produced for a non-moving party to survive summary judgment).

Josendis v. Wall to Wall Residence Repairs, Inc., 662 F.3d 1292 (11th Cir. 2011) (a verified complaint should be treated as a sworn statement for the purpose of summary judgment).

Atkins v. Salazar, 677 F.3d 667 (5th Cir. 2011) (before a court may enter a *sua sponte* order for summary judgment it must first provide the parties notice of this intention and allow the parties opportunity to respond).

Cooper v. Allied Barton Sec. Servs., 422 Fed.Appx. 33 (2nd Cir. 2011) (materials supporting or opposing a motion for summary judgment must be capable of being produced in a form that would be admissible at trial).

Cutting Underwater Techs. USA, Inc. v. Eni U.S. Operating Co., 671 F.3d 512 (5th Cir. 2012) (to survive a motion for summary judgment the non-moving party must come forward with more than a promise that it will later at trial prove the falsity of the movant's claims or facts).

Newell Rubbermaid, Inc. v. Raymond Corp., 676 F.3d 521 (6th Cir. 2012) (the standards for summary judgment under Rule 56, Fed. R. Civ. P., remain unchanged by the 2010 amendments).

Phelps v. State Farm Mut. Auto. Ins. Co., 680 F.3d 725 (6th Cir. 2012) (on summary judgment, courts must consider materials cited in supporting and opposing papers).

Hexcel Corp. v. Ineos Polymers, Inc., 681 F.3d 1055 (9th Cir. 2012) (sworn statements—i.e., affidavits, declarations, verified complaints—in support or opposition of a motion for summary judgment must be made on personal knowledge, not belief or speculation).

NOTES:

NOTES: _____
_____
_____
_____
_____
_____
_____
_____
_____
_____
_____
_____
_____
_____
_____
_____
_____
_____
_____
_____
_____
_____
_____
_____
_____
_____
_____
_____
_____
_____
_____
_____
_____
_____
_____
_____
_____
_____
_____

DUE PROCESS

Cline v. Frink Dairy Co., 274 U.S. 445, 465, 47 S.Ct. 681, 71 L.Ed. 1146 (1927) (the law must be precise enough to avoid "involving so many factors of varying effect that neither the person to decide in advance nor the jury after the fact can safely and certainly judge the result.").

Armstrong v. Monzo, 380 U.S. 545, 552, 85 S.Ct. 1187, 14 L.Ed.2d 62 (1965) (due process requires an opportunity to be heard at a meaningful time and in a meaningful manner; due process must be afforded before the deprivation of life, liberty, or property).

Grayned v. City of Rockford, 408 U.S. 104, 108, 92 S.Ct. 2294, 33 L.Ed.2d 222 (1972) (under the fair notice requirement, an ordinance is void for vagueness if a person of ordinary intelligence cannot reasonably interpret what is prohibited).

Kastigar v. U.S., 406 U.S. 441, 92 S.Ct. 1653, 32 L.Ed.2d 212 (1972) (where prisoner is compelled to speak at prison disciplinary hearing, that testimony would be precluded by the Fifth Amendment for use at a later criminal prosecution.)

Morrissey v. Brewer, 408 U.S. 471, 92 S.Ct. 2593, 33 L.Ed.2d 484 (1972) (a parolee is entitled to less than the full range of due process rights afforded a defendant at a criminal trial; however, at a minimum, due process requires, among other things, a written notice specifying the claimed parole violations and the right to cross-examine witnesses unless good reason exists to deny confrontation).

Gagon v. Scarpelli, 411 U.S. 778, __S.Ct.__, __L.Ed.2d__ (1973) (where parolee has requested counsel, and where substantial reasons or circumstances mitigate or refute a parole violation, the parole agency may, at its discretion, appoint counsel).

Wolff v. McDonnell, 418 U.S. 539, 94 S.Ct. 2963, 41 L.Ed.2d 935 (1974) (for disciplinary hearings that may potentially deprive an inmate of a liberty interest, prisoners are generally entitled to (1) twenty-four-hour advance written notice of a hearing on the claimed violation; (2) opportunity to be heard, including the opportunity to call witnesses and present evidence if consistent with institutional safety and correctional goals; and (3) written statement by the fact-finder detailing the evidence relied upon and the reasons for the disciplinary action).

Mathews v. Eldridge, 424 U.S. 319, 333, 96 S.Ct. 892, 47 L.Ed.2d 18 (1976) (due process requires an opportunity to be heard at a meaningful time and in a meaningful manner; citizens must be afforded due process before deprivation of life, liberty, or property).

Baxter v. Palmigiano, 425 U.S. 308, 96 S.Ct. 1551, 47 L.Ed.2d 810 (1976) (Fifth Amendment right to silence does not extend to prison disciplinary proceeding; prison officials may use the fact of silence against an accused inmate).

Meachum v. Fano, 427 U.S. 215, 225, 96 S.Ct. 2532, 49 L.Ed.2d 431 (1976) (prisoners' have no liberty interest in remaining at a specific facility, for the purposes of procedural due process).

Moody v. Daggett, 429 U.S. 78, 97 S.Ct. 274, 50 L.Ed.2d 236 (1976) (Fifth and Fourteenth Amendment due process protects parolees' significant liberty interests).

Vitek v. Jones, 445 U.S. 480, 494-96, 100 S.Ct. 1254, 63 L.Ed.2d 552 (1980) (concerning procedures used in determination of whether an inmate may be transfered from a prison to a mental hospital without consent, prisoners are generally entitled to (1) written notice; (2) opportunity to be heard; (3) limited right to present evidence and call and cross-examine witnesses; (4) written statements by the fact-finder concerning evidence and reasons; (5) limited right to assistance; and (6) notice of these rights).

Hewill v. Helms, 459 U.S. 460, 477, 103 S.Ct. 864, 74 L.Ed.2d 675 (1983) (prisoners confined in administrative segregation are entitled to periodic review to determine whether segregation remains appropriate).

Hudson v. Palmer, 468 U.S. 517, 104 S.Ct. 3194, 60 L.Ed.2d 447 (1984) (deprivations of property in state prisons do not violate due process unless state law fails to provide adequate post-deprivation remedies).

Ponte v. Real, 471 U.S. 491, __S.Ct.__, __L.Ed.2d__ (1985) (officials must give reason for refusing to call witness at prisoner disciplinary hearing, either on the hearing record or later in court, should decision be challenged in subsequent legal action).

Superintendent v. Hill, 472 U.S. 445, 454, 105 S.Ct. 2768, __L.Ed.2d__ (1985) (due process requires that "some evidence" support a decision to place a prisoner in segregation).

Daniels v. Williams, 474 U.S. 327, __S.Ct.__, __L.Ed.2d__ (1986) (negligence is not enough to support a due-process claim for property loss or damage; conduct must be intentional and abusive).

Patten v. North Dakota Parole Board, 783 F.2d 140 (8th Cir. 1986) (a protected liberty interest in parole can be created by state statutes, rules, or regulations).

Touossaint v. McCarthy, 801 F.2d 1080 (9th Cir. 1986), *cert. denied*, 481 U.S. 1069, __S.Ct.__, __L.Ed.2d__ (1987) (where a liberty interest is at stake, due process requires at a minimum the right to a non-adversarial hearing within a reasonable time, notice of charges, and the opportunity to be heard).

Bennett v. Arkansas, 485 U.S. 395, 108 S.Ct. 1204, 99 L.Ed.2d 455 (1988) (seizure of prisoner's federal Social Security benefits to help cover the cost of maintaining prison system held to be in conflict with federal law).

Domegan v. Fair, 859 F.2d 1059 (1st Cir. 1988) (prisoners have a protected liberty interest in receiving nutritionally adequate meals).

Kentucky Dep't of Corr. v. Thompson, 490 U.S. 454, 462-463, 109 S.Ct. 1904, 104 L.Ed.2d 506 (1989) (the Due Process Clause protects state-created liberty interests; for a state statute or regulation to create a liberty interest protected under the Constitution, two things must be true: (1) the law must set forth substantive predicates to govern official decision making, and (2) the law must contain explicitly mandatory language (i.e., a specific directive to the decision-maker that mandates a particular outcome if the substantive predicates have been met)).

Coffman v. Trickey, 884 F.2d 57 (8th Cir. 1989) (due process was violated because disciplinary charge failed to specify what rule was violated).

Washington v. Harper, 494 U.S. 210, 231, 235, 110 S.Ct. 1028, 188 L.Ed.2d 178 (1990) (concerning procedures used in determination of whether an inmate may be forcibly administered antipsychotic drugs, prisoners must generally be afforded: (1) notice of intent and hearing; (2) right to be present at hearing confirming psychiatrist findings; and (3) right to cross-examine witnesses), *overruled in part on other grounds by Sandin v. Conner*, 515 U.S. at 486.

Leonardson v. City of East Lansing, 896 F.2d 190, 196 (6th Cir. 1990) ("Vagueness may take two forms, both of which result in a denial of due process. A vague ordinance denies fair notice of the standard of conduct to which a citizen is held accountable. At the same time an ordinance is void for vagueness if it is an unrestricted delegation of power, which in practice leaves the definition of its terms to law enforcement officers, and thereby invites arbitrary, discriminatory and overzealous enforcement.").

Toussaint v. McCarthy, 926 F.2d 800 (9th Cir. 1990), *cert. denied*, __U.S.__, 112 S.Ct. 213, __L.Ed.2d__ (1991) (concerning placement in administrative segregation, prisoners are generally entitled to (1) notice of the charges or reason for the segregation; (2) informal non-adversarial hearing within a reasonable time after segregation; (3) opportunity to present views to the official determining whether to transfer the inmate to administrative segregation; and (4) meaningful periodic review concerning whether segregation remains appropriate (a review every 120 days is sufficient)).

Nicholson v. Moran, 961 F.2d 996 (1st Cir. 1992) (consent decree specifying disciplinary procedures created a protected liberty interest for prisoner to remain in general population).

Battle v. Barton, 970 F.2d 779 (11th Cir. 1992) (per curiam) (a prisoner's right to attend the disciplinary hearing is essential to due process protection, but is not absolute, i.e., there may exist exceptional circumstances).

Calhoun v. N.Y. State Div. of Parole Officers, 999 F.2d 647 (2nd Cir. 1993) (prisoners have a protected liberty interest in being released upon the expiration of their maximum term of imprisonment).

Reeves v. Pettcox, 19 F.3d 1060 (5th Cir. 1994) (prison officials violated due process because disciplinary procedures were undertaken without giving the prisoner fair warning or opportunity to know that his conduct was unlawful).

Sandin v. Conner, 515 U.S. 472, 115 S.Ct. 2293, 132 L.Ed.2d 418 (1995) (cause of action available for due process violation if prisoner can show deprivation of a protected liberty interest; such interests are generally limited to (1) actions that alter the prisoner's term of imprisonment; and (2) actions that impose an atypical and significant hardship in relation to the ordinary incidents of prison life).

Whitford v. Bolingo, 63 F.3d 527 (7th Cir. 1995) (concerning prisoner disciplinary proceedings, a confidential informant's reliability may be established by (1) the oath of the investigator as to the truth of his report containing the confidential information; (2) the corroborating evidence or testimony; (3) the official's statement on the record that the informant has an history of reliability; or (4) the *in camera* review of material documenting the investigator's determination of the informant's reliability).

U.S. v. Grandlund, 71 F.3d 507 (5th Cir. 1995) (the same due process rights protecting those facing revocation of parole apply to those facing revocation of supervised release).

Mahers v. Halford, 76 F.3d 951 (8th Cir. 1996) (prisoners are entitled to due process before they can be deprived of money received from outside sources).

Edwards v. Balisok, 520 U.S. 641, 117 S.Ct. 1584, 137 L.Ed.2d 906 (1997) (procedural defects in prisoner's disciplinary hearing may be challenged under § 1983, and a successful plaintiff is entitled to at least nominal damages if it's shown that insufficient hearing procedures violated due process, without also proving the result of the disciplinary hearing, as a substantive matter, was wrong, requiring the reinstatement of good-time credits, *id.* 520 U.S. at 645; claims alleging only *defective procedures* and *not* seeking reversal of disciplinary board decision and reinstatement of good-time credits are not barred by the standard under *Heck v. Humphrey* prohibiting § 1983 action that would necessarily imply the invalidity of conviction or sentence without a prior showing that the same has been invalidated).

Whitlock v. Johnson, 153 F.3d 380 (7th Cir. 1998) (faced with revocation of good-time credits, prisoners have a due process right to call witnesses in their defense).

Jurasek v. Utah State Hosp., 158 F.3d 506 (10th Cir. 1998) (a state may create more comprehensive due process protections for its residents than does the federal government).

City of West Covina v. Perkins, 525 U.S. 234, 119 S.Ct. 678, 142 L.Ed.2d 636 (1999) (due process requirement of advanced notice is necessary to ensure meaningful hearing).

U.S. v. Brierton, 165 F.3d 113 (7th Cir. 1999) (the "vagueness doctrine" prohibits the government from punishing people for conduct they reasonably could not have known was unlawful).

Brunsworth v. Gunderson, 179 F.3d 771 (9th Cir. 1999) (due process was violated when a prison disciplinary hearing board convicted prisoner of escape after a hearing at which no shred of evidence of the prisoner's guilt was presented, even if inmate demonstrated no cognizable liberty interest).

Frost v. Symington, 197 F.3d 348 (9th Cir. 1999) (due process requires officials to notify prisoner when withholding/censoring incoming mail).

Thomas v. McCaughtry, 201 F.3d 995 (7th Cir. 2000) (prisoners have a protected liberty interest in their good-time credit for due process purposes).

Cruz v. Gomez, 202 F.3d 593 (2nd Cir. 2000) (no due process claim stated when prisoner failed to show state law creating protected liberty interest).

Friedl v. City of New York, 210 F.3d 79 (2nd Cir. 2000) (withdrawal from work release may invoke due process protection).

U.S. v. Sanders, 211 F.3d 711 (2nd Cir. 2000) (due process prohibits the government from punishing people for lawful conduct).

Forbes v. Napolitan, 236 F.3d 1009 (9th Cir. 2000) (laws that criminalize conduct must not be vague as to any of their applications).

Prison Legal News v. Cook, 238 F.3d 1145 (9th Cir. 2001) (prisoners and publishers enjoy the First Amendment right that protects prisoners' receipt of standard mail, and such mail must be afforded the same procedural protection, with due process consideration, as other first-class mail and periodicals permitted by the prison).

Gaston v. Coughlin, 249 F.3d 156 (2nd Cir. 2001) (finding due process sufficient when prison informant had history of reliability and information constituted "some evidence" sufficient for imposition of disciplinary sanction).

Nat. Council of Resistance to Iran v. Dep't of State, 251 F.3d 192 (D.C. Cir. 2001) (due process requires an opportunity to be heard at a meaningful time and in a meaningful manner; due process must be afforded before deprivation of life, liberty, or property).

U.S. v. Sesma-Hernandez, 253 F.3d 759 (7th Cir. 2001) (parolees are entitled to written statement of facts relied on in decision to revoke parole).

Bieber v. Dep't of Army, 287 F.3d 1358 (Fed. Cir. 2002) (due process protections extend to administrative proceedings).

U.S. v. Evans, 318 F.3d 1011 (10th Cir. 2003) (due process requires statutes to specify in clear terms the conduct they prohibit).

Rem v. U.S. Bureau of Prisons, 320 F.3d 791 (8th Cir. 2003) (finding for the purposes of due process protection that prisoner had no liberty interest in his reputation and being labeled a drug trafficker).

Piggie v. Cotton, 342 F.3d 774 (7th Cir. 2003) (due process requires meaningful hearing, precluding officials involved with investigation or allegation of disciplinary charges from participating on board responsible for ultimate disposition of charges).

Luna v. Pico, 356 F.3d 481 (2nd Cir. 2004) (prisoner stated viable due process claim when prison officials punished prisoner based on bare accusation without supporting evidence).

White v. Lambert, 370 F.3d 1002 (9th Cir. 2004) (interstate transfer to private facility did not constitute due process violation, because prisoner had no protected interest in being housed in any specific prison).

Sira v. Morton, 380 F.3d 57 (2nd Cir. 2004) (due process requires disciplinary reports to specify sufficient facts to enable a reasonable person to understand the basis of a charge of misconduct and identify relevant evidence; and hearing officers are required to conduct independent evaluations of a confidential informant's credibility based on the totality of the circumstances).

Shakur v. Selsky, 391 F.3d 106 (2nd Cir. 2004) (prisoners must show both interference with a constitutionally protected liberty interest *and* insufficient deprivation procedures to state a cognizable due process claim).

Richards v. Dretke, 394 F.3d 291 (5th Cir. 2004) (finding no due process violation when multiple witnesses corroborated account of prisoner assault detailed in a confidential report, taken with the prisoner's own admissions, constituted "some evidence" sufficient for the imposition of disciplinary sanction).

Wilkinson v. Austin, 545 U.S. 209, 222-23, __S.Ct.__, __L.Ed.2d__ (2005) (prisoners retain the due process right to freedom from restraint which "imposes atypical and significant hardship on the inmate in relation to the ordinary incidents of prison life," but have no liberty interest in remaining at a specific facility for the purpose of procedural due process protection, unless transfer to another facility imposes an atypical and significant hardship).

King v. Federal Bureau of Prisons, 415 F.3d 634 (7th Cir. 2005) (although prisoners can be prohibited from conducting a business while incarcerated, prisoners cannot be prevented from protecting property interests already in existence at the time of incarceration).

Suprenant v. Rivas, 424 F.3d 5 (1st Cir. 2005) (prisoner alleged viable due process claim when prisoner was deprived of a meaningful disciplinary hearing because hearing officer demonstrated his bias by refusing to interview an alibi witness based on the preconceived notion that the witness would lie, and when the officer imposed disciplinary sanctions without waiting for the completion of internal investigation).

Wilson v. Jones, 430 F.3d 1113 (10th Cir. 2005) (disciplinary conviction resulting in prisoner's demotion to non-credit-earning status inevitably affected length of sentence and prisoner was entitled to due process protections).

Anderson v. Recore, 446 F.3d 324 (2nd Cir. 2006) (viable due process claim alleged when officials deprived plaintiff of notice of hearing and opportunity to be heard before revocation of pre-parole temporary release).

Trujillo v. Williams, 465 F.3d 1210 (10th Cir. 2006) (750 days in segregation probable atypical and significant hardship).

Hydrick v. Hunter, 466 F.3d 676 (9th Cir. 2006) (prison officials are required to afford prisoners due process protections before depriving privileges, including notice and a chance to be heard).

Lovelace v. Lee, 471 F.3d 174 (4th Cir. 2006) (for procedural due process claim, prisoner must show (1) deprivation of protected liberty interest, (2) atypical and significant hardship, and (3) constitutionally insufficient procedural safeguards).

Estate of DiMarco v. Wyoming Dep't of Corr., 473 F.3d 1334 (10th Cir. 2007) (prisoner failed to state viable due process claim when she had no protected liberty interest and prison officials did provided procedural protections).

Scruggs v. Jordan, 485 F.3d 934 (7th Cir. 2007) (prisoner did not state a due process claim when prison officials denied prisoner access to prison recordings, records, and witness because disciplinary board accepted prisoners account as accurate and evidence presentation would have been irrelevant, repetitive, and expensive).

Sickles v. Campbell County, 501 F.3d 726 (6th Cir. 2007) (when prison had interest in withholding funds from prisoner's account for booking fees and room and board costs, prisoner did not state a due process claim because of the small private interest of the prisoner, and because of the costly nature of instituting pre-deprivation procedures and when there existed a low risk of error in current process).

Dible v. Scholl, 506 F.3d 1106 (8th Cir. 2007) (prisoner alleged viable due process claim when disciplinary notice contained no information specifying victim, place, or date of alleged assault of another prisoner; prison had no legitimate interest in such lack of information, it would not have imposed an undue administrative burden, and deprived prisoner of information needed to marshal a defense).

Wilkins v. Timmerman-Cooper, 512 F.3d 768 (6th Cir. 2008) (video conference sufficient due process protection to enable parolee opportunity to observe and confront witnesses).

Hernandez v. Velasquez, 522 F.3d 556 (5th Cir. 2008) (prisoner found not to have a protected liberty interest in custodial classification and lockdown status for thirteen months; no serious harm caused and prisoners have no right to comfortable conditions).

Harbin-Bey v. Rutter, 524 F.3d 789 (6th Cir. 2008) (prisoner stated a possible due process claim when he alleged "indefinite" placement in administrative segregation).

Bonner v. Outlaw, 552 F.3d 673 (8th Cir. 2009) (officials violated due process when failing to notify prisoner that his packages had been rejected and notice would create no further burden on officials).

Carver v. Lehman, 558 F.3d 869 (9th Cir. 2009) (state law did not create liberty interest in early release because statute did not include language expressly establishing early release as a substantive right).

Marion v. Columbia Corr. Inst., 559 F.3d 693 (7th Cir. 2009) (240 days in segregation may constitute atypical and significant hardship).

U.S. v. Lloyd, 566 F.3d 341 (3rd Cir. 2009) (releasee entitled to due process protection of notice and right to confront witnesses when release revoked during hearing at which releasee was absent and revocation based on unreliable hearsay evidence).

Bandey-Bay v. Crist, 578 F.3d 763 (8th Cir. 2009) (per curiam) (officer's report constituted "some evidence" to support a finding that prisoner filed false report against officer).

Richardson v. Runnels, 594 F.3d 666 (9th Cir. 2010) (two weeks in administrative segregation did not create liberty interest for due process purposes).

Jennings v. Owens, 602 F.3d 652 (5th Cir. 2010) (sex offender conditions for parole did not create liberty interest for due process purposes where plaintiff had opportunity to contest sex-offender status).

Howard v. Werlinger, 403 Fed.Appx. 776 (3rd Cir. 2010) (due process does not mandate prisoners' right to confront evidence used against them in disciplinary proceedings).

Nevada Dep't of Corr. v. Greene, 648 F.3d 1014 (9th Cir. 2011), *cert denied* __U.S.__, 132 S.Ct. 1823, 182 L.Ed.2d 627 (2012) (requiring inmates to send home property no longer permitted for inmate possession does not violate due process, so long as inmates given notice of policy change and time to comply).

Perechini v. Callaway, 651 F.3d 802 (8th Cir. 2011) (when probation is granted or not, as a matter of official discretion, there is no liberty interest in probation for the purposes of due process).

Reedy v. Werholtz, 660 F.3d 1270 (10th Cir. 2011) (officials do not violate due process rights when requiring part of an inmate's earnings to be deposited in an account accessible only upon release, because government has legitimate interest in ensuring newly released offenders have funds).

Flowers v. Anderson, 661 F.3d 977 (8th Cir. 2011) ("some evidence" is sufficient to support an adverse finding in disciplinary proceedings).

Williams v. Hobbs, 662 F.3d 994 (8th Cir. 2011) (due process requires meaningful review to determine whether inmates should remain in ad. seg.; reviewing officials who had no intention of revoking prisoner's ad. seg. status, despite prisoner's exemplary behavior over the preceeding seven years, did not provide meaningful reviews).

Rosin v. Thaler, 417 Fed.Appx. 432 (5th Cir 2011) (prisoners have a protected property interest in the money placed in their inmate accounts).

Bogue v. Vaughn, 439 Fed.Appx. 700 (10th Cir. 2011) (due process does not mandate prisoners' right to confront evidence used against them in disciplinary hearings).

Osborne v. Williams, 444 Fed.Appx. 153 (9th Cir. 2011) (no due process claim stated where state Tort Claims Act would have provided adequate post-deprivation remedy for alleged wrongful confiscation of prisoner's property).

Carter v. Lawler, 446 Fed.Appx 420 (3rd Cir. 2011) (hearsay evidence is admissible in disciplinary proceedings).

Freeman v. Dep't of Corr., 447 Fed.Appx 385 (3rd Cir. 2011) (360 days of disciplinary confinement not atypical and significant hardship).

McDowell v. Litz, No. 10-4635, 2011 WL 816616 (3rd Cir. Mar. 10, 2011), *petition for cert. filed* (U.S. June 13, 2011) (unpublished) (prisoners have no protected liberty interest, for due process purposes, in institutional employment).

Bullard v. Scism, __U.S.__, 132 S.Ct. 1948, __L.Ed.2d__ (2012) (disciplinary hearing held after 3-day time limit for hearings did not violate due process rights; due process does not mandate such a 3-day limit and regulation did not create liberty interest).

Jimenez v. McQueen, 460 Fed.Appx 458 (5th Cir. 2012) (seven years of administrative segregation not atypical and significant hardship).

NOTES: _____
_____
_____
_____
_____
_____
_____
_____
_____
_____
_____
_____
_____
_____
_____
_____
_____
_____
_____
_____
_____
_____
_____
_____
_____
_____
_____
_____
_____
_____
_____
_____
_____
_____
_____
_____
_____
_____
_____
_____

NOTES: _____

EIGHTH AMENDMENT

Gregg v. Georga, 428 U.S. 153, 173, 183, __S.Ct.__, __L.Ed.2d__ (1976) (formally imposed punishment is cruel and unusual if it involves "the unnecessary and wanton infliction of pain" ["wanton" means malicious or un-called-for] such as punishment "totally without penological justification" or "grossly out of proportion to the severity of the crime"; upholding state's imposition of the death penalty).

Estelle v. Gamble, 429 U.S. 97, 97 S.Ct. 285, 50 L.Ed.2d 251 (1976) (provided the existence of "deliberate indifference," a prisoner's detention beyond a sentence constitutes cruel and unusual punishment).

Hutto v. Finney, 437 U.S. 678, 682, 685-87, 98 S.Ct. 2565, 57 L.Ed.2d 522 (1978) (confinement in prison or in isolation cell is punishment subject to Eighth Amendment scrutiny; punitive isolation in 8 x10 foot cell for more than thirty days with average of four, and sometimes ten or eleven, prisoners creates intolerable living condtions).

Rhodes v. Chapman, 452 U.S. 337, 101 S.Ct. 2392, 69 L.Ed.2d 59 (1981) (unnecessary infliction of pain is prohibited; however, harsh conditions and rough disciplinary treatment are part of the price that convicted persons must pay, finding Eighth Amendment not violated by population at 38% overcapacity [452 U.S. at 347-50]).

Youngberg v. Romeo, 457 U.S. 307, 102 S.Ct. 2452, 73 L.Ed.2d 28 (1983) (leaving prisoners handcuffed or chained in a cell is unconstitutionally restrictive).

Hudson v. Palmer, 468 U.S. 517, 104 S.Ct. 3194, 60 L.Ed.2d 447 (1984) ("[I]ntentional harassment of even the most hardened criminals cannot be tolerated by a civilized society.").

Akao v. Shimoda, 832 F.2d 119 (9th Cir. 1987) (per curiam) (prisoner alleged viable Eighth Amendment claim when overcrowding led to stress increase, tension, communicable disease, and prisoner violence).

Davenport v. DeRoberts, 844 F.2d 1310 (7th Cir. 1988), *cert. denied* __U.S.__, 109 S.Ct. 260, __L.Ed.2d__ (1989) (in-cell exercise and in-cell washbasin held inadequate; court issued injunction requiring five hours out-side recreation and three showers per week).

Grass v. Sargent, 903 F.3d 1206 (8th Cir. 1990) (per curiam) (no Eighth Amendment violation because prisoners have no right to smoke).

Lopez v. Robinson, 914 F.2d 486 (4th Cir. 1990) (prisoner alleged no viable Eighth Amendment claim though prison population in excess of 30% of designed capacity because no showing of adverse effects).

Wilson v. Seiter, 501 U.S. 294, 111 S.Ct. 2321, 115 L.Ed.2d 271 (1991) ("deliberate indifference" standard applies to prisoners' claims that conditions of confinement amount to cruel and unusual punishment; however, a "sufficiently serious" deprivation or injury must be shown).

Hudson v. McMillian, 503 U.S. 1, 112 S.Ct. 995, 117 L.Ed.2d 156 (1992) (even lacking serious injury, prisoners can maintain a suit under the Eighth Amendment for excessive force claims).

Helling v. McKinney, 509 U.S. 25, 34-35, 113 S.Ct. 2475, __L.Ed.2d__ (1993) (to state a claim of cruel and unusual punishment, prisoners need not wait for a deprivation or injury to occur if it can be shown that serious risk is inevitable).

LeMaire v. Maass, 12 F.3d 851 (9th Cir. 1993) ((1) exercise is one of the basic human needs protected by the Eighth Amendment; (2) lack of outside exercise for extended periods of time meets the requisite harm needed to satisfy the objective test for Eighth Amendment violations; (3) injunction mandating the installation of intercom system in disciplinary segregation unit, allowing inmates to summon for assistance, could be applied to all inmates, as a healthy inmate may have a medical emergency or be injured).

Tijerna v. Plentl, 984 F.2d 148 (5th Cir. 1993) (Eighth Amendment does not require serious injury to support a constitutional claim).

Farmer v. Brennan, 511 U.S. 825, 114 S.Ct. 1970, 128 L.Ed.2d 811 (1994) (noting that prisoners have the right to be free from cruel and unusual punishment, while directly addressing the appropriate standard for determining whether the Eighth Amendment is violated by inmate-on-inmate violence, discussing and rejecting an "objective standard" under which a prison official who was unaware of a substantial risk of harm to an inmate would nevertheless be held liable under the Eighth Amendment—even if the risk was obvious and a reasonable prison official would have been aware of it—officials must be aware of a risk to be held liable; deliberate indifference is sufficient for this purpose).

Housley v. Dodson, 41 F.3d 597, 599 (10th Cir. 1994) (in determining what constitutes adequate exercise requires consideration of the physical characteristics of the cell and jail and the average length of stay of the inmates; moreover, failure to provide inmates confined for more than a very short period with the opportunity for at least five hours a week of exercise outside cells "raises serious constitutional questions").

Boddie v. Schnieder, 105 F.3d 857 (2nd Cir. 1997) (sexual abuse may meet both the objective and subjective elements to an Eighth Amendment claim because such abuse can cause physical as well as psychological harm and such conduct shows sufficiently culpable state of mind).

May v. Baldwin, 109 F.3d 557 (9th Cir. 1997) (finding no Eighth Amendment violation when prisoner was denied outdoor exercise for short period of twenty-one days with no adverse medical effects shown).

Dixon v.Godinez, 114 F.3d 640 (7th Cir. 1997) (prison conditions, even if ordinarily not amounting to Eighth Amendment violations, may violate the Eighth Amendment if persisting over extended periods of time).

Hamilton v. Leavy, 117 F.3d 742 (3rd Cir. 1997) (prisoner alleged viable Eighth Amendment claim under *Farmer v. Brennan* when prison officials failed to take necessary protective steps because prisoner had institutional reputation as a "snitch" and history of violent acts against him).

Perkins v. Kansas Dep't of Corr., 165 F.3d 803 (10th Cir. 1999) (psychological pain can violate the Eighth Amendment).

Campbell v. Sikes, 169 F.3d 1353 (11th Cir. 1999) (inhumane prison conditions are prohibited under the Constitution, uncomfortable prisons are not).

Gregoire v. Class, 236 F.3d 413 (8th Cir. 2000) ("deliberate indifference" standard applies to prisoners' claims that conditions of confinement amount to cruel and unusual punishment).

Davis v. Rennie, 264 F.3d 86 (1st Cir. 2001) (prisoner may bring suit for use of excessive force under the Eighth Amendment).

DeSpain v. Uphoff, 264 F.3d 965 (10th Cir. 2001) (restricting prisoners to a single toilet flush per 36-hour period held unsanitary Eighth Amendment violation, even though officials forced to turn off toilet system after prisoner flooded housing unit).

Hope v. Pelzer, 536 U.S. 730, 122 S.Ct. 2508, 153 L.Ed.2d 666 (2002) (handcuffing prisoner to "hitching post" as punishment held violation of Eighth Amendment; guards not entitled to qualified immunity from claim for damages under § 1983).

Cantu v. Jones, 293 F.3d 981 (7th Cir. 2002) (prison officials must take measures to prevent inmate-on-inmate violence).

Calderon-Ortiz v. Laboy-Alvarado, 300 F.3d 60 (1st Cir. 2002) (prison officials must take measures to prevent inmate-on-inmate violence).

Torre-Viera v. Laboy-Alcarado, 311 F.3d 105 (1st Cir. 2002) (excessive use of tear gas on prisoners may reach level of Eighth Amendment violation).

Calhoun v. DeTella, 319 F.3d 936 (7th Cir. 2003) (prisoner alleged viable Eighth Amendment claim when strip search was made in the presence of female guards for the purpose of harassment).

Adams v. Perez, 331 F.3d 508 (5th Cir. 2003) ("deliberate indifference" standard applies to prisoners' claims that conditions of confinement amount to cruel and unusual punishment).

Trammell v. Keane, 338 F.3d 155 (2nd Cir. 2003) (prisoner did not alleged viable Eighth Amendment violation because disciplinary measure depriving prisoner of clothing, blanket, and mattress for several weeks and toilet paper for more than a week did not risk prisoner's health and safety).

Chandler v. Crosby, 379 F.3d 1278 (11th Cir. 2004) (prisoners denied air conditioning when temperatures in housing unit rose between 80-86 degrees did not violate Eighth Amendment; and occasional 90+ degree temperatures did not violate Eighth Amendment where other measures beside air conditioning used to mitigate effects of heat).

Watts v. McKinney, 394 F.3d 710 (9th Cir. 2005) (prisoner alleged viable Eighth Amendment claim when guard slammed prisoner's face into a wall and kicked him in the groin while handcuffed because such actions showed cruel and sadistic intention to harm another).

Harper v. Albert, 400 F.3d 1052 (7th Cir. 2005) (plaintiff must meet the "malicious and sadistic" standard in showing the requisite culpable mind of an excessive-force claim).

Purcell ex rel Estate of Morgan v. Toombs County, 400 F.3d 1313 (11th Cir. 2005) (viable Eighth Amendment claim not stated, though prisoner was beaten to death by other prisoner, because there existed no excessive risk of violence at the facility).

Trujillo v. Williams, 465 F.3d 1210 (10th Cir. 2006) (nutritionally adequate food must be provided for prisoners).

Brown v. Lippard, 472 F.3d 384 (5th Cir. 2006) (prisoner alleged viable Eighth Amendment claim when guard struck prisoner even though he was cooperating and unthreatening).

U.S. v. Miller, 477 F.3d 644 (8th Cir. 2007) (guard who struck and kicked prisoner restrained on ground violated Eighth Amendment because actions unwarranted and malicious).

U.S. v. Budd, 496 F.3d 517 (6th Cir. 2007) (prisoner alleged viable Eighth Amendment claim when guard slammed prisoner's head against a window frame, shoved him to the ground, and stepped on his back; prisoner was merely being obnoxious, posing no threat, and beating was not justified by any legitimate penological interest).

Irving v. Dormire, 519 F.3d 441 (8th Cir. 2008) (prisoner alleged viable Eighth Amendment claim when guards knowingly subjected prisoner to attack by another prisoner by opening his cell door).

Townsend v. Fuchs, 522 F.3d 765 (7th Cir. 2008) (prisoner alleged viable Eighth Amendment claim when prison officials forced him to choose between not showering or showering in a cell where his mattress got wet and was forced to sleep on the damp, moldy mattress).

Harbin-Bey v. Rutter, 524 F.3d 789 (6th Cir. 2008) ("routine discomfort" does not rise to the level of an Eighth Amendment violation, being part of the criminal penalty offenders pay; deprivation of a "life necessity" must be alleged).

Lockett v. Suardini, 526 F.3d 866 (6th Cir. 2008) (prisoner did not alleged viable Eighth Amendment claim because guards had legitimate interest in maintaining control and returning prisoner to cell, and minimal force was used in shoving, grabbing, and bending back two of prisoner's fingers).

Walker v. Bowersox, 526 F.3d 1186 (8th Cir. 2008) (prisoner beaten, prohibited water and toilet, forced to sit upright on bench for twenty-four hours stated Eighth Amendment claim because force used after prisoner was pacified).

Pierce v. County of Orange, 526 F.3d 1190, 1212-13 (9th Cir. 2008) (erroneously finding in favor of the County, "the district court relied exclusively on the fact that 'a group of detainees congregating in an open area containing weights and other equipment raises security concerns.' We agree that the County has considerable discretion to curtail access to exercise based on security concerns. *Bell*, 441 U.S. at 539 n. 23, 99 S.Ct. 1861. Here, however, the curtailment to ninety minutes weekly for inmates who otherwise spend the bulk of their time inside their cells reduces the amount of exercise to a point at which there is no meaningful vindication of the constitutional right to exercise for this entire category of detainees. The County has provided nothing more to justify this almost complete denial of exercise than a generalized reference to institutional security concerns. It has made no showing that such a severe restriction is reasonably related to satisfying those concerns.").

Levine v. Roebuck, 550 F.3d 684 (8th Cir. 2008) (force used in nurses' attempt to obtain urine from prisoner for drug test by inserting catheter did not rise to level of Eighth Amendment violation).

Wright v. Gourd, 554 F.3d 255 (2nd Cir. 2009) (no Eighth Amendment violation when guard grabbed prisoner without malice and no injury besides shortness of breath inflicted on prisoner).

Foster v. Runnels, 554 F.3d 807 (9th Cir. 2009) (prisoner denied sixteen meals in twenty-three days as discipline violated Eighth Amendment because measure unnecessary for officials' safety).

Fennel v. Gilstrap, 559 F.3d 1212 (11th Cir. 2009) (where prisoner was combative and twisted officer's arm, officer did not violate Eighth Amendment by kicking prisoner).

Smith v. U.S., 561 F.3d 1090 (10th Cir. 2009) (prisoner assigned to work in environment containing asbestos stated viable Eighth Amendment claim).

Giles v. Kearney, 571 F.3d 318 (3rd Cir. 2009) (guard who beat prisoner after he stopped resisting violated the Eighth Amendment).

Smith v. Ozmit, 578 F.3d 246 (4th Cir. 2009) (mere physical restraint did not violate the Eighth Amendment).

Lewis v. Downey, 581 F.3d 467 (7th Cir. 2009) (Eighth Amendment violated when prisoner who did not get out of bed was tasered by guard because level of force not justified).

Hendrickson v. Cooper, 589 F.3d 887 (7th Cir. 2009) (viable Eighth Amendment claim arose when guard attacked prisoner after an insult).

Wilkins v. Gaddy, __U.S.__, 130 S.Ct. 1175, __L.Ed.2d__ (2010) (whether prison officials acted with a culpable state of mind is key to an excessive-force claim, not whether the prisoner has suffered a certain degree of injury).

Norwwod v. Vance, 591 F.3d 1062 (9th Cir. 2010) (official immune to Eighth Amendment claim because safety concerns legitimate reason to deny prisoner outdoor exercise).

Santiago v. Walls, 599 F.3d 749 (7th Cir. 2010) (prisoner sprayed with pepper spray and yanked by handcuffs did not state Eighth Amendment violation, because measures not wantonly inflicted and were necessary to restore order after prisoner fought another prisoner).

Williams v. Jackson, 600 F.3d 1007 (8th Cir. 2010) (although causing only irritation to prisoner's eyes, removal of radiation shield from ultraviolet lamp by guards satisfied the objective injury requirement of an excessive-force Eighth Amendment claim).

Griffin v. Hardrick, 604 F.3d 949 (6th Cir. 2010) (where officer subdued detainee by knocking out legs, no Eighth Amendment violation because force within jail protocols).

Kaden v. Slykhvis, 651 F.3d 966 (8th Cir. 2011) (supervisor who acquiesced in the unconstitutional conduct of subordinates may be liable for deliberate indifference).

McCree v. Sherrod, 408 Fed.Appx 990 (7th Cir. 2011), *cert. denied* __U.S.__, 132 S.Ct. 269, 181 L.Ed.2d 158 (2011) (triple-celling inmates, in itself, insufficient to state a claim under the Eighth Amendment, without a showing of harm).

Ellis v. Pierce County, GA, 415 Fed.Appx. 215 (11th Cir. 2011) (deprivation of amenities such as television, phone access, social time, and hot water insufficient to state a claim under the Eighth Amendment).

Stewart v. Beard, 417 Fed.Appx. 117 (3rd Cir. 2011) (twenty-four-hour cell illumination in Restricted Housing Unit served legitimate security and safety concerns).

Webb v. Deboo, 423 Fed.Appx. 299 (4th Cir. 2011) (per curiam) (where overcrowding and sanitation issues could result in risk of inmates' harm, viable Eighth Amendment claim stated).

Williams v. Schreler, 436 Fed.Appx. 687 (7th Cir. 2011) (viable deliberate indifference claim stated when prisoner denied six meals on two consecutive days).

Gannaway v. Berks County Prison, 439 Fed.Appx. 86 (3rd Cir. 2011) (per curiam) (although diet of Nutraloaf allegedly made inmate ill, deliberate indifference claim not stated because inmate failed to notify defendants of his illness).

Richmond v. Settles, 450 Fed.Appx. 448 (6th Cir 2011) (six-day deprivation of toilet paper, basic hygiene items, running water, and showers insufficient to state a claim under Eighth Amendment).

Stewart v. Crawford, 452 Fed.Appx. 693 (8th Cir. 2011) (per curiam) (three hours out-of-cell exercise per week for segregated inmate sufficient under the Constitution where inmate's cell large enough for in-cell exercise).

Rice ex rel Rice v. Correctional Med. Serv., 675 F.3d 650, 665 (7th Cir. 2012) ("[P]rison officials have an obligation to intervene when they know a prisoner suffers from self-destructive tendencies.").

Guitron v. Paul, 675 F.3d 1044 (7th Cir. 2012) (bending of inmate's injured wrist insufficient to state excessive force claim when inmate refused to comply with an order to get against the wall).

Gomez v. Randle, 680 F.3d 859 (7th Cir. 2012) (viable Eighth Amendment claim stated if guard fired two shotgun rounds into inmate population to break up unarmed fight, hitting two inmates uninvolved with the fight; use of deadly force may not be justified).

Okaloosa County Bd. of County Com'rs, 456 Fed.Appx. 845 (11th Cir. 2012) (per curiam) (viable excessive force claim when guards knocked compliant, handcuffed woman to the ground and tased her sixteen times).

NOTES:

NOTES: _____
_____
_____
_____
_____
_____
_____
_____
_____
_____
_____
_____
_____
_____
_____
_____
_____
_____
_____
_____
_____
_____
_____
_____
_____
_____
_____
_____
_____
_____
_____
_____
_____
_____
_____
_____
_____
_____
_____
_____
_____
_____

EQUAL PROTECTION

F.S. Royster Guano Co. v. Virginia, 253 U.S. 412, 415, __S.Ct.__, __L.Ed.__ (1920) (under the Equal Protection Clause, "all persons similarly circumstanced shall be treated alike" by governmental entities).

Tigner v. Texas, 310 U.S. 141, 147, __S.Ct.__, __L.Ed.__ (1940) ("The Constitution does not require things which are different in fact or opinion to be treated in law as though they were the same").

McGowan v. Maryland, 366 U.S. 420, 425, 81 S.Ct. 1101, 6 L.Ed.2d 393 (1961) (establishing treatment that is different from those who are similarly situated is the first step in a successful equal protection claim); *Williamson v. Lee Optical of Oklahoma, Inc.*, 348 U.S. 483, 490, 75 S.Ct. 461, 99 L.Ed. 563 (1955) (same).

Lee v. Washington, 390 U.S. 333, __S.Ct.__, __L.Ed.2d__ (1968) (per curiam) (equal protection of laws extends to the incarcerated).

Graham v. Richardson, 403 U.S. 365, 372, __S.Ct.__, L.Ed.2d__ (1971) ("[C]lassifications . . . like those based on nationality or race, are inherently suspect and subject to close judicial scrutiny").

San Antonio Independent Sch. Dist. v. Rodriguez, 411 U.S. 1, 93 S.Ct. 1278, 36 L.Ed.2d 16 (1973) (dissimilar treatment of like groups must not only serve a legitimate governmental purpose but the means of treatment must actually serve that purpose).

City of Cleburne v. Cleburn Living Center, 473 U.S. 432, 105 S.Ct. 3249, 87 L.Ed.3d 313 (1985) (equal protection violation occurs when the government treats someone differently than another who is similarly situated).

Central Airlines, Inc. v. U.S., 138 F.3d 333 (8th Cir. 1988) (government officials must not apply the law in a discriminatory fashion).

Edmonson v. Leesville Concrete Co. Inc., 860 F.2d 1308 (5th Cir. 1988) (the principle of equal protection applies to governmental action in civil as well as criminal actions).

Jacobs, Visonsi & Jacobs Co. v. City of Lawrence, KS, 927 F.2d 1111 (10th Cir. 1991) (equal protection violation occurs when the government treats someone differently than another who is similarly situated).

Brown v. Zavaras, 63 F.3d 967 (10th Cir. 1995) (transsexual prisoners are not a suspect class for the purposes of equal protection, and therefore denial of estrogen treatment is subject to rational relation to legitimate penal concern, rather than strict judicial scrutiny).

Fraternal Order of Police v. U.S., 152 F.3d 998 (D.C. Cir. 1998) (an analysis of equal protection is substantially the same under the Fifth and the Fourteenth Amendments).

Webber v. Crabtree, 158 F.3d 460 (9th Cir. 1998) (prisoners are not suspect class for equal protection purposes).

Franklin v. D.C., 163 F.3d 625 (D.C. Cir. 1998) (non-English speaking inmates must be provided interpretors for essential communications such as medical requests and communication during parole hearings).

Rodriguez v. Cook, 169 F.3d 1176 (9th Cir. 1999) (indigent prisoners are not a suspect class for the purposes of equal protection).

U.S. v. Deering, 179 F.3d 592 (8th Cir. 1999) (equal protection prohibits selective enforcement of law, on basis of race).

Murell v. School Dist. No.1, Denver, Colo., 186 F.3d 1238 (10th Cir. 1999) (a denial of equal protection by a municipality, or any other person acting under color of state law, is actionable under § 1983).

Rouse v. Benson, 193 F.3d 936 (8th Cir. 1999) (prisoners enjoy the guarantees of equal protection).

Brown v. City of Oneonta, NY, 195 F.3d 111 (2nd 1999) (government should treat a person the same as others who are similarly situated).

Hilton v. City of Wheeling, 209 F.3d 1005 (7th Cir. 2000) (a person need not be a member of a protected group to qualify for equal protection).

Yates v. Stalder, 217 F.3d 332 (5th Cir. 2000) (absent a showing of legitimate penological interest, providing female prisoners better living conditions and job opportunities than male prisoners may constitute equal protections violation).

Morrison v. Garraghty, 239 F.3d 648 (4th Cir. 2001) (if religious items denied to Native Americans on basis of race alone, equal protection violation arises because policy not rationally related to legitimate interest).

Taylor v. Delatoore, 281 F.3d 844 (9th Cir. 2002) (PLRA's filing fee limitations serves legitimate governmental interest in curtailing frivolous prisoner suits and drain on judicial resources, and therefore does not violate equal protection).

Veney v. Wyche, 293 F.3d 726 (4th Cir. 2002) (policy prohibiting homosexual males from celling together while homosexual females permitted held not to violate equal protection of laws because rationally related to safety and security concerns).

Jackson v. State Bd. of Pardons & Parole, 331 F.3d 790 (11th Cir. 2003) (prisoners are not a suspect class for equal protection purposes).

Johnson v. California, 543 U.S. 499, 125 S.Ct 1141, 160 L.Ed.2d 949 (2005) (prison policy that makes distinctions based on race is subject to strict judicial review to determine whether the policy serves a compelling state interest and is narrowly tailored to serve and extend no further than that interest).

Phillips v. Girdich, 408 F.3d 124 (2nd Cir. 2005) (prisoner alleged viable equal protection claim when black prisoner was punished more harshly than white found in possession of drugs, and when prison officials used racial epithets).

Roubideaux v. N.D. Dep't of Corr. & Rehab., 570 F.3d 966 (8th Cir. 2009) (gender-based prison transfer did not violated equal protection of law, because decision rationally related to legitimate concerns of housing space).

Richardson v. Runnels, 594 F.3d 666 (9th Cir. 2010) (segregating and locking down African Americans in response to prison violence possibly violated equal protection when only few African American prisoners involved with disturbance).

Ra-o-kel-ly v. Johnson, 416 Fed.Appx 631 (9th Cir. 2011) (segregated inmates are not a protected class for Equal Protection purposes).

Daye v. Rubenstein, 417 Fed.Appx 317 (4th Cir. 2011), *petition for cert. filed* (U.S. May 5, 2011) (viable Equal Protection claim when black inmate alleged white inmates received more desirable task assignments).

Hearn v. Kennell, 433 Fed.Appx 483 (7th Cir. 2011) (prisoner failed to show intentional discrimination when officials provided Kosher meat but not halal meat).

Davis v. Prison Health Servs., 679 F.3d 433 (6th Cir. 2012) (gay inmate stated viable Equal Protections claim, alleging sexual orientation was motive behind termination for public-work assignment).

NOTES: _____

NOTES: _____

_____

_____

_____

_____

_____

_____

_____

_____

_____

_____

_____

_____

_____

_____

_____

_____

_____

_____

_____

_____

_____

_____

_____

_____

_____

_____

_____

_____

_____

_____

_____

_____

_____

_____

_____

_____

_____

_____

_____

_____

_____

EVIDENCE

Prudential Ins. Co. v. Gibraltor Fin. Corp., 694 F.2d 1150 (9th Cir. 1983) (survey evidence may be admissible under Fed. R. Evid. 807).

Superintendent v. Hill, 472 U.S. 445, 105 S.Ct. 2768, __L.Ed.2d__ (1985) ("some evidence" must support disciplinary board's decisions [472 U.S. at 455], though rule only requires decision not to be arbitrary and without support in the record [at 457]; prison guard's testimony that he saw defendants fleeing from area where inmate just attacked constituted "some evidence" [at 456-57]).

McRorie v. Shimoda, 795 F.2d 780 (9th Cir. 1986) ("custom" of constitutional violations may be inferred from officials' failure to properly investigate and sanction misconduct, because supervisors are charged with duty of investigating credible allegations of subordinates' misconduct).

Daubert v. Merrell Dow Pharmaceuticals, Inc., 509 U.S. 579, 581, 113 S.Ct. 2786, 2791, 125 L.Ed.2d 469 (1993) (*Daubert* sets forth a four-prong, yet non-exhaustive analytical framework for determining whether expert testimony is admissible under Rule 702 of the Federal Rules of Evidence).
    NOTE: In *Daubert* the Supreme Court set forth the proper analytical standard "for admitting expert scientific testimony in a federal trial." The Court rejected the more liberal standard embodied in Fed. R. Evid. 702 that the expert need only testify to "(1) scientific knowledge that (2) will assist the trier of fact to understand or determine a fact in issue." *Daubert*, 509 U.S. at 592, 113 S.Ct. at 2796. The Court stated that in order to "qualify as 'scientific knowledge,' an inference or assertion must be derived by the scientific method." *Id.*, at 590, 113 S.Ct. at 2795. The Court noted four non-exhaustive factors that would bear on this inquiry: (1) falsifiability, (2) peer review, (3) rate of error, and (4) general acceptance. *Id.*, 509 U.S. at 593-94, 113 S.Ct. at 2796-97.

Tome v. U.S., __U.S.__, 115 S.Ct. 696, __L.Ed.2d__ (1995) (holding that prior consistent out-of-court statements, normally admissible to rebut an allegation of improper motive for testifying, are inadmissible if the statement was made after the improper motive may have arisen).

City of Long Beach v. Standard Oil Co., 46 F.3d 929, 936 (9th Cir. 1995) (on appeal, a district court's ultimate evidentiary ruling to admit or exclude evidence is reviewed for "abuse of discretion"; finding abuse, there must also exist a prejudice or reversal is improper).
    NOTE: Trial courts have broad discretion in managing the introduction of evidence at trial; when a trial court's construction and interpretation of the actual law or rule governing evidence is to be reviewed *de novo* (over again; without deference to the trial court's interpretation), the trial court's management of evidence will not be disturbed unless there exists a harm to a party resulting from an abuse of judicial discretion.

Boyd v. Knox, 47 F.3d 966 (8th Cir. 1995) (circumstantial evidence can suffice to establish "deliberate indifference").

Woman Prisoners of D.C. Dep't of Corr. v. D.C., 93 F.3d 910 (D.C. Cir. 1996) ("custom" of constitutional violations may be inferred from officials' failure to properly investigate and sanction misconduct, because supervisors are charged with duty of investigating credible allegations of subordinates' misconduct).

Kumho Tire Co. Ltd. v. Carmichael, __U.S.__, 119 S.Ct. 1167, __L.Ed.2d__ (1999) (expands *Daubert* to include not only scientific experts, but also experts whose testimony is based on technical or other specialized knowledge).

Schledwitz v. U.S., 169 F.3d 1003 (6th Cir. 1999) (whether a witness is biased is always relevant).

Reynolds v. Green, 184 F.3d 589 (6th Cir. 1999) (hearsay within hearsay is only admissible if both levels of hearsay are permitted under a hearsay exception).

Schering Corp. v. Pfizer, Inc., 189 F.3d 218 (2nd Cir. 1999) (trustworthiness is a requirement for the admission of survey evidence).

U.S. v. Miles, 207 F.3d 988 (7th Cir. 2000) (evidence is unfairly prejudicial if it influences the jury to make a determination not on the evidence but on some improper basis).

U.S. v. Prigmore, 243 F.3d 1 (1st Cir. 2001) (expert testimony should not be offered for the singular purpose of making a conclusion of law).

Walker v. Bair, 257 F.3d 600 (6th Cir. 2001) (where evidence of damages was plaintiff's testimony of subjective injuries only, compensatory damages are improper).

U.S. v. Velarde-Gomez, 269 F.3d 1023 (9th Cir. 2001) ("physical evidence" includes a person's fingerprints, handwriting, vocal characteristics, stance, stride, gestures, or blood characteristics).

U.S. v. Jackson-Randolph, 282 F.3d 369 (6th Cir. 2002) (whether a witness would intentionally or unintentionally color his or her testimony for or against a party is a question of bias, and bias is always relevant to an evaluation of credibility).

Piptone v. Biomatrix, Inc., 288 F.3d 239 (5th Cir. 2002) (*Daubert* sets forth a four-prong, yet non-exhaustive analytical framework for determining whether expert testimony is admissible under Rule 702 of the Federal Rules of Evidence).

Briggs v. Terhuna, 334 F.3d 910 (9th Cir. 2003) (several unsupported findings irrelevant because parole board's decision based on "some evidence"), *overruled on other grounds by Hayward v. Marshall*, 603 F.3d 546 (9th Cir. 2010).

Johnson v. Karnes, 398 F.3d 868 (9th Cir. 2005) (circumstantial evidence is sufficient to show deliberate indifference).

Obrey v. Johnson, 400 F.3d 691 (9th Cir. 2005) (if the trial court has erred in excluding evidence, there must then be a presumption of prejudice, although the "presumption" can be rebutted by a showing that it is more probable than not that the jury would have reached the same verdict even if the evidence had been admitted).

Wisehart v. Davis, 408 F.3d 321 (7th Cir. 2005) (whether a witness has received a benefit (e.g., money, leniency, immunity) to secure his or her testimony speaks to potential bias and therefore is relevant to credibility, and may be explored on cross-examination).

U.S. v. Hamilton, 413 F.3d 1138 (8th Cir. 2005) (hearsay evidence is not admissible unless it falls under one of the hearsay exceptions).

U.S. v. Hall, 419 F.3d 980 (9th Cir. 2005) (the Confrontation Clause of the Sixth Amendment does not extend to include civil disputes).

U.S. v. Durham, 464 F.3d 976 (9th Cir. 2006) (a district court's construction or interpretation of the Federal Rules of Evidence, including whether certain evidence falls within the scope of a given rule, is reviewed *de novo*).
    NOTE: "*De novo*" means "anew"—without deference to the prior interpretation of the lower court.

U.S. v. Davis, 490 F.3d 541 (6th Cir. 2007) (it is within a court's discretion to exclude evidence of marginal relevance and significant prejudice).

Tassin v. Cain, 517 F.3d 770 (5th Cir. 2008) (a key witness who lies about an exchange or a potential benefit to secure his or her testimony undermines the integrity of the trial).

U.S. v. Seymour, 519 F.3d 700 (7th Cir. 2008) (evidence that was obtained in violation of a person's Constitutional rights cannot be used against the person for any purpose).

Pierce v. County of Orange, 519 F.3d 985, 1201 (9th Cir. 2008) (the district court did not abuse its discretion when it refused to admit class-member deposition testimony; class members incarcerated 100 miles from courthouse were not "unavailable" for the purposes of Fed.R.Evid. 804(a)(5), when plaintiffs did not follow requisite steps in attempting to subpoena witnesses).
    NOTE: If you intend to rely on the testimony of other inmates, it is required that the necessary steps are followed in issuing a subpoena *and* securing a transport order for their appearance at hearing or trial. If subpoena and transport order are reasonably pursued and it is still unlikely the incarcerated witnesses will be able to appear in court, they will likely be deemed "unavailable" for the purposes of Fed.R.Evid. 804, and their out-of-court statements may be admissible.

U.S. v. Quinones-Medina, 553 F.3d 19 (1st Cir. 2009) (funds for psychiatric expert properly denied where prisoner failed to connect psychological problems with reduced mental capacity).

NOTES:

NOTES:

FIRST AMENDMENT

Procunier v. Martinez, 416 U.S. 396, 94 S.Ct. 1800, 40 L.Ed.2d 224 (1974) (the public has a right to associate with prisoners).

Pell v. Procunier, 417 U.S. 817, 94 S.Ct. 2800, 41 L.Ed.2d 495 (1974) (the public has a right to associate with prisoners).

Elrod v. Burns, 427 U.S. 347, __S.Ct.__, __L.Ed.2d__ (1976) (First Amendment deprivations, regardless of how short the duration, constitute irreparable injury).

Murphy v. Missouri Dep't of Corr., 814 F.3d 1252 (8th Cir. 1987) (First Amendment held violated when mail prohibited from Aryan Nation because prison officials may not withhold mail unless literature advocates violence or is so racially inflammatory that it is likely to cause violence).

McCabe v. Arave, 827 F.2d 634 (9th Cir. 1987) (security and rehabilitation goals not reasonably related to prison ban of materials advocating racial purity but not encouraging prisoners to conduct illegal activity or violence).

Duaneutef v. O'Keefe, 98 F.3d 22 (2nd Cir. 1996) (First Amendment right of association not violated by ban of prisoner petitions where officials provided other methods for expression of grievances).

Chriceol v. Phillips, 169 F.3d 313 (5th Cir. 1999) (prison regulation prohibiting literature advocating racial violence held constitutionally permissible in furthering prison's security interests).

Croft v. Roe, 170 F.3d 957 (9th Cir. 1999) (any restriction on the flow of information to prisoners must relate to a legitimate penological interest, or risk offending the First Amendment).

Cooper v. Schriro, 189 F.3d 781 (8th Cir. 1999) (First Amendment claim stated because prison did not have legitimate penological interest in restricting all magazine access and other specific publications).

Lerman v. Board of Elections City of New York, 232 F.3d 135 (2nd Cir. 2000) (that some First Amendment activity remains unimpaired does not vindicate the unconstitutional impairment of other First Amendment activity).

U.S. v. Landham, 251 F.3d 1072 (6th Cir. 2001) (true threats are not protected by the First Amendment; speech that is vulgar or offensive is protected, however).

Jones v. Fitzgerald, 285 F.3d 705 (8th Cir. 2002) (First Amendment protects freedom of association and political belief).

Davis v. Goord, 320 F.3d 346 (2nd Cir. 2003) (First Amendment protects the pursuance of grievances).

Bahramour v. Lampert, 356 F.3d 969 (9th Cir. 2004) (ban of sexually explicit materials upheld in legitimate interest of curtailing sexual aggression and maintaining respect for authorities).

Cochran v. Veneman, 359 F.3d 263 (3rd Cir. 2004) (the right to refrain from speech or association is protected by the First Amendment).

Clement v. Cal. Dep't of Corr., 364 F.3d 1148 (9th Cir. 2004) (prison regulation prohibiting mail containing material download from the Internet held to be overly broad and not reasonably related to legitimate penological interest, thus in violation of the First Amendment).

Powell v. Alaxander, 391 F.3d 1 (1st Cir. 2004) (retaliation for exercise of First Amendment right is actionable under § 1983).

Jacklovich v. Simmons, 392 F.3d 420 (10th Cir. 2004) (absent legitimate penological interest to the contrary, prisoners have First Amendment right to receive information).

King v. Federal Bureau of Prisons, 415 F.3d 634 (7th Cir. 2005) (free speech necessarily entails freedom to read).

Beard v. Banks, 548 U.S. 521, 126 S.Ct. 2572, 165 L.Ed.2d 697 (2006) (applying *Turner* in upholding prison's regulation forbidding higher-security inmates access to print media as reasonably related to institutional security concerns; considering all four factors of *Turner* but noting "we believe that the first rationale itself satisfies *Turner*'s requirements" [126 S.Ct. at 2577-79]).

Borzych v. Frank, 439 F.3d 388 (7th Cir. 2006) (prison has legitimate security interest in ensuring safety and curtailing violence; therefore, First Amendment held not to be violated by prison's ban on racist literature).

Koutink v. Brown, 456 F.3d 777 (7th Cir. 2006) (outgoing letter depicting swastika and making reference to Ku Klux Klan lawfully confiscated because letter would diminish respectful human interaction inside and outside prison).

Jones v. Salt Lake County, 503 F.3d 1147 (10th Cir. 2007) (First Amendment right was not violated by prison's ban on sexually explicit material and technical publications covering weapons, contraband, and escape, as regulation is reasonably related to penological interest in maintaining security).

Singer v. Raemisch, 593 F.3d 529 (7th Cir. 2010) (officials had legitimate government interest in confiscating prisoner's role-playing-game materials, to prevent escapist fantasies and gang activity).

Nevada Dep't of Corr. v. Greene, 648 F.3d 1014 (9th Cir. 2011), *cert. denied* __U.S.__, 132 S.Ct 1823, 182 L.Ed.2d 627 (2012) (policy banning prisoner possession of typewriter held constitutional in light of reasonable goal of prison safety).

Woods v. Comm'r of the Ind. Dep't of Corr., 652 F.3d 745 (7th Cir. 2011) (upholding prison's ban on inmates' right to solicit pen-pals from pen-pal service companies because officials have legitimate interest in preventing inmates from defrauding the public).

Von den Bosch v. Raemish, 658 F.3d 778 (7th Cir. 2011), *cert. denied* __U.S.__, 132 S.Ct 1932, __ L.Ed.2d__ (2012) (prison officials had legitimate interest in banning articles containing false information about Wisconsin prison because information could potentially inflame prison population and discourage rehabilitation efforts).

Perry v. Secretary, Florida Dep't of Corr., 664 F.3d 1359 (11th Cir. 2011) (upholding prison's ban on inmates' right to solicity pen-pals from pen-pal service companies because officials have legitimate interest in preventing inmates from defrauding the public).

Tormasi v. Hayman, 443 Fed.Appx 742 (3rd Cir. 2011) (confiscation of patent application did not violate prisoner's First Amendment rights because prison officials had legitimate interest in prohibiting prisoner the commencement of a business while incarcerated).

Muson v. Gaetz, 673 F.3d 630 (7th Cir. 2012) (literature about drugs can be banned from prisons because administrators have rational interest in restricting prisoners from such information).

NOTES: _____

NOTES: _____

IMMUNITY

Dalehite v. United States, 346 U.S. 15, 34-36 __S.Ct.__, __L.Ed.2d__ (1953) (stating that the conduct protected by FTCA discretionary function exception (immunizing federal employees against liability) "is the discretion of the executive or administrator to act according to one's judgment of the best course. . . . It . . . includes more than the initiation of programs and activities. It also includes determinations made by executives or administrators in establishing plans, specifications or schedules of operations. Where there is room for policy judgment and decision there is discretion. It necessarily subordinates in carrying follows that acts of out the operations of government in accordance with official directions cannot be actionable" [footnotes omitted].).

Bivens v. Six Unknown Agents, 403 U.S. 388, 91 S.Ct. 1999, 29 L.Ed.2d 619 (1970) (federal government officials are not immune from claims arising from violations of constitutional rights).

Scheuer v. Rhoades, 416 U.S. 232, 94 S.Ct. 1683, 40 L.Ed.2d 90 (1974) (there is no "Eleventh Amendment immunity" for state officials sued in their individual capacities [416 U.S. at 237-38]; and the defense of qualified immunity is a question of "varying scope, . . . the variation being dependent upon the scope of discretion and responsibilities of the office and all the circumstances as they reasonably appeared at the time of the action on which liability is sought to be based. It is the existence of reasonable grounds for the belief formed at the time and in light of the circumstances, coupled with good-faith belief, that affords a basis for qualified immunity of executive officers for acts performed in the course of official conduct" [416 U.S. at 247-248].).

Imbler v. Pachtman, 424 U.S. 409, __S.Ct.__, __L.Ed.2d__ (1976) (grand jurors are absolutely immune from civil liability when acting within scope of duties).

Procunier v. Navarette, 434 U.S. 555, 98 S.Ct. 855, 55 L.Ed.2d (1978) (when motivated by malicious intent, prison officials are not immune from liabilities for deprivations of prisoners' constitutional rights).

Butz v. Economou, 438 U.S. 478, 507, 98 S.Ct. 2894, 57 L.Ed.2d 895 (1978) ("[I]n a suit for damages arising from unconstitutional action, federal executive officials exercising discretion are entitled only to the qualified immunity specified in *Scheuer* [supra], subject to those exceptional situations where it is demonstrated that absolute immunity is essential for the conduct of public business.").

Martinez v. California, 444 U.S. 277, __S.Ct.__, __L.Ed.2d__ (1980) (state law may not immunize public employees and entities from liability under § 1983).

Harlow v. Fitzgerald, 457 U.S. 800, 818, __S.Ct__, __L.Ed.2d__ (1982) (officials enjoy qualified immunity while performing discretionary functions, and will not be held liable for discretionary acts insofar as their conduct does not violate clearly established federal "rights of which a reasonable person would have known.").

Smith v. Wade, 461 U.S. 30, 103 S.Ct. 2606, 75 L.Ed.2d 632 (1983) (for acts taken in the course of official duty, prison officials may be held liable in civil rights action).

United States v. Varig Airlines, 467 U.S. 797, 813-814, __S.Ct.__, __L.Ed.2d__ (1984) (in determining whether the discretionary function exception of the FTCA stands to immunize a defendant, "it is unnecessary—and indeed impossible—to define with precision every contour of the discretionary function exception. From the legislative and judicial materials, however, it is possible to isolate several factors useful in determining when the acts of a Government employee are protected from liability by § 2680(a). First, it is the nature of the conduct, rather than the status of the actor, that governs whether the discretionary function exception applies in a given case. . . . Second, whatever else the discretionary function exception may include, it plainly was intended to encompass the discretionary acts of the Government acting in its role as a regulator of the conduct of private individuals.").

Kentucky v. Graham, 473 U.S. 159, 167 n.14, __S.Ct.__, __L.Ed.2d__ (1985) (states and state agencies are entitled to sovereign immunity "regardless of the relief sought.").

Mitchell v. Forsyth, 472 U.S. 511, 105 S.Ct. 2806, 86 L.Ed.2d 411 (1985) (Attorney General and I.R.S. agents do not enjoy absolute immunity).

Cameron v. I.R.S., 773 F.2d 126 (1985) (Attorney General and I.R.S. agents do not enjoy absolute immunity).

McRorie v. Shimoda, 795 F.2d 780 (9th Cir. 1986) (official-capacity suits are equivalent to suits against a government entity; and § 1983 liability lies against any official who personally deprives another person of a constitutionally protected right, provided a causal connection between personal conduct and deprivation, which can come by direct participation or by setting in motion a series of acts by others).

Forrester v. White, 484 U.S. 219, __S.Ct__, __L.Ed.2d__ (1988) (judges do not enjoy absolute immunity when acting in administrative rather than judicial role).

Felder v. Casey, 487 U.S. 131, 139, __S.Ct__, __L.Ed.2d__ (1988) ("[A] state law that [immunizes] government conduct otherwise subject to suit under Section 1983 is preempted, even where the federal civil rights litigation takes place in state court, because the application of state immunity would thwart the congressional remedy.").

Campbell v. Akansas Dep't of Corr., 155 F.3d 950 (8th Cir. 1988) (Eleventh Amendment shields DOC officials from suits for money damages brought against their official capacities).

Will v. Michigan Dep't of State Police, 491 U.S. 58, 71 n. 10, __S.Ct__, __L.Ed.2d__ (1989) (the Eleventh Amendment bars suits against the state or arms-of-state unless immunity is waived; but "[o]f course a state official in his or her official capacity, when sued for injunctive relief, would be a person under § 1983 because 'official-capacity actions for prospective relief are not treated as actions against the State.'"), *quoting Kentucky v. Graham*, 473 U.S. 159, 167 n.14, __S.Ct.__, __L.Ed.2d__ (1985); *Ex parte Young*, 209 U.S.123, 159-160, __S.Ct.__, __L.Ed.2d__ (1908).

Missouri v. Agyei ex rel. Jenkins, 491 U.S. 274, __S.Ct__, __L.Ed.2d__ (1989) (an award of attorney's fees is ancillary to an order of prospective relief, and therefore is not barred by Eleventh Amendment in suit against state officials).

United States v. Gaubert, 499 U.S. 315, 536-537, __S.Ct.__, __L.Ed.2d__ (1991) (in determining whether the discretionary function exception of the FTCA stands to immunize a defendant, "a court must first consider whether the action [in question] is a matter of choice for the acting employee. . . . [C]onduct cannot be discretionary unless it involves an element of judgment or choice. . . . Thus, the discretionary function exception will not apply when a federal statute, regulation, or policy specifically prescribes a course of action for an employee to follow. In this event, the employee has no rightful option but to adhere to the directive. . . . The [discretionary function] exception . . . protects only governmental actions and decisions based on considerations of public policy.").

Mireles v. Waco, 502 U.S. 9, __S.Ct__, __L.Ed.2d__ (1991) (per curiam) (judge enjoyed absolute immunity from claim arising from court's authorization to seize and force public defender into courtroom).

Hunter v. Bryand, 502 U.S. 224, __S.Ct__, __L.Ed.2d__ (1991) (questions of immunity should be resolved at the earliest possible stages of litigation).

Boretti v. Wiscomb, 930 F.2d 1150 (6th Cir. 1991) (prison nurse not entitled to qualified immunity when denying prisoner prescribed treatment because such compliance was not discretionary but ministerial).

Romero v. Kitsap County, 931 F.2d 624, 627 (9th Cir. 1991) (qualified-immunity test necessitates three inquiries: (1) the identification of the specific right allegedly violated; (2) the determination of whether that right was so "clearly established" as to alert a reasonable officer to its constitutional parameters; and (3) the ultimate determination of whether a reasonable officer could have believed lawful the particular conduct at issue—the first two inquiries are purely issues of law, but the third, though ultimately a legal question, may require some factual determinations, and the court may permit limited discovery concerning the reasonableness of conduct).

Burk v. Beene, 948 F.2d 489 (8th Cir. 1991) (a state may consent to be sued in federal court, waiving its sovereign immunity).

Hill v. Marshall, 962 F.2d 1209 (6th Cir. 1992) (for acts taken in the course of official duty, prison officials may be held liable in civil rights action).

Hays County Guardian v. Supple, 969 F.2d 111 (5th Cir. 1992) (Eleventh Amendment immunity does not bar state-law actions against state officials in their individual capacities).

Buckley v. Fitzsimmons, 509 U.S. 259, __S.Ct.__, __L.Ed.2d__ (1993) (whether immunity of either the absolute or the qualified type is available to shield an officer from civil liability is a question determined not on the officer's job title but on the function he or she preforms; and prosecutor is entitled to absolute judicial immunity for conduct occurring in course of duties as advocate for the state).

Elder v. Holloway, 510 U.S. 510, 114 S.Ct 1019, __L.Ed.2d__ (1994) (for the purposes of determining whether a defendant is entitled to qualified immunity, whether a federal right is clearly established is a question of law that is reviewed *de novo* on appeal; and appellate courts should use all relevant precedents, not only those presented to the district court by the parties; and immunity is not available to officials if "their conduct was unreasonable in light of clearly established law." [*id.*, U.S. at 511; S.Ct at 1021]).

Hunt v. Bennett, 17 F.3d 1263 (10th Cir. 1994) (Eleventh Amendment immunity does not bar state-law actions against state officials in their individual capacities).

Johnson v. Jones, 515 U.S. 304, 115 S.Ct. 2151, __L.Ed.2d__ (1995) (should immunity be denied to a defendant based on a finding that facts genuinely in dispute existed to be resolved at trial, denial of immunity is not appealable until the conclusion of the judicial proceedings, unless the denial of immunity is purely a question of law and not dependent on an ultimate finding of fact).

Archie v. Lanier, 95 F.3d 438 (1996) (judge was not absolutely immune from liability for action not associated with judicial capacity when stalking subordinate and potential employee).

U.S. v. Lanier, 520 U.S. 259, 270, 117 S.Ct 1219, 1230, __L.Ed.2d__ (1997) (the requirement that a violation must be of a "clearly established" law seeks to ensure that defendants "reasonably can anticipate when their conduct may give rise to liability," by attaching liability only if "[t]he contours of the right [violated are] sufficiently clear that a reasonable official would understand that what he is doing violates the right.").

Richardson v. McKight, 521 U.S. 399, 401, 117 S.Ct. 2100, 2102, 139 L.Ed.2d (1997) (private prison employees are not entitled to qualified immunity from prisoner's § 1983 suit).

Kalina v. Fletcher, 522 U.S. 118, __S.Ct.__, __L.Ed.2d__ (1997) (prosecutors do not enjoy shield of absolute immunity for conduct occurring outside the role of state advocate).

Crawford-El v. Britton, 523 U.S. 574, 118 S.Ct. 1584, 140 L.Ed.2d 759 (1998) (holding that (1) defendants bear the burden of invoking a qualified immunity defense, and (2) plaintiffs are not required to show "clear and convincing" evidence of retaliatory motive to survive summary judgment).

Sullivan v. Barnett, 139 F.3d 158 (3rd Cir. 1998) (there is no Eleventh Amendment immunity for state officials sued in their individual capacities).

Snyder v. Trepangier, 142 F.3d 791 (5th Cir. 1998) (when issues of material fact relative to immunity are unresolved, it is proper to leave immunity determination to the jury).

King v. Beavers, 148 F.3d 1031 (8th Cir. 1998) (all but the plainly incompetent government officer/agent who willingly violate the law are entitled to qualified immunity).

Stefanoff v. Hays County, TX, 154 F.3d 523 (5th Cir. 1998) (municipalities do not enjoy qualified immunity from civil rights actions).

Wilson v. Layne, 526 U.S. 603, 609, __S.Ct.__, __L.Ed.2d__ (1999) ("clearly established" does not mean that an official action is protected by qualified immunity unless the very action in question has previously been held unlawful, but it does mean that in light of preexisting law the unlawfulness must be apparent).

Alden v. Maine, 527 U.S. 706, 199 S.Ct. 2240, 144 L.Ed.2d 636 (1999) (state sovereign immunity does not bar all suits against state officers).

Miller v. City of Philadelphia, 174 F.3d 368 (3rd Cir. 1999) (investigative or administrative acts are not protected by doctrine of absolute immunity, because only acts closely associated with judicial process are protected).

Ttea v. Yslets Del Sur Pueblo, 181 F.3d 676 (5th Cir. 1999) (state sovereign immunity does not bar declaratory or injunctive relief against state actors).

Morris v. Lindau, 196 F.3d 102 (2nd Cir. 1999) (municipalities do not enjoy qualified or absolute immunity against § 1983 actions).

Schwenk v. Hartford, 204 F.3d 1187 (9th Cir. 2000) (official's claim of qualified immunity will be defeated if conduct was unlawful in light of pre-existing law).

Wilson v. Spain, 209 F.3d 713 (8th Cir. 2000) (municipalities may be held liable under § 1983 for acts committed by employees in violation of constitutional rights, provided such acts arise as result of a motivating municipal policy or custom).

Tapley v. Collins, 211 F.3d 1210 (11th Cir. 2000) (qualified immunity only protects government officials from suits against them in their individual capacities [i.e., against money damages, not injunctive relief]).

White v. Lee, 227 F.3d 1214, 1238 (9th Cir. 2000) ("[C]losely analogous preesixting case law is not required to show that a right was clearly established.").

Saucier v. Katz, 533 U.S. 194, 202, 208-09__S.Ct.__, __L.Ed.2d__ (2001) (under the objective analysis, an official is not entitled to qualified immunity "if it would be clear to a reasonable officer that his conduct was unlawful in the situation he confronted"), *overruled on other grounds by Citizens United v. FEC,* 130 S.Ct. 876 (2010).

Lee v. City of Los Angeles, 250 F.3d 668 (9th Cir. 2001) (municipalities may be held liable under § 1983 for official acts in violation of constitutional rights, provided such acts arise as result of a motivating municipal policy or custom).

Linder v. Calero-Portocarrero, 251 F.3d 178 (D.C. Cir. 2001) (federal agencies facing third-party subpoena cannot claim sovereign immunity to avoid judicial process).

Starlight Sugar, Inc. v. Soto, 253 F.3d 137 (1st Cir. 2001) (state and federal decisions may be considered when determining whether a constitutional right was "clearly established" for the purposes of qualified immunity).

Price v. Roark, 256 F.3d 364 (5th Cir. 2001) (although unlawful, conduct may still be protected by qualified immunity if mistake as to what the law requires is reasonable).

Gorman v. Easley, 257 F.3d 738 (8th Cir. 2001) (sovereign immunity protects the state and arms-of-state [e.g., executive departments], but not local governments [e.g., cities, counties, municipalities]).

Comstock v. McCrary, 273 F.3d 693 (6th Cir. 2001) (prison-contracted psychologist held "deliberately indifferent" to risk that prisoner would harm himself; no qualified immunity defense thus available).

Tellier v. Fields, 280 F.3d 69 (2nd Cir. 2001) (no qualified immunity available for those who willingly violate the law).

Lapides v. Bd. of Regents, 535 U.S. 613, __S.Ct.__, __L.Ed.2d__ (2002) (when the state caused the removal of state claim to federal court, such action constituted a waiver of Eleventh Amendment immunity).

Swift v. California, 384 F.3d 1184 (9th Cir. 2004) (parole officer held not absolutely immune when acting in an investigative capacity).

Adusaid v. Hillsborough County Bd. of County Comm'rs, 405 F.3d 1298 (11th Cir. 2005) (a county is a "person" for the purposes of a § 1983 action).

Geizler v. Longanbach, 410 F.3d 630 (9th Cir. 2005) (police officer not acting in judicial function, and therefore not entitled to absolute immunity, when coaching witness testimony at pretrial hearing).

LeClerc v. Webb, 419 F.3d 405 (5th Cir. 2005) (judges do not enjoy absolute immunity when acting in role of law enforcement rather than in their judicial role).

Wilson v. City of Boston, 421 F.3d 45 (1st Cir. 2005) (municipalities do not enjoy qualified immunity from § 1983 actions).

Mayorga v. Missouri, 442 F.3d 1128 (8th Cir. 2006) (absolute immunity to liability available to officials acting in the course of their duties as parole board members).

Root v. Liston, 444 F.3d 127 (2nd Cir. 2006) (prosecutor held absolutely immune when ordering an increase in defendant's bond).

Andrews v. Heaton, 483 F.3d 1070 (10th Cir. 2007) (judges and court staff held entitled to absolute immunity when dismissing civil suit).

Henry v. Purnell, 501 F.3d 374 (4th Cir. 2007) (all but the plainly incompetent government officer/agent who willingly violates the law are entitled to qualified immunity).

Hamilton's Bogarts, Inc. v. Michigan, 501 F.3d 644 (6th Cir. 2007) (state officials are considered "persons" for the purpose of a § 1983 action when plaintiff is seeking prospective injunctive relief, and Eleventh Amendment does not bar claim).

Scott v. Harris, 550 U.S. 372, __S.Ct.__, __L.Ed.2d__ (2007) (officials entitled to qualified immunity from liability when conduct, though mistaken, is reasonable under the circumstances).

Harris v. Hornhoust, 513 F.3d 509 (6th Cir. 2008) (prosecutors not entitled to absolute immunity when acting in investigatory capacity).

Johnson v. Dossey, 515 F.3d 778 (7th Cir. 2008) (prosecutor not absolutely immune from liability when acting in an investigative capacity and participating in a conspiracy targeting defendant).

DeMayo v. Nugent, 517 F.3d 11 (1st Cir. 2008) (when police officers did not act in an objectively reasonable manner, plaintiff stated cognizable § 1983 claim for damages against officers in their individual capacities).

Davenport v. Causey, 521 F.3d 544 (6th Cir. 2008) (finding officer entitled to qualified immunity, barring claim for damages brought against his individual capacity, because use of deadly force was not unreasonable).

Vives v. City of New York, 524 F.3d 346 (2nd Cir. 2008) (a state is not a "person" for the purposes of a § 1983 action).

Egolf v. Witmer, 526 F.3d 104, 111-12 (3rd Cir. 2008) (qualified immunity protects officers from liability if their mistakes are "reasonable mistakes," given the circumstances).

Walker v. Bowersox, 526 F.3d 1186 (8th Cir. 2008) (prisoner stated viable § 1983 claim for conditions of confinement violating the Eighth Amendment, and prison official are not entitled to qualified immunity against claim in their individual capacities).

Leary v. Livingston County, 528 F.3d 438 (6th Cir. 2008) (a reasonable officer would have known prisoner was in danger after rumor spread that plaintiff was a child molester, and officer not entitled to qualified immunity for failing to protect prisoner from inmate violence).

Walter v. Pike County, 544 F.3d 182 (3rd Cir. 2008) (question of qualified immunity immediately appealable without an ultimate determination of fact because question did not turn on disputed fact, but rather whether a right was clearly established).

Pearson v. Callahan, __U.S.__, 129 S.Ct. 808, 818, __L.Ed.2d__ (2009) (the two-prong test for determining whether qualified immunity is appropriate—i.e., whether a constitutionally protected right was violated and whether the transgressor reasonably should have been aware that the conduct was unlawful—is often a beneficial analysis, but it is not mandatory, and judges may "exercise their sound discretion in deciding which of the two prongs of the qualified immunity analysis should be addressed first in light of the circumstances of the particular case at hand.").

Foster v. Runnels, 554 F.3d 807 (9th Cir. 2009) (prisoners' right under Eighth Amendment to adequate meals is well established, and officer not entitled to qualified immunity for providing prisoner inadequate food).

Poirier v. Mass. Dep't of Corr., 558 F.3d 92 (1st Cir. 2009) (state and arms-of-state, including Department of Corrections, absolutely immune under Eleventh Amendment from § 1983 lawsuits, regardless of relief sought).
    NOTE: Injunctive relief is available against agents/employees in their official capacities as state officials.

Poolwa v. Marcantel, 565 F.3d 721 (10th Cir. 2009) (no immunity from suits brought against officials in their individual capacities where reasonable officer would have know conduct violated the Constitution).

Deville v. Marcantel, 567 F.3d 156 (5th Cir. 2009) (no immunity from suits brought against officials in their individual capacities where reasonable officer would have know conduct violated the Constitution).

Moldowan v. City of Warren, 578 F.3d 351 (6th Cir. 2009) (detective witness held absolutely immune from liability in claim arising from alleged perjury).

Faird v. Ellen, 593 F.3d 233 (2nd Cir. 2010) (prison officials are not entitled to qualified immunity from liability when officials should have known their conduct violated well-established federal right).

Jensen v. Wagner, 603 F.3d 1182 (10th Cir. 2010) (holding prosecutor absolutely immune to liability for alleged misrepresentation of facts to court and district attorney).

Colvin v. Carusu, 605 F.3d 282 (6th Cir. 2010) (prison chaplain acted reasonably for purposes of qualified immunity protection from liability when chaplain refused prisoner kosher meals after learning prisoner was Muslim).

Terry v. Hubert, 609 F.3d 757 (5th Cir. 2010) (a question of qualified immunity is immediately appealable if the question is of law, not of fact).

NOTES: _____

NOTES:

LIABILITY, DAMAGES & INJUNCTIVE RELIEF

Dalehite v. United States, 346 U.S. 15, 44-45, __S.Ct.__, __L.Ed.2d__ (1953) (the Federal Tort Claims Act requirement of 28 U.S.C. § 1346(b) that liability be based on a "negligent or wrongful act or omission" precludes "strict liability").

Bivens v. Six Unknown Agents, 403 U.S. 388, 91 S.Ct. 1999, 29 L.Ed.2d 619 (1970) (holding that (1) plaintiff may seek money damages under both *Bivens* and § 1983 action for violation of Fourth Amendment rights; and (2) private citizens may recover damages under *Bivens* for any injuries suffered as a result of a federal agent's violation of constitutionally protected rights).

Monell v. Dep't of Soc. Servs., 436 U.S. 658, __S.Ct.__, __L.Ed.2d__ (1978) (a municipality may not be held liable under § 1983 for the conduct of its officers, unless their conduct is the result of municipal policy or custom: "In particular we conclude that a municipality cannot be held liable soley because it employed a tortfeasor—or in other words, a municipality cannot be held liable under section 1983 on a respondent superior theory" [436 U.S. at 690 n.55].).

Lugar v. Edmondson Oil Co., 457 U.S. 922, 937, __S.Ct.__, __L.Ed.2d__ (1982) (private individuals have acted under the color of state law for the purposes of § 1983 action when (1) the claimed deprivation was caused by the exercise of a right or privilege created or imposed by the state or undertaken by a person for whom the state is responsible, and (2) the private party is fairly characterized as a state actor).

Smith v. Wade, 461 U.S. 30, 103 S.Ct. 1625, 75 L.Ed.2d 632 (1983) (prison guards may be held liable for punitive damages).

Pembaur v. City of Cincinnati, 475 U.S. 469, __S.Ct.__, __L.Ed.2d__ (1986) (municipality may be liable under § 1983 for unconstitutional conduct of final decision-maker, because officer possesses authority to establish municipal policy).

Memphis Community Sch. Dist. v. Stachura, 477 U.S. 299, 312-13, __S.Ct.__, __L.Ed.2d__ (1986) (damages awards cannot be based on the "abstract 'importance' of a constitutional right.").

Hewitt v. Helms, 482 U.S. 755, __S.Ct.__, __L.Ed.2d__ (1987) (court-ordered consent decree can form basis for an award of attorney's fees).

Texas State Teachers Ass'n v. Gatland Independanr Sch. Dist., 489 U.S. 782, __S.Ct.__, __L.Ed.2d__ (1989) (plaintiff is "prevailing party" when litigation has achieved a benefit sought in the lawsuit).

Hafer v. Melo, 502 U.S. 21, 112 S.Ct. 358, 116 L.Ed.2d 301 (1991) (state officials liable under § 1983 when action seeks damages against their individual capacities).

Farrar v. Habby, 506 U.S. 103, __S.Ct.__, __L.Ed.2d__ (1992) (most critical factor in award of attorney's fees is the degree of success obtained by the prevailing plaintiff).

Weaver v. Clarke, 45 F.3d 1253 (8th Cir. 1995) (finding that deliberate indifference in Eighth Amendment medical claim necessarily precluded a defense of qualified immunity).

Thompson v. Opeiu, 74 F.3d 1492 (6th Cir. 1996) (damages for emotional distress may be appropriate when suffering sleeplessness, anxiety, stress, marital problems, and humiliation).

Goff v. Burton, 91 F.3d 1188 (8th Cir. 1996) (affirming $2250 award at $10 a day for lost privileges resulting from a retaliatory transfer to a higher security prison).

Aversa v. U.S., 99 F.3d 1200 (1st Cir. 1996) (federal officials may be sued in their individual capacities for damages resulting from constitutional violation).

Bd. of County Comm'rs v. Brown, 520 U.S. 397, 404, __S.Ct.__, L.Ed.2d__ (1997) (to hold a municipality liable under § 1983, the plaintiff "must show that the municipal action was taken with the requisite degree of culpability and must demonstrate a direct causal link between the municipal action and the deprivation of federal rights").

Kerr v. Puckett, 138 F.3d 321 (7th Cir. 1998) (Prisoner Litigation Reform Act provision barring prisoners from bringing suit for mental or emotional injury without a prior showing of physical injury does not apply to suits filed by prisoners after they are released).

Ells v. University of Kan. Med. Center, 163 F.3d 1186 (10th Cir. 1998) (attorney's fees remained available where § 1983 settlement did not waive right to recover fees).

Wilson v. Layne, 526 U.S. 603, 119 S.Ct. 1692, 143 L.Ed.2d 818 (1999) (holding that (1) plaintiff may seek money damages under both *Bivens* and § 1983 action for violation of Fourth Amendment rights; and (2) private citizens may recover damages under *Bivens* for any injuries suffered as a result of a federal agent's violation of constitutionally protected rights).

Thomas v. Rouch, 165 F.3d 1137 (2nd Cir. 1999) (municipalities liable under § 1983 for employee acts in violation of the Constitution).

Ferril v. Parker Group, Inc., 168 F.3d 468 (11th Cir. 1999) (plaintiff bringing a civil rights claim may be compensated for psychological injuries as well as financial, property, or physical injury).

Rizzo v. Children's World Learning Centers, Inc., 173 F.3d 254 (5th Cir. 1999) (plaintiff prevailing under the Americans with Disabilities Act (ADA) may be awarded attorneys fees for both trial and appellate work).

Loyd v. Alaska Dep't of Corr., 176 F.3d 1336 (11th Cir. 1999) (injunctive relief should not be terminated without evidentiary hearing).

Jensen v. Lane County, 22 F.3d 570 (9th Cir. 2000) (to determine whether a private provider acted under the color of state law for the purposes of § 1983 liability, the court must consider whether there is a close nexus or joint action with the state, and that the action of the defendant may be fairly viewed as that of the state itself).

Marsh v. Butler County, AK, 225 F.3d 1243 (11th Cir. 2000) (deliberate indifference to serious medical needs necessarily precludes a defense of qualified immunity).

Edwards v. Johnson, 209 F.3d 772 (5th Cir. 2000) (federal agents may be sued via *Bivens* action for money damages arising from the violation of a constitutional right).

Baily v. Runyon, 220 F.3d 879 (8th Cir. 2000) (award of damages for emotional distress must be supported by evidence of genuine injury).

Daskalea v. D.C., 227 F.3d 433 (D.C. Cir. 2000) (upholding award of $350,000 in compensatory damages for mental and emotional distress, despite former prisoner's lack of permanent physical injury).

Hopwood v. State of Texas, 236 F.3d 256 (5th Cir. 2000) (nominal damages can support award of attorneys fees).

Cook County v. U.S. ex rel Chandler, 538 U.S. 199, 123 S.Ct 1239, __L.Ed.2d__ (2003) (municipalities cannot be held liable in punitive damages).

Buckhannon Bd. & Care Home, Inc. v. West Virginia Dep't of Health & Human Res., 532 U.S. 598, __S.Ct.__, __L.Ed.2d__ (2001) (court-ordered consent decree may form basis for award of attorney's fees, provided decree results in a change in relationship between parties), *superseded by statute as stated in Nulankeyutmonen Nkihtaq-mibon v. BIA,* 601 F.Supp.2d 337 (D. Me. 2009).

O'Rourke v. City of Providence, 235 F.3d 713 (1st Cir. 2001) (damages awarded by a jury will stand unless award is grossly excessive or shocks the conscience).

Fox v. General Motors Corp., 247 F.3d 169 (4th Cir. 2001) (damages awarded by a jury will stand unless award is grossly excessive or shocks the conscience).

Provost v. City of Newburgh, 262 F.3d 146 (2nd Cir. 2001) (holding that the $10,000 award of punitive damages was proper even though it was based on award of $1 nominal damages).

Armstrong v. Davis, 275 F.3d 849, 870 (9th Cir. 2001) (noting that a "few isolated violations affecting a narrow range of plaintiffs" does not provide a basis for system-wide injunctive relief).

Hope v. Pelzer, 536 U.S. 730, 122 S.Ct. 2508, 153 L.Ed.2d 666 (2002) (handcuffing prisoner to "hitching post" as punishment held to be violation of Eighth Amendment; guards not entitled to qualified immunity from claim for damages under § 1983)

Salinas v. O'Neill, 286 F.3d 827 (5th Cir. 2002) (damages for emotional distress may be appropriate when suffering sleeplessness, anxiety, stress, marital problems, and humiliation).

Higgins v. Beyer, 293 F.3d 683 (3rd Cir. 2002) (nominal damages available for procedural due process violation even though funds that were wrongfully seized from prisoner's account were later recovered).

Mitchell v. Horn, 318 F.3d 523 (3rd Cir. 2003) (PLRA's provision barring claims for mental or emotional damages, absent a showing of a non-*de minimis* physical injury, does not apply to claims for nominal and punitive damages, nor does it bar injunctive or declaratory relief; because such relief does not remunerate injury).

Calhoun v. DeTella, 319 F.3d 936 (7th Cir. 2003) (nominal damages are available for violations of constitutional rights).

Harden v. Pataki, 320 F.3d 1289 (11th Cir. 2003) (nominal damages are available without showing of an actual loss when constitutional rights are violated).

Shamaeizadeh v. Cunigan, 338 F.3d 535 (6th Cir. 2003) (damages for pain, suffering, embarrassment, and humiliation are recoverable under § 1983 action).

DiDorbo v. Hoy, 343 F.3d 172 (2nd Cir. 2003) (a purpose in awarding punitive damages is for deterrence, and that deterrence is directly related to what people can afford to pay).

Sallier v. Brooks, 343 F.3d 868 (6th Cir. 2003) (affirming jury award of $750 in compensatory damages for each instance of unlawful opening of legal mail).

Gwinn v. Awmiller, 354 F.3d 1211 (10th Cir. 2004) (no due process protection for conduct that only affects one's reputation).

Feliciano v. Rullan, 378 F.3d 42, 53-55 (1st Cir. 2004) (with respect to the limitations imposed by the PLRA, the court held that prospective injunctive relief remained necessary because "health care for inmates in Puerto Rican prisons remain constitutionally deficient"; however, the court noted that a "few isolated violations affecting a narrow range of plaintiffs" would not provide a basis for system-wide injunctive relief); *see also Armstrong v. Davis*, 275 F.3d 849, 870 (9th Cir. 2001).

Hayes v. Faulkner County, 388 F.3d 669 (8th Cir. 2004) (jail administrator acted under color of state law for the purposes of a § 1983 claim when deliberately indifferent to violations of detainee's due process rights).

Wagner v. City of Holyoke, 404 F.3d 504 (1st Cir. 2005) (award of nominal damages supported award of attorney's fees in § 1983 First Amendment claim).

Tarver v. City of Edna, 410 F.3d 745 (5th Cir. 2005) (psychological injuries can serve as a basis for § 1983 liability).

Benton v. Or. Student Assistance Comm'n, 421 F.3d 901 (9th Cir. 2005) (holding that plaintiff prevailed only insofar as an award of nominal damages for a § 1983 claim and was not entitled to an award of attorney's fees because no tangible result from litigation [i.e., no real change in status quo]).

Harris v. U.S., 422 F.3d 322 (6th Cir. 2005) (holding that (1) plaintiff may seek money damages under both *Bivens* and § 1983 action for violation of Fourth Amendment rights; and (2) private citizens may recover damages under *Bivens* for any injuries suffered as a result of a federal agent's violation of constitutionally protected rights).

Beedle v. Wilson, 422 F.3d 1059 (10th Cir. 2005) (if a private citizen was a willing participant in joint action with a state or its agents, he or she can be held liable under § 1983).

Springer v. Henry, 435 F.3d 268, 281-82 (3rd Cir. 2006) (award of $25,000 in punitive damages in retaliation case was held proper because defendant acted "recklessly, intentionally or maliciously").

Handberry v. Thompson, 446 F.3d 335 (2nd Cir. 2006) (with respect to the limitations imposed by the PLRA's narrow-relief provision, the court held the injunction ordering jail to provide educational services to prisoner was sufficiently narrow because it only extended to members of the plaintiff's class).

Menez-Soto v. Rodriguex, 448 F.3d 12 (1st Cir 2006) (in some contexts, emotional damages may be recoverable under § 1983).

Hydrick v. Hunter, 449 F.3d 978 (9th Cir. 2006) (a supervisor who participated in, or directed, or knew of and failed to act to prevent unlawful conduct, may be held liable for the constitutional violation of subordinates under § 1983, though there is no pure "respondent superior" liability under § 1983).

Elwood v. Drescher, 456 F.3d 943 (9th Cir. 2006) (*pro se* plaintiffs are not entitled to recover attorney's fees for personal work involved in litigating suit).

Humphries v. CBOCS West, Inc., 474 F.3d 387 (7th Cir 2007) (private actors may be held liable under § 1983).

P.N. v. Seattle Sch. Dist. No.1, 474 F.3d 1165 (9th Cir. 2007) (plaintiff held not prevailing party for the purposes of recovering attorney's fees despite significant change in status quo, because change was not ordered by the court).

Rossello-Gonzalez v. Acevedo-Vila, 483 F.3d 1 (1st Cir. 2007) (finding that defendants may not recover attorney's fees from plaintiff because action was not frivolous even if some of his claims were without merit).

Revis v. Meldrum, 489 F.3d 273 (6th Cir. 2007) (defendants entitled to attorney's fees when plaintiff alleged claim without evidentiary support; however, attorney's fees not appropriate when critical element to plaintiff's claim was absent, if error not obvious enough to render the claim frivolous).

Bogan v. City of Boston, 489 F.3d 417 (1st Cir. 2007) (compensatory damages arising under state and § 1983 claims constitutes a double recovery and are impermissible).

Gautreaux v. Chicago Hous. Auth., 491 F.3d 649 (7th Cir. 2007) (a plaintiff is a "prevailing party" when achieving substantial results embodied in court orders and has received substantial benefits from litigating his or her case).

Eeoc v. Convergy's Customer Management Group, Inc., 491 F.3d 790 (8th Cir. 2007) (plaintiff may seek compensatory damages under the Americans with Disabilities Act (ADA) for emotional distress).

Hutchins v. McDaniels, 512 F.3d 193 (5th Cir. 2007) (nominal and punitive damages available under PLRA even without a showing of physical injury).

Advantage Media, LLC v. City of Hopkins, 511 F.3d 833 (8th Cir. 2008) (preliminary injunction that merely maintained status quo insufficient to support recovery of attorney's fees).

Al-Amin v. Smith, 511 F.3d 1317 (11th Cir. 2008) (regardless of actual injury, nominal damages are available to successful plaintiff proving First Amendment violation).

People Against Police Violence v. City of Pittsburgh, 520 F.3d 226 (3rd cir. 2008) (when preliminary injunction provided plaintiffs with all the substantial relief they sought, forcing the city to revise legislation, altering the status quo, the prevailing plaintiffs were entitled to recover attorney's fees).

Alberto San, Inc. v. Consejo De Titulares Del Condominie San Alberto, 522 F.3d 1 (1st Cir 2008) (defendant not entitled to attorney's fees because plaintiff's claims not frivolous, unreasonable, or unfounded).

Welch v. Ciampa, 542 F.3d 927 (1st Cir. 2008) (plaintiffs must demonstrate link between a municipal policy and the unconstitutional acts of its officers in order to support a claim under § 1983; however, municipality may be liable under § 1983 for deprivation of federal right by a policymaker even if deprivation is a single incident rather than a result of established policy).

Pierce v. County of Orange, 526 F.3d 1190 (2008) (holding district court did not abuse its discretion when decertifying "damages class" of impaired pretrial detainees and rejecting statistical sampling as a useful tool for computing damages in this circumstance, because class size (estimated at 180,000) and array of variables related to claims, causation and damages are poorly addressed through sampling).

Mayfield v. Texas Dep't of Criminal Justice, 529 F.3d 599 (5th Cir. 2008) (PLRA bars compensatory damages where no physical injury is alleged; the bar applies to First Amendment claims).

Young Apartments, Inc. v. Town of Jupiter, 529 F.3d 1027 (11th Cir. 2008) (punitive damages available against officials in their individual capacities only, not official capacity).

Fegons v. Norris, 537 F.3d 897 (8th Cir. 2008) (punitive damages available when officials act with malice in depriving constitutional rights, and where necessary to deter future conduct).

Mesa v. Prejean, 543 F.3d 264 (5th Cir. 2008) (psychological injuries are actionable under § 1983).

De Jesus Nazario v. Rodriguez, 554 F.3d 196 (1st Cir. 2009) (plaintiff prevailing party for purposes of attorney's fees award, though received only punitive damages).

Garner v. Cuyahoga County Juv. Ct., 544 F.3d 624 (6th Cir. 2009) (defendant entitled to attorney's fees when plaintiff's claims frivolous).

Vallario v. Vandehely, 554 F.3d 1259, 1267-68 (10th Cir. 2009) (injunctive relief not proper where injunction would enjoin "wide range of behavior" for a class broadly framed in the complaint).

Tortu v. Las Vegas Metro Police Dep't, 556 F.3d 1075 (9th Cir. 2009) (plaintiff who suffered excruciating pain, humiliation, and embarrassment entitled to compensatory damages for officer's excessive force).

Unus v. Kane, 565 F.3d 103 (4th Cir. 2009) (defendant not entitled to attorney's fees because plaintiff's claims not frivolous, unreasonable, or unfounded).

Byrd v. Maricopa County Sheriff's Dep't, 565 F.3d 1205 (9th Cir. 2009 (under PLRA, prisoners must show physical injury to support an award in damages for mental and emotional harms).

Perez v. Westchester County Dep't of Corr., 587 F.3d 143 (2nd Cir. 2009) (plaintiffs entitled to attorney's fees because settlement altered legal relationship between plaintiffs and defendants by altering county's practices).

Hendrickson v. Cooper, 589 F.3d 887 (7th Cir. 2009) (where police officer acted with malice in harming prisoner in violation of Eighth Amendment, a $125,000 award in punitive damages proper).

Fox v. Vice, 594 F.3d 423 (5th Cir. 2010) (defendant entitled to attorney's fees because plaintiff knowingly filed claims with no basis in law and failed to participate in settlement negotiations).

Minix v. Canarecci, 597 F.3d 824 (7th Cir. 2010) (section 1983 claim of deliberate indifference to prisoners' medical need against municipality improper because no evidence to support allegation that inadequate medical care was caused by municipal policy).

Edgerly v. City &County of San Francisco, 599 F.3d 946 (9th Cir. 2010) (defendant entitled to attorney's fees when discovery revealed defendant uninvolved with arrest and search).

Guy v. City of San Diego, 608 F.3d 582 (9th Cir. 2010) (plaintiff properly awarded nominal damages in excessive-force suit against police),

NOTES:

NOTES: _____

MAIL & LEGAL MAIL

U.S. ex rel Milwaukee Social Democratic Pub. v. Burleson, 255 U.S. 407, 437, __S.Ct.__, __L.Ed__ (1927) (dissenting opinion) (Justice Holms observed: "[T]he use of the mails is almost as much a part of free speech as the right to use our tongues. . . ."); *see also **Blount v. Rizzi***, 400 U.S. 410, 416, __S.Ct.__, __L.Ed.2d__ (1970) (affirming this principle).

Procunier v. Martinez, 416 U.S. 396, 94 S.Ct. 1800, 40 L.Ed.2d 224 (1974) ((1) prisoners must be notified when officials refuse to send their letters, or if rejecting in-coming letters; (2) the author of a censored/confiscated letter must be afforded an opportunity to contest the decision; (3) complaints must be heard by a person other than the person who originally disapproved the letter; and (4) regulations censoring mail violate the First Amendment), *overruled in part by **Thornburgh v. Abbot***, 490 U.S. 401, 109 S.Ct. 1874, __L.Ed.2d__ (1989) (see *Thornburgh*, below).

Wolfish v. Levi, 573 F.2d 118, 130 (2nd Cir. 1978) ("The right to receive and send mail is unquestionably protected by the First Amendment"), *rev'd and rem'd on other grounds by **Bell v. Wolfish***, 441 U.S. 520, 99 S.Ct. 1861, 60 L.Ed.2d 447 (1979).

Upjohn Co. v. U.S., 449 U.S. 383, 389, 101 S.Ct. 677, 682, __L.Ed.2d__ (1981) ("The attorney-client privilege is the oldest of the privileges for confidential communications known to the common law. 8 J. Wigmore, *Evidence* section (McNaughton rev. 1961). Its purpose is to encourage full and frank communication between attorneys and their clients and thereby promote broader public interests in the observance of the law and administration of justice. The privilege recognizes that sound legal advice or advocacy serves public ends and that such advice or advocacy depends upon the lawyer's being fully informed by the client. As we stated last Term in *Trammel v. United States*, 445 U.S. 40, 51, 100 S.Ct. 906, 913, 63 L.Ed.2d 186 (1980): "The lawyer-client privilege rests on the need for the advocate and counselor to know all that relates to the client's reason for seeking representation if the professional mission is to be carried out." And in *Fisher v. United States*, 425 U.S. 391, 403, 96 S.Ct. 1569, 1577, 48 L.Ed.2d 39 (1976), we recognized the purpose of the privilege to be 'to encourage clients to make full disclosure to their attorneys.' The rational for this privilege has long been recognized by the Court, *see Hunt v. Blackburn*, 128 U.S. 464, 470, 9 S.Ct. 125, 127, 32 L.Ed. 488 (1888) (privilege 'is founded upon the necessity, in the interest and administration of justice, of the aid of persons having knowledge of the law and skilled in its practice, which assistance can only be safely and readily availed of when free from the consequences of the apprehension of disclosure.')").

Turner v. Safely, 482 U.S. 78, 107 S.Ct. 2254, 96 L.Ed.2d 64 (1987) (holding that certain restrictions on prisoners' mail do not violate the First Amendment, provided there exists a legitimate governmental interest).

Murphy v. Missouri Dep't of Corr., 814 F.3d 1252 (8th Cir. 1987) (First Amendment held violated when mail from Aryan Nation prohibited because prison officials may not withhold mail unless literature advocates violence or is so racially inflammatory that it is likely to cause violence).

Houston v. Lack, 487 U.S. 266, 108 S.Ct. 2379, 101 L.Ed.2d 245 (1988) (*pro se* prisoner filing a notice of appeal satisfies the time limit for filing if he delivers the notice to prison officials within the specified time; the "prison mailbox rule" is justified by the prisoner's dependance on the prison mail system and lack of counsel to assure timely filing with the court).

Thornburgh v. Abbot, 490 U.S. 401, 109 S.Ct. 1874, __L.Ed.2d__ (1989) (overruling the substantial-government-interest/least-restrictive-means standard embodied in *Procunier v. Martinez* in favor of the legitimate-government-interest standard embodied in *Truner v. Safely*; permitting prisons to censor inmate correspondence provided the four-prong test of *Turner* is satisfied, with the exception that *outgoing* mail is held to the less restrictive standard under *Procunier*, and the *Procunier* requirements still apply concerning notification and meaningful hearing concerning censored mail).

Lemon v. Dugger, 931 F.2d 1465 (11th Cir. 1991) (holding that (1) "special mail" may not be opened by prison officials outside the presence of the prisoner; (2) mail from prisoners directed to attorneys, state and federal officials, and media representatives qualify as "special mail"; and (3) prison officials who interfere with prisoners' legal mail violate both the right to access the courts and First Amendment rights to free speech).

Brewer v. Wilkinson, 3 F.3d 816 (5th Cir. 1993), *cert. denied*, __U.S.__, 114 S.Ct. 1081, __L.Ed.2d__ (1994) (prison officials opening "special mail" outside presence of addressee violated prisoners' right to access the courts and First Amendment rights to free speech).

Phelps v. U.S. Federal Government, 15 F.3d 735 (8th Cir. 1994) (prisoners retain First Amendment interest in receiving mail, and have a constitutional right to send and receive mail that may not be restricted except for legitimate penological interests).

Caldwell v. Amend, 30 F.3d 1199 (9th Cir. 1994) (*pro se* pleadings deemed filed on the date prisoner placed documents in prison's "legal mailbox," not the date of receipt by the court clerk).

Bell-Bay v. Williams, 87 F.3d 832 (6th Cir. 1996) (there exists a fundamental interest in preserving the confidentiality of prisoners' legal mail).

Croft v. Roe, 170 F.3d 957 (9th Cir. 1999) (any restriction on the flow of information to prisoners must relate to a legitimate penological interest).

Frost v. Symington, 197 F.3d 348 (9th Cir. 1999) (prisoners have Fourteenth Amendment right to receive notice when prison officials withhold incoming mail).

Altizer v. Deeds, 191 F.3d 540 (4th Cir. 1999) (prisoners' outgoing mail is lawfully subject to inspection for contraband); *see also Stow v. Grimaldi*, 993 F.2d 1002 (1st Cir. 1993) (same).

Prison Legal News v. Cook, 238 F.3d 1145 (9th Cir. 2001) (prisoners and publishers enjoy First Amendment right that protect prisoner receipt of standard mail, and such mail must be afforded the same procedural protection, with due process consideration, as other first-class mail and periodicals permitted by the prison).

Noble v. Kelly, 246 F.3d 93 (2nd Cir. 2001) (*pro se* prisoner satisfies the time limit for filing if he delivers the papers to prison officials within the specified time; the "prison mailbox rule" is justified by the prisoner's dependance on the prison mail system and lack of counsel to assure timely filing with the court).

Davis v. Norris, 249 F.3d 800 (8th Cir. 2001) (prisoners' First Amendment right protects against unjustified interference with mail, including photos).

Gomez v. Vernon, 255 F.3d 1118 (9th Cir. 2001) (affirming imposition of monetary sanctions on assistant Attorneys General who acquired and read privileged communications from prisoners' attorneys).

Dils v. Small, 260 F.3d 984 (9th Cir. 2001) (*pro se* pleadings deemed filed on the date prisoner placed documents in prison's "legal mailbox," not the date of receipt by the court clerk).

Sorrels v. McKee, 287 F.3d 1213 (9th Cir. 2002) (broad prison policy prohibiting books and magazines not purchased by prisoners themselves is unconstitutional).

Sulik v. Taney County, 316 F.3d 813 (8th Cir. 2003) (prison "mailbox rule" applies to *pro se* § 1983 claims).

Nasir v. Morgan, 350 F.3d 366 (3rd Cir. 2003) (finding legitimate penological interest in prohibiting former prisoner from communicating with current prisoner in the interest of preventing escape planning, future assaults, and other violent acts).

Harbin-Bey v. Rutter, 420 F.3d 571 (6th Cir. 2005) (holding regulation prohibiting mail depicting gang signs to be reasonably related to penological concerns under *Turner*).

Walker v. Jastremski, 430 F.3d 560, 563 (2nd Cir. 2005) (prison "mailbox rule" held not to apply if delay in filing "was attributable not to the vagaries of mails, nor to prison bureaucracy, but to the idiosyncrasies of the clerk's office").
NOTE: To be safe, file well before the end of the limitations period.

Jones v. Brown, 461 F.3d 353 (3rd Cir. 2006) (finding that, under *Turner*, inspecting legal mail outside of prisoner's presence was unreasonable).

Al-Amin v. Smith, 511 F.3d 1317 (11th Cir. 2008) (officials who open prisoner's legal mail outside his presence gave rise to viable First Amendment claim).

Brand v. Motley, 526 F.3d 921 (6th Cir. 2008) (despite district court's stamp on claim three days over one-year limitation, prison "mailbox rule" applied when prisoner signed and delivered claim to prison officials on last day of limitation period).

Riggins v. Clarke, 403 Fed.Appx. 292 (9th Cir. 2010), *cert. denied* , __U.S.__, 131 S.Ct 2118, 179 L.Ed.2d 911 (2011) (First Amendment not violated where prison had legitimate penological interest in prohibiting correspondence addressed to prisoners' chosen religious names and not the names under which they were committed to prison, in the interest of orderly administration of prison mail).

Wells v. Thaler, 460 Fed.Appx. 303 (5th Cir 2012) (blind inmate's right of free speech not violated where prison assistance in reading and writing letters necessarily abridges right to privacy, and where "intimate facts" subject to constitutional protection were not disclosed to others).

NOTES: _____

NOTES: _____
_____
_____
_____
_____
_____
_____
_____
_____
_____
_____
_____
_____
_____
_____
_____
_____
_____
_____
_____
_____
_____
_____
_____
_____
_____
_____
_____
_____
_____
_____
_____
_____
_____
_____
_____
_____
_____
_____
_____
_____
_____

MARRIAGE

Griswald v. Conn., 381 U.S. 479, __S.Ct.__, __L.Ed.2d__ (1965) (prisoners retain rights concerning decisions about family life).

Moore v. East Cleveland, 431 U.S. 494, __S.Ct__, __L.Ed.2d__ (1977) (cohabitation with relatives is a fundamental right protected by the Constitution).

Zablocki v. Redhail, 434 U.S. 374, __S.Ct__, __L.Ed.2d__ (1978) (marriage is a fundamental right protected by the Constitution).

Bd. of Directors of Rotary Int'l v. Rotary Club of Duarte, 481 U.S. 537, 545, __S.Ct__, __L.Ed.2d__ (1987) ("[T]he freedom to enter into and carry on certain intimate or private relationships is a fundamental element of liberty protected by the Bill of Rights.").

Turner v. Safely, 482 U.S. 78, 95-97, 107 S.Ct. 2254, 69 L.Ed.2d 64 (1987) (time and circumstances under which prisoners marry may yield to legitimate penological interests, but prohibiting prisoners from marrying other prisoners or civilians is an exaggerated response to penological interests unless officials find "compelling reasons" to prevent marriage).

Hernandez v. Coughlin, 18 F.3d 133 (2nd Cir. 1994) (prison officials may restrict the right to marital privacy providing a valid penological interest).

Gerber v. Hickman, 291 F.3d 617 (9th Cir. 2002) (prohibiting specimen for wife's artificial insemination deemed lawful because restriction is legitimate consequence of incarceration).

Powers v. Snyder, 484 F.3d 929 (7th Cir. 2007) (prison warden's decision to restrict visits from prisoner's wife held to constitute a viable First Amendment claim when restriction was allegedly in retaliation for an unspecified incident a decade earlier between the warden and prisoner).

Roe v. Crawford, 514 F.3d 789 (8th Cir. 2008) (right to marry may be restricted but not prohibited to prisoners).

NOTES: _____
_____
_____
_____
_____
_____
_____
_____
_____
_____
_____
_____
_____
_____
_____
_____
_____
_____
_____
_____
_____
_____
_____
_____
_____
_____
_____
_____
_____
_____
_____
_____
_____
_____
_____
_____
_____
_____
_____
_____
_____
_____
_____

NOTES:

MEDICAL

Estelle v. Gamble, 429 U.S. 97, 97 S.Ct. 285, 50 L.Ed.2d 251 (1976) (prisoners are entitled to medical care, provided by the government, as a fundamental principle under the Eighth Amendment's Cruel and Unusual Punishment Clause).

Roba v. U.S., 604 F.2d 215 (2nd Cir. 1979) (prisoner has a constitutionally protected right not to be transferred while he is in a life-threatening situation).

Ramos v. Lamm, 639 F.2d 559 (10th Cir. 1980) (prisoners are entitled to necessary mental health treatment).

Lee v. Downs, 641 F.2d 1117 (4th Cir. 1981) (prisoners must be protected from suicide and self-injury).

Woodall v. Fote, 648 F.2d 272 (5th Cir. 1981) (prisoners are entitled to necessary mental health treatment).

Johnson v. Clinton, 763 F.2d 326 (8th Cir. 1985) (claim against warden for cruel and unusual punishment cognizable when prisoner's life endangered by denying surgery for a hernia and forcing him to work beyond his physical ability).

U.S. v. DeCologero, 821 F.2d 39 (1st Cir. 1987) (adequate medical care is that which is on a level with modern medical science, provided within limits acceptable under the professional standards required of health services and medical providers); *see also* *Fernandez v. U.S.*, 941 F.2d 1488 (11th Cir. 1991).

West v. Atkins, 487 U.S. 42, __S.Ct.__, __L.Ed.2d__ (1988) (doctor of private medical company acted under color of state law for the purposes of a § 1983 claim).

White v. Napolean, 897 F.2d 103 (3rd Cir. 1990) (constitutional deliberate indifference can be shown by medical providers' persistence in an ineffective course of treatement); *see also* *Greeno v. Daley*, 414 F.3d 645 (7th Cir. 2005).

Gibson v. Mathews, 926 F.2d 532 (6th Cir. 1991) (prison officials' actions ultimately resulting in the inability to have abortion held not to violate the Constitution because federal regulation stating that officials should assist prisoners seeking abortion was not mandatory but discretionary).

Riggins v. Nevada, 504 U.S. 127, 112 S.Ct. 1810, 118 L.Ed.2d 479 (1992) (prisoners have a liberty interest against being forcibly medicated with psychotropic drugs).

McNeil v. U.S., 508 U.S. 106, 113 S.Ct. 1980, 124 L.Ed.2d 21 (1993) (the United States may be held liable under the Federal Tort Claims Act for medical malpractice).

Weaver v. Clarke, 45 F.3d 1253 (8th Cir. 1995) (qualified immunity is necessarily precluded in finding deliberate indifference to prisoners' serious medical needs in violation of the Eighth Amendment).

Boyd v. Knox, 47 F.3d 966 (8th Cir. 1995) ("deliberate indifference" by officials to prisoner's serious medical need may be established by circumstantial evidence).

Pennsylvania Dep't of Corr. v. Yeskey, 524 U.S. 206, 118 S.Ct. 1952, 141 L.Ed.2d 215 (1998) (the Americans with Disabilities Act (ADA) (42 U.S.C. §§ 12101-12213) applies to prisoners).

McElligott v. Foley, 182 F.3d 48 (11th Cir. 1999) (prison officials cannot insulate themselves from potential liability under the Eighth Amendment for acts or omissions reflecting deliberate indifference to serious medical needs of prisoners by instituting a policy of indifference).

Hall v. Thomas, 190 F.3d 693 (5th Cir. 1999) (the Americans with Disabilities Act (ADA) (42 U.S.C. §§ 12101-12213) applies to prisoners).

Hinson v. Edmond, 192 F.3d 1342 (11th Cir. 1999) (privately employed prison physician not acting as government official for purposes of qualified immunity).

Marsh v. Butler County, AK, 225 F.3d 1243 (11th Cir. 2000) (qualified immunity is necessarily precluded in finding deliberate indifference to prisoners' serious medical needs in violation of the Eighth Amendment).

Garcia v. S.U.N.Y. Health Servs. Cen. of Brooklyn, 280 F.3d 98 (2nd Cir. 2000) (deliberate indifference or intentional discrimination are necessary to support a damages claim under Americans with Disabilities Act or the Rehabilitation Act).

Closs v. Weber, 238 F.3d 1018 (8th Cir. 2001) (prisoners have a liberty interest against being forcibly medicated with psychotropic drugs).

Domino v. Texas Dep't of Criminal Justice, 239 F.3d 752 (5th Cir. 2001) (just as a "serious medical need" may exist for a physical condition, so may a "serious medical need" exist for psychological or psychiatric treatment).

Lee v. City of Los Angeles, 250 F.3d 668, 691 (9th Cir. 2001) (the Americans with Disabilities Act, 42 U.S.C. § 12132(1), definition of "public entity" includes "any department, agency, special purpose district, or other instrumentality of a state or states or local government").

Comstock v. McCrary, 273 F.3d 693 (6th Cir. 2001) (prison-contracted psychologist held "deliberately indifferent" to risk that prisoner would harm himself; no qualified immunity defense was thus available).

Barns v. Gorman, 536 U.S. 181, 122 S.Ct. 2097, __L.Ed.2d__ (2002) (injunctive relief and compensatory damages are available under the Americans with Disabilities Act and the Rehabilitation Act, but not punitive damages).

Thompson v. Davis, 295 F.3d 890, 896 (9th Cir. 2002) ("Drug addiction that significantly limits a major life activity is a recognized disability under the ADA," but this qualification protects only those addicts not currently using illegal drugs and who have completed or are in the process of completing supervised drug rehabilitation programming).

Graham ex rel Estate of Graham v. County of Washtenaw, 358 F.3d 377 (6th Cir. 2004) (prison officials cannot be held liable for following through with treatments medically prescribed for inmates, even if such prescriptions are erroneous).

Woodward v. Corr. Med. Servs. of Illinois, 368 F.3d 917 (7th Cir. 2004) (Eight Amendment deliberate-indifference claim stated for prison's failure to treat mental health needs).

Spruill v. Gillis, 372 F.3d 218 (3rd Cir. 2004) (prison officials cannot be held liable for medical mistreatment unless they have reason to believe, or actual knowledge of, mistreatment or non-treatment and failed to act).

Walker v. Horn, 385 F.3d 321 (3rd Cir. 2004) (employee of private medical company acted under color of state law for the purposes of a § 1983 claim).

Johnson v. Karnes, 398 F.3d 868 (9th Cir. 2005) (prison officials' knowledge of prisoners' serious medical needs may be inferred from circumstantial evidence).

Crow v. Montgomery, 403 F.3d 598 (8th Cir. 2005) (mere negligence is insufficient; a sufficiently culpable mind must be shown to demonstrate that defendant was deliberately indifferent).

Johnson v. Wright, 412 F.3d 398 (2nd Cir. 2005) (prison officials who disregarded risk to prisoner's health by denying treatment recommended by prison doctor held liable under Eighth Amendment).

Greeno v. Daley, 414 F.3d 645 (7th Cir. 2005) (claim stated against prison nurse under Eighth Amendment who allegedly deprived prisoner of medication despite deteriorating health condition).

Mata v. Saiz, 427 F.3d 746 (10th Cir. 2005) (prisoner who had heart attack after reporting chest pain and denied medical treatment stated cognizable Eighth Amendment claim).

U.S. v. Georgia, 546 U.S.151, 126 S.Ct. 877, __L.Ed.2d__ (2006) (if conduct violates both the Americans with Disabilities Act and the Constitution, compensatory damages should be available).

Vaugn v. Greene County, 438 F.3d 845 (8th Cir. 2006) (finding no cognizable due process claim because pretrial detainee showed no evidence that prison officials knew the extent of his medical needs).

Jett v. Penner, 439 F.3d 1091 (9th Cir. 2006) (Eighth Amendment deliberate-indifference claim stated when prison delayed two weeks to treat prisoner's broken thumb and more than three months for follow-up treatment).

Feeney v. Corr. Med. Servs., Inc., 464 F.3d 158 (1st Cir. 2006), *cert. denied* __U.S.__, 128 S.Ct.105, 169 L.Ed.2d 75 (2007) (prisoners are entitled to treatment by medical specialists).

Easter v. Powell, 467 F.3d 459 (5th Cir. 2006) (prison nurse held liable under Eighth Amendment for refusing to adhere to prisoner's prescribed treatment, knowing prisoner had heart condition, experiencing chest pains, and did not have prescribed medication).

Erickson v. Pardus, 551 U.S. 89, 127 S.Ct. 2197, __L.Ed.2d__ (2007) (when prison officials denied medical treatment for prisoner's life-threatening liver condition, deliberate-indifference claim was stated).

Edwards v. Snyder, 478 F.3d 827 (7th Cir. 2007) (when prisoner was forced to wait two days for treatment of dislocated finger, deliberate-indifference claim was stated).

Ruiz-Rosa v. Rullan, 485 F.3d 150 (1st Cir. 2007) (deliberate indifference not found when doctor may have prescribed wrong antibiotic and pretrial detainee died because doctor had no knowledge that substantial risk of serious harm existed).

Lockett v. Suardini, 526 F.3d 866 (6th Cir. 2008) (prisoner's allegation that nurse failed to treat medical condition after altercation with guards found not to violate the Eighth Amendment because injuries were minor and nurse saw him twice within a twenty-four-hour period).

Brown v. D.C., 514 F.3d 1279 (D.C. Cir. 2008) (prisoner stated Eighth Amendment claim when prison officials failed to transfer him to a hospital, despite doctors' order to do so and prisoner's complaint of pain).

Gibson v. Moskowitz, 523 F.3d 657 (6th Cir. 2008) (Eighth Amendment violation when prisoner died of dehydration caused by psychiatric medication and psychiatrist ignored symptoms of dehydration).

Dickworth v. Ahmad, 532 F.3d 675 (7th Cir. 2008) (under the Eighth Amendment, states have an affirmative duty to provide medical care to prisoners).

Martinez v. Beggz, 563 F.3d 1082 (10th Cir. 2009) (although knowing detainee was intoxicated, officials did not know detainee had heart condition, which resulted in fatal heart attack, and therefore were not deliberately indifferent to medical need).

Giles v. Kearney, 571 F.3d 318 (3rd Cir. 2009) (no Eighth Amendment claim when prisoner with punctured lung taken to hospital after twenty-four-hour period because officials not deliberately indifferent to medical need).

McRaven v. Sander, 577 F.3d 974 (8th Cir. 2009) (viable Eighth Amendment claim when nurse failed to detect drug overdose because assumed detainee intoxicated but did not check blood work for alcohol poisoning).

Smith v. Smith, 589 F.3d 736 (4th Cir. 2009) (prisoner stated viable Eighth Amendment claim when medical treatment delayed by prison nurse who tore up doctor's order).

Harper v. Lawrence County, 592 F.3d 1227 (11th Cir. 2010) (officials violated due process when ignoring warnings that detainee needed medical treatment, resulting in death by alcohol withdrawal).

Farid v. Ellen, 593 F.3d 233 (2nd Cir. 2010) (inconsistent hepatitis C treatment was at most negligent and did not rise to level of Eighth Amendment violation).

Grayton v. McCoy, 593 F.3d 610 (7th Cir. 2010) (no Eighth Amendment violation; prison nurses only negligent when ignored prisoner with heart condition complaint of chest pains; nurses were not deliberately indifferent).

Baribeau v. City of Minneapolis, 596 F.3d 465 (8th Cir. 2010) (per curiam) (confiscation of pretrial detainee's prosthetic leg by prison officials held rationally related to security interests).

Nelson v. Shuffman, 603 F.3d 439 (8th Cir. 2010) (viable Eighth Amendment claim when prison psychologist prescribed treatment that was never provided to prisoner).

Flanory v. Bonn, 604 F.3d 249 (6th Cir. 2010) (prisoner who was denied toothpaste for 337 days stated viable Eighth Amendment claim when dental problems arose and ignored by officials).

Thomas v. Cook County Sheriff's Dep't, 604 F.3d 293 (7th Cir. 2010) (officials violated due process when failing to act on numerous medical requests submitted on behalf of detainee before detainee eventually died of meningitis).

Berry v. Peterman, 604 F.3d 435 (7th Cir. 2010) (prison doctor and nurse violated Eighth Amendment when denied prisoner treatment of extremely painful toothache that later necessitated root canal).

Fields v. Smith, 653 F.3d 550 (7th Cir. 2011), *cert. denied* __U.S.__, 132 S.Ct. 1810, 182 L.Ed.2d 616 (2012) (Gender Identity Disorder is a serious medical condition, and prison officials violate the Eighth Amendment when they fail to adequately treat inmates with GID, which may include treatment such as hormone therapy and sexual reassignment surgery).

Smith v. Knox County Jail, 666 F.3d 1037 (7th Cir. 2012) (per curiam) (five-day delay in treating inmate who suffered attack by another inmate stated viable Eighth Amendment medical deliberate indifference claim where attack resulted in pain, bleeding, vomiting, eye damage and dizziness).

Paine v. Cason, 678 F.3d 500 (7th Cir. 2012), *as amended on denial of reh'g and reh'g en banc* (May 17, 2012) (prisoners are not entitled under the Constitution to have their time of confinement extended in order to receive medical care).

Snow v. McDaniel, 681 F.3d 978 (9th Cir. 2012) (a reasonable jury could find denial of surgery by non-treating, non-specialist physicians medically unacceptable under the Eighth Amendment).

Finn v. Haddock, 459 Fed.Appx. 833 (11th Cir. 2012) (prison officials cannot be deliberately indifferent to medical needs they do not know about).

Wells v. Thaler, 460 Fed.Appx. 303 (5th Cir. 2012) (where prison officials attempted but failed to locate Braille and audio resources for visually impaired prisoner, and where other prisoners qualified and available as readers, no violation of ADA arose).

NOTES: _____
_____
_____
_____
_____
_____
_____
_____
_____
_____
_____
_____
_____
_____
_____
_____
_____
_____
_____
_____
_____
_____
_____
_____
_____
_____
_____
_____
_____
_____
_____
_____
_____
_____
_____
_____
_____
_____
_____
_____
_____

NOTES:

MOOTNESS

County of Los Angeles v. Davis, 440 U.S. 625, 99 S.Ct. 1379, 59 L.Ed.2d 642 (1979) (civil cases involving the violation of law become moot if (1) there is no reasonable expectation that the alleged violation will recur, and (2) if interim relief or events have completely and irrevocably eradicated the effects of the alleged violation).

Boag v. MacDougall, 454 U.S. 364, 364-65, __S.Ct.__, __L.Ed.2d__ (1982) (per curiam) (damages claims are not mooted by transfer from facility).

Murphy v. Hunt, 455 U.S. 478 472, 102 S.Ct. 1181, 71 L.Ed.2d 353 (1982) (civil cases involving the violation of law become moot if (1) there is no reasonable expectation that the alleged violation will recur, and (2) if interim relief or events have completely and irrevocably eradicated the effects of the alleged violation).

Beyah v, Coughlin, 789 F.2d 986 (1986) (transfer from prison may have mooted claim for "declaratory and injunctive relief" concerning that facility, but did not moot claims for compensatory and punitive damages).

Norman-Bloodsaw v. Lawrence Berkley Laboratory, 135 F.3d 1260 (9th Cir. 1998) (mere voluntary cessation of illegal conduct does not moot the case).

DiGore v. Ryan, 172 F.3d 454 (7th Cir. 1999) (a case becomes moot if no controversy persists between the parties).

AT&T Communications of Southwest v. City of Austin, 235 F.3d 241 (5th Cir. 2000) (a case becomes moot if no controversy persists between the parties).

Herman v. Holiday, 238 F.3d 660 (5th Cir. 2001) (prisoner's Eighth Amendment claim for injunctive relief concerning exposure to asbestos rendered moot when prisoner transferred to a different facility).

Cantrell v. City of Long Beach, 241 F.3d 674 (9th Cir. 2001) (demonstrating mootness is a heavy burden).

Al Najar v. Ashcroft, 273 F.3d 1330 (11th Cir. 2001) (a case becomes moot if no controversy persists between the parties).

Davis v. N.Y., 316 F.3d 93 (2nd Cir. 2002) (despite transfer, injunctive relief may still be available where conditions persist at new location).

Goodwin v. C.N.J., Inc., 436 F.3d 44 (1st Cir. 2006) (a legally cognizable interest in the outcome of an action must persist, or the case becomes moot).

Salahuddin v. Gourd, 467 F.3d 263 (2nd Cir. 2006) (prisoner's claim for injunctive relief becomes moot when prisoner transferred to another facility that does not pose same concerns forming basis of complaint).

Incumaa v. Ozmint, 507 F.3d 281 (4th Cir. 2007) (plaintiff's claim for injunctive relief became moot when prisoner transferred to another facility, even though challenged publications ban "similar" to ban at new location).

Jacobs v.Clark County School Dist., 526 F.3d 419 (9th Cir. 2008) (claim for even nominal damages prevents mootness).

Burkey v. Marberry, 556 F.3d 142, 148 (3rd Cir. 2009) (claim is moot if there is no "continuing injury" likely to be favorably redressed).

Ortiz v. Downey, 561 F.3d 664 (7th Cir. 2009) (where no realistic possibility that prisoner would be returned to facility and subjected to alleged unconstitutional conditions, claim for prospective relief was rendered moot).

Cardinal v. Metrish, 564 F.3d 794 (6th Cir. 2009) (prisoner claim moot when transferred to another facility that provided proper religious diet).

NOTES: _____

NOTES:

PHONES

Duran v. Elrod, 542 F.2d 998 (7th Cir. 1976) (prison officials must provide inmates access to enough phones so as to make phone use practicable).

Feeley v. Sampson, 570 F.2d 364 (1st Cir. 1978) (inmates have a right to access phones, and imposition of severe limitations on this right raises constitutional questions).

Benzel v. Grammer, 869 F.2d 1105 (8th Cir. 1989) (prison regulation prohibiting prisoners housed in segregation from calling non-attorney, non-relatives held justified by prison security and rehabilitation concerns).

Murphy v. Walker, 51 F.3d 714 (7th Cir. 1995) (per curiam) (suspension of phone privileges may violate Sixth Amendment if revocation impedes right to access counsel).

U.S. v. Workman, 80 F.3d 688 (2nd Cir. 1996) (monitoring and recording of prisoners' calls held not to violate the Constitution when policy is published in inmate handbook and signs posted).

Pope v. Hightower, 101 F.3d 1382 (11th Cir. 1996) (prison policy limiting phone numbers that prisoners may call to ten held justified restriction to reduce criminal activity and harassment).

U.S. v. Morin, 437 F.3d 777 (8th Cir. 2006) (monitoring and recording of prisoners' calls held not to violate the Constitution when inmates provided adequate notice).

Almahdi v. Bourque, 386 Fed.Appx. 260 (3rd Cir. 2010) (*Bivens* claim not stated where prisoner incurred a 180-day suspension of phone privileges for disciplinary purposes).

Holloway v. Magress, 666 F.3d 1076 8th Cir. 2012), *petition for cert. filed* (U.S. Apr 25, 2012) (phone rate increase for state profit does not violate the Constitution where inmates have alternative means to communicate via visits and mail).

NOTES:

NOTES: _____
_____
_____
_____
_____
_____
_____
_____
_____
_____
_____
_____
_____
_____
_____
_____
_____
_____
_____
_____
_____
_____
_____
_____
_____
_____
_____
_____
_____
_____
_____
_____
_____
_____
_____
_____
_____
_____
_____
_____

PRELIMINARY INJUNCTIONS & TROS

Stenberg v. Cheker Oil Co., 573 F.2d 921 (6th Cir. 1978) (a preliminary injunction is an extraordinary remedy that should only be granted if the movant carries the burden of persuasion).

Brenda v. Grand Lodge of Internat'l Ass'n of Machinists & Aerospace Workers, 584 F.2d 308 (9th Cir. 1978) *cert. dismissed*, 441 U.S. 937, __S.Ct.__, __L.Ed.2d__ (1979) (the "alternative standard," as opposed to the traditional standard, for preliminary injunctive relief requires the moving party to demonstrate either (1) a combination of probable success on the merits and the possibility of irreparable injury, or (2) that serious questions are raised and the balance of hardships tips sharply in its favor).

Los Angeles Memorial Coliseum Commission v. national Football League, 634 F.3d 1197 (9th Cir. 1980) ("irreparable injury" is defined as an actual and concrete harm, or the imminent threat of an actual and concrete harm).

Enterprise Int'l, Inc. v.Corporacion Estatal Petrolera Ecutoriana, 762 F.2d 464 (5th Cir. 1985) (a preliminary injunction is an extraordinary remedy; it should not be granted routinely, but only when the plaintiff, by a clear showing, carries her burden of persuasion on each of the required elements).

In re DeLorean Motor, Inc. v. Fisher, 755 F.3d 1223 (6th Cir. 1985) (the four elements a court must consider in whether to grant a preliminary injunction are "[f]actors to be balanced, not prerequisites that must be met").

Cassim v. Bowen, 824 F.2d 791 (9th Cir. 1987) (the "traditional standard" considered in determining whether to issue a preliminary injunction requires that (1) the moving party will suffer irreparable injury if the relief is denied; (2) the moving party will probably prevail on the merits; (3) the balance of potential harm favors the moving party; and (4) the public interest favors granting relief).

Caribbean Marine Services Co. v. Baldridge, 844 F.2d 668 (9th Cir. 1988) (a threat is not "imminent" if based upon remote possibilities or mere speculation).

Bradley v. Pittsburgh Board of Education, 910 F.2d 1172 (3rd Cir. 1990) (a court is not obligated to hold a hearing on a motion for preliminary injunction when the movant has not presented a colorable factual basis to support the claim on the merits or the contention of irreparable harm).

International Jensen, Inc. v. Metrosound U.S.A., 4 F.3d 819 (9th Cir. 1993) (a preliminary injunction under Rule 65 of the Federal Rules of Civil Procedure may be granted if the moving party satisfies either the (1) "traditional standard" or (2) "alternative standard" of law).
    NOTE: *See Washington v. Reno* and *Cassim v. Bowen* for "traditional standard," and see *Brenda v. Grand Lodge of Internat'l Ass'n of Machinists & Aerospace Workers* for the "alternative standard."

Stanley v. University of S. Cal., 13 F.3d 1313 (9th Cir. 1994) (when a party seeks a preliminary injunction, the court must deny such relief unless the facts and law clearly favor the moving party).

Washington v. Reno, 35 F.3d 1093 (6th Cir. 1994) (to grant a preliminary injunction, a court must consider: (1) whether there is a strong or substantial likelihood of movant being successful on the merits of the claim; (2)

whether the movant has established irreparable harm; (3) whether the issuance of a preliminary injunction would cause substantial harm to others: and (4) whether the public interest is served by the issuance of the injunction).

NOTES:

NOTES: _____

PRETRIAL DETAINEES

Bell v. Wolfish, 441 U.S. 520, 535, 537, 99 S.Ct. 1861, 60 L.Ed.2d 447 (1979) (pretrial detainees "are protected by the Fourteenth Amendment's Due Process Clause, as well as specific substantive guarantees of the federal Constitution, such as the First and Eighth Amendments. . . ." Moreover, under "the Due Process Clause, detainees have a right against jail conditions or restrictions that 'amount to punishment.'").

Campell v. Cauthon, 623 F.3d 503 (8th Cir. 1980) (holding that pretrial detainees are generally entitled to one hour of exercise outside their cells daily if they spend more than sixteen hours in their cell).

Lock v. Jenkins, 641 F.2d 488 (1981) (finding the importance of dayroom access increases as the length of time the pretrial detainee spends in the cell increases and the size of the cell decreases).

City of Revere v. Massachusetts General Hospital, 463 U.S. 239, 244, __S.Ct.__, __L.Ed.2d__ (1983) (pretrial detainees are entitled to adequate medical care).

Riggins v. Nevada, 504 U.S. 127, 135, 112 S.Ct. 1810, 118 L.Ed.2d 479 (1992) (pretrial detainees may not be forcibly administered antipsychotic drugs without the prior finding that (1) medication is medically appropriate, (2) less intrusive alternatives have been considered, and (3) treatment is essential for the detainee's safety or the safety of others).

Alvarez-Machain v. U.S., 96 F.3d 1246 (9th Cir. 1996) (pretrial detainees' rights are distinct from convicted prisoners' rights because the government cannot punish a pretrial detainee).

Payne for Hicks, v. Chuchich, 161 F.3d 1030 (7th Cir. 1998) (pretrial detainees may not be punished, because detainees have not been found guilty of a crime).

Higgs v. Carver, 286 F.3d 437 (7th Cir. 2002) (pretrial detainee stated viable claim when prison officials segregated inmate in retaliation for filing a lawsuit).

Calderon-Ortiz v. Laboy-Alvarado, 300 F.3d 60 (1st Cir. 2002) (prisoner alleged viable deliberate-indifference claim when detainee was sodomized by other prisoners and officials knew of potential for harm yet failed to adequately classify and house plaintiff).

Napier v. Preslicka, 314 F.3d 528 (11th Cir. 2002) (PLRA's provision barring claims for emotional distress absent a showing of physical injury applies to pretrial detainees).

Sell v. U.S., 539 U.S. 166, 180-83, __S.Ct.__, __L.Ed.2d__ (2003) (state may forcibly administer antipsychotic medication to render detainee competent to stand trial upon finding that (1) important government interests are at stake; (2) involuntary medication will significantly further those state interests; (3) involuntary medication is necessary to further those interests; and (4) medication is medically in the detainee's best interest).

Tilman v. Prator, 368 F.3d 521 (5th Cir. 2004) (the strictures of *Sandin* apply to convicted but unsentenced prisoners).

Hartsfield v. Colburn, 371 F.3d 454 (8th Cir. 2004) (pretrial detainees are entitled to at least as much protection under the Fourteenth Amendment as convicted prisoners are under the Eighth Amendment).

Hayes v. Faulkner County, 388 F.3d 669 (8th Cir. 2004) (jail administrator acted under color of state law for the purposes of § 1983 claim when deliberately indifferent to violations of detainee's due process rights).

Daniels v. Woodside, 396 F.3d 730 (6th Cir. 2005) (pretrial detainee did not allege a viable due process claim when he was placed in twenty-four-hour lockdown, deprived shower and personal hygiene products, because he had expressed suicidal thoughts and government had legitimate interest in preventing suicide).

Hart v. Sheahan, 396 F.3d 887 (7th Cir. 2005) (pretrial detainees may not be punished, except for jail infractions, because detainees have not been found guilty of a crime; and possible due process claim stated when detainees could not get the attention of guard for ten minutes while detainee was attacked by cellmate and guard provided no reason for delay).

Hydrick v. Hunter, 449 F.3d 978 (9th Cir. 2006) (for the purposes of due process determination, paroled, detained, and convicted prisoners have liberty interest in avoiding unwanted administration of antipsychotic drugs).

Kahle v. Leonard, 477 F.3d 544 (8th Cir. 2007) (pretrial detainees are entitled to at least as much protection under the Fourteenth Amendment as convicts are under the Eighth Amendment).

Stevenson v. Carroll, 495 F.3d 62 (3rd Cir. 2007) (the strictures of the *Sandin* due process analysis do not apply to pretrial detainees).

Williams v. Rodriguez, 509 F.3d 392 (7th Cir. 2007) (the Due Process Clause provides at least as much protection for pretrial detainees as the Eighth Amendment provides convicted prisoners).

Pierce v. County of Orange, 526 F.3d 1190, 1211 (9th Cir. 2008) (when determining whether legitimate, non-punitive reasons for a policy exist pertaining to pretrial detainees, a "court should not . . . blindly [defer] to [officials'] bare invocation of security concerns" without requiring some evidence that prison policies are based on legitimate penological justifications).

Pierce v. County of Orange, 526 F.3d 1190 (9th Cir. 2008) (county jail failed to reasonably accommodate mobility-impaired and dexterity-impaired pretrial detainees, in violation of the Americans with Disabilities Act).

Grieveson v. Anderson, 538 F.3d 763 (7th Cir. 2008) (officials who failed to intervene when detainee assaulted by other prisoners may give rise to deliberate-indifference claim under the Fourteenth Amendment).

Byrd v. Maricopa County Sheriff's Dep't, 565 F.3d 1205 (9th Cir. 2009) (pretrial detainees entitled to at least as much protection under Fourteenth Amendment as convicted prisoners enjoy under Eighth Amendment).

Clouter v. County of Contra Costa, 591 F.3d 1232 (9th Cir. 2010) (where detainee hanged himself after removal from suicide protection the day before, viable due-process claim arose because detainee made several suicide threats).

Baribeau v. City of Minneapolis, 596 F.3d 465 (8th Cir. 2010) (per curiam) (confiscation of pretrial detainee's prosthetic leg by prison officials held rationally related to security interests).

Minix v. Canarecci, 597 F.3d 824 (7th Cir. 2010) (pretrial detainees entitled to at least as much protection under Fourteenth Amendment as convicted prisoners enjoy under Eighth Amendment).

Morris v. Zefferi, 601 F.3d 805 (8th Cir. 2010) (transporting prisoner in dog cage where other non-punitive transport method available may violate due process).

Simmons v. Navajo County, 609 F.3d 1011 (9th Cir. 2010) (officials not deliberately indifferent to medical need when detainee committed suicide because preventative precautions were taken).

NOTES: _____

_____

_____

_____

_____

_____

_____

_____

_____

_____

_____

_____

_____

_____

_____

_____

_____

_____

_____

_____

_____

_____

_____

_____

_____

_____

_____

_____

_____

_____

_____

_____

_____

_____

_____

_____

_____

_____

_____

_____

NOTES:

PRISONER LITIGATION REFORM ACT (PLRA)

Felker v. Yurpin, 518 U.S. 651, 116 S.Ct. 2333, 135 L.Ed.2d 827 (1996) (petition for writ of *habeas corpus* is not a "civil action" for the purposes of the PLRA; *habeas* petitions are not bound by the strictures of the PLRA).

Reyes v. Keane, 90 F.3d 676 (2nd Cir. 1996) (petition for writ of *habeas corpus* is not a "civil action" for the purposes of the PLRA; *habeas* petitions are not bound by the strictures of the PLRA).

Garrett v. Hawk, 127 F.3d 1263 (10th Cir. 1998) (holding that Federal Tort Claims Act is not "available" to prisoner pursuing *Bivens* claim against individual prison staff; therefore, the FTCA notice of claim procedure does not apply and need not be exhausted).

Kerr v. Puckett, 138 F.3d 321 (7th Cir. 1998) (PLRA provision barring prisoners from bringing suit for mental or emotional injury without a prior showing of physical injury does not apply to suits filed by prisoners after they are released).

Rivera v. Allin, 144 F.3d 719 (11th Cir. 1998) (claims dismissed as frivolous, malicious, or for failing to state a claim upon which relief may be granted before the enactment of the PLRA count as strikes for PLRA's three-strikes provision).

Gibbs v. Cross, 160 F.3d 962 (3rd Cir. 1998) (prison withholding medical care to prisoner who became ill after breathing particulate matter emitted from a cell vent held sufficient to qualify under the "imminent danger" exception to the "three strikes" provision of the PLRA).

Pischke v. Litscher, 178 F.3d 497 (7th Cir. 1999) (prisoners still have constitutional rights which can be vindicated by suits under § 1983 for damages or injunctive relief, but the requirements of the PLRA must be adhered to).

Miller v. French, 530 U.S. 327, 331, 120 S.Ct. 2246, 147 L.Ed.2d 326 (2000) (the PLRA "establishes standards for the entry and termination of prospective relief in civil actions challenging prison conditions").

Jenkins v. Haubert, 179 F.3d 19 (2nd Cir. 1999) (should there exist separate internal complaint and/or appeal protocols for particular issues, then the specialized system must be exhausted instead of the inapplicable grievance system; holding that appeal of disciplinary conviction satisfied the exhaustion requirement).

Rumbles v. Hill, 182 F.3d 1064 (9th Cir. 1999), *cert. denied,* 528 U.S. 1074 (2000) (language of the PLRA, as well as the language of the pre-PLRA version of section 1997e, indicate that Congress did not intend prisoners to exhaust state tort claim procedures in addition to internal prison grievances).

U.S. v. Jones, 215 F.3d 467 (4th Cir. 2000) (PLRA applies to civil actions, including post-conviction actions for return of property).

Boivin v. Black, 225 F.3d 36 (1st Cir. 2000) (PLRA's provisions capping attorneys' fees held not to deny access to courts because it only restricts access to attorneys who are unwilling to accept lowers fees).

Booth v. Churner, 532 U.S. 731, 121 S.Ct. 1819, 149 L.Ed.2d 958 (2001) (subsection (a) of 42 U.S.C. § 1997(e) [PLRA] requires prisoners to complete prison administrative remedies before suing over prison conditions, even when prisoner is seeking only money damages not recoverable through such administrative process; yet prisoners need not list and then exhaust tentative demands for such relief, for the applicability of the exhaustion requirement turns on whether the grievances system will address the prisoner's complaint, not whether it provides the remedy that the prisoner prefers).

Richardson v. Spulock, 260 F.3d 495 (5th Cir. 2001) (should there exist separate internal complaint and/or appeal protocols for particular issues, then the specialized system must be exhausted instead of the inapplicable grievance system, and filing an "administrative" appeal rather than the required "disciplinary" appeal did not exhaust).

Strong v. David, 297 F.3d 646, 649 (7th Cir. 2002) ("no administrative system may demand that the prisoner specify each remedy later sought in litigation—for *Booth v. Churner* . . . holds that § 1997e(a) requires each prisoner to exhaust a process and not a remedy.").

Porter v. Nussle, 534 U.S. 516, 122 S.Ct. 983, 152 L.Ed.2d 12 (2002) (subsection (a) of 42 U.S.C. § 1997(e) [PLRA] requires prisoners to complete prison administrative remedies before suing prison officials under federal law, because the exhaustion requirement was created "to reduce the quantity and improve the quality of prisoners suits; to this purpose, Congress afforded corrections officials time and opportunity to address complaints internally before allowing the initiation of a federal case" [534 U.S. at 524-25]; PLRA applies to suits involving prison conditions, and the phrase "prison condition" applies "to all inmate suites about prison life, whether they involve general circumstances or particular episodes, and whether they allege excessive force or some other wrong" [534 U.S. at 532].).

Webb v. Ada County, 285 F.3d 829 (9th Cir. 2002) (PLRA provision capping awards for attorney's fees applies to post-judgment efforts to enforce relief granted in original judgment).

Mitchell v. Horn, 318 F.3d 523 (3rd Cir. 2003) (PLRA's provision barring claims for mental or emotional damages, absent a showing of a non-*de minimis* physical injury, does not apply to claims for nominal and punitive damages, nor does it bar injunctive or declaratory relief; such relief does not remunerate injury).

Dannenberg v. Valadez, 338 F.3d 1070 (9th Cir. 2003) (PLRA cap on attorney's fees awardable to the successful plaintiff does not apply when the court orders injunctive relief as well as damages).

Ciarpaglini v. Saini, 352 F.3d 328, 330 (7th Cir. 2003) (when prison officials discontinued prisoner's medication for panic disorder and ADHD, resulting in serious physical symptoms, claim was found sufficient under the "imminent-danger" exception to the PLRA's "three strikes" provision).

Healy v. Wisconsin, 65 Fed.Appx. 567 (7th Cir. 2003) (dismissal of a claim as frivolous, malicious, or for failing to state a claim upon which relief can be granted counts as a strike and is counted as another strike if dismissal is unsuccessfully challenged on appeal).

Riccardo v. Rausch, 375 F.3d 521 (7th Cir. 2004) (prison officials cannot hear and decide a grievance on the merits then later seek dismissal of a subsequent lawsuit on non-exhaustion grounds for failing to strictly comply with grievance procedures); *see also* ***Gates v. Cook***, 376 F.3d 323 (5th Cir. 2004); ***Spruill v. Gillis***, 372 F.3d 218

(3rd Cir. 2004); *Ross v. County of Bernalillo*, 365 F.3rd 1181 (10th Cir. 2004); *Pozo v. McCaughtry*, 286 F.3d 1022 (7th Cir.), *cert. denied*, 537 U.S. 949 (2002).

Chandler v. Crosby, 379 F.3d 1278 (11th Cir. 2004) (finding that the PLRA's exhaustion requirement does not apply to every member represented in a class action; it is sufficient that the named plaintiff(s) exhausted available remedies).

Lira v. Herrera, 427 F.3d 1164 (9th Cir. 2005) (PLRA requires dismissal of only those claims not fully exhausted when complaint alleges both exhausted and un-exhausted claims).

Burrell v. Powers, 431 F.3d 282 (7th Cir. 2005) (prisoner did not exhaust all administrative remedies when failing to appeal denial of grievance; dismissal of claim held proper).

Norton v. City of Marietta, 432 F.3d 1145 (10th Cir. 2005) (former prisoners need not exhaust administrative remedies before bringing § 1983 action because PLRA exhaustion provision does not apply to persons no longer incarcerated).

Woodward v. Ngo, 548 U.S. 81, 126 S.Ct. 2378, 165 L.Ed.2d 368 (2006) (the exhaustion requirement under the PLRA requires that prisoners observe all administrative deadlines and requirements concerning the exhaustion of available remedies).

Skinner v. Govorchin, 463 F.3d 518 (6th Cir. 2006) (100% deduction from prisoner account for filing fee and court costs impermissible; PLRA allows for 20% only).

Butler v. Dep't of Justice, 492 F.3d 440 (D.C. Cir. 2007) (dismissal of prisoner complaint for failure to prosecute does not count as a strike towards the PLRA's "three strikes" provision).

George v. Smith, 507 F.3d 605 (7th Cir. 2007) (each claim of a multi-claim, multi-defendant lawsuit counts as an individual strike towards the "three-strike" provision of the PLRA).

Fields v. Oklahoma State Penitentiary, 511 F.3d 1109 (10th Cir. 2007) (when grievances dismissed for failure to comply with administrative grievance procedures, prisoner failed to exhaust remedies because he did not attempt to re-file grievances in compliance with policy).

Jones v. Bock, 549 U.S. 199, 127 S.Ct. 910, 166 L.Ed.2d 798 (2007) (PLRA does not require an inmate to plead and demonstrate complete exhaustion of administrative remedies before filing a lawsuit.)
       NOTE: Generally, administrative remedies must be exhausted before a suit; however, under this case it's the defendant's burden to show a failure to exhaust, not the prisoner's.

Whitington v. Ortiz, 472 F.3d 804 (10th Cir. 2007) (finding that prisoner exhausted available administrative remedies because prison officials failed to respond to grievance in a timely manner).

Tarari v. Hues, 473 F.3d 440 (2nd Cir. 2007) (dismissal of premature appeal not considered strike under PLRA's three-strikes provision, because appeal not frivolous and procedural defect curable).

Okoro v. Hemingway, 481 F.3d 873 (6th Cir. 2007) (whether prisoner failed to exhaust all administrative remedies for the purposes of the PLRA is an affirmative defense the defendants must raise, prisoners need not specifically demonstrate exhaustion as a prerequisite to state a claim).

Andrews v. Cervantes, 493 F.3d 1047 (9th Cir. 2007) (policy that did not screen for contagious diseases constituted an imminent threat for PLRA purposes).

Davis v. Kan. Dep't of Corr., 507 F.3d 1346 (10th Cir. 2007) (complaint that asserted no possible legal theory under which plaintiff could proceed, properly dismissed as frivolous and counted toward PLRA's three-strikes provision).

Polanco v. Hopkins, 510 F.3d 152 (2nd Cir. 2007) (prisoner failed to demonstrate risk of injury from exposure to mold in prison shower or from alleged unjust institution of disciplinary measures for the purposes of the "imminent-danger" exception to the "three-strikes" provision of the PLRA).

Pierce v. County of Orange, 526 F.3d 1190, 1204 n.12 (9th Cir. 2008) (noting that the PLRA *only* provides for the termination or modification of prospective relief, not for vacating prior judgments), *citing Inmates of Suffolk County Jail v. Rouse*, 129 F.3d 649, 662 (1st Cir. 1997).

Ammons v. Gerlinger, 547 F.3d 724 (7th Cir. 2008) (a prisoner who has received three strikes under the PLRA must inform the court of this fact).

Griffin v. Arpaio, 557 F.3d 1117, 1120 (9th Cir. 2009) ("A grievance need not include legal terminology or legal theories unless they are in some way needed to provide notice of the harm being grieved").

McLean v. U.S., 566 F.3d 391 (4th Cir. 2009) (claim dismissed without prejudice not a strike, because claim could be revived by competent pleading).

Malik v. D.C., 574 F.3d 781 (D.C. Cir. 2009) (prisoners cannot be expected to exhaust administrative remedies that do not exist; PLRA inapplicable).

Parker v. Conway, 581 F.3d 198 (3rd Cir. 2009) (PLRA does not violate equal protection, because attorney-fee cap rationally related to government interest).

Espinal v. Goord, 588 F.3d 119 (2nd Cir. 2009) (where description of misconduct in grievance reasonably identified parties to whom claim related, PLRA exhaustion requirement held inapplicable because prisoner included new defendants in lawsuit).

Johnson v. Rowley, 569 F.3d 40 (2nd Cir. 2009) (claim of religious discrimination not exhausted, because raised at an intermediate stage of prison grievance process, not at the outset).

Nunez v. Duncan, 591 F.3d 1217 (9th Cir. 2010) (where prisoners adhere to grievance policy when exhasusting their claims but where the actions of prison officals cause the remedy process to go uncompleted, the failure to exhaust may be excused).

Dillon v. Rogers, 596 F.3d 260 (5th Cir. 2010) (whether administrative remedies have been duly exhausted should not be resolved by a jury; the court should hold evidentiary hearing on the matter).

Keup v. Hopkins, 596 F.3d 899 (8th Cir. 2010) ((1) prison officials waived exhaustion defense when failing to raise it at trial; (2) PLRA cap limiting award of attorney's fees to 150% of judgment applied to award of nominal damages, awarding $1.50 in attorney's fees).

Reed-Bey v. Pramstaller, 603 F.3d 322 (6th Cir. 2010) (prison officials could not raise exhaustion defense when they decided prisoner's grievance on its merits despite its procedural failings).

Harvey v. Jordan, 605 F.3d 681 (9th Cir. 2010) ((1) prisoners must file institutional grievances within time limits of administrative policy; (2) prisoners are not required to appeal a grievance when satisfied with the grant of relief achieved at intermediate stages of grievance process).

Little v. Jones, 607 F.3d 1245 (10th Cir. 2010) (where administrators prevented prisoner from completing grievance process, defendants we precluded from raising failure-to-exhaust defense).

Messa v. Goord, 652 F.3d 305 (2nd Cir. 2011) (whether administrative remedies have been exhausted is a matter for the judge, not a jury, to resolve).

Williams v. Hobbs, 662 F.3d 994 (8th Cir. 2011) (where injuries were not a direct result of lengthy stay in administrative segregation, prisoner's due process claim for damages failed for lack of showing of physical injury).

Pavey v. Conley, 663 F.3d 899 (7th Cir 2011) (verbal complaint insufficient to exhaust administrative remedies where policy required inmate to submit complaint form).

Barkley v. Ricci, 439 Fed.Appx. 119 (3rd Cir. 2011) (inmate failed to appeal grievance and thus did not exhaust administrative remedies).

Thomas v. Parker, 672 F.3d 1182 (10th Cir. 2012) (claim dismissed in part for failing to state a claim and in part for failure to exhaust counted as a strike under the PLRA).

NOTES: _____

NOTES: _____

PRIVACY, SEARCH & SEIZURE

Houchins v. KQED, Inc., 438 U.S. 1, 5 n.2, __S.Ct.__, __L.Ed.2d__ (1978) ("[I]nmates in jails and prisons retain certain fundamental rights of privacy; they are not like animals in a zoo to be filmed and photographed at will by the public or by media reporters, however 'educational' the process may be for others.").

Bell v. Wolfish, 441 U.S. 520, 99 S.Ct. 1861, 60 L.Ed.2d 447 (1979) (courts should consider the degree to which searches invade the personal privacy of pretrial detainees and degree of abusiveness, considering (1) scope of intrusion, (2) manner in which the search is conducted, (3) justification for the search, and (4) place of search; the Court stated: "The test of reasonableness under the Fourth Amendment is not capable of precise definition or mechanical application. In each case it requires a balancing of the need for the particular search against the invasion of personal rights that the search entails. Courts must consider the scope of the particular intrusion, the manner in which it is conducted, the justification for initiating it, and the place in which it is conducted" [411 U.S. at 559].).

Lee v. Downs, 641 F.2d 1117 (4th Cir. 1981) (male guards may pat- and strip-search female inmates if justified by emergency circumstances, in which case male guards may also access prison areas where they would see female inmates use toilet and shower facilities).

Hudson v. Palmer, 468 U.S. 517, 528, 104 S.Ct. 3194, 60 L.Ed.2d 447 (1984) (the Fourth Amendment is not violated by prison officials who conduct random cell searches; prison security outweighs prisoners' privacy interests).

U.S. v. Cohen, 796 F.2d 20, 24 (2nd Cir. 1986) ("An individual's mere presence in a prison cell does not strip away every garment cloaking his Fourth Amendment rights, even though the covering that remains is but a small remnant.").

Kent v. Johnson, 821 F.3d 1220 (6th Cir. 1987) (viable Fourth Amendment claim when male prisoner exposed to female guards who were given unrestricted access to all areas of housing unit without legitimate reason).

Covino v. Patrissi, 967 F.2d 73 (2nd Cir. 1992) (regulation requiring random visual body cavity searches of prisoners held justified in light of security concerns).

Stewart v. McGinnis, 5 F.3d 1031 (7th Cir. 1993) (when state provided adequate post-deprivation remedy, prison officials' confiscation of prisoner's property did not rise to a constitutional violation).

Jordan v. Gardener, 986 F.2d 1521 (9th Cir. 1993) (if avoidable, male guards may not infringe upon female inmates' right to personal privacy).

Hays v. Marriott, 70 F.3d 1144 (10th Cir. 1995) (strip search of male prisoner viewed by 100 officials, including females, violated Fourth Amendment).

Moore v. Carwell, 168 F.3d 234 (5th Cir. 1999) (prisoner alleged viable Fourth Amendment claim when the absence of exigent circumstances and existence of readily available alternative to multiple strip and body-cavity searches may have rendered searches unreasonable).

Doe v. Delie, 257 F.3d 309 (3rd Cir. 2001) (prisoner's right of privacy over medical records may be overridden provided a legitimate governmental interest).

Hill v. McKinley, 311 F.3d 899 (8th Cir. 2002) (prisoner alleged viable Fourth Amendment claim when prison officials allowed restrained female prisoner to be exposed naked, spread-eagle before male guards for substantial amount of time).

Wiley v. Serrano, 37 Fed.Appx. 252 (9th Cir. 2002) (invasive searches such as rectal or vaginal cavity searches may be justified if (1) prison staff have reasonable cause to search the inmate; (2) the search serves a valid penological interest; and (3) the search is undertaken in a reasonable way).

Wood v. Hancock Sheriff's Dep't., 354 F.3d 57 (1st Cir. 2003) (regulation permitting the strip search of prisoners after contact visits held justified in light of risk of smuggling contraband).

Nicholas v. Goord, 430 F.3d 652 (2nd Cir. 2005) (prison held to have a legitimate penological interest in drawing blood samples to create DNA-indexing system), *overruled on other grounds by U.S. v. Amerson*, 483 F.3d 73 (2nd Cir. 2008).

Louis v. Nebraska Dep't of Corr. Servs, 437 F.3d 697 (8th Cir. 2006) (prison held to have a legitimate penological interest in performing periodic urinalysis to prevent unauthorized drug use).

Shell v. U.S., 448 F.3d 951 (7th Cir. 2006) (informants may be planted in cell or housing unit without violating the Fourth Amendment); *see also U.S. v. White*, 401 U.S. 745, 91 S.Ct. 1122, 28 L.Ed.2d 453 (1971).

Hydrick v. Hunter, 466 F.3d 676 (9th Cir. 2006) (viable Fourth Amendment claim alleged when prisoners were forced to publicly strip and personal property was arbitrarily taken).

Iqbal v. Hasty, 490 F.3d 143 (2nd Cir. 2007) (repeated body-cavity searches used as punishment violates Fourth Amendment), *rev'd on other grounds by Ashcroft v. Iqbal*, __U.S.__, 129 S.Ct. 1937, __L.Ed.2d__ (2009).

Hydrick v. Hunter, 500 F.3d 978 (9th Cir. 2007) (public strip search and property seizure may have been arbitrary and unjustified under the Fourth Amendment), *vacated on other grounds*, __U.S.__, 129 S.Ct. 2431, __L.Ed.2d__ (2009).

Wilson v. Collins, 517 F.3d 421 (6th Cir. 2008) (mouth swab of convicted felons held constitutional in creating DNA index).

Byrd v. Maricopa County Sheriff's Dep't, 565 F.3d 1205 (9th Cir. 2009, *reh'g en banc granted* 583 F.3d 673 (9th Cir. 2009), *and on reh'g en banc* 629 F.3d 1135 (9th Cir. 2011), *cert. denied* 2011 WL 1231308 (U.S. 2011) (en bank) (where female prison cadet touched male inmate's genital area during a pat-search, viable Fourth Amendment claim was stated).

Sanchez v. Pereira-Castillo, 590 F.3d 31 (1st Cir. 2009) (where less intrusive search measure created doubt of possession of contraband, exploratory abdominal surgery held to violate prisoner's Fourth Amendment right to privacy).

Nunez v. Duncan, 591 F.3d 1217 (9th Cir. 2010) (random searches of prisoners returning from work detail permitted under Fourth Amendment).

Jackson v. Herrington, 393 Fed.Appx. 348 (6th Cir. 2010), *cert. denied* __U.S.__, 131 S.Ct. 1479, 179 L.Ed.2d 316 (2011) (facility policy of routine strip-searches of all incoming transferred prisoners does not violate the Constitution).

Spencer v. Roche, 659 F.3d 142 (1st Cir. 2011), *cert. denied* __U.S.__, 132 S.Ct 1861, 182 L.Ed.2d 643 (2012) (x-ray taken to determine if inmate concealed package of crack cocaine in his anal cavity held not to violate Fourth Amendment because reason for the search and manner in which it was carried out were reasonable).

Watson v. Secretary, Penn. Dep't of Corr., 436 Fed.Appx. 131 (3rd Cir. 2011) (per curiam) (repeated strip-searches wherein prison staff made derogatory remarks and squeezed prisoner's penis and testicles constituted viable Fourth Amendment claim).

Gannaway v. Berks County Prison, 439 Fed.Appx. 86 (3rd Cir. 2011) (per curiam) (Fourth Amendment claim not stated where inmate publicly strip-searched in gym because was permitted to wear shorts).

Florence v. Bd. of Chosen Freeholder of County of Burlington et al, 566 U.S.__, 132 S.Ct. 1510, 182 L.Ed.2d 566 (2012) (slip opinion) (there is no mechanical way to determine whether intrusions on an inmate's privacy are reasonable, but "the need for a particular search must be balanced against the resulting invasion of personal rights" [slip op. at 6]; however, correctional officers have legitimate security interests in conducting body cavity searches of detainees admitted to a jail's general population, even for detainees arrested for minor offenses, and reasonable suspicion that a detainee is concealing contraband is not required [slip op. at 10, 19]).

Haskell v. Harris, 669 F.3d 1049 (9th Cir. 2012) (policy requiring collection of DNA samples from all adult prisoners arrested for felonies held constitutional).

NOTES:

NOTES:

RELIGION

Cantwell v. Connecticut, 310 U.S. 296, __S.Ct.__, __L.Ed__ (1940) (the First Amendment Free Exercise of Religion Clause absolutely protects the right to believe in a religion, but it does not absolutely protect all conduct associated with a religion).

Everson v. Board of Education, 330 U.S. 1, 15, 67 S.Ct. 504, 511, 91 L.Ed. 711, 723 (1947) (neither a state nor the federal government may set up a church, nor can they pass laws which aid one religion, aid all religions, or prefer one religion over another).

Presbyterian Church in United States v. Mary Elizabeth Blue Hall Mem'l Presbyterian Church, 393 U.S. 440, 89 S.Ct. 601, 21 L.Ed.2d 685 (1969) (question of an ecclesiastical nature should not be submitted to a court, as this would destroy the doctrine of separation of church and state).

Lemon v. Krutzman, 403 U.S. 602, 612-613, 91 S.Ct. 2105, 2111, 29 L.Ed.2d 745, 755 (1971) (whether a government practice violates the the Establishment Clause is analyzed under a three-part test: (1) it "must have a secular legislative purpose"; (2) its "primary effect" must be one that neither advances nor inhibits religion; and (3) it "must not foster an excessive government entanglement with religion"); s*ee, e.g., Zelaman v. Simmons-Harris*, 536 U.S. 639, 688-70, 122 S.Ct. 2460, 2476, 153 L.Ed.2d 604, 627-28 (2002); *compare with Lee v. Weisman*, 505 U.S. 577, 587, 112 S.Ct. 2649, 2655, 120 L.Ed.2d 467, 480-81 (1992) (here the Supreme Court did not apply the *Lemon* test when rejecting school policy permitting the invitation of the clergy to say prayers at school graduation ceremonies, instead applying a bright-line rule focusing on whether policy coerces participation of the unwilling).

Cruz v. Beto, 405 U.S. 319, 322 n.2, 92 S.Ct. 1079, 31 L.Ed.2d 263 (1972) (per curiam) ("[R]easonable opportunity must be afforded to all prisoners to exercise the religious freedom guaranteed by the First and Fourteenth Amendments").

Wisconsin v. Yoder, 406 U.S. 205, 215-16, 92 S.Ct. 1526, 1533, 32 L.Ed. 15, 25 (1972) (beliefs that are merely moral or philosophical in nature are not enough to state a First Amendment claim; only religious beliefs are protected).

Mawhinney v. Henderson, 542 F.2d 1, 3 (2nd Cir. 1976) (holding that inmates in "punitive segregation and keeplock" could not be denied participation in chapel services simply and only on the basis of their classification; individualized determinations of the "necessity of their exclusion" were required).

Sequoyah v. Tenn. Valley Auth., 620 F.2d 1159 (6th Cir. 1980) (orthodoxy is not a factor in determining whether the First Amendment protects a person's religious beliefs).

Thomas v. Review Bd. of Indiana Employment Sec. Division, 450 U.S. 707, 101 S.Ct. 1425, 67 L.Ed.2d 624 (1981) (it is not for courts to decide the validity of a plaintiff's religious beliefs).

Africa v. Pennsylvania, 662 F.2d 1025, 1032 (3rd Cir. 1981) (in determining whether a prisoner's beliefs are religious in nature, the court asks (1) whether the beliefs address "fundamental and ultimate questions"; (2)

whether the religion is "comprehensive in nature," consisting of a belief system as opposed to an isolated teaching; and (3) whether there are "formal and external signs" [recognizable symbolism]).

O'Lone v. Estate of Shebazz, 482 U.S. 342, 107 S.Ct. 2400, 96 L.Ed.2d 282 (1987) (holding that prisoners retain their free exercise of religion rights in prison; however, prison rules which prohibited Muslim inmates from engaging in Friday afternoon prayer services were reasonable, relying in part on the fact that practitioners were allowed "alternative means" to practice their religion, being able to participate in other weekly religious services).

Patrick v. LeFerre, 745 F.2d 153, 159 (2nd Cir. 1984) (federal law protects beliefs if believer "conceives of the beliefs as religious in nature.").

Faird v. Smith, 850 F.2d 917 (2nd Cir. 1988) (finding right to free exercise of religion not violated when prison confiscated tarot cards and prisoner supplied no evidence that his sincerely held beliefs mandated their use).

Employment Div., Dep't of Human Resources of Oregon v. Smith, 494 U.S. 872, 887, 110 S.Ct. 1595, 108 L.Ed.2d 876 (1990) ("It is not within the judicial ken to question the centrality of particular beliefs or practices to a faith, or the validity of particular litigants' interpretations of those creeds.").

Ferguson v. C.I.R., 921 F.2d 588 (5th Cir. 1991) (all sincerely held religious beliefs are protected by the Establishment Clause, and courts may not delve into the validity of such beliefs).

Kreisner v. City of San Diego, 1 F.3d 775 (9th Cir. 1993) (if the purpose of a government practice or statute is to endorse religious custom or viewpoint, it violates the Establishment Clause).

Alston v. DeBruyn, 13 F.3d 1036 (7th Cir. 1994) (holding that it was improper for the district court to assume that limits on an inmate's access to religious services were justified based on the inmate's placement in administrative segregation).

Brown v. Borough of Mahaffey, PA, 35 F.3d 846 (3rd Cir. 1994) (the First Amendment forbids the government from intentionally burdening religious worship).

Barghout v. Bureau of Kosher Meat and Food Control, 66 F.3d 1337 (4th Cir. 1994) (the government must take a neutral stance on questions of religion).

American Life League, Inc. v. Reno, 47 F.3d 642 (4th Cir. 1995) (the Free Exercise Clause does not permit the government to adopt laws designed to interfere with religious belief or practice).

Helland v. South Bend Community School Corp., 93 F.3d 327 (7th Cir. 1996) (state-supported activities must not be used for religious indoctrination).

City of Boerne v. Flores, 521 U.S. 507, 536, 117 S.Ct. 2157, 2172, 138 L.Ed.2d 624, 649 (1997) (Religious Freedom Restoration Act of 1993 (RFRA), 42 U.S.C. § 2000bb, *et seq,* overruled insofar as it applied to the states).

NOTE: the RFRA can still be used by federal prisoners. *See, e.g., **Gonzales v. O Centro Espirita Beneficente Uniao do Vegetal**,* __U.S.__, 126 S.Ct. 1211, 1216-17, 163 L.Ed.2d 1017, 1027 (2006) ("Under

RFRA, the Federal Government may not, as a statutory matter, substantially burden a person's exercise of religion, 'even if the burden results from a rule of general applicability' § 2000bb-1(a).").

Koenick v. Felton, 190 F.3d 259 (4th Cir. 1999) (separation of church and state precludes the government from overtly endorsing a religion or religion in general, though it may recognize religion or a religious holiday).

Spies v. Voinovich, 173 F.3d 398 (6th Cir. 1999) (prohibition against Zen Buddhist chanting group and possession of certain religious items held rationally related to security concerns).

Love v. Reed, 216 F.3d 682 (8th Cir. 2000) (merely because a prisoner is struggling with the tenets of a religious belief system does not forfeit protection of free exercise on insincerity grounds).

Levitan v. Ashcroft, 281 F.3d 1313 (D.C. Cir. 2002) (right to free exercise of religion may be violated when prison prevented prisoners from consuming small amounts of wine as part of Catholic sacrament without reasonable penological interest).

DeerHeide v. Suthers, 286 F.3d 1179 (10th Cir. 2002) (First Amendment protects right to religion-based diet).

Williams v. Morton, 343 F.3d 212 (3rd Cir. 2003) (religious equal protection claim failed when Muslim prisoners were provided with vegetarian meals rather than Halal meals with meat because policy legitimate in light of prisons fiscal concerns and security).

McEachin v. McGuinnis, 357 F.3d 197 (2nd Cir. 2004) (prisoners may not be disciplined for refusing to perform task in violation of their religious beliefs).

Freeman v. Texas Dep't of Criminal Justice, 369 F.3d 854 (5th Cir. 2004) (religious claim based on equal protection failed because prisoner could not show prison policy to be intentionally discriminatory).

Murphy v. Missouri Dep't of Corr., 372 F.3d 979 (8th Cir. 2004) (finding prison to have legitimate security concern in prohibiting group religious service advocating Caucasians as superior race; no First or Fourteenth Amendment violation).

Yerushalayim v. U.S. Dep't of Corr., 374 F.3d 89 (2nd Cir. 2004) (RLUIPA does not create a cause of action against the federal government or its correctional facilities [RLUIPA applies, rather, to state governments and state correctional facilities]).

DeHart v. Horn, 390 F.3d 262 (3rd Cir. 2004) (considering penological interest in conserving resources, First Amendment held not violated when single Buddhist prisoner was denied religion-based diet because accommodating dietary requirements would be too burdensome on state resources).

Adkins v. Kaspar, 393 F.3d 559, 567 (5th Cir. 2004) (to pursue a claim for violations of religious rights under RFRA or RLUIPA, plaintiff must show (1) that the government has in fact burdened a "religious exercise," and (2) that the burden is "substantial"; this established, it is upon the government to show a "compelling state interest" in imposing the burden, and that it is implemented by the "least restrictive" measure).

Searles v. Dechant, 393 F.3d 1126 (10th Cir. 2004) (centrality of tenet is not the touchstone but sincerity in belief of tenet is; constitutional violation when prison inhibited non-central religious expression).

Cutter v. Wilkinson, 423 F.3d 579 (6th Cir. 2005) (RLUIPA creates a private cause of action for institutionalized and incarcerated persons who allege that a state government has substantially burdened their religious conduct).

Cutter v. Wilkinson, 544 U.S. 709, 715-16, 125 S.Ct.2113, __L.Ed.2d__ (2005) (RLUIPA's provision relating to institutionalized persons (42 U.S.C. § 2000cc-1(b)(1)-(2)) applies only to state programs or activities receiving federal financial assistance or affecting interstate commerce).

Warsoldier v. Woodford, 418 F.3d 989, 994 (9th Cir. 2005) (the "compelling state interest" test under RFRA or RLUIPA replaces the stricter "legitimate penological interest" test embodied in *Turner v. Safely*, for religious claims brought under RFRA or RLUIPA).

Kaufman v. McCaughtry, 419 F.3d 678 (7th Cir. 2005) (atheism is protected under the Constitution because it takes a position on religion, on the existence and importance of a supreme being, and when prisoner's belief was sincerely held).

Borzych v. Frank, 439 F.3d 388, 390 (7th Cir. 2006) (religious practices may be lawfully restricted by prison officials provided the government has a legitimate penological interest to do so, e.g., to maintain security, order, discipline, safety, etc.; however, under RLUIPA prisons that receive federal funding may not substantially burden a prisoner's religious exercise without a "compelling state interest"; finding a compelling interest, the steps taken must be the "least restrictive means" in furthering that interest).
     NOTE: This standard is also used in federal prisoners' claims under RFRA.

Boles v. Neet, 486 F.3d 1177 (10th Cir. 2007) (providing no security concerns, prison officials refusal to permit Jewish prisoner to wear religious attire during transport from prison to hospital was unreasonable under *Turner*).

Baranowski v. Hart, 486 F.3d 112 (5th Cir. 2007) (finding prison's refusal to hold weekly Jewish services and provide kosher meals was reasonable under *Turner,* and finding no equal protection violation when certain groups were permitted greater access to prison chapel considering demand and need of groups requesting chapel services).

Kay v. Bennis, 500 F.3d 1214, 1220 (10th Cir. 2007) (the "genuine and sincere" belief in the use of religious items—not the necessity of the items—is sufficient to state a claim for which relief may be granted).

Americans United for Separation of Church and State v. Prison Fellowship Ministries, 509 F.3d 406, 415 (8th Cir. 2008) (whether the Establishment Clause is violated by a faith-based program depends on whether the program (1) indoctrinates recipients with religion; (2) defines program recipients by their adherence to religion; or (3) causes the government to become excessively entangled in matters of religion).

Green v. Solan Co. Jail, 513 F.3d 982 (9th Cir. 2008) (RLUIPA requires the government to meet a higher burden of proof than the rational-basis test of *Turner v. Safely*).

Koger v. Bryan, 523 F.3d 789 (7th Cir. 2008) (prisoners' religious rights clearly established; official not entitled to qualified immunity).

Mayfield v. Texas Dep't of Criminal Justice, 529 F.3d 599 (5th Cir. 2008) (finding the First Amendment not violated when Odinist prisoners were denied (1) runestones for risk of potential gambling and gang-related dangers, and when denied (2) group religious services because belief advocated racial segregation and Caucasian supremacy, and because of security concerns).

Kaemmerling v. Lappin, 553 F.3d 669, 680 (D.C. Cir. 2008) (plaintiff's *pro se* complaint properly dismissed because it failed to allege "substantial burden on his exercise of religion").

Gladson v. Iowa Dep't of Corr., 551 F.3d 825 (8th Cir. 2009) (Wiccan holiday celebration restricted to three hours by prison officials held lawful).

Rendelman v. Rouse, 569 F.3d 182 (4th Cir. 2009) (individual capacity suits are not available under the RFRA or the RLUIPA).

Hodgson v. Fabin, 376 Fed.Appx. 592 (8th Cir. 2010) (safety and security dangers in allowing prisoners to smudge and burn incense were sufficient to support prison policy banning these practices).

Riggins v. Clarke, 403 Fed.Appx. 292 (9th Cir. 2010), *cert. denied*, __U.S.__, 131 S.Ct. 2118, 179 L.Ed.2d 911 (2011) (First Amendment not violated where prison had legitimate penological interest in prohibiting correspondence addressed to inmates' religious names and not the names under which they were committed, in the interest of orderly administration of prison mail).

Sossamon v. Texas, __U.S.__, 131 S.Ct. 1651, 179 L.Ed.2d 700 (2011) (RLUIPA does not permit suits for money damages against states or individuals, but suits seeking prospective relief against states and official capacity of state agents only).

DeMoss v. Crain, 636 F.3d 145 (5th Cir. 2011) (recording of religious services that were conducted out of presence of volunteers and officers did not violate RLUIPA nor the First Amendment; prisoner was not forced to significantly alter his religious observances, and policy rational in light of security concerns).

Maddox v. Love, 655 F.3d 709 (7th Cir. 2011) (viable claim under the First and Fourteenth Amendments exists where prison officials disparately allocate resources to favored religious groups, in discrimination of other sects).

Burnett v. Jones, 437 Fed.Appx. 736 (10th Cir. 2011) (temporary or incidental restrictions on prisoner's religious practices do not substantially burden his expression of religion).

Sharp v. Johnson, 669 F.3d 144 (3rd Cir. 2012), *cert. denied*, No. 08-2174 2012 WL 1657210 (3rd. Cir. Feb 9, 2012) (RLUIPA does not permit suits against individuals, but states and state capacities only).

NOTES: _____
_____
_____
_____
_____
_____
_____
_____
_____
_____
_____
_____
_____
_____
_____
_____
_____
_____
_____
_____
_____
_____
_____
_____
_____
_____
_____
_____
_____
_____
_____
_____
_____
_____
_____
_____

NOTES: _____

RETALIATION

Smith v. Campbell, 250 F.3d 1032 (6th Cir. 2001) (actionable claim stated when prisoner is retaliated against for exercising his/her Constitutional rights).

Higgs v. Carver, 286 F.3d 437 (7th Cir. 2002) (pretrial detainee stated viable claim when prison officials segregated inmate in retaliation for filing a lawsuit).

Walker v. Thompson, 288 F.3d 1005 (7th Cir. 2002) (prison officials retaliating against a prisoner for exercising right to use law library by refusing to allow him exercise outside of cell constituted cognizable claim under § 1983).

Keenan v. Tejeda, 290 F.3d 252 (5th Cir. 2002) (limitations on or retaliation for exercising right of speech is prohibited by the First Amendment).

Atkinson v. Taylor, 316 F.3d 257 (3rd Cir. 2003) (retaliation claim stated when prisoner alleged that officials placed him in administrative segregation, denied access to legal materials, food, and harassed him for filing lawsuit).

Bruce v. Ylst, 351 F.3d 1283 (9th Cir. 2003) (prisoner's retaliation claim stated when officials effectively "chilled" his First Amendment right to file prison grievances; sufficient under § 1983).

Nei v. Dooley, 372 F.3d 1003 (8th Cir. 2004) (inmate stated viable claim of retaliation for filing civil rights lawsuit, based on allegations of denial to access prison law library).

Powell v. Alaxander, 391 F.3d 1 (1st Cir. 2004) (claims of retaliation for exercise of First Amendment rights are actionable under § 1983).

Rhodes v. Robinson, 408 F.3d 559 (9th Cir. 2005) (allegation of retaliatory action when officials withheld and destroyed property, threatened transfer, and assaulted prisoner for filing prison grievances and lawsuit stated viable claim, chilling prisoner's First Amendment rights, even though his rights were not necessarily silenced).

Siggers-El v. Barlow, 412 F.3d 693 (6th Cir. 2005) (viable retaliation claim was stated when prison transferred prisoner to another facility, affecting ability to visit and pay attorney).

Fogle v. Pierson, 435 F.3d 1252 (10th Cir. 2006) (actionable claim stated when prisoner is retaliated against for exercising his/her Constitutional rights).

Simpson v. Nickel, 450 F.3d 303 (7th Cir. 2007) (viable retaliation claim stated when prison retaliated against prisoners for exercising First Amendment right to petition in redress of grievances).

Lockett v. Suardini, 526 F.3d 866 (6th Cir. 2008) (retaliation claim was not stated when alleged retaliatory action was in response to "insolent" behavior and speech that is not constitutionally protected).

Nelson v. Shuffman, 603 F.3d 439 (8th Cir. 2010) (prisoner who filed abuse and neglect claim against prison doctor and was then deprived of privileges, placed in inadequate ward and isolated, stated viable retaliation claim under First Amendment).

Brown v. Lirios, 391 Fed.Appx. 539 (7th Cir. 2010), *cert. denied*, __U.S.__, 131 S.Ct 841, 178 L.Ed.2d 571 (2010) (no retaliation claim stated; prisoners' conduct must be protected by the First Amendment and refusal to follow legitimate prison regulation is not protected activity.)

Silva v. DeVittorio, 658 F.3d 1090 (9th Cir. 2011) (where prisoner's legal papers were confiscated in order to prevent his testimony against officials, prisoner stated viable retaliation claim).

King v. Zamiara, 680 F.3d 686 (6th Cir. 2012) (officials' actions, motivated in part to punish inmate for filing grievance, that ultimately resulted in inmate's increased security-level classification constituted retaliation, in violation of the First Amendment).

Gomez v. Randle, 680 F.3d 859 (7th Cir. 2012) (inmate transferred to facility that housed known enemies in retaliation for filing grievances stated viable First Amendment claim).

NOTES:

NOTES: _____

STATE & FEDERAL COMPLAINTS

U.S. v. Classic, 313 U.S. 299, 326, __S.Ct.__, __L.Ed.2d__ (1941) (a person acts under color of state law for the purposes of § 1983 when the power misused is "possessed by virtue of state law and made possible only because the wrongdoer is clothed with the authority of state law.").

Screws v. U.S., 325 U.S. 91, 92-93, __S.Ct.__, __L.Ed.2d__ (1945) ("It is clear that under 'color' of law means under 'pretense' of law. Thus acts of other officers in the ambit of their personal pursuits are plainly excluded. Acts of officers who undertake to perform their official duties are included whether they hew to the line of their authority or overstep it. If, as suggested, the statute was designed to embrace only actions which the State has authorized, the words 'under color of state law' were hardly apt words to express the idea.").

Haines v. Kerner, 404 U.S. 519, 92 S.Ct. 594, 30 L.Ed.2d 652 (1972) (*pro se* litigants' pleadings are to be construed liberally and held to a less stringent standard than pleadings drafted by lawyers; if a court can reasonably interpret *pro se* pleadings to state a cognizable claim on which litigant could prevail, it should do so despite failure to cite proper legal authority, confusion of legal theories, poor syntax and sentence structure, or litigant's unfamiliarity with pleading requirements). *See, e.g.,* ***Boag v. MacDougall***, 454 U.S. 364, 102 S.Ct. 594, 70 L.Ed.2d 551 (1982); ***Fazzomo v. Northeast Ohio Corr'l Center***, 473 F.3d 229 (6th Cir. 2006); ***Gomez-Diaz v. U.S.***, 433 F.3d 788 (11th Cir. 2005).

Preiser v. Rodriguez, 411 U.S. 475, 499-500 __S.Ct.__, __L.Ed.2d__ (1973) (section 1983 "action is [the] 'proper remedy' for state prisoner making constitutional challenge to conditions of prison life, but not fact or length of custody"; *habeas corpus* is the proper remedy to challenge the fact of or duration of imprisonment).

Paul v. Davis, 424 U.S. 693, 700-01, __S.Ct.__, __L.Ed.2d__ (1976) (section 1983 claim improper when alleging only state tort claim implicating only state law).

Chapman v. Houston Welfare Rights Org., 441 U.S. 600, __S.Ct.__, __L.Ed.2d__ (1970) (federal district courts have original jurisdiction over claims brought under § 1983).

Carlson v. Green, 446 U.S. 14, 18-19, __S.Ct.__, __L.Ed.2d__ (1980) (prisoners may seek redress of constitutional deprivations by the actions of persons acting under color of federal law directly under the constitution, though such *Bivens*-type actions are not permitted "when defendants show that Congress has provided an alternative remedy which it explicitly declared to be a substitute for recovery directly under the Constitution and viewed as equally effective.").

Maher v. Gagne, 448 U.S. 122, __S.Ct.__, __L.Ed.2d__ (1980) (federal district courts have original jurisdiction over claims brought under § 1983 only when a substantive right allegedly violated is protected under the Constitution or federal statute proving for civil rights).

Gillespre v. Civiletti, 629 F.2d 637 (9th Cir. 1980) (although both § 1983 and § 1985 are civil rights statutes, they have different origins: § 1983 is based upon the Fourteenth Amendment and thus concerns deprivation of rights that are accomplished under state law; § 1985 is derived from the Thirteenth Amendment, and covers all deprivations of equal protection of the laws and equal privileges and immunities under the laws, regardless of its source).

Lugar v. Edmondson Oil Co., 457 U.S. 922, 937, __S.Ct.__, __L.Ed.2d__ (1982) (private individuals have acted under color of state law for purposes of § 1983 action when (1) claimed deprivation was caused by exercise of right or privilege created or imposed by the state or undertaken by a person for whom the state is responsible, and when (2) the private party is fairly characterized as a state actor, acting with or under significant aid from state officials, though not an actual officer of the state).

A&A Concrete, Inc. v. White Mountain Apache Tribe, 676 F.2d 1330 (9th Cir. 1982) (claims for conspiracy to deprive civil rights under §§ 1985(2) and 1985(3) require the element of class-based animus).

Tower v. Glover, 467 U.S. 914, __S.Ct.__, __L.Ed.2d__ (1984) (plan to deprive constitutional rights of client by appointed counsel conspiring with state officials possible activity under color of state for purposes of § 1983).

Noll v. Carlson, 809 F.3d 1446 (9th Cir. 1987) (*pro se* litigant bringing a civil rights action *in forma pauperis* is entitled to five procedural protections: (1) process issued and served; (2) notice of any motion made by the defendant or the court to dismiss the complaint, and the basis for the motion; (3) opportunity to at least submit a memorandum in opposition; (4) in the event of dismissal, a statement of the grounds for the decision; and (5) opportunity to amend the complaint to overcome the deficiencies, unless it clearly appears the deficiencies cannot be overcome by amendment).

West v. Atkins, 487 U.S. 42, __S.Ct.__, __L.Ed.2d__ (1988) (doctor of private medical company acted under color of state law for the purposes of a § 1983 claim); *see, e.g., Walker v. Horn*, 385 F.3d 321 (3rd Cir. 2004) (same).

Burk v. Beene, 948 F.2d 489 (8th Cir. 1991) (a state may consent to be sued in federal court, waiving its sovereign immunity).

Albright v. Oliver, 510 U.S. 266, __S.Ct.__, __L.Ed.2d__ (1994) (section 1983 provides a vehicle for asserting federal rights; it is not a source of federal rights).

Livadas v. Bradshaw, 512 U.S. 107, 132-33, __S.Ct.__, __L.Ed.2d__ (1994) (section 1983 remedies are available for violations of federal law except when the federal statute is not intended to give rise to liability under § 1983).

Cook v. Texas D.O.C. Justice Planning Dep't, 37 F.3d 166 (5th Cir. 1994) (holding that (1) § 1983 action is the appropriate vehicle for recovering damages resulting from illegal administrative procedures; that (2) § 1983 action is the appropriate vehicle for challenging unconstitutional parole procedures; and that (3) prior convictions held void in prior appellate court decision should not be considered in determining parole eligibility).

Falcon v. U.S. Bureau of Prisons, 52 F.3d 137 (7th Cir. 1995) (prisoner seeking a change in length or level of confinement must use a writ of *habeas corpus*; prisoner who seeks anything else must use a civil rights action).

Livadas v. Bradshaw, 520 U.S. 329, 340-41, __S.Ct.__, __L.Ed.2d__ (1997) (an enforceable federal right under § 1983 is created when (1) Congress intended the statutory provision to be of benefit to the plaintiff; (2) when the statute uses mandatory language imposing an unambiguous obligation on the states; and (3) when the statue is not so vague that enforcement would "strain judicial competence").

Edwards v. Balisok, 520 U.S. 641, __S.Ct.__, __L.Ed.2d__ (1997) (section 1983 claim improper when successful challenge to disciplinary procedures would necessarily imply the invalidity of disciplinary decision affecting length of sentence).

Bruns v. National Credit Union Admin., 122 F.3d 1251 (9th Cir. 1997) (Federal Tort Claims Act does not exclude *Bivens* claims).

Duffy v. Wolfe, 123 F.3d 1026 (8th Cir. 1997) (*Bivens* and § 1983 actions are almost identical, except *Bivens* lies for the recovery of damages against federal officials, while § 1983 lies against state actors).

Hillside Enterprises, Inc. v. Continental Carlisle, Inc., 147 F.3d 732 (8th Cir. 1998) (federal courts are required to accept the interpretation of state law by the highest court of the state).

Whitley v. Hunt, 158 F.3d 882 (5th Cir. 1998) (*Bivens* claims may only be brought against federal government agents in their individual capacities, not against federal government agencies themselves).

Boguslavsky v. Kaplan, 159 F.3d 715 (2nd Cir. 1998) (*pro se* litigants are allowed some degree of flexibility in pleading an action).

Washington v. Doley, 173 F.3d 1158 (9th Cir. 1999) (courts have broad discretion to consolidate separate actions pending in the same district, and such consolidation, when challenged, will be reviewed for abuse of discretion); *see also Investor's Research Co. v. U.S. Dist. Court for Cent. Dist. of Cal.*, 877 F.2d 777 (9th Cir. 1989) (same).

Frost v. Symington, 197 F.3d 348 (9th Cir. 1999) (*pro se* litigant's pleadings must be construed liberally in favor of plaintiff on motion for summary judgment).

Barwood, Inc. v. D.C., 202 F.3d 290 (D.C. Cir. 2000) (violations of state law are not cognizable under § 1983 without independent constitutional violations).

Berg v. County of Allegheny, 219 F.3d 261 (3rd Cir. 2000) (plaintiff must demonstrate a deprivation of a federal right by a person acting under color of state law to make a *prima facie* case under § 1983).

McDade v. West, 223 F3d 1135, 1140 (9th Cir. 2000) (holding that when a government employee "invok[es] the power of [his or her] office to accomplish the offensive act," that act "clearly related to the performance of official duties," and the employee acted under color of state law for the purposes of a § 1983 action).

Corr'l Servs. Corp. v. Malesko, 534 U.S. 61, __S.Ct.__, __L.Ed.2d__ (2001) (*Bivens* actions may not be brought "against private entities acting under color of federal law" [534 U.S. at 66]—in this case "against a private corporation operating a halfway house under contract with the Bureau of Prisons" [*id.*, at 63]).

Petrey v. City of Toledo, 246 F.3d 548 (6th Cir. 2001) (unlike states, municipalities such as cities can be sued directly under § 1983).

Boyce v. Ashroft, 251 F.3d 911 (10th Cir. 2001) (federal prisoners challenging their convictions, sentences, or administrative decisions to revoke good-time credits, must use a writ of *habeas corpus*; prisoners raising constitutional claims regarding transfers to administrative segregation, exclusion from prison programs, suspension of privileges or other prison decisions falling under the definition of conditions of confinement, must use a § 1983 or *Bivens*).

Augon v. Commonwealth Ports Auth., 316 F.3d 899 (9th Cir. 2003) (section 1983 applies to the Commonwealth of the Northern Mariana Islands).

Farese v. Scherer, 342 F.3d 1223 (11th Cir. 2003) (prisoner stated cognizable claim under § 1985 for conspiracy to intimidate parties to lawsuits; complaint sufficiently alleged all elements of standing: injury, intimidation, causation, and likelihood of relief).

Muhammad v. Close, __U.S.__, 124 S.Ct. 1303, __L.Ed.2d__ (2004) (prisoners may sue a prison official under § 1983 over a confrontation and subsequent disciplinary charge without first exhausting state or federal *habeas corpus* remedies, provided the claim doesn't implicate conviction or length of sentence).

Rodi v. S. New Eng. Sch. of Law, 389 F.3d 5 (1st Cir. 2004) (*pro se* complaints are to be construed liberally and dismissed only if there exists no hope of success).

Wilkinson v. Dotson, 544 U.S. 74, __S.Ct.__, __L.Ed.2d__ (2005) (claims asserting procedural defects in reaching a prisoner's conviction, not the fact of conviction, are not barred by the favorable termination requirement of *Heck*).

City of Rancho Palos Verdes v. Abrams, 544 U.S. 113, __S.Ct.__, __L.Ed.2d__ (2005) (where Congress created an express and private means of redress within a statute itself, § 1983 is then unavailable because Congress did not intend to leave open a more expansive remedy under § 1983).

Glaus v. Anderson, 408 F.3d 382 (7th Cir. 2005) (federal prisoners suing under *Bivens* may sue officials only in their individual capacity).

Beedle v. Wilson, 422 F.3d 1059 (10th Cir. 2005) (nurse's aide did not act under color of state law for purposes of § 1983 when sexually assaulting patient at county hospital).

Simpson v. Nickel, 450 F.3d 303 (7th Cir. 2006) (section 1983 claim challenging the fact or duration of incarceration accrues when the incarceration ends).

Kaba v. Stepp, 458 F.3d 678 (7th Cir. 2006) (court liberally construed complaint to state a claim for negligence under the Federal Tort Claims Act, though complaint failed to specifically allege a claim under the FTCA).

Savory v. Lyons, 469 F.3d 667 (7th Cir. 2006) (it is not required that an action brought under § 1983 be first exhausted in state courts; *habeas corpus* petitioners must, however, exhaust state remedies as a prerequisite to federal action).

Wilkie v. Robbins, __U.S.__, 127 S.Ct. 2588, 2598, __L.Ed.2d__ (2007) ("[T]he decision whether to recognize a *Bivens* remedy may require two steps. In the first place, there is the question whether any alternative, existing process for protecting [a constitutionally recognized] interest amounts to a convincing reason for the Judicial Branch to refrain from providing a new and freestanding remedy in damages. But even in the absence of an alternative, a *Bivens* remedy is a subject of judgment: "the federal courts must make the kind of remedial deter-mination that is appropriate for a common-law tribunal, paying special heed, however, to any special factors counseling hesitation before authorizing a new kind of federal litigation" [citations omitted].).

Jackson v. Jackson, 475 F.3d 261 (5th Cir. 2007) (an *habeas corpus* petition is the proper vehicle for prisoners challenging the fact of conviction; an action under § 1983 is the proper vehicle for prisoners challenging condi-tions of confinement).

Porter v. White, 483 F.3d 1294 (11th Cir. 2007) (section 1983 claim for due process violation did not accrue for the purposes of civil action until conviction was vacated).

Woods v. Buss, 496 F.3d 620 (7th Cir. 2007) (section 1983 is the proper vehicle to challenge lethal injection protocol).

Powers v. Hamilton County Public Defender Com'n, 501 F.3d 592 (6th Cir. 2007) (where public defender's conduct is systematic and administrative and in state's interest, conduct is under color of state law).

Longoria v. Dretke, 507 F.3d 898 (5th Cir. 2007) (holding that the district court properly dismissed plaintiff's *pro se* complaint concerning First Amendment claims; even construed liberally, complaint must raise contentions to preserve the cause of action).

Americans United for Separation of Church and State v. Prison Fellowship Ministries, Inc., 509 F.3d 406 (8th Cir. 2007) (private parties given power to incarcerate, treat, and discipline prisoners acted under color of state law for § 1983 purposes).

Aguilar v. U.S. Immig. and Customs Enforcement, 510 F.3d 1 (1st Cir. 2007) (civil-rights remedy under § 1983 encompasses violations of rights secured by federal statutory as well as constitutional law).

Chmielinski v. Mass. Office of the Comm'r of Prob., 513 F.3d 309 (1st Cir. 2008) (state remedies [i.e., state court civil actions] need not be exhausted as prerequisite to § 1983 action in federal court).

Jackson v. Brown, 513 F.3d 1057 (9th Cir. 2008) (public defender executing "traditional function" of *vior dire* and closing arguments not acting under color of state law for purposes of § 1983).

Mora v. City of Gaithering, 519 F.3d 216 (4th Cir. 2008) (section 1983 complaint for lack of due process not complete unless state fails to provide due process; due process implicated not in deprivation of right but in inad-equacy of post-deprivation state remedies).

Perez-Acevedo v. Rivero-Cubano, 520 F.3d 26 (1st Cir. 2008) (section 1983 applies to Puerto Rico).

Harrison v. Ash, 539 F.3d 510 (6th Cir. 2008) (prison nurses contracted to county acted under color of state law for § 1983 purposes).

James v. Richman, 547 F.3d 214 (3rd Cir. 2008) (federal courts should not abstain from § 1983 actions where state policy has created a *de facto* exhaustion requirement, because state remedies need not be exhausted as prerequisite to § 1983 action in federal court).

Aschroft v. Iqbal, __U.S.__, 129 S.Ct. 1937, __L.Ed.2d__ (2009) (although prisoners may bring *Bivens* actions against federal officers for deprivation of rights implied under the Constitution, such implied causes of action are disfavored; therefore, the Court extends *Bivens* liability to new contexts or to new categories of defendants reluctantly).

Smith v. U.S., 561 F.3d 1090 (10th Cir. 2009) (*Bivens* actions not precluded by Inmate Accident Compensation Act; but § 1983 actions preempted because IACA creates exclusive remedy for prisoners to obtain relief for injury occurring during work duty).

Reams v. Irvin, 561 F.3d 1258 (11th Cir. 2009) (section 1983 complaint improper when adequate state remedies not exhausted before commencement of procedural due process claim).

Bonner v. Perry, 564 F.3d 424 (6th Cir. 2009) (section 1983 claim for sexual abuse accrued at the time of injury).

Cooper v. Postal Service, 577 F.3d 479 (2nd Cir. 2009) (private religious organization preforming traditional state function of postal service acted under color of state law for §1983 purposes).

Grier v. Klem, 591 F.3d 672 (3rd Cir. 2010) (claim cognizable where § 1983 claim would grant prisoner access to DNA evidence, because mere access to evidence would not necessarily invalidate conviction [*see Heck v. Humphrey*]).

Payne v. Peninsula Sch. Dist., 598 F.3d 1123 (9th Cir. 2010) (exhaustion of state remedies prerequisite to § 1983 complaint when federal law specifically preempts § 1983, creating exhaustion requirement).

Minneci v. Pollard, __U.S__, 132 S.Ct 617, 181 L.Ed.2d 606 (2012) (private persons who violate federal rights while acting under the color of federal law, though not liable under Bivens, may be held liable in state court under common-law tort actions).

Florer v. Congregation Pidyon Shevuyim, N.A., 639 F.3d 916 (9th Cir. 2012) (private entities providing chaplain services to prisoners are not government actors and do not act under color of state law for purposes of § 1983 or RLUIPA).

NOTES: _____

NOTES: _____
_____
_____
_____
_____
_____
_____
_____
_____
_____
_____
_____
_____
_____
_____
_____
_____
_____
_____
_____
_____
_____
_____
_____
_____
_____
_____
_____
_____
_____
_____
_____
_____
_____
_____
_____
_____
_____
_____
_____

VISITATION

Procunier v. Martinez, 416 U.S.396, 94 S.Ct.1800, 40 L.Ed.2d 224 (1974) (paralegals and law students working under an attorney have a derivative right to visit inmates in their housing facilities).

Ruiz v. Estelle, 679 F.2d 1115, 1154-55 (5th Cir. 1982), *cert.denied*, 460 U.S. 1042, __S.Ct.__, __L.Ed.2d__ (1983) (affirming injunction prohibiting censorship of attorney-client mail, and ensuring confidential attorney-client visitation).

Block v. Rutherford, 468 U.S. 576, 586, __S.Ct.__, __L.Ed.2d__ (1984) (upholding Los Angeles County Jail ban on all contact visits because "[t]hey open the institution to the introduction of drugs, weapons, and other contraband. Visitors can easily conceal guns, knives, drugs, or other contraband in countless ways and pass them to an inmate unnoticed by even the most vigilant observers. And these items can readily be slipped from the clothing of an innocent child, or transferred by other visitors permitted close contact with inmates.").

O'Bryan v. County of Saginaw, 741 F.2d 283 (6th Cir. 1984) (prohibition of contact visits lawful because contact visits not constitutional right).

Thorne v. Jones, 765 F.2d 1270 (5th Cir. 1985) (prison officials found to be justified in denying the visitation of prisoner's mother when she refused to consent to a strip-search before visiting, and when prison officials had reliable information that prisoner was receiving drugs through visiting).

Robinson v. Palmer, 841 F.2d 1151 (D.C. Cir. 1988) (prohibition on wife's visitation was justified when prisoner's wife caught attempting to smuggle marijuana into prison, and when prisoner had other means of communication with his wife).

Martin v. Tyson, 845 F.2d 1451 (7th Cir. 1988) (per curiam) (policy prohibiting detainees contact visits, limiting number of visitors per detainee, and visit lengths held constitutional because of jail's small size and number of detainees in occupancy).

Casey v. Lewis, 4 F.3d 1516 (9th Cir. 1993) (regulation prohibiting high-security prisoners from contact visits with attorneys held not to constitute a violation right of access to courts).

Mann v. Reynolds, 46 F.3d 1055 (10th Cir. 1995) (finding that without reasonable security concerns the prison could not justify policy prohibiting death-row and high-security prisoners from contact visits with attorneys).

Spear v. Sowders, 71 F.3d 626 (6th Cir. 1995) (prison officials may not search a visitor who objects, without giving the visitor the opportunity to end the visit and depart).

Bazzetta v. McGinnis, 286 F.3d 311 (6th cir. 2002) (prisoners have a right to visiting, and the ability of inmates to make phone calls and send and receive letters is insufficient substitute for visitation), *rev'd on other grounds* 539 U.S.126, 123 S.Ct. 2162, 156 L.Ed.2d 162 (2003)..

Overton v. Bazzetta, 539 U.S. 126, 123 S.Ct. 2162, 156 L.Ed.2d 162 (2003) (prison regulation requiring children to be with a family member or legal guardian during visitation was rationally related to legitimate penological interest, under the *Turner* standard, to protect child visitors from harm and to prevent future crime).

Gerber v. Hickman, 291 F.3d 617 (9th Cir. 2002) (en banc) (prisoners retain the right to visit under the First Amendment, but the right may be limited provided a legitimate government purpose).

Wirsching v. Colorado, 360 F.3d 1191 (10th Cir. 2004) (prison regulation prohibiting sex-offenders from visitation with children does not violate First Amendment because of legitimate penological concern in protecting the child and rehabilitation of prisoner).

Victoria W. v. Larpenter, 369 F.3d 475, 485 n.6 (5th Cir. 2004) (prohibition on contact visits for pretrial detainees held to serve valid security interests when non-contact visits are permitted [citing *Block*, 468 U.S. at 588, *supra*]).

Bazzetta v. McGinnis, 430 F.3d 795 (6th Cir. 2005) (finding regulation to serve a legitimate penological interest when prisoners are prohibited visitation upon guilty finding of substance abuse charges).

Samford v. Dretke, 562 F.3d 674 (5th Cir. 2009) (per curiam) (threats to mother formed legitimate reason to prevent visits with prisoner's children).

Fulton v. Goord, 591 F.3d 37 (2nd Cir. 2009) (under the Americans with Disabilities Act, disabled persons have a right to "reasonable accommodation" that would enable visiting with incarcerated family members, and housing inmate in facility very distant from disabled family member, making her unable to visit her husband, may violate the ADA).

Dunn v. Castro, 621 F.3d 1196 (9th Cir. 2010) (prisoners do not possess an absolute right to visitation and suspension of visitation privileges as a disciplinary measure for violation of prison rules is constitutional).

Burnett v. Jones, 437 Fed.Appx. 736 (10th Cir. 2011), *cert. denied*, __U.S.__, 132 S.Ct. 1546, 182 L.Ed.2d 178 (2012) (contact visits may legitimately be restricted for high security inmates).

Pfender v. Secretary, Penn. Dep't of Corr., 443 Fed.Appx. 749 (3rd Cir. 2011), *cert. denied*, __U.S.__, 132 S.Ct. 2403, __L.Ed.2d__ (2012) (prison had rational interest in preventing inmate's visits with wife, who officials suspected of giving inmate photo of prison complex).

Bilka v. Farrey, 447 Fed.Appx. 742 (7th Cir. 2011) (prison officials had legitimate security interest in preventing smuggling of contraband when denying visits between prisoner and former prison employee).

Towery v. Brewer, 672 F.3d 650 (9th Cir. 2012), *cert. denied*, __U.S.__, 132 S.Ct. 1656, 182 L.Ed.2d 250 (2012) (death-row inmates entitled to contact visits with legal counsel, even on day of execution).

Lopez v. Brewer, 680 F.3d 1068 (9th Cir. 2012) (death-row inmates entitled to contact visits with legal counsel, even on day of execution).

NOTES: _____
_____
_____
_____
_____
_____
_____
_____
_____
_____
_____
_____
_____
_____
_____
_____
_____
_____
_____
_____
_____
_____
_____
_____
_____
_____
_____
_____
_____
_____
_____
_____
_____
_____
_____
_____
_____
_____
_____
_____

NOTES: _____

APPENDIX

SELECTED AMENDMENTS TO THE U.S. CONSTITUTION

AMENDMENT 1 (religious and political freedom): Congress shall make no law respecting an establishment of religion, or prohibiting the free exercise thereof, or abridge the freedom of speech, or of the press; or of the right of the people to assemble, and to petition the government for a redress of grievances.

AMENDMENT 2 (right to bear arms): A well-regulated militia, being necessary to the security of a free state, the right of the people to keep and bear arms, shall not be infringed.

AMENDMENT 3 (quartering solders): [Omitted.]

AMENDMENT 4 (unreasonable searches and seizures): The right of the people to be secure in their persons, houses, papers, and effects, against unreasonable searches and seizures, shall not be violated, and no warrants shall issue, but upon probable cause, supported by oath or affirmation, and particularly describing the place to be searched, and the persons or things to be seized.

AMENDMENT 5 (criminal actions - provisions concerning - due process of law and just compensation clauses): No person shall be held to answer for a capital, or otherwise infamous crime, unless on a presentment or indictment of a grand jury, except in cases arising in the land or naval forces, or in the militia, when in actual service in time of war or public danger; nor shall any person be subject for the same offense to be twice put in jeopardy of life or limb; nor shall be compelled in any criminal case to be a witness against himself, nor be deprived of life, liberty, or property, without due process of law; nor shall private property be taken for public use, without just compensation.

AMENDMENT 6 (rights of the accused): In all criminal prosecutions, the accused shall enjoy the right to a speedy and public trial, by an impartial jury of the state and district wherein the crime shall have been committed, which district shall have been previously ascertained by law, and to be informed of the nature and cause of the accusation; to be confronted with the witnesses against him; to have compulsory process for obtaining witnesses in his favor, and to have the assistance of counsel for his defense.

AMENDMENT 7 (trial by jury in civil cases): In suits at common law, where the value in controversy shall exceed twenty dollars, the right of trial by jury, shall be preserved, and no fact tried by a jury, shall be otherwise re-examined in any court of the United States, than according to the rules of common law.

AMENDMENT 8 (bail - punishment): Excessive bail shall not be required, nor excessive fines imposed, nor cruel and unusual punishments inflicted.

AMENDMENT 9 (rights retained by people): The enumeration in the Constitution, of certain rights, shall not be construed to deny or disparage others retained by the people.

AMENDMENT 10 (rights reserved to states or people): The powers not delegated to the United States by the Constitution, nor prohibited by it to the states, are reserved to the states respectively, or to the people.

AMENDMENT 11 (suits against states - restriction of judicial power): The judicial power of the United States shall not be construed to extend to any suit in law or equity, commenced or prosecuted against one of the United States by citizens of another state, or by citizens or subjects of any foreign state.

AMENDMENT 12 (election of President and Vice President): [Omitted.]

AMENDMENT 13: Section 1 (slavery prohibited): Neither slavery nor involuntary servitude, except as a punishment for crime whereof the party shall have been duly convicted, shall exist within the States, United States, or any place subject to their jurisdiction.

 Section 2 (power to enforce article): Congress shall have power to enforce this article by appropriate legislation.

AMENDMENT 14: Section 1 (citizenship - due process of law - equal protection): All persons born or naturalized in the United States, and subject to the jurisdiction thereof, are citizens of the United States and of the state wherein they reside. No state shall make or enforce any law which shall abridge the privileges or immunities of citizens of the United States; nor shall any state deprive any person of life, liberty, or property, without due process of law; nor deny to any person within its jurisdiction the equal protection of the laws.

 [Sections 2-4 omitted.]

 Section 5 (power to enforce article): The congress shall have power to enforce, by appropriate legislation, the provisions of this article.

RECOMMENDED READING

A Jailhouse Lawyer's Manual, Columbia University School of Law, 435 West 116th Street, New York, NY 10027 (Comprehensive soft-bound guide to prisoners' rights, which contains sections covering post-conviction, *habeas corpus*, and criminal appeal proceedings.)

Black's Law Dictionary, West Group, 610 Opperman Drive, P.O. Box 64526, St. Paul, MN 55164-0526 (Don't underestimate the utility of a law dictionary. *Black's Law Dictionary* comes in many versions, but for the resource-limited prisoner, the cheaper, soft-bound Pocket Edition is a reasonable option, and worth the investment.)

Federal Civil Rules Handbook, West Group, 610 Opperman Drive, P.O. Box 64526, St. Paul, MN 55164-0526 (Contains detailed discussions on the federal civil rules, and provides up-to-date interpretive annotations and citations—very handy.)

Georgetown Law Journal Annual Review of Criminal Procedure, the Georgetown Law Journal Association, 600 New Jersey Avenue N.W., Washington D.C. 20001 (Covers mostly federal criminal procedure, but includes a prisoners' rights section accompanied by numerous, current case citations—inexpensive for prisoners and a good source for new cases.)

Nolo's Deposition Handbook, by Paul Bergman and Albert Moore, Nolo, 950 Parker Street, Berkeley, CA 94710 (Covers the deposition process, who may be deposed, and provides strategies.)

Prison Legal News, P.O. Box 1151, Lake Worth, FL 33460 (Excellent monthly newsletter; contains articles discussing current events in the world of prisoners' rights and criminal procedure—inexpensive and *highly* recommended.)

Rights of Prisoners, West group, 610 Opperman Drive, P.O. Box 64526, St. Paul, MN 55164-0526 (Probably *the* most comprehensive treatise available on prisoners' rights, but expensive. Published in three hard-bound volumes and annually supplemented.)

Represent Yourself in Court: How to Prepare and Try a Winning Case, by Paul Bergman and Sara Berman-Barrett, Nolo, 950 Parker Street, Berkeley, CA 94710 (Covers the *pro se* process of civil litigation, from planning and filing, thru trial, with a bit on appeals—though directed at the free-world populace, it is quite useful for the prisoner litigant as well.)

The Bluebook: A Uniform System of Citation, Harvard Law, Attention Business Office, Bluebook Orders, Harvard Law Review Association, Gannett House, 1511 Massachusetts Avenue, Cambridge, MA 02138 (Exhaustive guide to legal citation and writing.)

GLOSSARY

Ab ante: Before; in advance of.

Ab antecendente: Beforehand.

Ab antiquo: From antiquity.

Ab initio: From the beginning.

Abatement: A reduction or termination.

Abdication: Surrender an office, power, or right.

Abjudicate: Considered wrong or derogated by a court judgment.

Abridge: To shorten; reduce.

Abrogation: Repeal of a law.

Absque hoc: Without this.

Accrue: To come due; to mature.

Acquiescence: Passive compliance or conduct from which consent may be implied.

Act: (1) to do something; (2) public law.

Acta diurna: Daily records; event journals.

Acta publica: Of general knowledge and concern.

Act in pais: A matter not of record; judicial act preformed out of court.

Actio: An action or cause of action.

Action: Court proceeding to enforce a right or punish a wrong.

Actual injury: An actual, measurable loss or detriment, as opposed to, for example, an injury to the right of freedom of speech where the injury is to the right itself.

Actus reus: Guilty act (physical act of a crime).

Ad damnum: To the damage (of the plaintiff).

Addendum: Additional document or supplement.

Ad diem: On the day.

Ad hoc: For this (for this particular purpose).

Ad infinitum: Continuing indefinitely.

Ad interim: In the meantime.

Adjectives: Words or phrases that modify nouns.

Adjective law: The body of law and rules of procedure by which substantive law is given effect.

Adjudge: To decide judicially.

Adjudicate: To make a formal judgment or decision.

Adjudication: A judgment.

Adjuration: A promise or swearing of an oath.

Ad litem: For the suit.

Administrative law: The (1) statutes creating agencies, (2) agency-made rules and regulations and administrative opinions, and (3) legal principles governing the acts of public officials.

Admissibility: Of the ability to be entered into evidence at hearing, trial, or other proceeding.

Admissions: A discovery tool by which a party may require its adversary to admit or deny the validity of a matter.

Ad nauseam: To the point of disgust (redundant, repetitive).

Ad respondendum: To answer.

Ad satisfaciendum: To satisfy.

Adverbs: Words that modify verbs, adjectives, or other adverbs expressing a relation of place, time, circumstance, manner, cause, degree, etc.

Ad vitam: For life.

A fortiori: By the stronger force or logic (even more so).

Affiant: One who makes an affidavit.

Affidavit: A sworn written statement.

Affirm: To agree with the opinion of a lower court.

Aforesaid: Previously mentioned or described.

Alderman: A member of a city's legislative body.

Alias: Otherwise known as.

Aliter: Otherwise.

Aliunde: From another place or source.

A.L.R. (American Law Reports): Selected cases published with annotations discussing the law (West Group publishes six series, A.L.R., A.L.R. 2nd, A.L.R. 3rd, A.L.R. 4th, A.L.R. 5th, A.L.R. Fed).

Ambiguity: Uncertain meaning.

Amend: To change.

Amicus curiae: Friend of the court (commonly refers to non-party briefings).

Am.Jur. (American Jurisprudence): A legal encyclopedia published by Lawyer's Cooperative Publishing.

Am.Jur.2d (American Jurisprudence Second): A legal encyclopedia published by Lawyer's Cooperative Publishing.

Ancient documents: Writings older than thirty years.

Animo: With intent.

Animo et corpore: By the intent and act.

Animus: The intention in which something is done.

Annotation: A footnote in a writing.

Annul: To void, nullify, or abolish.

Ante: Before.

Ante-date: To date an instrument or document or other writing with a time before its execution or creation.

A pais: At issue.

A posteriori: From the later point of view; effect to cause.

Appellant: The party who is appealing the decision from a lower court.

Appellee (or Respondent): On appeal, the person supporting the decision for the lower court.

Appendix: A section, table, or additional material at the end of a book or document.

Appurtenances: Things or rights necessary but subordinate or incidental to a principle thing.

A priori: From what is before (deducing from self-evident principles).

A quo: From which.

Arbitrary: Determined at a person's discretion, rather than by rule or policy.

Arbitration: A method for resolving a legal dispute by a neutral third party, whose decision is binding.

Archives: The place where records are keep; the records themselves.

Arguendo: In arguing.

Array: The group of persons called for jury service.

Arrest of judgment: The court's refusal to render judgment after a verdict because the verdict is wrong in view of the facts.

Article (art.): Subdivision of a written or published document.

Assets: Property of any description having monetary value.

Assumpsit: An action to recover damages for breach of an oral or simple contract.

Attest: To witness or testify.

Attorney General: The chief legal officer or prosecutor of the federal government or state.

Autre: Another.

Avails: Profits.

Aver: To assert or verify or prove.

Award: To grant or adjudge to.

Barter: Exchange of goods rather that money.

Base: Inferior or subordinate; foundation; impure.

Beyond reasonable doubt: The highest burden of proof, used in criminal cases.

Bicameral: Of two houses or chambers, as in our American bicameral legislature of an upper and lower chamber.

Bilateral contract: A contract containing mutual provision between the parties; this is, obligations on both sides of the contract.

Bill: Proposed legislation.

Bill of particulars: A detailed statement of a party's cause of action or a prosecutor's information.

Bill of sale: Written evidence of a sale or transfer of title.

Bill number: The number issued to a bill of proposed legislation.

Bill of Rights: The first ten amendments to the U.S. Constitution (now including the Thirteenth and Fourteenth Amendments)

Blackmail: Extortion.

Bona fide: Without fraud or deceit; genuine.

Bona vacantia: Property with seemingly no owner.

Bond: A written obligation under government seal; a certificate or evidence of debt.

Boycott: Persons combining in an effort to withhold services and to prevent others from the same.

Brief: A written statement setting forth legal contentions and points of authority.

Burden of proof: The obligation of a party to prove disputed facts.

By-laws: Rules and regulations adopted for operation and management.

Canon: A fundamental rule or principle.

Canons of statutory construction: Rules developed to aid in uniform statutory interpretation.

Capricious: Unpredictable or impulsive behavior.

Caption: Information at the head of a legal document, containing the name of the court, parties, docket or file number, and description of the purpose of the document.

Carte blanche: An instrument or other form signed in blank, with the conditions or terms to be filled in; the phrase "carte blanche" has also come to mean "unlimited authority."

Case law: Rules and principles of law developed by judicial decisions.

Causa proxima: The direct or proximate cause.

Cause of action: Matter or grounds upon which a legal action may be brought.

CC (cc or c.c.): Carbon copy (used to indicate that another party has been sent a duplicate).

Cede: To surrender: to give up on.

Certificate: A signed statement authenticating or assuring something.

C.F.R. (Code of Federal Regulations): Official publication of federal agency regulations.

Challenge: To dispute, object, or otherwise take exception to.

Chattel (personal chattel): Movable belongings.

Chilling effect: The resulting effect when a law or practice discourages the exercise of a constitutional right.

Circuitry of action: An unnecessarily roundabout or indirect proceeding to attain what is desired.

Circumstantial evidence: Evidence that proves facts indirectly or by inference.

Cite: To quote or refer to supporting authority.

Citation signals: Abbreviations, words, or phrases that signal information, treatment, history about the accompanying citation.

Civil action: An enforcement of a private right.

Civil law: The law of civil or private rights, as opposed to criminal or administrative law.

C.J.S. (Corpus Juris Secundum): A legal encyclopedia published by West Group.

Claim: A demand or assertion of a right.

Clear and convincing evidence: Evidence showing that a thing still to be proved is highly probable or certain within reason (this is a greater burden of proof than the "preponderance of evidence" but less than "reasonable doubt").

Closing arguments: A litigant's summary and conclusions about the evidence presented at trial, spoken at the end of evidence presentment, before the jury or judge retires to deliberate on the matter.

Code: A system of carefully arranged and officially promulgated law.

Codify: To include in the Code.

Coercion: Compelling one against his or her will by superiority authority or other force.

Cognovit: A defendant's admission of no defense and consent to judgment.

Collateral: Indirect, additional, or related to.

Color of law: With the appearance of legal right or function, but without actual legal basis.

Comity: The willingness of courts to abide the law of other states or countries.

Common law: The body of law derived by judicial decisions, rather than by legislative enactment.

Common pleas: A court with jurisdiction over civil actions.

Compensatory damages: Monetary relief sufficient to compensate for or replace a loss.

Complaint: A formal pleading initiating a lawsuit.

Complainant: A party who has initiated a lawsuit.

Concise: Short; succinct.

Conclusion: The portion of a legal document concluding the author's argument and request for relief or action.

Concurrent: At the same time; having the same authority or contributing to the same thing.

Congress: The federal legislature, both the Senate and the House of Representatives.

Conjecture: A guess or notion based on slight evidence.

Connivance: Intentional oversight or consent to the unlawful act of another.

Consanguinity: Blood relationship.

Consent judgment (consent decree): A judgment based on an agreement between the parties, rather than on an adjudication.

Consequential damages: Damages arising incidentally to the act of a party.

Consideration: Essential to a legal contract, the benefit to the promisor or loss to the promisee.

Consolidation: To unite.

Conspiracy: An agreement between two or more people to do an unlawful act.

Constitution: A document setting out the structure, function, powers of government, and rights of the people.

Constitutional convention: An assembly of delegates come together at the beckon of the legislature to frame, revise, or amend a constitution.

Constitutional law: The body of law dealing with the structure, function, powers of government, and rights of the people.

Construction: The interpretation of the meaning of a constitution, statute, regulation, will, other instrument, or oral agreement.

Constructive: Inferred or implied.

Contempt: Disregard or disobedience of a public authority such as a judge.

Contingency: A possible or expected event or happening.

Continuance: Postponement.

Contra: Contrary or opposite to.

Contract: An agreement between two or more parties to do or not do something.

Contributory negligence: The personal negligence of an injured party which contributed to its own damages or injury.

Conversion: The wrongful appropriation of another's goods.

Co-obligor: A person bound in a mutual obligation with others.

Coram nobis: Before ourselves (a review of some matter sought in the same court).

Coram non judice: Done without jurisdiction.

Coram vobis: In your presence.

Corollary: A proposition that naturally follows from a proven proposition.

Corporal: Of the body; physical.

Corporation: An artificial entity established in law to preform a purpose.

Corporeal: Tangible.

Corpus delicti: Body of the crime (the facts of the matter, or the material substance on which the crime was based).

Corroborating evidence: Additional evidence supporting or confirming evidence already given.

Costs: Monetary award to the successful party for expenses incurred in prosecuting or defending a case.

Costs de incremento: Cost awarded by the court in addition to those awarded by the jury.

Count: An individual statement, by itself a sufficient cause of action.

Counterclaim: A defendant's claim used in opposition of or reduction to a plaintiff's claim.

Counterfeit: Unlawful reproduction of an original.

Counter-plea: A plea made in reply to another plea.

Court Rules: Rules promulgated by the jurisdiction's highest court, directing proper procedural conduct in civil and criminal matters, and in evidentiary matters.

Creditor: The person to whom a debt is owed.

Criminal Law: The body of law specifically created by legislation forbidding certain acts as offensive to the public, state, or federal government.

Cross-action: A cause of action against a plaintiff stated in defendant's plea or answer.

Cross-complaint: A plea or complaint filed by a defendant against another defendant or a third party.

Cui bono: Whom may profit by the action.

Culpable: Blameworthy.

Cum: Together with.

Cum onere: Subject to the burden, charge, or incumbrance.

Cumulative: Additional.

Curia: A court of justice.

Custom: Established in law by long usage.

Cy pres: "As near as" (a rule of construction whereby the intention of the maker of an instrument is followed as closely as possible when it would be impossible or illegal to carry it out literally).

Damage: Loss or injury to person or property.

Damnum absque injuria: Wrong for which no legal remedy exists.

De bene esse: Conditional or subject to future exception.

Debtor: One who owes a debt.

Declaratory relief: The declaration by a court that specific conduct is unlawful.

Decree nisi: A decree that becomes absolute except on the contingency of some happening or if cause is shown against it.

De facto: Something that exists as a matter of fact (usually applied to corporations without a legal charter).

Default: Failure to preform a duty or obligation.

Default day: The final day for a defendant to answer a complaint.

Default judgment: Judgment in favor of the plaintiff when a defendant fails to appear and make a defense.

Defendant: The party opposing a legal action.

Dehors: Outside of, beyond the scope of; foreign to the record.

De jure: As a matter of law; by right.

Delegate: To appoint or authorize; a person appointed.

Delictum: A wrong; a tort.

Demand letter: A letter demanding a specific response from the party receiving the letter.

De minimis: Concerning trifles (unimportant, insignificant matters or details).

Demurrer: To wait or stay (motion to dismiss, stating that even if the facts are true as alleged, they are insufficient to maintain a cause of action in law).

De nova: Anew; over again.

Deponent: One who makes a deposition.

Deposition: An out-of-court session in which a witness is examined and recorded.

Derogation: Partial nullification.

Dictum: An authoritative rule, opinion, or maxim.

Digest: An alphabetically and topically arranged collection of case headnotes.

Dilatory: Tending to cause delay (usually applying to motions challenging an action based on jurisdiction or other defenses that don't speak to the merits of the claim).

Diligence: The care and attention expected of a person in view of particular events or conditions.

Direct evidence: Proof given by a witness with firsthand knowledge about a principle fact in dispute.

Directed verdict: A verdict given by a jury according to the result specified by the judge.

Disclaimer: The renouncement of a title or interest or cause of action.

Disclosure: To reveal facts, things, or documents.

Discovery: The process by which the parties to an action disclose material relevant to, or that could reasonable lead to materials relevant to a proceeding.

District Attorney: The officer representing a state or the federal government in a specified judicial district.

Docket number: A number assigned a case by the court clerk.

Doctrine: A legal principle that is widely accepted and utilized.

Due process: (1) Procedural due process: the minimum legal requirements of procedure and hearing required before the deprivation of life, liberty, or property; (2) substantive due process: that the Fifth and Fourteenth Amendments require the government to be fair and reasonable in furthering legitimate governmental goals.

Duces tecum: Bring with you.

E.g.: For example.

Eo instante: In that very instant.

Eo nomine: By or under that name.

Ejusdem generis: Of the same kind or class (canon of construction holding that general words or phrases should be interpreted to include values or items as those listed with respect to the words of general meaning.

Elements: Preconditions to the operation of a statute, law, or form of relief.

Emolument: Advantage or gain coming as a result of holding an office.

En autre doit: In the right of another.

En banc: On the bench (all the judges participating).

Encl. (or enc.): Abbreviation for "enclosed."

En fait: In fact.

Enjoining: Prohibition by judicial order.

En masse: In mass; the whole.

Enjoin: To direct, forbid, or restrain.

Equity: Fair.

Equitable: Just; fair.

Error: Mistaken judgment as to fact or law.

Eschew: To avoid.

Estoppel: A bar against asserting a claim or right.

Et al: And other people.

Et non: And not.

Et sequitor (et seq.): That which follows (subsequent pages or sections).

Et sic: And so.

Ex abundanti cautela: From an abundance of caution.

Ex ante: From before (based on assumption; a prediction).

Exculpate: Tending to establish innocence.

Ex delicto: Resulting from a crime or tort.

Executive Branch (agency, department): The branch of government concerned with administering and furthering the law (President, governors, administrative departments).

Executive order: A statement of executive policy issued by the chief executive (President, governors).

Executive proclamations: Chief executive's statement commemorating a public event (not a law or order).

Exemplary damages: Damages to compensate for particularly wrongful conduct.

Ex facie: From the face of it (apparently or evidently).

Ex facto: From the fact (in consequence of the fact or action).

Exhibit: A document, record, or thing introduced as evidence.

Exhaustive: Complete and detailed; unabridged.

Ex maleficio: By an illegal act or misconduct.

Ex officio: By virtue or of the authority implied by office.

Exonerate: To free from responsibility.

Ex parte: From the part (something for one party only, usually without notice to other parties).

Ex post facto: After the fact of a matter.

Express: Clear and definite.

Expressio unius est exclusio alterius: Canon of construction requiring that the inclusion of one thing implies the exclusion of another.

Expunge: To erase or destroy (as in to expunge a criminal record).

Ex relatione (ex rel.): On the relation of (suit brought by the government upon the application of a private person).

Extrajudicial evidence: Facts not directly under judicial view, including those facts that may be inferred.

Extrinsic evidence: Evidence that is not properly before the court.

Facias: That you cause.

Fed. Appx. (Federal Appendix): An unofficial reporter series published by West Group containing "unpublished" decisions (decisions not designated for official publication in the Federal Reporter) from the federal circuit courts of appeal.

Federal Register: A daily publication of agency activities (e.g., opinions, rules, notices, etc.).

F, F.2d, F.3d (Federal Reporter, First, Second, and Third Series): A reporter publishing U.S. Circuit Court decisions.

F.Supp., F.Supp.2d (Federal Supplement, First and Second Series): A reporter publishing U.S. District Court decisions.

Fed.R.Civ.P. (Federal Rules of Civil Procedure): Court rules governing civil actions in trial courts.

Fiduciary: Related to a thing upon which a trust is founded; a trustee.

Foreclosed: Prevented.

F.R.A.P. (Federal Rules of Appellate Procedure): Court rules governing appeals in appellate courts.

F.R.E. (Federal Rules of Evidence): Court rules governing evidence in federal civil and criminal matters.

Friendly suit: A suit entered into by the parties upon a matter of common interest.

Good faith: Sincere and honest.

Gratis: For free; without reward.

Gross: A total sum; flagrant or shameful.

Guardian ad litem: A person appointed to guard a ward for the duration of the pending action.

Habeas corpus: A writ used to preserve personal freedom, ordering a custodian to produce a person in custody for the court, so that judicial inquiry can be made as to the legality of confinement.

Habeas corpus ad testificandum: The habeas corpus petition used to produce a prisoner for in-court testimony.

Harmonizing: Resolving conflicting sources of law.

Headnotes: An editor's summary of a point of law or holding contained in a case.

Hearsay evidence: Evidence derived from what others have said or written, rather than evidence given by someone who has firsthand experienced of the matter.

History: The treatment of a case on appeal and/or remand.

Hornbooks: Textbooks on a single legal subject.

House of Representatives: One of two chambers (houses) of the U.S. legislature, comprised of numerous state representatives elected to serve two-year terms.

Hypothetical question: An assumed or actual situation or set of facts used as a basis for forming a conclusion that may be applied to other facts or situations of a similar nature.

Ibiden (ibid or ib): In the same.

Id est: That is.

I.e.: That is.

Illicit: Unlawful or unauthorized.

Immaterial: Of insignificance or not bearing on important matters.

Impeach: To challenge or discredit.

Imprimus: First of all.

Imputed: Something attributed to a person because of an association with another.

In autre droit: In another's right.

In camera: In a chamber (under private judicial review, without spectators).

Inchoate: Incomplete or imperfect.

Incorporeal: Having no physical body; intangible.

Inculpate: To accuse or to implicate.

Incur: To suffer a liability or expense.

Indefeasible: That which cannot be defeated or undone.

In delicto: In fault.

Indemnification: Compensation for loss or damage sustained.

In derogation of common law: Legislation altering the common law.

Indicia: Indication.

Indirect evidence: Circumstantial evidence.

Inequity: Unfair.

Infamous: Having a bad reputation.

Infect: To contaminate.

Infer: To conclude or draw inferences from a set or pattern of facts.

In forma pauperis: In the manner of a pauper (indigent person exempt from court fees and costs).

Infra: Below.

In genere: The same kind.

Inherent: The essence or characteristic of a thing; a vested right or privilege.

In hoc: In respect to this.

In infinitum: Indefinitely.

In initio: In the beginning.

Injunction: A court order commanding or preventing some action.

In jure: In law or in right.

Injuria: Injury.

Injuria absque damno: Injury without damage (a legal wrong that does not support a lawsuit because there was no harm).

Injury: The violation of personal rights, to which the law provides a remedy.

In limine: At the beginning (a matter presented to a judge (usually evidentiary) before or during trial).

In lieu of: Instead of.

In loco: Instead of.

Innuendo: By hinting (an indirect suggestion).

In pais: Outside of court or without legal authority.

In pari delicto: Equally at fault.

In pari materia: Canon of statutory construction requiring that statutes related to the same subject matter should be read consistently.

In praesenti: At present.

In personam: Against a person (involving personal rights or obligations).

In re: In the matter of; in regard to.

In rem: Against a thing (generally pertaining to the rights of a person over a thing).

Instanter: Without delay.

Instrument: A document evidencing an act or agreement (e.g., a contract).

Inter alia: Among other things.

Inter alios: Among other people.

Interim: In the meantime.

Interim order: A preliminary order made before the outcome of the suit.

Interlineation: Written into an instrument before or after execution.

Interlocutory: Something that is temporary or that has intervened after the commencement but before the end of a suit.

Interrogatories: A discovery tool by which a party may require an adversary to submit written answers in response to interrogative questions.

In toto: In the whole.

Intra: Within.

Intra vires: Within the power or authority.

Introduction: Portion of a document stating the authors purpose in creating the writing.

In vacuo: "In a vacuum" (out of context).

Invited-error estoppel: The common law doctrine precluding a party from appealing a matter, even if technically a legal error, if it had consented to or even caused the error.

Ipsa dixit: He said it himself (something asserted but not proven).

Ipso facto: By the fact itself (that is, by the nature of a thing or situation).

IRAC (Idea, Rule, Application, and Conclusion): A method of legal formatting and analysis consisting of stating the idea or issue involved, the rules/laws controlling the matter, applying those rules/laws to the idea/issue, and stating a succinct conclusion.

Irrelevance: Inapplicable to the matter at issue.

Irreparable injury: An injury that cannot be remedied by money damages, but is remediable by injunction.

Joint action: An action prosecuted or defended by more than one party together.

Joint liability: Liability shared by two or more parties.

Judgment: The decision of a court.

Judicial Branch: The branch of a government dealing with the interpretation of law as applied to a set of facts (i.e., courts).

Judicial notice: A court's acceptance, without requiring proof, of an indisputable fact.

Jurisdiction: Authority or power over a matter.

Jurisprudence: The study of legal principles as a legal science.

Jurist: A legal scholar or expert.

Jus: Right or law; fairness.

KeyCite: Westlaw's automated service for researching the history and treatment of a case, statute, regulation, etc.

Key Numbers: Numbers indicating digest topics.

L. (Ln. or l.): Line (lines: *ll.* or *LL* or *Ls*).

Latent: Not apparent; hidden.

Law reviews and journals: Student written and produced publications containing articles on current legal topics.

Laying a foundation: The process by which evidence is introduce, demonstrating admissibility with respect to the facts at issue, or having to do with the credibility of a witness.

L.Ed. (Supreme Court Reporter, Lawyer's Edition): Lawyers Cooperative Publishing's unofficial reporter of Supreme Court decisions.

L.Ed.2d (Supreme Court Reporter, Lawyer's Edition Second Series).

Legislation: The creation and enactment of law.

Legislative branch: The branch of a government charged with creating laws.

Legislature: A body of representatives whose job is to make laws.

Lex: The law.

LEXIS: Internet legal research service.

Liability: A person's or entity's legal obligation, accountability, or responsibility to another person or to society.

Liberty: The freedom or right or power to do or not do something without restriction.

Liberty interest: An interest protected by the due process clause of state and federal constitutions.

License: Permission or privilege.

Licet: Not forbidden by the law.

Lien: An encumbrance or right to hold property until a debt has been paid.

Limitation: Restriction.

Lineal: In a line.

Liquidate: To pay off or lessen; to make a determination.

Lis pendens: "Pending suit" (the doctrine by which a court has jurisdiction over property involved in a suit until a final determination.)

Lite pendente: While the suit is pending.

Litigant: A party to a suit or other action.

Local action: Action capable of being brought in one county only.

Local court: A court with jurisdiction in a particular district only.

Locus delicti: The place where a tort or injury occurred.

Loose-leaf services: Legal publications that are in the form of easily updated three-ring binders.

Loss: Injury or damage or destruction to something.

Magistrate: An inferior judge; a public officer invested with judicial power

Maintenance: Meddling with or perpetuating a suit in bad faith.

Maladministration: Wrongful administration.

Malfeasance: A wrongful act.

Malice: Intent to commit a wrong.

Malicious prosecution: Prosecution of a civil or criminal action without probable cause and with malice.

Malo animo: With malice or wrongful intent.

Malpractice: Negligence on the part of a professional, such as a doctor or lawyer.

Malum: Bad or wicked.

Malum prohibitum: Something bad prohibited by law.

Mandamus: We command (a writ used to compel official conduct).

Marriage: The civil status created in the legal union of two people for life.

Material fact: A fact that is significant or essential to a matter at hand.

Matter in issue: A point or question in dispute.

Matter of fact: Some truth or occurrence that can be proved by one or more of the five bodily senses.

Matter of record: A fact proved by a record.

Maxim: A rule or principle universally regarded as reasonable or correct.

Measure of damages: The method or rule used for computing the extent of damages.

Mediation: A non-binding method of resolving a dispute involving a neutral third party to facilitate negotiations.

Medical jurisprudence: Medical rules and principles as applied to legal questions.

Memorandum: (1) An informal document outlining an issue; (2) a party's written statement of its legal arguments and points of authority.

Mens rea: Guilty mind (criminal intent or recklessness).

Merits: The subject and substance of a legal matter, rather than matters of procedure, forms, or technicalities.

Mesne: In the middle; between.

Mini-digests: Concise digests in case reporters digesting only decisions appearing in a single volume.

Minutes: A summarizing record of what happened during a court proceeding.

Misfeasance: A lawful act preformed in an unlawful manner.

Misjoinder: The improper joining of two or more parties in a lawsuit who do not share a joint interest; the improper combining of two or more distinct causes of action not permissibly joined in law.

Misnomer: A mistake in naming a person, place, or thing.

Mispleading: Mistake or omission of something crucial or critical to a complaint or defense.

Misrepresentation: Causing another to believe a fact or condition that is not true or correct.

Mistake of fact: Mistake about a fact in existence, or mistake as to the existence of a fact that does not exist.

Mistake of law: Mistaken conclusions as to the legal effect concerning the facts of the matter.

Mistrial: A trial wherein final judgment cannot be rendered because of some fundamental error in the proceedings.

Mitigation: To make less severe, as proper in light of the circumstances.

Modus: Mode or manner or form of something.

Moiety: One half.

Moratorium: The legal suspension of enforcement of a law, liability, or debt.

Motion: A request posed to a court asking for a ruling or order.

Multifarious: Improper joining of distinct matters or causes in an action; improper joining of parties in an action.

Multiplicity of actions: Different, unnecessary suits brought against a defendant regarding the same issue.

Municipal: Concerning a town or city and its government.

Municipal corporation: District inhabitants incorporated into political subdivision of a state.

Municipal courts: Inferior courts of limited jurisdiction over criminal and civil matters, operating in municipalities.

Municipal ordinance: A municipal law applicable within the municipality's jurisdiction.

n.: Footnote (footnotes: *nn.*).

Negate: To deny; to nullify.

Negative averment: A negative fact asserted as a positive.

Negligence: The breach of a duty to act or refrain from acting (in the manner of a reasonably prudent person) to the injury of another.

Negotiation: Debate and arrangement of terms in a business transaction.

Net: The remaining sum after subtracting all charges and deductions.

Nihil (nil): Nothing.

Nihil dicit: "He says nothing" (judgment against a defendant who fails to answer or otherwise respond to a complaint).

Nihil est: "There is nothing" (the sheriff's return when unable to serve a writ).

Nisi: Unless.

Nolle (or nolo) prosequi: To abandon (to abandon a suit or prosecution).

Nolle (or nolo) contendere: I will not contend.

Nominal damages: A small amount of money damages (usually $1.00) awarded when a legal injury is suffered but there is no substantial loss or injury to be compensated.

Non compos mentis: Not master of one's mind (insane or incompetent).

Nonfeasance: The failure to act when there exists a legal duty to do so.

Non joinder: Omission of a party necessary to an action.

Non obstante: Notwithstanding.

Non obstante veredicto: Notwithstanding the verdict.

Non prosequitur: He does not prosecute (a judgment against a plaintiff who fails to pursue a pending suit).

Non-resident: One who is not a legal resident of a jurisdiction.

Non sequitur: It does not follow (not a logical conclusion or inference).

Noscitur a sociis: It is known by association (a canon of construction holding that a meaning of a word or phrase should be interpreted by the words immediately surrounding it).

Nonsuit: Judgment against a plaintiff when unable to prove the case or otherwise cannot proceed to trial on the merits.

Nota bene: Careful or special notice.

Notary public: A person authorized by the state to attest and authenticate a written instrument.

Notice: Legal notification.

Notice of Appeal: A document filed with the trial/hearing court notifying the court, its clerks, and the parties that a litigant intends to appeal a case.

Noun: A word indicating a person, place, or thing.

Novelty: The quality of being new, original, or unusual.

Nudum pactum: A naked agreement, not enforceable in court.

Nul tiel record: The plea asserting that a plaintiff has based an action on a record that does not exist.

Null: Does not exist or is not valid.

Nullity: Something that is of no effect.

Nunc pro tunc: "Now for then" (indicating that something is presently done that should have been done in the past, or has the effect of having been done in the past).

Nunquam: Never or nowhere.

Obiter dictum: Something said in passing (judicial comment not directly pertaining to a decision, and thus making no precedent, but may still be persuasive).

Objections: A party's interjection that it disagrees with some course of action.

Oblique: Indirect.

Obloquy: Blame.

Official: Of a public office.

Official publication: Legal materials that are published/sanctioned by the government, as opposed to a proprietary organization's private publication.

Onus probandi: (or simply "onus") burden of proof.

Open court: A court convened in public (as opposed to in chambers).

Opening statements: A litigant's initial statements to a jury or judge at the commencement of a trial, before the presentation of evidence.

Oral argument: Oral, in-court presentation of a litigant's arguments.

Order: A command or direction.

Ore tenus: By word of mouth (orally).

Organic law: A law considered to be fundamental, primary.

Overbreadth doctrine: Holding that a statute may not be so broadly written that it deters or "chills" free expression, even if the statute prohibits acts that may be legitimately forbidden.

Overreaching: Acting beyond what is appropriate; straying from a prescribed function.

Overruled: The rejection by a court of due jurisdiction of law or prior judicial precedent.

Oyer: To hear.

p. or pg.: Page (pages: *pp.* or *pgs*).

Panel: A list of potential jurors.

Parallel citations: Two or more citations indicating separate locations for the same legal material.

Par: Equal.

Par. or para.: Paragraph.

Pari delicto: A fault shared equally.

Pari passu: In equal measure or degree.

Party: A person or entity involved or interested in a proceeding.

Patent: Obvious.

Peculation: A party's unlawful appropriation of money or property entrusted to its care by another.

Pecuniary: Regarding money.

Penal: Punishable.

Pendente lite: While the action is pending (during the litigation process).

Per annum: By the year.

Per capita: Divided equally among individuals; in relation to people taken individually.

Per curiam: Opinion by the whole court, as opposed to a single, authoring judge.

Per diem: By the day.

Peremptory challenge: The right to exclude a juror during the jury selection process for no particular reason.

Perjury: The willful statement of an untruth while under oath.

Perpetual injunction: An injunction ordered after final adjudication that will continue to have force indefinitely.

Perpetuating testimony: The right to reduce a witness's testimony to a written transcript for later use in court should the witness become unavailable.

Perquisites (perk): Benefits or profits of an office, gained in addition to salary.

Per se: In or by itself.

Personality: Personal property, as distinct from real property (real estate).

Petit jury: A jury of twelve or less, as distinct from a grand jury.

Petition: A written application or initial pleading to an authority or court.

Petition for rehearing: A request that the appellate court re-hear the issue.

Petition for Review: A request that a state's highest court review a decision of a lower appellate court.

Plaintiff: The complaining party seeking redress or relief.

Plaintiff in error: The party who prosecutes a writ of error in a higher court, unsatisfied by the lower court's judgment.

Pleading: A formal document in a lawsuit setting forth or responding to a claim.

Pocket parts: Soft-bound supplements in the back of legal research books.

Popular Name Table: A table cross-referencing the common names of statutes with their official citations.

Positive evidence: Same as direct evidence.

Post diem: After the day.

Post litem motam: After commencing the suit.

Power: The right or ability.

Power of attorney: Authority to act as agent or attorney for another.

Praecipe: An order to a court clerk to issue summons or some other writ.

Precatory: Advisory; recommended.

Precedent: A rule of law made by a court when interpreting statutes, rules, or other precedent.

Preclude: Prevent.

Preconditions: Conditions that must be satisfied before a statute will operate.

Predicate: The thing, opinion, or matter upon which something is based and offered.

Prejudice: Inclination to decide or regard a matter for personal reason rather than for honest belief; affect (negatively).

Preliminary: Of an action or event preceding or done in preparation for something more important.

Preliminary injunction: A temporary injunction issued before or during trial to prevent irreparable injury.

Preponderance of the evidence: The standard of proof required in most civil trials; finding for the party with the most evidence in its favor, if only in a slight amount.

Prerogative: A right, power, privilege, or immunity of one's office.

Prescription: Establishing rules; a right to or over a thing.

Presumption: Taken as true without further proof.

Pre-trial conference: A conference, held by a court and the parties to an action, to prepare for trial.

Prima facie: Sufficient to establish a fact or presumption unless rebutted.

Prima facie evidence: Evidence sufficient to establish a fact unless rebutted by additional evidence.

Primary sources: Materials containing the letter of the law (e.g., statutes, constitutions, regulations).

Principle: A fundamental or primary rule or law from which others may develop.

Privilege: A legal right, immunity, or exemption of a person or class.

Privity: A relationship between two or more parties that is recognized by law.

Probative fact: A fact proving a material or ultimate fact.

Pro bono: For the public good.

Procedural law: Rules that direct the steps and order for having a right or duty enforced.

Process and service: A summons or writ officially served upon a person or entity.

Proclivity: Tendency, inclination, or propensity.

Proctor: A person appointed to conduct or manage a matter on the part of another.

Procuration: The appointment of one to act on behalf of another.

Production requests: A discovery tool by which a party to an action may request the disclosure or production of documents, things, or to inspect a thing or a place.

Profert: An offer made by a party to produce documents.

Proffer: To offer; to make a showing.

Pro forma: For form (made or done as a formality, or of a formatted description).

Pro hac vice: For this particular purpose.

Prolixity: Unnecessary facts.

Promulgate: To announce; to put into legal force.

Prong: Each of more than one separate points or elements that must be met as a precondition to the application of a law or rule (see "Element").

Pronoun: A word used as a substitute for a noun (e.g., *I, you, he, anybody*).

Proper noun: A name or title.

Pro persona (pro per): On one's own behalf.

Property in custodia legis: Property in legal custody or within the jurisdiction of a court.

Propria persona: In his own person.

Proprietary: Of or relating to an owner or ownership.

Propriety: The state or quality of conforming to conventionally accepted standards of behavior or morals.

Propter: Because of.

Pro rata: By rate or proportion.

Prorogation: Putting off until later.

Proscription: Being prohibited.

Pro se: On one's own behalf (without a lawyer).

Prospective: Expected or expecting to be something particular in the future.

Pro tanto: To the extent.

Pro tempore (pro tem): For the time being; temporary.

Prothonotary: The clerk of the court.

Provisional: Temporary.

Proxy: One who acts on the part of another.

Prudent: Acting with or showing care and thought for the future.

Public corporation: A corporation created for public benefit or use (e.g., schools, cities, etc.).

Puis: Afterwards.

Punitive damages: Damages awarded in punishment or deterrence of a deceitful, reckless, or malicious act or omission.

Purview: The scope of or the influence or concerns of something.

Putative: Believed or assumed.

Qua: In the capacity of (in another's place).

Quamidu: Until.

Quantum: An amount.

Quare: Wherefore.

Quash: To void or dismiss.

Quasi: Near; almost.

Quasi-delict: A tort caused without intent to injure.

Quasi-judicial: Concerning questions or matters that may be heard and decided by an executive or administrative department.

Qua surpa: As above.

Quid pro quo: Something for something (thing exchanged for another thing).

Quo animo: With purpose.

Quoad: As far as.

Quoad hoc: As to this.

Quoad vide: Refer to another part.

Quorum: The number of people necessary to vote or make decisions.

Ratio decidendi: Why a decision is made; the reason.

Re: Regarding.

Real evidence: Physical, tangible evidence.

Real injury: Injury resulting from an act, not words.

Rebuttal: The time allowed to a party to present evidence contradicting the other party's evidence.

Rebuttable presumption: An inferential presumption from facts that may be overcome by contrary evidence.

Rebutter: A defendant's pleading in reply to a plaintiff's surrejoinder.

Recall of witness: The act of calling a witness to give further testimony.

Receiver pendente lite: One appointed to control a fund or property while litigation continues.

Recess: A break in a proceeding.

Reciprocal: Given in return; shared.

Reckless: To persist with an action while aware of and disregarding the possibility of a harmful consequence to another.

Recorder: A person appointed to keep records that must be kept according to law.

Recoupment: Reducing financial losses by legal or equitable right.

Recourse: A source of help; the right to hold one secondarily liable when the one primarily liable is in default.

Recover: To regain; to succeed.

Redress: To set right; satisfy.

Reducto ad absurdum: Demonstrating the fallacy of an argument by showing that it leads to an absurdity.

Redundant: Unnecessary.

Referendum: Offering legislation for final ratification or rejection by vote of the citizens.

Regional reporters: Reporters publishing state appellate court decisions in a limited region of the U.S.

Register: The official record of events as they occur.

Regulation: A policy directing the conduct of an administrative agency.

Rejoinder: The defendant's answer to the plaintiff's reply or replication.

Release: The willful relinquishment of a right or legal claim.

Relevancy: The correlation between evidence and case-specific facts.

Remand: To send back to the court from which it came.

Remedial: Corrective.

Remittitur: The act of returning jurisdiction of a case to a lower court after reversal or remand by the higher court.

Remote: Distant; loosely connected to.

Removal of cause: The transference of a case from one court to another, especially from a state court to a federal court.

Renunciation: To forego or abandon a right or claim.

Repeal: To revoke.

Repleader: A court order that the parties re-plead their cases from another point of view.

Reply: A plaintiff's pleading in response to a defendant's answer.

Report: A formal account or statement of facts.

Representation: Statements or actions suggesting or implying the existence of some fact.

Rescind: To void or cancel.

Res gestae: Actions or words considered to be intrinsically related to some matter.

Residuary: Remaining after the greater part has gone.

Residuum: Leftover.

Res ipsa loquitur: Self-evident; presumed to be true.

Res judicata: A thing adjudicated (definitively settled by judicial decision).

Res nova: New thing (undecided issue of law).

Res nullius: Something without an owner.

Respondeat superior: The superior responds (the notion that a superior should answer for the acts of a subordinate).

Respondent: The defendant; on appeal, the party who answers.

Restatement: Legal treatise published by the American Law Institute describing the law in a given field.

Retainer: The preliminary or initial fee intended to secure the services of an attorney or other professional.

Retaining lien: The lien possessed by a professional upon a client's assets or property.

Retraxit: The in-court renunciation of a claim, foreclosing future action on that matter.

Retroactive: Taking effect from a date in the past.

Retrospective: Looking at or considering a past event.

Retrospective law: A law impacting a right or claim or transaction that has occurred before the enactment of the law.

Return: The written statement of one who has executed or served a writ or process or court order.

Return day: The day when process or writ is to be returned and when the defendant must make an appearance.

Reverse: The reversal of a lower court's opinion by a court of appeals.

Review: To re-examine.

Right of action: The legal right to bring a lawsuit.

Rule nisi: A rule that will become final unless cause is shown why it should not.

Rules of court: Regulations governing practice and procedure in court.

S (or ss.): *Scilicet* ("to wit").

Sanction: To ratify or permit; to punish.

Sans: Without.

Scienter: With knowledge (the part of a pleading alleging a defendant's knowledge of a crime or tort).

Scintilla: Very small; the least part.

S.Ct. (Supreme Court Reporter): West Group's unofficial reporter of Supreme Court decisions.

Secondary evidence: Evidence substituted and acceptable upon a showing that the original or primary evidence is lost or destroyed.

Secondary sources: Legal research materials interpreting or discussing the law.

Sect. or §: Section (sections: §§).

Self-regarding evidence: Words, conduct, physical expressions, behavior, or mannerism of a party or the party's witness that influences the credibility of evidence to the party's benefit ("self-serving," or "self-saving) or detriment ("self-disserving").

Semper: Always.

Senate: The 100-member upper house of the bicameral U.S. legislature, as opposed to the lower House of Representatives, with each member of the Senate serving a six-year term.

Separation of powers: Each branch of the government is independent, and may not intrude on the duties of the other branches.

Seriatim: Severally; sequential; in series.

Service: Notification or delivery.

Set aside: To disregard, annul, or void.

Set-off: A cross-claim by a defendant that reduces or discharges a plaintiff's claim.

Severable: Dividable.

Several actions: Separate actions that may not be joined.

Several liability: Liability that is separate from another's liability.

Shepard's Citations: Volume-bound lists of citations to legal materials, indicating citations to earlier materials, and showing treatment and history of those materials.

Sheypardizing: To trace the history and treatment of legal materials.

Sic: So; thus.

[sic]: Used to indicate that irregularity or error in a quoted material actually appearing in the original passage.

Similiter: "Likewise" (a term indicating that a party has accepted an issue of fact as offered or represented by the opposing party).

Sine: Without.

Sine die: Without time limit.

Sine qua non: Without which not (an indispensable condition or thing).

Situs: Site; location.

Slander: Spoken defamation, as opposed to written defamation (libel).

Speculative damages: Damages that cannot be measured or are so uncertain that they will not be awarded.

SS (or ss.): *Subscripsi* (signed below).

Stare decisis: To stand by prior decisions (the requirement that courts abide with the precedent of prior rulings).

Statement of facts: The portion of a legal document describing the facts upon which the document is based.

Statute: A law passed by the legislature.

Stay: Stop; pause.

Stipulation: Agreement between opposing parties.

Straw man argument: A tenuous, exaggerated, or hypothetical argument that an advocate establishes for the purpose of disproving it.

Strict Liability: Liability that does not depend on negligence or intent to harm, but that is based only on the breach of an absolute duty to make something safe.

Strike out: To eliminate material in a pleading, instrument, document, or record.

Sua sponte: Of its own volition.

Subagent: One who works or acts on the behalf of an agent.

Subordination of perjury: The crime of causing another to commit perjury.

Substantive issues: Involving the merits of a court action.

Sub judice: Under a judge (at bar; before the court).

Sub nom: Under the name (as a citation signal, indicates a change in the names of the title of the case).

Subpoena: A writ commanding an appearance in court.

Subpoena duces tecum: A writ commanding that items be brought to court.

Substantive law: All laws except those pertaining to legal remedy and method of redress.

Sui generis: Of its kind or class.

Summons: A writ issued by a court comanding the appearance of a defendant to answer a civil clam.

Suo nomine: In his own name.

Supersedeas: A writ to suspend court proceedings and to prevent judgment.

Supra: Above.

Supreme Court: The highest court in the United States; also the name of the highest court in most states.

Surrebuttal: A party's response to the other party's rebuttal.

Surrebutter: The plaintiff's pleading in response to the defendant's rebutter.

Surrejoinder: The plaintiff's pleading in response to the defendant's rejoinder.

Syllabus: A summary of content.

Tax: Government enforced contribution, used to support the government.

Tax lien: A government lien on property.

Temporary Restraining Order: A type of preliminary injunction temporarily requiring someone to act or refrain from acting in a certain manner.

Tender: An offering in order to satisfy an obligation such as a debt or judgment.

Terra firma: Land.

Testimony: Statements given under oath.

Third parties: Those who are not legally interested in a court action, instrument, or contract.

Threshold: The lower limit; the minimum limit for something to occur.

Tithes: Funds or property given to a religious institution in accordance with religious tenants.

Toll: To stop the running of; to abate; to annul (such as to stop the running of a statute of limitations—to toll the statute).

Tort: A legal wrong giving rise to a civil cause of action.

Tort-feasor: One who has committed a tort.

Tortious: Wrongful; injurious.

Transcript: A written record of a hearing, trial, deposition, or other proceedings.

Transitory action: A lawsuit that may be filed wherever a defendant can be found.

Traverse: To delay or deny.

Treatises: Literature written by scholars on varying topics of law.

Trespass: Generally, an unlawful act of force against a person or property.

Trespass vi et armis: "By force of arms" (an action to recover damages for injury to person or property).

Trust: The care and possession of real or personal property for the benefit of another.

Ultimate fact: A fact or issue to be finally decided by a jury or judge, in view of the evidence presented; that which must ultimately be resolved.

Ultra: Beyond or above.

Ultra vires: Beyond the granted or legal powers.

Una voce: Unanimously.

Undue influence: Inappropriate influence or control over another.

Unites States Circuit Courts of Appeal: Federal court of appeals with jurisdiction over a specific region, sitting above federal district courts but below the U.S. Supreme Court.

United States District Courts: Federal trial courts.

United States Supreme Court: The highest federal court, comprised on nine justices.

Unofficial publications: Legal materials (e.g., statutes, case law, etc.) published by private companies.

U.S.C. (United States Code): Official publication of federal statutes.

U.S.C.A. (United States Code Annotated): West Group's unofficial publication of federal statutes.

U.S.C.S. (United States Code Services): Reed's unofficial publication of federal statutes.

U.S.L.W. (United States Law Week): A newspaper weekly reporting activity in federal courts.

Usque: Insofar as.

Vacate: To annul or void.

Vagueness doctrine: Based on the Due Process Clause, holding that criminal statutes must be clear in their intent, so as to provide clear warning to the people.

Vel non: Or not.

Venire: The group of persons called for jury service.

Venireman: One summoned for jury service.

Venue: The proper place to pursue a lawsuit, because it is the place where the contested matter occurred.

Verdict: The jury's decision.

Vest: To take effect

Veto: The act of the chief executive officer declining to enact a law passed by the legislature.

Vindictive damages: Punitive or exemplary damages.

Vis.: *Videlicet* (namely; in other words).

Vis major: An inevitable occurrence.

Voir dire: "Speak the truth" (the preliminary examination of potential jurors).

Waiver: A knowing and willful relinquishment or denial of a right or cause of action.

Wanton: To be indifferent to the consequences to others, while unreasonably or maliciously risking harm.

Ward: One within the control and protection of another.

Warden: Guardian; the chief administrator of a prison.

Warranty: An assurance or promise to the truth or extent of a matter.

Without prejudice: Retaining right or privilege.

Writ: A written order authorized in law by authority of the state or sovereign.

Writ of certiorari: A request to appeal a decision to the highest court in a jurisdiction, usually to the U.S. Supreme Court.

Writ of error: A writ from a court of appeal to a lower court, allowing for the review of the record to correct possible errors.

Writ of execution: The writ used to impose a final judgment.

NOTES: _____
_____
_____
_____
_____
_____
_____
_____
_____
_____
_____
_____
_____
_____
_____
_____
_____
_____
_____
_____
_____
_____
_____
_____
_____
_____
_____
_____
_____
_____
_____
_____
_____
_____
_____
_____
_____

NOTES: _____

INDEX

INDEX

Made in United States
Troutdale, OR
07/29/2024